QUALITY IMPROVEMENT USING STATISTICAL PROCESS CONTROL

Quality Improvement Using Statistical Process Control

Lawrence S. Aft, PE
Southern College of Technology

HARCOURT BRACE JOVANOVICH, PUBLISHERS
Technology Publications

San Diego   New York   Chicago   Austin   Washington, D.C.
London   Sydney   Tokyo   Toronto

For Susan

About the Cover: design by Carol Conway; photo courtesy Siemens Energy and Automation, Roswell, Georgia

ISBN: 0-15-574103-9
Library of Congress Catalog Card Number: 87-82395
Printed in the United States of America

Preface

The United States is at an economic crossroads, and the path that must be followed is one that leads to continual quality improvement. Those organizations that embrace this philosophy will ultimately be successful in world markets. Continual quality improvement does not just happen. There must be a method, a structured approach, and one such approach is the use of statistical process control, or SPC.

Statistical process control is a problem-solving methodology that works best when it is part of a quality improvement process. SPC has been around for a long time; the statistical methods it uses were developed during the 1920s. However, these statistical methods, by themselves, do not bring about needed quality improvements. Rather, they are brought about by management teams. Statistics is merely the *tool* that helps identify and solve quality problems, which eventually results in productivity growth.

This book is the result of much quality improvement work with many organizations. It was prepared to demonstrate the use of basic statistical concepts in helping to solve quality and productivity problems. The statistics and statistical methods presented are not rigorous; at best they can be described as intuitive. An understanding of these procedures is essential for the long-term economic health of American business and industry.

The text was written with many audiences in mind. Top management must understand the need for its involvement in the quality improvement process, and managers at all levels must at least understand the relationship of quality improvement and SPC. Technically oriented personnel must grasp the process orientation that is the key to improvement, and even college students must be led to see process improvement as part of the overall competitive business strategy.

The first part of the book explains the continuous improvement philosophy, and the second illustrates the application of the intuitive statistical analysis. Colleges of engineering, engineering technology, and business must begin to require courses dealing with quality improvement principles. Quality is everyone's responsibility.

This book would not have been possible without the assistance of a number of people and organizations. The people provided the contact and the organizations provided the opportunity for applying the principles presented here. In no particular order these include, from Amoco Foam Products Company—Val Fisher, Tim Gavin, and Clarinda Bell; from the Defense Logistics Agency/Defense Contracts Administration Service Region, Atlanta—Ed Palmer and John Thompson; from Ciba Vision—Chris Lynch and Kitty Murphy; and from Georgia Marble Company—Matt Graves and Dewey Rhodes. Other individuals who assisted or supported in some fashion include Jim Kling and John Linn at Southern Tech. I also owe a special thanks to my able secretaries Judy Brooks and Gerrie Kriner and to my wife, Susan, and my children, Steven and Dana. They put up with me while I was writing and rewriting.

Finally, I hope that you will, after reading the text, remember the following:

1. Quality improvement is more than numbers—statistics is a tool.
2. Quality improvement is a management responsibility.
3. Quality improvement is essential for economic well being.

LAWRENCE S. AFT

Also by Lawrence S. Aft, available from Harcourt Brace Jovanovich:

Production and Inventory Control

Emphasizing scheduling, forecasting, planning, and inventory control procedures, this book provides an introduction to Production and Inventory Control for business management and technology students and for practitioners.

Contents

CHAPTER 3
QUALITY AND PRODUCTIVITY   25

CHAPTER 4
PROCESS ORIENTATION   36

CHAPTER 5
THE ENTIRE PROCESS   56

CHAPTER 6
DEFINING EXPECTATIONS   67

CHAPTER 7
IDENTIFYING PROBLEMS 76

CHAPTER 8
PARETO ANALYSIS 85

CHAPTER 9
CAUSE AND EFFECT ANALYSIS 97

CHAPTER 10
GROUP PROBLEM SOLVING 108

CHAPTER 19
IMPLEMENTING THE PHILOSOPHY   295

CHAPTER 20
CASE STUDIES   309

QUALITY IMPROVEMENT USING STATISTICAL PROCESS CONTROL

CHAPTER 1

Introduction to Statistical Process Control

One of the toughest parts about adopting a philosophy of quality may be convincing employees that you really mean it this time.   [54: 37]

Donald R. Beall
Rockwell International Corporation

1.1   INTRODUCTION

For many years the United States was the unchallenged leading supplier of manufactured goods. When the United States flexed its economic muscle, there was no competition. That has changed, and changed dramatically.

A checklist of many leading industries in the United States might be eye-opening. All the following were at one time dominated by American companies.

- **Automobiles:** GM, Ford, and Chrysler no longer dominate. The Japanese, German, Korean, Swedish, and even Yugoslavian and Spanish car makers have captured over half of annual car sales.

- **Steel:** A look at the unemployment statistics for cities such as Gary, Indiana, Youngstown, Ohio, and Pittsburgh, Pennsylvania, only confirms that Japanese, Korean, and European steel manufacturers are becoming principal sources of this important raw material.

- **Electronics:** The home electronics market is led by Japanese companies such as Sony. There are relatively few U.S. producers left in the competitive market. Examine the newspaper ads and Sony, Panasonic, Sharp, JVC, NEC, Sanyo, and Toshiba are featured. You can count on the fingers of one hand the number of U.S.-owned companies still producing electronics in this country.

- **Musical instruments:** The name in pianos these days seems to be Yamaha.

- **Clothing:** Recently, Congress saw a flurry of proposed legislation designed to protect American textile and clothing manufacturers from foreign imports. The shoe industry, once the backbone of the Northeast, has virtually disappeared from the land. Most zippers are Japanese produced or produced in plants owned by the Japanese.

- **Photocopy:** Would it surprise you to discover that Xerox is not the world's largest photocopier manufacturer? Ricoh is the largest selling brand of copy machine.

- **Watches:** The Seiko watch from Japan is the best seller. There are not many U.S.-made watches available. There are even fewer schools teaching the art of watchmaking.

- **Ship repair:** Not suprisingly, at this point we find that the U.S. Navy is having some of its rework (maintenance) done by foreign countries, Japan in the Far East, Germany in Europe, and Israel in the Middle East. According to one career Naval officer, "They do the rework better and cheaper." On a closely related product, "Foreign suppliers are now manufacturing vast amounts of the key components for United States weapons systems, including Navy combat vessels, aircraft, tanks, communication networks, missiles, electronic components, even ammunition." [195: 37]

The list goes on to include items such as microwave ovens, medical equipment, computer chips, athletic equipment, optics, robots, oceangoing ships, and electric motors. All these products share some common characteristics. "They are attractive, complex, products of high technology, demanded in high volume—just the type of products for which a company would like to be a leader in design and manufacture. They are also products in which U.S. share of the worldwide market dropped by 50 percent during the past decade." [22: 46] An interested visitor to Japan will frequently hear Japanese acquaintances say, "'Well, I'd like to buy American goods, but, well you know . . .' and the sentence trails off with a shake of the head and a knowing smile." [195: 8A]

According to *Insight,* "Today more than 70 percent of the goods produced in the United States are in direct competition with foreign merchandise. Should the rate of productivity continue as it is, the U.S. competitive posture, both domestically and abroad, can only decline." [37: 10]

1.2 THE PROBLEM

The following appeared in the Toronto *Sun* on April 25, 1983.

Apparently the computer giant, IBM, decided to have some parts manufactured in Japan as a trial project. In the specifications they set out that the limit of defective parts would be acceptable at three units per 10,000. When the delivery came in there was an accompanying letter. 'We Japanese have hard time understanding North American business practices. But the three defective parts per 10,000 have been included and are wrapped separately. Hope this pleases.' [196: 6]

The preceding section, as well as the incident IBM reported, contains some disturbing information. What happened? Why did it happen? How did it happen? Just what did happen, anyway? A number of people have focused on the problem. Let's listen to what some other people have said. Their comments should put the problem into perspective.

According to Douglas D. Danforth, Chairman of Westinghouse Electric Corporation, "I find that leading companies world wide make total quality their priority, and they consistently apply it to building increasing customer value." [11: 15]

According to W. Edwards Deming, "The trouble is American managers don't know where to look for waste, so they blame the decline in productivity and quality on the workers and on international competition." [7: 14]

According to the American Productivity Center in Houston, Texas,

In the American consuming public there is a lack of awareness of the seriousness of U.S. quality problems and corporate leadership often subjugates long-term quality improvements to the short-term pressures of meeting schedules and reducing costs. Workers read the signals from management and operate accordingly. [2: 1]

When management actions show that the major objective is to deliver on time rather than deliver conforming material, the workers know what counts. When profits become the overriding objective, the workers understand what drives the organization.

Charles C. Harwood, President of Signetics Corporation, succinctly states the problem: "our quality people were responsible for quality, and everyone else was responsible for output. Our quality people were policemen." [19: 26]

Former Commerce Secretary Malcolm Baldrige blames the problem in no small part on industry managers. He said,

"After World War II we were the overall leaders in world management. We lived off that leadership while the rest of the world was rebuilding, but we were blinded by the success American industry enjoyed during the population boom of the 1950s and 1960s . . . management rested on its laurels. [81: 10]

The 1986 survey of industrial engineers conducted by the Institute of Industrial Engineers included the following comment, suggested by over 62 percent of the practicing IE's surveyed. "Management's failure to understand how productivity can be improved ranks highest on the list of major obstacles to productivity improvement." [83: 71]

Another official in President Reagan's cabinet, Deputy Treasury Secretary Richard Darman, lashed out at the business establishment, charging that "bloated, risk-averse, inefficient and unimaginative corporate bureaucracies were hurting U.S. competitiveness." [81: 9]

Two recently released national surveys are almost as frightening. In the 1986 Gallup/ASQC survey of top business executives "three out of four top executives believe that employee attitude is a very serious detractor of quality in American business—considerably higher than any other factor mentioned." [73: 48] A Boston University marketing department survey of workers found that only 22 percent said they trusted management. The workers also felt that what little training they received from management did not fit their real needs. [168: 1c, 16c] No further comment is necessary on these results.

What happened? At one time we were king of the mountain. Without competition there was no need to improve. We could say to our customer, "Take it or leave it." That attitude is understandable when you are on top and when you are the only player in the game. "When it comes to product quality, American managers still think the competitive problem is much less serious than it really is." [98: 7] It may not be the wisest attitude, but it is understandable.

Why did it happen? There are two major reasons for the attitude, and the fall from the top of the mountain. First, we got greedy. When you are in front it's easy to do. Remember the Hare in "The Tortoise and the Hare?" As Kay R. Whitmore, President of Kodak said, "You don't get there just because you used to do it; you get there because you keep working at it." [53: 23] The second reason was short-sightedness. Too much emphasis on the short-term picture. Top corporate officials have been judged on the latest rate-of-return figures. Production managers have been evaluated on how well they meet schedules and how far under budget they operated. As a result, improvements were often delayed or canceled so as not to affect rate of return, schedule, or budget.

In a survey reported in the *Harvard Business Review,* two-thirds of the Japanese supervisors and managers believed that product quality, not cost, schedule, or productivity, was the top priority. Yet at almost 82 percent of U.S. companies managers and supervisors believed that the top priority was meeting the production schedule. [98: 10]

How did it happen? Nobody set out to intentionally bring productivity and quality down. The system just evolved. But once in place, it generated enough inertia to make it extremely difficult to change.

What did happen? We lost sight of our goal. We believed we could stay on top by doing what we always had. The figures, although constantly changing, show dramatically that we could not.

Now what? Do we give up? Throw in the towel? Become an entirely service-based economy? OF COURSE NOT. We can look at what our competition did and do what they did. We can look at what American companies like Corning and Ford and Nashua have done. We can learn from their successes and failures. And we can do it even better. The first step is to define our objective, which has to be improving quality. This will lead to the improvement of productivity.

1.3 QUALITY DEFINED

The United States has many different definitions of quality. There is no national, industry, or even plant agreement as to what it means. Quality definitions are confused by slogans like "do it right the first time," "zero defects," "corporate commitment," "excellence plus," and so on. In most applications, quality has been a stated destination, a goal. The philosophy L.P. Sullivan, Chairman of the American Supplier Institute, espouses is in tune with the Japanese system. "Quality should have an operational definition of reducing waste, and thereby improving quality. In other words, quality cannot be the end objective, but a means to achieve lower manufacturing costs." [15: 32] W. E. Deming, who provided much leadership to Japan as they began their quality improvement process, states, "Improve quality and your costs go down . . . if costs go down and quality goes up, you capture the market." [16: 23] Tom Peters and Nancy Austin, in *A Passion for Excellence,* state, "quality is, above all, about care, people passion, consistency, eyeball contact and gut reaction." [59: 98] Kaoru Ishikawa, the internationally acclaimed Japanese quality expert, defines quality control as follows: "To practice quality control is to develop, design, produce and service a product which is most economical, most useful, and always satisfactory to the consumer." [58: 44] Poor quality is easy to identify because we have all experienced it. It can be described as

> undesirable results due to unwanted or unexpected variations in the services received. The degree of deficiency will be different but we've all encountered it in hotels, restaurants, rental cars, appliance repairs, home maintenance, and many others. It is usually not an out and out failure, just a completely unsatisfactory situation as measured by our own personal expectations and standards.   [183: 406]

Based on their comments and similar thoughts from many other individuals, the following definition of quality is offered for use throughout this book.

QUALITY IS CONSISTENCY AT THE TARGET VALUE.

Quality, under this definition, certainly means conformance to specifications. Quality, under this definition, certainly means fitness for use. Quality, under this definition, is measurable with common statistical procedures that are relatively easy to use.

The goal of any quality program in any organization is to continue to improve by reducing the variability around the target. The less variability there is, the more consistency there will be. This will lead to the ultimate goal of increasing productivity. Let's use a short example to illustrate this.

Figures 1–1 and 1–2 show the results of the inspection of some quality characteristic produced by two different processes. Process 1, as shown in Figure 1–1, meets the specifications. It just meets the Figure 1–1 specifications, and it certainly does conform to the requirements. Process 2, as shown in Figure 1–2, also meets

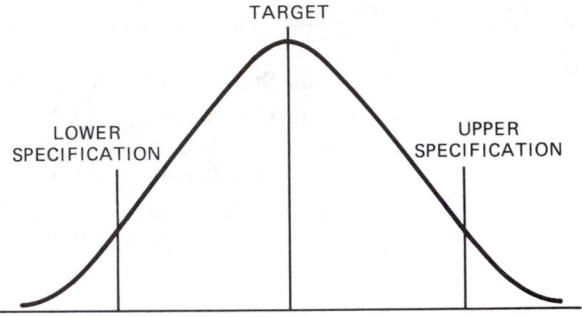

FIGURE 1–1 Process with Relatively Large Variation

the specifications. But in Figure 1–2, process 2 shows more of its values closer to the target. If this product were steel, for example, the material produced by process 2 would be more uniform, the characteristic more predictable, and the product would be more desirable than that produced by process 1.

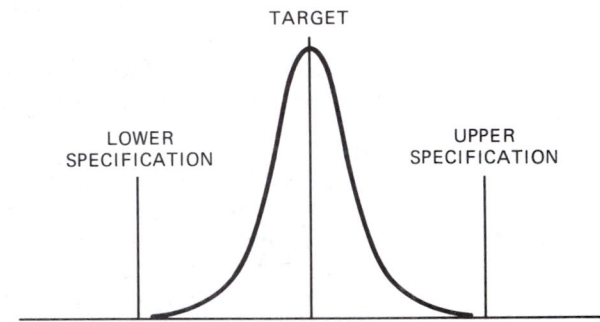

FIGURE 1–2 Process with Relatively Small Variation

Obviously, product produced by process 2 is better than that produced by process 1. But, according to our definition of quality, we have not yet done our job. Our goal is to produce consistently at the target. Total consistency would be every single value on the target.

1.4 STATISTICAL QUALITY CONTROL

The history and development of statistical process control is linked to the development of statistical quality control. Most of the groundwork for SQC was performed by units of the Bell Telephone System.

> By 1922, the work of the Inspection Department in the Western Electric Company was becoming well defined. The inspection of telephone products had been extended to factories of the Automatic Electric Company and the Stromberg-Carlson Company. Visiting inspectors made periodic inspections on material repaired at 27 distributing houses and at many non-Western Electric manufacturers' plants. [25: 5]

This work was carried on, led by individuals at the Bell Labs, such as W. A. Shewhart and Harold F. Dodge. The effort of these men, plus people such as Joseph Juran and W. Edwards Deming, led to the publication in 1956 of Western Electric's *Statistical Quality Control Handbook*.

While the Bell System was developing the principles of statistical quality control for use in its manufacturing operations, World War II gave the United States a tremendous opportunity to apply these principles. With the rapid expansion of industry to meet the war efforts, staffed primarily by untrained personnel, quality of final products was at risk. Training in statistical quality control was mandatory to support the war effort, and "One particular series of courses was set up in a number of training centers throughout the United States. These courses focused on the use of statistical quality control in industry, and topics such as control charts and acceptance sampling plans were taught." [25: 7]

These efforts were short-lived, initially, because the war came to an end. Without pressure or foreign competition, American industry had little motivation to invest in quality control. What did exist was primarily inspection—detecting mistakes after they had been committed. Quality control became, in most instances, synonymous with inspection.

1.5 STATISTICAL PROCESS CONTROL

Statistical process control, or SPC, is the name often given to the ongoing process of continuing to improve quality. SPC would better be defined as the statistical and problem-solving measures used for continuously improving quality. And **by continuing to improve quality, we mean continuing to reduce the variability about our target.** Statistical process control starts with a management commitment for continuous improvement. SPC is a compilation of tools and techniques that helps define problems, identify critical characteristics, and develop a procedure to collect and analyze data that depict the processes that will eventually result in the product. Finally, the improvement process that uses SPC works at developing an environment that puts everyone in the organization on the same team, trying to solve the problems that cause the variability within the processes and products. Statistical process control is, in a nutshell, both a problem-solving procedure and a philosophy.

As a problem-solving procedure, statistical process control consists of a set of analysis tools that helps to identify problems, potential causes of the problems, actual causes of the problems, and ways to evaluate changes to the processes that may be part of the overall scheme of continuous improvement. Specifically, SPC as part of the improvement process uses checklists, Pareto analysis, cause–effect diagrams, flow charts, basic descriptive statistics, control charts, and group problem-solving techniques to help solve problems. These tools are easily mastered and can be used by employees at all levels of the organization.

Effective use of statistical process control requires management to adopt a new philosophy. First, a commitment must be made to continuous improvement. This includes training everyone in the fundamentals of this philosophy. Throughout this book, we will continue to refer to this commitment. It is the key to making SPC work. Statistical process control cannot be viewed as just another program to improve quality. To achieve our definition of quality (consistency about the target value), continuous improvements must be made to constantly reduce variability. Improvement with statistical process control is not a short-term "fix." The Japanese companies that adopted this improvement philosophy in the early 1950s did not begin to make significant inroads into the world markets for at least a decade. Many Japanese companies have begun to operate in the United States. Tom Peters found, in his ongoing study of successful organizations, the following:

> One of the scariest numbers I've seen is the dollars spent for training at the Nissan assembly plant in Smyrna, TN. Depending on whose numbers you look at, between $52 and $65 million was spent for training before they produced the first truck. That's $15,000 a head. Can you imagine the response from an old line company if you asked for $65 million for training? The sad part is that nobody would even have the audacity to ask for it. It would never occur to them to even think that boldly. If they did, the controller would say, "You want to put all that money into people that will leave and work for someone else?" [12: 18]

Even now these companies are still committed to and using statistical process control for quality improvement.

> Management believed that the most important and promising strategy for success was to improve the quality of products. Production of high-quality goods at low cost was thought to be the key to winning international competition, and corporations systematically mobilized their human and physical resources to achieve this goal. [57: 56]

The second element of the philosophy is that quality improvement must be viewed as everybody's job. The statement of Koji Kobayashi, CEO of Japan's NEC Corporations, is typical of the attitude required to make the SPC quality improvement philosophy work. "[It is] necessary for all functions of a company to participate . . . in order to effectively carry out this concept [SPC]." [13: 10] Quality has to be viewed as prevention of defects before they occur rather than detection after the fact. Everyone at every stage must be actively and willingly involved in this process. Everyone must feel the responsibility.

Implementing the quality improvement philosophy marks a major change for many organizations. Such a significant change is not easy. External pressures, such as profit margins, and internal pressures, like meeting the schedule, can be compelling reasons to back down from the commitment. There is no simple way to make the improvement philosophy using SPC work.

The analytical techniques are easy to learn. Their use will help—a little. But their use has been known for years, since the 1920s, and by themselves they have not worked. Without complete commitment from everyone within the organization, they will not work.

1.6 CONCLUSION _____

For the first time there is a real awareness that we are in a major crisis, that an era has ended. You certainly see it among governors, who are acutely aware that the number of truly middle class jobs, particularly for noncollege graduates, are diminishing . . . we are entering a major crisis with no easy answers. [89: 11A]

Statistical process control is not a new concept. Deming has been teaching the concept since his Stanford courses during World War II. Although unsuccessful in this country initially, his words were readily accepted and implemented in Japan in the 1950s. His work has been carried on and expanded by others, including both academicians and industrial practitioners. These individuals have been both U.S. citizens and Japanese. The names include, but are not limited to, Eugene Grant, Joseph Juran, Philip Crosby, and Kaoru Ishikawa.

The importance of continuing process improvement cannot be overemphasized. Quality improvement—**continuous quality improvement**—is everybody's job. From the top executive to the production worker, the goal must be quality improvement. Improving quality will increase productivity.

This book will thoroughly explain the statistical process control concepts and illustrate the basic tools necessary to make it work. The key, though, the shoes necessary for running the race, is management commitment. With it, the tools will work.

So it is with quality improvement using statistical process control. By committing to improve for now—and forever—an organization will be able to continue to compete. U.S. managers have traditionally viewed quality as a defensive strategy to control costs. Quality now has to be viewed, as Harvard professor David Garvin said in a recent interview, as ''a competitive strategy that will separate the winners from the losers.'' [100: 65]

CHAPTER 2

The Philosophy of Statistical Process Control

Because all of the best intentions in the world won't assure quality if you don't have the right tooling in a product line, or if you don't provide the proper environment for the people.   [29: 16]

Robert Anderson
Rockwell International

2.1 INTRODUCTION

A recent survey, published in *Quality Progress* [27: 14], asked some very interesting questions directed toward all types of departments and all levels of management. Some of the questions were:

- Does your department ever reject anything?
- Do rejects stay rejected?
- Are you ever surprised that a reject got through?
- Do you learn anything from rejects?
- Does corrective action ever result from rejects?
- Do you know if any customers were lost for quality reasons?

Without commenting on specific answers to these questions, let us instead discuss two important points these questions raise. First, all the questions deal with rejects—discovering mistakes after the fact. Although the original survey had many more questions, the same common thread tied most of them together.

Second point: if the answer to the first question was yes, who is responsible? If the answer to the second was no, who is responsible? Depending on the answers to the rest of the questions in the listing, who is responsible?

According to a widely circulated newspaper survey, the headline indicated, AUTO EXECS FAULT EMPLOYEES FOR LACK OF QUALITY. The attitude expressed in the article about the survey was, "No matter how you design, plan and execute a product, it can only be as good as the people who are building it."

Does this agree with our answers about the responsibility for defects? Let us answer one more question. True or false: people do not want to do good work. Obviously, the answer to this is false. People want to do a good job. Do any of us ever set out to intentionally make mistakes? Of course not. But does your department ever reject anything? The reason for the rejects is that mistakes were made— perhaps mistakes in methods, perhaps mistakes in materials, perhaps mistakes made by machines, or, certainly, perhaps mistakes made by people.

Mistakes happen. They will never be completely eliminated. It is the responsibility of management to minimize the opportunity for mistakes to occur. This can best be accomplished not through blaming workers, but by management adopting and implementing a philosophy incorporating statistical process control management concepts.

2.2 STATISTICAL PROCESS CONTROL MODEL: GETTING STARTED

The philosophy of statistical process control is one of **continuous improvement.** While later chapters will discuss each major component in detail, this chapter will present the executive summary of this continuous improvement process.

As has already been emphasized, the key to making SPC work starts at the top. Permit an analogy to build the model. We have stated that SPC is a continuous process. Once it starts it never stops. Lacking a perpetual motion machine, the process needs some form of constant power to maintain its momentum. Now to the analogy. This form of power, the engine, is management's commitment to the philosophy and management's creation of the environment in which the process will work. As we begin developing our model, let's show management commitment as the engine or driving force for quality improvement using SPC. Figure 2–1 starts the model.

Management commitment encompasses several key concepts. First among these is the realization that once the engine is started there can be no shutting it off. Statistical process control is not just another program. Programs, by their very nature, imply that there is a beginning and an end. Most organizations have been victim to many programs, especially in the quality area. Traditionally, these have all been marked by gigantic hoopla at the beginning. The program then runs for a while and, before we know it, it's time for another program. It doesn't take long for people to take the attitude, "Here comes another one, wonder if they really mean it this time." As the quote that opened Chapter 1 stated, you have to make employees believe that you really mean it this time.

For statistical process control to work, management cannot permit it to be viewed as just another program. SPC must mark a fundamental change in the way

MANAGEMENT
COMMITMENT

FIGURE 2–1 Management Commitment: Engine That Drives SPC

the organization operates. This is the foundation for a successful improvement program.

"Now just a minute," you're saying. "That is all fine and good for you to say, Mr. Author. You don't have to run our company. You don't have to meet schedules, you don't have to come in on budget, you don't have to meet payrolls." Yes, it is easy for me to say. I never promised that it would be easy. But I'm not alone. Listen, for instance, to Kay R. Whitmore, President of Kodak. "Quality is one of those things that, if you don't continuously do something about it, you are very quickly perceived to be uninterested." [53: 23] Making a commitment is never easy. Let us temporarily digress.

What is a commitment? Without resorting to the dictionary, let us try to answer that with another question. Have we made any commitments in our own personal lives? Probably. How about our marriage? Do we enter marriage expecting failure? Do we go to great lengths to make it work? Are there still some social stigmas for marriages that don't work and end in divorce? What about religion? Are we committed to our faith or do we keep changing religions when a new one comes along?

When we are committed to something, we do indeed go to great lengths to make it work. We don't let the little things throw us. We stick it out, through thick and thin, or as some wedding vows state, "for better or worse."

End of digression. We now stand ready to embrace the quality improvement philosophy that uses statistical process control. This has many names. We are ready, whatever the name, to embark on the process of continuous improvement. Are we committed? Are we willing to change the way we have always done things? This includes a willingness to invest in machinery and improved methods at the expense of short-term profit. This means, as we will see, a willingness to give credibility to suggestions from all levels. This also means an acceptance of the fact that we may not meet our production schedule if the quality is not at the level it needs to be.

Above all, adopting the philosophy means changing the way we have traditionally thought and managed. As the philosophy unfolds, we will see that we are all responsible. Every individual in the organization must understand that we all gain or we all lose at once. It isn't management's company. As Chapter 1 indicated, if we all don't row in the same direction, then surely we will sink under the weight of the competition.

Continually improving quality performance must become a cornerstone of corporate policy. The idea, in explicit terms, of what quality means to the long-term success of the organization must be stated and demonstrated. No matter what the wording of the policy, it has to boil down to the "consistent in-line implementation of quality achievement throughout the organization. . . . " [14: 19]

An essential part of this quality policy is the establishment of specific quality goals. Management must continually emphasize achievement toward these quality standards. To achieve these standards, management must not only make available the necessary technology, but must, in the words of Kaoru Ishikawa,

> Assemble information cncerning quality and QC and specify, in concrete terms, the priority policies in regard to quality. Establish "priority of quality" and "quality first" as the basic policy, and determine long-term goals for quality standards. This must be done in concrete terms and with an international perspective.   [58: 125]

Many organizations have developed quality policies. Often these have been accompanied by a big to-do. Then nothing happens. The policy has often been the result of management fear. "A crisis atmosphere has developed in the last few years, and upper managers genuinely want to improve. But . . . they're quite susceptible to the idea that they can solve their problems by exhorting their subordinates through slogans." [18: 33] Stating that continuous quality improvement is the organization's business policy is but the first step. To carry this out, to implement the philosophy, calls for extensive training of all level of personnel. It is a major responsibility of management to provide that training.

Management commitment is the engine that drives this continuous improvement process. The commitment isn't easy. But the commitment has to be there. It has to be at the top of the organization. Chapter 19 will discuss, in more detail, some suggestions as to how this philosophy can be adopted and implemented so that it works. But bear in mind, it is not easy. There are no quick fixes.

2.3   PROCESS DEFINITION

Statistical process control is the process of continuous improvement. The second key element in the philosophy is the recognition and definition of the process orientation. Before improvement can begin, the organization's activities must first be viewed as interrelated processes. The output of the first process is the input of the next, and so on. The end product or service produced by the organization is the output of the interrelationships of all these processes. Viewing the operations as a series of processes, these processes must then be described and defined.

We cannot logically determine ways to improve a process until we understand the process. Whether as simple as hammering a nail into a piece of wood or as complicated as extruding rolls of plastic foam, the process must be defined.

Many processes, unfortunately, are not even understood by the operators responsible. Their knowledge is limited to button pushing or raw material loading, without knowing the ramifications of what happens inside the "black box," so to speak, that is the process. And yet, in light of the auto industry survey described earlier in this chapter, these very uninformed operators are the first ones to be blamed whenever anything goes wrong. Based on personal observations, most operators want to know what is happening in their process. If they knew, and if they knew how it influenced the rest of the processes, then maybe, just maybe, they could improve the process.

Many tools have been developed to facilitate process definition. Again, in Chapter 4 we will learn how to use the flow chart or flow process chart. This is simply an organized and systematic way to list the steps found in any process.

Earlier we started an analogy that viewed management commitment as the engine that drives the continuous improvement process. To continue the analogy, the process definition becomes the first stage in this cycle of continuous improvement that is driven by management commitment. Figure 2–2 illustrates this.

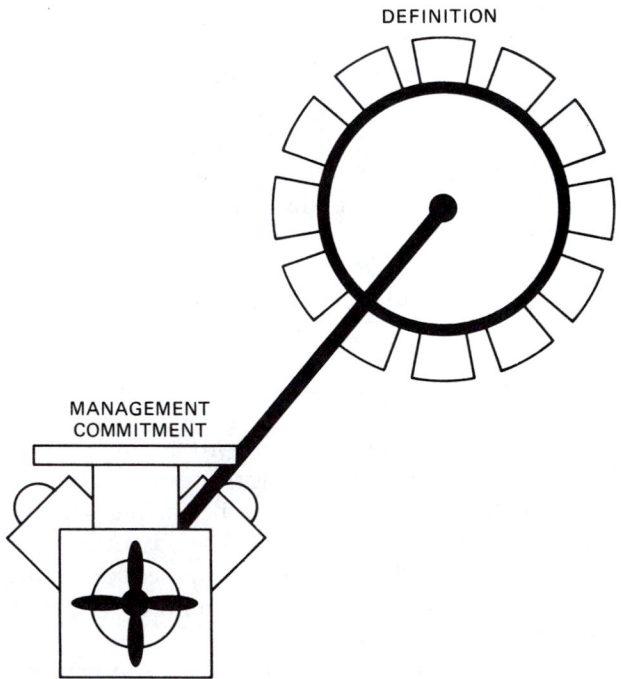

FIGURE 2–2 Process Definition: First Cog in Process Improvement

2.4 PROCESS CHARACTERISTICS

After the process has been defined, a very tangible result is that the inputs and outputs will have been identified. And, as part of the definition process, certain of these inputs and outputs will have been identified as critical to the process. The critical inputs are those that are essential for the process to perform as desired. These can range from correctly filled out requisition forms to proper raw material from stock to proper instructions. These inputs guide the actual operation of the process. If the inputs are wrong, for example, the wrong quantity is requisitioned, or if the improper instructions are given, for example, requesting the wrong blood test in a lab, then the output of the process will be flawed. As the data-processing people so succinctly state, "garbage in, garbage out."

It is necessary, then, as part of statistical process control, to identify these key process characteristics. Most processes have many inputs, but only certain key or critical inputs. These must be identified before any action can be taken to improve the process. While some may be obvious, other key inputs may be more difficult to identify. It is helpful at this stage of SPC implementation to gather all knowledgeable and affected parties to discuss and identify the critical inputs. Tools such as brainstorming, cause/effect diagrams, and Pareto charts are extremely helpful in reaching a consensus as to what the critical inputs actually are.

Remembering that, so to speak, everyone sinks or swims together, it is important at this time to accept everyone's thoughts regarding key inputs. The people closest to the process are most likely to know what they need to do their job—perform their process—correctly. However, broader knowledge is also needed to identify the impact of an early process input to a much later step in the process.

Identifying process characteristics, specifically key process inputs, is the second stage in our continuous improvement process. Figure 2–3 illustrates the introduction of this piece to our model of the improvement philosophy. Remember, the process is driven by management commitment.

2.5 MONITORING AND CONTROLLING THE PROCESS

After the key process characteristics are identified, or at least those believed to be key, these characteristics have to be monitored to determine if the process is in control. In the SPC sense, monitoring the process means collecting data about the process to get a picture of how it performs with relationship to its target and specifications and how it performs over time.

Data, or information about the process, are collected by the operator. These data should be both the traditional inspection results that have always been available and measurements of key process characteristics such as temperatures, pressures, material feeds, and so on.

Each characteristic will vary. The data will show this variation. Two types of variation might be present.

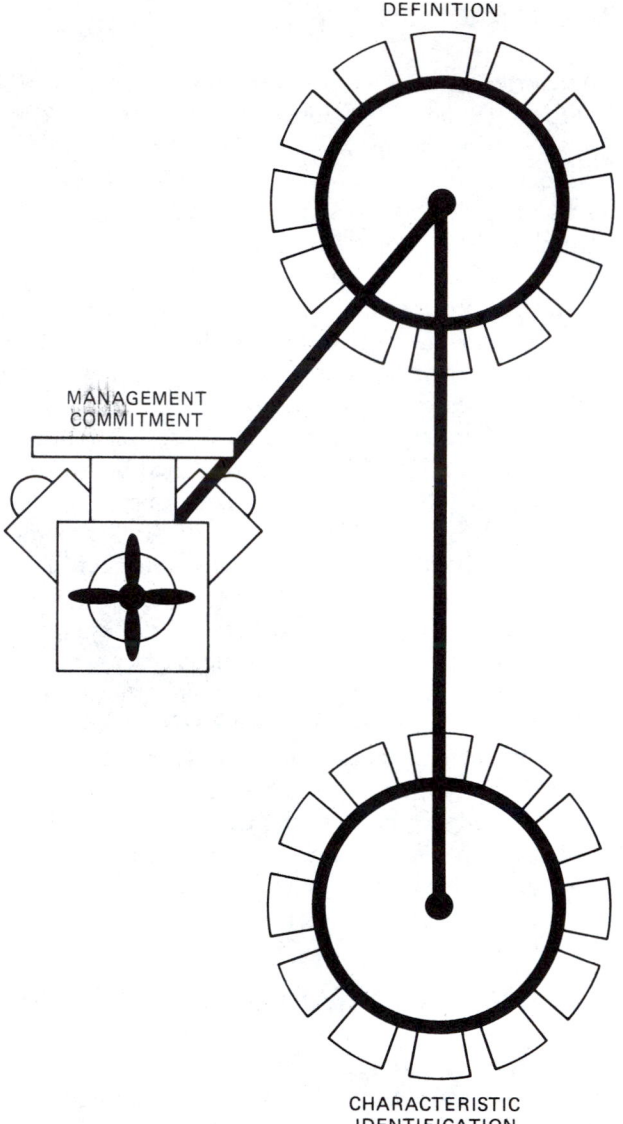

FIGURE 2-3   Process Characteristics: Before Control Is Possible Baselines must be Defined

The first is normal variation. This is present in every process and is characteristic of every process. There are no exceptions. Remember from Chapter 1, the goal of statistical process control is to reduce the amount of this type of variation that is present, eventually approaching zero variation.

The second type of variation we will call abnormal variation. This is variation that is due to unusual causes. When it does occur, there is one or, more generally, several causes. Chapter 11 will discuss variation in more detail.

A process is said to be stable when only normal variation is present. Collecting process data, when graphed according to the time the data were observed, will show the type of variation that is present. This graph is called a control chart or, more specifically, a run chart. When a process is shown to be stable, that is, **when only normal variation is present,** the process can be viewed as being **in control.**

Just because a process is in control, though, doesn't mean we are satisfied. A process that is in control can have some significant problems. One potential problem might be that the process is nowhere near the desired target value. Plotting the data by frequency of occurrence in a histogram will show this relationship. A related problem, also shown by the histogram, is that even though the process may be centered on target the normal variation present may be too large for the specifications. When this situation exists, the process is not capable of producing all of its output within the needed or desired specification limits. When a process is not capable, the percentage of output that will be produced outside the limits can be determined statistically and appropriate adjustments made until the process can be improved. One manufacturer, for example, knew its process was capable of producing to within plus or minus 12 of the target value. Since the specification required that the product be within plus or minus 10, the appropriate adjustment was short-term sorting of nonconforming material until the process could be improved. A stable process may not be a good process.

Descriptive statistics can be calculated that will summarize the location and variability of any process. These numbers, which are easily calculated, provide a common language for describing the results of monitoring a process.

Both analysis tools, the run chart and histogram (and the related descriptive statistics), are necessary for identifying what is happening to a process. Using only one can result in some missing information and missed opportunities for improvement. For example, a histogram by itself might show that a process is centered and the variability is normal. However, when a run chart for the same data is examined, a different picture may result. Look, for example, at the data summarized in Figures 2–4 and 2–5. While the histogram in Figure 2–4 shows the process is centered at the target value and between specifications, the run chart shown in Figure 2–5 indicates that the process was deteriorating as time passed. Monitoring the data as they are being collected can prevent a problem from occurring or show a problem as it starts to develop.

Comparing charts for two or more processes, monitored during the same overall time frame, can show the relationship between two characteristics. Often one characteristic, as it varies, will cause variation in another. Increasing a temperature, for instance, may increase a pressure further along in the process. Discovering these interrelationships can help to identify causes of variation. In one plant, everytime the operator made an adjustment to one input, an hour later another characteristic became unstable. By monitoring these process characteristics using the tools described, this was obvious and the excessive operator adjustment ceased.

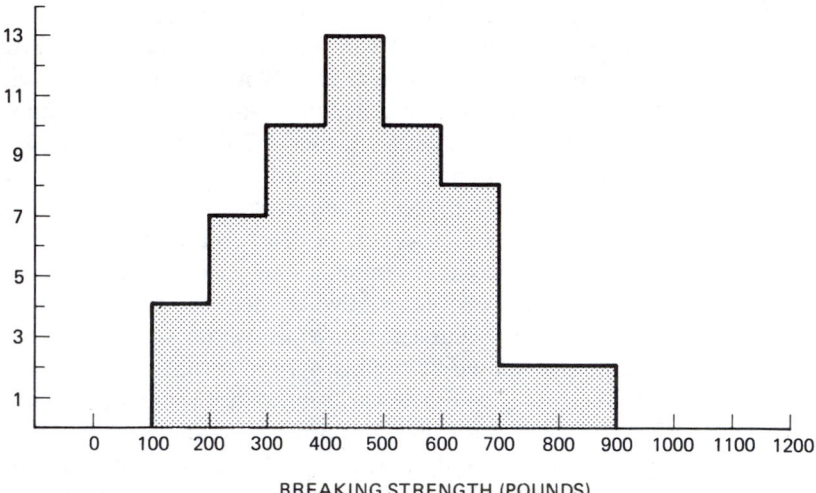

BREAKING STRENGTH (POUNDS)

FIGURE 2–4 Sample Histogram

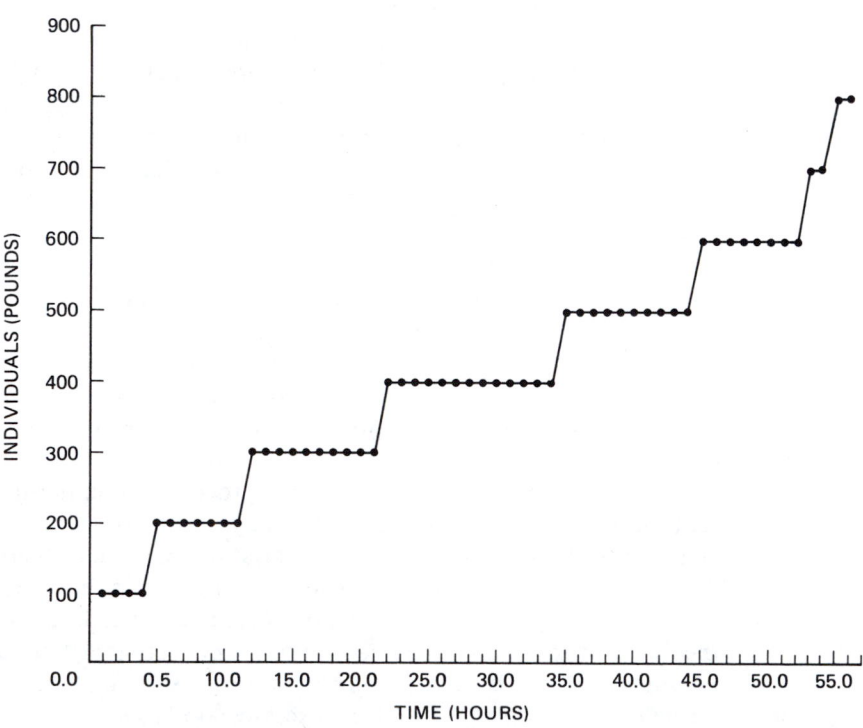

TIME (HOURS)

FIGURE 2–5 Sample Run Chart

Monitoring and controlling the process provides base-line data about the stability and variability of the process. "All systems exhibit variability. Knowing how to tell if a variation is a signal that something is wrong, or is simply part of the expected variation, distinguishes the good manager from the inept." [190: 26] Information gathered here provides information for beginning the improvement process. As such, it forms the next link in our process improvement cycle, as shown in Figure 2–6.

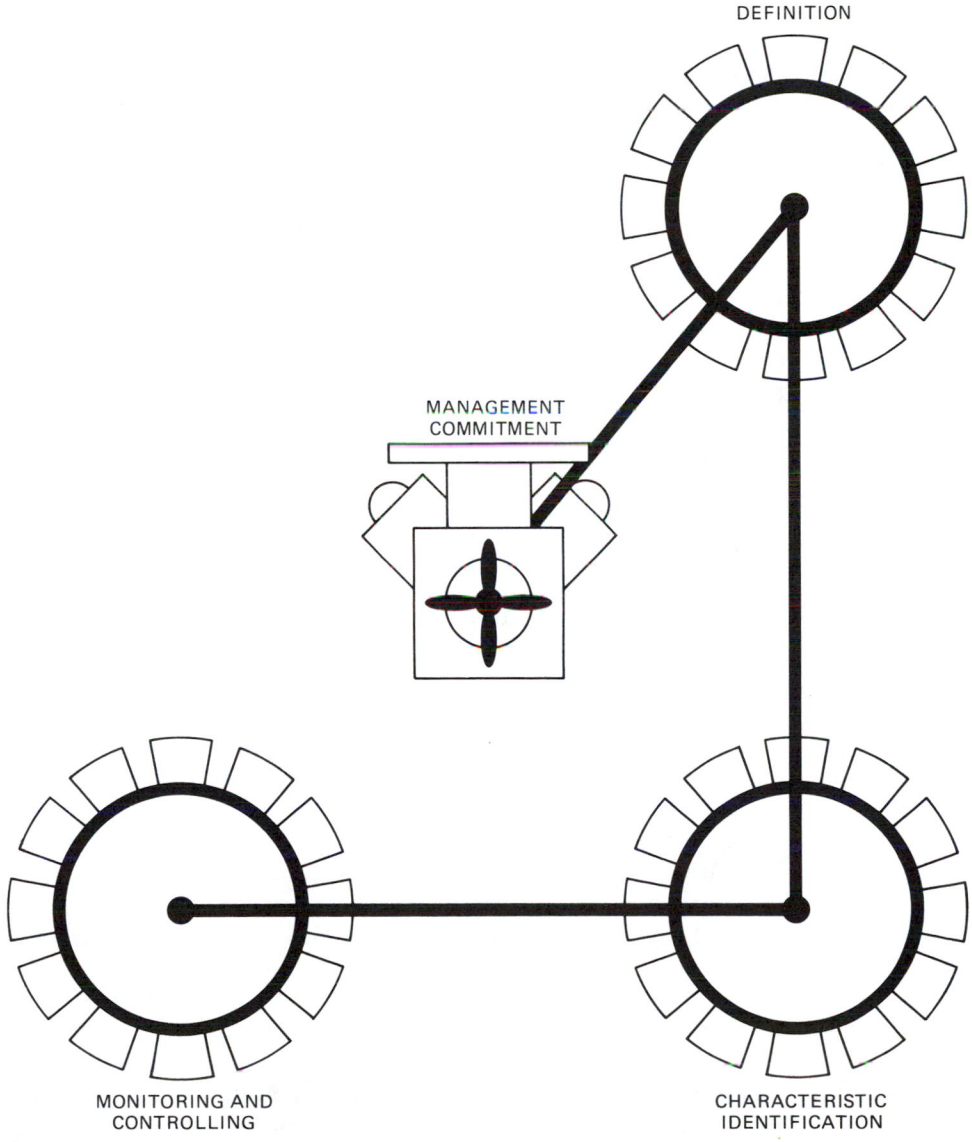

FIGURE 2–6 Process Monitoring: Establishing the Current Condition

2.6 IMPROVING THE PROCESS

When the process is monitored and found to be in control, then the improvement process can begin. As we have defined it in our statistical process control philosophy, **improving the process means reducing the variability.** This is perhaps easier said than done.

There are two facets to improving the process. First is the identification of improvements. Second is management's willingness to commit the resources to improve. Both Deming and Juran indicate that approximately 85 percent of the problems encountered can be rectified only through management action. [5: Q3] We are back to management commitment to improvement.

Sometimes quality improvements cost significant amounts of money. But if the desire to improve is genuine, if the commitment really exists, the necessary investment must be made. Many companies have verified the accuracy of this statement: *Quality improvement is an investment, not a cost.*

Example 2.6.1 Most authorities agree that the cost of quality is usually somewhere between 10 and 20 percent of sales. Assume that a company's annual sales are $10,000,000. Assume also that the company's cost of quality is 10 percent of sales, or $1,000,000. If the company spends $50,000 the next year to fix, in a preventive way, a quality problem so that the cost of quality is reduced a mere 2 percent, the cost of quality for the company is now 8 percent of sales, of $800,000. Before the investment in quality improvement was made, the cost of quality was $1,000,000. As a result of the $50,000 investment, there is a $200,000 cost savings or profit increase. The cost of fixing the process, the quality improvement, was an investment. And how many investments can return four times their value in just one year? ∎

The process monitoring tools, run charts and histograms, identify when excessive variation is present, a target is not being hit, or specifications are not being met. Then the expertise of those involved with the process has to be used to identify potential solutions, along with technical experts who have studied the process in detail. Sometimes these solutions jump out, other times they have to be coaxed out. Sometimes the people who do the process know what has to be done to improve it. Then the data collected provide the information necessary to justify the improvement. Suddenly, management is given a presentation in its own language.

Brainstorming sessions, creativity training, cause/effect diagrams, and Pareto analysis are some of the methods used to generate ideas for process improvement when the solution doesn't jump out. Generally, a group or team of employees, sometimes called an SPC team or a process improvement team, is formed to work on the problem. This team established for the problem at hand consists of people with knowledge and expertise in the area. Typically, these groups include production operators, supervisors, maintenance personnel, and technical experts. The group identifies, evaluates, and recommends solutions to these problems.

For statistical process control to work, these recommendations then have to be given serious consideration by management and, for the most part, implemented. If a team recommends purchasing a new machine, modifying an old, or changing a process, management must give the proposal the same chance one of their own would have. If the team has done its homework, then management has to be committed to following up. Sometimes this may affect the company's bottom line. It may cost "big bucks" to fix a problem, but if the desire is to improve, the investment must be made.

The analogy that began this chapter, using management commitment as the engine to drive the SPC quality improvement process, is almost complete. Figure 2–7 shows the complete improvement cycle. One time around the loop or one revolution of this cycle will result in process improvement. Each time around the circle will get us closer to our goal of increasing consistency at the target value. But we cannot stop there.

2.7 CONTINUING THE PROCESS

To become competitive and to remain competitive, we must keep this process going. It is management's job to provide the motivation and the resources to keep it moving. Imagine, if you will, the quality improvement process shown in Figure 2–7 to be a wheel. Management gets the wheel started. Management keeps it going. As this wheel rolls, it can pick up momentum. As the wheel rolls, it will continually get closer to the goal of an entirely consistent product. But, as with any rolling wheel, it can easily be tripped over. It will require a single-minded adherence to purpose to approach this goal.

Much of the remaining material in this text concerns the development and implementation of these basic elements of the statistical process control philosophy. Although it is easy to write about the need for management commitment, it is often harder to demonstrate that commitment. Suggestions will be made to help with this part of the process.

The concept of identifying the process variables must, of course, be preceded by a complete understanding of the process concept. Fundamental to this is accepting that many nonmechanical aspects of work can also be viewed as processes and can be continually improved in the same fashion. Processing paperwork, performing laboratory tests, and manufacturing paper products all can be viewed as processes with characteristics that can be monitored and controlled.

The statistics necessary for control are not necessarily difficult. The concepts and techniques will be explained and amply illustrated. The emphasis will be on reducing the process variability. Statistical process control, will achieve the improvement through reducing the variability of each process.

This reduction will result from tapping all sources of expertise about the process. Not just engineers, but everybody has ideas about improvement, including supervisors, maintenance personnel, quality assurance representatives, and production operators. Seeking out the ideas takes some skills, and these will be explained.

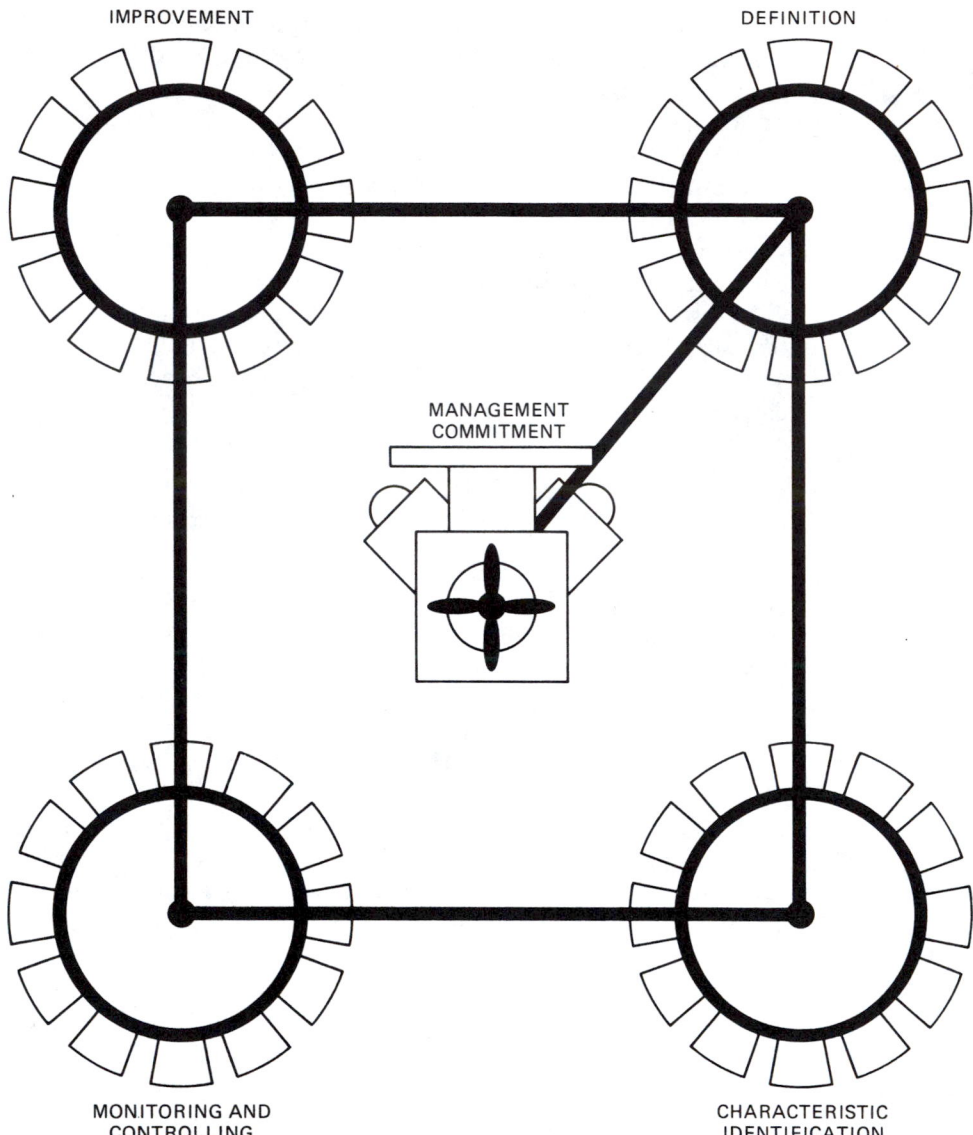

FIGURE 2–7 Process Improvement: Completing and Beginning the Cycle Again

Along with the presentation and illustration of the SPC tools, the book will also continue to emphasize the philosophy. SPC is, for many organizations, a new way of doing business. It marks a change in the corporate culture. For it to really work, the quality improvement philosophy that uses statistical process control, the entire culture and attitudes within the organization, must change.

By continually preaching, we hope that this philosophy becomes a part of the daily business life of the reader. All organizations must become committed to this new philosophy. It must extend through all parts of our society. Not only must businesses adopt this, but government and educational establishments as well. It cannot be viewed only as a quality philosophy, but rather it must be viewed as a complete operational philosophy.

2.8 CONCLUSION

This philosophy works. But it is not without some potential failure points. Robert Reid, writing in *Quality,* suggested the following Pitfalls to Successful SPC. [5: Q4] Our discussion will amplify these pitfalls.

Many organizations have tried SPC and then backed away. Some of the reasons given for backing away include:

- **Lack of top management support.** Management supported the program but was not committed. Cheerleading is fine, but not enough to keep the continuous improvement process working.

- **Lack of middle management support.** Middle managers have perhaps the most difficult adjustment to make regarding SPC. They give up authority to make changes to those closer to the process. Change is always difficult, and for many of these mid-level managers it is almost impossible. To protect their territory, they don't share the commitment that is required. *Middle managers are the most frequently overlooked personnel when SPC is installed within an organization.* Great pains are taken to win over top management and extensive training is provided to production workers. The people in the middle are neglected.

- **Commitment in only one department.** Each organization is a series of interconnected processes, with the output of one process being the input for the next. Improving just one small part of a complex system way, in fact, confuse and disrupt more than it helps. SPC must be an organization-wide commitment.

- **Haphazard approach.** Some organizations have only taken parts of the philosophy, typically the process monitoring ones. No other action is taken and the system doesn't improve, resulting in frustration. The monitoring will help, maybe as much as 15 percent, but certainly not anywhere near as much as SPC is cracked up to help.

- **Incompetent training.** The failure to train all employees in the proper use and interpretation of statistics does not give the process a chance to work.

- **Short-term evaluation.** Despite our statement that a commitment to statistical process control is forever, many organizations want these long-term improvements right now. Remember, it took the Japanese a long time. And they are still working at it.

- **No testing of incoming materials.** A process is only as good as its inputs. SPC won't turn garbage into gold.
- **Overselling.** Deming refers to "intant pudding." He says there is no instant pudding. Many people in an organization become disappointed when there are not many improvements right away. SPC is a process of making many small improvements that eventually add up to a big improvement.

Although there are pitfalls, the results can be positive. Let us end this chapter on a positive statement. Ford Motor Company, since seriously adopting statistical process control in 1980, achieved by 1984 a 59 percent reduction in consumer complaints on their new cars. [16: 21]

"Business is now so complex and difficult and the survival of firms so hazardous, in an environment increasingly unpredictable, competitive, and fraught with danger, that a company's continued existence depends on the day-to-day mobilization of every ounce of intelligence." [190: 25] That intelligence includes the use of statistical process control for improving quality.

CHAPTER 3

Quality and Productivity

There is no such thing as an acceptable level of nonconformance.   [36: 37]

Terry Sargent
Westinghouse Electric Corporation

3.1   INTRODUCTION

There is a clear relationship between quality and productivity. **As quality improves, productivity increases.** The reason is simple: as quality improves, there will be less defective or scrap material produced. More acceptable product will be produced with the same amount of resources. The output increases with no increase in the required amount of input. Producing acceptable product always costs less than producing unacceptable product.

This basic theorem is at the heart of the need for statistical process control. Relatively small increases in quality can cause dramatic increases in productivity. And producing acceptable product (read quality product) does not cost any more than producing unacceptable product. The phrase that was used, quality product, is somewhat elusive. Quality is a perception. "Because consumers do not always possess complete information about a product's attributes, they must frequently rely on indirect measures when comparing brands." [99: 41]

When a better quality product is produced, the amount of rejected and reworked material will be reduced. Although we traditionally think in terms of manufacturing, it can also apply to service industries. "All the checks issued in this country today include the magnetic ink character recognition code, known as E-13B. Yet not all these checks can be used. When the attempt is made, computers reject them as unreadable. The problem is serious enough so that the Bank Administration Institute estimates that [in] 1980, faulty checks . . . cost the country's banks a whopping $435 million a year in rework." [107: 227]

Having stated the relationship between quality and productivity, the remainder of this chapter will present two examples illustrating the principle. The first, a hypothetical situation, shows dramatically what can happen. The second is an actual case study, as reported in a nationally circulated publication.

3.2 REWORK AND PRODUCTIVITY

A small manufacturing company produces its product using a process that has 10 successive operations. The management is justifiably proud that they are operating at a level that gives them 97 percent acceptable quality at each step of the process. Furthermore, they are able to rework 90 percent of the material that does not meet specifications.

Annual sales for the finished product are a modest 100,000 units a year. Each unit sells for $11.00. Materials for each unit cost $4.50, and, for discussion's sake, we will assume that this is added equally in $0.45 increments at each of the 10 production steps. The unit labor cost is $3.50, with $0.35 being spent at each step in the process. Products that are reworked cost $4.00, on the average, for each repair.

A quick analysis might lead us to believe that the company is making a tidy profit, what with sales revenue of ($11 per unit) × (100,000 units) = $1,100,000. Material expenses of ($4.50 per unit) × (100,000 units) = $450,000 added to labor expenses of ($3.50 per unit) × (100,000) units give a total cost of $800,000. This leaves a profit of $300,000, or 27.3 percent of sales. Not a bad return on sales of $1,100,000. However, this analysis does not take into account the impact quality and rework play.

To understand the financial drain that is placed on the company, let us first look at the process. Although the process is producing 97 percent good or acceptable material at each step, it is producing 3 percent unacceptable or nonconforming material at each step as well. This means only 97 of every 100 parts produced on operation 1 will make it to operation 2. Similarly, only 97 percent of those will survive for operation 3. Carrying this through all 10 operations means the production will be as shown in Table 3–1.

Fewer than 74 units will be available for sale for every 100 units started. Under these conditions, sales will not be 100,000 units, but rather 73,740. With this sales level, the revenue will only be $811,140 at the $11 per unit selling price. With total costs still at $800,000 (presuming the defects are found in the typical final inspection step), the $11,140 profit is not nearly as enticing, providing only a 1.39 percent return on the sales dollar. It would be more profitable for the organization to put the money in a savings account.

Obviously, the company should do something. There are three options that readily come to mind. In option 1, additional units can be produced to drive sales back up to 100,000 units. In option 2, defective units can be reworked, and then sold. The third option involves improving the quality performance at each step of the process. Let's examine the implications of each.

TABLE 3-1
Cumulative Impact of 3 Percent Defective Material

Operation	Units/100 Surviving after Processing
1	97.00
2	94.09
3	91.27
4	88.53
5	85.87
6	83.30
7	80.80
8	78.37
9	76.02
10	73.74

Option 1. To increase the final production of acceptable product up to the desired level of 100,000 units, the production at each succeeding step must reflect the 3 percent loss due to quality problems. Thus, to have 100,000 acceptable units after operation 10, we must have more than that available for the operation. Specifically, the 100,000 units that are required represent 97 percent of the product entering that step. This can be expressed using the simple algebraic relationship

$$100,000 = 0.97X_{10}$$

where X_{10} is the number of units required at the beginning of operation 10. Solving this equation for X results in the value of $X = 103,093$. To account for the anticipated 3 percent loss of product, 103,093 units must enter operation 10.

This means there must be 103,093 units available after operation 9. Similar math yields the result

$$103,093 = 0.97X_9$$

with $X_9 = 106,282$. Table 3-2 lists all the values for the 10 operations.

TABLE 3-2
Material Required at Each Operation to Guarantee 100,000 Available after Last Operation, 3 Percent Defective Material

Operation	Units Required Entering Operation
10	103,093
9	106,282
8	109,569
7	112,569
6	116,452
5	120,054
4	123,767
3	127,595
2	131,542
1	135,611

By processing more units at each operation, the organization incurs more material cost and more labor costs. The additional costs are shown in Table 3-3. As indicated in the table, the total cost for 100,000 acceptable (good, conforming) units is $949,538.55. The 100,000 units bring in $1,100,000 and the resulting profit is $150,461.35, or 13.7 percent of sales.

Option 2. Remembering that 90 percent of the defective material can be reworked, at a cost of $4.00 per unit per rework, the following analysis results. With 3 percent defective at each step of the process, only 73,740 good units, or 26,260 defective units, were produced. If 90 percent of these could be repaired or reworked at each step at the $4.00 per unit per operation cost, then Table 3-4 shows the available production after each step. The rework cost will be

$$(\$4.00)(26,636) = \$106,544$$

Total revenue will be based on the 91,771 good units. At $11 per unit, these will bring in a total of $1,009,481. Total cost will be the original $800,000 plus the rework cost of $106,544, for a total of $906,544. Profit will be $102,973, or 10.2 percent of sales.

Thus far, both options 1 and 2 provided an increase in both actual dollars and the percentage return as a function of sales. The third alternative is to improve the quality at each step of the process. While SPC can bring dramatic improvements, for the sake of this example, let's not get greedy. A small improvement in quality, say 2 percent, can have a dramatic impact on overall performance. Let us assume, for this example, that the cost of this improvement is a $25,000 investment by management in improving part of the process, perhaps by sponsoring an SPC training course.

Option 3. Increasing the quality 2 percent at each step of the process will result in a significant increase in the quantity of acceptable product produced by

TABLE 3-3
Additional Material and Labor Costs to Guarantee 100,000 Sales, 3 Percent Defective Material

Operation	Material Cost	Labor Cost	Total Cost
10	$46,391.85	$36,082.55	$ 82,474.40
9	47,826.90	37,198.70	85,025.60
8	49,306.05	38,349.15	87,655.20
7	50,831.10	39,535.30	90,366.40
6	52,403.40	40,758.20	93,161.60
5	54,024.30	42,018.90	96,043.20
4	55,695.15	43,318.45	99,013.60
3	57,417.90	44,658.25	102,076.15
2	59,193.90	46,039.70	105,233.60
1	61,024.95	47,463.85	108,488.80
			$949,538.55

TABLE 3–4
Material Available after Rework, 3 Percent Defective Material

Operation	Number Entering	Defectives	No. Reworked	Available
10	92063	2919	2627	91771
9	97626	2928	2635	92063
8	97920	2937	2643	97626
7	98215	2946	2651	97920
6	98510	2955	2660	98215
5	98806	2964	2668	98510
4	99103	2973	2676	98806
3	99401	2982	2684	99103
2	99700	2991	2692	99401
1	100000	3000	2700	99700
			26636	

the process. Table 3–5 tabulates these numbers. Output will be 90,440 units, yielding a revenue, at the $11 per unit selling price, of $994,840. The materials and labor cost is still $800,000, and the cost of improving the process is $25,000, for a total cost of $825,000. The $169,840 profit represents a 17.1 percent return on sales. This is the best yet.

If 90 percent of the defects can still be repaired, at the same $4 per unit, the number offered for sale will be increased by $(0.9)(100,000 - 90,440) = 8,604$ to a total of 99,044. This would increase revenue to $1,089,484 and cost to $859,416. The resulting profit of $230,068 represents a return of 21.1 percent of sales.

Improving process quality at each step of the operation yields dramatic improvements in the productivity, and, most importantly, the bottom line reflects the improvement. For products that have more dependent operations than those illustrated in this example, the result are more dramatic. Table 3–6 illustrates the net quality for a number of different combinations of sequential operations and quality levels.

TABLE 3–5
Impact of 1 Percent Defective Material

Operation	Parts per 100 Surviving after Processing
1	99.00
2	98.01
3	97.03
4	96.06
5	95.10
6	94.15
7	93.20
8	92.27
9	91.35
10	90.44

TABLE 3–6
Final Product Quality, Percent Acceptable Available

No. of Operations	Quality at Each Successive Operation (%)					
	80	*90*	*95*	*99*	*99.9*	*99.99*
5	32.76	59.05	77.38	95.10	99.50	99.95
10	10.73	34.87	59.87	90.44	99.00	99.90
15	3.52	20.59	46.33	86.00	98.51	99.85
20	1.15	12.16	35.85	81.79	98.02	99.80
25	0.37	7.18	27.74	77.78	97.53	99.75
50	0.00	0.52	7.69	60.50	95.12	99.50
100	0.00	0.00	0.59	36.60	90.48	99.00

Theoretically, it seems to work. An increase in quality results in an increase in productivity. The following example, reprinted with permission of *Quality Progress,* shows that quality improvement is a natural partner to cost reduction and productivity improvement.

3.3 QUALITY + PRODUCTIVITY + COST = PROFIT

QUALITY + PRODUCTIVITY + COST = PROFIT*

Quality improvement is a natural partner to cost reduction and productivity improvements, a case history shows.

Harry E. Williams

Early in 1981, the management of Stacoswitch concluded that the company needed a modern program to improve product quality in order to meet current market conditions and to assure continued growth for the company.

But before any company can launch a program to improve productivity and quality, or lower its costs, it must arrive at a clear definition of what each of thse terms means, and how they will be measured, in order to assure maximum cooperation. Quality, if thought of as just good or bad, would provide very little to be measured in specific numerical terms. Therefore, management defined quality as "conformance to the requirements." This approach allowed the company to make numerical measurements of progress and enabled it to track variances and plot overall trends. The cost of quality was reduced to one set of variables called "quality costs." The company measured the quality effort in terms of what "conformance to the requirements" really cost; to put it another way, the company tried to determine the cost of doing things wrong.

Productivity measurements offered another type of challenge. A gross measure of "sales per employee" might seem reasonable until you examine the effect of a price increase or other data, such as employee terminations. Therefore, management adopted two different

*Reprinted with permission of the American Society for Quality Control.

measurements: the number of units or end items produced in each direct labor hour; and the value of sales for each direct labor hour worked.

Costs were evaluated using the total costs to produce and deliver an average-size lot of end items that were all similar in configuration and in performance requirements. Short or long runs (large or small lot sizes) were carefully monitored: the smaller lot sizes of parts and materials can cause some cost increases, as well as an excessive number of set ups; larger lots (greater-than-standard lot sizes) might seem to have lower run costs than average lots.

After spending a considerable amount of time gathering base-line data, we saw that if any dramatic improvements were to be made at the profit line, three programs had to be developed and implemented simultaneously: productivity improvement, quality improvement, and cost reduction.

The goal of the quality improvement program was to re-educate supervisors, managers, and lead personnel about the importance of manufacturing parts, subassemblies, and deliverable end items in accordance with the requirements: engineering drawings and specifications. We started a department supervisor who had the fewest number of rejections. Supervisors had all received badges that read, "We do it right or we don't do it at all"; supervisors with

ACCEPTANCE RATE TRENDS
(PERCENT ACCEPTED)

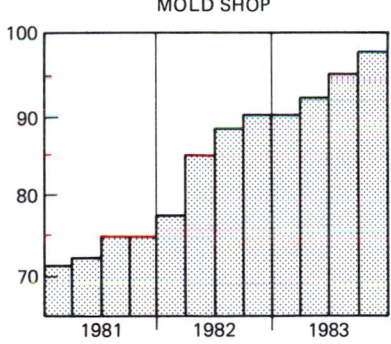

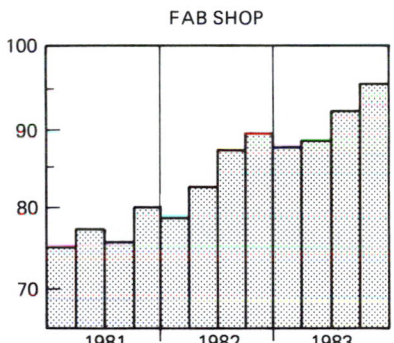

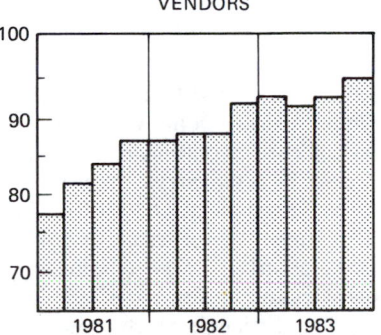

the lowest number of rejections received gold stars for their badges. Supervisors soon took pride in being able to achieve the fewest number of rejections, and requests for refurbished tooling, drawing changes, and capital equipment increased notably.

The "let's do it right the first time" attitude was very contagious, and once the manufacturing supervisors saw the relationships of quality, productivity, and costs, we immediately observed positive changes.

We took the same approach with suppliers, except that in this case, each one was invited to discuss the unnecessary costs to both parties when a rejection occurred in receiving inspection. What we learned from these discussions was invaluable.

The yields increased from each manufacturing department, and often 100% acceptance was achieved. Vendors' rejection rates fell, as did customer returns. As the cost of quality continued steadily downward, a portion of these costs could now be channeled into prevention techniques in order to avoid known pitfalls in the manufacturing process. The prevention of variances is cost effective and forms an essential element in a quality improvement program.

We began our cost reduction program at the same time as we began our quality improvement efforts. We started by investigating the areas of highest cost as determined by the cost collection system in effect at the time. Care was taken to *avoid* tampering with the design of the parts or final assembly. We zeroed in on tooling improvements, handling methods, the flow of materials, tumbling and trimming costs, and the overall working environment of the operators performing all of the manufacturing activities.

Our products use many injection-molded parts and stamping as an integral portion of their design. For this reason, we have developed extensive capabilities in plastic injection-molding equipment and its associated tooling. In addition, various sizes of punch presses and precision dies are used to support material requirements and to manufacture short-run, complex parts.

The mold shop increased its output by 17% and during the same period reduced direct labor costs by 50%. The refurbishment and modification of molds to run automatically, rather than with an operator in attendance, was one major factor. The need to trim parts was also reduced by 60%. Acceptance rates were maintained at 98% to 100%.

The fab shop (machine shop) followed the same policies as the mold shop and kept the punch-press dies and equipment in tip-top condition. Periodic part inspections and preventive maintenance for tooling and equipment resulted in a 21% increase in output, with a 29% reduction in direct labor costs. The acceptance rates averaged in excess of 96%.

The assembly department increased unit output by 14% and achieved a reduction in personnel of 31%. Final inspection costs were also reduced because the responsibility for conformance (in addition to schedule and cost) was vested in the operator performing the work, not the inspector.

During the same period that these accomplishments were being achieved, the need for overtime diminished to a point where it is almost nonexistent. A reduction in overtime costs of 91% was achieved as output, confidence, and pride steadily increased.

The increases in productivity were the result of reducing operating costs, supplying the proper tools and equipment, and providing an unmistakable understanding of what was expected in department performance. It is very important to define exactly what is expected from the manufacturing supervisors, not in terms of job descriptions and job specifications (we have these and use them), but in simple everyday language. Our company's expectations from an equilateral triangle which shows attitude, attendance, and ability in equal balance.

QUALITY, COSTS, AND PROFITS
GROSS PROFIT TRENDS

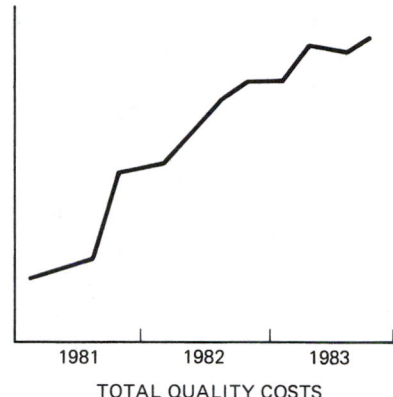

TOTAL QUALITY COSTS

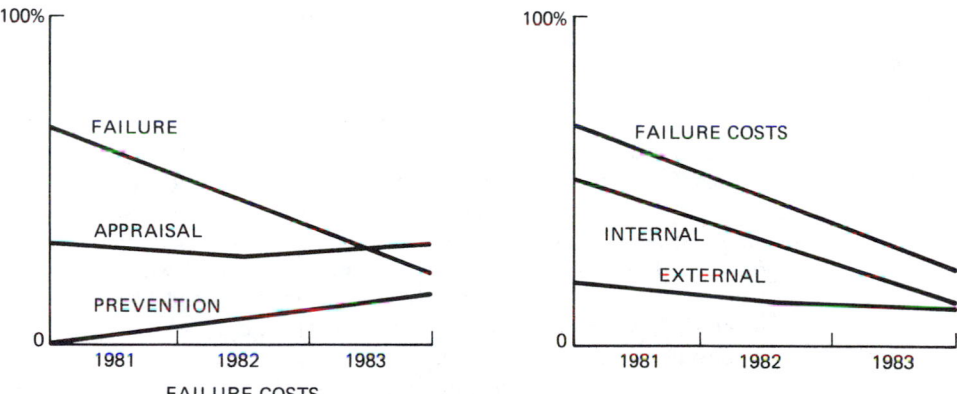

The employee with the greatest ability is of little value if he or she won't willingly support the department (and company) in achieving its goals, and of course, if he or she is absent.

Furthermore the message that quality, cost, and schedule are specific, measurable performance requirements, and are to be in equal balance for maximum effectiveness, must be clearly established. We applied that principle first to our suppliers, and then took the message to our supervisors. The lowest cost item is of little value if the item does not meet the requirements, and if the item is not available when needed. The most expensive item is not always the best; the cheapest item may not cost the least.

Finally, we found that morale had a strong influence on productivity. While we were carrying out programs to increase quality and productivity and to reduce costs, the maintenance department was also busy painting work and office areas, improving the lighting, installing air conditioners, and covering the work benches with white formica. The shops were laid out more efficiently, and the normal flow of materials was revised so that material flowed in a straight progression rather than crisscrossing several times. New furniture was acquired for the employees' lunchroom and the assembly departments, the yards were cleaned up, and better offices were constructed where needed. Several reorganizations were also accomplished; each recognized an outstanding performer. As the plant output increased, the rejection rates decreased, and the overall plant improvements became more apparent. The entire company's performance improved almost in direct proportion.

Our emphasis on quality, productivity, and costs produced impressive results.

- The number of personnel in the eleven operations departments was reduced by over 30% through attrition and transfer.
- The value of shipments or sales was increased by 36%.
- Manufacturing-caused scrap was reduced to almost zero—about 0.1%.
- Quality costs were reduced by 21% in the second year, and by an additional 13% in the third year.
- The productivity measurements showed an increase of 27% in "sales by direct labor hour," and an 8% increase in "unit output by direct labor hour."
- The gross profits rose by 124%; significantly, our managers and supervisors participated in the profit.

The other benefits that accompanied these major gains were also noteworthy. They include: reduced employee turnover and absenteeism; fewer engineering hours for support time to manufacturing; increased cross-training of operators and lead personnel; improved equipment utilization and tooling accountability; fewer "setups" and reworks during manufacturing runs; better vendor relations and improved vendor delivery and quality; increased cash flow and decreased loans; fewer part shortages and less "workaround" time; reduced inventory and better part accountability, less factory scrap and fewer negative variances in manufacturing; fewer department disputes and operating problems; reduced lead time for deliveries to customers; better customer service as a result of being on schedule.

Significant gains are possible in the areas of quality, productivity, and costs when every employee knows how and why these gains will be achieved. Each one, however, must understand his or her role and be rewarded accordingly as the improvements become a reality.

3.4 CONCLUSION

As our theorem stated, productivity increases as quality improves, and the examples verified that there is a direct relationship between quality and productivity. Robert Anderson, Chairman of Rockwell International, drew the best conclusion possible. "It's just a direct link: If the quality of the product is right, the rest of the plant is running well. People are motivated, the customer is happy, there is not a lot of scrap, there is not a lot of rework—the plant is running the way it ought to run." [29: 16]

EXERCISES

Use the following data to answer the indicated questions. A small manufacturing plant has four sequential operations. The quality level, in terms of percentage defective at each operation, is 4 percent. Shown in the table is the unit labor and material cost. Eighty percent of the defective material produced by this plant can be reworked at a cost of $22.00 per unit per rework operation. The company would like to sell 50,000 units a year. The suggested selling price of the unit is $48.00. The cost of improving the quality of the process from 4 to 2 percent defective is $50,000, and the cost of improving the quality of the process from 4 to 1 percent defective is $125,000.

Step	Labor Cost	Material Cost
1	$3.00	$5.00
2	2.00	5.00
3	1.00	2.00
4	4.00	2.00

1. Under current conditions, what percentage of sales is "profit" if no rework is performed?

2. Under current conditions, what percentage of sales will profit be if rework is performed?

3. If the quality is improved to 2 percent defective and no rework is performed, what percentage of sales will profit be?

4. If the quality is improved to 1 percent defective and no rework is performed, what percentage of sales will profit be?

5. If the quality is improved to 2 percent defective and rework is performed what percentage of sales will profit be?

6. If the quality is improved to 1 percent defective and rework is performed, what percentage of sales will profit be?

CHAPTER 4

Process Orientation

Our program has become much more prevention intensive—not inspection intensive. It's become much more planning—and process intensive as opposed to product intensive.   [54: 39]

Paul Wondrasch
AT&T

4.1 INTRODUCTION

As the tool for our quality improvement philosophy, statistical process control was carefully selected. All three words have important meaning. In this chapter we will look at process as it applies to SPC and continuous quality improvement.

It is a basic principle of SPC that all aspects of a business can be viewed as a process. Successful companies, such as IBM, have placed their quality improvement efforts on the process. According to Edward Kane of their corporate staff, "Quality focus on the business process refers to the quality effort to improve the effectiveness, efficiency, and adaptability of those business processes—complex, cross-functional processes typified by few measurements and unknown limits." [10: 25]

The term process, as used here, will be defined as a transformation. There are many kinds of processes: changing aluminum into aircraft parts, changing plastic pellets into plastic foam cups, changing customer needs into specific requirements, changing patients' blood into information to aid an M.D. in diagnosing the condition, order entry, billing, personnel data systems, inventory control, production control, procurement, and so on. Every activity in each organization can be viewed as being a process.

Some of the processes listed are simple. Some are complex. All have four common elements.

First are inputs. These can be raw materials, words, or even human blood. Second is the transformation or action that is performed on these inputs. This "magic" can be a forming operation, an encoding operation, an interpreting action, or anything that will alter the input. The third element is the output. This is what results after the transformation. Outputs can be finished products that are ready to use or, more likely, outputs are inputs to the next process.

The fourth characteristic of a process is one of extreme importance.

> Of prime importance . . . is an *owner*. In processes that cross several departments, the owner is essentially a middle manager—the person accountable for achieving the end result of the series of operations. The owner is fully responsible for yield, cost, and quality as well as schedule. In addition, he or she has to balance the process to the targets set on these characteristics. [108: 303]

In manufacturing organizations the ownership is usually clearly defined. In the service sector this really needs work.

Figure 4–1 illustrates a generic process.

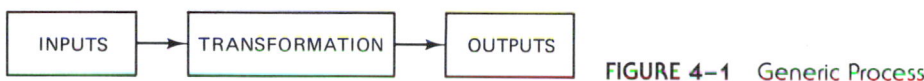

FIGURE 4–1 Generic Process

Statistical process control encourages us to view all activities as process. These processes are the smallest components or transformations that we can define. When all the processes of an organization are linked together, they form a large-scale or extended process.

For instance, a company such as Lockheed or Boeing may describe their processes as making airplanes. Extended inputs would be customer specifications. The transformation would be airplane making. The extended output would be the airplanes. Figure 4–2 illustrates this. The process can either be that general or much more specific, such as buffing a bearing that is part of a landing gear assembly. There the input would be an unbuffed bearing, the transformation the buffing, and the output the buffed bearing. Figure 4–3 shows this.

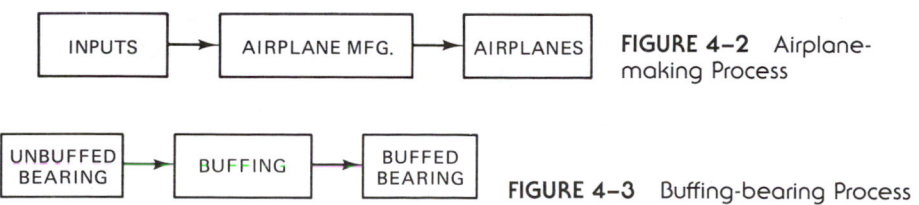

FIGURE 4–2 Airplane-making Process

FIGURE 4–3 Buffing-bearing Process

For SPC analysis and the process of continuous improvement, a process as large as the airplane-making example would be meaningless. Instead, the process must be improved at each minute transformation, such as the buffing operation. When each individual process is improved, in light of its interrelationship with all the other processes, then the overall final product produced by all the subprocesses will be of improved quality.

Before jumping too far ahead, a standardized methodology must be used to identify the inputs and outputs to the process and to describe the activities found within the process. This process orientation sets the stage for the eventual process improvement that is part of the statistical process control cycle.

4.2 PROCESS CHARACTERISTICS

We have described a process as a transformation with inputs and outputs. It is appropriate at this point to define a process a bit more precisely. We will do that by listing four characteristics that are necessary for a process to exist.

The first of these characteristics is that the inputs be measurable. Whether these inputs are pounds or pressures or temperature, they should be characteristics that can be measured in some fashion. An input must be measurable to be a candidate for improvement.

Second, the process transformation must add value to the product. In some fashion, the process must add to the input. There would be no need for the process if the change did not add something to the input. For example, removing metal burrs from a bearing make the bearing more valuable, as does encoding checks so that they can be electronically processed at a later step in the process.

The third characteristic of a process is that the outputs of the process be measurable. The output of one process serves as the input for the next. As with the inputs, if the outputs cannot be measured, then they cannot be controlled and improved. The deburred bearing should have a smoother surface, a characteristic that is definitely measurable.

The fourth characteristic that defines a process is that the process should be an activity that is repeated. For process characteristics to be measured, controlled, and improved, the process must occur on a "regular" basis. With the goal of reducing process variability, we have to direct our efforts toward those events that have variability that can be measured, controlled, and reduced. One-time activities are not suitable candidates for the effort involved since there will be no performance history nor future to be concerned with.

The point at which the inputs begin and the point at which the outputs end must be clearly defined. Then ownership of the process can be more easily established.

The key to continuous improvement, though, is the input to the process. When we reduce the variability of the inputs, we will automatically reduce the variability of the outputs. Less variability (around the target) will lead to better quality. Therefore, we will look in more detail at the inputs to the process.

4.3 PROCESS INPUTS

Initially, we will describe generic processes. Later, via examples, we will illustrate processes with more specific details. The generic process has five general classifications of inputs. These are people, equipment, material, procedures, and environment.

People, or personnel, are the trained and qualified operators of the process. They can be machine operators, skilled crafts people, or mere button pushers. The key words used to describe people are trained and qualified. For a process to perform properly and be a candidate for improvement, the people "doing" the process have to know what they are doing and be able to "do it" as it should be done. A key part of the people input is the training that the workers receive. This should be ongoing training that focuses not only on job skills, but on SPC and other problem-solving and developmental areas as well.

Equipment is the hardware or machines required for the transformation. It can be a sophisticated, computer-assisted machine, or it can be a complex processing station such as a plastic extrusion machine, or it can be as simple as a sewing machine or a typewriter or even a hand tool. A key word to remember regarding the equipment is that it should be appropriate for the transformation process. Using pliers is inappropriate for fastening a nut when a wrench would be a better choice.

Material is whatever it is that will be transformed by the process. It is also the output of the preceding process. Material can be completely raw material, such as the sand that is used to make glass, or it can be a travel form awaiting a supervisor's approval, or it can be two subassemblies awaiting assembly into a finished product.

Procedures are the methods followed during the transformation. They are the steps involved in taking the input and transforming it into the desired output. The method should be current and well defined and used by all the personnel who are inputs to the process. A key to the procedures input is consistency. The same method should be used by all the people all the time. To use an industrial engineering phrase, the method should be standardized, and, to use another IE term, it should be the "best" method.

The final input is the environment. This is a broad enough term to include just about everything else, including temperature, humidity, airflow, noise, vibration, ambience, and anything else we would like to add to the listing. This can be quite important. As one case study will show, a critical input to the process involved the temperature of a raw material. By controlling the temperature of that material, the overall variability of the product declined and the quality improved. "Unless we better control the environment in which the machines and people work, much of the data coming from the typical shop environment could be very misleading." [63: 120]

The rest of the process diagrams within this chapter will show the process inputs augmented by people, equipment, material, procedures, and environment.

4.4 THE TRADITIONAL QUALITY IMPROVEMENT PROCESS _____

Now that we have a grasp for what a process is, it is time to see how it relates to statistical process control. We have mentioned a number of times that we improve quality by reducing variability about the target. At least that is what we stated as our goal.

But that is not the way that industry has traditionally looked at quality improvement. Quality control has primarily been concerned with the outputs of the process. In many organizations the quality function is synonymous with inspection and consists only of inspection. The purpose of inspection is to find the defects *after* they have been produced. Inspectors are considered to be doing their job properly only if they find defects.

When defects are found, action is taken on the product, either via the reject route, where in effect the inspector says ''Gottcha!'', or via the rework route. In both instances the action is after the fact. The typical result of this type of quality process is that the management says, ''You have too many rejects, don't let it happen anymore.'' The people responsible for producing the rejects typically get into trouble. Management blames the workers for producing the defects. The attitude is one of ''if you did the job right you wouldn't make any mistakes.'' This sounds logical, but there are many times when even a properly performed job is not acceptable. Thus, when the inspectors find the defects, they are complimented, while those who produced the defects, for whatever reasons, are in the proverbial dog house. Quality control has played the role of the policeman. Figure 4–4 shows this traditional quality improvement process. (Chapter 18 will discuss process capability and the operator's responsibility for defects.) Note the closed loop of inspection, defect detection, and action on the product. **Success for this system is finding defects.**

Inspection doesn't necessarily find all the defects. No inspection system is 100 percent foolproof. Sometimes the organization that has produced the product does not find all the nonconforming material. When that occurs the customer often finds the defect via his inspection process. The customer uses resources to find defects that should not be present.

The customer, as policeman, might be happy, though. At least he knows that his inspection system is working. It is indeed catching the defects that the vendor is trying to slip by. Finding the defects just confirms what the customer already thinks about the vendor.

Figure 4–5 shows this traditional quality improvement process. Note the closed loop of inspection, defect detection, and action on the product. **Success for this system is finding defects.** And not even the customer's inspection will be 100 percent effective. Some nonconforming material will enter the customer's process as defective material.

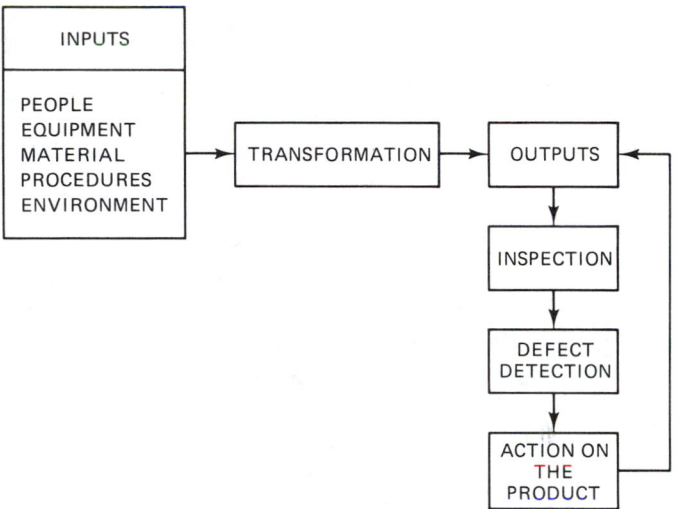

FIGURE 4–4   Traditional QC Process with In-House Defect Detection

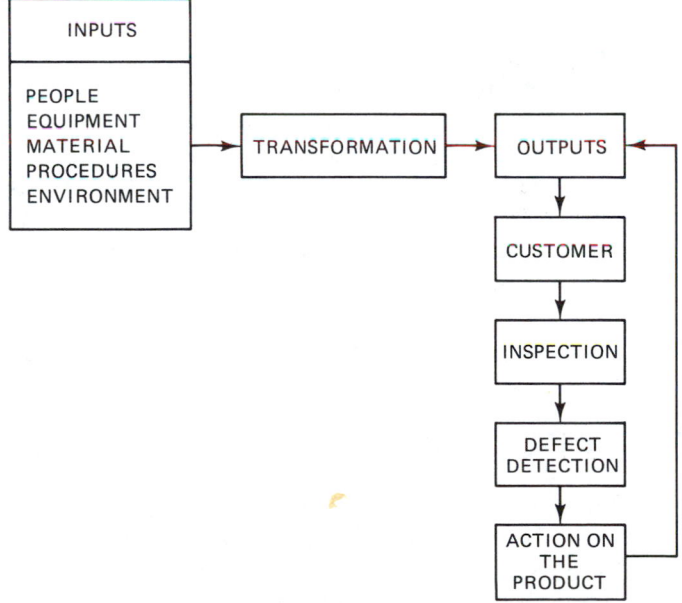

FIGURE 4–5   Traditional QC Process with Customer Defect Detection

4.5 PROCESS CONTROL OF QUALITY

The traditional method of controlling quality, the policeman's role, sets up the closed loop of action only on the product and only after the fact. Process control of quality approaches quality from the **prevention** orientation, not the detection mode. SPC views the role of quality as being before the fact. Our goal is to prevent the defect from being produced. Then there will be no need to inspect for it afterward, because it won't exist. Every part of the process is keyed toward prevention. Actions are all designed to prevent problems from occurring.

Process control of quality begins with the inputs to the process. It begins with the people, equipment, material, procedures, and environment. As these are added to the process, they are sampled for their conformance to requirements. They are monitored not only for the conformance, but also for trends. Remember that our goal is to continually reduce the variability around the target. The information from this sampling is used, in the prevention mode, for improving the process. This improvement comes from reducing the variability of the inputs to the process and by improving the transformation process. If all the inputs to the process are nearly the same and if all the inputs to the process are performing exactly on their specified target, then the chance that the transformation will affect them all the same is increased tremendously. Figure 4–6a shows the impact of sampling on the process inputs.

Inputs, though, are not the only part of the process that is to be sampled. The transformation itself must be monitored on a regular basis. The consistency of this part of the process must be checked and variations to the target must be continuously reduced. This reduction of variation will also lead, as Figure 4–6b indicates, to process improvement.

Thus far, two-thirds of the process has been sampled, the inputs and the transformations. It is also important to monitor the outputs of the process as well. Sampling the outputs not for the purpose of defect detection, but for variation, will also lead to prevention of future defects by reducing variability. This will also lead to process improvement. Figure 4–6c completes the diagram that depicts process control of quality. Note that this is a closed loop. Improvements are always routed through the inputs to the process and the transformation act. This is where improvement occurs. Finding defects after they have been produced is not productive.

4.6 PROCESS DESCRIPTION

Thus far, we have described a process in generic terms. Naturally, all processes have inputs, transformations, and outputs. But for us to understand processes better, we have to be able to define the process in terms that can be used to aid in process improvement. Fortunately, industrial engineers have been using a flow process chart for many years to describe processes. The flow process chart uses a standard set of symbols to identify the sequence of activities that make up any process. The symbols

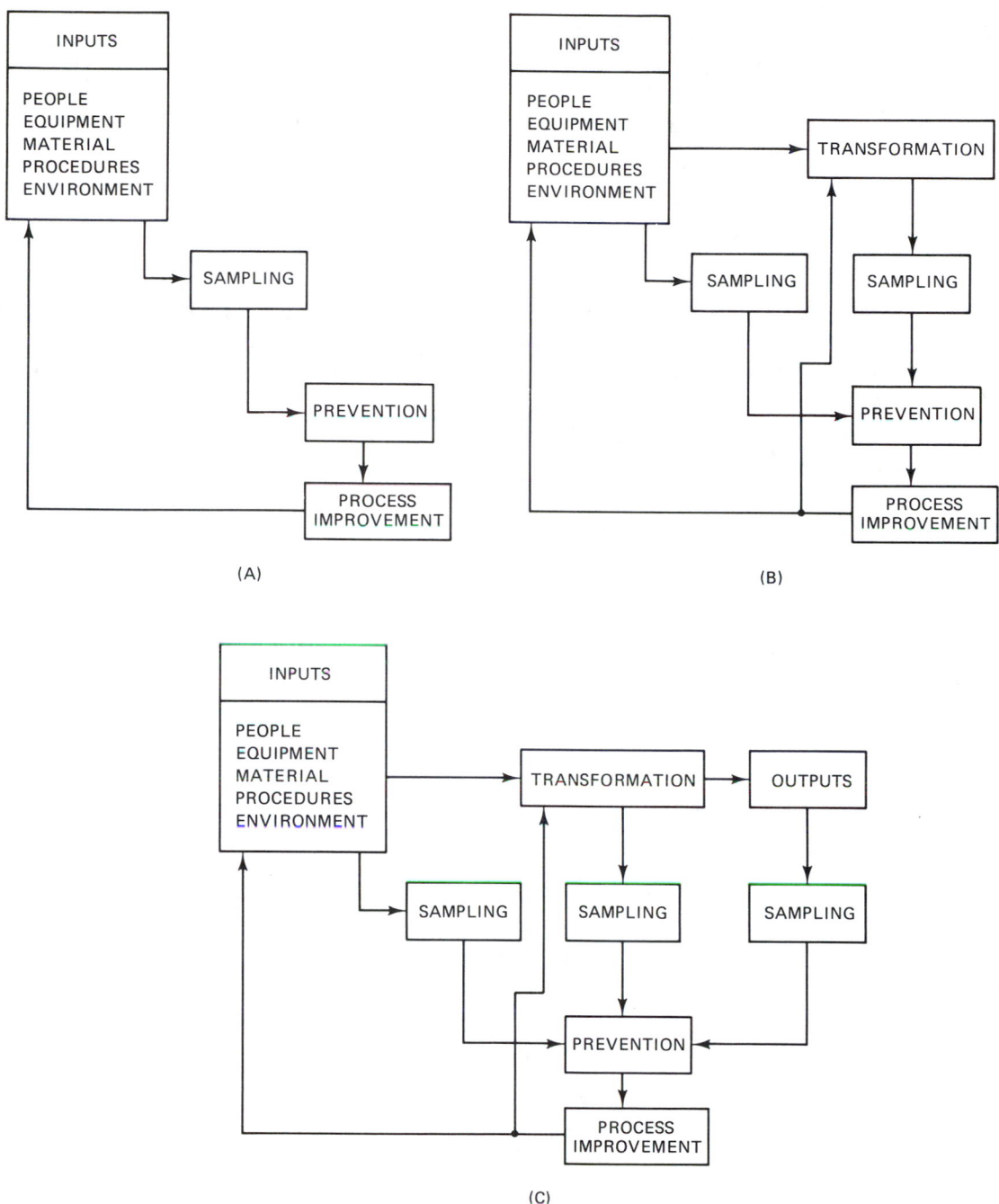

FIGURE 4–6 Process-oriented Quality: (a) Inputs; (b) Transformation; (c) Outputs

and their standard definitions are included in this section. One additional symbol is most helpful in describing processes from a quality improvement perspective and is also included in the listing. Also included will be two examples using the process flow diagram. The symbols in Figure 4–7 are defined as follows:

- The **operation** occurs when an object is changed in one or more of its characteristics. An operation may be as large as our airplane transformation, or it may be a step in the transformation. Operations can be as diverse as driving a nail, deburring a bearing, encoding a check, or approving a travel reimbursement form.

- The **transportation** occurs when an object is moved from one location to another. A transportation is not reported as a separate operation if it occurs as an integral part of an operation. Examples of transportations include moving material with lift trucks, by hoists, by people power, or electronically via computers and telephone modems.

- An **inspection** is the examination of an object for conformance with some specification. This can be a simple visual check for part ID or proper count, the reading of a temperature gauge, or the sophisticated electronic test that many of today's products must endure.

- A **delay** occurs when the next planned operation does not take place as planned. A delay can be material waiting in a queue at a work station to be processed, material waiting to be shipped after it has been processed, or paperwork waiting to be processed.

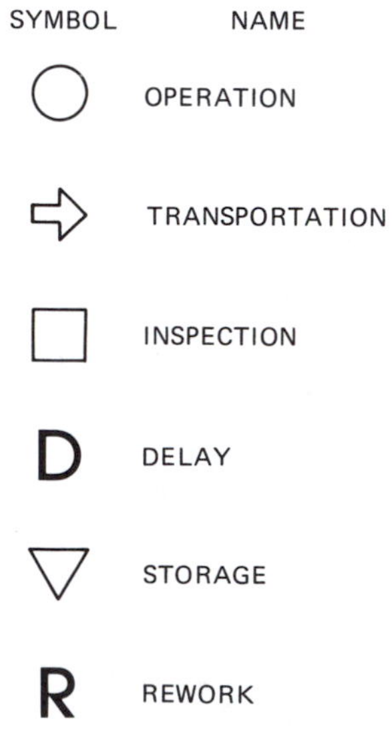

SYMBOL	NAME
◯	OPERATION
⇨	TRANSPORTATION
▢	INSPECTION
D	DELAY
▽	STORAGE
R	REWORK

FIGURE 4–7 Process Flow Symbols

- A **storage** takes place when material is kept under some type of control so that its withdrawal requires authorization. Examples of storage include bulk material in storage, finished goods in the warehouse, precious metals in a vault, or personnel records in a secure file.

- The **rework** operation occurs whenever any of the operations has to be performed over because it did not conform to standards the first time it was performed. Rework can occur after an inspection, or it can be the result of an operator noting that the process did not perform as it should have the first time.

When two or more operations occur simultaneously, the symbols are shown on top of each other. This situation is known as a **combined operation.** Typical of this instance is when an operation and an inspection occur at the same time.

The value to us of the flow process diagram is not so much in identifying the symbols, but in forcing us to list the activities that are part of the job. When we write down every step of the process, we start the process of identifying the nature of the inputs and outputs that are required to complete the process.

As we look at the following example, we will construct the flow diagram, but our analysis will focus on the inputs and outputs to the process charted.

Example 4.6.1 The first of the examples that will be used to illustrate the use of the process flow diagram will be an everyday job that many readers have probably performed many times. That is the task of waxing the family automobile. Let us first describe the process in a narrative. We will then show it as a process by identifying its inputs, the transformation, and the outputs, and, finally, we will show it in detail on the process flow diagram.

This process will begin after the car has been washed and dried. The car, ready to be waxed, is sitting in the garage waiting. The ambitious car owner, who we will call the waxer, enters the garage, locates the wax on the shelf, locates the applicator on the shelf, shakes the wax, and opens the pouring spout. Wax is then applied to the entire vehicle. After the entire car is waxed, the wax is capped, and the applicator and the wax are stored on the shelf. The waxer then checks to make sure that the wax has dried. Once this is affirmed, the waxer then takes a clean, soft rag and proceeds to rub the dried wax off the car. After this is done, she stands back to admire her work when she notices that she missed a spot. She then proceeds back to that spot and rubs the wax off the spot she missed. The waxer finishes the job by returning the soft, clean rag to storage.

While the preceding paragraph was a very short narrative, it contains sufficient information to describe the process. Then inputs to the process, in our terminology, are as follows:

Inputs

- The **people** input is our esteemed waxer.
- The **equipment** used is the wax applicator and the clean, soft rag.

- The **material** used is the wax and the car.
- The **procedures** used are not formal, but the method included applying the wax to the car, allowing it to dry, and then rubbing it off.
- The **environment** input was the garage and the controlled light and temperature conditions typically found in a garage. Most waxes caution against applying in direct sunlight and under conditions of extreme heat or extreme cold. The environment of the garage controlled against those extremes.

Transformation

- The **transformation** in this process was changing the car from a clean but unwaxed state to a waxed condition.

Outputs

- The **output** of this process is a brighter car and a better protected car. This output has added value to the car, not only in extending the life of the finish, but the intrinsic value of giving the waxer a bright car to drive around in.

This transformation certainly meets all the conditions of a process. The inputs are measurable. For example, the amount of wax applied can be measured, as can the environmental conditions, such as air temperature in the garage. The transformation adds value. A waxed car certainly has more intrinsic value than an unwaxed one. The output of the process, a brighter car and better protected car are also measurable. The entire process will undoubtedly be repeated many times, so it fits that condition for being deemed a process. And as a candidate for improvement, certainly many of the input variables can be monitored, controlled, and then improved to give more consistent results. Let us look at the inputs to the process and determine what some of the critical characteristics of these might be.

- The people input is the waxer. What characteristics must the waxer have in order to do her job properly? She must be properly trained. She must have the strength to apply the wax and rub it off. She must have the motivation to apply the wax. She must have the time to perform the process.
- Equipment used is the applicator and the wiping rag. What are the characteristics required of these inputs? Perhaps they include cleanliness, size, and availability.
- Material used includes the wax and the car itself. Characteristics of these inputs that might be necessary for the process to perform as it should include, for the wax, the quantity, consistency, prior coatings, and maybe the surface temperature would be important.
- Procedures that might be important are methods of applying the wax, i.e., in circular strokes, and methods of wiping the wax off to assure maximum lustre and protection.

- Environmental inputs include light, temperature, and humidity. These all could be critical. There are undoubtedly some limits on the temperature and humidity that make the application of wax impossible.

Our discussion is certainly not complete. It is presented merely to illustrate how the inputs are identified and then questioned to develop a list of potential critical characteristics. The same type of analysis can take place with the outputs. This information can then be used to identify those characteristics that can and or should be monitored and controlled as we work toward improving the process. Figure 4–8 shows the process flow diagram. Each operation, transportation, inspection, delay, storage, and rework is indicated by the appropriate symbol. Two points to note about the diagram. First, the operator was charted, not the car or the wax. In every diagram of this type, we must select a person or thing and chart what happens to that person or thing. Everything must be expressed using that reference point. Second, numerous opportunities are present for improving this process. It is not our intent here to show how to improve a process. We only want to learn how to use the diagram to document an existing process and to start us thinking about the nature of the inputs and outputs that are important to the process. Figure 4–9 provides a form that is useful in describing the process flow. ■

PROCESS: Car Waxing	OBJECTIVE: Waxed Car	DATE: 11-19-96
DESCRIPTION		
Locate wax on shelf		
Locate applicator on shelf		
Shake wax		
Open wax		
Vehicle waxed		
Wax closed		
Wax stored on shelf		
Applicator stored on shelf		
Check to see if wax dry		
Obtain clean dry rag		
Rub wax off		
Admire work		
Rub missed wax off		
Return rag to storage		

FIGURE 4–8 Process Flow Diagram for Example 4.6.1

Example 4.6.2 This second example of the flow process diagram shows the technique used on the installation of a quality improvement program. It is reprinted as part of this example. ■

PROCESS FLOW

NAME OF PROCESS _____

OBJECTIVE OF PROCESS _____

CHARTED BY _____ DATE _____ PAGE ___ OF ___

DESCRIPTION

FIGURE 4–9 Generic Process Flow Diagram

INTEGRATING CUSTOMER SATISFACTION INTO DAILY WORK*

James C. Walden

Customer Satisfaction

There is a great deal of talk these days about satisfying the customer, so much that one would think that the customer was once totally abandoned. At Florida Power and Light we don't feel that we have ever abandoned the customer, but these days we are thinking about the customer from a very different perspective. We have come to discover that we have several "customers" that can be broadly classified into two categories, **external** and **internal.**

The "external" customer in our case is the ratepayer and the ultimate judge of the quality of our service. We, like many other companies, are conducting extensive surveys to determine what the ratepayer values most. These surveys are becoming increasingly more significant in the policymaking process. However, from my perspective as head of the fossil power production department, our department employees do not routinely deal with the public and, therefore, can easily lose sight of their personal contribution to satisfying customer's needs.

Now that we have matured in the Quality Improvement Team cycle we have been asking ourselves the following questions. How does an organization go about getting every individual employee to sincerely embrace a **Customer Orientation** attitude? Furthermore, how can you create the environment that results in each employee personally applying the quality improvement concepts to his own everyday work? How do you transfer the use of the quality improvement concepts from Quality Teams to each individual employee? These are the questions I intend to address.

We think the answer lies in getting back to basics—people talking to people! More specifically, each employee sitting down and negotiating face to face with his next "internal" customer. So what is different about this? Don't we talk to each other? Yes, we communicate with one another but more often than we would care to admit, our focus has not always been on satisfying the needs and reasonable expectations of our internal customers. It is easy to get comfortable with what you do and forget why you are doing it. To assure that these negotiations produce the desired focus on building quality into the product we are utilizing a formalized process (Figure 1).

Quality in Daily Work

A complete explanation of the flow chart in Figure 1 is beyond the scope of this paper. However, I will give some examples of how the groundwork is being laid to assure this process is implemented in the fossil power production department.

At the department level, we are conducting routine meetings with our primary internal customers. These meetings are attended by manager-level personnel from both departments. The major difference in these meetings now is the way in which issues are discussed. The dialogue has shifted from simply solving problems to identifying those activities that are key to long term quality and then negotiating valid requirements among these managers. All the managers have been trained in the process of Figure 1.

A specific example involves one of our prime suppliers, the Power Plant Engineering Department. When we began these meetings with Engineering, we were not extremely happy with the products we were receiving. We were confident that if we could only get them to see our problems, everything would be resolved. Not surprising, they felt we were not always reasonable and we did not always give them the support they needed to turn out a quality product. With outside facilitation, we began to realize that both departments had a lot to do about the problems with which we were complaining.

The significant breakthrough came when both Departments decided to quit placing blame and started defining just what each expected out of the other. The key processes involved in producing and implementing an engineering package were broken down and the departments negotiated specific accountabilities on which they could agree and support. We found that within a specific work process, our department was frequently the supplier and Engineering was the customer. For instance, we were the supplier of valid specifications for the project. If the field people do not adequately describe the problem and all the related constraints (valid requiremnts), then it should not be a big surprise to us that the engineering package does not meet our needs. This was an application of Quality in Daily Work (QIDW). We did

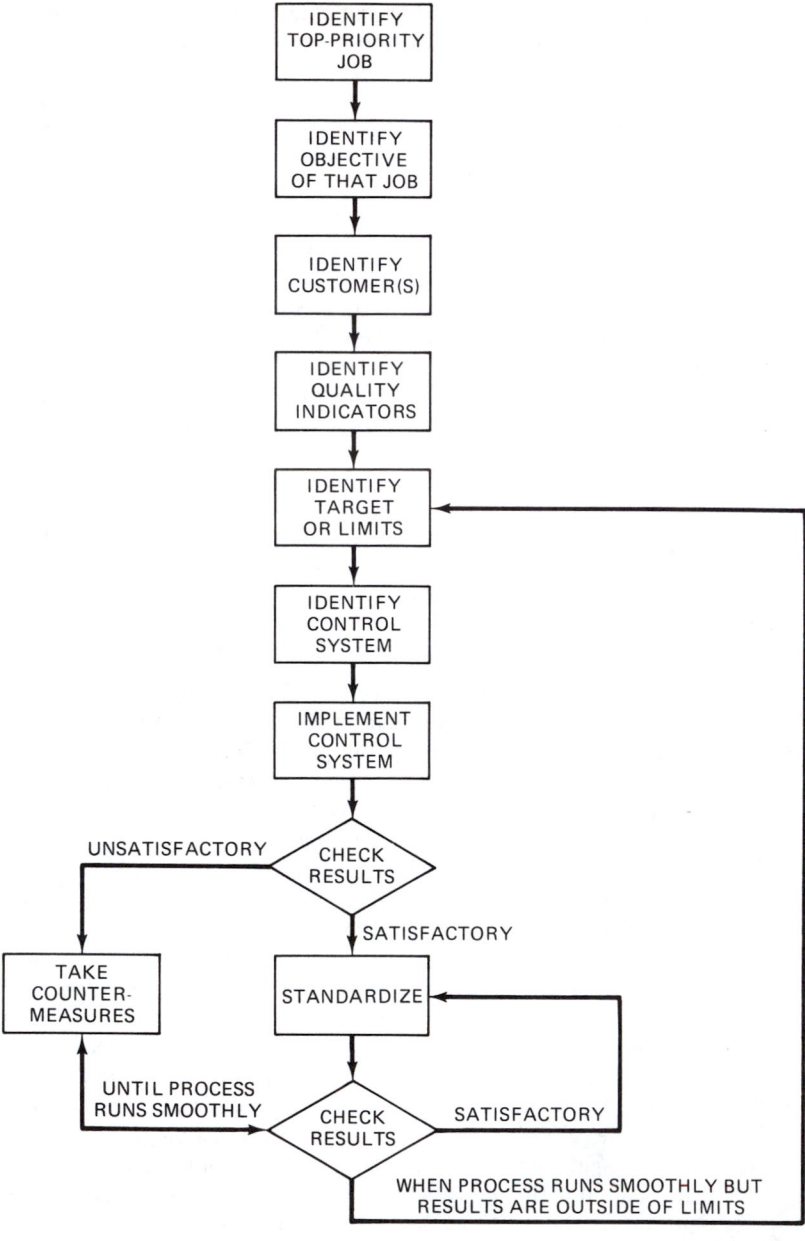

not know it by this term at the time. We learned the hard way, that to realistically and permanently change these attitudes we needed a formal process. Sitting down and talking is necessary, but it is not sufficient. Some formal process comparable to that outlined in Figure 1 is required to keep the negotiations properly focused and assure the appropriate quality improvement techniques are utilized.

Once the ice was broken at the department management level, the engineers and operating personnel began communicating with each other in a more positive and productive way. We currently have a team consisting of personnel from the Engineering Department, the Power Plants and our Power Plant Services group that are working on improving the engineering package request method. It is significant to note that these people could immediately see the benefit of the QIDW process and began conducting meetings on their own.

An example at the plant level illustrates how the individual employee is personally involved in the process. Following a training seminar, we asked the participants to identify their own products, select one they wanted to improve, and ask their primary "customer" for input. The clerks, as a group, identified that one of their products (receiving report) had an excessive error rate. Error reports from the Accounts Payable Department (their customer) indicated the receiving reports were leaving the plant with errors. The Accounts Payable clerk could not do the job of paying the vendor unless the receiving reports had all the correct information.

After studying the problem, the plant clerk contacted the Accounts Payable clerk and discussed the problem. While the Accounts Payable clerk did not want to accept any errors, she indicated that if the error rate could be cut from 4% to 1% then she would be pleased. The clerks set a realistic goal of 2% and then **committed to** correct the deficiency. The valid requirements were already documented in a company procedure so the primary task was to find out where the process was breaking down. Some of the causes found and resolved were lack of familiarity with the procedure, rushing through the report to get it out, and improperly submitted (to the clerks) source documents. Individual clerks interviewed material receivers to determine why the receiving invoices were not being completed correctly.

As a result of this effort, existing procedures have been made more usable by converting them to check lists and the affected employees have a much better understanding and appreciation of the receiving report preparation process for which they are personally responsible. The end result is that within three months the error rate was reduced to zero and has consistently been less than 1%.

You might say this is a very simplistic process, just **common sense,** and you would be correct. How far do each of your employees (management and subordinates) go to really satisfy their internal customers' needs and reasonable expectations? We have found this process to be a practical method for **implementing and standardizing practices that are common sense** but not **consistently applied.**

Why Do This?

We said at the beginning that we were searching for a way to link each employee to satisfying the external customer; to show how he relates to the corporate objectives and, more specifically, to provide the environment and the structure that supports and requires each employee to apply quality improvement techniques in their daily work. This application of the concept, "the next process is your customer," is one way for the individual to become more personally involved in improving the work process for which he has personal responsibility. It is a practical way to institutionalize the use of quality improvement techniques.

As our people begin to shift to a customer orientation focus and critically review some of their output, we see them completely eliminating many tasks that do not in any way contribute to organizational goals. For example, a participant in a Customer Orientation training class was matching each of his personal products with his primary internal customer. He discovered that he was routinely preparing a report for which there was no customer. The person and reason for the report no longer existed. However, this conscientious employee was diligently preparing, photocopying, and distributing this report that was immediately relegated to the trash can. Worse than that, some of these reports were being filed and maintained (but never read) by others. How many of your employees are engaged in efficiently producing products that do not have a customer? How many of them **know** they are producing products with the wrong specifications but are frustrated by a management system that does not encourage or allow them to make meaningful changes?

Once the customer and the employee (supplier) have agreed on the valid requirements of the product, the supplier breaks down the work process (flow charting) and isolates the most significant problem areas. We have seen that, at this stage, obsolete or inadequate procedures are often identified. In many cases a standardized written procedure does not exist for a critical step in a process and the production of a quality product relies solely on one person's memory. The QIDW process forces these "critical to quality" steps to surface so that they can be corrected and standardized.

The greatest payoff comes when the individual employee begins to take control of his own process and applies the quality improvement concepts on a daily basis. Gains from the use of complicated (and seldom used) techniques are insignificant compared with the results obtained when the individual makes a personal commitment to improve his products.

Making It Happen

The concepts I have been discussing are not new. We have received substantial counseling from many experts including Dr. Juran, Dr. Deming and the Japanese Union of Scientists and Engineers. The real challenge to all of us is how do we implement the concept in our own environments? The flow chart in Figure 1 depicts the process we are using, but how do you really turn the employees (this includes management) on to ensure successful implementation?

Laying the Groundwork. Prepare the management of that work group (plant, division, etc.). Conduct orientation sessions that reshape the concept of the customer. The extent of this orientation will depend on the depth of knowledge of these key leaders in quality concepts. Spread the orientation out and give the participants time to accept the new concepts before giving them the task of implementation. Select key management personnel to participate in the development of the final training package and involve them in the training sessions. The more stakeholders there are involved, the quicker the acceptance.

Training. The training modules that we are presently using address two main areas, **people issues** and the **basics of process control.**

The People Issues. We are asking our employees to exhibit behaviors to which they are unaccustomed. We are asking them to look at their job from a totally different perspective. Their initial reaction is "what is in it for me?" We think this is a valid question and one that must be addressed if you expect to get commitment to applying the formal process. Training modules have been developed that address:

- Win–win negotiations
- Teamwork
- Trust
- Humanizing the customer
- Effective listening

The Basics of Process Control

- Inputs/processes/outputs
- Valid requirements
- Customer/supplier relationship
- Determining wants and needs
- Quality indicators
- Basic problem solving techniques

Our Quality Improvement Teams provide a substantial knowledge base of quality improvement skills. They are an integral part of our Quality Improvement Program. Besides contributing to a teamwork environment, they provide a continuous supply of employees trained in quality improvement skills.

Pitfalls

Laying the Groundwork. We are talking about a fundamental shift in thinking about the way we approach our job. If the management behavior on the job does not complement the concepts being taught in the class, there is little hope that the concepts will become institutionalized. Not all of our managers have the same understanding and enthusiasm for what we are trying to accomplish and why. This is why we have included key management personnel in the development and delivery of the training.

Skimping on Training. We have seen a direct correlation between the level of enthusiasm by the participants and the **degree** of training. There is a significant shift in participant attitude following the win–win and the customer/supplier relationship modules of training. We have found this training very effective in generating participant interest to learn and try the concept.

We continue to get numerous complaints over new terminology and concepts. This frustration is a very real barrier to the application of the newly learned concepts. New terminology is unavoidable and only through adequate training and constant **reinforcement** have we been able to reduce this frustration. The reinforcement aspect is another reason for involving key management personnel in the training. If they do not reinforce the concepts, including the use of the terminology in routine meetings, it will not become a part of daily work.

Reaction to Criticism of Past Management Practices. The participants very quickly point out that you are asking them to do things that "management" does not practice. This is a valid point since we are all learning and practicing these new concepts at all levels in the organization. A defense of past behavior will not be accepted and a candid response is required if credibility is to be maintained. These "tests of sincerity" come very early in the training (trust exercises).

Picking the Wrong People for the Pilot. There will be many obstacles for the pilot group to overcome and this is not the time to involve someone who is looking for excuses to prove this will not work. In order to build a critical mass support for these concepts, it is essential that positive thinkers are selected for the pilot applications. These are the people who will recognize the benefit and have demonstrated from past performance that they can "make it happen" regardless of the obstacles. During the pilot, word will spread rapidly throughout the work group. These positive thinkers will be the future promoters of the concepts throughout the work unit.

Follow-up. Like anything else that is a fundamental shift in the way you do business, a lot of energy is required to reshape the work environment. This process is not something you do in **addition** to your regular work. It is the **way** you will do your work. To implement it will take a tremendous amount of energy and leadership. If you are not prepared to follow through on reshaping the work environment and you do not have the support of top management to fully implement a quality improvement program, I recommend that you do not start.

Summary

At Florida Power and Light we are reshaping the Corporate Objective setting process to conform to the customers' needs. If we truly expect to satisfy the customers' needs and be profitable, we must go beyond just writing objectives. We need a method to link each employee in the organization to the Corporate Objectives in order to meet the customers' needs. Buzzwords in a Corporate statement do not mean much to the individual in the field.

We have reclassified our customers into the categories of **external** and **internal.** By concentrating on satisfying the needs and reasonable expectations of his internal customer, each employee will eventually be linked to satisfying the external customer.

Focusing on satisfying the needs and valid requirements of the internal customer is a practical method for integrating customer satisfaction into daily work. Implementing this process is a matter of getting back to basics, people talking to people. The **process** is required to assure that quality improvement techniques are used as a framework to guide these ''negotiations.'' Through this **structured** approach, the individual is required to apply quality improvement techniques on a daily basis. This is one way to transfer the use of the quality improvement skills learned during Quality Improvement Team activity to ''on the job activities.''

Extensive training is required to implement this method. The Quality in Daily Work process is part of our Management system and requires the direct involvement of management to implement. It requires tremendous effort and leadership to successfully implement.

We think it is worth the effort and necessary, if we are to remain competitive in a rapidly changing environment.

Example 4.6.3   The process orientation fits many organizations, not just traditional manufacturing. The health-care field has what it calls the laboratory testing system. It can be viewed as a typical process with inputs, transformations, and outputs. The inputs to the laboratory testing system include doctors' clinical questions, specimens, such as blood samples, methods and technology, and people. The transformations done at labs are the tests themselves, which seek to determine the nature of the inputs. The results are varied, depending on the desired outputs. Health-care-quality professionals group the outputs into four categories.

1.   *Informational* outputs. These include the test results and their interpretation. They are used as inputs to what might be seen as the next step in the process, treatment of the patients.

2.   *Behavioral* outputs. These reflect the nature of the decision, the confidence the customer has in the results, and the resultant action.

3.   *Health effect.* Medical concepts such as morbidity, mortality, and even reduction in anxiety are possible outputs in this area.

4. *Externalities.* The impacts that the outputs of this process have regarding cost, legal liability, and even patient discomfort have to be considered.

Some of the inputs to this process are more critical than others. Some of the outputs are more critical than others. While we won't assess the criticality of them, the same type of evaluation regarding this can be used for improving this process or system. ■

4.7 CONCLUSION

The process orientation is one key to implementing the statistical process control philosophy for quality improvement. Every activity within the organization must be viewed as a process. Each process has its inputs, consisting of people, materials, methods, machines, and the environment, its transformations, and its outputs. It is critical that we remember that the output of each process is the input for the next process. The result of all these processes will be the end product or service that the organization offers.

The initial objective of SPC is to identify the critical inputs to each process and reduce the variability of those inputs about their respective target values. As time goes by, the objective is to identify every input to every process and reduce the variability of each input about its respective target value. Once this is done, the process repeats and repeats and repeats. The ultimate objective is that there be no variability for any of the inputs to any of the processes. Then a completely consistent output will result.

> An internal Ford communication dated March 3, 1983 included a quality definition that reflects our company's commitment to achieve worldwide quality leadership. This letter says, in part,
>> Employees (and suppliers) must begin to think of the quality of the processes that produce them. In this regard, we should focus on methods to reduce the variability of process output, not just meeting specifications. We need a commitment to quality . . . supported by an ongoing effort to reduce the variability within our processes. Importantly, our approach must be based on a philosophy of never ending improvement . . . [signed by D. E. Petersen, President, Ford Motor Company.] [8: 20]

As we work toward the elimination of variation in our processes, we must always remember that no process sits entirely by itself. Each process is part of an interconnected system. Chapter 5 will examine these extended relationships.

CHAPTER 5

The Entire Process

The real benefit was realized when the customer's particular requirements for processing and/or for use were identified and satisfied.   [32: 15]

Bob Kukla
National-Standard Company

5.1   INTRODUCTION

In Chapter 4, we described a process. All processes have inputs, transformations, and outputs. We also indicated that every task, whether it was glass making, order processing, or even waxing a car, could be viewed as a process. A third major point we made was that the entire business system could be viewed as a series of related processes. Even if these individual processes were not physically close, they were closely interrelated. **The output for one process is the input for the next.** No process stands by itself.

This chapter is called The Entire Process. For discussion's sake, and to provide a framework for building this concept, we will first discuss those processes that are internal to the company. As the role of each is discussed, remember that they are linked to each other via the output/input relationship. The figures presented will show this, but it is the key concept that we want to remember from this chapter. Chapter 6 will discuss defining those outputs and inputs.

5.2   INTERNAL PROCESS

Every organization views itself as having a primary mission, the major product or service produced by that organization. Whether that mission is to produce airplanes, evaluate blood samples, or provide statistical training, that is what we will refer to as the basic process. This mission, or process, requires that the organization take some inputs, transform them in some fashion, and turn out some output.

While the broad perspective is quite useful, we want to narrow this down a little bit. The basic process, which we will show in Figure 5-1, is affected by many other processes that occur within and without the organization. The following sections will discuss the role of each of these. Remember, the output from some of these processes serves as input to the basic process. Remember, also, that the output from the basic process also serves as the input to some of these related processes.

5.2.1 Purchasing

A standard definition for the purchasing function might be as follows. Purchasing is the process of obtaining goods and services. As defined, purchasing is a process. Let us first look at the inputs, transformations, and outputs of this process.

Purchasing is responsible for procuring the raw materials needed for the basic process and all the other processes within the organization, as well. To perform its job, purchasing must know what has to be purchased. Typically, this information is transmitted via some form of requisition. This requisition must include certain information if purchasing is to complete its process. As a bare minimum, the purchasing process requires information such as material identification (e.g., part number), quantity required, date required by, quality specifications, and an authorization to acquire the material for the organization.

After receiving this information, the purchasing process transforms the input into the acquired material. While this is being done, some outputs will be generated. These outputs include first and foremost the actual material that is required. Also among the outputs will be payment and other accounting information. Some information may be sent to the inventory control function.

The basic process, to continue to operate, must have the material. Purchasing, to perform its process, must have information from the basic process. Figure 5-2 shows this two-way interrelationship.

While we are not done with purchasing yet, since purchasing receives inputs from sources other than the basic process, we want to look next at one of the other outputs of the basic process.

5.2.2 Distribution

Distribution is the process of taking the final product and getting that product to the customer. The input to the process is the product that is turned out by the basic

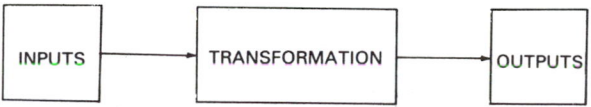

FIGURE 5-1 Basic Transformation Process

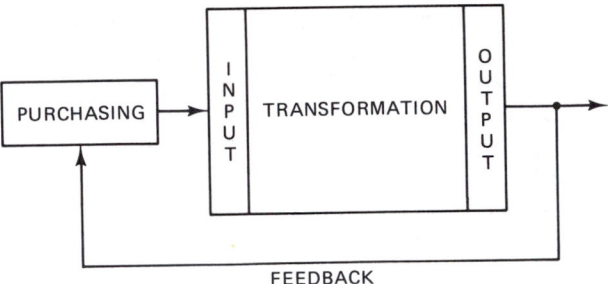

FIGURE 5–2 Extending the Process: Purchasing

process. The transformation is moving the product from the location where it is the output of the basic process to where it is the input for the customer. This can be another manufacturing facility, where the output of a subassembly is incorporated into another firm's final assembly, another processing plant where the output is a raw material, or a distribution center or final user.

To do its job, perform its process, distribution must have, first and foremost, a product to distribute. To distribute the product, it also must know who and where and how and when and what and how many. As you can see, there are many other inputs to the distribution process. This concept of interrelationships can't be avoided.

To answer who, information is necessary from sales. But sales must also provide information to the basic transformation process so that process knows how many to make, the specific characteristics required, the delivery date, and so on. At this point we had best pause and identify what we set out to do in this section, identify what we will call the **internal process.** As shown in Figure 5–3, the internal process includes the purchasing process, the basic transformation process, and the

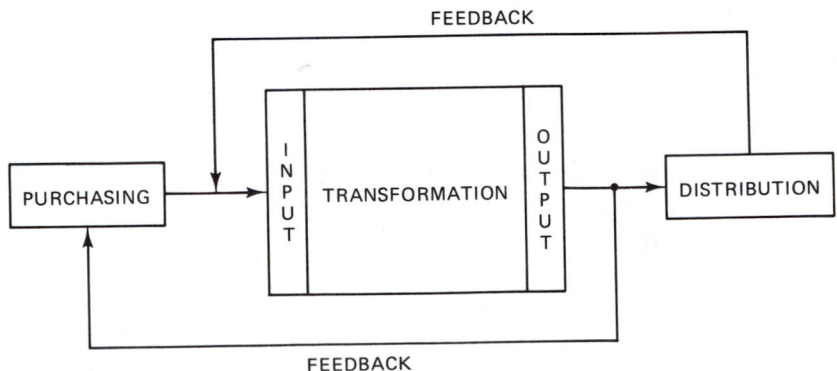

FIGURE 5–3 Extending the Process: Distribution, the Internal Process

distribution process. Since these share many of the same inputs, we will show these as one block in future diagrams.

5.3 INTERNAL PROCESS INPUTS

Purchasing, transformation, and distribution form the basic internal process for most organizations. These three processes are affected by some very significant processes within the organization. For these three functions to perform, they need information from engineering, human resources, finance and accounting, and sales or marketing. The role of each of these process inputs is first defined.

Engineering, as we will describe it, has several functions. One is research and development. Determining what new products might be produced, can be produced, and might be salable are some of the processes that engineering performs. Each of these, remember, is a process in its own right, with inputs, transformations, and outputs. Engineering also performs what might be called product engineering, which includes the preparation of drawings and material specifications. It also includes the process engineering function, involving the specification of the basic transformation process that will produce the product that the organization will distribute.

Human resources provides the individuals and the training for those individuals that are required to operate the various transformation processes. Whether they are skilled electronics maintenance technicians, less skilled machine operators, or unskilled materials handling personnel, the proper people with the proper skills are an essential input to the basic internal process of the organization. Human resources must have certain information to complete its process. It must know skill levels, quantities, pay levels, and so forth. Again, while providing people for sales, human resources needs information from sales to complete its job. As Figure 5–2 shows, every process not only gives its output to the next process in line, but it also receives input from just about every process in line as well.

Finance and accounting keep track of the money. They pay the bills, so this process has to know who is owed money. It also has to approve payment of the money. To pay the bills, finance also needs the input of money, which comes from the sales of the product. But sales needs money to operate. Each process effects every other process in some way.

Sales and marketing are responsible for providing paying customers for the output of the internal process. They must have a product to sell that not only meets the customers' requirements, but also is what the customer really wants. To do that, engineering must provide that product conceptually, human resources must provide the people to convert the concept to reality, purchasing must provide the materials that will perform to the specifications, finance must pay for the materials, the basic process must be in place to transform these into the desired product, and distribution must get it to the customer when it is needed. Talk about your basic interrelationships. And remember, all these are within the organization. Figure 5–4 summarizes this process relationship between the internal process and these internal sources of inputs (and outputs.)

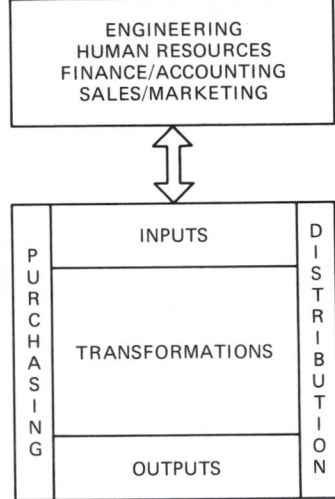

FIGURE 5-4 Extended Process: Other Internal Impacts

5.4 EXTERNAL PROCESS RELATIONSHIPS: THE CUSTOMER

Thus far, all the relationships have been internal to the organization. Most companies, since they don't operate in a vacuum, must be concerned with the external inputs and outputs that they deal with.

The most obvious of the external output recipients is the customer. As we have established already, satisfying both the stated needs and the real needs should be the major objective when the product is supplied to the customer. Written specifications are usually the minimum required. As in school, it is possible to pass by just meeting the minimum requirements, but the better job offers go to students who consistently exceed the minimums. A students are more sought after than C students. To do more than just meet the minimums, the real needs of the customer must be identified.

During a seminar with 40 company presidents, Tom Peters and Nancy Austin, authors of *A Passion for Excellence,* found that everyone present, all 40 presidents, stated that long-term customer satisfaction was top priority. When asked a follow-up question about how to assure that this occurred and whether or not this was even measured, none of the presidents could respond and state what method was used. [59: 87]

A number of successful companies do employ a way to monitor the output of their process and generate input to improve that process. The following paragraphs will summarize some suggestions for evaluating the customer portion of the extended process.

First and foremost, it must be realized that interaction with customers is twofold. The programs of customer relationships must provide a measure of how well we are doing in our customers' eyes and must also provide input for improving our process. Let us look now, via the following example, at how one specific company, National Standard Company through its Specialty Products Division, handles this dual procedure.

Example 5.4.1 | We began our effort at the customer's location, outlining what our effort included. We made presentations to the highest level of management at each location because the program required a customer commitment for the necessary time and participation. . . . We identified items that were good candidates for improvement because of potential cost savings or production improvements. A monthly status report was prepared by our quality function to assure that all items were being tracked.

The design team was notified of items selected and scheduled meetings with customers. This team included representatives from marketing, technical, and manufacturing. It is difficult for a sales representative to go in and discuss only the needs of the customer, so the design team would accompany the sales representative to the customers' sites.

We requested that each customer advise us of a date to observe his operations and meet with his personnel, including production operators and supervisors. The effort required a relationship of trust between the buyer and seller if we were to do more than just work with specifications.

The initial meetings were very important. They allowed us to review the customers' processing, and the customers' employees were contacted to discuss their problems and concerns.

Once problems or needs were identified, our design team was in a better position to investigate and analyze. Armed with information, we could determine what should or could be done to meet the customer requirements. [32: 16] ∎

Some organizations go even further than this by developing programs that quantify customer perceptions. One such program was developed by Walker Marketing in Indianapolis. [55: 47–49] Their principles for developing this structured of a feedback system include the following:

1. Sample both long-term and new customers.
2. Design the program to be continuous in nature.
3. Track customer's repurchase intent and willingness to recommend your company to another person, as well as the customer's perception of quality.
4. Make the survey comprehensive so that it includes all the products and services offered.
5. The statistical analysis of the data should provide information regarding both the relative importance of attributes, as well as your organization's performance on those attributes.
6. Give the customer an avenue for identifying specific problems.

7. Use the results of the survey through mechanisms such as quality review sessions, incentive plans, and use by internal quality assurance administrators.

All organizations can and should use these customer surveys. All organizations must know their customer's requirements and expectations. They must know their own abilities and requirements so they can communicate that information to their suppliers. It does not have to be limited to manufacturing. Even service organizations, like colleges, should survey their customers.

For example, the *Criteria for Accrediting Programs in Engineering Technology,* published by the Accreditation Board for Engineering and Technology, specifically states, "An accreditable program must demonstrate employer satisfaction with recent graduates, graduate satisfaction with employment, career mobility opportunities, appropriate starting salaries and appropriate job titles." [65: 9] The customers of the education programs, the employers, and the graduates must demonstrate satisfaction in order for programs to be certified as meeting accreditation standards.

Figure 5–5 shows the addition of the customer to the process. As Peter Drucker has written, quality is what the customer sees as value and nothing else. [34: 15] Robert Tallon, president of Florida Power and Light, said, "Our quality program has taught us, among other things, that we must be customer driven, that we must put aside our egos and let the customer be in charge—and if there's one thing that customers demand today, it's quality." [95: 37] The customer is not the only external part of the process, though. On the other end of the system is the supplier, or vendor.

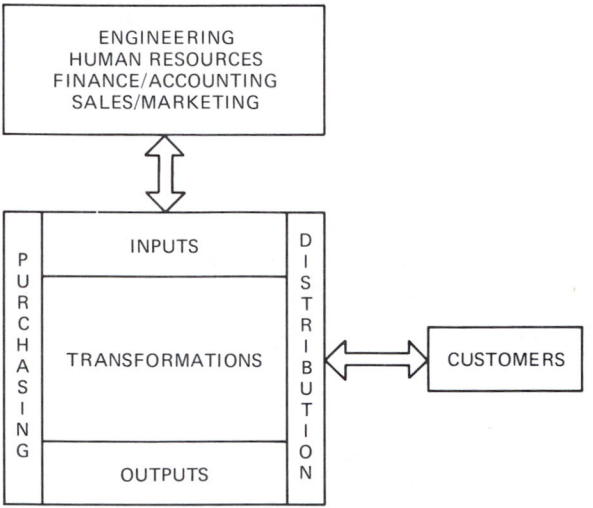

FIGURE 5–5 Extension of the Process to Include Customers

5.5 EXTERNAL PROCESS RELATIONSHIPS: THE SUPPLIER _____

Our organization must have the same relationship with our suppliers that we have with our customers. Our vendors give us inputs, the raw materials that are used in our transformation process. Without communication of our expectations to our vendors, there can be no improvement.

> In Japan there has been a tendency to view the vendor/vendee relationship as a long term relationship that is not subject to market price changes. This relationship is then nurtured and guided into becoming a tool for quality improvement, productivity improvement, and cost reduction for both the vendor and vendee. [51: 212]

There are many areas that must be shared between customer and supplier. To establish this long-term relationship, we must evaluate the vendor's ability to meet our needs and our requirements. Before entering into one of these relationships, we must be sure that the vendor is capable of providing the inputs we require. While many lengthy dissertations have been written about vendor evaluation, the following summarizes some of the key areas where expectations and requirements must be known.

- **QUALITY** activities. Vendor abilities regarding items such as test equipment, inspection procedures, control procedures, sampling plans, and all related procedures must be known by the customer so that judgment can be made concerning the vendor's ability to meet customer requirements.

- **MANUFACTURING** information. Included in this category are items such as production capacity, available equipment, process capabilities, and the potential for growth or expansion. We have to know if the vendor can produce what we need.

- **TECHNICAL** information. Information concerning design procedures, research and development capability and commitment, and available technical assistance tell us even more about the vendor's ability to meet our requirements.

- **SERVICE** to the customer. Just as important as meeting requirements initially is the ability of the supplier to continue to work with the customer after the sale. Information about the handling of complaints, the availability of service, the availability of spare parts, and the serviceability of the product are key pieces of information. Customers will often be willing to pay a premium price for the perception of quality products and quality service.

- **PERSONNEL** data. The relative experience, training, and even number of employees will have a significant impact on the quality of the product provided.

- **FINANCIAL** information. Even if an organization is capable of meeting our requirements, it must have the financial stability to remain in business to service us on a continuing basis. A complete financial evaluation of the organization is essential.

- **OTHER** information. Besides all the technical data, there are other, non-quantifiable pieces of information that help shade the evaluation of vendors. These include items such as general reputation, overall stability, organization, and just a general subjective feeling.

Vendor relationships used to be rather simple and straightforward. They were characterized by such features as

purchased goods were natural or semiprocessed natural materials; the quality of these materials was notoriously variable . . . written specifications were rudimentary; tolerances were wide by today's standards . . . the product was used independently rather than as part of a broad system design [and] the need for interchangeability was minimal. Buyer and vendor were usually in the same geographic locality and the feedback loop was short. [Finally] the shows were small, and all vendor relations, whether on quality matters or otherwise, were usually conducted by the two proprietors and . . . were long-lived, extending commonly over the life span of the proprietors involved.   [50: 10]

They are no longer so simple. Today the key word is interdependence. Products are much more complex, and, for a variety of reasons, there is considerably more subcontracting. Vendors and customers have to cooperate. Both have a vested interest in the ultimate success of the final output from the process. The vendor has to be sure that the product meets the needs of the customer. The vendor has to understand and be able to meet those needs and requirements. This customer must, then, as the supplier for the next process, understand the needs and requirements of the next customer. Everyone can do a better job when they know what is expected of them.

To make this happen requires communication. This does not always happen. ''In the overwhelming number of cases the vendor does not know what his product will be used for—he does not ask, and the vendee/engineer does not volunteer the information.'' [51: 212] To remedy situations such as these, Juran suggests a process that he calls joint quality planning. [50: 12–13] This includes basic of communications and cooperation such as:

- Clearly stating the meaning of specifications
- Defining all key terms and phrases to set up a common language
- Using standard methods of measurement
- Establishing compatible procedures and data systems
- Avoiding duplication of test facilities, inspection, and test programs

Suppliers and customers are key parts of our extended process. Figure 5–6 shows the current status of our extended process. This includes our basic internal process as well as the extension to customers and suppliers.

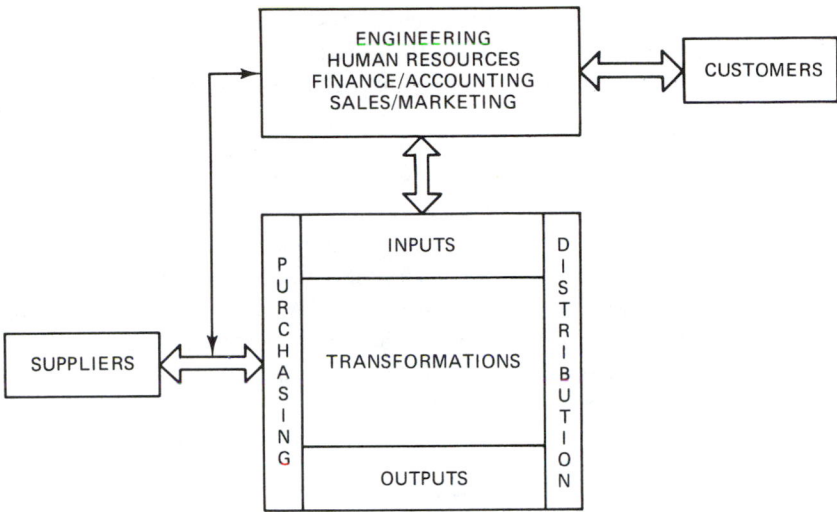

FIGURE 5-6 Extension of the Process to Include Suppliers

Even this does not complete the picture. Our extended process does not operate in a vacuum. Other forces affect the process.

5.6 EXTERNAL FORCES

There are four additional forces that work on the process. These are the competition, the government, unions, and finally, the investors. The following paragraphs
will briefly examine the impact each has on the process.

The competition of the free market is one of the strengths of our system. As
the old cliché goes, build a better mousetrap and the world will beat a path to your
door. There will always be someone out there who thinks that he or she can do
what you are doing, only better, or faster, and, of course, cheaper. Sometimes that
competition is local, sometimes it is international. Competition serves the role of
forcing us to continue to improve the process. If we don't get better and keep getting
better, then eventually we will cease to exist.

The government imposes many conditions or restrictions on the operation of
businesses. These restrictions include everything from health and safety laws to wage
payment policies. Our internal processes must respond to these requirements. If the
government is a customer, then it imposes many additional requirements. (*Note:* It
is not the intent or purpose of this book to delve into the many Mil-Specs, such as
9858a, that govern this type of relationship.)

If a union represents the workers, then the union has some say as to the nature
and operation of the transformation processes. Improvement of the process includes

demonstrating and convincing the union that a more productive organization is, in the long term, a benefit for the union's members. It also has to be remembered that the main reason people join unions is for the job security that unions attempt to provide.

Last, but certainly not least, are the investors or owners of the organization. The bottom line for the investors is making a return on their investment. The following quote from the mission statement of the Ford Motor Company states this most emphatically. "Our mission is to improve continually our products and services to meet our customers' needs, allowing us to prosper as a business and to provide a reasonable return for our stockholders, the owners of our business." [17: 1a] Quality may be job 1 at Ford, but they remember the reason that Ford is in business. That reason is first and foremost to stay in business. That can be accomplished only through making a profit.

5.7 CONCLUSION

Figure 5-7 completes our model of the process. The basic internal process is dependent on internal support functions as well as the relationship with customers and suppliers. The entire process is affected by external forces.

Within all these process relationships is the feedback loop. While it is important to identify this continuing series of processes, it is just as important to be able to define the requirements and needs so that they can be measured and improved. Chapter 6 will deal with defining the expectations and expressing them in such a way that the measurement and improvement process can begin.

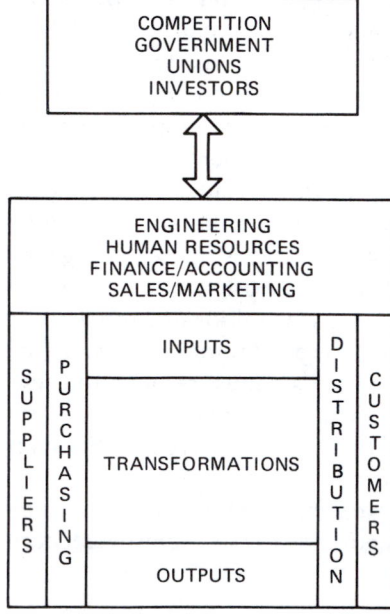

FIGURE 5-7 Other External Influences on the Process

Defining Expectations

When you can measure what you are
speaking about and express it in numbers
you know something about it, but when you
cannot measure it, when you cannot
express it in numbers, your knowledge is of
the meager and unsatisfactory kind.   [68]
Lord Kelvin

6.1   INTRODUCTION

Ronald D. Snee, the 1986 recipient of the American Society for Quality Control's Shewhart Medal, in his acceptance speech, said, "We must adopt the view of 'In God We Trust, others must have data,' for without data, everyone is an expert. Issues that generate great disagreement and controversy are usually those where little factual data exist." [33: 26] When expectations and reality do not coincide, then there is a pressing need for measurement. Before problems exist, to be consistent with our SPC philosophy of prevention, in which characteristic identification is a major cog, there should be a definition of the data that will be used to monitor, control, and ultimately evaluate the process.

Defining expectations involves three phases. The first of these is process related, involving the identification, at each step of the process, of the supplier and the customer for that particular operation. The second phase is agreement between each supplier and customer on the key input and output characteristics that affect the process transformation. The third phase is specifying the proper terms and characteristics so that the process inputs and outputs can be consistently measured.

6.2 EXTENDED PROCESS IDENTIFICATION

Within the complete extended process is a complex system of subprocesses. The output from one process is the input to the next process in the system. Whether we are talking about the supplier and our purchasing process, the customer and our marketing process, or any process in between, this relationship of output to input exists.

At each of these interfaces the supplier and the customer must be identified. For example, the stockroom may be the supplier for the assembly line, the automatic screw machine may be the supplier for the fastening operation, or the finance department may be the supplier for travel expense reimbursement. In each case the customer needs something that the supplier provides.

The process identification requires that analysis of each of these subprocesses takes place. This analysis must be performed both by the customer and the supplier for each process.

The first step for developing measurement expectations is the identification of the supplier for each process. The individual who is responsible for the process or subprocess must identify the source of the inputs for the process. For example, in the stockroom instance, the supplier for the assembly line is not just the stockroom, but an individual who furnishes stock to the assembly line from the stockroom.

Once the supplier is identified, two analysis tasks are necessary. First, the expectations for the input must be specified. Second, the actualities of the inputs currently received must also be described.

While the customer is identifying this information, the supplier should also be specifying the customer for his outputs. The analysis tasks awaiting the customer are similar to those of the supplier. The supplier should list expectations regarding the outputs of the process as they relate to the particular customer under consideration. The supplier should also list the actualities regarding the outputs of the process.

An example should clarify this first phase.

Example 6.2.1   At Aft Tech, a renowned center of technology education, students receive grade reports at the end of each term. The registrar at Aft Tech is responsible for the process that prepares and distributes these grade reports to the students.

The input required of this process is the final course grades from each instructor for each student. Thus the supplier for the registrar, who is the customer, is the faculty member.

To complete his process, in order to provide the grade report to the student, there are certain expectations the registrar has regarding the input to the grade-creation process. In no particular order, these include:

- A grade for every student in every course
- Grades submitted on the proper form

- Grades submitted on time
- Exception reports for nonstandard grades
- Legible writing on grade reports

Examining the preceding term's grades, the registrar discovered the following actualities:

- Missing grades for some students
- Missing grades for entire courses
- Grades submitted on old forms
- Grades submitted on nonstandard forms
- Grades submitted late
- No exception report filed with nonstandard grades
- Illegible handwriting on grade report forms
- Unsigned grade report forms

As part of the analysis, the supplier for this process, the faculty member, also has to identify the expectations and the realities of this interface. Regarding course grades at the end of the term, the instructor must recognize that the immediate customer for the output of this process is the registrar. The faculty member, To provide grades to the registrar, has the following expectations:

- A complete and accurate class roll will be provided.
- A proper form for recording course grades will be provided.
- Exception report forms will be provided.
- These forms will be provided in a timely fashion so that they can be completed when grades are determined.
- There will be sufficient time between the end of the term and the due date for grades for a proper evaluation of student performance to occur.

The realities or actualities of the system as it existed at Aft Tech were, in the perspective of the faculty member, somewhat different.

- Missing names were noted on some grade report forms.
- Extra names were found on some grade report forms.
- Grade report forms were inconsistent from course to course.
- No exception report forms or instructions for use were provided with the grade report forms.
- Grade report forms were not provided until two hours before they were due.
- Grade report forms were due 12 hours after the last final exam was scheduled.

This completes the first step of process identification. As can be seen, some problems appear to be present. We will return to this situation in the next example after step 2 of this process is explained. ■

In example 6.2.1 we saw that there were some marked inconsistencies between the expectations and actualities of the customer and the supplier. In many organizations the net effect of these inconsistencies is a lot of ill will. The registrar at Aft Tech probably would have less than nice things to say about the faculty regarding grade reports. The comments might sound like, ''How can I get the grades out if the faculty don't cooperate?'' The faculty might also have a few things to say about the unreasonable registrar.

This is more pronounced if we are talking about the business world. Listen to what four leading corporate executives say about this definition of customer requirements.

Claude I. Taylor, chairman of the board of Air Canada says, ''Meeting the needs of the customer has to be our primary objective because the competition is just too fierce. We can't be satisfied with what we think is good; customers will tell us by their indifference that, despite our definitions, we don't measure up to their standards and their needs.'' [93: 30]

Robert Tallon, president of Florida Power and Light, states it this way. ''Our quality program has taught us, among other things, that we must be customer-driven, that we must put aside our egos and let the customer be in charge—and if there's one thing that the customers demand today, it's quality.'' [95: 37]

Renowned quality consultant Armand Feigenbaum puts it this way: ''These [quality leveraged companies] achieve success because they have built in a clear customer oriented management process throughout the organization. People understand the process, believe in it, and want to be a part of it.'' [94: 33]

Finally, Richard L. Thomas, president of First Chicago Company, the holding company for the First National Bank of Chicago, says, ''We must remind ourselves again and again that the customer is paramount and we must act accordingly . . . the customer is our highest priority.'' [92: 27]

Sitmar Cruises regularly measures the responses of its customers to its service. ''A probing 200-item questionnaire distributed to each guest at the end of each cruise is Sitmar's approach to keeping tabs on passenger attitudes about almost everything. President John P. Bland describes the questionnaire as a key tool in helping Sitmar retain its 'tradition of excellence.' Quick computer analysis of answers leads to quick management action to assume quality. . . . '' [213: 21]

The customer and the customer's expectations are critical. Whether it's manufacturing or service, we must deliver what the customer perceives as being a quality product or service. Nothing else will do.

This has set the stage for the second step of this phase. Once the expectations and actualities for the customer and the supplier have been identified, the customer and the supplier must sit down and communicate about the inputs and outputs necessary for the overall process to carry on so that the ultimate consumer is satisfied with the ultimate output of the process. The customer and the supplier must agree on what is needed.

According to Phil Crosby, "at least half of quality problems are caused by not clearly stating what the requirements are." [45] The customer must inform the supplier what is needed, what is critical for the next process to be completed. The supplier must also inform the customer what is needed to satisfy the expectations of the customer. Armed with this information, the expectations of both parties will be on the way toward an improving process.

Example 6.2.2 Returning to the hallowed halls of Aft Tech, let us eavesdrop on the discussion between the registrar and the faculty. (D will stand for the dean, R for the registrar, and F for the faculty.)

D: I have called you together today so that we can mutually define expectations of outputs and inputs of the grade reporting process. Let us start with the registrar. Please tell the faculty what you need in order to prepare grade reports for the students.

R: I need grades for every student in every course on the proper form. If there is an exception, such as an incomplete, I need a record of the reason for the incomplete. These must be to me as soon as possible after the end of the term.

F: That is certainly quite a list of demands. Why do you need the grades on *your* form?

R: If all the grades come in on the same form, my clerical staff will know what to look for and where to look for it. They will not have to be concerned about the procedure for entering the grade on the students' complete record.

F: Why do you need grades for every student?

R: The grade reports, or report cards, are generated by a computer program. This will not work unless there is an entry for every student in every course. One missing grade will prevent every student from receiving his or her final grade.

F: Why do you need a reason for an incomplete? It is my prerogative to assign grades and I don't have to give anybody my reasons.

D: Let me answer that one. You might get hit by a car on your way home tonight. If you do, we need a way to determine when the student has completed the requirements for the course. By filling out an exception report, you are providing backup for the unexpected.

F: Our next question. Why do you need the grades so darn fast after the end of the term? It takes a while to grade the work and figure course averages. Sometimes you want the final grades within 12 hours. That is unreasonable.

R: We need the grades before the next term starts. One time each year we need the grades within 12 hours, and that is only because the faculty has decided to have the graduation ceremonies 24 hours after final exams are over. If we don't have the grades ready, we don't know who is eligible to take which classes or who is even still eligible to remain in school.

F: How can we get grades in if there are erroneous names on our grade report forms?

R: That is a good point. To give you a correct grade reporting form, you have to inform me if the preliminary rolls are correct. You do that and I will give you an accurate grade reporting form. But you have to let me know who is and who isn't attending your classes. I will be glade to provide you with a corrected roll. While we are at it, what else do you need in order to get the grades to me on time?

We could listen some more, but it should be obvious that the registrar and the faculty are starting to communicate. Before the discussion is over the registrar will know what the faculty need to provide the grade reports on time, and the faculty will know what the registrar needs to perform his process. ■

Each process has this potential for communication between customers and suppliers. Once a supplier knows the customer's expectations, then the supplier should work with his suppliers to make sure that these expectations are known.

Thus far we have examined the first two phases of expectation definition. We have identified expectations and have come to common agreement between supplier and customer as to what those expectations are. These common expectations provide the building block for the third phase, the definition of a characteristic that can be monitored and controlled.

6.3 MEASUREMENT CHARACTERISTICS

Deming refers often to what he calls operational definitions. These operational definitions are an explicit statement of the measurable characteristics of processes. They are a result of the internal process objectives, for example, the requirement that grades at Aft Tech be available prior to the next term, and the expectations that have been agreed on by the customer and the supplier. This definition process yields measurement characteristics.

It is these measurement characteristics that show us how we are doing and provide a base for determining whether or not we are improving. As a condition for defining measurement characteristics, we have to desire to monitor or measure that particular characteristic. We will assume that to be a precondition for the rest of this process.

The process of developing the measurement characteristic begins with a performance objective and a customer expectation. This performance objective/expectation provides the basis for determining what will be measured. For example, the agreement at Aft Tech might be that accurate grade reports be furnished to the faculty.

Once this objective is specified, then the measurement characteristic for this can be developed. This objective should be expressed in general terms. This means that adjectives describing the performance should be dropped. Also, there should be no specification of desired outcomes. Thus accurate grade reports should be stated, in measurement terms, as roster errors.

Specifically, after the discussions between the faculty and the registrar, this should be defined as a class roster showing all and only the students enrolled in each course for credit. Similarly, the reporting of the grades in a timely fashion is another objective that could be agreed on. Timely, being a modifier, suggests that the characteristic that might be important is the lateness of the grades. This could further be defined as the number of hours past the deadline that the grades are received by the registrar.

The characteristic must be expressed so that data can be collected. If data cannot be collected, then the objective must be restated.

Remembering that the precondition for defining measurement characteristics is that the process is to be monitored, the next step in this phase of identification is the development of a sampling procedure or scheme. While later information will describe sampling in more detail, the general characteristics of the sampling methodology are as follows.

The samples should be viewed as rational subgroups. Whatever is logical for the process under investigation should be used. If the process normally produces a product in subgroups of 12, then 12 would be a rational sample.

The samples should be taken at reasonable times. There is always a trade-off between desire and cost. These two have to be balanced. We would like as much information as possible; but when the cost of obtaining that information is too high, we have defeated our purpose.

The number of samples to examine should be large enough to give us sufficient information about the process. A sample taken one time will not tell us anything about variability over time. The overall quantity produced by the process and the potential for change are determining factors for the number of samples. Sometimes every item produced should be sampled; other times as few as 1 out of every 1000 produced is sufficient.

After the sampling scheme is determined, the appropriate measuring device must be specified. Both the customer and the supplier should be measuring the characteristic with the same hardware. The hardware can be as sophisticated as a computer analyzer or as simple as a child's ruler. The measuring device can be built into the process or it can be a separate piece of equipment.

Some measuring equipment is relatively complicated and the measurement technique has to be spelled out in detail. Many organizations have detailed test procedures that guide whoever is responsible for performing the measurement through every step that is required. Other measuring equipment, such as the ruler, requires little or no instruction in its formal use.

The final step in this phase is the actual collection of data. These data describe the process. Chapters 11 and 12 will describe the use of data, through some basic statistical analysis, to draw conclusions about the performance of the process. Later chapters will introduce even more powerful analysis procedures that use the results of the data collected via this measurement process.

At this point, an example should clarify the use of the third phase of the definition process.

Example 6.3.1 An airplane manufacturer purchases its landing gear hubs from a subcontractor. One expectation that the customer and supplier have agreed on is that these hubs for the landing gears should be round. The general characteristic that they have agreed to monitor and control is hub roundness.

At this point in their discussion they were ready to start collecting data on hub roundness, but found that they could not measure hub roundness. They had no idea what they meant by hub roundness. Their definition, the operational definition of the characteristic in Deming's terms, was not appropriate. It was time to go back and try to identify a better way to define what they meant by hub roundness.

After some thought, they realized that round hubs would have the same diameter at any point on the circumference. Therefore, the characteristic that they were really concerned about was hub diameters and not hub roundness. Specifically, they were concerned about the distance through the center of the hub from one edge to the other. This can be measured and compared with some arbitrary criterion to determine whether or not the hubs are round.

This is part of the measuring procedure. The customer and supplier agree to select five hubs at random from each day's production. A standard caliper will be used to measure the diameter. These measures will be taken at 30-degree intervals about the circumference of each hub. These six diameters will be averaged and the range (the difference between the largest and smallest values) calculated. If the average is within 0.001 of the specification and the range is no larger than 0.007, then they will agree that the hub is round.

Subsequent data collected provided information as to the suitability of the process that produced the hubs. As long as the data reflected the roundness of the hubs, there could be no misunderstanding about the quality of the hubs regarding this characteristic. ■

Many times, individuals involved in a process will, at this point, say something like this: "The methodology is fine and dandy but it won't work on my job even if it does for other jobs. My process is unique. It does not have anything that can be measured." This just is not the case. While examples from manufacturing are readily apparent, such as rework dollars, scrap dollars, error rates, arrival rates, and so on, there are characteristics that can be easily measured in other disciplines as well.

Looking first at quality assurance itself, there are measures of performance, such as the percentage of lots rejected by mistake, time required for improvements to be made, and time required to react to engineering changes. Accounting can measure number of late payments, time to make a payment, billing errors, number of incorrect entries, number of payroll errors, and time required to process invoices. Data processing can measure the time required to prepare specific reports, the number or percent of late reports, the number of coding errors, the number of rewrites on programs that are required, the number of user errors identified, and so on.

Marketing can evaluate, numerically, the accuracy of their forecasts, the number of order entry errors, the number of errors made in writing contracts, and the processing time for contracts. Purchasing can evaluate the time required to receive an order, the time required to process an order, down time due to late deliveries of ordered material, the dollars invested in excess inventory, and similar factors. [85: 43]

These lists, while relatively short, are representative of the kinds of data that can be collected. The statement made earlier simply represents laziness on the part of the person making the statement.

6.4 CONCLUSION

Knowing what to measure and how to measure are keys to improving the performance of each process. The cooperation we illustrated between the customer and the supplier so that the supplier could meet the customer's expectations is a key component in developing the characteristic definitions.

As we saw, we began our definition process with the expectations that were critical to the customer. We made an assumption that the customer would automatically know what was or what was not important or critical to the process. This is a big assumption and it is not always correct to make this big an assumption.

There will be many times when we know we have a problem with the process, but we don't know what is causing the problem. We don't really know where to look to even begin defining the measurements that will help us to monitor and later control the process. When this is the case, there are several procedures that have been developed that make the identification of critical characteristics if not easier, then more systematic. These include check sheets, Pareto charts, cause and effect diagrams, and project improvement teams.

The next section of the text will examine these in some detail. Remember, as you read about them, that their purpose is to help us to identify the characteristics that are critical to the continuous improvement of our processes. An early caution will warn us to remember that these techniques are a means to an end and not an end in themselves. After the discussion of these "aids to definition," the fourth part of the book will examine the analysis of the data that are collected for the critical characteristics.

CHAPTER 7

Identifying Problems

Consistent in-line implementation of the specifics of quality achievement throughout the organization is the big opportunity for many companies today.   [18: 33]
A. V. Feigenbaum

7.1   INTRODUCTION

Every organization has problems. They can range from too much rework to inconsistencies in output to too much variability in processing time. Statistical process control is a problem-solving procedure that helps us to identify and then solve the problems that are present in every process. Regardless of the process, we can view every problem as one of too much variation about the desired target characteristic.

This section of the book will examine a set of techniques initially described in Ishikawa's *Guide to Quality Control* [79]. This chapter will illustrate problem identification techniques, specifically brainstorming and what is known as the check sheet. Chapter 8 will examine the analysis tool known as the Pareto chart. Chapter 9 will carry the analysis one step further, through the use of the cause and effect, or fishbone, or Ishikawa diagram. Chapter 10 will suggest a way for these valuable techniques to be used by any organization via the project improvement team.

As you will discover during the course of the next several pages, these techniques are not difficult to learn. Nor are they difficult to implement. The key to their success is that they have the potential to involve everyone in the organization in the improvement process. The effectiveness of the techniques requires only a familiarity with the process, not necessarily a familiarity with statistical process control.

This section will present some generic examples using the problem identification methodologies. The last section of the book will present some real-life examples that include the application of these procedures.

7.2 BRAINSTORMING

"Brainstorming is the most popular technique used . . . because it opens the door to increased spontaneity, creativity, enthusiasm, and humor. Brainstorming is the practical application of the concept of synergy: the whole is richer than any of its component parts." [60: 100] Brainstorming, explained in its most basic way, is using a group of individuals to stimulate the production of ideas. As assumption underlying the use of brainstorming is that people want to create ideas. As it applies to SPC, brainstorming will be used in three areas:

- Identification of potential problems
- Identification of potential causes of problems
- Identification of potential solutions to problems

Brainstorming takes the old cliché "two heads are better than one" and expands on it. If two heads are good, then three or five, or even fifteen heads are even better. Brainstorming, as an idea-generating mechanism, is almost always more effective that trying to generate ideas alone.

There have been many fine discussions of brainstorming (see, for example, [69] or [60]). This section of the chapter will focus on two aspects of brainstorming, the creative process and the procedure for brainstorming.

Part and parcel of every dissertation ever written on brainstorming is the instruction *be creative*. The journalist Bill Moyers provided the following statement, "[Creativity is] . . . any thinking process which solves problems in an original and useful way. It begins by letting down your shield. Stop being self-conscious—afraid of playing the fool—and be open to experience." [60: 102]

Some characteristics of creativity have been suggested and include such advice as:

1. Results come from making an effort to concentrate on creativity.
2. Creative thinking must be practiced.
3. Part of being creative is the ability to fail.
4. Imagination is based on previous experiences.

Unfortunately, many people tend to think that they cannot be creative. They throw up roadblocks and prejudge all their own ideas. Brainstorming is a technique that helps to overcome this bar to creativity. The brainpower of the people involved with the process is a powerful force that we have to learn to use.

Brainstorming, or organized creativity, is most effective when there is some organization to the activity. The first step in the brainstorming process is the identification of the topic that will be brainstormed. Before this chapter ends, we will explore the problems that exist at a typical workplace. A brainstorming session for this would logically be focused on *quality and productivity problems within the department*. The better defined the topic is the more effective the brainstorming will be.

After the topic is defined, the idea generation begins. It is important to remember the following general points about the ideas generated. First, no criticism of any idea can be permitted. No matter how wild the idea is, it is accepted. Second, no evaluation is made of any idea during the brainstorming. Third, self-judgments should not be permitted. Fourth, personalities should not enter the process, especially if the topic being discussed is the quality or productivity of the department. The objective of brainstorming is the quantity, not the quality, of ideas presented.

Each idea, as it is presented, should be written down, preferably on a flip chart or board for all to see. Provide sufficient space for all possible ideas that may be forthcoming. Don't arbitrarily limit the number of ideas by limiting the writing space.

The generation of ideas can proceed in many different ways. Your author has found that one very effective method, especially with a "shy" group, is to ask each member of the brainstorming group, in order, to suggest an idea. Each member is limited to one idea per turn. Each member is encouraged to build or piggyback on the preceding idea.

The leader of the brainstorming session plays a key role. Some points to remember for the leader of the session include:

- No idea is stupid.
- For some members, speaking out during a brainstorming session will be their first attempt at speaking in public; the leader must be patient and welcome and encourage their ideas.
- Good-natured laughter should be encouraged to enhance the climate for creative activity.
- Exaggeration should be encouraged. It may add humor and it certainly adds a creative stimulus to the process.

After the group has exhausted their supply of ideas, it is time to clarify any items on the list of ideas that are not clear. Everyone should leave the brainstorming session fully understanding what every item means. At this time, any ridiculous ideas are tossed away. This is a tedious process and can result in some hurt feelings, so some care is called for in developing the edited list of ideas.

Example 7.2.1   As a frequent presenter of seminars, the author is subject to many different varieties of coffee. No matter where the seminar is given, the quality, or lack subjective quality, of the coffee served provides numerous comments. Quality, the goodness or badness or inconsistency from pot to pot, provides a useful vehicle for demonstrating the use of brainstorming.

As we identify it, the topic for this brainstorming session is, "What is causing the bad taste in the coffee?'' Initially, the responses given by the group include the following:

- It is too strong.
- It is too weak.
- It is bitter.

This initial line of responses is quickly exhausted. The leader of the session must then focus on each of these three points suggested. The question is then put to the group, ''Why is the coffee too strong?'' Again, a list of possible responses results:

- Not enough water
- Too many grounds
- Coffee measure incorrectly calibrated
- Coffee too fresh
- Coffee too old
- Too finely ground coffee
- Perked too long
- Operator's taste
- Operator's lack of skill
- Coffee maker dirty
- Coffee maker broken
- Filter used incorrectly
- Filter not used
- No allowance for water absorbed in grounds
- Water too cold
- Water too warm

A similar list could be generated, with perhaps similar responses, for the question about why the coffee is too weak or too bitter. As can be seen, the list grows relatively quickly.

As we will be using brainstorming in statistical process control, the objective will be to either identify problems, identify causes, or identify solutions. We will now examine the use of brainstorming in identifying problems.

7.3   CHECK SHEETS

As indicated in the preceding section, in a typical brainstorming situation we will be examining the identification of potential (and real) quality and productivity problems in a specific department. Brainstorming will identify potential problems. Many of these problems will be suggested because they have just recently occurred. This is normal. People remember what happened most recently. They don't always remember what happens most often. The check sheet identifies the relative frequency with which problems occur.

Building on the brainstorming, the check sheet is a simple device to list and tabulate the problems as they occur during a given period of time. Figure 7–1 shows a typical blank form for a check sheet. This form is used for collecting the information.

There are several key areas within the typical check sheet. Each serves as a column heading on the check sheet. These are the identification of potential problems, the way-to-measure section, the when-to-measure, and the count/tally section.

The first column, the characteristics, problems, defects, or undesirable effects column, is a complete listing of all the potential problems that the brainstorming

IDENTIFICATION INFORMATION:			
			DATE:
CHARACTERISTICS PROBLEMS DEFECTS UNDESIRABLE EFFECTS	WAY TO MEASURE	WHEN TO MEASURE	COUNT/TALLY

FIGURE 7–1 Sample Check Sheet: Data Collection

came up with, along with some extra space for those problems that occur that nobody could remember during the brainstorming. The statement of the problem should be short, concise, and easily understood by everyone who will be filling out the check sheet. There can be no room for misinterpretation.

The second column is a brief description of the way the characteristic is measured or identified. The term or phrase used should be meaningful to those who will be collecting the data. For example, the term used can be as simple as "micrometer" or in company jargon such as "LFE reading." **A key part of the way-to-measure section of the check sheet is the identification of exactly what constitutes a problem.** The definition of acceptable ranges is necessary before the data collection begins.

The third column suggests that frequency of measurement of the characteristic. Sometimes every unit produced is checked. Often, especially with continuous processes that turn out large quantities of some type of bulk material, every unit cannot be checked. Some of the characteristics may be checked for on a regular basis. When this is the case, the timing has already been established as a part of normal inspection procedures. The particular value may normally be recorded every 2 hours, and this would be an appropriate time. Other problems may be noted when they occur. When different time phases are used, the summarization of the data will have to reflect this difference.

The fourth column is the count or tally section. This indicates how many times the particular characteristic or problem occurred. The data are recorded with the simple tally mark.

After the data are collected, they are summarized. A form such as the one shown in Figure 7–2 is useful for this. When different time periods are used for collecting data, using the relative frequency is a convenient way to standardize the reporting of the number of occurrences. If defects are recorded when they occur, these defects should be segregated from the other classes of defects. The ranking of defects is useful in identifying the most frequently occurring problems.

When improving a process, it makes sense to try to fix the big problems first. Deming said it quite succinctly: "Think big . . . work on the big problems. If you work on the little problems we'll all be lost." [16: 28]

The following example shows the use of a check sheet for identifying problems.

Example 7.3.1 A foundry was producing castings. These castings, unfortunately, were subject to a number of quality problems. In an effort to improve their process, the foundry decided to implement an SPC program. Before any improvements could be made to the process, the problems had to be identified.

A group of employees, supervisors, engineers, maintenance technicians, and quality assurance personnel was formed to come up with some potential problems. As a result of their brainstorming session, some potential problems were identified. These included the following:

- Blemishes on the surface
- Chips on the surface

IDENTIFICATION INFORMATION:			DATE:
CHARACTERISTICS PROBLEMS DEFECTS UNDESIRABLE EFFECTS	COUNT/ TALLY	TOTAL	RANK ORDER

FIGURE 7–2 Sample Check Sheet: Data Summary

- Broken appendages
- Burrs
- Missing holes
- Wrong material
- Dirt and foreign particles present
- Extra holes

In this particular instance, each casting must be checked for each of these potential problems. All the characteristics, with the exception of the wrong-material defect, are visual checks. The wrong material is a lab test that must be run on special equipment.

The check sheet for data collection is set up as shown in Figure 7–3. Once the sheet is set up, the data can be collected. For a period of one week, beginning on the date shown, the group marked down every time each problem occurred. Figure

IDENTIFICATION INFORMATION: CAST PRODUCTS SAND MOLD DEPARTMENT		DATE: JAN 5-12	
CHARACTERISTICS PROBLEMS DEFECTS UNDESIRABLE EFFECTS	WAY TO MEASURE	WHEN TO MEASURE	COUNT/TALLY
			MARK IF PRESENT
SURFACE BLEMISHES	VISUAL	EACH UNIT	
CHIPS ON SURFACE	VISUAL	EACH UNIT	
BROKEN APPENDAGES	VISUAL	EACH UNIT	
BURRS	VISUAL	EACH UNIT	
MISSING HOLES	VISUAL	EACH UNIT	
WRONG MATERIAL	LAB TEST	EACH UNIT	
DIRT PRESENT	VISUAL	EACH UNIT	
EXTRA HOLES	VISUAL	EACH UNIT	

FIGURE 7-3 Check Sheet for Example 7.3.1

7-4 summarizes the tally marks, indicating that the most frequently occurring defect is blemishes on the surface. The rank order column shows the ranking of the other problems. The check sheet has identified the most frequently occurring problems. Now the foundry has a place to start their process of continuous improvement. ∎

7.4 CONCLUSION

The techniques of brainstorming and the check sheet are useful tools for identifying a starting place in process improvement. They are simple to use and take advantage of the knowledge everybody in the work force has about the process. The results gathered from the check sheet have the additional advantage of being data collected by the workers.

IDENTIFICATION INFORMATION: CAST PRODUCTS SAND MOLD DEPARTMENT			DATE: JAN 5-12
CHARACTERISTICS PROBLEMS DEFECTS UNDESIRABLE EFFECTS	COUNT/ TALLY	TOTAL	RANK ORDER
SURFACE BLEMISHES		86	1
CHIPS ON SURFACE		53	3
BROKEN APPENDAGES		9	4
BURRS		61	2
MISSING HOLES		2	6 [TIE]
WRONG MATERIAL		1	8
DIRT PRESENT		7	5
EXTRA HOLES		2	6 [TIE]

FIGURE 7-4 Check Sheet Summary for Example 7.3.1

The check sheet provides the raw data to document the existence of problems that everybody always knew about. When most workers are asked what the problems are, they can generally respond accurately. But sometimes management is reluctant to listen to the worker. The techniques presented in this chapter, and expanded on in Chapter 8, provide valuable mechanisms for presenting this information in a fashion that will be useful as a foundation or starting point for process improvement.

CHAPTER 8

Pareto Analysis

*The vital few are everywhere, but
masquerading under a variety of aliases.
[78: 49]*

J. M. Juran

8.1 INTRODUCTION

The check sheet described in Chapter 7 provided a mechanism for recording the actual defects or problems as they occurred in the operation of the process. This is useful information, but it is not summarized for effective use.

The Pareto principle is based on the work of the Italian economist, Vilfredo Pareto. He studied the distribution of wealth and found that a minority of the population controlled a majority of the wealth. This can be effectively used in problem analysis to separate the significant few from the trivial many.

The Pareto chart is a graphical representation of the relative frequency with which various problems occur. Generally, the descriptive statistical device called the histogram is used to present the information. This chapter will describe the uses of Pareto charts, explain the methodology of constructing the charts, and illustrate the use of the analysis procedure to identify quality problems.

Figure 8–1 shows a typical Pareto chart. Section 8.3 will explain the methodology used to construct a chart such as this.

8.2 USES FOR PARETO ANALYSIS

Ishikawa, in his *Guide to Quality Control*, suggests several quality-related uses for Pareto charts. [79: 42–50] The Pareto chart is the first step to making quality improvements. The check sheet identifies the problems, but the chart itself, by showing

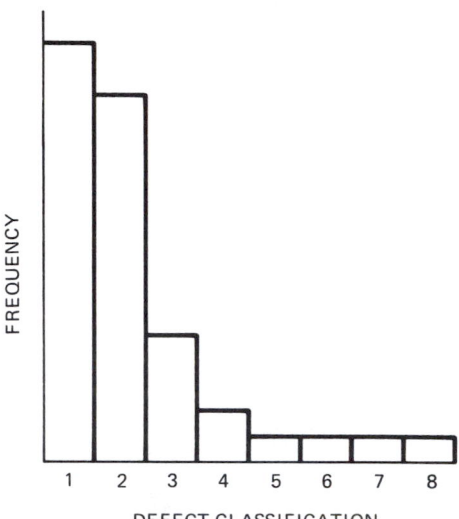

FIGURE 8–1 Sample Pareto Chart

the relative frequency of the problems, clearly identifies the major or significant problems that face the organization. According to the Pareto principle, the significant few, the major problems, will appear with the most frequency. Usually two or three problems occur much more frequently than the others. The chart will show this and guide everyone in the organization to focus improvement efforts on what are obviously the serious problems.

Reducing the number of times the critical problem occurs is the goal.

> Experience has shown us that it is easier to reduce a tall bar by half than to reduce a short bar to zero. . . . Because we have to produce results with limited capacities, manpower and time, we must cooperate to achieve improvements by concentrating on the worthy targets, that is, the item or items represented by the tallest and taller bars of the Pareto diagram. [79: 45]

The Pareto analysis, by the graphic way it presents the information, brings ready agreement to the priority of action.

A second use for Pareto charts is that they can be applied to all areas, all processes within an organization. The diagrams don't have to be limited to defect classification. They can also show items such as number of hours spent on certain repair projects, dollars spent on certain budget items, numbers of different types of accidents occurring, and so forth. The ABC inventory management policy of identifying high-value inventory items is based on just this type of analysis.

The third use for the charts is as a measure of improvement. After the problems have been identified and steps taken to improve the processes that are causing the problems, additional data collection would show that the size of the bars is shrinking. ''Generally, if improvement measures are taken, and proven effective, the order of the bars will change.'' [79: 49]

8.3 CONSTRUCTING PARETO CHARTS

The Pareto chart is similar to the descriptive statistical tool known as the histogram. Histograms are bar charts that show the quantity, frequency, or relative frequency with which some characteristic occurs.

Histograms have two sides. The horizontal scale usually indicates the different characteristics possible. For example, there might be a separate marking for each defect classification that might occur. Generally, each classification is of equal width. Sometimes we get carried away and refer mathematically to the base of the histogram as the x axis.

The vertical side of the histogram shows the quantity of that particular characteristic that is present. Sometimes this is expressed as an actual count, such as number of dollars; some times it is expressed as a relative frequency or percentage. For example, if the chart is recording defects, it may be more meaningful to express the results as ''this defect occurred 34 percent of the possible times it was checked for.'' If we continue to be carried away with technical names, the vertical scale has the mathematical name of y axis.

Example 8.3.1 A check sheet for defects for a sand mold department was compiled in Example 7.3.1. That sheet is reproduced here as Figure 8-2. Construct a histogram showing the defects and the number of times each defect occurred.

The first step is to construct the horizontal axis. This is shown in Figure 8-3. Note that each defect classification is shown in the order in which it appeared on the check sheet. Also note that each defect classification has the same width. These are usually called classes or cells.

The second step is to construct the vertical axis. This shows the actual count or number of times each defect occurred. The most any defect occurred was 86 times, while the least was 1 time for ''wrong material.'' The scale for frequency should reflect the entire range of potential values. In this instance, a major division of 10 has been selected, primarily because it is simple and convenient. Figure 8-4 shows the addition of the vertical axis to the histogram.

The third step in developing the histogram is drawing a rectangle for each defect classification. The base of the rectangle is the width of the cell on the horizontal scale. The side of the rectangle goes to the frequency for that defect. Figure 8-5 shows the first of these rectangles, or bars. Figure 8-6 completes the histogram for the sand mold department.

The formal completion of the histogram might include any appropriate identifying information, such as department, dates, and so on. ∎

Pareto charts are similar to histograms, but they have one distinct difference. **The Pareto chart arranges the bars of the histogram in descending order.** The cate-

IDENTIFICATION INFORMATION: CAST PRODUCTS SAND MOLD DEPARTMENT			DATE: JAN 5-12
CHARACTERISTICS PROBLEMS DEFECTS UNDESIRABLE EFFECTS	COUNT/ TALLY	TOTAL	RANK ORDER
SURFACE BLEMISHES		86	1
CHIPS ON SURFACE		53	3
BROKEN APPENDAGES		9	4
BURRS		61	2
MISSING HOLES		2	6 [TIE]
WRONG MATERIAL		1	8
DIRT PRESENT		7	5
EXTRA HOLES		2	6 [TIE]

FIGURE 8–2 Sand-mold Department Check Sheet Summary

gory with the largest frequency is placed first, the second largest second, and so on. This focuses attention on the major cases.

Example 8.3.2 Use the information presented in Example 8.3.1 to develop a Pareto chart for the check sheet information developed in the sand mold department.

Figure 8–6 is most of the way there. All that remains is placing the rectangles of the historgram in rank order. Since the check sheet of Figure 8–2 listed the rank order, it is easy to develop the Pareto chart (Figure 8–7).

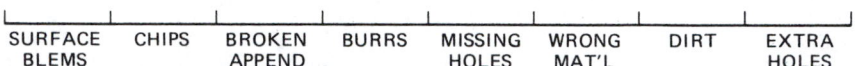

| SURFACE BLEMS | CHIPS | BROKEN APPEND | BURRS | MISSING HOLES | WRONG MAT'L | DIRT | EXTRA HOLES |

FIGURE 8–3 Sand-mold Histogram: Horizontal Axis

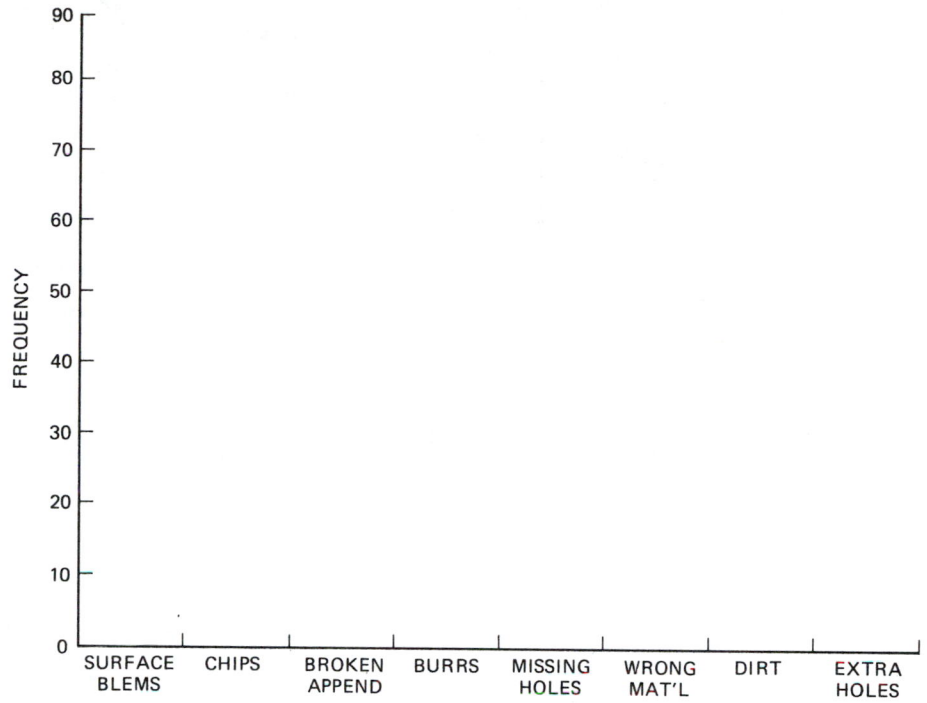

FIGURE 8–4 Sand-mold Histogram: Vertical Axis

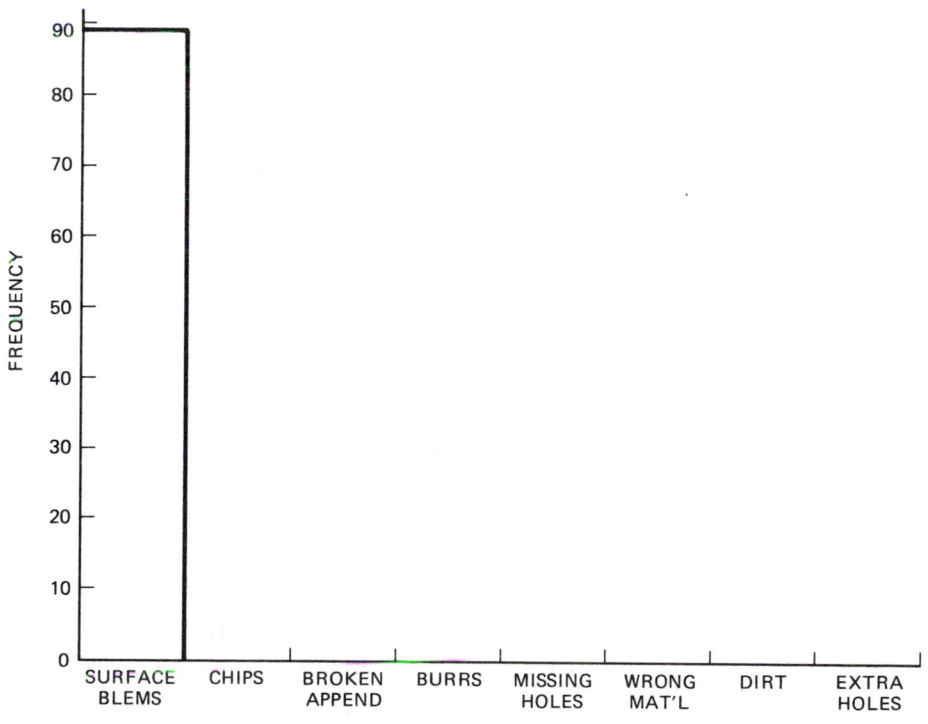

FIGURE 8–5 Sand-mold Histogram: First Bar

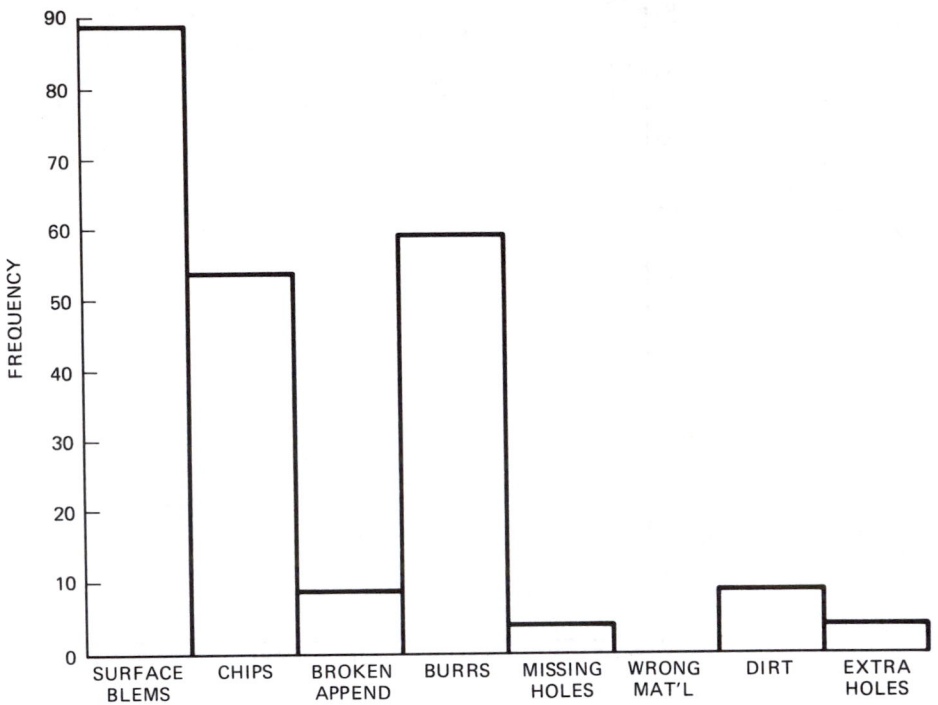

FIGURE 8-6 Sand-mold Histogram

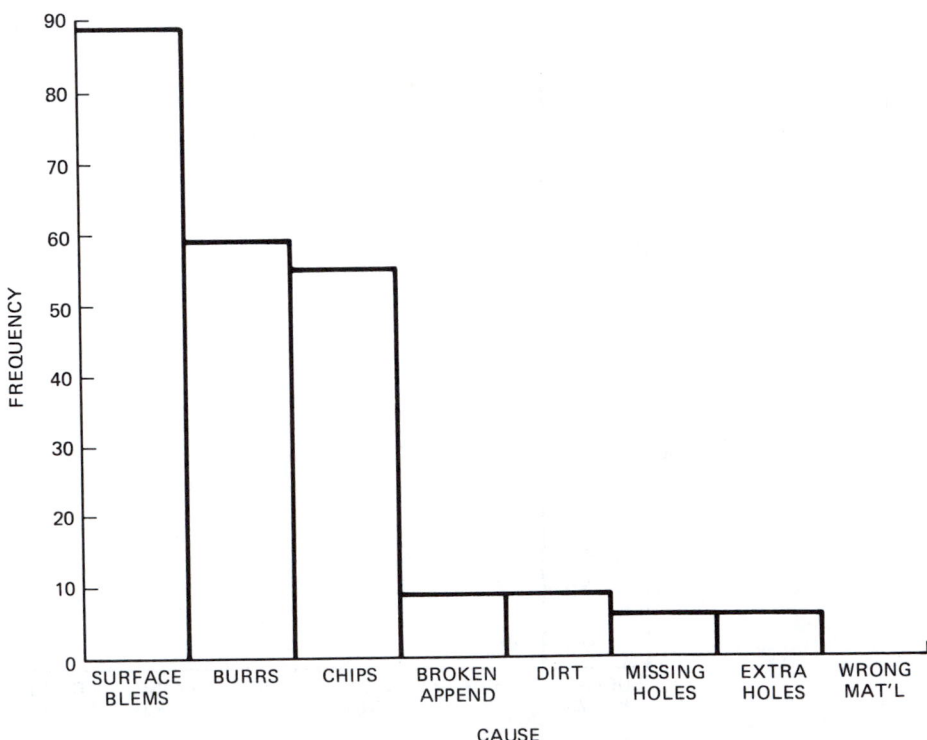

FIGURE 8-7 Sand-mold Pareto Chart

As can be seen, most of the defects appear to be caused by only three of the potential causes. Attention can now be focused on improving the process that has led to creating surface blemishes, burrs, and chips on the surface.   ■

Example 8.3.3   A manufacturing company has been collecting information about its vendors. This information, while not comprising a check sheet in the same sense that the employee-generated data forms are, serves the same purpose as a check sheet in capturing information about a process. In this instance the process is the receipt of purchased material. The information, as summarized, appears in Figure 8-8. Rank ordering the vendors by number of lots rejected, results in the order shown in Figure 8-9.

Figure 8-9 has a major drawback, though. The rank ordering does not take into account the total number of lots submitted. Vendor C appeared to be the best, with only 2 rejected lots. But that is 2 lots out of a possible 9. Vendor G appears to be the worst, but again, the number may be deceiving. Nine rejections out of a possible 133 is a lot better percentage than 2 rejections out of a possible 9.

A better way of looking at these data, for which each category has a different number of possible occurrences, is by looking at the relative frequency (percentage), rather than absolute or observed frequency. This gives all the data a common denominator, so to speak. Figure 8-10 compiles this relative frequency and revises the rank order for each of the vendors based on the relative frequency of rejected lots. This revised information is used to construct the Pareto chart shown in Figure 8-11. This chart identifies those vendors who are having the most problems meeting this company's criteria.   ■

Sometimes Pareto charts are drawn to show the cumulative effect of each classification. The relative percentage for each occurrence is expressed as a percentage of the total problem. Example 8.3.4 will show this for the data collected and analyzed in Example 8.3.3.

Vendor ID	Number of Submissions	Number of Rejections
A	42	4
B	51	7
C	9	2
D	87	7
E	38	5
F	79	6
G	133	9
H	72	8
I	49	6
J	59	7

FIGURE 8-8   Vendor Data

Vendor ID	Number of Submissions	Number of Rejections	Rank Order
A	42	4	2
B	51	7	5
C	9	2	1
D	87	7	5
E	38	5	3
F	79	6	4
G	133	9	7
H	72	8	6
I	49	6	4
J	59	7	5

FIGURE 8–9 Vendor Data Rank Order

Example 8.3.4 Figure 8–11 showed the relative percentages of each vendor's lots that were rejected. To develop a cumulative Pareto chart, we must determine what percentage of the total rejects each vendor was responsible for. Figure 8–12 takes the original data and the rank ordering shown in Figure 8–11 and calculates the percentage of total rejects attributable to each vendor. These percentages are then accumulated, so that by adding in the percent for the last (best) vendor the total becomes 100 percent. These cumulative percents are then graphed, usually as a histogram, as a cumulative Pareto chart. Sometimes a bar chart is not used and a line graph is. When this is the case, the same information is available, but it looks just a little bit different. Figure 8–13a shows the bar graph version of this chart. Figure 8–13b shows the line chart of the same data.

In both charts, the more frequently appearing problem appears first, and the graph tends to tail off as it approaches the end. The only difference is one of presentation styles. In terms of guiding the analysis, both charts, the cumulative and non-cumulative, show the same information. ■

8.4 CONCLUSION

Pareto charts and the accompanying Pareto analysis identify the most significant problems. In terms of data analysis, the chart provides a convenient summarization

Vendor ID	No. Submission	No. Rejection	Percent Rej.	Rank
A	42	4	9.5	4
B	51	7	13.7	9
C	9	2	22.2	10
D	87	7	8.0	3
E	38	5	13.2	8
F	79	6	7.6	2
G	133	9	6.8	1
H	72	8	11.1	5
I	49	6	12.2	7
J	59	7	11.9	6

FIGURE 8–10 Vendor Data Rank Order by Percent

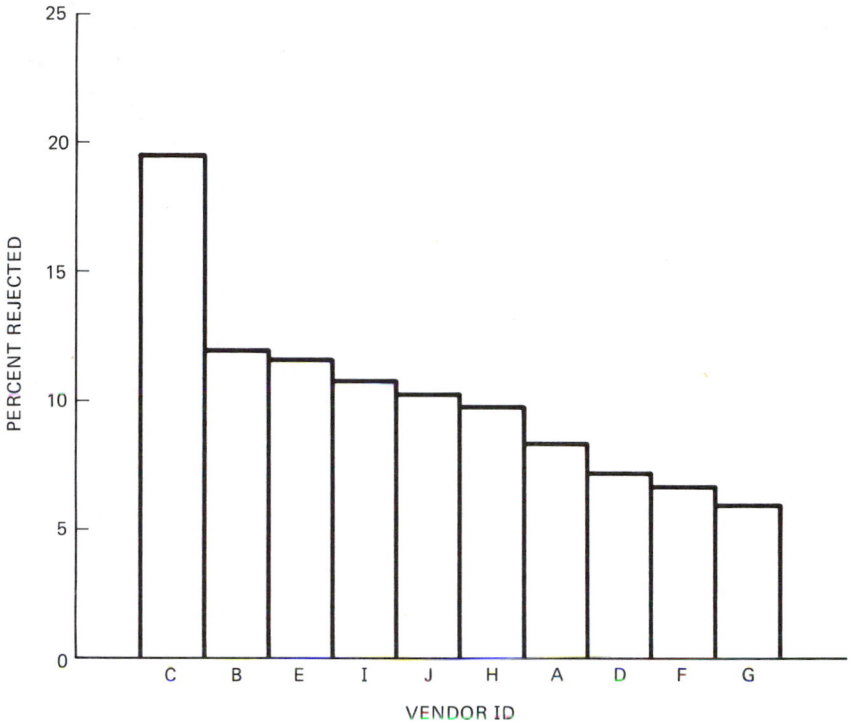

FIGURE 8–11 Vendor Data Pareto Chart

tool. It highlights the most frequently occurring problems and directs attention toward them.

Besides problem identification, there are a number of other applications of this analysis procedure. The following is a partial listing of some of the other applications of Pareto analysis. Many of them relate directly to the cost of quality. [80: 257–258]

Vendor ID	Percent Rej.	Cumulative Percent	Rank
C	19.1	19.1	10
B	11.8	30.9	9
E	11.4	42.3	8
I	10.5	52.8	7
J	10.2	63.0	6
H	9.6	72.6	5
A	8.2	80.8	4
D	6.9	87.7	3
F	6.5	94.2	2
G	5.8	100.0	1

FIGURE 8–12 Vendor Data Rank Order by Cumulative Percent

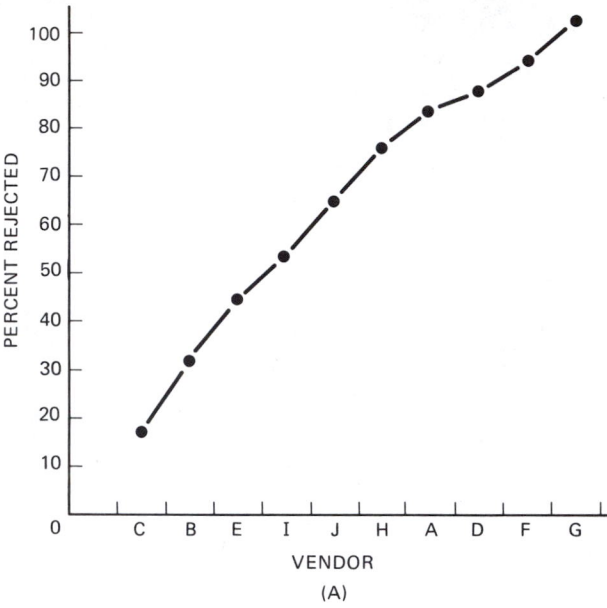

(A)

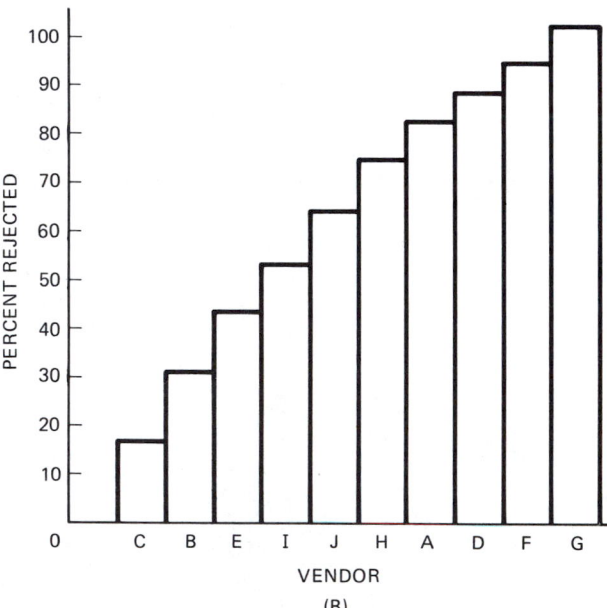

(B)

FIGURE 8–13 (a) Cumulative Pareto Line Graph; (b) Cumulative Pareto Bar Chart

- Analysis of losses by material identification numbers. This is very useful for purchased goods.

- Analysis of losses by type of product. For example, the particular type of component, such as fastener, may be causing the bulk of the quality-related problems.

- Analysis of losses by the specific process that causes the problem. More problems may be resulting from one process, such as electroplating, than from any other process.

- Analysis of losses by the vendor or supplier of the material. As the example showed, sometimes certain vendors cause more of the problems than others.

- Analysis by cost of the product. More attention might be paid to those parts that have a higher dollar value, either in actual material cost or in value added by the process.

- Analysis by method of failure. The way in which a particular product fails may indicate a significant problem that requires attention.

Once the vital problems have been identified, regardless of their nature, the next step in the SPC process is to identify potential causes of the problems. Chapter 9 will discuss the cause/effect, Ishikawa, or fishbone diagram. This is a useful analytical tool for finding potential problems to the process.

EXERCISES

The following are situations where Pareto analysis might be useful.

1. Aft-Tech has kept careful records regarding the number of rejects in each of its manufacturing facilities during the last month. These records require summarization before presentation to management. Prepare a Pareto chart for this information.

Plant	Number of Units Produced	Rejects
Atlanta	4800	341
Boise	3100	309
Cleveland	5450	379
Detroit	4444	333
Eugene	1250	150
Fresno	5050	404
Greenville	2800	310
Hahira	400	27
Indianapolis	6660	460
Juneau	1875	166
Kendell	3200	289
Lawrence	4000	201

2. The Aft-Tech Machine Works has recorded reject rates for each of its manufacturing departments. Use Pareto analysis to determine which department(s) requires the most improvement.

Department	Reject Rate (%)
Lathe	3.0
Mill	9.5
Bore	4.3
Ream	3.8
Broach	5.5
Saw	4.4
Grinding	5.3
Lapping	4.1
Honing	2.9
Microstoning	3.0
Forge	8.8

3. Quality costs for Aft-Tech's subassembly plants has been collected on a plant by plant basis for the past year. Prepare a Pareto chart for this information.

Plant	Total Quality Cost	Total Cost
Mobile	$145,000	$4,500,000
Nashville	222,000	5,300,000
Orleans	278,000	5,950,000
Paducah	312,000	6,250,000
Quincy	340,000	3,975,000
Roanoke	367,000	6,725,000
Seattle	378,000	6,900,000
Tarrytown	421,000	7,230,000
Unadilla	439,000	7,555,000
Victoria	490,000	8,120,000
Washington	505,000	9,500,000
Yakima	600,000	9,980,000

CHAPTER 9

Cause and Effect Analysis

Since you can't get quality out of a jar or off the shelf, you have to create it yourself within the context of your corporate culture. [76: 571]

James R. Houghton
Corning Glass Works

9.1 INTRODUCTION

The check sheet described in Chapter 7 helps to identify potential quality or process problems. Pareto analysis, discussed in Chapter 8, highlights the most frequently occurring and usually the most pressing problems. This is very important. However, merely identifying the problem will not improve the process. Identifying and convincing everyone in the organization of the major quality problems will not solve them.

A methodology is required that will help to identify potential causes of the problem. One such methodology that is appropriate is known as the cause and effect diagram or the Ishikawa diagram in honor of its developer, or sometimes as the fishbone diagram since the resulting shape of this analytical tool often takes the form of a fishbone.

Ishikawa, in his *Guide to Quality Control* [79], discusses the development of many different types of these diagrams. We will concentrate our work on but one of these to illustrate the application of this most useful technique.

The use of this analytical tool is generally quite popular. As we will see, the diagram is relatively simple to use. It provides an opportunity to involve all the individuals associated with a process in the actual problem-solving process. The construction of the diagram is intriguing as each participant immediately sees the result of his or her contribution. The diagram does get results. As the cases presented at the end of the text show, "problems tackled by cause and effect analysis have a remarkable success record." [60: 107]

9.2 METHODOLOGY

The cause and effect diagram is a picture that shows the relationship between the problem under consideration and its potential causes and the potential causes of the potential causes. Section 9.3 will suggest the steps required to construct this diagram. It should be noted that the construction and use of the diagram and analysis is much more effective with groups than as an individual tool.

The first step is to identify the problem that is to be considered. This is the "effect" that we will try to find the cause for. The effect is generally shown within a box at the far-right side of the diagram. A long arrow leads into the box, providing a connection for the causes with the effect. Figure 9–1 shows this for a generic problem. The source of the problem should be the Pareto analysis performed after the problem data were collected. As a group problem-solving technique, the cause and effect diagrams are often drawn on a blackboard or flip chart. That provides a picture for everyone within the group to see and to add to.

The second step in constructing the diagram involves the identification of potential major causes of the problem. These are shown on the diagram as major branches leading into the main arrow or spine of the cause and effect diagram. Figure 9–2 shows this addition.

These major potential causes can often be generalized to one or more of the following:

- **Machinery.** The equipment available to perform the process. Whether it is a typing process that involves a typewriter or word processor, or a machine tool, the cause of the poblem may be directly related to the machine or equipment used. Broken machinery and worn-out machinery are typical causes of problem.

- **Material.** Another major input to any process is the material used. The transformation can be only as good as the material received. If there is a quality problem with the material or if incorrect or substandard material is used, there will be the potential for quality problems. Specifically, material that does not meet the standards of the particular process will cause quality problems.

- **Methods.** The procedures and steps followed while the job is being performed can have a significant impact on the quality. Using a wrong or inconsistent method can be a serious problem.

FIGURE 9–1 Cause and Effect Diagram, Step 1 ———————————→ PROBLEM

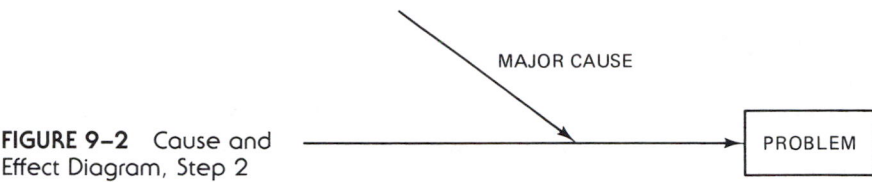

FIGURE 9–2 Cause and Effect Diagram, Step 2

- **Manpower.** The last of these common major causes may be the people actually performing the work. They may not be qualified, they may not have been trained, or they may not even been told the requirements of their process.

The four potential causes described, machines, material, methods, and manpower, are often referred to as the "4M's." The 4M cause and effect diagram is one of the most frequently used versions. Even if additional potential causes are identified, such as the environment, the 4M structure provides a good starting point for analysis. Figure 9–3 shows a typical 4M version of the cause and effect diagram.

The third step leading to a complete cause and effect diagram is the identification of possible submajor causes that might contribute to the major causes. For example, using the 4M approach, a major cause might be manpower. A submajor cause could be training. Similarly, contributing to the major cause of machine could be a worn tool. Figure 9–4 shows the cause and effect diagram, in the 4M format, showing major and now submajor causes. Note how the major arrow represents a trunk and the submajor causes limbs. We might go further and say the submajor causes look somewhat like branches.

The fourth step, and possibly the fifth, sixth, and so on, is the addition of more contributing causes. Calling the next level sub-submajor starts to become awkward. But the skeleton of the cause and effect diagram continues to expand until it looks like a bare tree or an x-ray of a fish. Hence the name fishbone diagram that

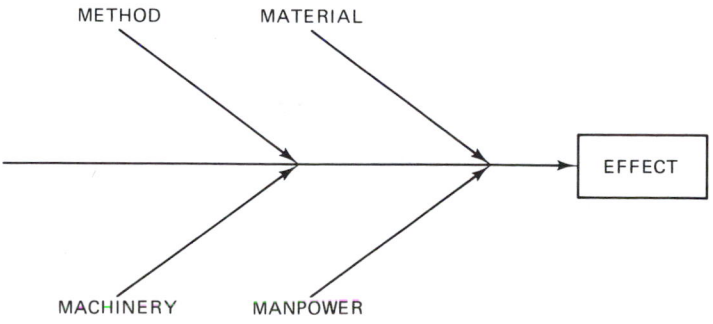

FIGURE 9–3 4M Cause and Effect Diagram

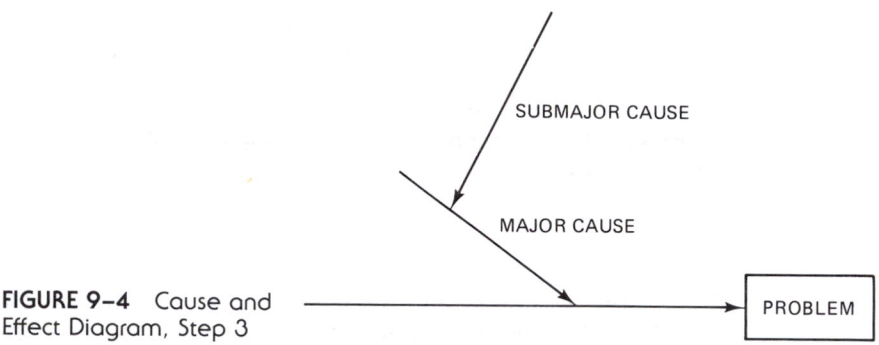

FIGURE 9-4 Cause and Effect Diagram, Step 3

is sometimes affixed to this analytical tool. Figure 9-5 shows a completed structure. Figure 9-6 shows a fishbone diagram for a quality problem in a foundry.

The fifth step in our process is to look, with our group, at the completed diagram. At this point we should continue brainstorming in an effort to identify additional causes that may have been overlooked the first time around. Sometimes just wondering *what if,* or *how come,* or *why* will stimulate additional potential causes.

At this point it is wise to take a break and let the work already completed have an opportunity to sink in, so to speak. After a resting period, the process should resume, with the sixth step. This is identifying the most likely causes. The group that is performing the cause and effect analysis should have extensive knowledge of the process. Based on the group's experience, one or more most probable causes can be identified. The group leader at this point has the task of bringing the group discussion to a consensus about the most probable causes. Even though the group may be in agreement at this point about what it thinks the major cause is, it still must not rule out the others.

After this consensus is reached, the cause and effect analysis is temporarily completed. At this point we must begin to monitor the process to determine if,

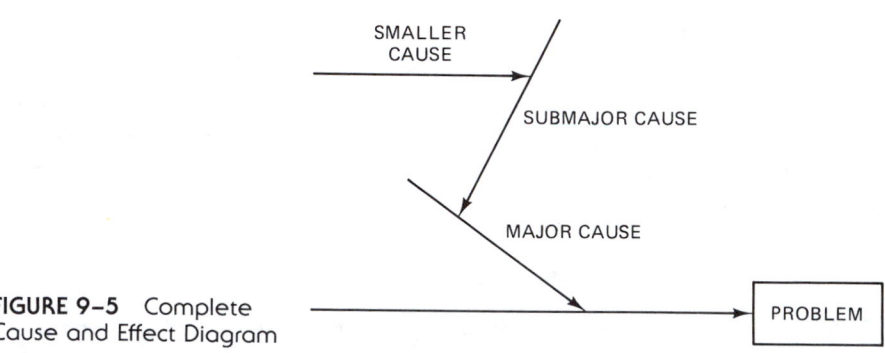

FIGURE 9-5 Complete Cause and Effect Diagram

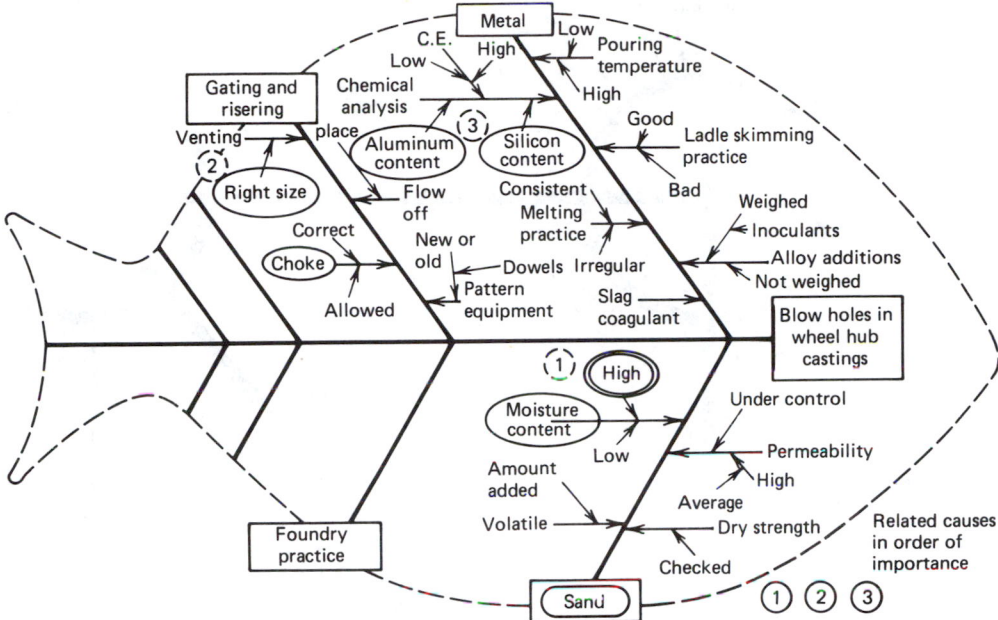

FIGURE 9–6 Fishbone Diagram (Source: Sinha, M.N. and W.O. Willborn, *The Management of Quality Assurance*, John Wiley & Sons, Inc., New York, 1985. Reprinted with permission)

indeed, we have found the cause of the quality problem. This involves data collection and some fundamental statistical analysis. (These procedures will be explained in later chapters in sufficient detail to allow their use.)

At this point we have reached the next cog in our statistical process control model. As Figure 9–7 shows, we are now ready to begin the process monitoring and control phase. Before we do that, we will conclude this chapter with the actual construction of a cause and effect diagram.

9.3 APPLICATION

A serious quality problem has disrupted the food service operations at Aft-Tech. The toast served at the recent executive breakfast was burned. No check sheet was required to identify this problem, no Pareto analysis was needed to determine which effect needed to be investigated. The president was embarrassed by the blackened wheat toast and not only wants to know why, but wants to make sure that this never happens again.

The corporate quality assurance manager, when told of the problem, viewed this as an outstanding opportunity to use one of the corporation's statistical process control analysis tools, the cause and effect diagram.

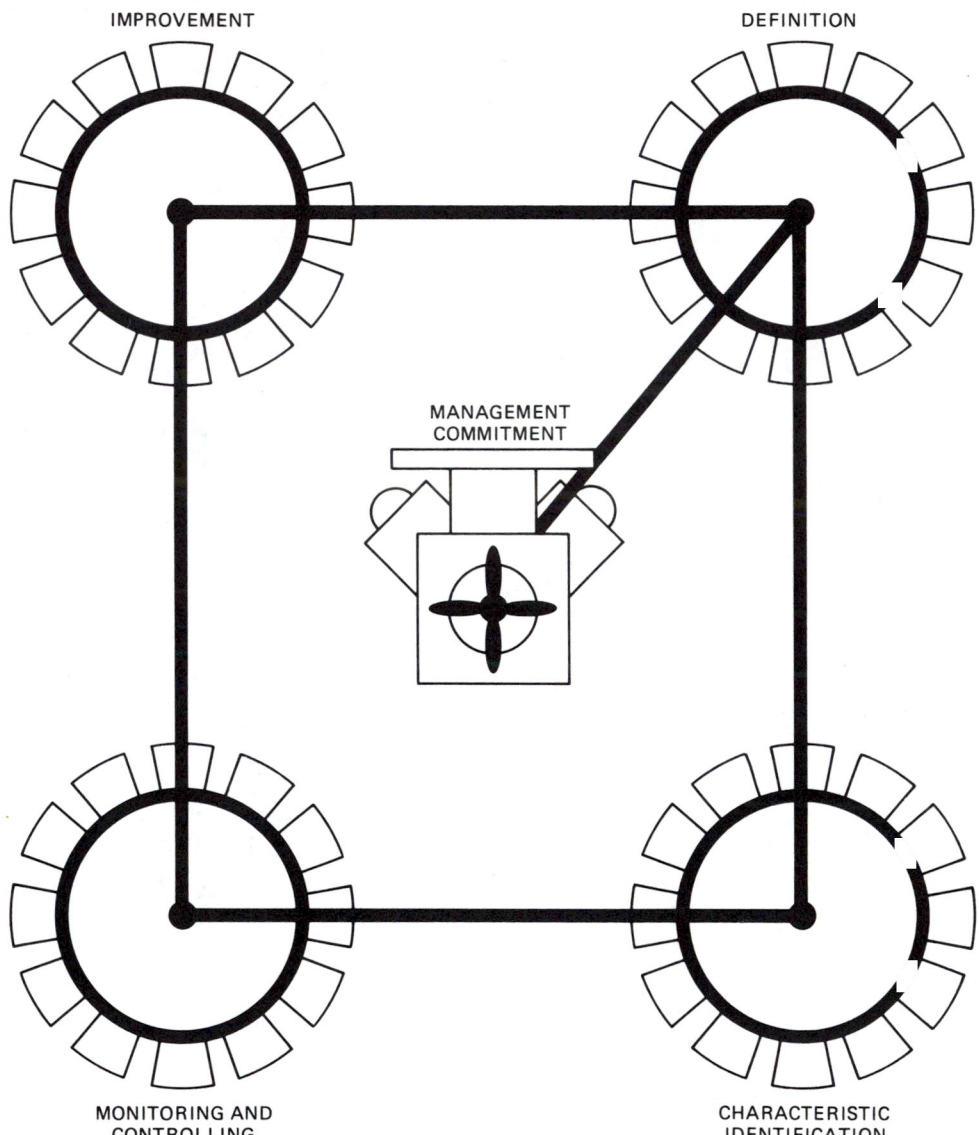

FIGURE 9–7 SPC Model

She immediately formed a group, consisting of the pastry chef, the pastry assistant, the purchasing agent, the dining room supervisor, the table waiter, and the stores manager. These individuals all know the toast-making process or are involved in some phase of it. This group, with the QA manager serving as leader, immediately set to work trying to determine the cause of this disastrous situation.

```
                                                                    ┌─────────┐
──────────────────────────────────────────────────────────────────▶│ BURNED  │
                                                                    │ TOAST   │
                                                                    └─────────┘
```

FIGURE 9–8 C/E Burned-toast Problem

Using a flip chart to record the information gathered, the group identified *burned toast* as the effect that needed remedying. Figure 9–8 shows the start of the diagram. Then, using the 4M approach, major potential causes were cited for each of the four factors. These were enumerated as follows:

Major Cause
Machinery: toaster
Method: Procedure for making golden toast
Manpower: assistant pastry chef
waiter
Materials: bread
butter

After these major causes were identified, as they related to the burnt toast problem, they were added to the cause and effect diagram as shown in Figure 9–9.

The serious analysis now began. For each of the major possible causes, contributing potential submajor causes were identified, and contributing sub-submajor causes, and so forth, were suggested. These are listed next and then added to the fishbone diagram.

Major Cause	Submajor Cause	Sub-submajor Cause
Machinery	Heats too long	Timer defective
		Timer set wrong
	Heats too hot	Defective thermostat
		Defective insulation
		Mislabled thermostat
	Bread too close to heating coils	
	New toaster	Not broken in
Method	Too much heat specified	New model toaster
		No specs yet
	Too much time specified	New model toaster
		No specs yet
Manpower	Lack of training	
	Lack of experience	
	Personal preference	
	Lack of attention	Attending other tasks
	Defective order	Misunderstanding of term
Materials	Thicker bread	New vendor
		Mislabeled
	Frozen bread	Too many wheat orders
	Different brand	Quick toasting
	Prebuttered bread	
	Mistaken bread	Mispackaged

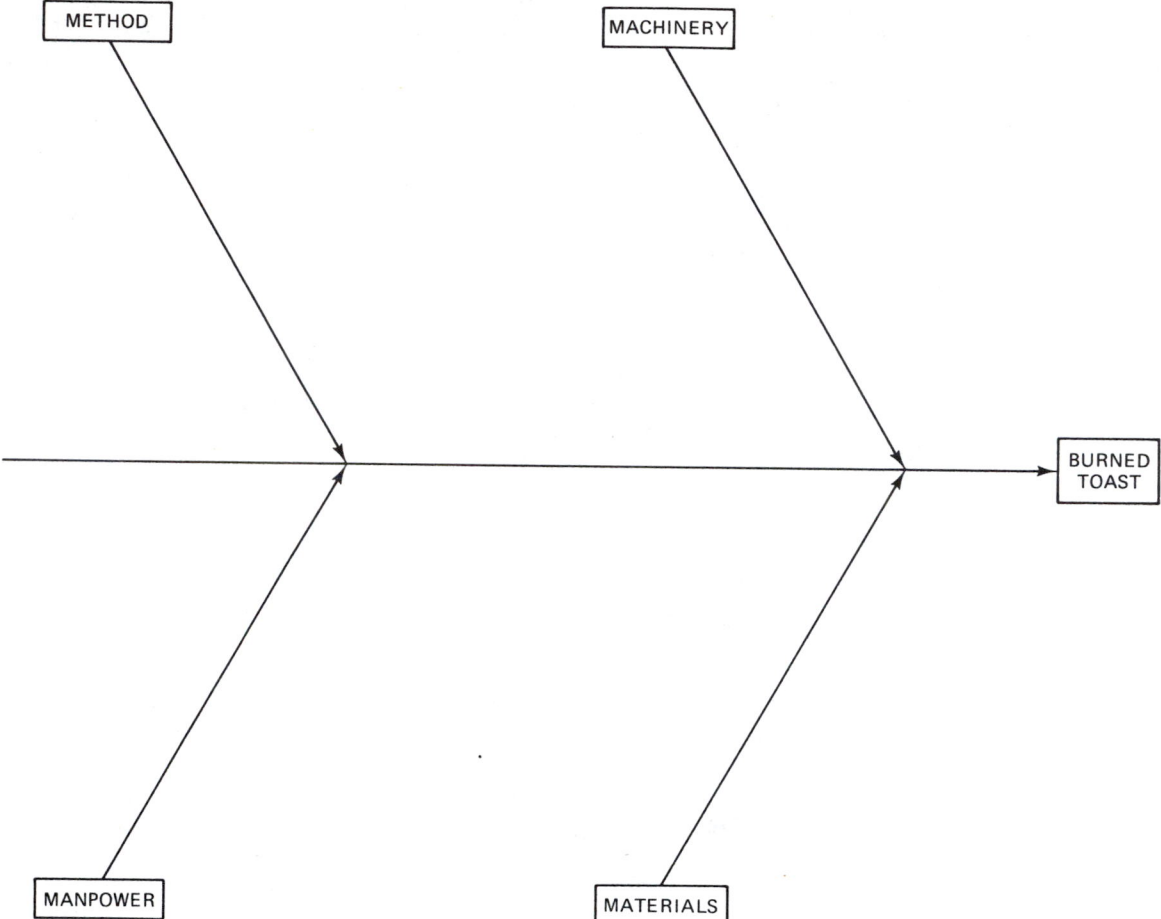

FIGURE 9–9 4M for Burned-toast Problem

Figure 9–10 shows the "completed" cause and effect diagram. Each major cause has a number of additional contributing causes. Each of these causes is potentially the reason for the burnt toast. After the group has completed the diagram, the next task is the identification of the most likely possible cause or causes.

In this application, several potential causes were identified as being most likely. These were defective timer, lack of attention, and thicker bread. These were noted by circling on the cause and effect diagram, as shown in Figure 9–11.

While the discussion was underway, the question of environmental factors came up. The possibility of factors such as relative humidity and room temperature were suggested as possible causes of the problem. The relative humidity was thought to be a serious possibility, and that, along with other environmental factors such as

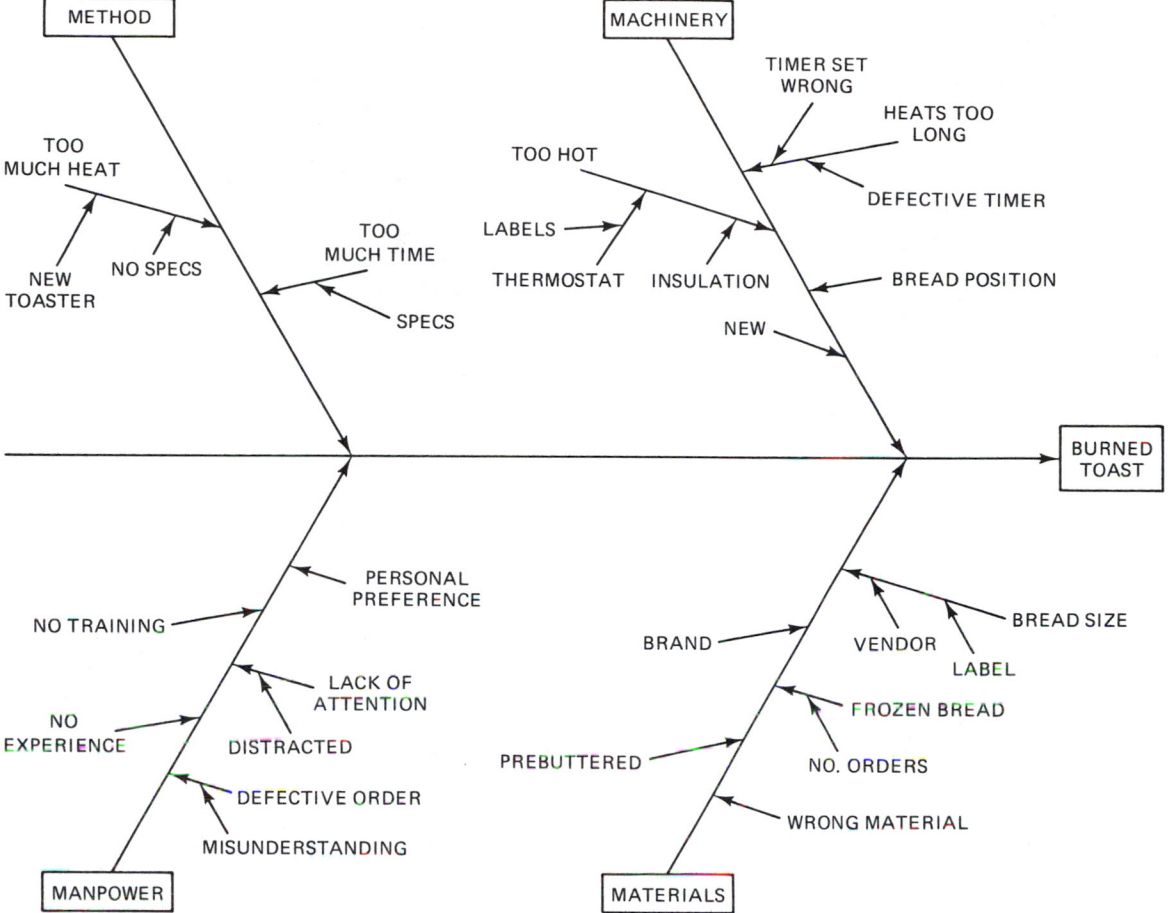

FIGURE 9–10 Expanded C/E for Burned-toast Problem

airflow, was added to the diagram. The final diagram is shown in Figure 9–11, with the four most probable causes identified with circles.

9.3.1 Misapplication

The cause and effect diagram can be a useful tool in identifying potential causes of problems. It can also be misused as well. A well-constructed and helpful diagram has the general appearance of a fish skeleton. Sometimes other patterns emerge after the diagram has been constructed. The following series of figures will show what some of these look like and what they represent.

When a cause and effect diagram looks like the one shown in Figure 9–12,

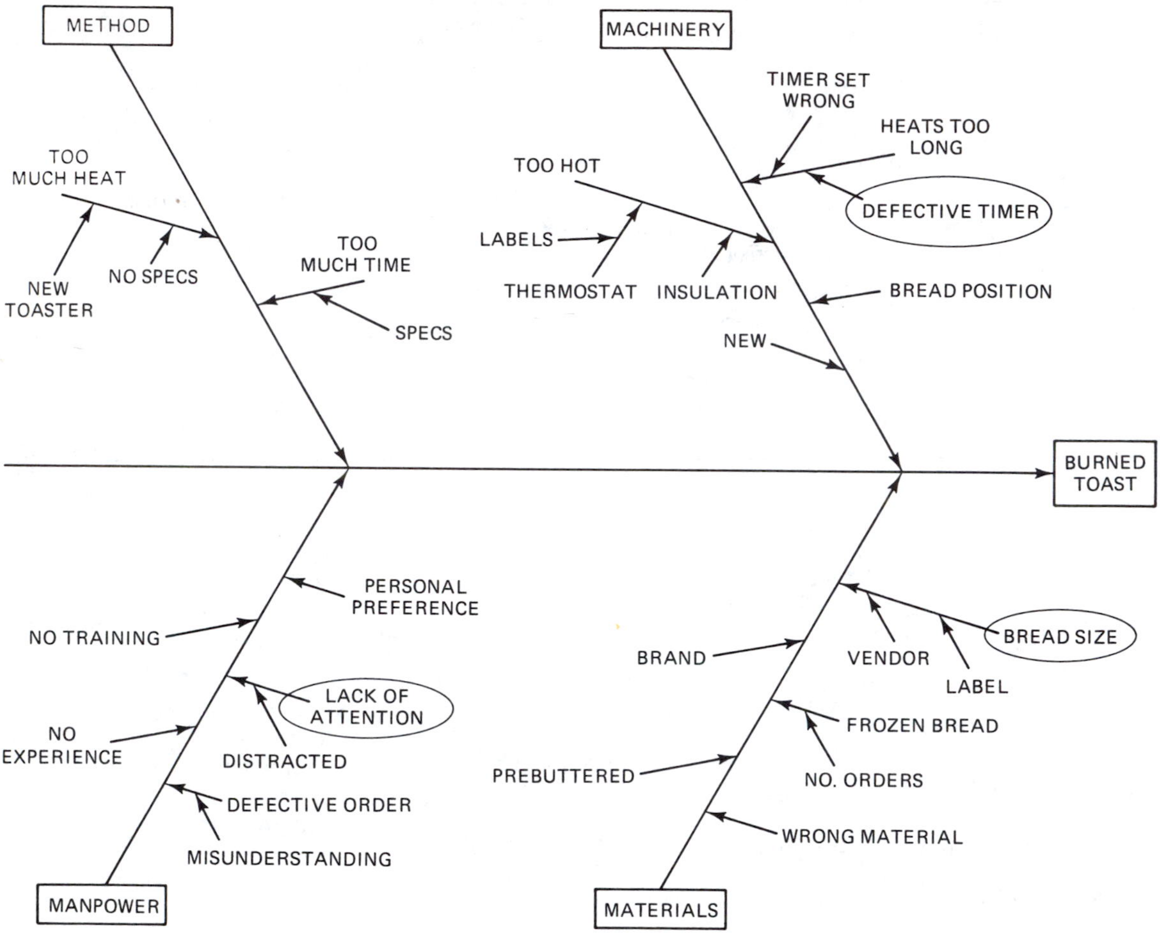

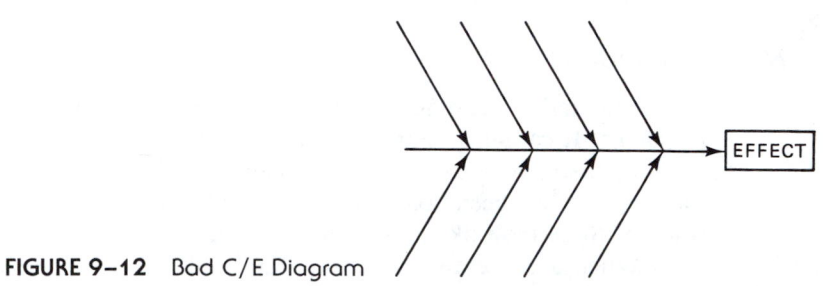

FIGURE 9–11 Final C/E for Burned-toast Problem

FIGURE 9–12 Bad C/E Diagram

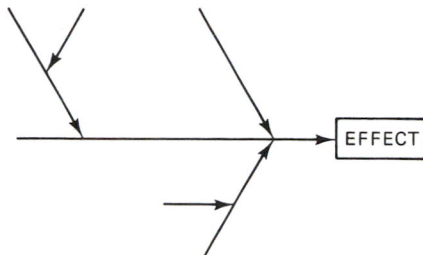

FIGURE 9–13 C/E Diagram
with Too Few Causes

then it probably means that the knowledge of the process is very shallow. The suggestions mean that the people doing the analysis don't really understand what they are doing or how it relates to the rest of the process.

Although Figure 9–13 shows a diagram in the proper form, the limited number of causes and subcauses limits the effectiveness of the diagram in identifying potential causes to the quality problem. Figure 9–6 is an example of a good diagram that identifies many potential causes. Another excellent example is presented in Case Study 1 in Chapter 20.

9.4 CONCLUSION

The next step in the improvement process would be to collect data about these process characteristics to determine if any of them are indeed the cause and, if so, what the best method of improving the process would be to eliminate the problem of the burnt toast. This requires statistical analysis information that will be presented beginning with Chapter 11.

Before moving on to the statistical portion of statistical process control, the monitoring and controlling part of our SPC model, we will take a slight detour. In Chapter 8 we mentioned problem-solving groups. These are extremely effective when developed and used properly.

Chapter 10 will present an overview of group problem-solving methods as they relate to process improvement. The references cited will povide the reader with ample opportunities to pursue other more detailed work on groups.

CHAPTER 10

Group Problem Solving

Team participation should never occur until the management team is totally participating in the improvement process, if you don't want the employees to believe they are being manipulated. [85: 87]

> **H. J. Harrington**
> **IBM Corporation**

10.1 INTRODUCTION

William E. Brock, a Secretary of Labor in the Reagan administration, stated

> Industry must be concerned with real, honest to goodness labor involvement—worker involvement in the company, I think those firms that are going to be successful, and those that are successful today, are firms that pay a great deal of attention to the human qualities of their work forces in terms of offering their employees career success and keeping them happy. [82: 27]

Virtually all successful quality improvement programs share, as a common bond, worker involvement in the improvement process. We have mentioned it often within the text. Before going any further, we should examine exactly what we mean, within the context of statistical process control, regarding employee groups.

Before defining employee groups, though, a couple of thoughts about employee involvement. F. James McDonald, president of General Motors, when talking about the use of teams, made the statement, "As far as I'm concerned, it's the only way to operate the business—there isn't any other in today's world." Tom Peters, coauthor of *In Search of Excellence*, has said, "The major failure of American business is seeing the employee as a part of the problem instead of part of the solution." [85: 86]

We can learn from the Japanese experience, both in Japan and at organizations in this country.

> Japanese managers treat their employees as resources that, if cultivated, will yield economic returns to the firm. Firms invest in training for all employees and emphasize development of a labor force skilled in a variety of jobs. All workers are assumed to be capable and desirous of contributing to the firm and are made to feel like fully contributing members. [128: 38]

10.2 EMPLOYEE TEAMS

A variety of different types of teams is used by employers in an attempt to use the contributions that employees can make to the organization. These have generally fit into the following general categories: departmental improvement teams, quality circles, process improvement teams, and task forces.

Briefly, a departmental improvement team involves all members of a department. They work on a continuing basis to solve problems that arise regarding the department's operation. A quality circle is "a group of volunteer workers, from the same group, who usually meet for an hour each week to discuss problems, investigate causes, recommend solutions, and take corrective action when authority is in their purview." [70: 356] Quality circles differ from departmental teams in that the circles focus more on quality problems as they relate to one specific area.

A process improvement team is created to address quality, productivity, and waste problems that involve a major process within the organization. The process invariably crosses departmental lines and requires input from many different functional organizations. The creation and operation of this team is consistent with the SPC philosophy.

A task force is usually created to deal with a major problem. The top management selects experts who work at putting out a major fire that in some way threatens the operation of the entire organization. Generally, service on a task force is performed in lieu of the employee's regular job.

Figure 10–1 summarizes the operation and structure of the four types of employee involvement groups. This chapter will focus on the process improvement team because of its close link with the statistical process control philosophy that we have developed.

10.3 PROCESS IMPROVEMENT TEAMS

Process improvement teams, or just teams in the context of this chapter, are groups of employees who meet regularly to discuss problems that relate to specific processes. These teams investigate the causes of problems, collect data about the process-related problems, and recommend corrective action to improve the process.

The members of the team come from different departments that are associated with the process. A typical team might consist of production operators, supervisors,

Characteristics	Department improvement teams	Quality circles	Process improvement teams	Task forces
Membership	Department members	Department members	Selected members of work-related departments	Selected members based on experience
Participation	Mandatory	Voluntary	Mandatory	Mandatory
Management direction	Moderate	Minimal	Moderate	High
Problem selection	By group	By group	By group	By management
Solution urgency	Moderate	Low	Moderate	High
Scope of activity	Within department	Within department	Interdepartment	Interdepartment
Identification of solution	By members	By members	By members	By members
Schedule pressure	Moderate	Minimal	Moderate	High
Activity time	Short meetings, long period	Short meetings, long period	Short meetings, long period	Long meetings, short period, no other assignment
Process facilitator	Optional	Encouraged	None	None
Implementation	By members	By members	By members	By others

FIGURE 10-1 Employee Group Characteristics (Source: Harrington, *The Improvement Process*, McGraw-Hill Book Company, New York, Reprinted with permission)

inspection personnel, process engineers, product engineers, and representatives from accounting, purchasing, and marketing. Sometimes there is even a member from the quality assurance department.

The process improvement team uses the techniques of SPC to identify problems and potential causes. Statistical techniques relating to process monitoring and control are used to isolate and eliminate the real contributing causes to the process problems. "Once an in-depth analysis of process problems and causes has been made, it takes very little effort to 'estimate' predictions of possible improvement efforts on the various elements that affect current process capability." [87: 32]

Process improvement teams do involve many of the organization's workers in assuming responsibility for the continuous improvement of the process. The members of the team do see that their efforts and their insights provide concrete suggestions for changes to the process that result in improving quality, and as a result, naturally, improving productivity.

On the other hand, these teams are not something that top management need be afraid of. With the demonstration of commitment by management to changing the organization's culture to the continuous improvement philosophy, the teams are merely part of that overall process. They are another resource. Process improvement teams are also not a management program. Management may be part of the groups, but management does not own the teams.

The teams cannot be viewed as a cure-all. Just by forming the teams, there is no guarantee that there will be instant success. As a result of monitoring and controlling the process, the group may discover that the process is doing as good as it can. This may not be the desired answer to the problems of the process. Any improvement may involve massive changes to the transformation process. The suggestions from the teams may not be popular.

Despite the potential limitation, process improvement teams have an enviable track record. Case Study 1 in Chapter 20 describes the activities of one such team working on the process. The results, while not spectacular, certainly demonstrate the usefulness of this type of team.

Section 10.4 discusses the operation of these groups. For managers and workers unfamiliar with group processes, problems often arise. There are changes in attitude, philosophy, and corporate culture involved in using groups to solve problems that were at one time entirely the responsibility of management and the technical support staff. New ways of thinking have to be used. But, as you read the suggestions regarding successful group operations, remember, "The most important underlying force at this point is the 'commitment' being demonstrated. . . ." [87: 32]

10.4 TEAM OPERATION

A number of helpful hints for managing all types of groups have been suggested over the years. This section is an amalgamation of those thoughts that, in the author's experience, have been most productive and have led to quality and productivity improvements. At the end of the chapter, a brief bibliography on groups is provided.

The first point we will make regards the composition of the group. The group *must* be representative of all the people involved with the process. If it is too top heavy with management, then it is viewed as a management group. If first-line supervision is left out, it will be viewed as a conspiracy against the supervisors. If too many engineering or technical people are involved, they may impose their preconceived notions on the other group members. The team members should want to be on the team and participate in the process. The process improvement team will not be successful if the members don't want to do their job as a team member.

A second consideration is the identification of the group leader. This person should, naturally, have an interest in the process and some knowledge, but not necessarily expert knowledge, of the process. The leader should have knowledge of the SPC tools that the group will use, such as check sheets, Pareto analysis, cause and effect diagrams, and statistical quality control. The leader should be respected by the other members of the group and should be able to foster a team spirit in the group. The leader does not necessarily have to be a member of management.

A third and very important point is that the group needs an early success. The initial problem should be carefully selected so that there is a good chance that the activities of the group or team will lead to a quality and productivity improvement. Later projects may or may not have the same chance of success. A key task that the process improvement team can perform is ruling out potential causes.

Groups succeed or fail based on the participation of the members of the group. The following barriers to participation have been developed and are presented as a guide. [63: 228]

1. **Poor communication.** Channels of communication in the organization inhibit the free flow of information and opinions or the sharing of results and costs.

2. **Theory X discipline.** In Douglas McGregor's theory X management style, motivation and discipline are based on threats of punishment, and the only rewards are the removal of the threat.

3. **Short-term shortsightedness.** If all rewards are based on short-term production quotas or short-term profit, everybody's job becomes a short-term experience and the one is involved in the company's long-term future.

4. **CEO mind reading.** The perception throughout the company of top management's true thinking and philosophy will control people's actions, regardless of the reality of what is on the CEO's mind—unless he or she communicates his or her thoughts effectively.

5. **Weak management commitment.** Suspicions that management is not sincere and will not back you when the going gets tough will kill any initial enthusiasm, particularly for long-term programs. (Chapter 19 discusses commitment in more detail.)

6. **Autocratic environment.** If the record shows decades of autocratic controls on decision making, it is only natural to assume this will continue, despite any statements from management to the contrary.

7. **Lack of middle management support.** They are the key in any organization and if they are not supportive, despite any coercive efforts by top management, any new participative program will fail.

8. **Wrong leadership.** The wrong facilitator or leader or coordinator will doom the process improvement team. If a person is picked because of availability rather than suitability, one improperly trained or without "people" skills, the program will die.

9. **Union opposition.** Unions are naturally threatened by the formation of groups, and if you don't bring them in early, you won't get another chance—the program will fail.

10. **Poor preplanning.** The use of SPC and particularly the use of process improvement teams represent a major shift in company philosophy. This demands what can best be called a PR program to fully explain to everyone exactly what the intent is, what the timetable is, who is initially involved, who the coordinators are, and what is expected from each person in the organization, even if they are not a member of the team initially.

Even with good participation, there can be failure. Some of the more frequently cited reasons for failure of the process improvement teams include the following. [85: 106–107]

First is the **lack of time.** Typical of the specific reason is the response, "I'm too busy fixing it to keep it from happening again." Second is the **lack of ownership.** This is indicated by the "it's not by job" syndrome. What has to be understood is that it is everybody's job to continue improving the process. Ducking responsibility is shortsighted.

Third is the **lack of recognition**. Management has traditionally rewarded only the proper performance of the individual at his or her job. If time is taken to help one of the other workers, the individual's own performance, especially regarding production, will suffer. Granted that in the long term having better inputs to your process will improve your performance, it is difficult to get that message through to the people evaluating performance.

A fourth roadblock is the **errors will happen** belief. If we believe that anything other than our organization's actions control the outputs of our process, then we will have problems. Self-fulfilling prophecies, especially regarding mistakes, can be the ruination of a company. A fifth problem is **ignorance of the importance of the problem.** If people forget the concept of the extended process, then actions taken at one point can have dire consequences way down the line. A burr left on a fastener may cause a catastrophic failure if that fastener is used to keep a wing on an airplane.

Sixth is the belief that **no one can do anything** about the problem anyway. The solution may be costly, but there is almost always a solution. A seventh problem to effective team operation is the **schedule versus quality** trade-off that just about every manager is faced with making at some point. The quality of the output is remembered long after the relief of making the schedule is forgotten. Eighth is the problem of **people trying to protect themselves.** If individuals are more concerned with self-perservation than doing the job, the improvement process is doomed. Carried to the ultimate, the old line, "She never makes a mistake—she never does anything," fits the situation. If a member of the process improvement team decides that the cause is his or her part of the process, then we will never solve the problem.

One last difficulty is offered, and this is **headhunting by management.** If this is all management wants, then there will be no improvement. If this is what management wants, there can be no doubt about the level of commitment present.

Despite the potential problems and barriers that we have just discussed, process improvement teams are effective. The next section describes some of the advantages that accrue to organizations that effectively utilize these teams.

10.5 TEAM ADVANTAGES

Some advantages of using teams to attempt to solve process-related quality problems have already been mentioned. The following listing summarizes and expands on these. [84: 101–102]

1. Because of combined disciplines, the scheme ensures that a total cause and effect analysis can be made. The proper formation of the group or team, with

representatives from most portions of the extended process, provides the necessary expertise.

2. As expert professionals, team members require no education and training to become effective. They already know the process. The only education or training necessary is in the SPC procedures.

3. Since the team understands the total process and its interaction, team decisions can optimize total efficiency and minimize suboptimization. The team looks at the entire process and not just the microscopic part that each member normally deals with.

4. Links between functions are provided and are united by common goals. The increased communication is positive, whether it is between internal customers and suppliers or between the organization and its customers and suppliers.

5. Waste and cost can be effectively reduced. Quality will improve, and our theorem states that as quality increases so does productivity.

6. If implemented before the process design is complete, the process improvement team is an effective way of preventing problems from occurring. We want to focus on the prevention of problems and not on detecting them after the fact.

7. The team members become acquainted with the total business concept. The sooner everyone in an organization realizes that they are all part of the extended process, the sooner they can begin the process of continuous improvement.

We would be remiss if we did not also report some disadvantages of using these teams. The list is not nearly as long. The teams require time for meetings, time for data collection as part of process monitoring, and time for data analysis and interpretation. This is time away from regular activities for the team members. Sometimes the team discussions become specialized and some of the members cannot follow. When this is the case, the use of time is again questioned.

There are many reported instances of significant improvements caused by process improvement teams. Some have been reported to increase productivity by as much as 300 percent. Case Study 1 in Chapter 20 illustrates the operation of one such team at a manufacturing plant. The productivity improvement there speaks for itself.

10.6 CONCLUSION

The use of process improvement teams does not guarantee that all process problems will immediately disappear. The use of process improvement teams cannot substitute for management commitment to the continuing process of never ending improvement. Let me repeat. **The most important underlying force is the commitment.** [87: 32] Process improvement teams, though, are extremely useful in identifying potential process problems and using the fundamental data collection and analysis techniques of statistical quality control.

The following section of the text will present these statistical concepts. The material presented will not attempt to be a thorough or complete statistical quality control text. Rather, the material presented will be just enough so that all individuals involved in statistical process control can understand the concepts that make SPC so effective at improving quality. A bibliography of statistical quality control books will be presented at the end of the next section.

SELECTED REFERENCES

The following is a partial listing of texts and articles that provide more insight into the operation of process improvement teams.

Cole, Robert E., "Learning from the Japanese: Prospects and Pitfalls," *Management Review,* September 1980.

Deming, W. E., and Gray C. S., "Japan: Quality Control and Innovation," *Business Week,* July 20, 1981.

Gryna, Frank M., *Quality Circles—A Team Approach to Problem Solving,* Amacom, New York, 1981.

Harrington, H. J., *The Improvement Process,* McGraw-Hill, New York, 1987.

Hayes, Robert, "Why Japanese Factories Work," *Harvard Business Review,* July/August 1981.

Ishikawa, Kaoru, *Guide to Quality Control,* Asian Productivity Organization, Tokyo, 1976.

Ouichi, William G., *Theory Z—How American Business Can Meet the Japanese Challenge,* Addison-Wesley, Reading, MA.

Squires, F., "A New Role for the Quality Circle," *Quality,* August 1981.

"Involved People Making the Difference in Manufacturing," *Modern Materials Handling,* January 20, 1982.

CHAPTER 11

Variability

Today, the real payoff comes from applying the proven manufacturing control and feedback techniques to all key activities in the business and treating the entire company as a complex process that contains many subprocesses, only one of which is the process that produces the products sold to the customer. [85: 136]

H. James Harrington
IBM

11.1 INTRODUCTION

Thus far, according to the statistical process control model we have developed, we have discussed the need for management commitment for the program to work. This is the key, and we must not forget it. As this commitment is secured, then we proceed to define our operation as a process. It makes no difference what product is produced, whether it is a manufactured part or a service, it is produced as a result of a process, actually a series of related processes. Each miniprocess has its inputs, transformations, and outputs. For each process, whether it is mini or macro, there are suppliers and customers. The customers have expectations regarding their input. These expectations are identified, and the critical ones noted.

At this point, according to the model, we are ready to begin monitoring and controlling these processes. To do this, we first measure the variability of the process. Our objective, the goal of continuous improvement, remember, we have stated as continually reducing the variability of the process.

Before we can talk about monitoring and controlling processes, we must understand how to measure variability. Before we can do that, we must understand variability. That is the purpose of this chapter.

11.2 NORMAL VARIATION

Every process has some amount of variation. Neither people or nor machines can perform any action exactly the same way everytime it is performed. That is a fact. Think of some activity that you perform many times and are very skilled in. Think of signing your name. On a sheet of blank paper or even in the margin of this book sign your name 10 times in a row. The last signature will look somewhat different from the first. Even if we were to program an industrial robot to sign its name, we would not be able to get exactly the same pattern everytime. There would be small differences.

Normal variation is present in every process. "One characteristic of modern manufacturing is that no two pieces are ever made exactly alike. The variations may be small, as in the case of gage blocks which have been guaranteed to two-millionths of an inch." [61: 347] The variation may be much larger and visible to the naked eye. But the fact remains that normal variation is present in every process. The fact that tolerances are specified for measurements is evidence that this variation is expected.

This normal variation has many causes. It is almost always due to a combination or interaction of the inputs to a process, coupled with the transformation process. Even inputs that have virtually no variability may, when placed in contact with other inputs to the process, develop some variability. For example, the combination of certain gases with certain raw materials at certain temperatures and pressures will cause reactions that vary slightly everytime they occur. They may be within given ranges, but they still vary some from interaction to interaction. This variability is usually random in nature, although the specific process may dictate its general shape.

Normal variability may be caused, in a typical manufacturing environment, by such items as slight variation in raw material, occasional machine vibration, and human variability. Slight changes in environmental conditions may also affect the process.

Besides being present all the time, **normal variation is predictable.** The shape, size, and general location of the variability can all be measured and used to describe the expected output of the process. Later in this chapter we will look at a relatively simple way to describe the variability that is present in a specific process.

11.3 ABNORMAL VARIATION

We called the variation that is always present in every process normal variation. Logic would imply, then, that there must be abnormal variation as well. There is. What we will call **abnormal variation is any unusual or unexpected occurrence.** Abnormal variation is due to a special cause or set of causes. These special causes do not usually occur. These special causes of abnormal variation are always assignable to some specific action or set of actions. Sometimes, though, it is difficult to pinpoint what the specific causes are.

Some typical causes of abnormal variation include defective material, improper setup, untrained operators, tool wear, careless operators, and even weather conditions. For example, a sudden lightning strike during a thunderstorm can cause severe problems for a process.

Abnormal variation is not predictable. Although we will learn ways to determine when abnormal variation is happening, we generally cannot predict ahead of time when it will occur. We may, for example, have some idea that lightning may strike during a thunderstorm in July or August, but would we necessarily even be anticipating it during January? Even if we were expecting it, there is no exact way yet to predict where it will strike.

11.4   DESCRIBING VARIATION

Thus far in this chapter we have stated that variation is always present in every process. We have also stated that there are two types of variation, normal and abnormal. By using a simple statistical tool, the frequency distribution, we can obtain a picture of the nature of the variability present in the measurements we are collecting.

The frequency distribution is a simple graph, related closely to the frequency histogram that we used in conjunction with Pareto analysis in Chapter 8. The frequency distribution shows the number of times a given measurement value, or range of measurement values, occurs within the sample of data that are being recorded. It is nothing more than a tally.

The following examples are offered as an illustration of a frequency distribution.

Example 11.4.1   In anticipation of a visit to a local game of chance a young student of statistical process control wanted to determine the nature of variation that was present in a pair of dice that he was going to use. To do this, he elected to roll the pair of dice and record the value that came up after each roll. To simplify this, he put an x above the number each time it showed. The resultant data about the variability are summarized in Figure 11–1. From this frequency distribution the dice player was able to draw three conclusions. First, the most frequently occurring or most likely value to show up on any roll would be a 6, 7, or 8. This shows the location of the measurements. Second, many more of the outcomes were near the center. As a matter of fact, of the 87 values he recorded, over half were either a 6, 7, or 8. The third conclusion that could be drawn, based on the observed values, was that all the expected measurements were between 2 and 12. This is an indication of the total possible variability of this dice-rolling process. The values 2 and 12 also indicate the limits of the normally expected variation. (Naturally, in this type of process, the outer limits are mandated by the process itself, but not all processes have this characteristic.) If a value of 13 had been recorded, there would have been a very surprised young man.

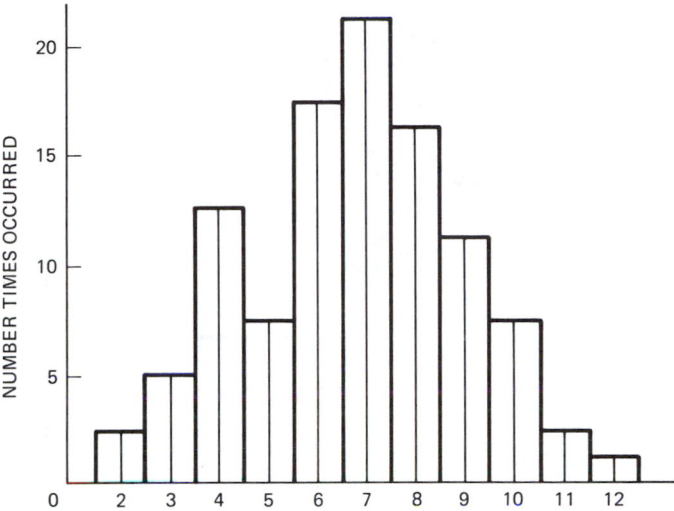

FIGURE 11-1 Sample Process Frequency Distribution

The distribution in Figure 11-1 shows what would be expected if only normal variation were present. The prospective dice player could now plan strategy according to this because the outcomes of tossing the dice should be predictable. ■

Example 11.4.2 Our young man decided to visit the local game of chance before actually wagering any money on the outcome. Surreptitiously, he recorded some measurements of the outcome of the dice toss and developed the frequency distribution shown in Figure 11-2. This figure does not look quite like Figure 11-1. Something has happened to the process. In the language that we have developed in this chapter, the something that has happened is the appearance of abnormal variation. The location of the outcomes seems to have shifted. It is further to the right. The most likely outcomes are no longer 6, 7, or 8, but rather 7 and 11. No longer are most of the values clustered around the center. This too has shifted to the right. The spread or limits have remained the same. While we may not be expert dice rollers, the examination of these two figures does indicate that something has happened. The abnormal variation may be due to a pair of loaded dice being introduced, it may be due to the incredible luck of the dice roller, or it may be due to some other factor. What we have seen, though, is a change in the process, and, before we continue, we should try to assign the reason or set of reasons that caused this change in the pattern of variability. ■

Our two examples show us how the frequency distribution can give us information regarding the nature of the variability for a process. The frequency distribution showed us the general location of the data we collected, it showed us the general shape, and it established limits for the process based on the observed data.

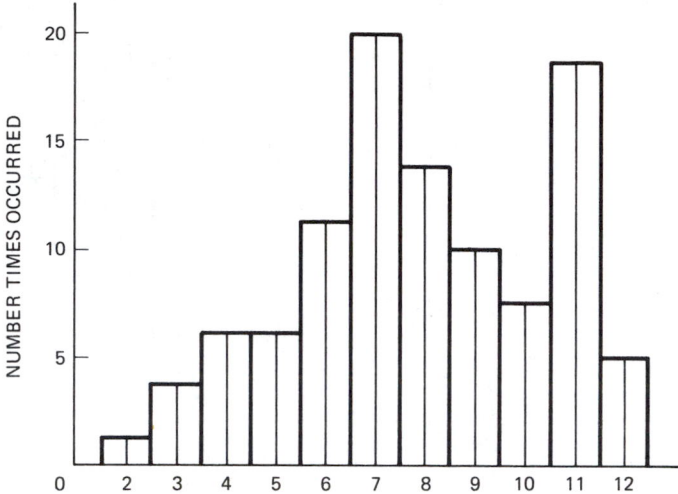

FIGURE 11-2   Sample Process Frequency Distribution: Abnormal Variation

One last example for the dice-rolling process will look at a slight variation on the data-collection process.

Example 11.4.3   We will once again look at the dice-rolling process. Only this time, instead of rolling just one pair or two dice, we will roll four dice and divide the total in half. This should speed up our data-collection process. The results of this are shown in Figure 11-3. We can once again draw three conclusions about the distribution shown.

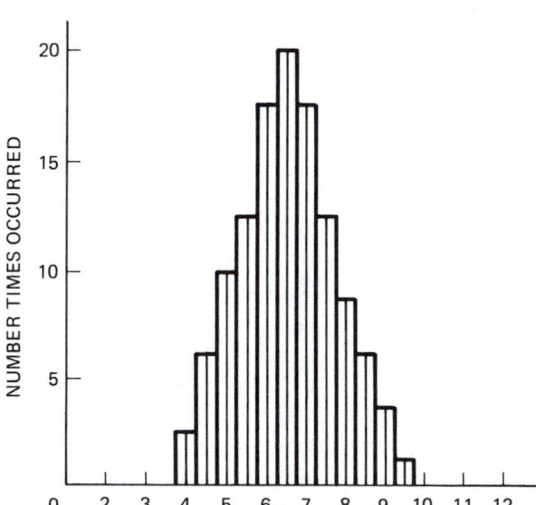

FIGURE 11-3   Sample Process Frequency Distribution with Process Modification

These conclusions will be stated in terms of comparison with the distribution shown in Figure 11–1.

The most likely results this time are 6, 6.5, and 7. When just two dice were used, there were no 0.5's recorded. The distribution is still much higher in the middle and still gets smaller as it tails off. This shape, though, almost looks like it fits a bell-shaped curve. Figure 11–4 superimposes a bell-shaped curve over the frequency distribution to illustrate this. It is not a perfect fit, but it is rather good. The total variability has been reduced. The smallest calculated average we recorded was 4 and the largest was 9.5. This total span was 5.5, or half of what we experienced when just two dice were rolled. When we roll multiple dice, in order to obtain the average of two, we would have needed a 1 to appear on each of the four dice. The chance of this happening is rather slim. Thus, if we think about it, we should not be too surprised to find, as the number of trials we use increases or our sample size increases, that the overall width of normal variability decreases. If we rolled 10 dice, for example, and divided the total showing by 5, the only way we could get a 2 would be to have ten 1's show up. The chances of that happening are almost non-existent. ∎

The preceding example made a point that needs to be emphasized. As the number of samples or trials increases, the total normal variability generally decreases. We will discuss this in more detail later.

11.5 VARIATION AND MANAGEMENT ACTION

We have identified the two types of variation that can be present in a process. These are normal and abnormal. We know that normal variation exists. When we rolled

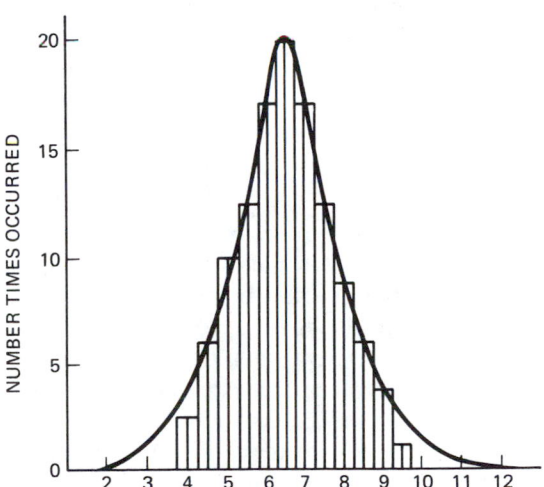

FIGURE 11–4 Sample Process Frequency Distribution with Bell-shaped Curve

the dice in the preceding examples, we expected different values to appear. We would have suspected something strange if we always got the same value. The interaction of the two dice produced a different value, depending on the number showing on the face of each of the dice. We saw that abnormal variation can occur.

Whenever variation is present in a process, and that is all the time, our philosophy states that it requires some management action. Futhermore, each different type of variation requires a different type of management action. The SPC philosophy that we have developed, the one of continuous improvement, requires that we reduce and continue to reduce the variability within the processes.

Let us look first at abnormal variation. As we know, abnormal variation is variation that normally is not present in a process. As a result, when it does occur, the assignable cause or causes must be tracked down. If this abnormal variation is detrimental to the process, then we must eliminate it. If it is positive, then we must identify it and try to repeat it.

Abnormal variation requires an investigatory approach. We must play detective and try to determine what was happening to the process when the abnormal variation occurred. We want to identify each of the special or assignable causes that were present at that time. These are often known by the individuals who are closest to the process, the operators. Elimination of the causes of abnormal variation usually requires that action be taken by these individuals to identify and remove this type of variation.

Many studies have shown that only about 15 percent of all quality problems are due to abnormal causes. This means that only about 15 percent of the quality problems can be identified and fixed by those closest to the process. Example 11.5.1 will illustrate some typical management actions that take place when variation is present.

Now for normal variation. Remember, this is the variation that is always present in a process. The limits of this variation are a function of the process itself. In our dice-rolling example we knew that the smallest value we could have would be a 2 and the largest would be a 12. That is what the process could do. We would not ever expect a 1 or a value larger than 12.

The only way we could expect to change this normal variability of the process is to change the process. The only way we would never expect to find a value as low as a 2 as the sum of rolling 2 dice would be by removing the 1's from the dice, or at least one of the dice. Similarly, when we discuss business processes we see the same type of action being required.

The only way to reduce normal variation is for management to take action on the process. If there is too much variability in the density of material that is being produced by a process, and the process is operating such that only normal variability is present, then only management can take action to change the process. This may involve purchasing better raw materials, providing more training for the operators, or providing a new machine to transform the material. To expect the operator to do this without this type of action would be ridiculous.

The same studies that indicated that abnormal variation was responsible for

15 percent of quality problems also indicated that abnormal variation is responsible for 85 percent of quality problems. The normal variation is responsible for the products not being able to perform according to expectations. Normal variation is part of every process and is described by every process. It can be reduced only by changing the process and/or the inputs to the process. And that change can be done only by management action.

Example 11.5.1 A demonstration of management action taken regarding process variability is often shown via a simulation known as the White Bead Company. This example will explain this demonstration and show the relationship of management action and variability.

A company is formed for the purpose of manufacturing white beads. The simulated manufacturing process is a large box containing white beads and red beads. There are usually about 25 percent red beads in the box. As the story unfolds, the plant manager/owner employs production operators and two quality control inspectors so that 200 percent inspection can be performed. The production operators are charged with producing 50 white beads a day. These are "produced" by using a paddle that will scoop up 50 of the beads. The inspectors count the number of red beads each operator produces and then record that number.

Before production begins, the manager carefully states the White Bead Company's "Quality Philosophy," develops a mission statement calling for **quality first** and **no red beads,** and carefully instructs each production worker in the proper methods and techniques, using all the latest in training aids, including photos demonstrating the work properly completed. Workers are asked to make their objectives (i.e., from an MBO program) no red beads. Workers are shown quality motivational signs, such as Zero Defects, which are posted in the training room. The workers are also sometimes given quality improvement buttons and even asked to sign a quality pledge. Each of these motivational techniques is carefully explained to the entire training group. Similarly, the manager carefully explains to the inspectors what their jobs are and how they have to contribute. When production begins, the first day's production is, naturally, laced with red beads. After the first day the manager gathers his workers and gives them a "pep" talk, telling them that they have to do better. The talk may include references to international competition and the need for economic survival. The talk usually ends with everyone agreeing to do better or try harder.

The second day of production is sometimes highlighted by a worker improving the performance of the preceding day. When this happens, the manager promptly rewards the worker, usually with a happy face or other similar award. Sometimes the worker is asked to give the rest of the workers a pep talk or testimonial. Workers who do not do as well are admonished and urged to try harder. At the end of the second day, red beads are still being produced. Another company meeting results and the workers are really encouraged and cajoled into trying to do better. The manager really makes a big point about he necessity to improve quality or else.

The third day yields similar production and quality results. Sometimes the workers will try to cheat—they will try to individually pick off the red beads. Sometimes the workers will try to bribe the inspectors. Regardless, though, at the end of the third day it looks bleak for the White Bead Company. At that point, management informs the workers that it has tried to be nice, but that in light of the drastically reduced market share the company must make some drastic move. Overhead is cut by laying off some of the inspectors. It is parenthetically pointed out that when there is a quality problem the quality manager is often the first to go. Workers are sometimes yelled at and always threatened with the loss of their jobs unless things improve. Perhaps the plant manager is even faced with the loss of his or her job as well.

Despite all these efforts, the fourth day's production is not any better than that of the first three. At that point the axe is lowered and the plant is closed. The plant manager tearfully bids each loyal employee farewell and gives a talk about how hard we tried and how sorry he is that they mutually let each other down.

The leader, who was also the manager, then recounts all the actions: the slogans, the motivation, the joint objective setting, the quality buttons, the 200 percent inspection, the incentives, and so forth. He then asks the group what happened. The response is usually of the nature, "There was no way we could produce only white beads. The container was loaded with red beads." When questioned again about what should have been done to improve quality, the response is often, "We need to get a container with no red beads."

That statement leads to the point that the simulation tries to make. The leader asks how the red beads can be removed, and receives the answer that **"management must remove the red beds."** Management provides the "production facility" and only management can provide one without any red beads. Everything else is peripheral to the management action.

An analysis of the data that the inspectors collected shows that the number of red beads found each day is well within the bounds of the expected, normal variation for the process. It can be pointed out that the yelling and threatening performed during the simulation is not unusual. Managers often discipline for actions that the workers have no control over. That is an unfortunate fact that only education can change.

The simulation concludes with a restatement of the results. The only way to produce a quality product, the only way to produce all white beads, is the get the red beads out. ■

11.6 CONCLUSION

Every process has a certain amount of variability. There is no way to escape that fact. Normal variation will always be present. Sometimes abnormal variation sneaks into a process. This can and should be removed.

When only normal variation is present in a process, we say that the process is stable. As we work toward our goal of continuous improvement, we must, as a first step, assure that the process is stable. Once the process is stable, we can begin the improvement process.

We mentioned three characteristics of variation in this chapter, three conclusions we can draw about the measurements we collect from any process characteristic. We can draw conclusions about location, spread, and shape. Chapter 12 will introduce some basic concepts that are necessary to statistically describe these basic characteristics. Future chapters will show how to use these statistics to make predictions about the performance of a process and how to evaluate any changes made to the process.

We also stated most emphatically that the responsibility for reducing normal variation lies with management. Only by changing the process can normal variation be reduced. Any other actions will be wastes of time and have only minimal impact on improvement.

EXERCISES

Use the following data to construct frequency distributions. Then use those distributions to answer the questions:

a. What is the location of the distribution?

b. What is the spread of the distribution?

c. What is the shape of the distribution?

1. The following are readings collected on landing gear diameters.

4.56	4.59	4.27	4.71	4.35
4.46	4.51	4.59	4.88	4.70
4.78	4.29	4.47	4.49	4.57
4.61	4.88	4.62	4.60	4.50
4.59	4.55	4.56	4.53	4.39
4.33	4.66	4.39	4.29	4.52
4.68	4.51	4.46	4.56	4.60
4.71	4.81	4.55	4.58	4.51
4.44	4.59	4.59	4.59	4.72

2. The following are the number of errors found on sales orders processed by the accounting department.

5	3	5	1	6	7
6	7	5	2	4	6
3	8	4	3	5	5
9	3	6	4	7	8
0	9	6	5	5	3
8	2	7	5	6	4
4	1	6	6	5	5
6	1	5	8	6	8
5	8	5	4	5	9
10	5	9	3	6	0

CHAPTER 12

Basic Measurement Statistics

Statistics don't solve problems. They identify where the problems are and point managers and workers towards solutions.   [45]
William Conway

12.1 INTRODUCTION

Statistics are powerful *tools,* but they are only one of many *tools* that are available for helping to solve quality problems. Most applications of statistics require that the individual using them have extensive formal training. But there are some basic statistical measures that greatly assist in the analysis of the data collected while processes are being monitored.

These statistics were mentioned in Chapter 11. They include measures of location, measures of variability, and measures of shape.

This chapter will present a practical approach to the use of these statistics, rather than a theoretic or even academic approach.

The victory of statistical methods in industry really represented a compromise between "pure" statistics and the practical realities of industrial situations. Statistical methods, as actually practiced in total quality control, do not represent an exact science. Their character is strongly influenced by human relations factors, technological conditions, and cost considerations.   [61: 346]

12.2 HISTOGRAMS

We have already used histograms in our analysis of Pareto charts. Histograms show, via a bar graph, the frequency distribution of various characteristics. These bar graphs are very useful in describing and summarizing various characteristics. By way of review, the following example will construct a histogram and illustrate how we can use the histogram to intuitively estimate measures of location, shape, and variability.

Example 12.2.1 The baked goods division of Aft-Tech, known as Aft Baked, decided to monitor the process for a line of pastries that they were having problems with. After collecting data on check sheets, performing Pareto analysis, and developing a cause and effect diagram, they decided that one potential cause of the half-baked pastries was the temperature of the oven. As a result, they decided to monitor that process input and see if and how they could improve it. They collected the data shown in Figure 12–1 over a one-week period. Hourly readings were selected as being the most convenient for the operators to obtain. After the data were collected, a frequency distribution was developed showing the relative number of readings at each temperature level. This is shown in Figure 12–2. This was then used to construct the bar chart or histogram shown in Figure 12–3. This histogram can then be used to get a "feel" for the descriptive statistics that have been mentioned.

Regarding the location of the data, the histogram appears to be centered somewhere around 375 or 376. The variability of spread of the data is between 369 and 381. This is a range of 12 degrees. The shape is generally higher in the center and tapers off near the outer limits of the observed data.

The histogram can be compared with the specifications for the baking process to let Aft Baked know how they are doing. A check of records indicates that the recipe for this pastry calls for a temperature of 373 degrees with an allowable range of ±3 degrees. If this is superimposed on the histogram, as is shown in Figure 12–4, then we can see, very obviously, that Aft Baked has problems.

These problems are twofold. First, they are missing their target value. Second,

TIME:	0800	0900	1000	1100	1200	1300	1400	1500	1600
TEMP:	375	377	376	378	380	372	375	377	376
TIME:	0800	0900	1000	1100	1200	1300	1400	1500	1600
TEMP:	372	373	374	375	376	377	378	372	373
TIME:	0800	0900	1000	1100	1200	1300	1400	1500	1600
TEMP:	375	377	378	374	375	375	375	376	381
TIME:	0800	0900	1000	1100	1200	1300	1400	1500	1600
TEMP:	369	379	376	374	375	377	378	379	374
TIME:	0800	0900	1000	1100	1200	1300	1400	1500	1600
TEMP:	373	374	376	377	378	379	374	377	380

FIGURE 12–1 Temperature Data

Temperature	Number of Readings
369	1
370	0
371	0
372	3
373	3
374	6
375	8
376	6
377	7
378	5
379	3
380	2
381	1

FIGURE 12-2 Sample Frequency Distribution

they have too much variability in the process. This is useful information. They immediately know how much they have to raise the temperature and they also know that, as the process currently exists, they must expect the normal process variability to extend beyond specification limits.   ■

While the histogram gives a good estimate of the three characteristics we want to know, it is still an estimate. There are statistics that we can calculate, or have an inexpensive calculator calculate, that will give us the exact value of these descriptive pieces of information.

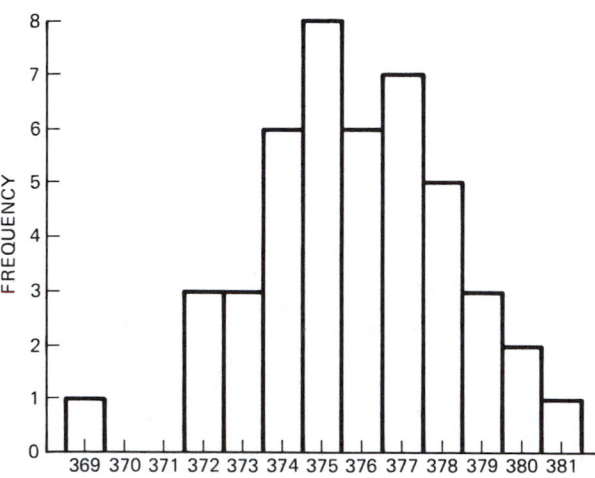

FIGURE 12-3 Sample Frequency Histogram

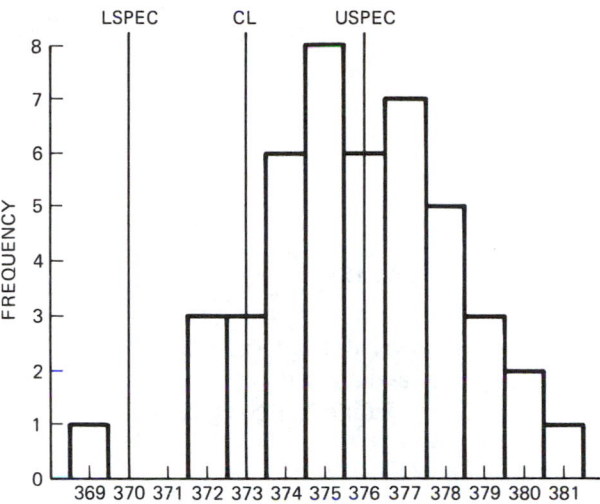

FIGURE 12–4 Histogram with Specifications

12.3 MEASURES OF CENTRAL TENDENCY

The term average is usually used to describe the central tendency or location of the center of the data. There are generally assumed to be about half of the values above the average and half below the average. The average, though, is a generic term. There are three statistics that give information about the central tendency for data. These are the arithmetic mean, the median, and the mode.

The arithmetic mean is the average that most of us use all the time. It is the value we used, starting probably in second grade, to determine how we were doing in school. **The arithmetic mean is the sum of the values in the sample divided by the number of values in the sample.** It is the most commonly used average, and most of the time, unless we state otherwise, we use the arithmetic mean as our measure of central tendency.

Example 12.3.1 A student at Aft-Tech, in partial fulfillment of course requirements in a compensation administration course, conducted a salary survey outside the local professional baseball stadium. His results, shown in ascending order in Figure 12–5, were somewhat surprising. The last sample shown was, obviously, one of the participants in the contest. To calculate the arithmetic mean, we must find the total of the salaries. These add up to be $720,000. Dividing by the nine sample values, we determine this mean to be an even $80,000. ■

The second measure of central tendency that we can calculate is the median. **The median is the middle value in a sample of ascending or descending data. There**

Sample	Annual Salary
1	$20,000
2	20,000
3	25,000
4	25,000
5	25,000
6	25,000
7	30,000
8	30,000
9	520,000

FIGURE 12–5   Salary Data

are as many values above the median as below it. For a sample with an even number of values, the median is the arithmetic mean of the two middle values. There are times when the median is a much better indicator of central location than the arithmetic mean is.

Referring back to the preceding example, we saw that the average salary was $80,000 when we used the arithmetic mean. This might not really be representative nor the best estimate of the salaries present in the stadium on that particular day. The one large salary seems to have an undue effect on the average.

Example 12.3.2 Determine the median salary for the data shown in Figure 12–5. Examining these data, which has been put in ascending order for us, we note that there are nine values. The middle value will be the fifth value. Counting from the top down, we determine that the fifth value down is $25,000. This is the median value. It is perhaps a better indicator of the location of the salary data.   ∎

The median is not overly influenced by one piece of data that may be caused by abnormal variation. There is, as we know, a special or assignable cause for the large salary. We must keep that value in the data because it is legitimate, but it does have a tremendous impact on our description if we use the wrong descriptive statistic.

The third measure of location is the mode. **The mode is the most frequently occurring value within a sample of data.** If two values occur most frequently, we say that the data are bimodal. If there are three or more, we use the expression multimodal. As with the median, the mode sometimes gives a better indication of location than does the much more frequently used arithmetic mean. Let us refer once again to the salary data in Figure 12–5.

Example 12.3.3 A frequency distribution for the data would show that there are two values of $20,000, four at $25,000, two at $30,000, and one at $520,000. Obviously, the most frequently occurring value is $25,000. The mode for these data, which is the same as the median, is $25,000.   ∎

The mode is a useful estimate of location when there are individual values located relatively far from the center of the distribution.

Example 12.3.4 Calculate the mean, median, and mode for the temperature data shown in Example 12.2.1 and reproduced here as Figure 12-6. The data appeared to be centered around 375 or 376, as the histogram in Figure 12-3 showed.

The arithmetic mean is the sum of all the temperature readings divided by the total number. For the 45 readings in Figure 12-6, the total is 16,911. Dividing this by 45 gives the arithmetic mean, the value of 375.8 degrees.

The median is the middle value. The middle value for this example of 45 will be the 23rd one when the data are put in ascending or descending order. Figure 12-7 shows this for the 45 values. As the figure shows, this is 376.

The mode, or most frequently occurring value, is readily apparent from the histogram of Figure 12-3. The mode will be the largest or highest bar in the histogram. In this case, 375 is the most frequently occurring value. ∎

The results for this example show that the arithmetic mean, median, and mode are all very close. This is often the case. For the remainder of this text, *we will use the arithmethic mean exclusively for calculating the average* or measure of location or best estimate for a sample of data. We will use the symbol, $\overline{X}$ to identify the mean of average for any sample data. We will use the letter n to identify the number of pieces of data that are in a sample.

By establishing these symbols, we can verbally communicate information about certain process characteristics. Going back to the temperature data, knowing that the average temperature is 375.8 degrees, as compared with the target value of 373 degrees, immediately lets us know that we are centered above the desired value. This will also indicate to us that we are going to have more than half of our values above the desired value.

TIME:	0800	0900	1000	1100	1200	1300	1400	1500	1600
TEMP:	375	377	376	378	380	372	375	377	376
TIME:	0800	0900	1000	1100	1200	1300	1400	1500	1600
TEMP:	372	373	374	375	376	377	378	372	373
TIME:	0800	0900	1000	1100	1200	1300	1400	1500	1600
TEMP:	375	377	378	374	375	375	375	376	381
TIME:	0800	0900	1000	1100	1200	1300	1400	1500	1600
TEMP:	369	379	376	374	375	377	378	379	374
TIME:	0800	0900	1000	1100	1200	1300	1400	1500	1600
TEMP:	373	374	376	377	378	379	374	377	380

FIGURE 12-6 Temperature Data

Temperatures in Ascending Order	
#	
1	369
2	372
3	372
4	372
5	373
6	373
7	373
8	374
9	374
10	374
11	374
12	374
13	374
14	375
15	375
16	375
17	375
18	375
19	375
20	375
21	375
22	376
23	376 ← MEDIAN VALUE
24	376
25	376
26	376
27	376
28	377
29	377
30	377
31	377
32	377
33	377
34	377
35	378
36	378
37	378
38	378
39	378
40	379
41	379
42	379
43	380
44	380
45	381

FIGURE 12–7 Rearranged Temperature Data

12.4 MEASURES OF VARIABILITY

While the average tells us location, which may be the most useful of all pieces of information to know, we also want to know how widely dispersed or spread out the data are. The average by itself, while transmitting important information, does not give a complete picture of the process characteristics.

In statistical process control applications, we generally use two measures of variability. One of these is the range; the other is the standard deviation.

The range is the difference between the largest and smallest values within a sample. It is relatively easy to calculate and requires no advanced math abilities.

Example 12.4.1 Determine the range of the data in the sample salary data shown in Figure 12–5. The largest value in the sample is the pro athlete's salary of $520,000. The smallest is the $20,000 reported by one of the fans. The difference between these, the range, is $500,000. ∎

The range is a quick way to estimate the variability of sample data. Obviously, as this example shows, the range can be tremendously affected by the one value. There is a trade-off between this liability and the obvious ease in calculation. The symbol we use for the range of a sample is R.

A more sophisticated measure of process variability is the standard deviation. This is a mathematical measure of variability of each data point about the mean. Specifically, **the standard deviation is the square root of the average of the squared deviations of each point from the mean.** The symbols commonly used for standard deviation are either the Greek letter sigma, σ, or the letter s. (These symbols have precise statistical meanings that should be adhered to, but in common practice they are often ignored.) Often the symbol is followed by a subscripted x, which indicates that this is the standard deviation for individuals.

The standard deviation can be calculated using the following formula; however, in practice the standard deviation is usually determined either by a computer or with a built-in function found on many calculators. Note that the $n - 1$ term in the denominator of the calculation is the result of some work done by statisticians.

$$S_x = \sqrt{\frac{\sum\limits_{i=1}^{n} (x_i - \bar{x})^2}{n - 1}}$$

The name standard in standard deviation implies a special significance. It means that when we know the standard deviation it gives us special information about the data that it describes. According to a special statistical relationship, known as *Chebyshev's inequality,* the amount of area under any distribution that is farther away from the mean than k standard deviation units is less than $1/k^2$. This means that, **regardless** of the shape of the distribution, there will always be at least

75 percent of the values within two standard deviations of the mean and at least 88 percent of the values within three standard deviations of the mean.

If the values are normally distributed, that is, if the pattern reflects the bell-shaped curve, then these percentages become very important. Then, within one standard deviation of the mean there will be about 68 percent of the values, within two standard deviations of the mean there will be 95.5 percent of the values, and within three standard deviations of the mean will be approximately 99.7 percent of all possible or expected values. Figure 12–8 shows this relationship. This is extremely useful information when we try to make predictions about future performance.

Example 12.4.2 Determine the range and standard deviation for the temperature data in Figure 12–1. The calculation of the range is straightforward. The largest value in the sample is 381 and the smallest is 369. The difference between these is the range of 12 degrees.

To calculate the standard deviation, the first step requires that the difference between each value and the mean be calculated. This is shown in Figure 12–9a. Remembering that the mean for this example is 375.8, this difference, for the value of 369, is 6.8. After this is completed, the differences are squared. This is shown in Figure 12–9b. The squares are then summed, as Figure 12–9b also shows. This total is divided by the number of values in the sample minus 1, or 44 for this example. The square root of this is then calculated, giving the standard deviation for this sample of 45 temperatures. The entire formula, with the values from Figure 12–9b inserted, is

$$s = \sqrt{\frac{264.11}{44}} = 2.45$$

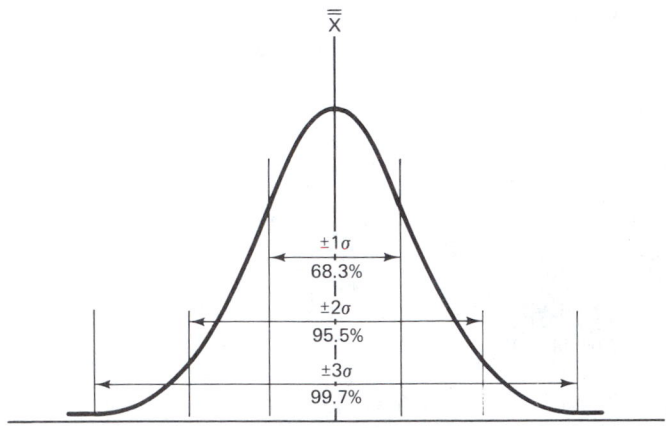

FIGURE 12–8   Normal Curve

x	$x - \bar{x}$		$(x - \bar{x})^2$
369	6.8		46.24
372	3.8		14.44
372	3.8		14.44
372	3.8		14.44
373	2.8		7.84
373	2.8		7.84
373	2.8		7.84
374	1.8		3.24
374	1.8		3.24
374	1.8		3.24
374	1.8		3.24
374	1.8		3.24
374	1.8		3.24
375	.8		.64
375	.8		.64
375	.8		.64
373	.8		.64
375	.8		.64
375	.8		.64
375	.8		.64
375	.8		.64
376	.2		.04
376	.2		.04
376	.2		.04
376	.2		.04
376	.2		.04
376	.2		.04
377	1.2		1.44
377	1.2		1.44
377	1.2		1.44
377	1.2		1.44
377	1.2		1.44
377	1.2		1.44
377	1.2		1.44
378	2.2		4.84
378	2.2		4.84
378	2.2		4.84
378	2.2		4.84
378	2.2		4.84
379	3.2		15.64
379	3.2		15.64
379	3.2		15.64
380	4.2		17.64
380	4.2		17.64
381	5.2		27.04
		$\Sigma =$	264.11

(a)

(b)

FIGURE 12–9 (a) Standard Deviation Calculation, Part 1; (b) Part 2

12.5 MEASURES OF SHAPE

The most commonly occurring shape is the normal or bell-shaped curve. Because of the relationship between the standard deviation and the percentage of values found between the one, two, and three sigma limits, we naturally would like for all of our data to be normally distributed. When that is the case, we can predict the expected proportions between standard deviations and the mean. Section 12.7 illustrates a way to find these expected proportions for any normally distributed sample or population.

While making assumptions can be dangerous, we often, by looking at the histogram, decide that the data collected appear to be normally distributed and proceed accordingly. This can be misleading. Statisticians have developed many formal tests for normality, including the Chi square goodness of fit test. These tests should be used whenever there is any doubt.

There is another way to assure normality when dealing with relatively large samples of data. This is by using smaller samples from the entire population or universe. There is an important statistical rule that helps remove the risk. This is called the **central limit theorem.** This fundamental rule states the following:

1. For a relatively large number of samples, no matter what the original shape of the data, the distribution of sample averages will always be normally distributed.

2. The relationship between the standard deviation for the distribution of individuals and the distribution of sample averages will be

$$S_{\overline{x}} = \frac{S_x}{\sqrt{n}}$$

where $S_{\overline{x}}$ = standard deviation of the sample averages
S_x = standard deviation of the individual values
n = sample size

The central limit theorem is extremely important regarding the validity and confidence we have in control charts. This theorem also provides us a way to always be certain about the shape of our distribution.

The frequency distribution can also give us some additional information about the nature of the information we have collected and want to analyze. Making judgments about the location, spread, and shape can be useful. Figure 12–10A shows a distribution that appears to be located on the target and within specifications and is normally distributed.

Figure 12–10B also shows some sample data that are located on target and within specifications, but the shape indicates that perhaps the data are reflective of two distributions.

Figure 12–10C shows data that are centered below the target and spread to fit

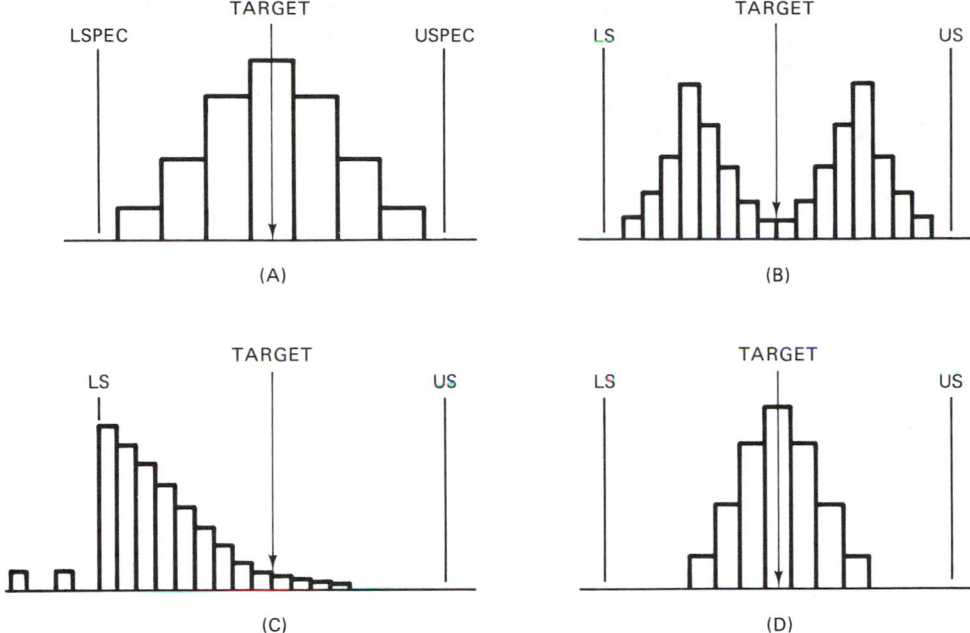

FIGURE 12–10 Sample Distribution for Interpretation

almost within the specifications. The data appear to be merely half of a normally shaped distribution, though. The data have been truncated, though, perhaps via inspection. The inspection process caught almost every nonconforming item, but not quite all of them. There are still some that made it past the screening.

Figure 12–10D shows data that are centered on target and spread well within specification limits. The shape of this is normal as well. Obviously, from a management point of view, this is the type of situation we like to see.

12.6 ADDITIONAL STATISTICAL CALCULATIONS

We have now addressed the three major statistics necessary to describe data, the measures of location, spread, and shape. Two additional statistics provide useful information. These are the grand average and the average range.

The grand average is designated via the symbol $\bar{\bar{x}}$. It is the average of the sample averages. By itself it gives the best estimate of location for the data. Because it averages, arithmetically, the sample averages, it removes some of the effects that a single value may have on our estimate of location.

The average range, another arithmetic average, is represented by the symbol $\bar{R}$. As with the grand average, the average range removes some of the effects that a single far-out value has on our estimate of variability.

Example 12.6.1 Refer again to the data in Figure 12–1, shown again as Figure 12–11. The data this time, though, will be viewed as being daily samples, with nine values in each sample. The average for each of these five samples and the range are shown in Figure 12–12. The grand average is the sum of these sample averages divided by the number of sample averages.

$$\overline{\overline{x}} = \frac{1878.9}{5} = 375.78$$

This is, with allowance for rounding, the same as the average of all the individuals.

The average range is the sum of the sample ranges divided by the number of sample ranges.

$$\overline{R} = \frac{38}{5} = 7.6$$

The interested reader may want to take this opportunity to check out the central limit theorem's second provision. The standard deviation of the five sample averages is 0.814. Remembering that the standard deviation for individuals was 2.45, and using a sample size of 9, we see that 2.45/9 = 0.817. Not bad for a small number of samples. ■

12.7 NORMAL CURVE PROBABILITIES

Just about every statistics book includes an extensive section on calculating normal curve probabilities. A normal curve probability, for our use, is the proportion of

TIME:	0800	0900	1000	1100	1200	1300	1400	1500	1600
TEMP:	375	377	376	378	380	372	375	377	376

TIME:	0800	0900	1000	1100	1200	1300	1400	1500	1600
TEMP:	372	373	374	375	376	377	378	372	373

TIME:	0800	0900	1000	1100	1200	1300	1400	1500	1600
TEMP:	375	377	378	374	375	375	375	376	381

TIME:	0800	0900	1000	1100	1200	1300	1400	1500	1600
TEMP:	369	379	376	374	375	377	378	379	374

TIME:	0800	0900	1000	1100	1200	1300	1400	1500	1600
TEMP:	373	374	376	377	378	379	374	377	380

FIGURE 12–11 Temperature Data

Day	Average Temperature	Range
1	376.2	8
2	374.4	6
3	376.2	7
4	375.7	10
5	376.4	7
	1878.9	38

FIGURE 12–12 Daily Temperature Summaries

values that we would expect to find between any two points under a normally distributed sample.

To calculate specific values, we take advantage of the work of a famous statistician by the name of Gauss. The table that he developed is included as Appendix A to this book. He determined the proportions for a normally distributed population with a mean of 0 and a standard deviation of 1. We convert our sample data via a relationship that has come to be called the z transform. It looks like the following equation:

$$z = \frac{x - \bar{\bar{x}}}{\dfrac{s_x}{\sqrt{n}}}$$

When used in conjunction with the table in Appendix A, we can determine the proportion of values between any point and the grand average of the sampled data. The following example will illustrate the use of the z transform.

Example 12.7.1 Using the temperature data that we have been following throughout this chapter, calculate the following. Remember that the data had a grand average of 375.8 and a standard deviation of 2.45. We sampled the temperatures in subgroups of size 9.

(a) What proportion of sample average temperatures will be expected to be found between 374 and the mean? This corresponds to the drawing in Figure 12–13a.

The z transform is calculated as

$$z = \frac{374 - 375.8}{\dfrac{2.45}{\sqrt{9}}}$$

$$= 2.20$$

The negative sign merely indicates that the point is to the left of the mean. This value is then located in the z column in the table in Appendix A. This corresponds

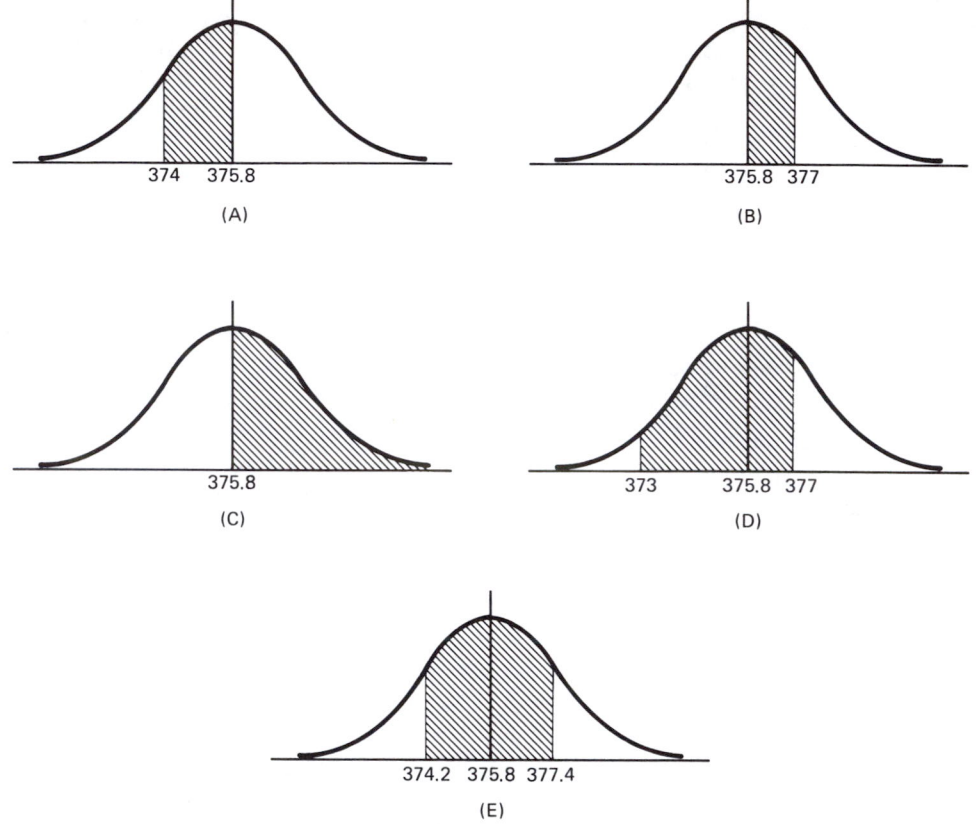

FIGURE 12-13 Normal Probability for (a) Example 12.7.1a; (b) Example 12.7.1b; (c) Example 12.7.1c; (d) Example 12.7.1d; (e) Example 12.7.1e

to a value of 0.4861. We would expect to find 48.61 percent of the sample averages between 374 and the mean.

(b) What proportion would we expect to find between 377 and the mean? This corresponds to the drawing in Figure 12–13b.

The z transform calculation is

$$z = \frac{\dfrac{377 - 375.8}{2.45}}{\sqrt{9}}$$

$$= +1.47$$

Using Appendix A again, we read the value 0.4292. This means that 42.9 percent of the values would be expected to fall between the sample average of 377 and the grand average.

(c) What proportion would we expect to find greater than the mean? Figure 12–13c shows this situation. Without even using the z transform, we can readily see that *half* of the values are larger than the grand mean.

(d) What proportion would we expect to find between 373 and 377? Figure 12–13d indicates that this is the combination or addition of the proportions we found in parts a and b. Thus, to determine this proportion, we simply add the 0.4861 of part a to the 0.4292 of part b, giving a total of 0.9153 or 91.53 percent.

(e) What proportion would we expect to find between 377.4 and 374.2? Figure 12–13e shows this situation.

This requires the calculation of two z values, one for each point. First we calculate z for 377.4.

$$z = \frac{\dfrac{377.4 - 375.8}{2.45}}{\sqrt{9}}$$

$$= +1.96$$

This corresponds to a value of 0.475. Similarly, the z transform for the other point, 374.2, gives a z value of

$$z = \frac{\dfrac{374.2 - 375.8}{2.45}}{\sqrt{9}}$$

$$= -1.96$$

This also gives a table value showing that 47.5 percent of the values are expected between this sample and the grand mean. The sum of these is 0.95 or 95 percent. ■

12.8 CONCLUSIONS

The basic statistics presented in this chapter are fundamental to the understanding of data analysis. The techniques presented are not difficult to master. They rely as much on intuition as theory. Hopefully they are "user friendly" statistics.

These simple statistical methods by themselves are not sufficient to make any individual an expert in statistical analysis. For that, someone well trained in statistical methods is required. But these simple analysis tools can provide the basis for an understanding and the eventual improvement of each of our processes. This type of statistical training should be required knowledge for every employee in every organization. Without this basic knowledge, we can go no further with process monitoring, controlling, and improvement.

Symbol	Description
x	Individual Values or Measurements
$\bar{x}$	Sample Average
$\bar{\bar{x}}$	Grand Average
R	Sample Range
$\bar{R}$	Average Range
S_x	Sample Standard Deviation for Sampled Individuals
σ_x	Sample Standard Deviation for Population of Individuals
$S_{\bar{x}}$	Sample Standard Deviation for Distribution of Sample Averages

FIGURE 12–14   Statistical Symbol Summary

Figure 12–14 summarizes the symbols that we used, along with a cursory definition of the terms to which they refer. These simple concepts will prove to be extremely powerful as we analyze data and make recommendations and management decisions.

EXERCISES

1. Construct a frequency distribution or histogram for the following data:
   (a) The average times to failure for a missile guidance component were recorded as follows. The time is in hours.

4.1	4.6	4.2	4.7	4.9	4.7	4.6	4.8
4.2	4.4	4.6	4.8	4.7	4.5	4.3	4.1
4.4	4.4	4.5	4.5	4.6	4.5	4.6	4.4
4.8	4.1	4.4	4.6	4.5	4.5	4.3	4.7
4.6	4.7	4.7	4.6	4.7	4.6	4.6	4.5
4.7	4.4	4.4	4.3	4.5	4.5	4.6	4.5

   (b) The weather bureau collected the following barometric pressure each 2 hours for a period of 4 days.

Time	Day			
	1	2	3	4
0100	29.95	30.01	29.95	29.91
0300	29.86	29.91	29.85	29.94
0500	29.94	30.00	29.65	30.08
0700	29.91	29.89	29.25	30.14
0900	30.00	30.04	28.95	30.18
1100	30.05	29.92	28.85	30.16
1300	30.08	30.02	28.65	30.10
1500	30.14	29.98	29.05	29.84
1700	30.10	29.89	29.18	29.88
1900	30.11	30.01	29.56	30.07
2100	30.02	30.00	30.04	29.94

(c) An SPC instructor collected the following class grades for a period of several terms.

Term 1	Term 2	Term 3
88	74	77
84	78	78
91	82	79
77	86	80
86	90	77
85	88	78
70	92	79
78	82	80
94	72	77
66	62	72
85	52	82
82	77	81
70	87	80
74	91	79

2. Use the data in Problem 1 to calculate the arithmetic mean and range for each sample of data presented.

CHAPTER 13

Introduction to Control Charts

The chief reason we measure and chart and analyze is to bring about improvement. The information we're generating from this process gives us an early warning that something is amiss and allows us to take corrective actions faster. [92: 28]

Richard Thomas
First Chicago Corporation

13.1 INTRODUCTION

In Chapter 12 we learned about some basic statistics that permit us to draw some conclusions about how our process is performing. By constructing a frequency distribution or histogram, we were able to estimate location, spread, and shape. The location and spread can be better defined with statistics, such as the mean, standard deviation, and range.

The measure of location can be compared with target or nominal specification limits to determine how the process is performing relative to the desired target. The measures of variability can be compared with the upper and lower tolerance or specs limits to determine, approximately, whether or not the process is capable of meeting the requirements.

One factor is missing in this analysis. The distribution is constructed, the histogram drawn, and the statistics calculated after the fact. It is all *historical data,* so to speak. It is all, also, summary data.

What we need, in addition to this important historical data, is an analysis of how the process is performing over **time**. Processes often change over time. If we can examine the performance of a process as time goes by, then we can start to detect any changes that might be occurring.

The tool that will show us this information is known as the control chart. The control chart is the tool that we will use to monitor and control the process. And the "we" that is used here is each and every one of us. Whether we are an operator on the production line or a corporation president, there are characteristics that we can monitor. The most effective use of the control chart is as a tool for each of us to use on our own processes.

This chapter will discuss the basic concept of control and will examine a very simple type of control chart, the run chart. The following chapters will describe specific types of control charts, including those for variables or measurement characteristics, individuals, and attributes, or countable characteristics.

13.2 THE CONCEPT OF CONTROL

The control chart is used to monitor the processes that have been determined to be critical. Important characteristics of these processes have been converted to measurement characteristics; we are now ready to begin an ongoing monitoring process to determine if the characteristics are stable, important to the performance of the process, and capable of being improved.

Process monitoring is performed to identify and quantify the type of variation that is present in a process. Some amount of normal variation will always be present. Sometimes abnormal variation will be present. The monitoring process shows us which type is present and how much of that type is present.

If a process shows abnormal variation, the first step is to identify it. The second step is to remove it and guide the process to stability. If a process shows only normal variation and is stable, then the process of improvement can begin.

The important point to remember is that a process is in control when only normal variation is present. **When a process is in control, the process is not necessarily producing the output that is desired.**

Example 13.2.1   Very often, when visiting with a business client, the author has been met with initial resistance to the use of these types of process-monitoring tools. The standard response takes the format, "The control chart may be fine and all for a process that changes over time, but when ours goes bad, it goes all at once. We have instantaneous failure." This will usually be followed by showing an inspection report such as the one in Figure 13–1. In this case the inspection involved checking one dimension with a go-nogo gage. As the results show, the first eight samples all were OK and passed. The ninth was not. This clearly shows that the process is subject to the so-called instantaneous failure. Right! Had the inspection information, the dimension being checked, been recorded and then graphed as a function of time, the instantaneous failure excuse would go right out the window. Figure 13–2 indicates that the first eight readings, while all meeting specifications, showed an obvious downward trend.

The question should be raised as to whether, based on this analysis, if the last two or three parts should even have been made without changing the process in

	Inspection Results	
Sample Number	Accept	Reject
1	X	
2	X	
3	X	
4	X	
5	X	
6	X	
7	X	
8	X	
9	X	
10		X

FIGURE 13-1 Instantaneous Failure Inspection Results

some fashion. Instantaneous failure may exist, but more often than not it is merely an excuse to avoid performing the process monitoring that is necessary as a first step in process improvement. ∎

13.3 CONTROL LIMITS

Control limits numerically define the bounds of normal variability for each process. They identify the limits within or between which we would expect to find virtually all the values when only normal variation is present. The process sets its own control limits. *Arbitrarily changing control limits without changing the process is a meaningless exercise.* The control limits don't drive the process, they merely reflect the current state of the process.

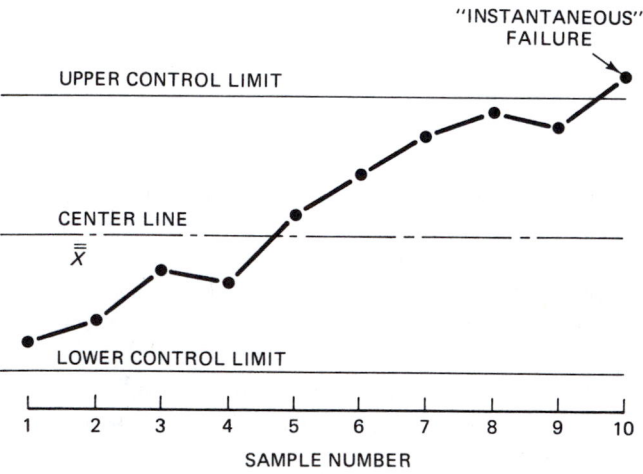

FIGURE 13-2 Instantaneous Failure Run Chart

Generally, when we refer to control limits, we are talking about three-sigma control limits. The three sigma refers to normally distributed samples and populations. In Chapter 12 we showed that, when the data are normally distributed, approximately 99.7 percent of all possible points will be within plus or minus 3 standard deviations of the mean. Unless stated otherwise, we will always mean this type of control limit; 99.7 percent of the possible values is certainly, and traditionally has reflected, the expected limits of normal variation. While it is possible to have a value fall outside of these limits due to normal or random causes, it is not very likely.

When all the measurements we make for a certain process characteristic fall between the control limits, we tentatively say that the process is in control. Whenever a value falls outside of the control limits, we say that the process is out of control. (In Chapter 17 we will examine some other factors that help us to interpret control charts.)

When a process is in control, only normal variation is present. The process is stable. When a process is out of control, abnormal variation has entered the picture. The process is no longer stable.

As we have indicated, when the process is stable, it can be improved only through management action on the process. When it is unstable, it can often be returned to stability by those closest to the process.

Example 13.3.1 A process in a data-processing department involves the coding of and transferring of information from sales reports to the computer data base. This process is performed by a data-entry clerk. Her work is periodically checked by people and the errors reported. Figure 13–3 shows the results of a recent month's audits of the clerk's work.

The target for this characteristic, naturally, is 0 errors. Realistically, this may not be possible. Figure 13–4 shows a frequency histogram for the data. The mean and standard deviation for this sample are, respectively, 6.57 errors per day and 3.12 errors. Our preliminary analysis of this information is that, obviously, we are seeing more errors than we would like. Also, the expected normal variability is approximately $\pm(3)$ (3.12) or ± 9.36 errors per day. That means we would expect a day with as few as 0 errors or as many as 15.93. Our system is stable, even if we are not pleased with the location.

Although we may be stable, think how the supervisor might react, especially upon seeing a day with 14 errors. The initial reaction would be to reprimand or discipline the clerk. Fourteen just seems like too many mistakes. Instead of reprimanding the clerk, the supervisor should work with all levels of management to improve the system that is producing the errors. Perhaps more training is needed. Perhaps a better format for the initial information would be useful. The responsibility lies with management and the process. Despite these warnings, though, and even if the supervisor understands SPC and the concept of control limits, the natural inclination is to yell at the worker, to blame the worker for producing results that are to be normally expected. ■

Date	Number of Errors
1–1	8
2	9
3	5
4	9
5	3
8	11
9	8
10	9
11	5
12	5
15	7
16	6
17	9
18	14
19	4
22	3
23	1
24	6
25	6
26	4
29	7
30	2
31	10

FIGURE 13–3 Audit Results

Control charts show the control limits graphically. Pictures are much easier to interpret than numbers. Figure 13–5 shows the makeup of a typical control chart. Note the special abbreviations used on the figure: UCL for upper control limit, LCL for lower control limit, and CL for center line.

13.4 SAMPLING

After the measurement characteristic has been identified, data must be collected. This generally involves sampling. A sample is a collection of events or measurements used to analyze the performance of a process. Samples are sometimes called subgroups.

There are a number of different ways to collect sample data. One sampling scheme is called random sampling. In random sampling, items are selected so that each item has the same chance of being selected. Another commonly used sampling scheme is consecutive sampling. In this instance, items are sampled in the order they are produced. Other ways to sample, such as stratified sampling, are also used. Most good statistics books have explanations of the basic types of sampling methodologies. For process control, we will generally use either random or sequential sampling.

Determination of the actual sampling scheme depends on several factors and has several characteristics. First, the sample should be rational. A rational subgroup

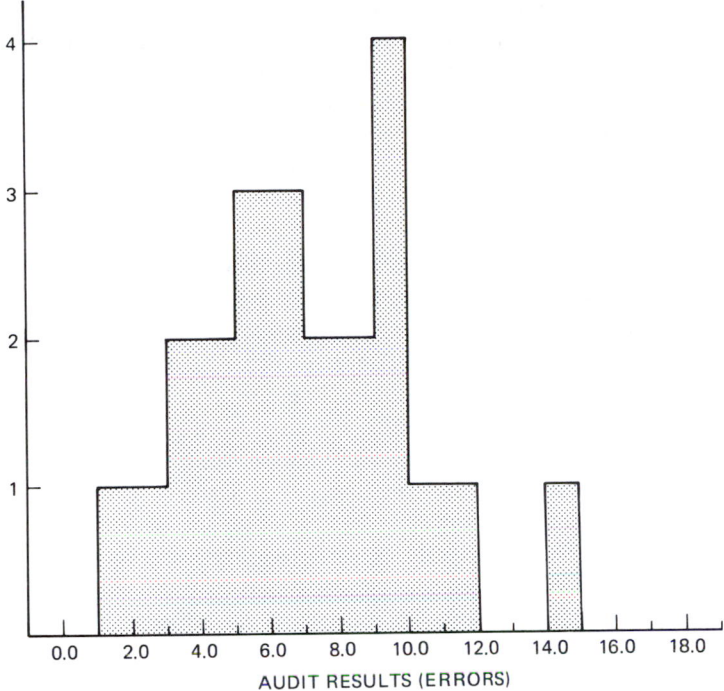

FIGURE 13-4 Audit Frequency Distribution

CONTROL CHART COMPONENTS

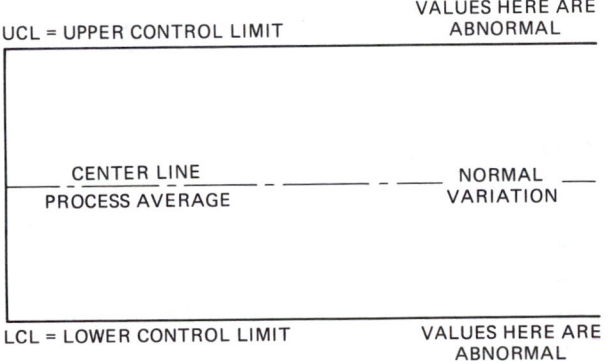

FIGURE 13-5 Typical Control Chart

is one that is believed to be free from abnormal variation. All members of the rational sample should be obtained under similar conditions.

The sample size is determined by the nature of the process and the type of chart being constructed. Certain processes have logical sample sizes. For example, a mold for a certain product may produce four units at a time. Four would be a logical sample size for this process. Some low-production-rate processes, building airplanes for example, might have the need for a sample size of 1, with every item being sampled.

The frequency of sampling as we monitor the process depends on the cost and difficulty of obtaining the sample and the expected frequency with which we expect the process to change. Destructive tests will naturally demand that fewer units be sampled and tested. The ease with which the data can be obtained also influences how often we will sample. There may be logical breaks in the work, or times when other information is also collected, that make for a logical and reasonable sampling frequency. Some processes change so rapidly that observations must be made every few minutes. Other processes are relatively stable and hours may go by between the need for sampling.

The number of samples required, while a function of the accuracy and confidence desired, is often determined by the experience of the analyst. It should be sufficient to allow all sources of variation to appear. It is often a matter of judgment, but as a general guideline the following sample-size suggestions are offered.

For variables charts, there should be a minimum of 50 total readings, with 100 being the suggested level. The more sample readings, the better the results will be, though a point of diminishing returns is eventually reached. For attributes charts, a minimum of 20 readings is suggested, but, again, the more readings we have before determining control limits, the better off we will be.

One caution about sampling at this point. Sometimes, when individuals record a sample reading, they can't believe their eyes. This might be called the "Oh Fudge" syndrome. The inspector collects the data, looks at them and says, "Oh Fudge, That can't be correct!" The information is then discarded because it did not match the expectations of the person collecting it. All information must be recorded and used in the initial analysis of the process unless there is obvious abnormal variation present. To do otherwise will bias the data and information collected.

13.5 RUN CHARTS

The simplest of all control charts is the run chart, sometimes called the individual measurements chart. The run chart shows the progress of a monitored characteristic as a function of time. On the x axis we show time, and on the y axis we show the actual measurement or attribute that has been collected for that time. We also provide a space for the noting of any comments about the process. A change of material, a substitute operator, a fork lift wreck, or anything else could be a source of abnormal variation. A brief note would clue in the analyst if the process has to be investigated at a later time. An examination of the actual pattern of data points may also indicate that the process is not behaving normally.

Example 13.5.1 Let us refer again to the temperature data from our baking example in Chapter 12, which are reproduced in Figure 13-6. To refresh our memories, there data appeared to be normally distributed, were centered at 375.8 degrees, and had a standard deviation of 2.45 degrees. The target value for this process was 373 degrees, and the specification limits were 370 and 376 degrees. This process was not meeting specifications at the time the data were collected.

Part of the monitoring and controlling process involves the construction of the control chart or, in this case, the run chart. The run chart for the 45 values is shown in Figure 13-7. An examination of the run chart might point out some interesting information that was not obvious just by looking at the raw data. As we move from left to right across the chart, we notice that, almost everytime the temperature approaches the upper specification limit there is an immediate drop of several degrees. We also notice that this appears to be a pattern that is repeated several times. This suggests three possible problems with the process.

First, there might be a problem with the thermostat or temperature controller maintaining a constant temperature. It may be in need of preventive maintenance, recalibration, or replacement. Second, some operator adjustment may be taking place. The operator may be watching the temperature indicator and turning the temperature way down everytime it reaches the upper specification limit. This is often done. Studies have shown that this type of **overcontrol can increase process variability to as much as twice the normal** variability if the process were left alone. [117: 28] Chances are the operator has never been properly trained or the supervisor is being negligent in his or her duty. A third possibility might be that someone is opening the door to check on how everything is going, just like we do with our home ovens. When the door is opened, the heat rushes out and there are significant fluctuations in the temperature within the oven. ■

TIME:	0800	0900	1000	1100	1200	1300	1400	1500	1600
TEMP:	375	377	376	378	380	372	375	377	376
TIME:	0800	0900	1000	1100	1200	1300	1400	1500	1600
TEMP:	372	373	374	375	376	377	378	372	373
TIME:	0800	0900	1000	1100	1200	1300	1400	1500	1600
TEMP:	375	377	378	374	375	375	375	376	381
TIME:	0800	0900	1000	1100	1200	1300	1400	1500	1600
TEMP:	369	379	376	374	375	377	378	379	374
TIME:	0800	0900	1000	1100	1200	1300	1400	1500	1600
TEMP:	373	374	376	377	378	379	374	377	380

FIGURE 13–6 Temperature Data

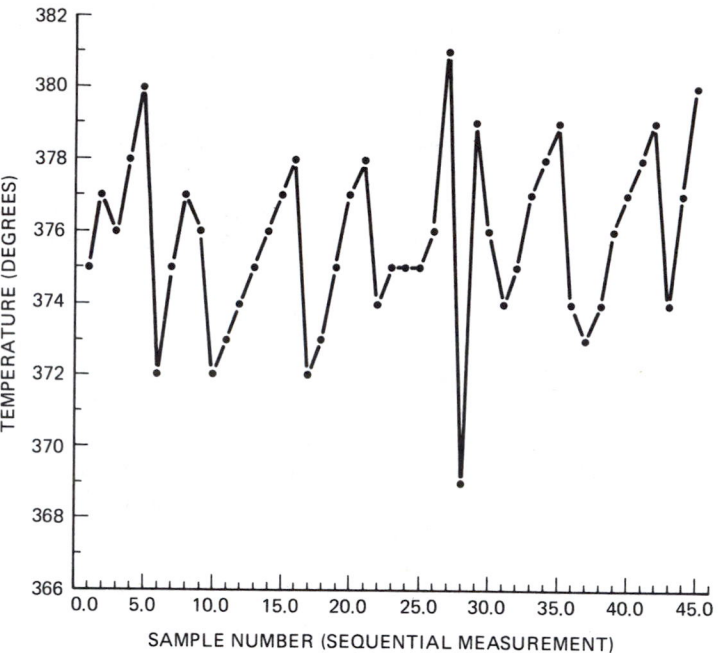

FIGURE 13-7 Temperature Data Run Chart

These potential sources of the inability to meet the temperature specification are correctable. The responsibility for correcting them lies with management. The worker cannot be expected to replace a defective controller nor is the worker responsible for overadjusting unless training has taught the worker that this is an improper method. ■

The run chart shows us how the process is changing over time. It is extremely effective when each operator, the individual responsible for each process, maintains his or her own chart. Then the changes that take place are immediately obvious. However, when this is done, there is a danger that the chart can be misinterpreted.

Example 13.5.2 An operator on an assembly line has been keeping records, every 15 minutes, of the fill weights of certain containers of a common household product. Although the containers are filled automatically, the operator is responsible for adjusting the process and monitoring the process throughout the workday. Figure 13–8a shows the first 2 hours worth of readings and the target specification value for desired fill weight. Note that the values are shown on the chart under the time and directly aligned with the point on the graph.

Let us imagine that at this point the supervisor happens by on her normal walk

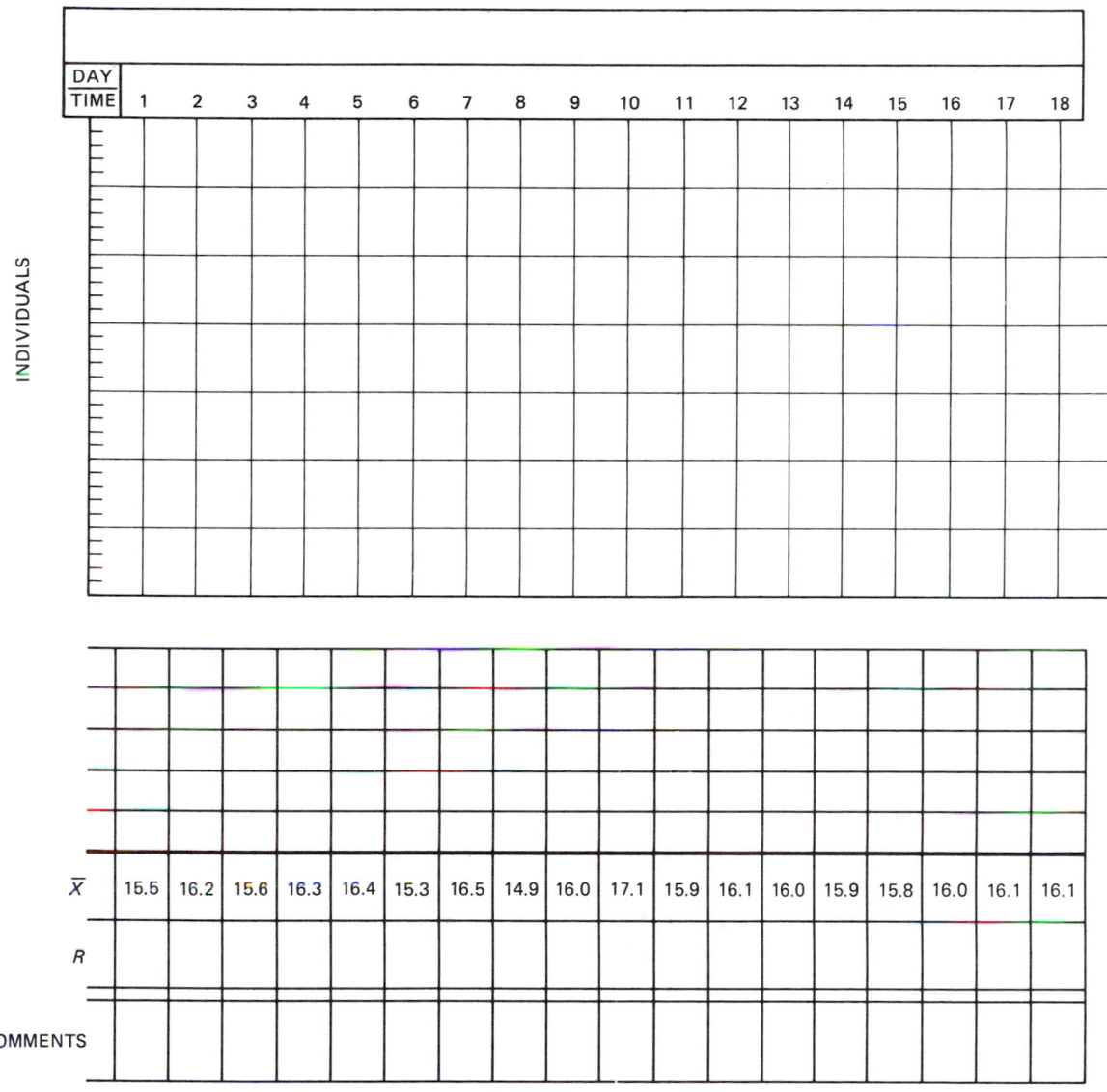

FIGURE 13–8 (a) Fill Weight Run Chart, Part 1

(cont.)

around the department. She happens to notice the low value that was just recorded. A typical reaction **might** be, "You better watch out. We can't shortchange the customer." The operator hears that, but doesn't worry, since, as Figure 13–8b shows, the next reading has come back up. Well, unfortunately, the next reading, all by itself, is where shown in Figure 13–8c. At the time the supervisor is on her way back

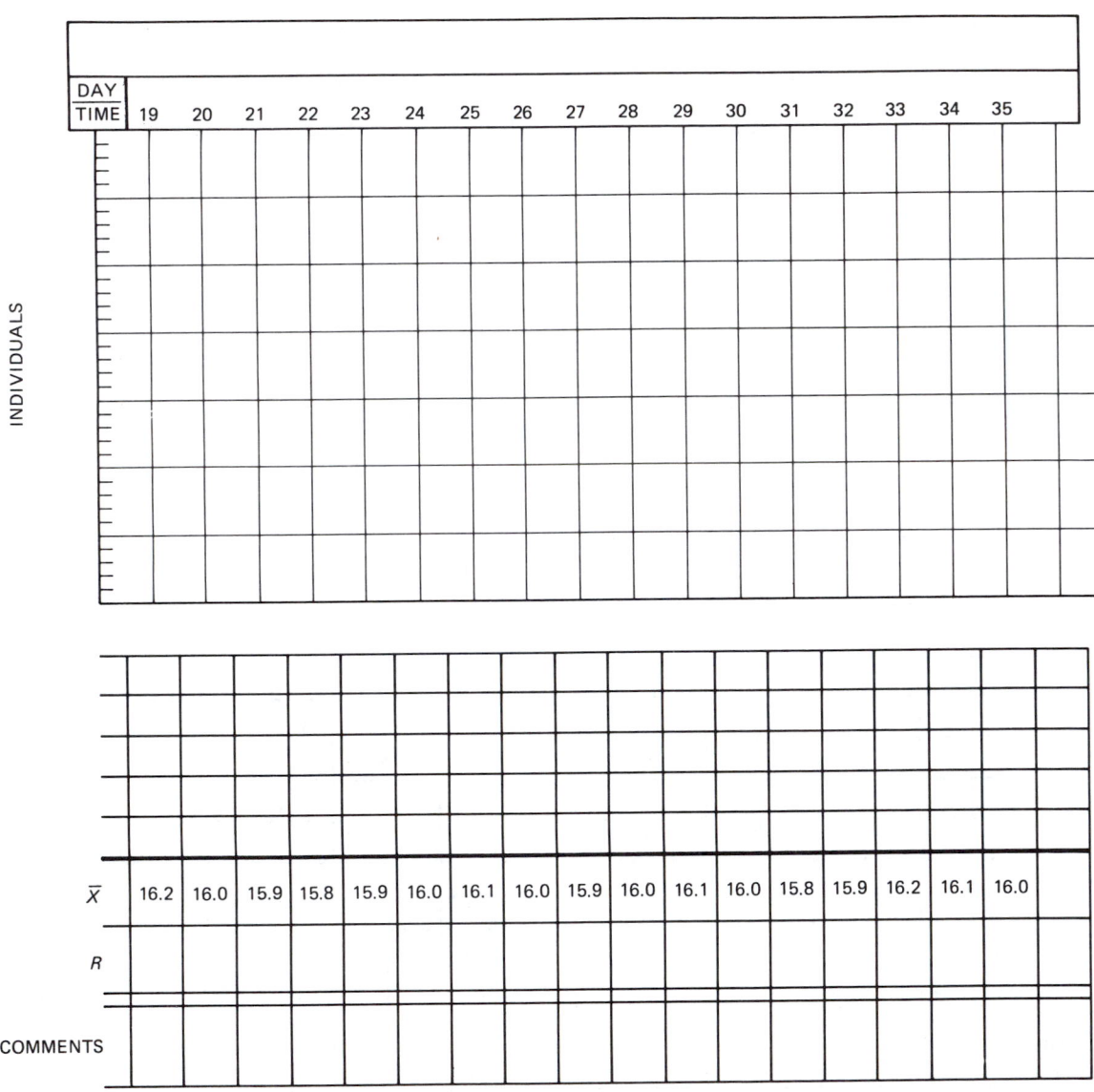

FIGURE 13-8a (*Continued*)

from the morning walk around, and she checks the run chart and sees the high value shown in Figure 13-8c. A typical reaction **might** be, "Now you've done it. You're giving the product away. First you're too low and now you're too high. You better get your act together or else." Being a prudent operator, Figure 13-8d shows the run chart for the next 2 or 3 hours. The operator made sure that there would be no

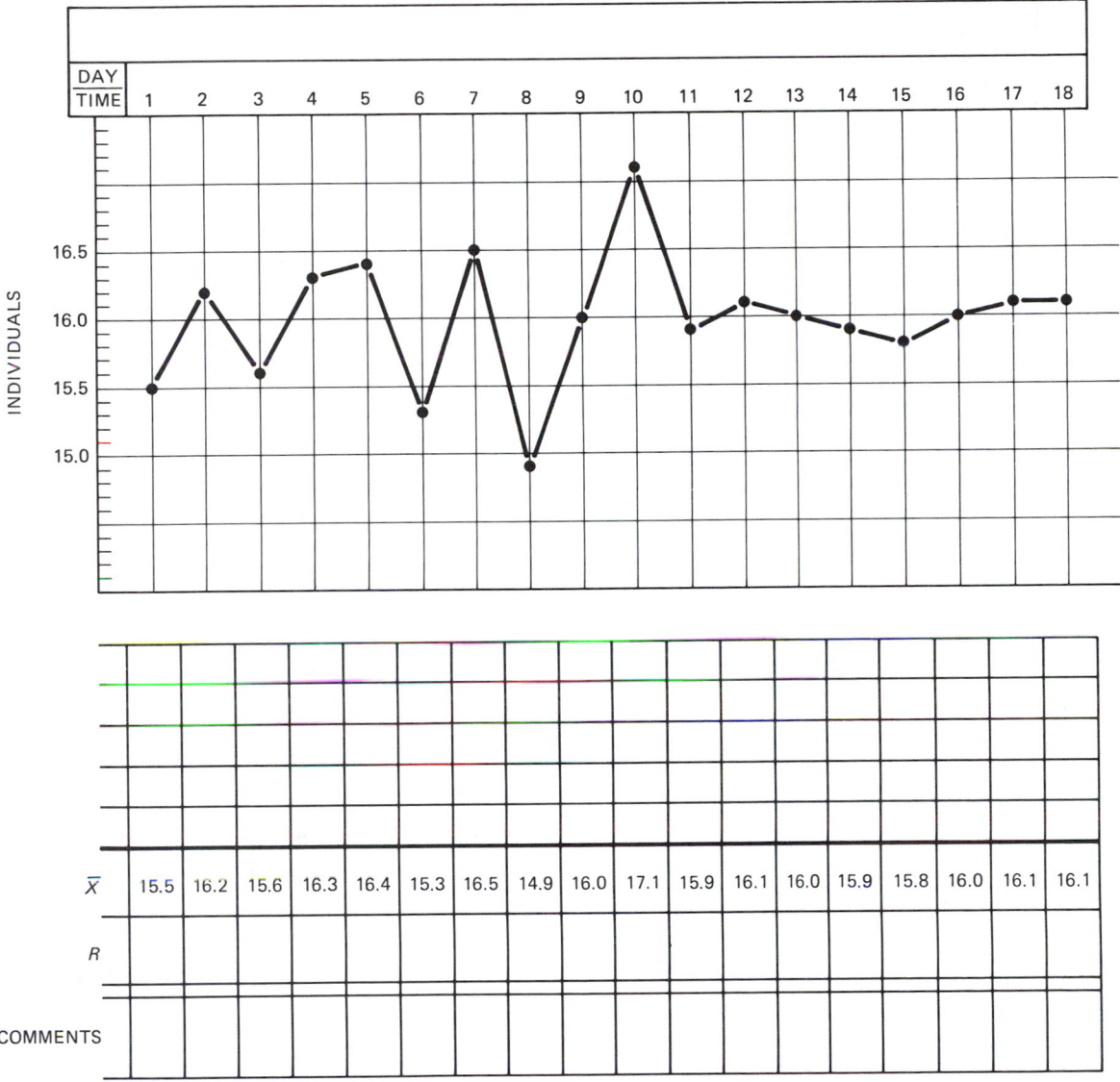

| $\overline{X}$ | 15.5 | 16.2 | 15.6 | 16.3 | 16.4 | 15.3 | 16.5 | 14.9 | 16.0 | 17.1 | 15.9 | 16.1 | 16.0 | 15.9 | 15.8 | 16.0 | 16.1 | 16.1 |

FIGURE 13-8 (b) Fill Weight Run Chart, Part 2   (*cont.*)

more static from the supervisor. The workday is long enough without that kind of hassle.   ■

Obviously, the preceding example showed an abuse of the run chart. Let's look at the same data handled correctly.

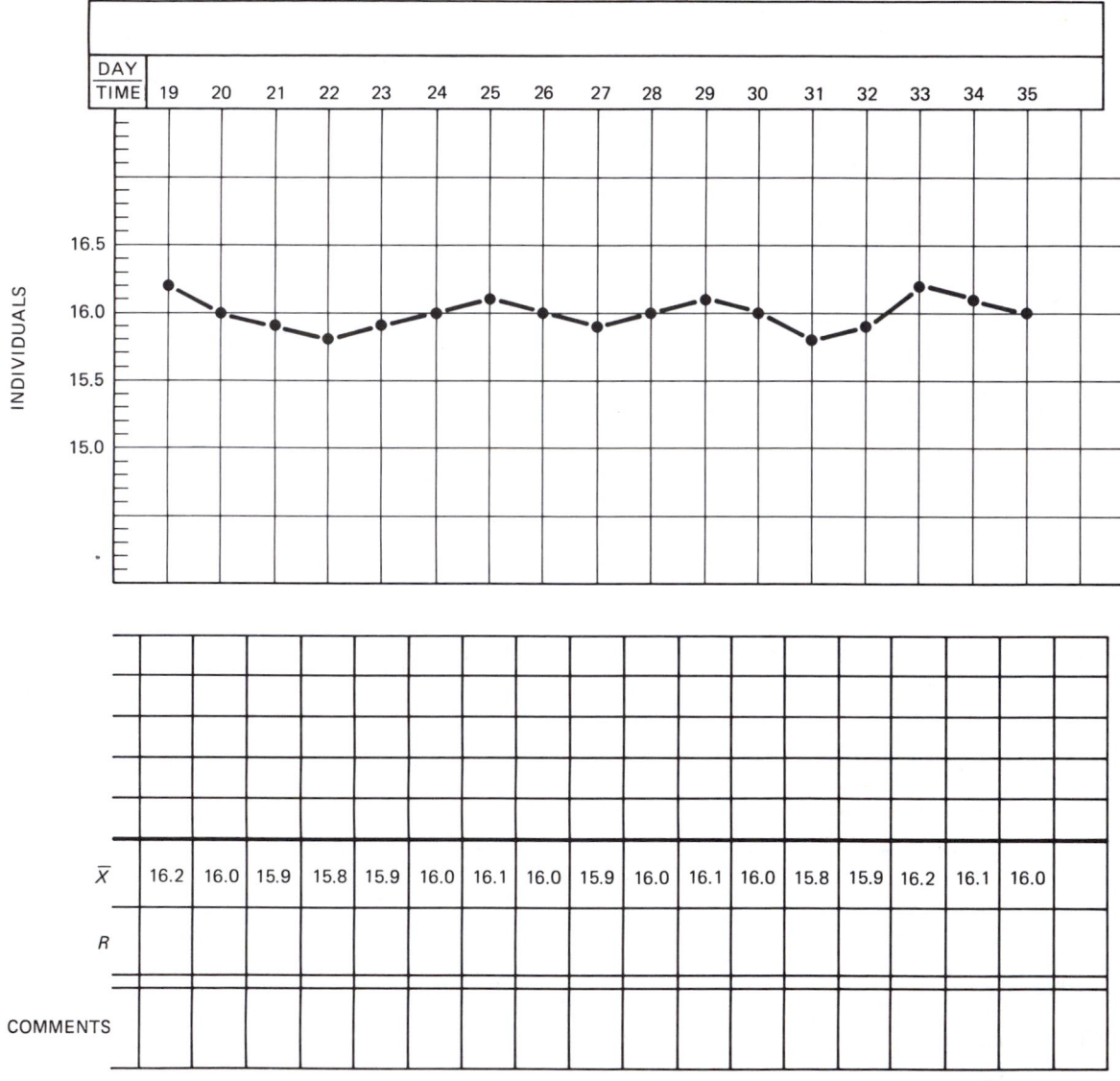

FIGURE 13–8b (*Continued*)

Example 13.5.3 A preliminary statistical analysis shows that the average value for these data is 16.0 ounces and the standard deviation is 0.40 ounces. We can't ask much more than that regarding being centered on target. The histogram for the data, shown in Figure 13–9, shows that the data appear to have a normal shape.

Calculating three sigma control limits for these fill weights yields an upper

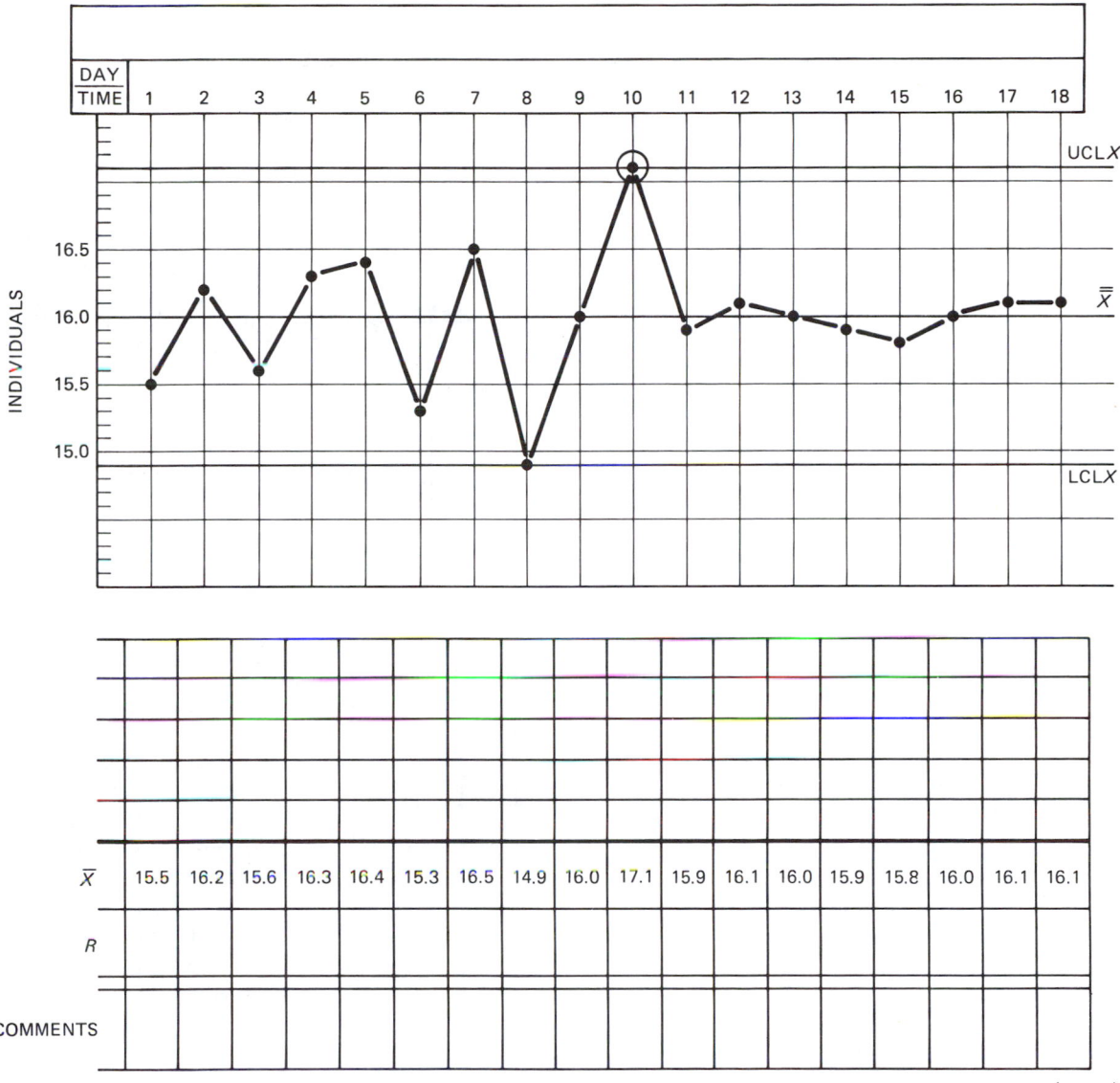

FIGURE 13-8 (c) Fill Weight Run Chart, Part 3

(*cont.*)

limit of approximately 17.2 and a lower limit of approximately 14.8. Both the values that the supervisor questioned, the 14.9 and the 17.1, fall within the control limits and should have been normally expected. (The remainder of the values, generated by fear, *might* be suspect or *might* be legitimate.) Assuming that the values are genuine readings, an examination of the run chart shown in Figure 13-8d indicates

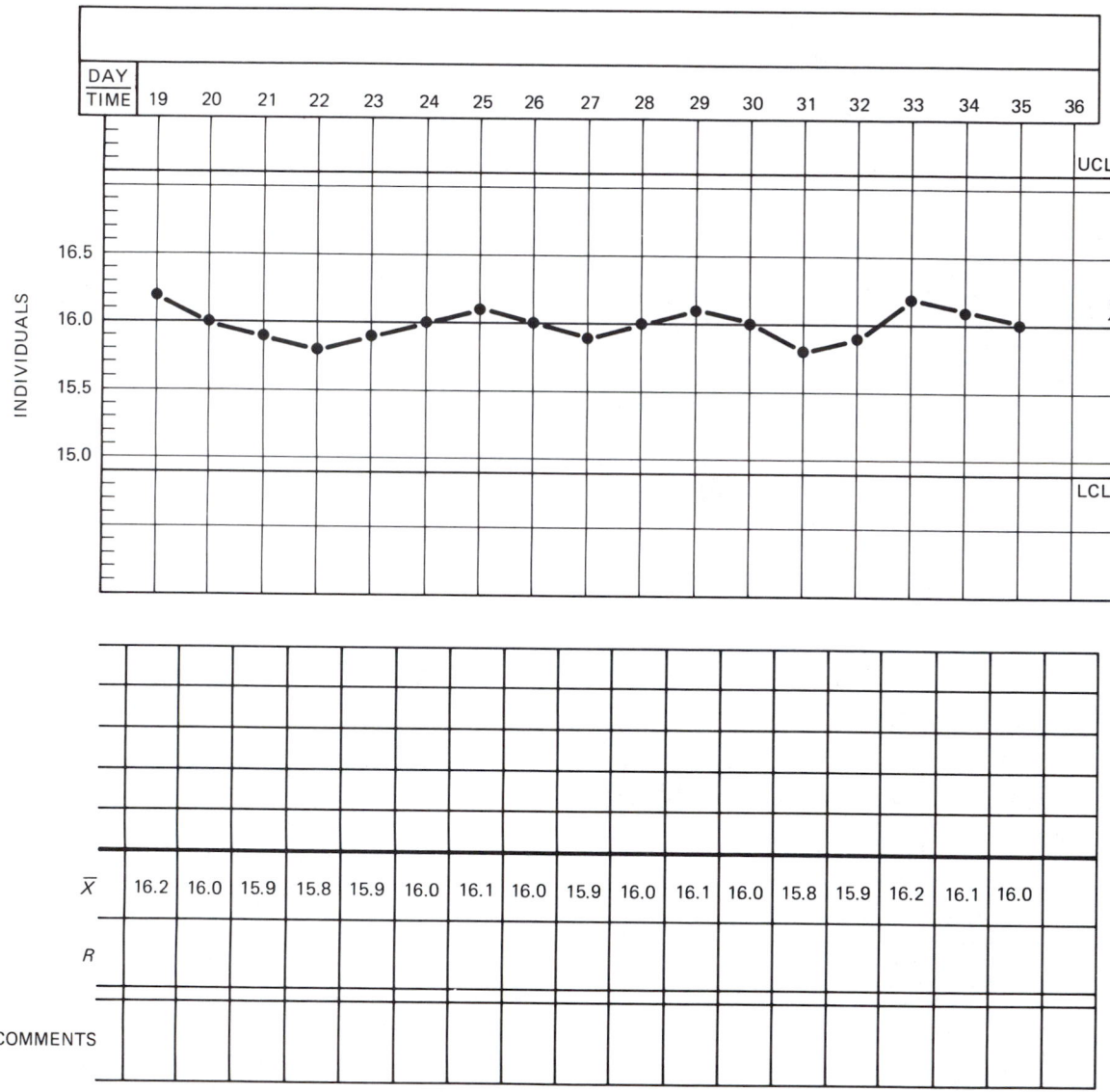

FIGURE 13–8c (*Continued*)

that the process is in control and nothing unusual seems to be happening. The operator should look for any unusual values, but the process is, in reality, performing very consistently. ■

Example 13.5.4 This last example will once again illustrate the power of the run chart in identifying a possible problem with the process. Figure 13–10 shows some feed rates for mate-

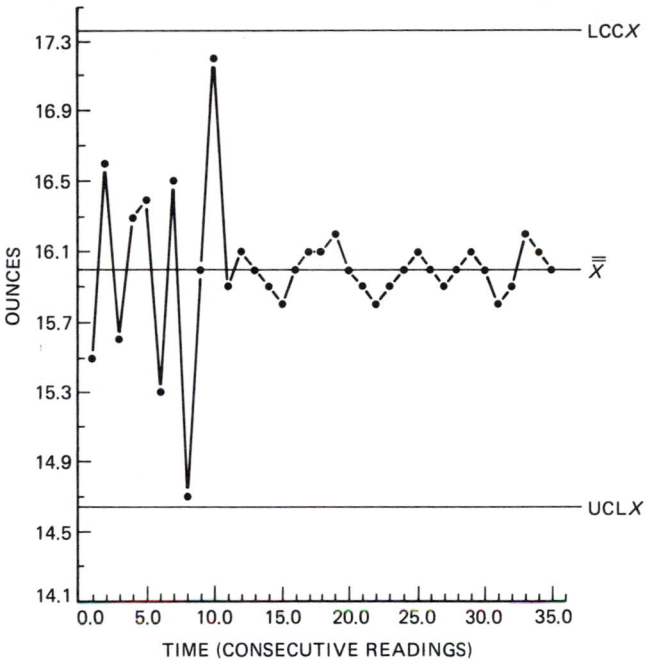

FIGURE 13-8 (d) Fill Weight Run Chart, Part 4

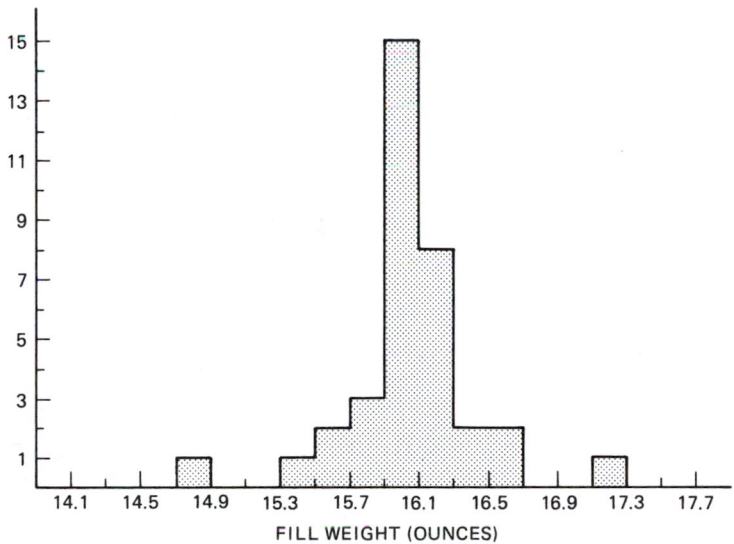

FIGURE 13-9 Fill Weight Histogram

Sample #	Rate	Sample #	Rate
1	1.6	26	3.1
2	2.1	27	3.1
3	2.2	28	3.1
4	2.2	29	3.2
5	2.2	30	3.2
6	2.3	31	3.3
7	2.5	32	3.3
8	2.5	33	3.3
9	2.5	34	3.4
10	2.6	35	3.4
11	2.6	36	3.4
12	2.7	37	3.5
13	2.7	38	3.6
14	2.8	39	3.7
15	2.8	40	3.7
16	2.8	41	3.8
17	2.8	42	3.8
18	2.8	43	3.9
19	2.9	44	4.0
20	2.9	45	4.0
21	2.9	46	4.0
22	3.0	47	4.0
23	3.0	48	4.0
24	3.0	49	4.1
25	3.1	50	4.3

FIGURE 13–10   Feed Rate Data

rial moving through a press. The target value for the feed rate is 3.0 and the minimum acceptable value is 1.5, while the upper acceptable value is 4.5. The data are arranged in a frequency histogram and the result is shown in Figure 13–11. The preliminary analysis of the values indicates that they are centered at about 3.0, have a range of 2.7, and appear to be normally distributed. A calculation of the mean shows the arithmetic average is actually 3.11 and the standard deviation is 0.61. Further evaluation would lead us to believe that, if the process is stable, and so far the information seems to indicate that it is stable, all the normal variation would be expected to be between 1.28 and 4.94. However, before jumping to any conclusions, we should first develop the run chart. This is shown in Figure 13–12. ∎

Obviously, there is a problem. There is an ever increasing trend. This is not normal. Action should be taken immediately to discover the special cause or causes of this abnormal variation. The operator may be very helpful at this point in determining the indicated course of action that should be taken. After all, the operator is closest to the process and should have the first best guess. This might be caused by some component wearing out or a control device slipping. Whatever, **the run chart gave**

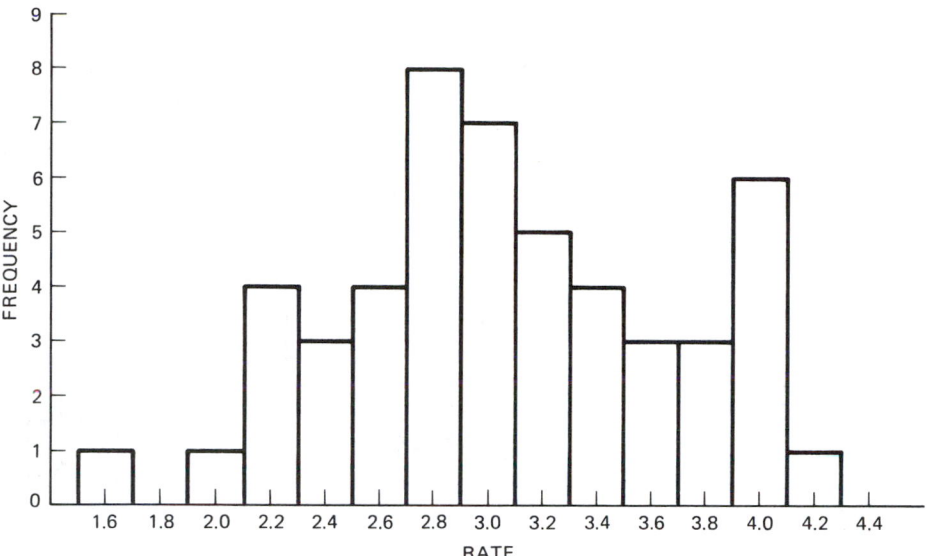

FIGURE 13-11 Feed Rate Histogram

us the indication that something was amiss before we actually produced any nonconforming material.   ■

13.6 CONCLUSION _____

Whenever we elect to collect data regarding a process, we gain tremendous insight
about the process when we look at the data as a function of time. Changes, patterns,
or any unusual "looks" to the data can give us an indication that the process is
changing or needs to be changed.

More sophisticated charts, such as control charts for averages and ranges, percentage defective, number of defects, and standard deviations can provide additional insight. And when coupled with information about target or nominal values,
specification limits, and our basic descriptive statistics, we are well equipped to begin monitoring, controlling, and improving the processes that produce our product.

Any critical input characteristic can be measured. Any critical output characteristic can be measured. Once these have been measured, they can be viewed in the
context of the control chart.

Control charts provide us with a continuing way to monitor our processes. As
we monitor more of the inputs and outputs, we will continue to improve the consistency. We always need to remember our definition of quality from the first chapter,
and that is the constant reduction of variability. As we proceed toward this goal,

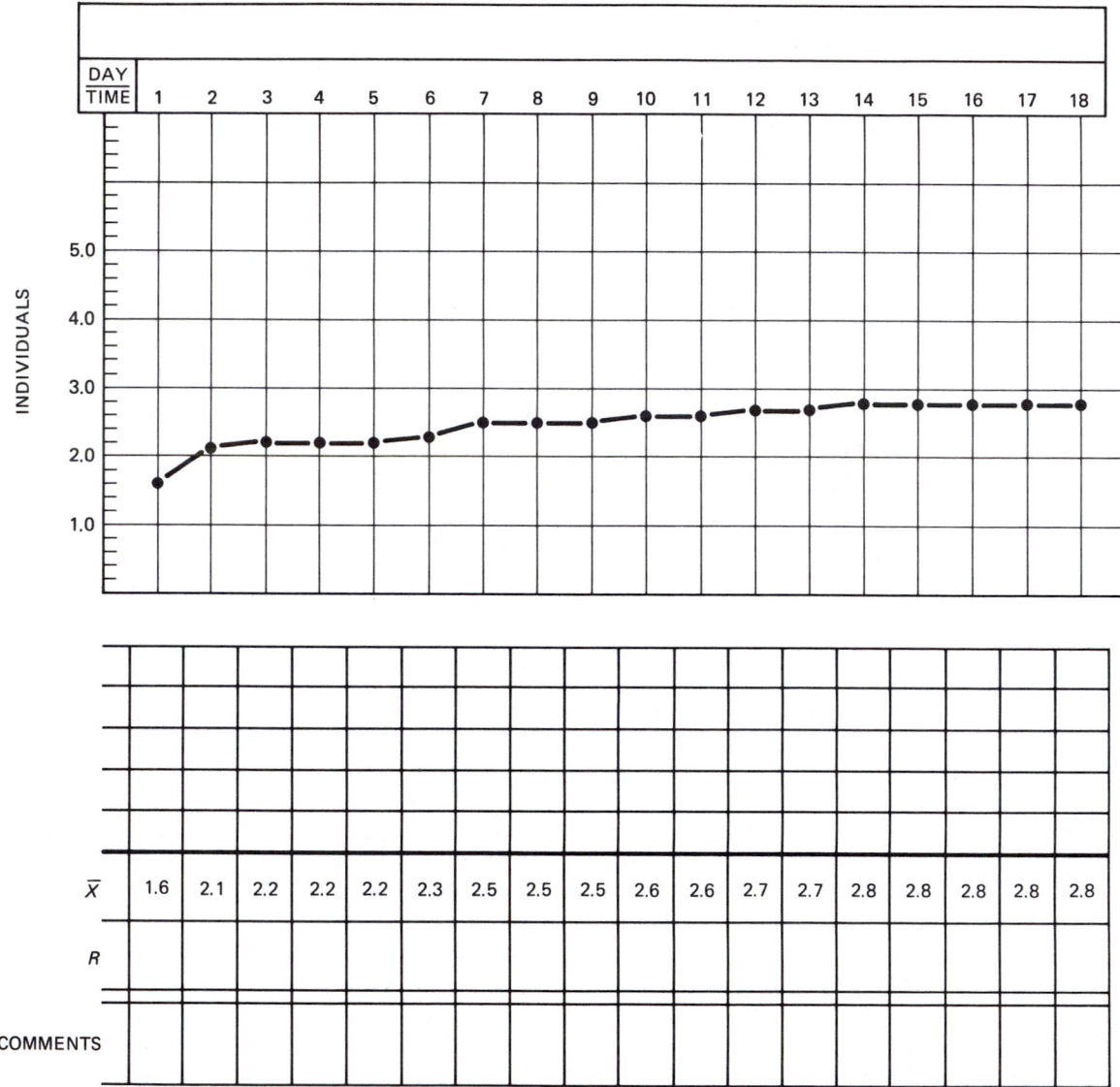

FIGURE 13–12 Feed Rate Run Chart

we would expect to continually reset our limits as we improve our process. Figure 13–13 shows how we would like our process control charts to look over time. Control charts also provide us with a common language. When everyone in the organization understands the concept of control and the use of the charts in achieving it, we are that much closer to our goal. Remember the customer–supplier relationships we

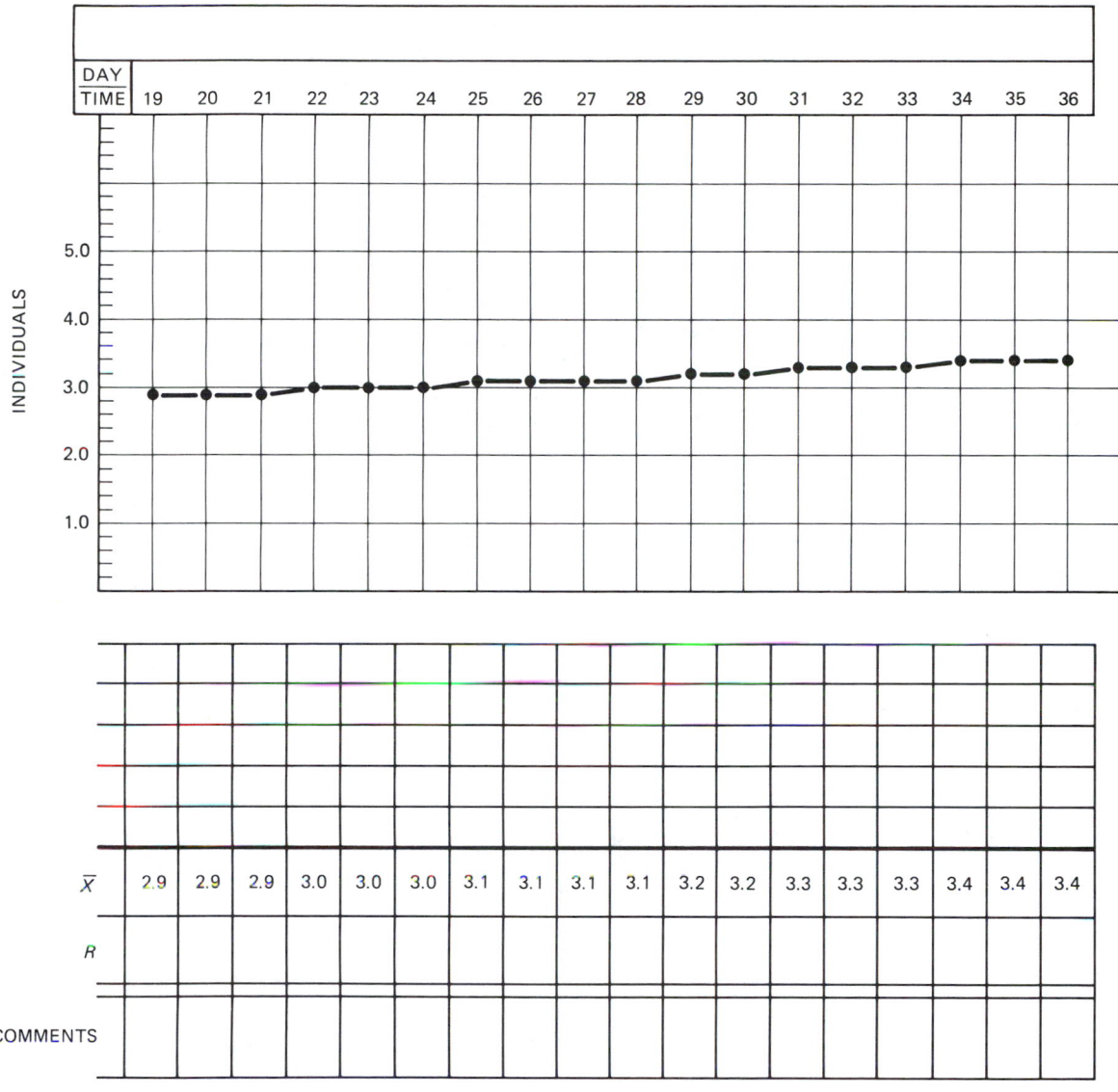

FIGURE 13–12 (*Continued*)   (*cont.*)

discussed earlier. From a financial aspect, control charts help us to reduce the amount of inspection required and will help to reduce the cost of rejections. [120: 27] Finally, control charts will help us to differentiate between the special causes, the abnormal variation, and the regular or normal causes. To improve, we must eliminate all special causes and work on reducing the normal variation.

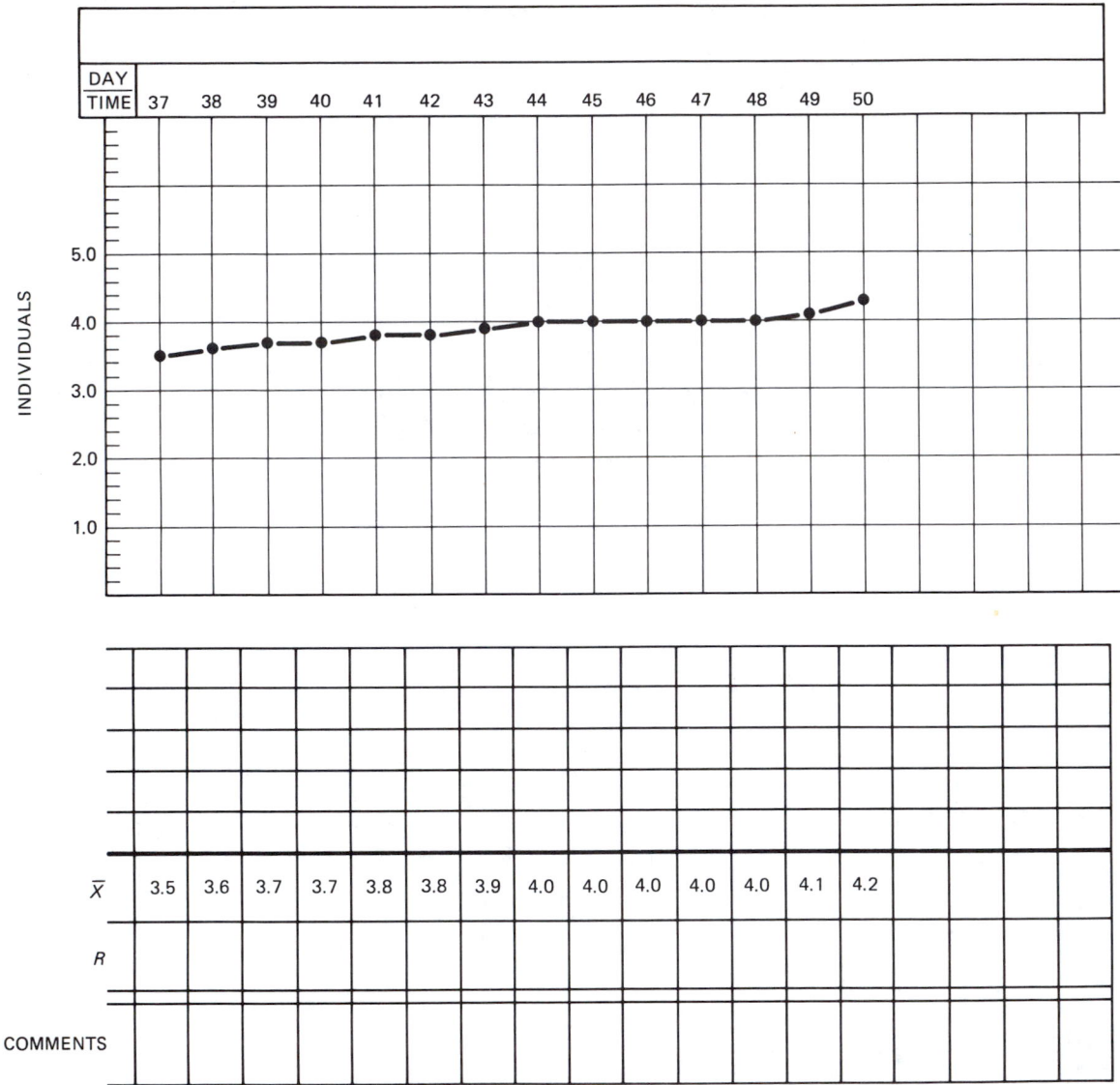

FIGURE 13–12 (*Continued*)

One final word of caution. The control charts by themselves will not solve problems. Like all other statistical methods, they will only help to identify the problems as they occur. But knowing when the problem occurs is a tremendous advantage. For their application to be successful, there must be management commitment to process improvement.

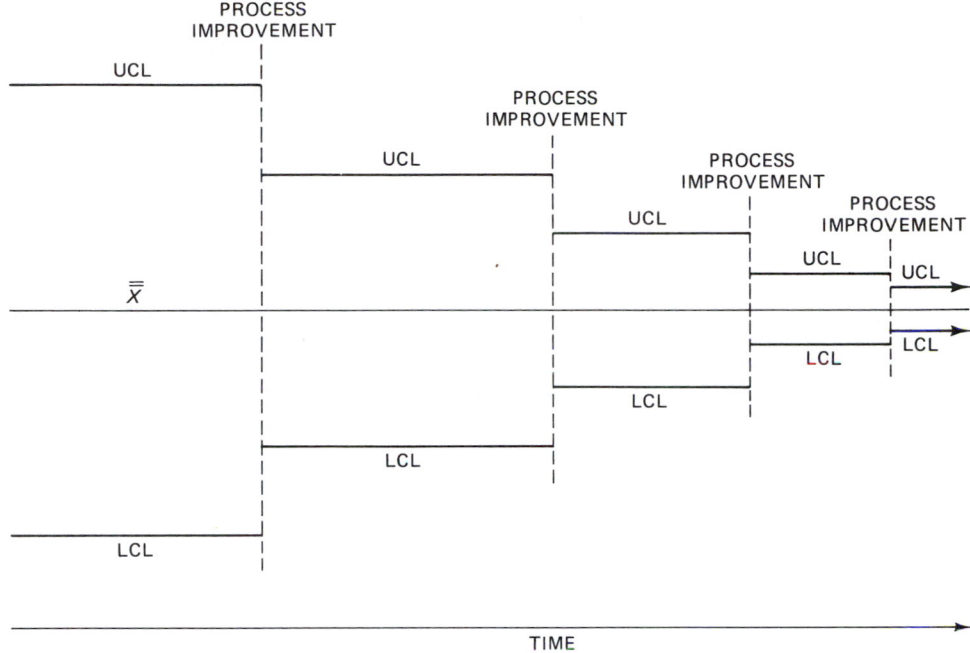

FIGURE 13-13   Control Charts over Time

EXERCISES

Prepare a run chart from the information given.

1. Tire inflations were checked after installation at an auto assembly plant. The data are as follows:

Sample	Value (psi)	Sample	Value (psi)
1	15	11	23
2	22	12	11
3	18	13	13
4	28	14	17
5	56	15	24
6	10	16	26
7	12	17	16
8	20	18	22
9	25	19	27
10	29	20	21

2. Chicken Little Poultry Farm collected information on the number of chickens that died each day from heat stress during June.

Date	Number	Date	Number
1	55	16	62
2	65	17	65
3	60	18	57
4	63	19	63
5	55	20	52
6	58	21	81
7	61	22	68
8	64	23	64
9	70	24	62
10	57	25	57
11	56	26	55
12	54	27	60
13	61	28	54
14	58	29	58
15	59	30	52

3. The following data were collected on the diameters of 30 compact disc center holes. The target is 1.5 mm.

Sample	Value (mm)	Sample	Value (mm)
1	1.4	14	1.5
2	1.7	15	1.3
3	1.5	16	1.1
4	1.2	17	1.4
5	1.8	18	1.6
6	1.5	19	1.7
7	1.3	20	1.5
8	1.6	21	1.4
9	2.0	22	1.5
10	1.7	23	1.6
11	1.5	24	1.2
12	1.5	25	2.6
13	1.9	26	1.8

4. A munitions manufacturer has developed a new propellant charge. Tests under simulated use conditions have produced the following velocities for a targeted fill weight of 45 units.

Sample	Velocity	Sample	Velocity
1	55	13	55
2	53	14	52
3	60	15	65
4	49	16	65
5	54	17	49
6	59	18	58
7	45	19	57
8	100	20	53
9	32	21	45
10	55	22	49
11	49	23	70
12	50	24	63

SELECTED REFERENCES

The following is a partial listing of statistical quality control texts or texts with significant sections about SQC. Any of these will explain, in detail, the theory and application of statistical methods to quality control. The publication dates are not shown because many of the books are being continually revised and the reader should, naturally, want to use the latest edition of any text.

Aft, L., *Fundamentals of Industrial Quality Control,* Addison-Wesley, Reading, Mass.

Braverman, J., *Fundamentals of Statistical Quality Control,* Reston (Prentice-Hall), Englewood Cliffs, N.J.

Burr, I., *Elementary Statistical Quality Control,* Marcel-Dekkar, New York.

Duncan, A., *Quality Control and Industrial Statistics,* Irwin, Homewood, Ill.

Grant, E., and R. Leavenworth, *Statistical Quality Control,* McGraw-Hill, New York.

Hansen, B., *Quality Control,* Prentice-Hall, Englewood Cliffs, N.J.

Juran, J. (editor), *Quality Control Handbook,* McGraw-Hill, New York.

Montgomery, D., *Statistical Quality Control,* Wiley, New York.

Shewhart, W., *Economic Control of Quality of Manufactured Product* (Available from American Society for Quality Control, Milwaukee, Wisc.).

Wadsworth, H., K. Stephens, and B. Godfrey, *Modern Methods for Quality Control and Improvement,* Wiley, New York.

Western Electric Company, *Statistical Quality Control Handbook,* AT&T (Available from American Society for Quality Control, Milwaukee, Wisc.).

CHAPTER 14

Control Charts for Variables

The secret of Japan's success is an unrelenting, some might say fanatical, adherence to what amounts to a de facto national industrial policy. That policy is quality first. [118:11]

Dana Cound
DiversiTech

14.1 INTRODUCTION

Chapter 13 introduced the concept of the control chart. This is an extremely powerful statistical tool. Control chart methodology was originally developed by Shewhart and his colleagues at Bell Labs during the 1930s. His landmark work, *ECONOMIC CONTROL OF QUALITY OF MANUFACTURED PRODUCT,* originally published in 1931, was republished by the American Society for Quality Control in 1980.

This chapter will examine the construction and use of two of the three sigma control charts that Shewhart developed, the charts for ranges and averages. These are charts for variables.

Before we discuss variables and the control charts that monitor these processes, it will be useful to once again define what we mean by control. This time, though, let use the words of Shewhart:

A phenomenon will be said to be controlled when, through the use of past experience, we can predict, at least within limits, how the phenomenon may he expected to vary in the future. Here it is understood that prediction within limits means that we can state, at least approximately, the probability that the observed phenomenon will fall within the given limits. [120: 6]

As our discussion in Chapter 13 indicated, the control limits indicate the limits of the normal or random variation. **The control limits that we will learn to calculate in this chapter have no direct relationship with the specifications** for the process. Ideally, a process should be both in control and within specifications. The relationship of specifications to control limits is discussed in greater detail in Chapter 18.

14.2 VARIABLES AND ATTRIBUTES

The control charts that we will examine in this chapter, and the next four for that matter, are charts for variables. As we will use the term, a variable is a characteristic that we can measure. A variable can take on any value within a given set of limits. The value that we can measure is limited only be the precision of our measuring equipment. Temperatures, pressures, diameters, and electrical resistance all are examples of variables.

The control charts that we will examine in Chapter 16 deal with attributes. Attributes are characteristics that are countable, but not measurable. An attribute either exists or it doesn't. Typical attributes that are commonly used include proportion defective and number or defects or errors.

Generally, we obtain more information about the performance of the process from measuring variables. Some characteristics, such as number of errors, must be counted. Attribute analysis can lead to the instantaneous failure mode, we discussed in Chapter 13.

Given the choice, it is recommended that variables charts be used whenever possible to monitor processes. It is easier to see trends develop and identify potentially helpful corrective actions before problems occur. Attribute charts generally track problems after they have occurred.

14.3 PROCEDURE FOR CONSTRUCTING CHARTS

This section will identify the procedure that is recommended for the construction of charts for ranges and averages. We will stress that the charts are tools for monitoring the process and improving the process. When used properly, these charts can help to prevent problems.

The first step in constructing a chart for ranges and averages is to determine the characteristic to be monitored. This is selected either as the result of a Pareto analysis, from a process flow analysis and discussions with the process' customers, or from a cause and effect diagram analysis.

After the characteristic is identified, the sample size is determined. To effectively use the Shewhart relationships, the sample size is recommended to be between 2 and 10 items. The guiding principle here will be whatever fits the process, whatever is reasonable. The frequency of sampling is also considered at this point. It should fit the process and not overly interfere with the other work being performed by the operator, who should be the data collector. Again, the guiding word is reasonable.

Once the sampling scheme is developed, sufficient initial data should be collected to give meaningful results. A commonly accepted number is a minimum of at least 50 individual readings. with 100 being better and 200 even better than that. Any and all unusual occurrences should be noted on the data-collection form. An example of a typical variables chart data-collection form is shown in Figure 14–1.

After the data have been collected, the initial calculations are performed. The average for each sample is calculated, as is the range. This is also recorded. The grand average and the average range are the next statistics to be calculated.

Next, the sample ranges and sample averages are graphed or plotted on the appropriate charts. Generally, the individual ranges and averages are connected with a solid line. This will help to show patterns later during analysis. The grand average and the average range are drawn in to identify the location of the process.

At this point, the limits for ranges are calculated. Note that we calculate the limit for ranges first. Our concern throughout this text has been for the reduction of variability. It is logical, then, to make sure that **the process variability, as represented by the ranges, is the first characteristic that is examined for control.** The formulas for control limits for ranges are shown next.

$$\mathrm{UCL}R = D_4\overline{R}$$

$$\mathrm{LCL}R = D_3\overline{R}$$

The values for D_4 and D_3 are known as Shewhart control chart constants and appear in Appendix B, as well as in Figure 14–2. The values of these constants depend on the initial sample size. This must remain constant throughout the analysis.

After the limits for ranges have been calculated, they should be drawn on the chart for ranges. Each sample range should be checked to see if the values fall between the upper and lower control limits. If a sample range is not between the limits, then we should determine if there is an assignable or special cause for this abnormal variation. Often the notations made during the data-collection process will determine if there is a special reason. **If there is a special cause for a sample being outside the limits that sample should be discarded.**

If this is the case, then the grand average and the average range must be recalculated. Following that, the control limits for ranges must also be calculated again. The sample ranges are then compared with the "new" limits, which are also drawn on the chart. If any of the remaining ranges are out of control, the process is repeated. If not, then a broken line is used to connect the points around the deleted range.

Control limits for averages are calculated after we are convinced that the ranges are stable. The formulas for the three sigma limits for averages are shown next. Again, the constant value, A_2, comes from the work that Shewhart did.

$$\mathrm{UCL}\overline{X} = \overline{\overline{X}} + A_2\overline{R}$$

$$\mathrm{LCL}\overline{X} = \overline{\overline{X}} - A_2\overline{R}$$

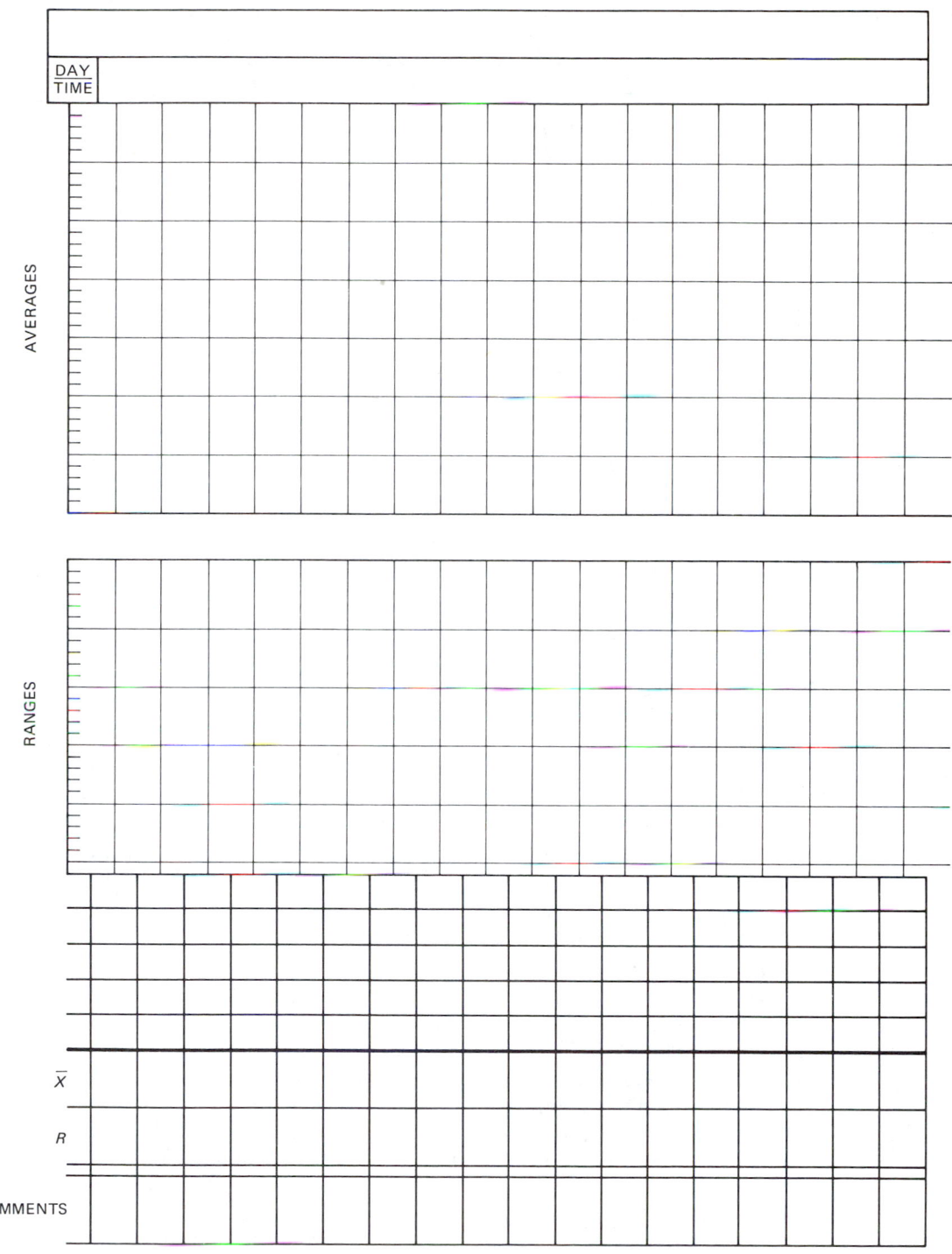

FIGURE 14–1 Typical Variables Control Chart Form

n	A_2	D_3	D_4	d_2
2	1.88	0	3.27	1.128
3	1.02	0	2.57	1.693
4	.73	0	2.28	2.059
5	.58	0	2.11	2.326
6	.48	0	2.00	2.534
7	.42	.08	1.92	2.704
8	.37	.14	1.86	2.847
9	.34	.18	1.82	2.970
10	.31	.22	1.78	3.078

Copyright, ASTM, 1916 Race Street, Philadelphia, PA 19103. Reprinted with permission.

FIGURE 14-2 Shewhart Control Chart Constants

After the limits for averages have been calculated, they should be drawn on the chart for averages. Each sample average should be checked to see if the values fall between the upper and lower control limits. If a sample average is not between the limits, then we should determine if there is an assignable or special cause for this abnormal variation. Often the notations made during the data-collection process will determine if there is a special reason. As with the ranges, if there is **special/identifiable cause** for the abnormal variation, then the sample should be discarded.

If this is the case, then the grand average and the average range must be recalculated. Following that, the control limits for ranges must also be calculated again. The sample ranges are then compared with the "new" limits, which are also drawn on the chart. If any of the remaining ranges are out of control, the process is repeated. If not, then a broken line is used to connect the points around the deleted range. Then the limits for averages are recalculated. The sample averages are then compared with the "new" limits, which are also drawn on the chart. If any of the remaining averages are out of control, the entire process is repeated. If not, then a broken line is used to connect the points around the deleted average.

At this point, the process is said to be in control. This means that only normal variation is present. A process must be in control before we can begin improving it. No mention has been made about whether or not material being produced conforms to specifications.

That is the procedure. Section 14.4 will look at some examples of the process.

One last point of emphasis, though. The process, once it is in control, generally will require continuing monitoring. This should be done by the operator. As soon as abnormal variation occurs, the operator should first recognize it and, second, initiate action to remove it. Looking at the data after the fact, a day or week or even a month later, will not help to control the process. Chapter 17 will illustrate some of the common control chart interpretation techniques.

14.4 CONTROL CHART APPLICATIONS

This section includes three example problems. The first of these explains, step by step, all the activities required to construct control charts for ranges and averages.

The second presents the data and works through the calculations with a minimum of narrative. Additional problems are provided in the exercise section at the end of the chapter.

Example 14.4.1 A furniture factory is producing assemble-it-yourself bookcases. For the shelves to fit properly with the shelf supports, the width of each shelf must have little variation.

To see how they are doing, the furniture factory has collected some shelf widths. Due to the nature of the shelf-width-making process, the process was sampled at random three times every hour for a period of 3 days. This gave the sample width measurements, to the nearest centimeter, shown in Figure 14–3. The nominal or target for these data is 20 centimeters. We note that on the first day of data collection the saw broke at 1:00. We also note that at 2:00 on the third day the saw was sharpened.

The average and range for each sample is calculated and shown in Figure 14–4. The average range for the data is determined to be 2.89 and the average of all the individuals, the grand average, is 19.49 cm. These values, along with the sample ranges and sample averages, are shown in Figure 14–5.

The control limits for averages are calculated using the sample average range of 2.89.

$$UCLR = D_4\overline{R}$$

$$UCLR = (2.57)(2.89) = 7.42$$

$$LCLR = D_3\overline{R}$$

$$LCLR = (0)(2.89) = 0$$

These are added to the control chart and shown in Figure 14–6. Preliminary examination indicates that the sample range for the 1:00 sample on the first day is out of control. This should not be surprising, since we did note that the saw broke at that point. This special cause, the breaking of the saw, is sufficient reason to thrown out that particular point. Since that is the only point that is out *of* the limits, the average range and the average average are recalculated. The new R is 2.65 and the new X is 19.46. the new average range is used to recompute the control limit for ranges.

$$UCLR = (2.57)(2.65) = 6.82$$

$$LCLR = (0)(2.65) = 0$$

The new limits are drawn on the chart as shown in Figure 14–7. It now appears that the ranges are in control. Our attention can now be directed to the sample

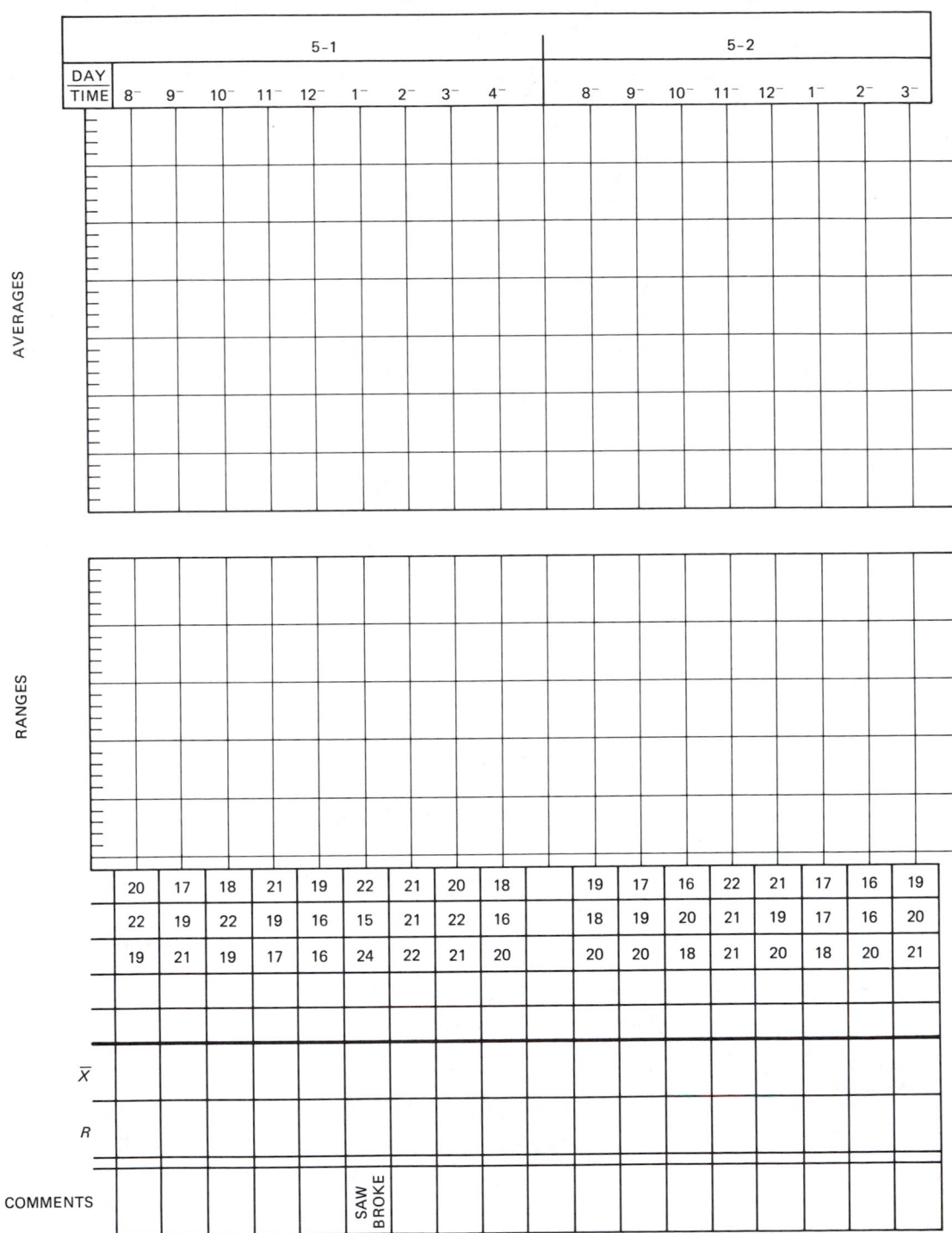

FIGURE 14-3 Data for Example 14.4.1

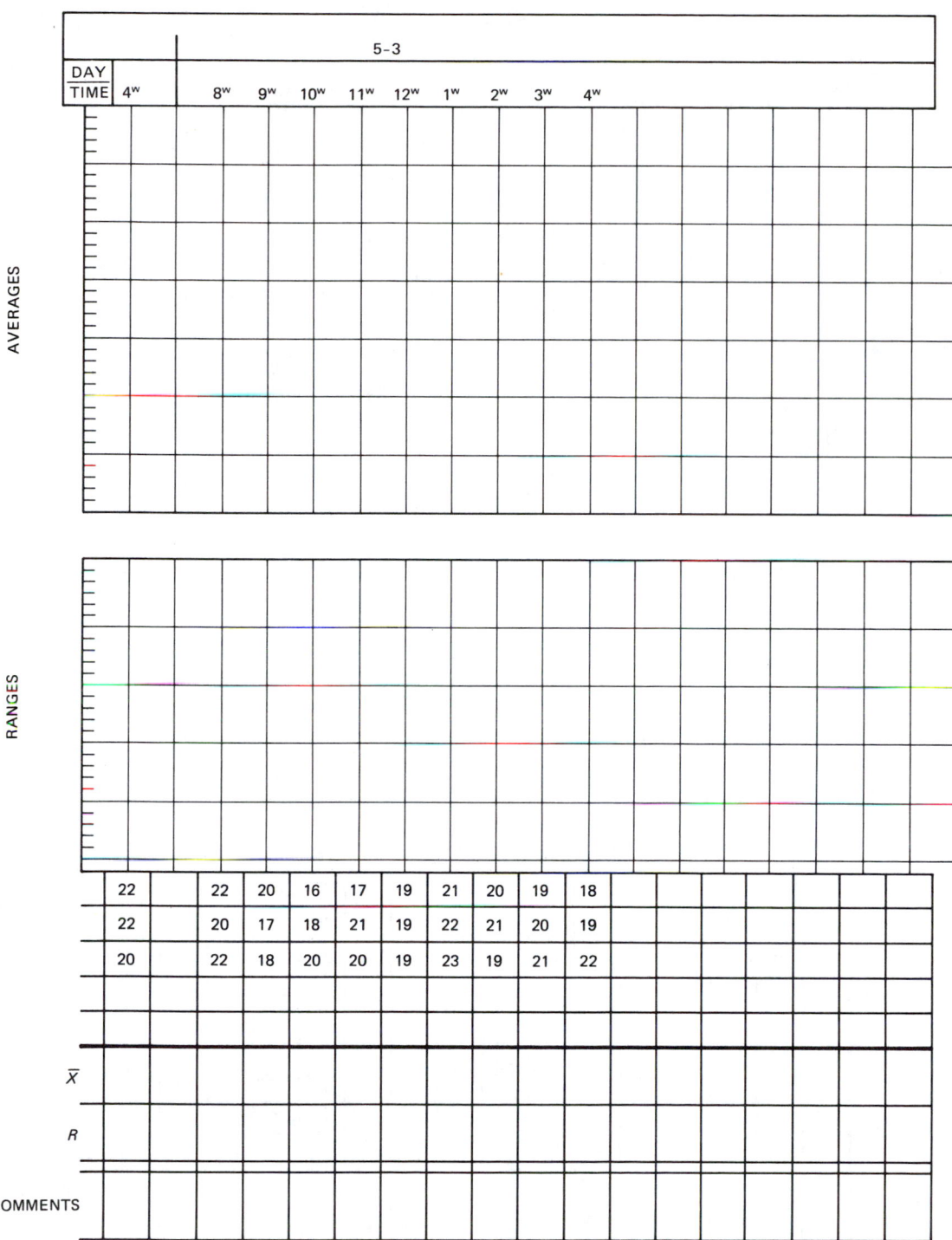

FIGURE 14-3 (*Continued*)

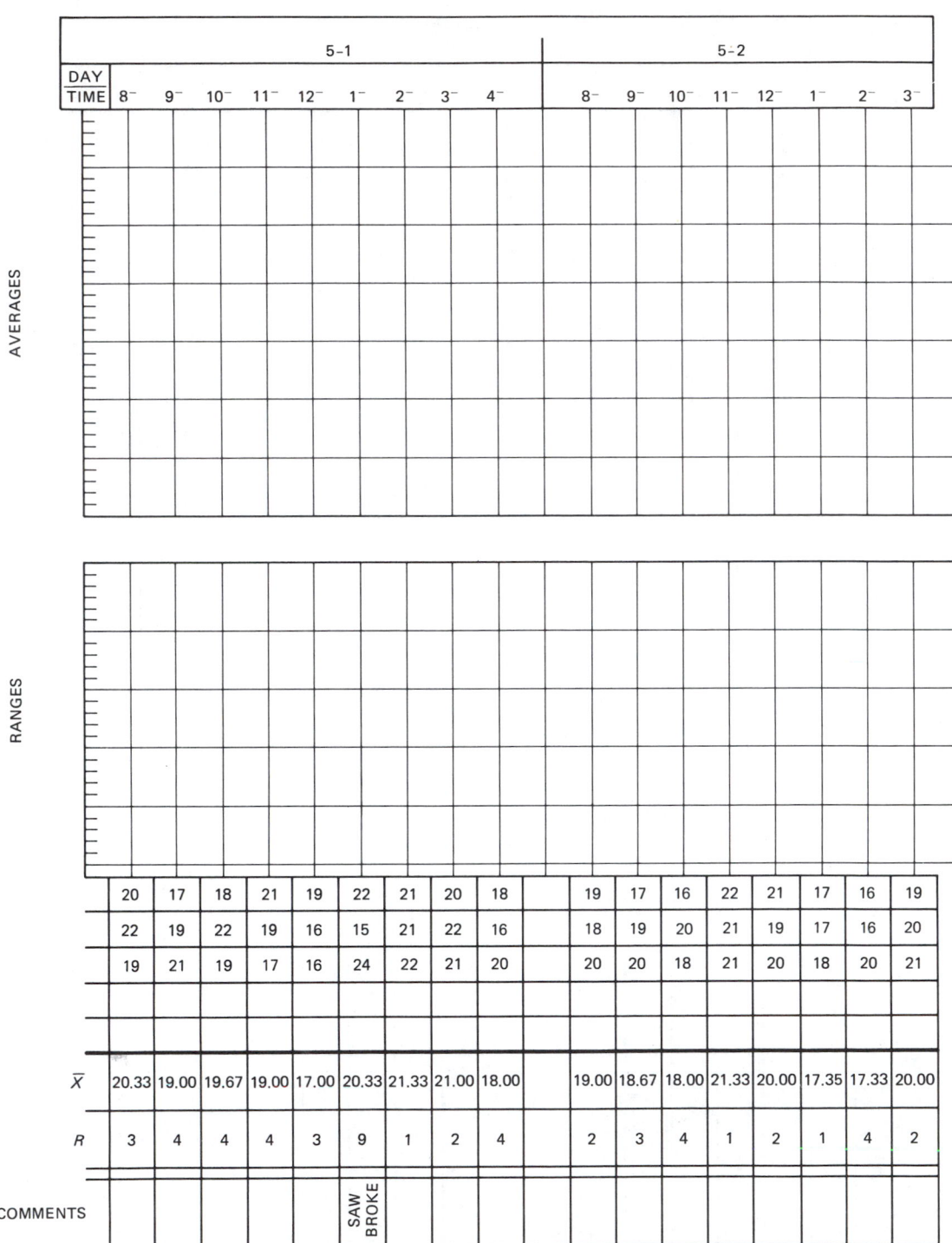

FIGURE 14-4 Average and Range for Example 14.4.1

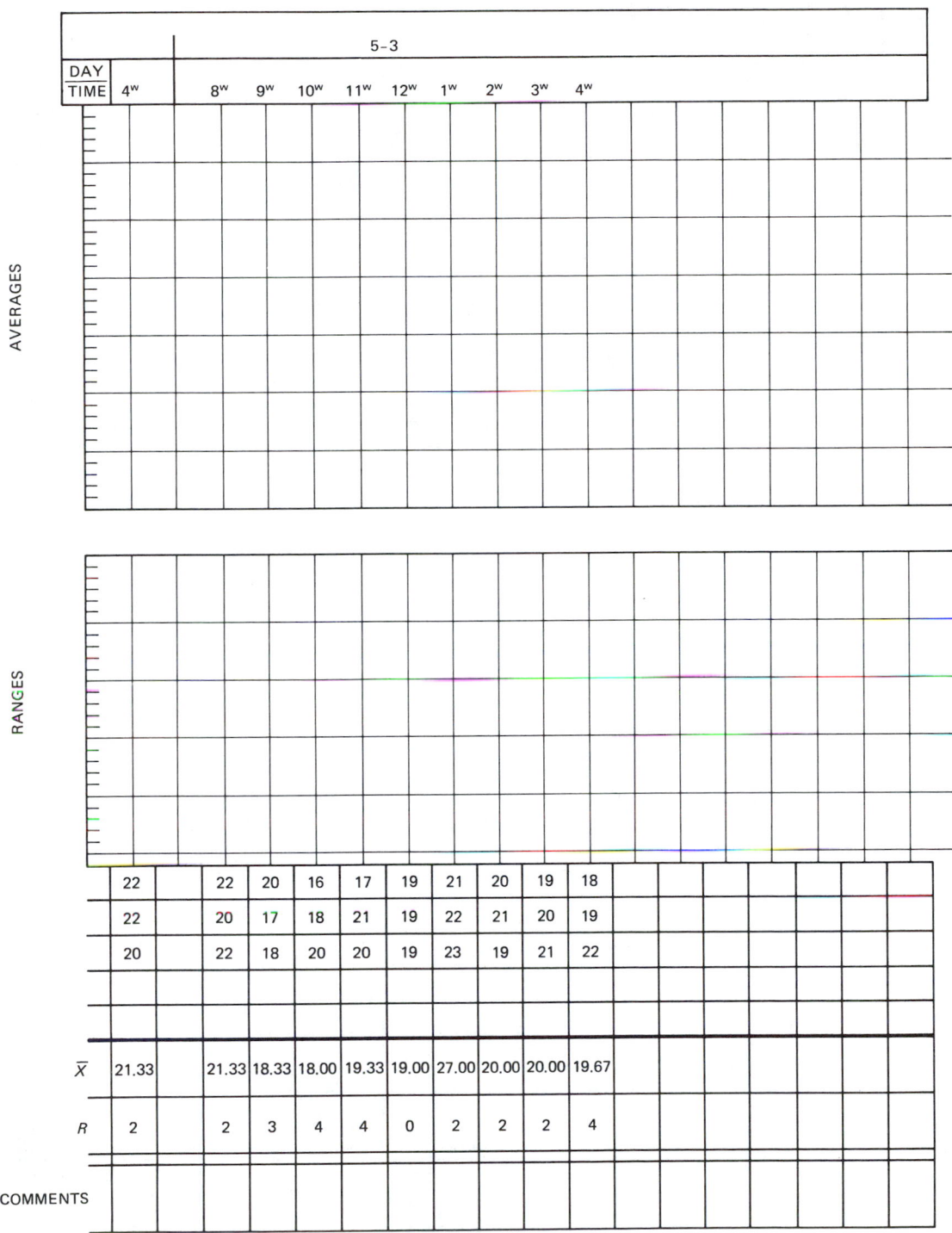

		5–3																		
DAY TIME	4ʷ	8ʷ	9ʷ	10ʷ	11ʷ	12ʷ	1ʷ	2ʷ	3ʷ	4ʷ										

AVERAGES

RANGES

	22		22	20	16	17	19	21	20	19	18									
	22		20	17	18	21	19	22	21	20	19									
	20		22	18	20	20	19	23	19	21	22									
$\overline{X}$	21.33		21.33	18.33	18.00	19.33	19.00	27.00	20.00	20.00	19.67									
R	2		2	3	4	4	0	2	2	2	4									
COMMENTS																				

FIGURE 14–4 (*Continued*)

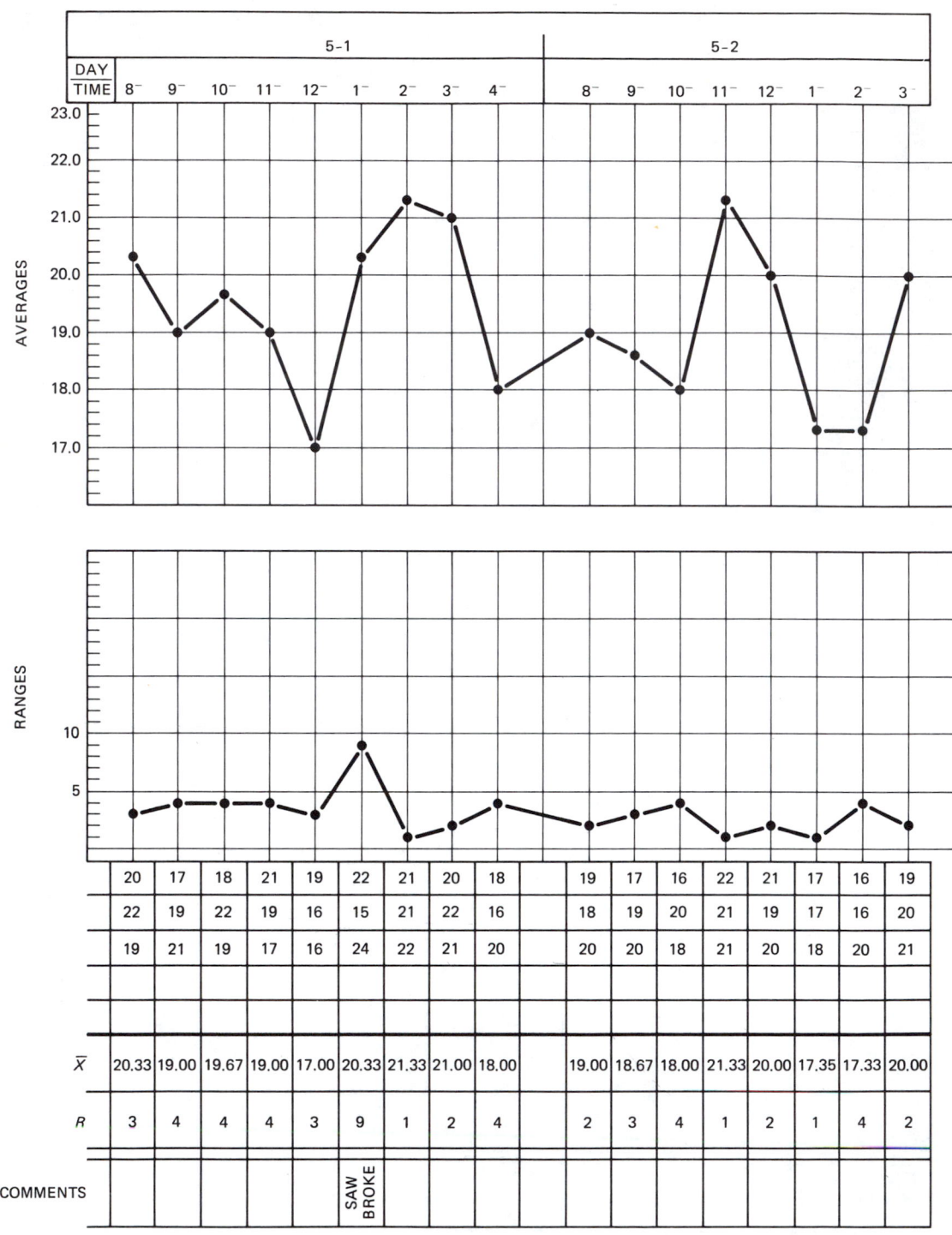

FIGURE 14-5 Initial Plot for Example 14.4.1

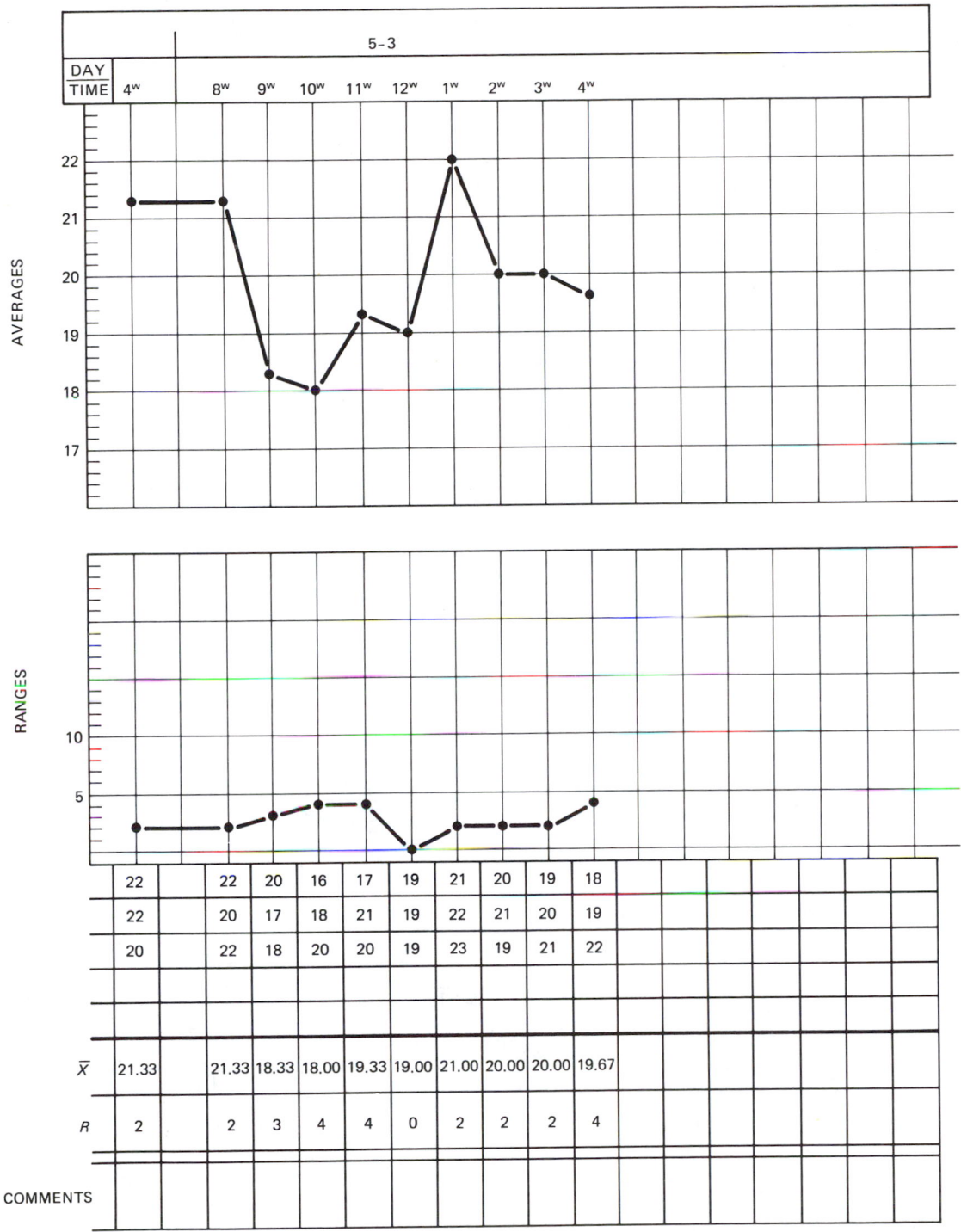

FIGURE 14-5 (*Continued*)

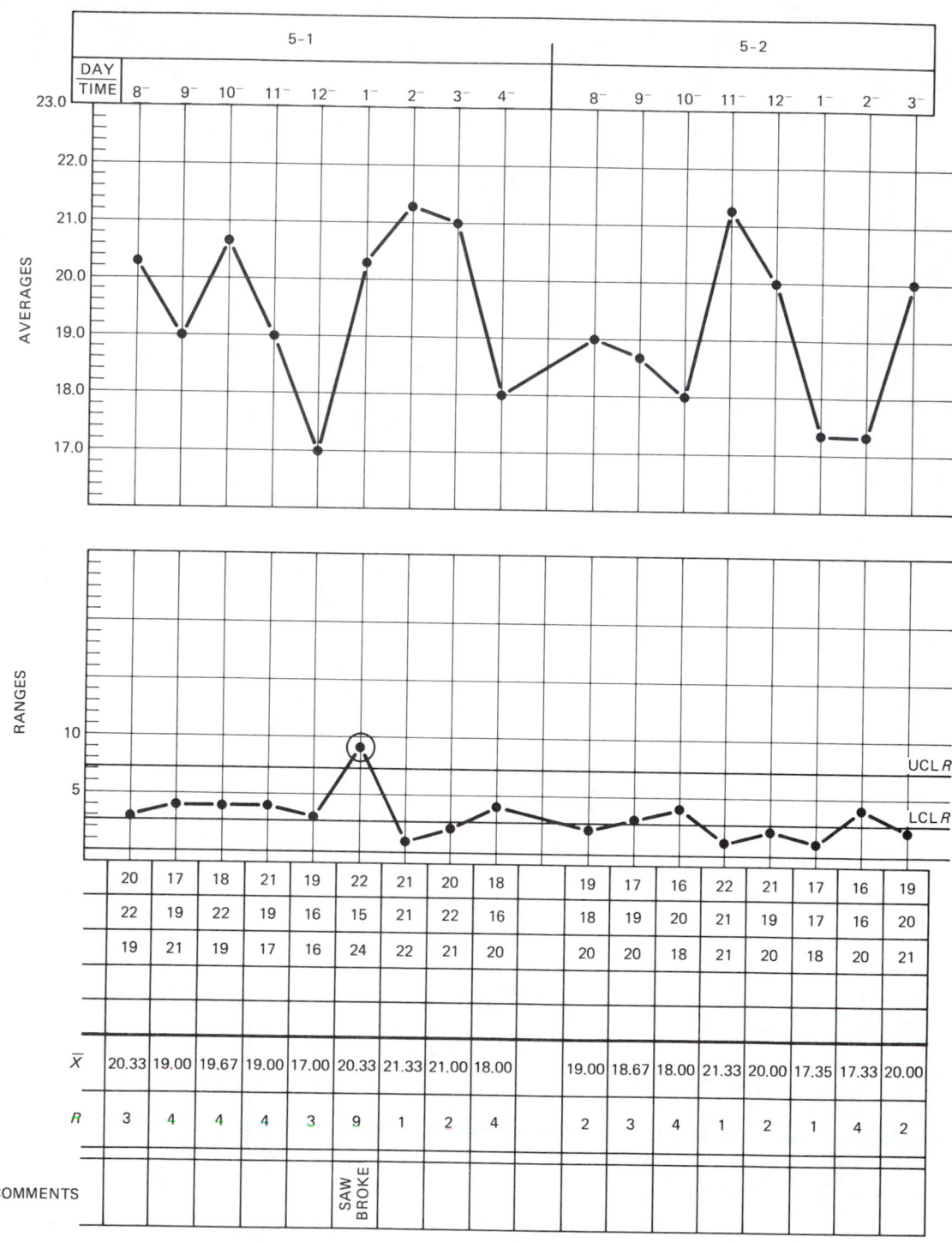

FIGURE 14–6 Initial Limits for Example 14.4.1

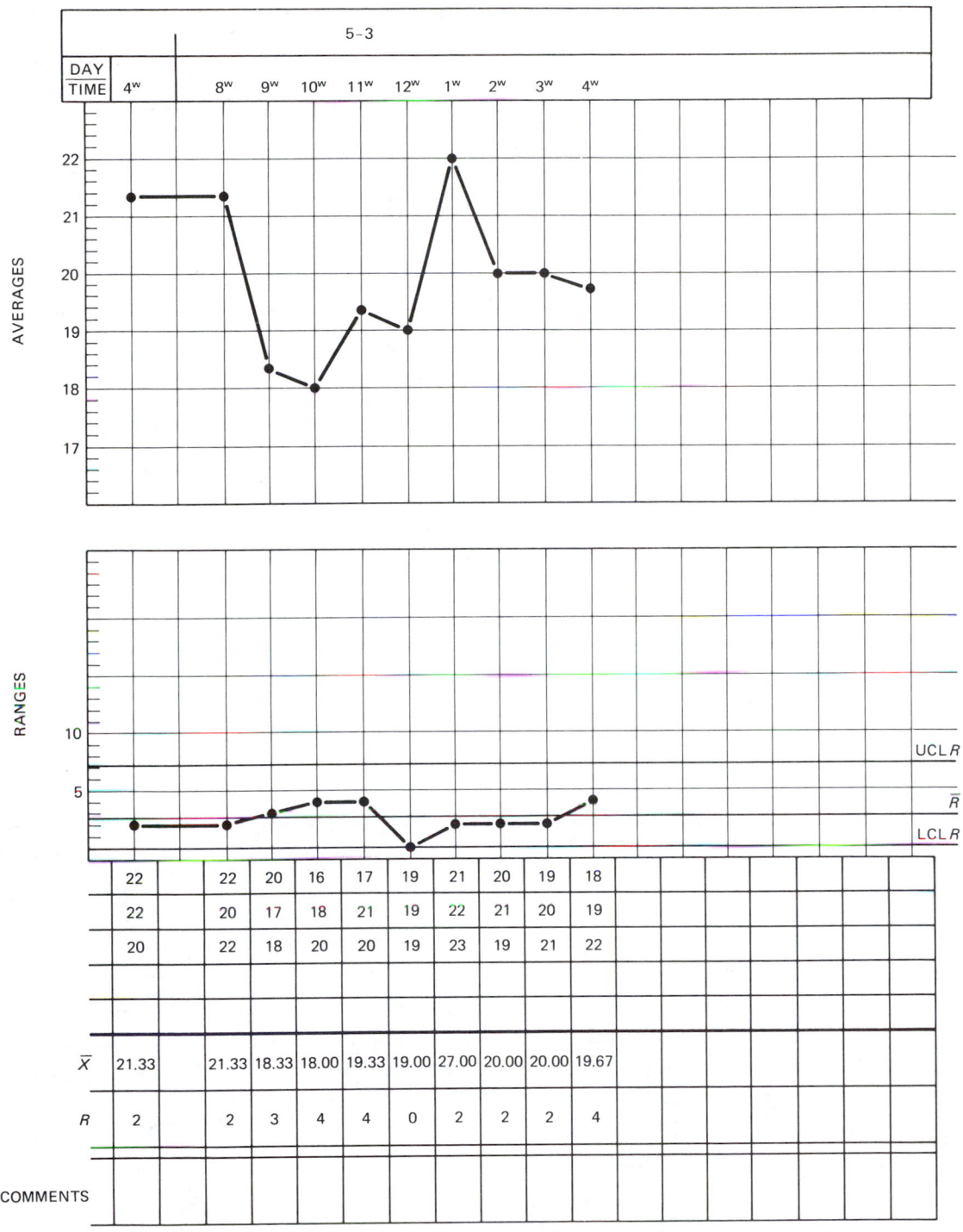

FIGURE 14-6 (*Continued*)

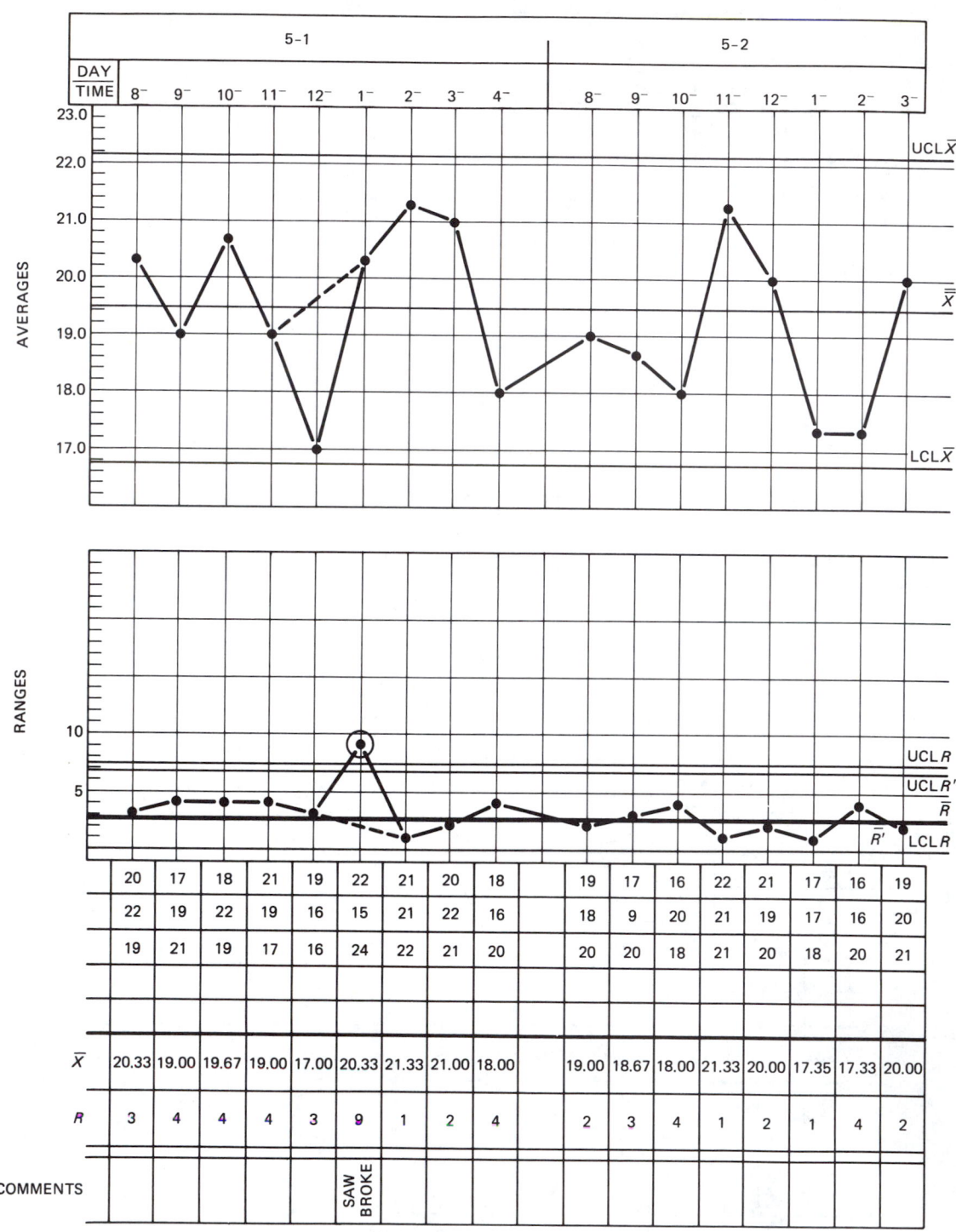

FIGURE 14-7 Revised Limits for Example 14.4.1

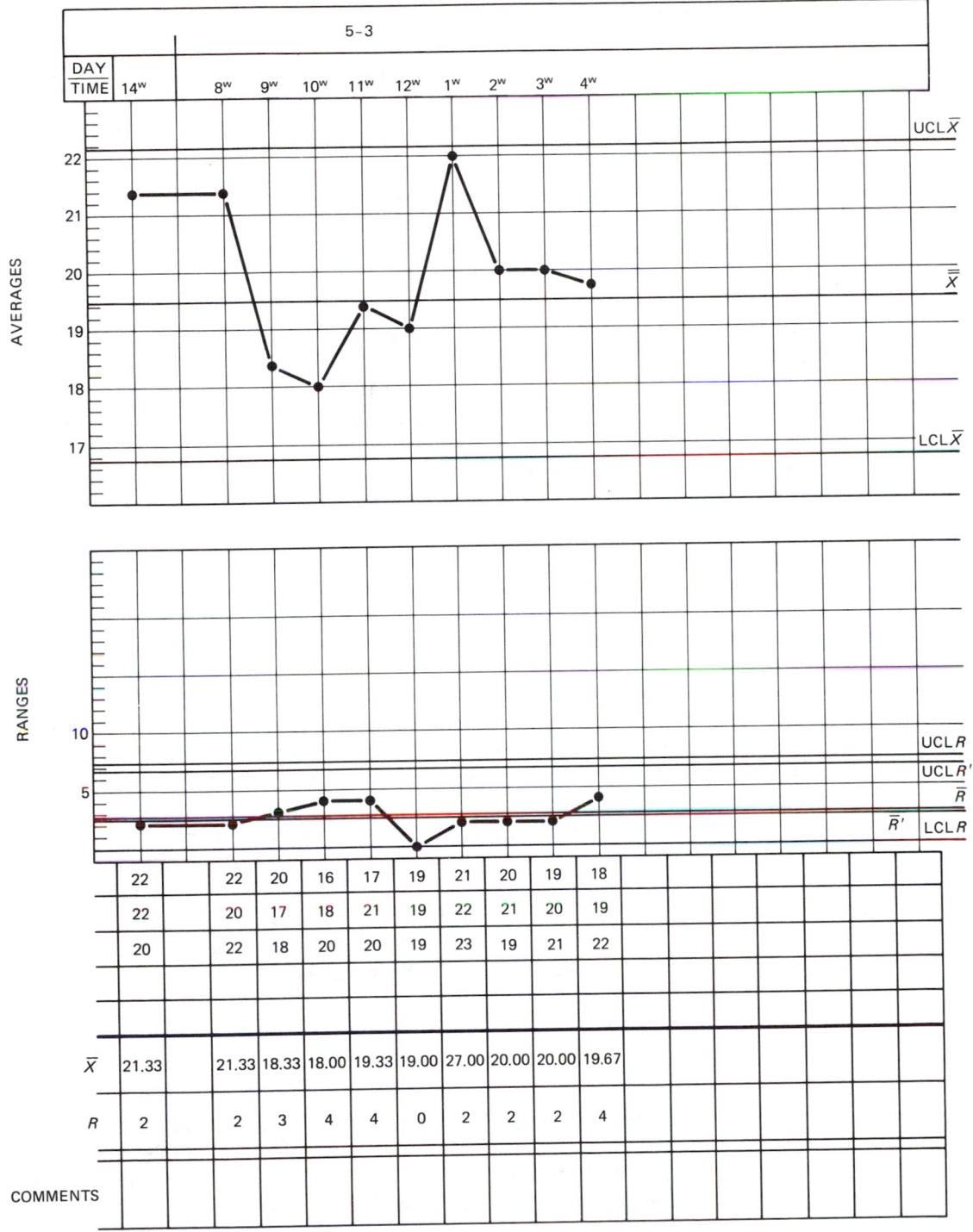

FIGURE 14-7 (*Continued*)

averages. Using the "new" average range and grand average, these limits are calculated.

$$\text{UCL}\overline{X} = \overline{\overline{X}} + A_2\overline{R}$$

$$\text{UCL}X = 19.46 + (1.02)(2.65) = 22.16$$

$$\text{LCL}\overline{X} = \overline{\overline{X}} - A_2\overline{R}$$

$$\text{LCL}X = 19.46 - (1.02)(2.65) = 16.76$$

Adding these to the control chart in Figure 14–7 shows that the sample averages are all in control. The process that produces the shelves is consistently producing shelves with average widths between 16.76 and 22.16 cm. This is located a little bit below the desired value of 20 cm. Whether too many of the shelves are too wide or not wide enough has not been addressed. What we do know is that at this time the process is stable. At the least, we would expect the operator to continue to sample three shelves each hour and record the sample range and sample average on the chart and react to any changes in the process that may occur. If necessary, and of course it is *always* necessary, the amount of variability in the process should be reduced by modifying the process in some way. ∎

Example 14.4.2 A manufacturer of water hoses identified a critical characteristic the inside diameter of the hoses. The nominal value is 0.5 inch and the specifications require that the diameter be between 0.505 and 0.495 inch.

Figure 14–8 shows data collected for the process that forms the diameter. The data are collected on the bottom of a typical control chart data-collection sheet. Due to the nature of the process, a sample of size 4 was selected, and 20 samples of 4 were collected.

The average for each sample and the range for each sample are shown in Figure 14–9. The average range and the grand average are 0.00825 and 0.501, respectively. Figure 14–10 shows the sample averages and the sample ranges, along with their respective averages as they have been added to the control chart form.

The control limits for the ranges are calculated using the average range of 0.00825 and the $n = 4$ values from the Shewhart constants.

$$\text{UCL}R = 0.0186$$

$$\text{LCL}R = 0$$

These are added to the control chart and shown in Figure 14–11.

The 10:00 sample on the second day indicates that the sample range is out of control. Checking back to the data-collection form, we note that there was a belt break at that time. This is a special cause and justifies tossing out the sample values. Recomputing the average range gives a revised value of 0.00742. The revised grand

	DAY	11-7					11-8					11-9				
	TIME	8⁻	10⁻	12⁻	2⁻	4⁻	8⁻	10⁻	12⁻	2⁻	4⁻	8⁻	10⁻	12⁻	2⁻	4⁻
AVERAGES																
RANGES																
		0.502	0.501	0.496	0.499	0.492	0.502	0.501	0.500	0.503	0.496	0.499	0.502	0.501	0.506	0.503
		0.506	0.502	0.496	0.503	0.502	0.503	0.490	0.499	0.501	0.502		0.506	0.499	0.503	0.501
		0.498	0.501	0.501	0.504	0.506	0.498	0.514	0.498	0.504	0.500	0.493	0.498	0.503	0.501	0.497
		0.501	0.496	0.500	0.496	0.497	0.499	0.502	0.501	0.500	0.498	0.504	0.507	0.504	0.500	0.494
$\overline{X}$		0.502	0.500	0.498	0.501	0.499	0.501	0.502	0.500	0.502	0.499	0.500	0.503	0.502	0.503	0.499
R		0.008	0.006	0.005	0.009	0.014	0.005	0.024	0.003	0.004	0.006	0.011	0.009	0.005	0.006	0.009
COMMENTS							BELT BROKE									

FIGURE 14-8 Average and Range for Example 14.4.2

(*cont.*)

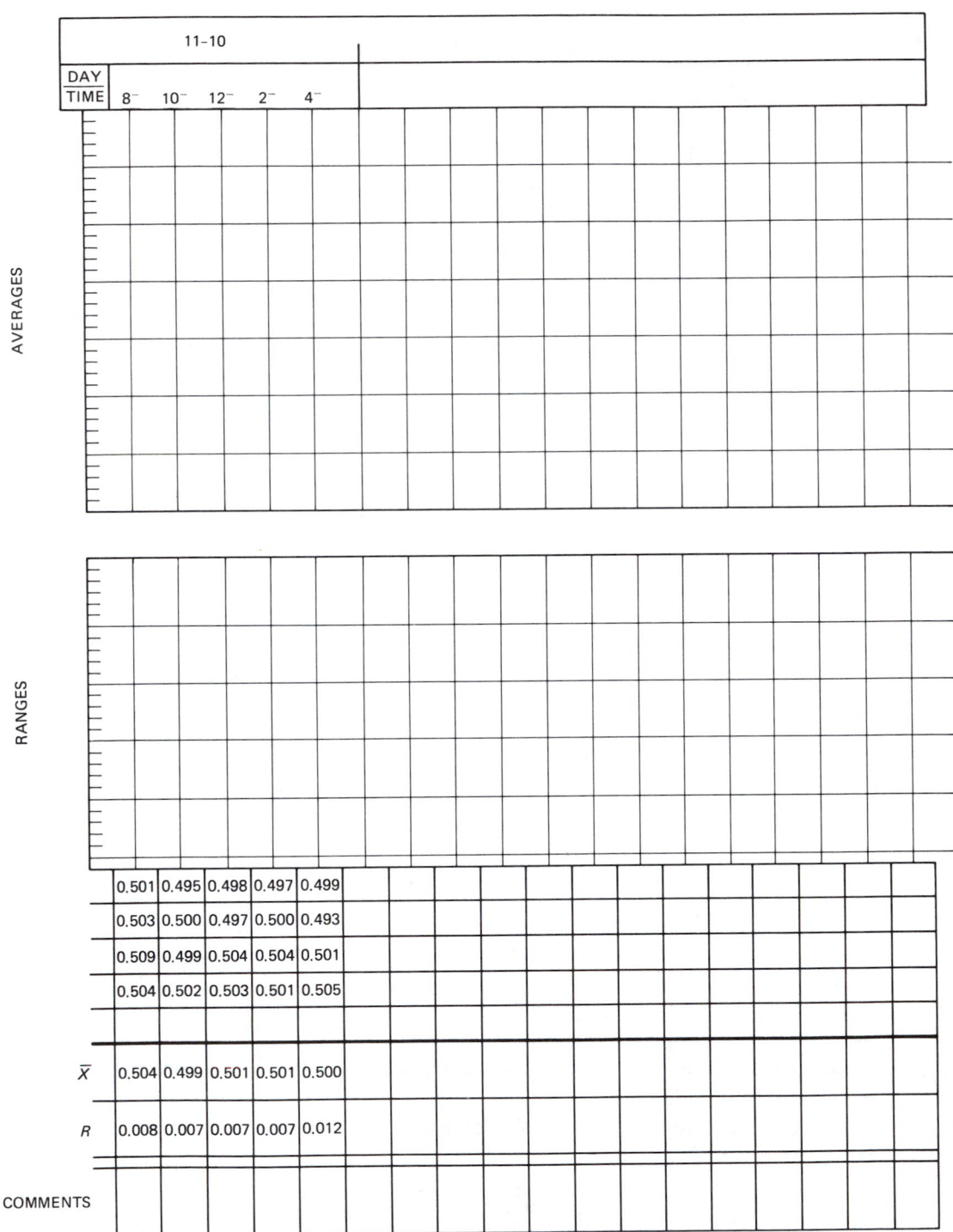

FIGURE 14-8 (*Continued*)

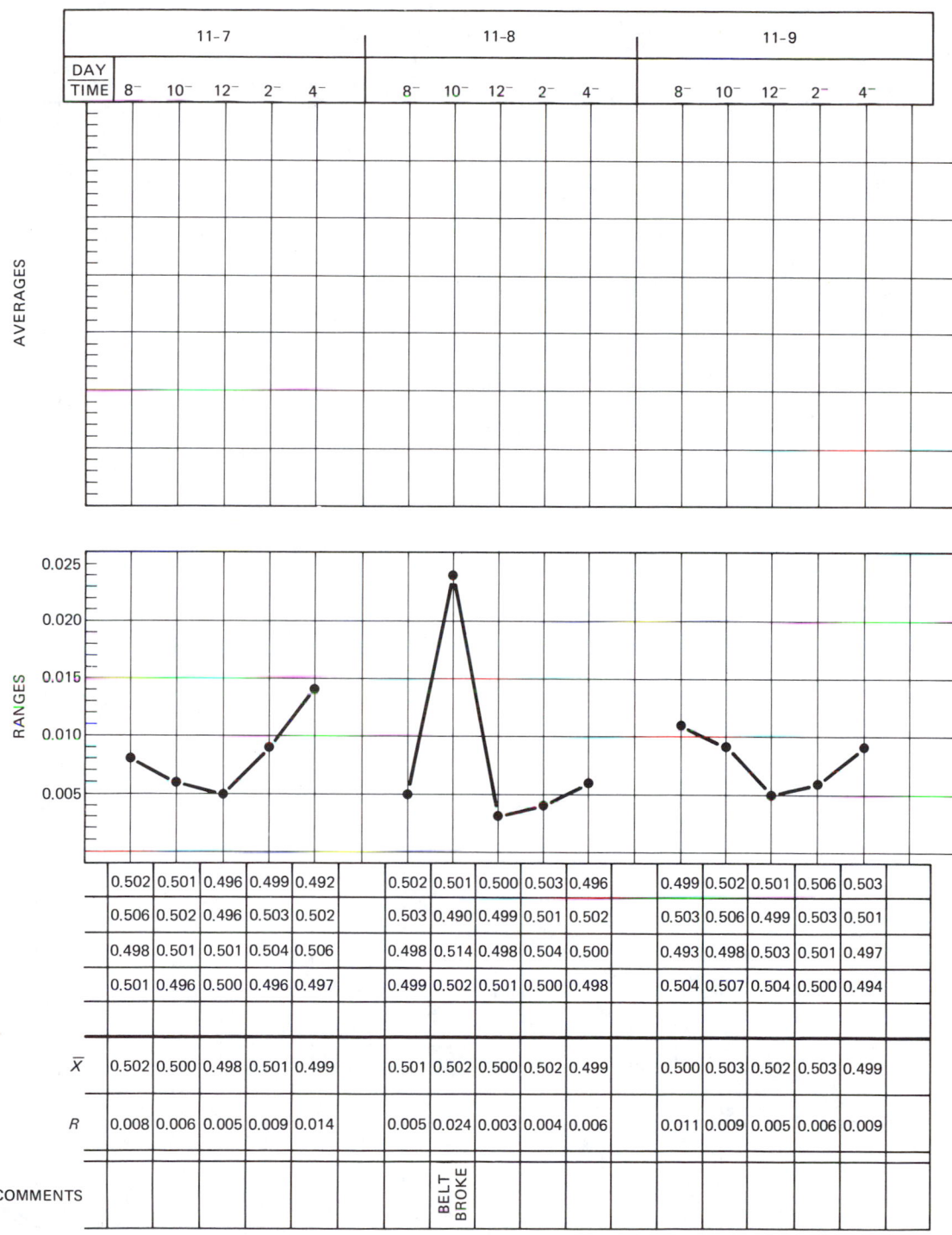

FIGURE 14–9 Initial Plot for Example 14.4.2, Part 1

(*cont.*)

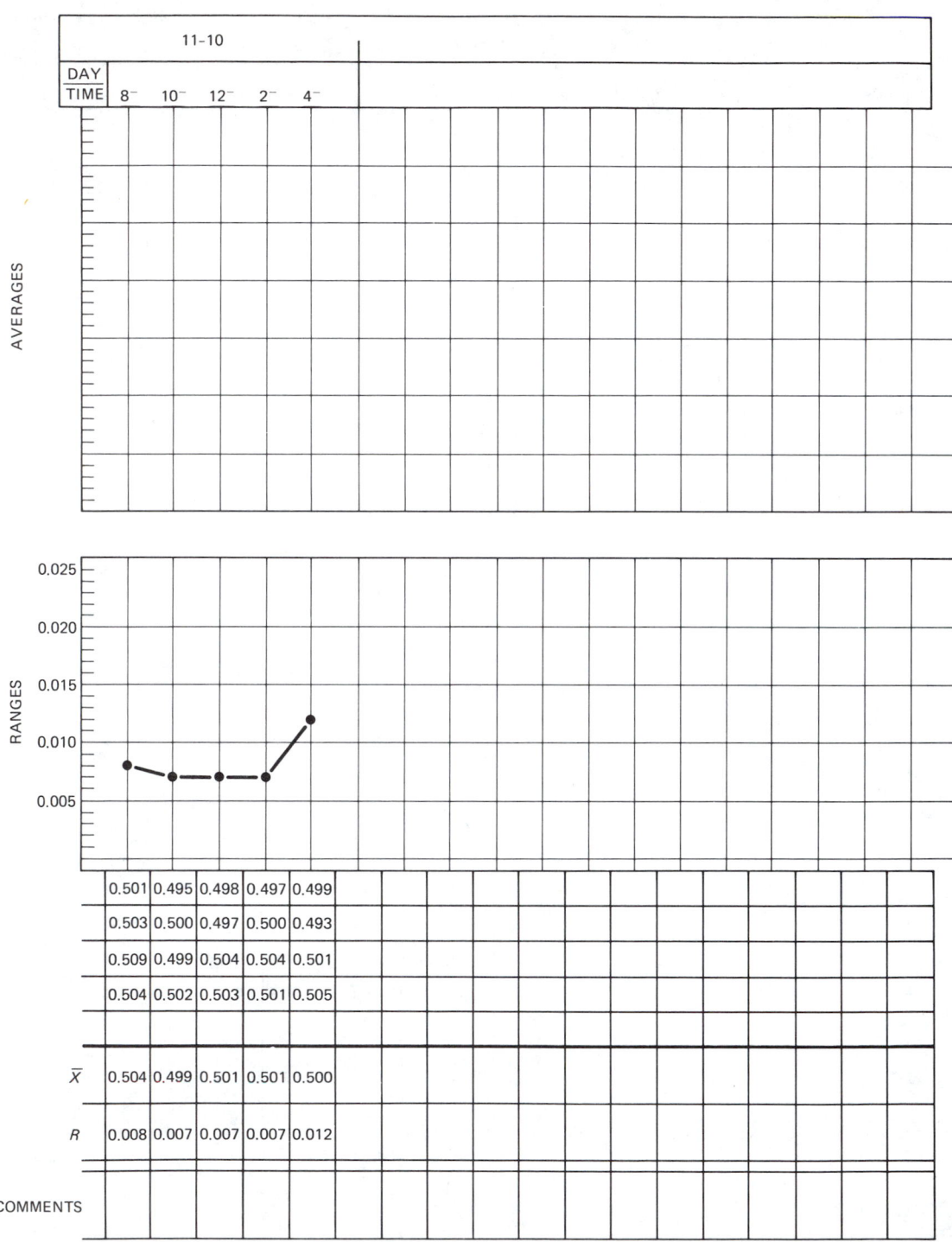

FIGURE 14–9 (*Continued*)

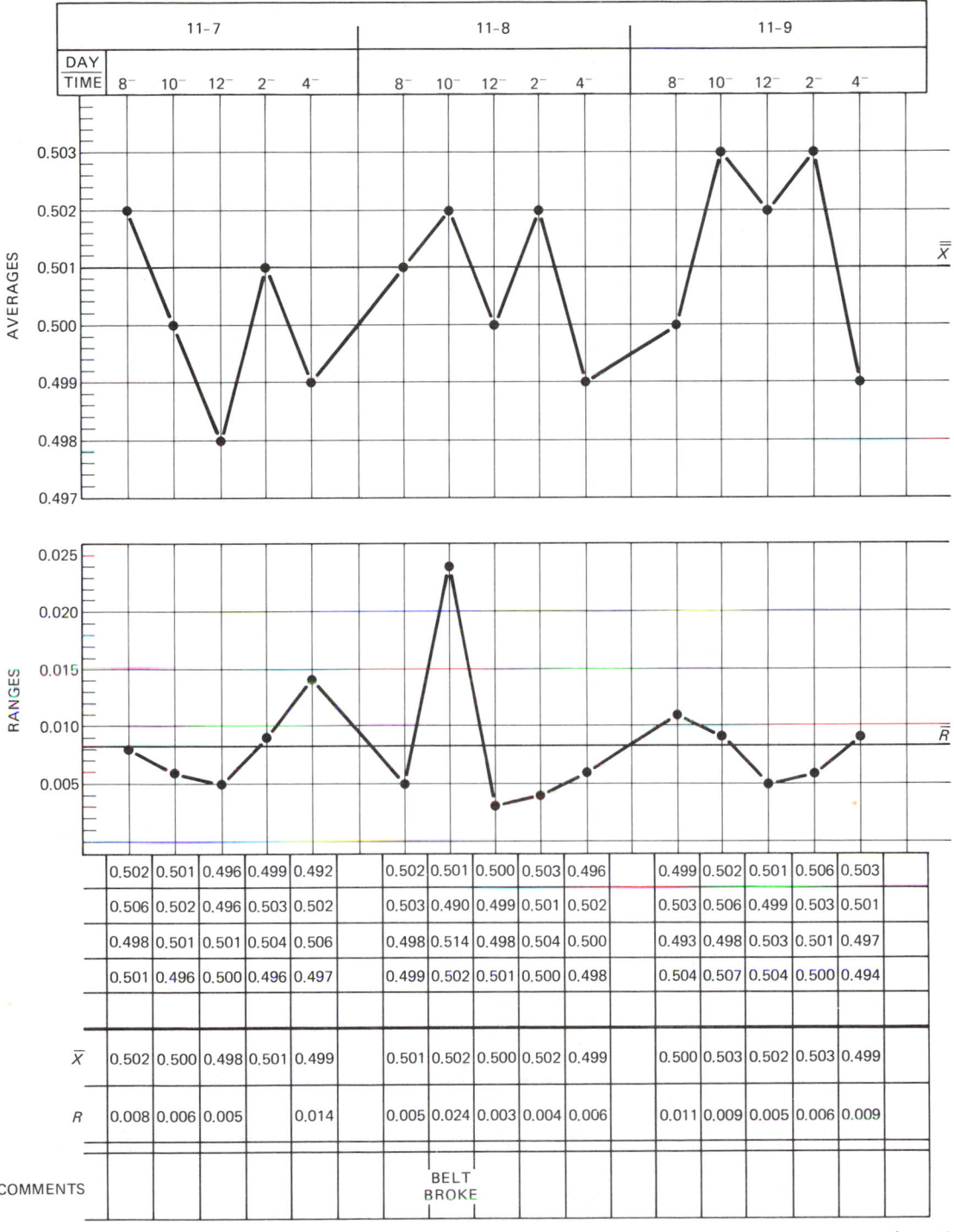

FIGURE 14–10 Initial Plot for Example 14.4.2, Part 2

(*cont.*)

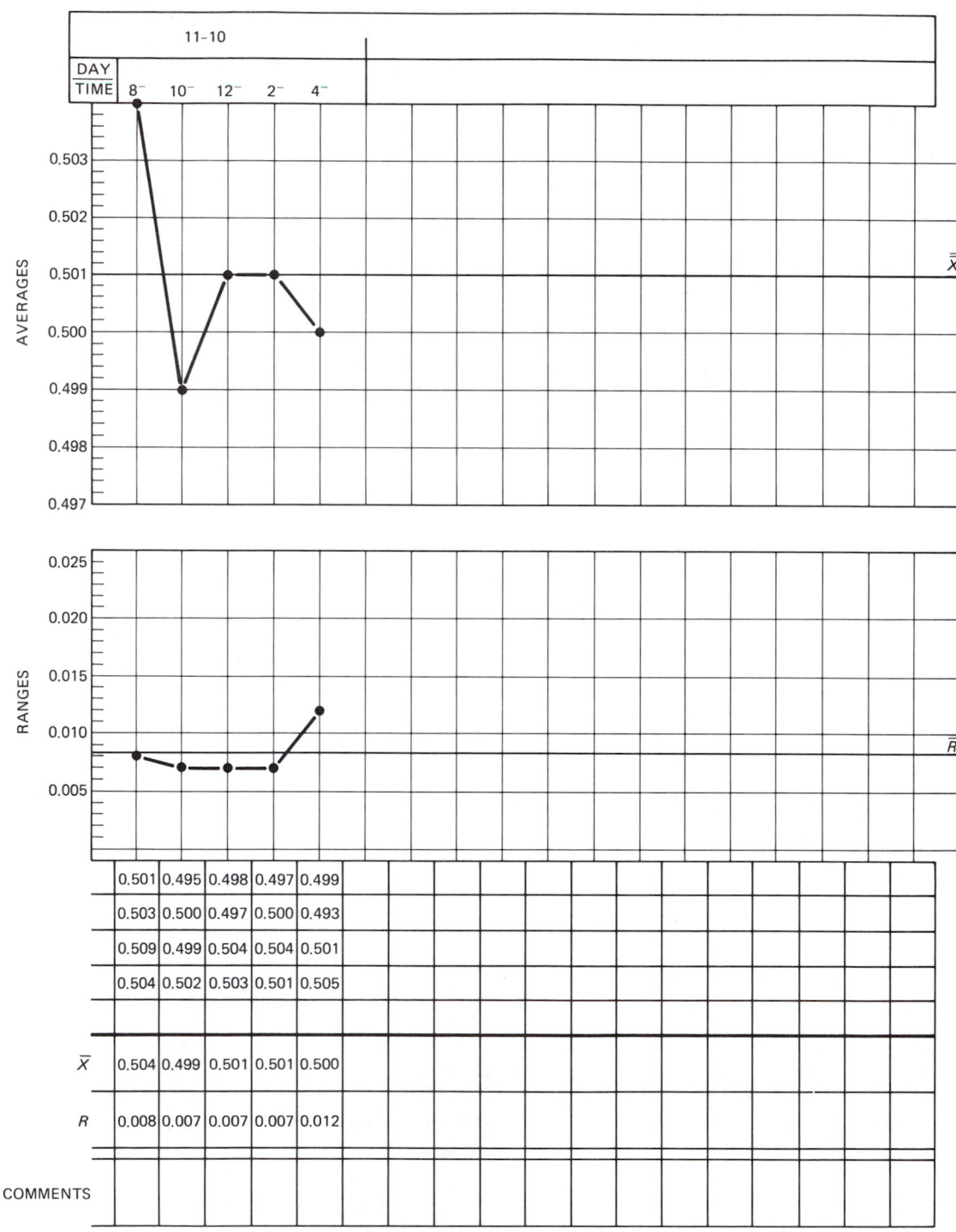

FIGURE 14–10 (*Continued*)

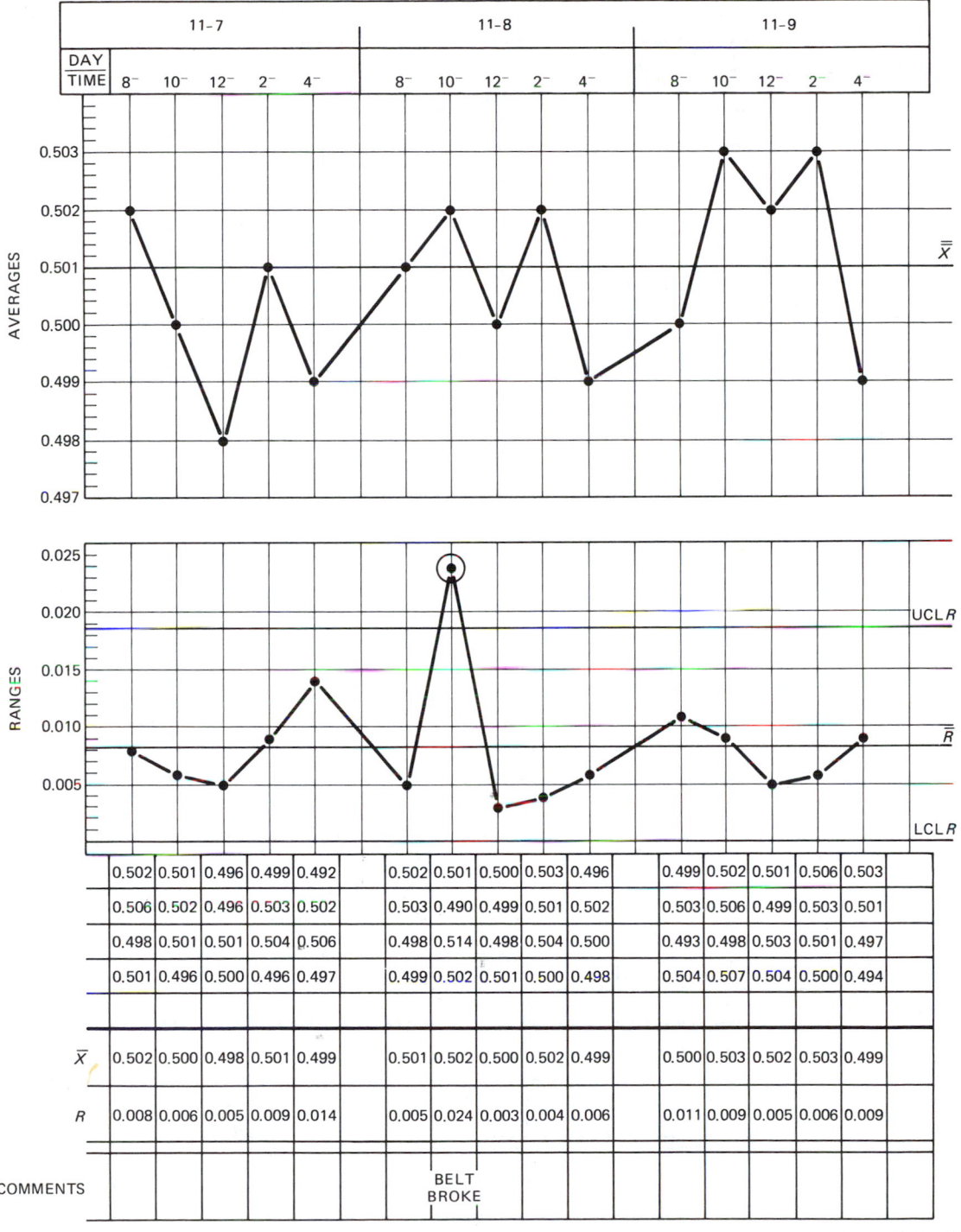

FIGURE 14–11 Initial Limits for Example 14.4.2

(cont.)

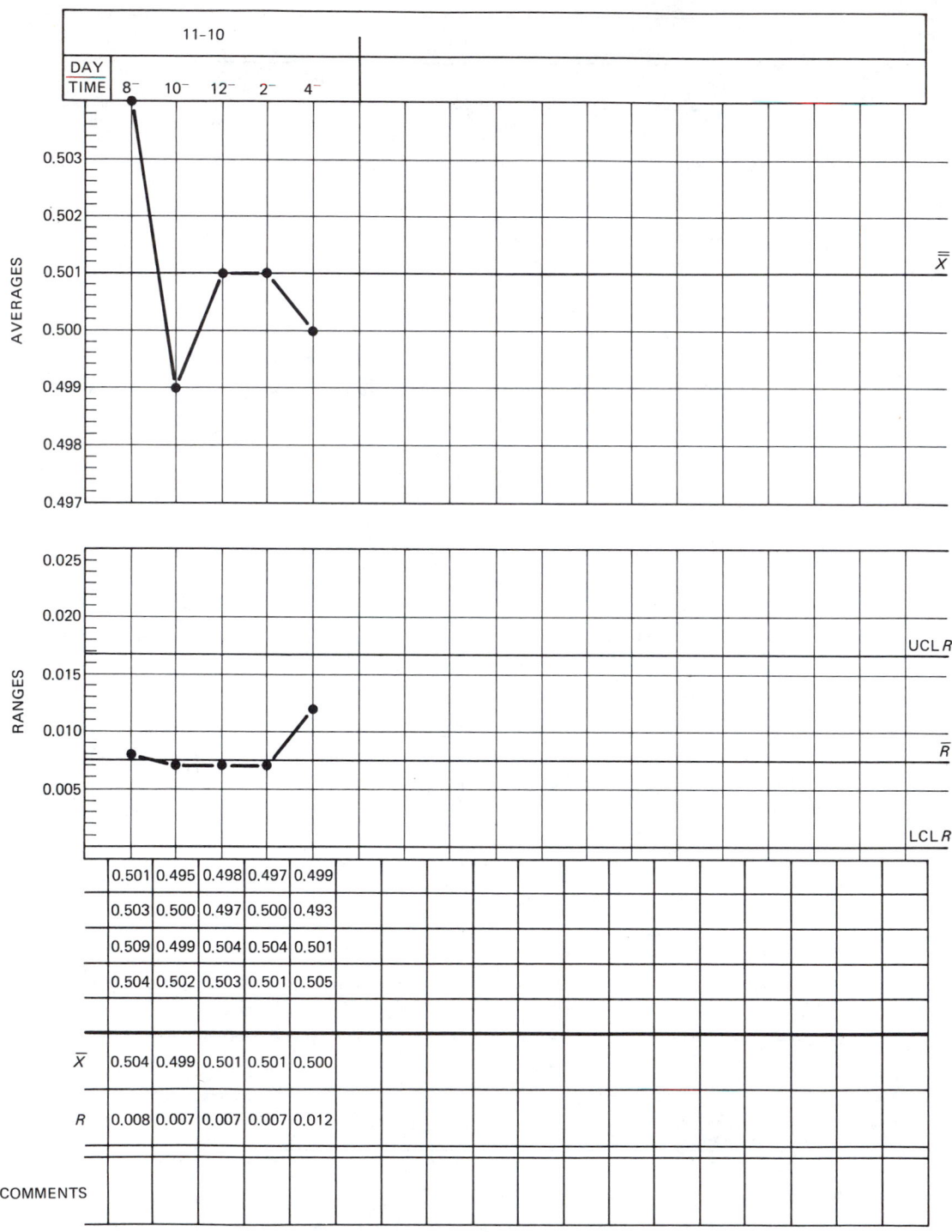

FIGURE 14-11 (*Continued*)

average is still 0.501. The "new" control limits for ranges are determined using the revised average range.

$$UCLR = 0.0168$$

$$LCLR = 0$$

These values, along with the new averages, are shown in Figure 14–12. All the sample ranges are within the limits, and, at least regarding variability, we can say that the process is stable.

The control limits for averages are calculated next.

$$UCL\overline{X} = 0.5064$$

$$LCL\overline{X} = 0.4956$$

All the sample averages, as Figure 14–12 shows, are in control. The process is stable. If we refer back to our specification limits for the process, we remember that we needed all the individuals to fall between 0.495 and 0.505. Examining the initial hose diameters, it is obvious that the diameters do not meet the specifications. Yet knowing now that the process is stable, that the process is in control, we know that the only way to meet specifications is to improve the process in some fashion such that the variability will be reduced. (Changing the specifications would work, if the change is justified and will not alter the operating characteristics of the hose or alter the expectations of the next customer in the extended process.) No amount of exhorting the workers, no amount of inspection, nothing except improving the process will improve the quality. We can certainly develop inspection plans to screen out many of the defects, especially since we are able to use some statistical knowledge of predict the expected number or percentage of defectives, but that does not guarantee that we will meet specifications. This process, as it is presently operating, is not capable of meeting the specifications. ■

Example 14.4.3 The output of one textile process is yarn that should have a breaking strength of 85; at least, that is the target. Customer complaints have indicated that this is not always the case, and the organization has decided to collect some data about the process in order to monitor, control, and improve what they are doing. The test involved is a destructive test. Material is produced on five lines, so it was rationally decided that a sample of 5 should be taken daily for a period of 3 weeks. (That meant that one sample a day would be taken and the five specimens broken to determine the strength.) These data are shown in Figure 14–13, which also shows the range for each sample and the average for each of the 15 samples. Other calculations initially established

$$\overline{R} = 6.33$$

$$\overline{X} = 84.9$$

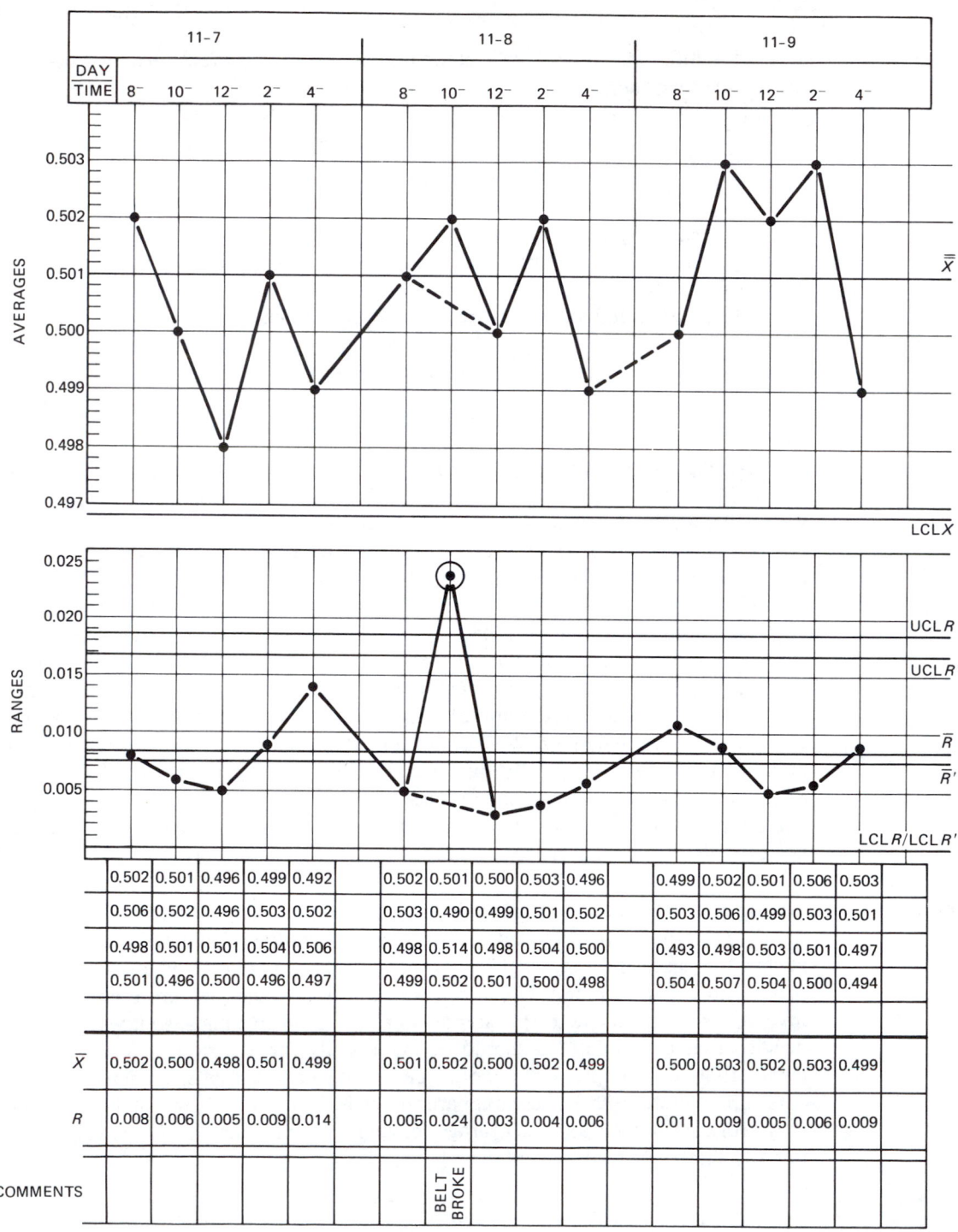

FIGURE 14–12 Revised Limits for Example 14.4.2

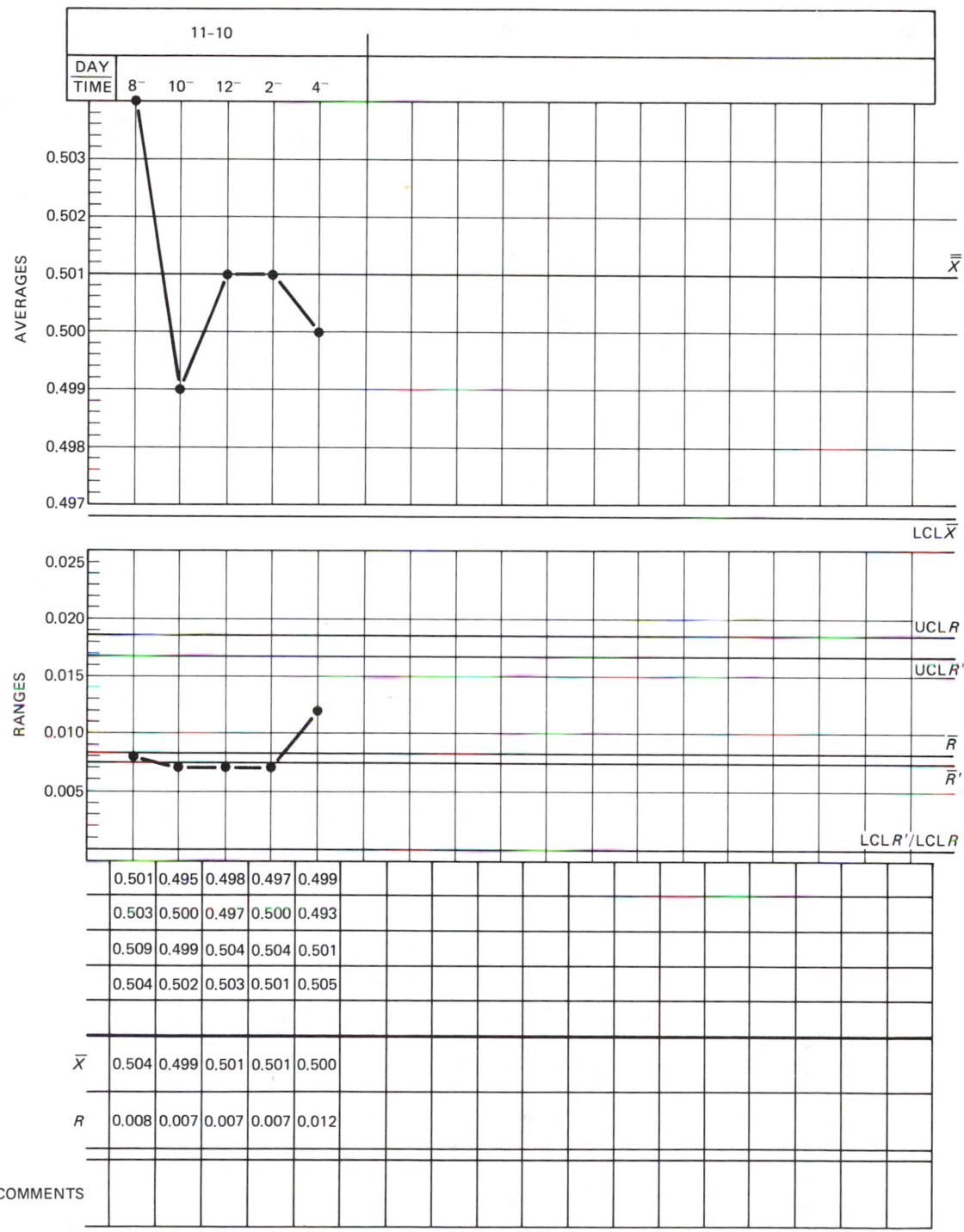

FIGURE 14-12 (*Continued*)

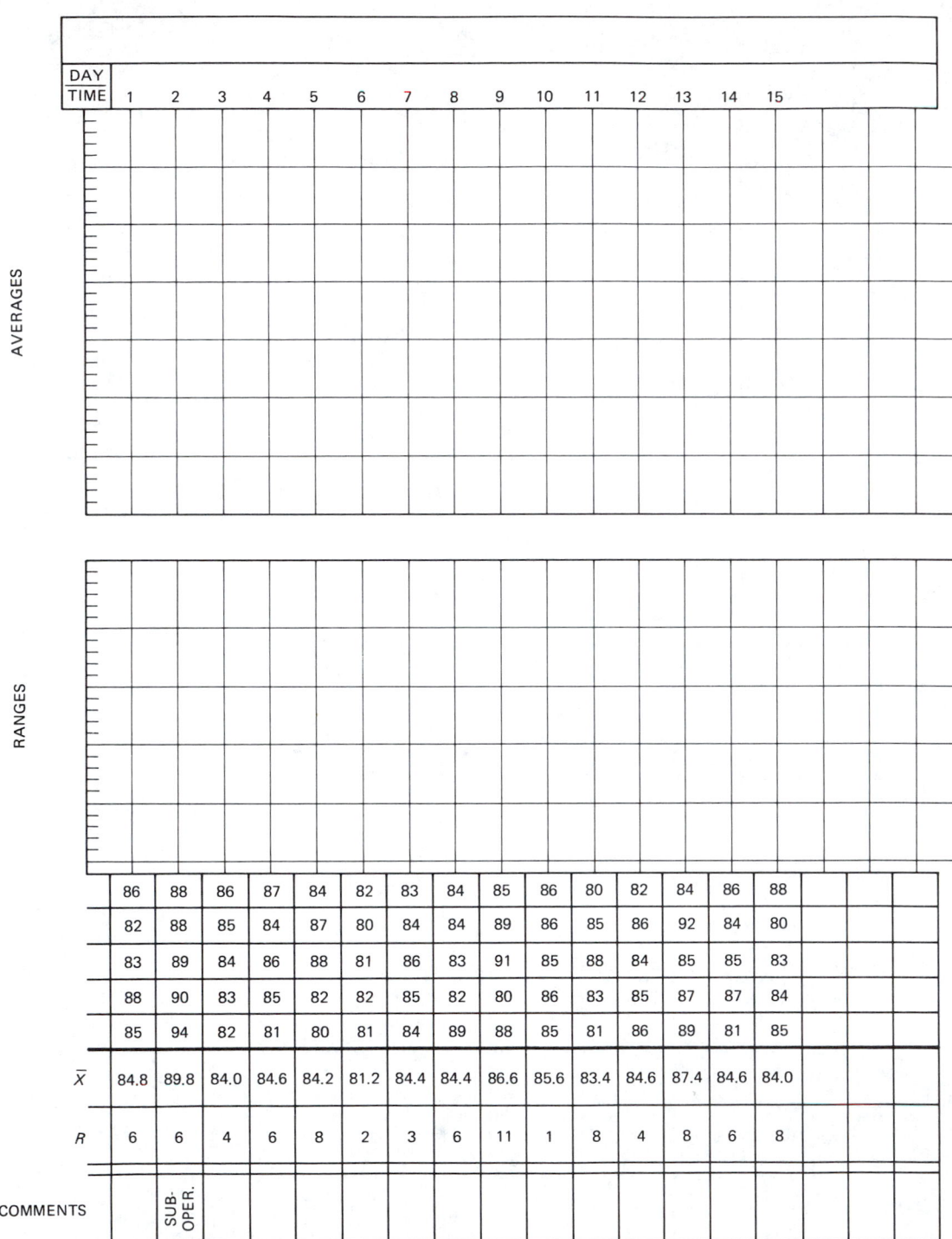

	DAY/TIME	1	2	3	4	5	6	7	8	9	10	11	12	13	14	15			
		86	88	86	87	84	82	83	84	85	86	80	82	84	86	88			
		82	88	85	84	87	80	84	84	89	86	85	86	92	84	80			
		83	89	84	86	88	81	86	83	91	85	88	84	85	85	83			
		88	90	83	85	82	82	85	82	80	86	83	85	87	87	84			
		85	94	82	81	80	81	84	89	88	85	81	86	89	81	85			
$\overline{X}$		84.8	89.8	84.0	84.6	84.2	81.2	84.4	84.4	86.6	85.6	83.4	84.6	87.4	84.6	84.0			
R		6	6	4	6	8	2	3	6	11	1	8	4	8	6	8			
COMMENTS		SUB-OPER.																	

FIGURE 14–13   Data for Example 14.4.3

The average range was used to calculate control limits for ranges, which, along with the measures of location, are shown on Figure 14–14.

$$\text{UCL}R = 13.36$$

$$\text{LCL}R = 0$$

All the sample ranges are in control. The control limits for averages indicate that

$$\text{UCL}\overline{X} = 88.57$$

$$\text{LCL}\overline{X} = 81.23$$

When these are added to the chart in Figure 14–15, we see that the sample for day 2 is out of control. The indication that there was a substitute operator on that day is reason to delete that sample from the calculations and analysis. The new average range is 6.26 and the new grand average is 84.6. Recalculating the limits for ranges results in

$$\text{UCL}\overline{R} = 13.41$$

$$\text{LCL}\overline{R} = 0$$

These are plotted in Figure 14–16. All the sample ranges are still in control. The new limits for averages and the revised average range and revised grand average are also shown in that figure. The revised control limits for averages are

$$\text{UCL}\overline{X} = 88.29$$

$$\text{LCL}\overline{X} = 80.91$$

These are added to Figure 14–16. Analyzing the control chart of Figure 14–16 shows that all the sample averages now fall within the control limits. The process is stable.

The yarn still may be breaking at too low a strength, but that is a function of the process, not the result of any abnormal variation within the process. The process must be improved to improve the breaking strength. This can be done either through raising the target value or by reducing the variability within the process. Raising the target may provide a short-term fix of the problem. Reducing the variability is the way to continuous improvement. ∎

14.5 CONCLUSION

This chapter introduced the concept of the control chart to variables, specifically to the average and the range. Some key points to remember. The control chart shows the limits of normal variation. The control chart shows abnormal variation. When used as a process-monitoring tool, the control chart will show when action is to be taken at the point of the operation.

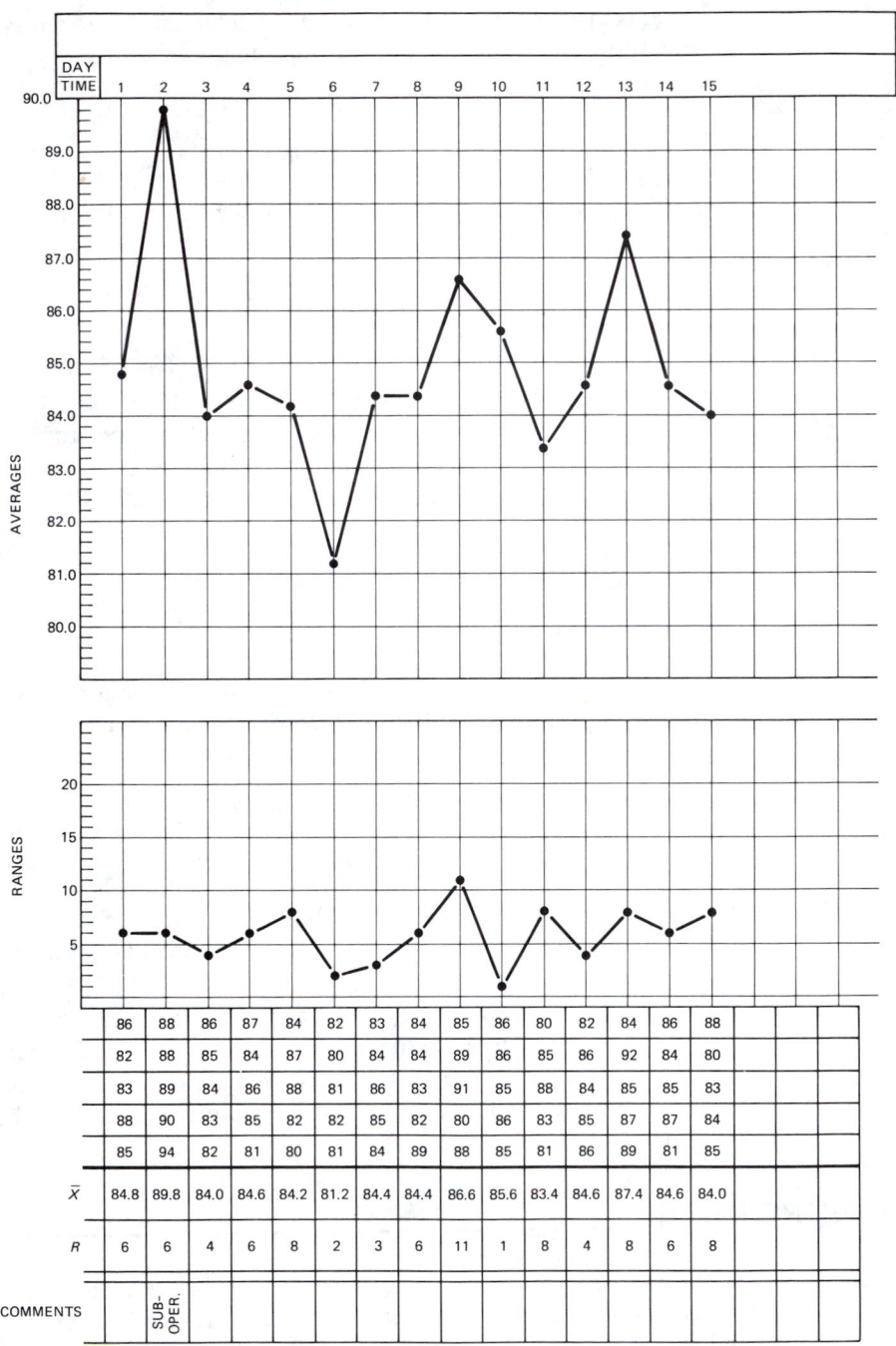

FIGURE 14–14   Initial Plot for Example 14.4.3

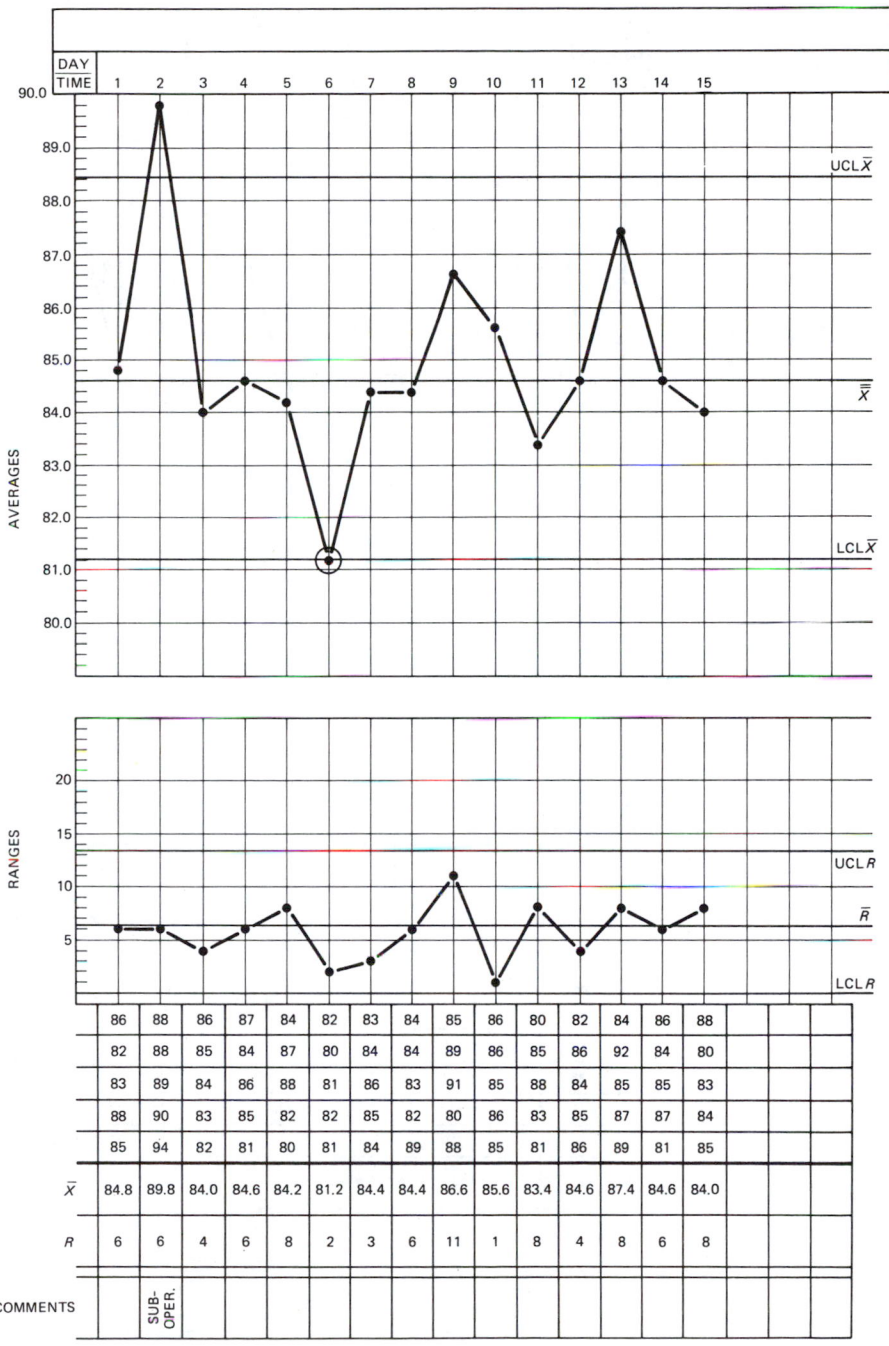

FIGURE 14–15 Initial Limits for Example 14.4.3

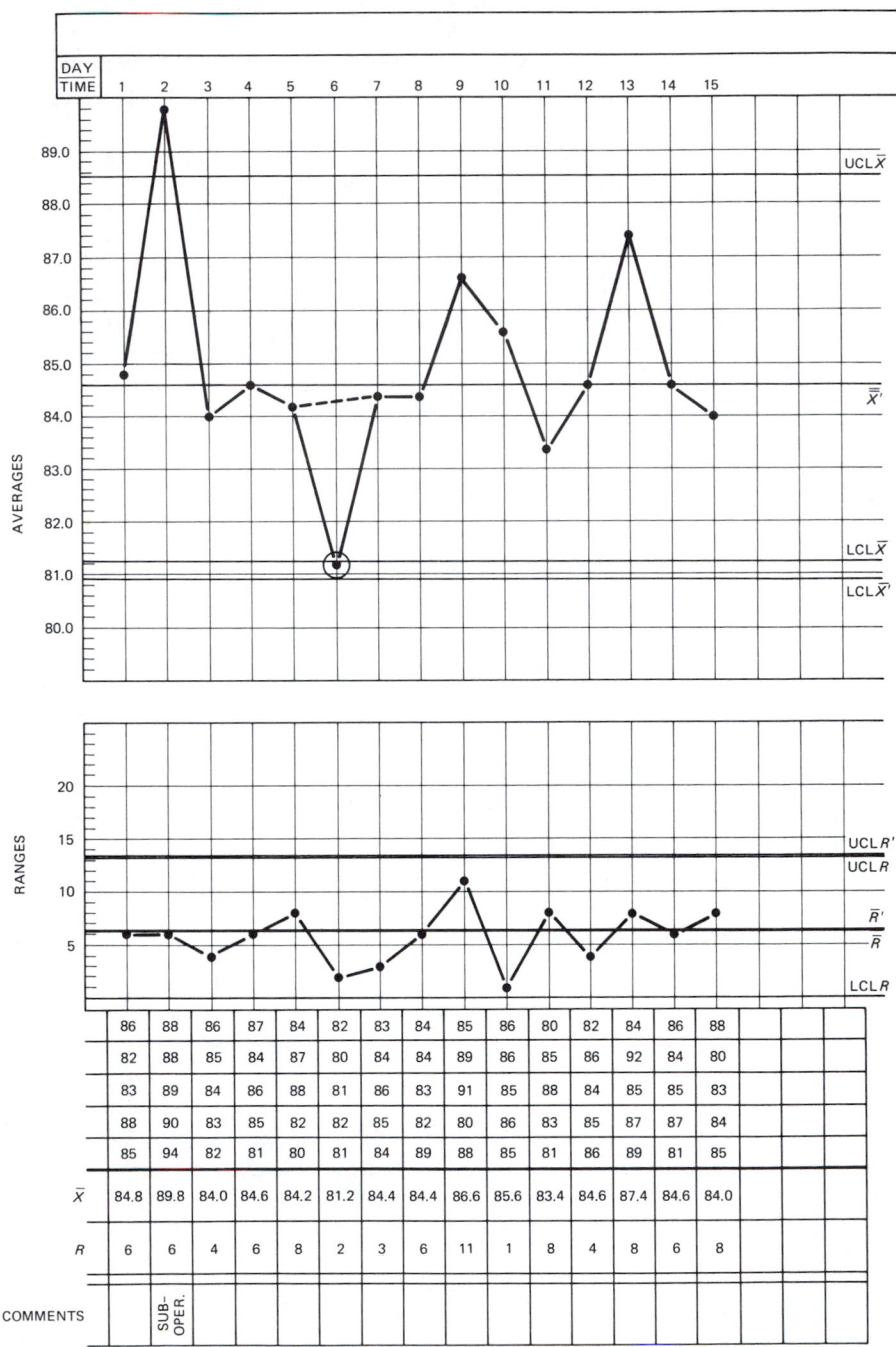

FIGURE 14–16   Revised Limits for Example 14.4.3, Part 1

The control chart is determined by the process. The process does not respond to a change in control limits; rather, the process responds to changes in the inputs and to changes in the transformation. The control limits only reflect the process. The results will remain useful only as long as the process does not change. If there is a change to the process, then the limits will also change.

Chapter 15 continues the discussion of charts for variables, focusing on charts for individuals. Chapter 16 introduces two of the charts for attributes and one discussing the interpretation of control charts.

EXERCISES

Determine control limits for ranges and averages for the following sets of data. Recompute limits where appropriate.

1. Deviations from the nominal specification value have been recorded hourly for a punch-press-produced part. Samples of 4 were selected and the deviation *above* spec in 0.001 inch was recorded as follows.

Sample	1	2	3	4	5
1	6	2	3	1	2
2	3	6	2	5	1
3	2	3	1	3	2
4	4	4	3	4	1
5	2	5	4	2	3
6	1	2	3	4	4
7	3	2	4	5	1
8	2	4	6	6	3
9	4	6	1	6	5
10	3	4	2	5	4
11	1	2	4	5	4
12	4	1	3	4	3
13	9	0	0	9	15
14	3	2	6	1	4
15	2	2	4	3	3
16	4	3	3	3	2
17	5	6	2	5	4
18	4	5	2	4	1
19	4	4	4	2	3
20	6	3	5	1	5
21	5	4	4	1	6
22	3	5	3	3	4
23	1	1	2	2	2
24	3	2	1	4	5
25	2	5	4	6	4
26	5	3	5	3	1
27	6	2	3	4	3
28	4	2	2	2	2
29	3	4	1	4	4
30	2	3	1	5	6

2. The Cheap Tire Company has collected sequential data regarding the time required to apply white letters to its GIT radial tire. These data, in 0.01 minute, were recorded as follows.

Sample	I	II	III	IV
1	5	5	2	3
2	1	3	2	2
3	3	4	2	1
4	4	2	3	4
5	2	1	3	0
6	2	4	0	3
7	2	4	5	1
8	4	1	3	6
9	4	1	3	1
10	0	3	3	2
11	0	3	4	3
12	1	1	1	4
13	4	0	4	4
14	3	1	1	3
15	1	2	4	1
16	2	3	5	5
17	1	5	1	2
18	0	0	4	1
19	2	3	4	1
20	1	5	4	2
21	0	3	1	2
22	5	1	4	4
23	0	3	3	2
24	3	2	4	3
25	20	2	3	0
26	3	2	1	4
27	2	3	1	2
28	0	3	7	1
29	0	0	2	4
30	2	4	3	3

3. A well-known television fund raiser needed to raise $1,000,000 for her favorite charity. The collections during the first month are listed for four outlets.

Day	Location			
	1	2	3	4
1	5	4	5	6
2	8	7	7	3
3	3	2	3	8
4	2	3	4	4
5	7	8	9	8
6	4	3	2	7
7	14	9	2	1
8	9	7	2	4
9	6	7	1	5

Day	Location			
	1	2	3	4
10	4	7	9	5
11	3	7	8	7
12	6	5	4	9
13	7	6	3	4
14	9	9	9	3
15	1	2	8	1
16	3	4	4	8
17	7	6	7	7
18	8	9	7	2
19	8	9	2	1
20	4	4	9	8
21	4	4	9	6
22	2	3	1	5
23	3	3	8	9
24	7	7	7	4
25	9	8	1	21
26	8	1	4	7
27	0	0	0	4
28	4	3	2	1
29	8	1	1	8
30	2	9	8	0

4. A printed circuit board manufacturer measured the percent of acid used in the etching solution for boards produced on each of its lines. These data are shown for a period of 30 days.

Sample	Line 1	Line 2	Line 3
1	2	1	0
2	1	0	1
3	1	2	0
4	3	3	4
5	4	4	3
6	3	2	1
7	5	16	8
8	1	4	2
9	3	1	1
10	0	4	1
11	1	4	3
12	3	2	4
13	2	1	3
14	4	0	1
15	0	0	0
16	1	2	2
17	1	1	1
18	4	2	3
19	2	2	1
20	5	3	0
21	3	4	4

(cont.)

Sample	Line 1	Line 2	Line 3
22	3	3	1
23	4	3	3
24	3	2	1
25	0	0	1
26	3	4	3
27	0	4	5
28	1	0	4
29	0	1	2
30	1	2	4

CHAPTER 15

Control Chart for Individuals

Statistical quality control is a proven and essential tool for getting at the variability that governs quality consistency. To be effective, statistical control must operate within the overall total quality management process rather than as an end in itself. [18: 34]

A. V. Feigenbaum

15.1 INTRODUCTION

There are times, when monitoring a process, when it is not practical to collect data for several sample values at one time. The individuals or x chart is commonly used in situations such as the following:

- The study of process or product variables for which it is difficult, uneconomical, or impractical to obtain several measurements during a short period (a rational subgroup); and it is impractical to use averages and ranges charts.

- Accounting, clerical, or other commercial data, such as ratios, efficiency, expenditure, and quality costs, [25: 191]

- In situations when there is a very short run. This is typical of job-shop operations.

Since the sample size in this instance is 1, the range poses a special challenge to compute. As the chapter will explain, the concept of a moving range will be used. This chapter, as with the preceding, will focus first on the method of constructing the charts and, second, work through several examples to illustrate the concepts.

As with the charts for averages and ranges, the control limits used will identify the bounds of natural or normal variation present in the process. Since individual values will be used, the assumption will be made that the process is normally distributed. This has to be checked first with, at the very minimum, a histogram of the data. We will proceed now with what can best be called control charts for individuals and moving ranges.

15.2 MOVING RANGES

Samples of size 1 cannot have any variability within the sample. This is obviously impossible. The variability that we measure and monitor when we construct the charts for individuals is the variation between two successive samples. We measure this with the absolute value of the difference between two successive sample values.

This difference is the moving range, or just plain range. We still use a designation of R for this range. we also use a sample size of 2, since we are taking the difference between the current value and the preceding one.

Example 15.2.1 Shown are five sample pressures measured on a gas line.

Observation	Pressure
1	8
2	6
3	9
4	7
5	3

The range, or difference, between the second and the first values observed is the difference between 6 and 8, or 2. For observations 3 and 2, the difference is 9-6, or 3. The rest of the moving ranges are tabulated next.

Observation	Pressure	Range
1	8	—
2	6	2
3	9	3
4	7	2
5	3	4

Note that there is no range for the first observation. This is a penalty we pay for using the moving range. We have one fewer range than we have observations. We must remember this when we calculate the average range. ∎

15.3 METHOD FOR CONSTRUCTING THE CONTROL CHART

The first step in constructing a chart for moving ranges and individuals is to determine the characteristic to be monitored. As with the charts for ranges and averages, this is selected either as the result of a Pareto analysis, from a process flow analysis and discussions with the process' customers, or from a cause and effect diagram analysis.

After the characteristic is identified, the sampling scheme is determined. To use the Shewhart relationships, the sample size is defined as being 2. The guiding principle regarding number of samples to observe before setting limits will be whatever fits the process, whatever is reasonable. Generally, a minimum of 20 individual measurements should be recorded, although, as always, the more observations the better the results will represent the process being monitored. The frequency of sampling is also considered at this point. It should fit the process and not overly interfere with the other work being performed by the operator, who should be the data collector. Again, the guiding word is reasonable.

Once the sampling scheme is developed, sufficient initial data should be collected to give meaningful results. Any and all unusual occurrences should be noted on the data-collection form. An example of a typical individual's chart data-collection form is shown in Figure 15–1.

After the data have been collected, the initial calculations are performed. The average for each sample is the sample value. The range is calculated as the moving range discussed in Section 15.2. This is also recorded.

The grand average and the average range are the next statistics to be calculated. Remember that the divisors for the grand average and average range calculations are different.

Next, the sample ranges and individuals are graphed or plotted on the appropriate charts. Generally, the individual ranges and individual observations are connected with a solid line. This will help to show patterns later during analysis. The grand average and the average range are drawn in to identify the location of the process.

At this point, the limits for ranges are calculated. Note that we calculate the limits for ranges first. Our concern throughout this text has been for the reduction of variability. It is logical, then, to make sure that **the process variability, as represented by the ranges, is the first characteristic that is examined for control.** The formulas for control limits for ranges are

$$\text{UCL}R = D_4\overline{R}$$

$$\text{LCL}R = D_3\overline{R}$$

The values for D_4 and D_3 are known as Shewhart control chart constants and appear in Appendix B, as well as in Figure 15–2. The values of these constants are set at 2 for this type of moving range chart. This must remain constant throughout the analysis.

After the limits for ranges have been calculated, they should be drawn on the chart for ranges. Each sample range should be checked to see if the values fall between the upper and lower control limits. If a sample range is not between the

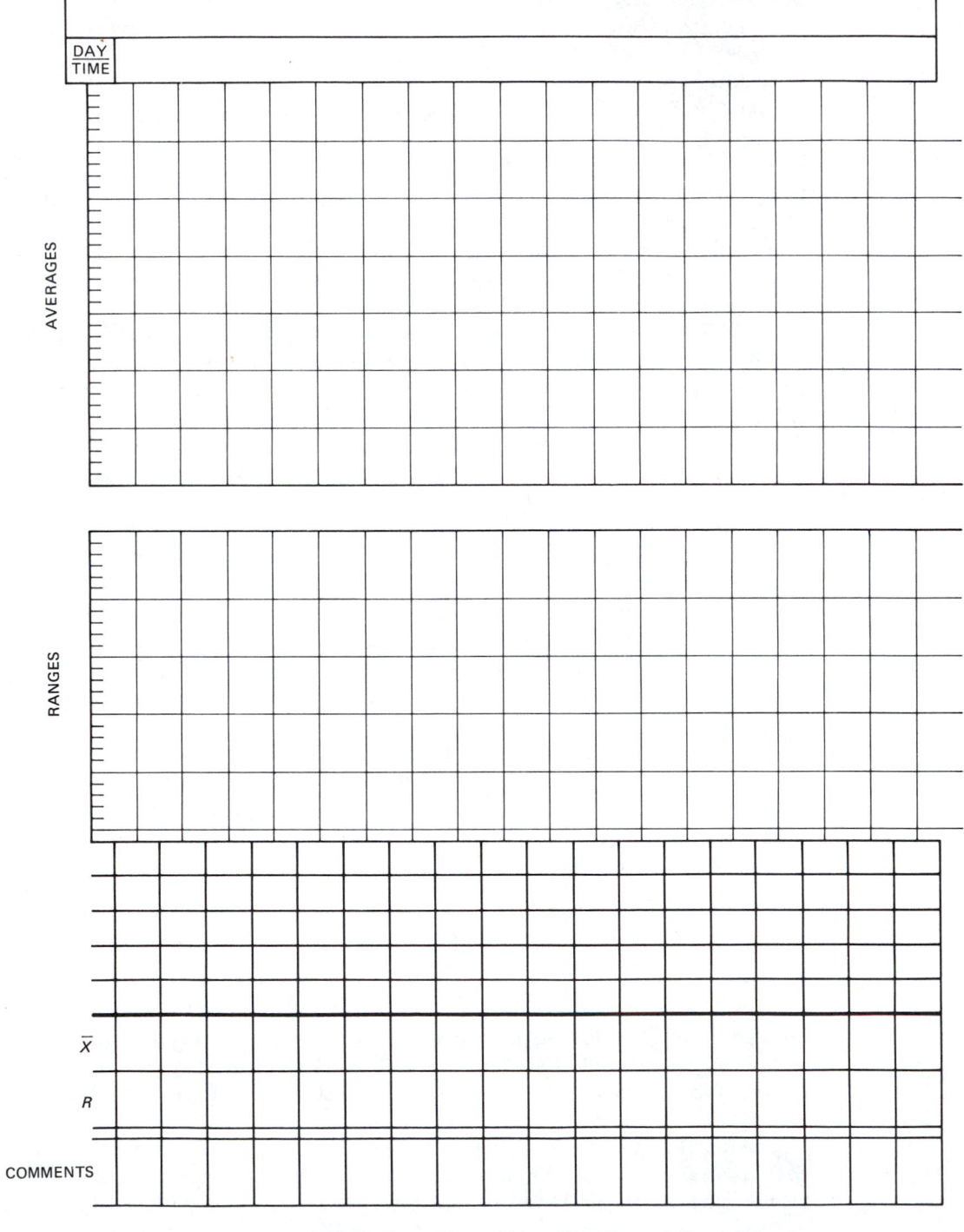

FIGURE 15–1 Typical Variables Control Chart Form

n	A_2	D_3	D_4	d_2
2	1.88	0	3.27	1.128
3	1.02	0	2.57	1.693
4	.73	0	2.28	2.059
5	.58	0	2.11	2.326
6	.48	0	2.00	2.534
7	.42	.08	1.92	2.704
8	.37	.14	1.86	2.847
9	.34	.18	1.82	2.970
10	.31	.22	1.78	3.078

Copyright, ASTM, 1916 Race Street, Philadelphia, PA 19103. Reprinted with permission.

FIGURE 15–2 Shewhart Control Chart Constants

limits, then we should determine if there is an assignable or special cause for this abnormal variation. Often the notations made during the data-collection process will determine if there is a special reason. **If there is a special cause for a sample being outside the limits, that sample should be discarded.**

If this is the case, then the grand average and the average range must be recalculated. Following that, the control limits for ranges must also be calculated again. The sample ranges are then compared with the "new" limits, which are also drawn on the chart. If any of the remaining ranges are out of control, the process is repeated. If not, then a broken line is used to connect the points around the deleted range.

Control limits for individuals are calculated after we are convinced that the ranges are stable. The formulas for the three sigma limits for averages are

$$\text{UCL}X = \overline{\overline{X}} + \frac{3\overline{R}}{d_2}$$

$$\text{LCL}X = \overline{\overline{X}} - \frac{3\overline{R}}{d_2}$$

Again, the constant value, d_2, comes from the work that Shewhart did.

After the limits for individuals have been calculated, they should be drawn on the chart for individuals. Each sample observation should be checked to see if the values fall between the upper and lower control limits. If a sample observation is not between the limits, then we should determine if there is an assignable or special cause for this abnormal variation. Often the notations made during the data-collection process will determine if there is a special reason. As with the ranges, if there is a special/identifiable cause for the abnormal variation, then the sample should be discarded.

If this is the case, then the grand average and the average range must be recalculated. Following that, the control limits for ranges must also be calculated again.

The sample ranges are then compared with the "new" limits, which are also drawn on the chart. If any of the remaining ranges are out of control, the process is repeated. If not, then a broken line is used to connect the points around the deleted range. Then the limits for averages are recalculated. The sample individuals are then compared with the "new" limits, which are also drawn on the chart. If any of the remaining averages are out of control, the entire process is repeated. If not, then a broken line is used to connect the points around the deleted individual.

At this point, the process is said to be in control. This means that only normal variation is present. A process must be in control before we can begin improving it. No mention has been made about whether or not material being produced conforms to specifications.

That is the procedure. Section 15.4 will look at some examples of the process.

One last point of emphasis, though. The process, once it is in control, generally will require continuing monitoring. This should be done by the operator. As soon as abnormal variation occurs, the operator should first recognize it and, second, initiate action to remove it. Looking at the data after the fact, a day or week or even a month later, will not help to control the process. Chapter 17 will illustrate some of the common control chart interpretation techniques.

15.4   EXAMPLES

Example 15.4.1   A destructive test was performed on a component and the time to failure, in hundredths of a minute, was recorded. Figure 15–3 shows these data, on the standard chart form, for the 30 readings that were collected. As explained in Section 15.3, after the data are collected, the moving range for each set of points is calculated. This is shown in Figure 15–4.

The average of the individuals and the average range are calculated next. For the individuals,

$$\overline{X} = \frac{227}{30} = 7.57$$

For the ranges,

$$\overline{R} = \frac{81}{29} = 2.79$$

The points are plotted in the ranges and individuals charts, respectively, and the central lines are drawn on the charts in Figure 15–5.

The variability or consistency of the ranges is checked first. These control limits are calculated using the formulas shown in Section 15.3.

$$UCLR = D_4\overline{R} = (3.27)(2.79) = 9.12$$
$$LCLR = D_3\overline{R} = 0$$

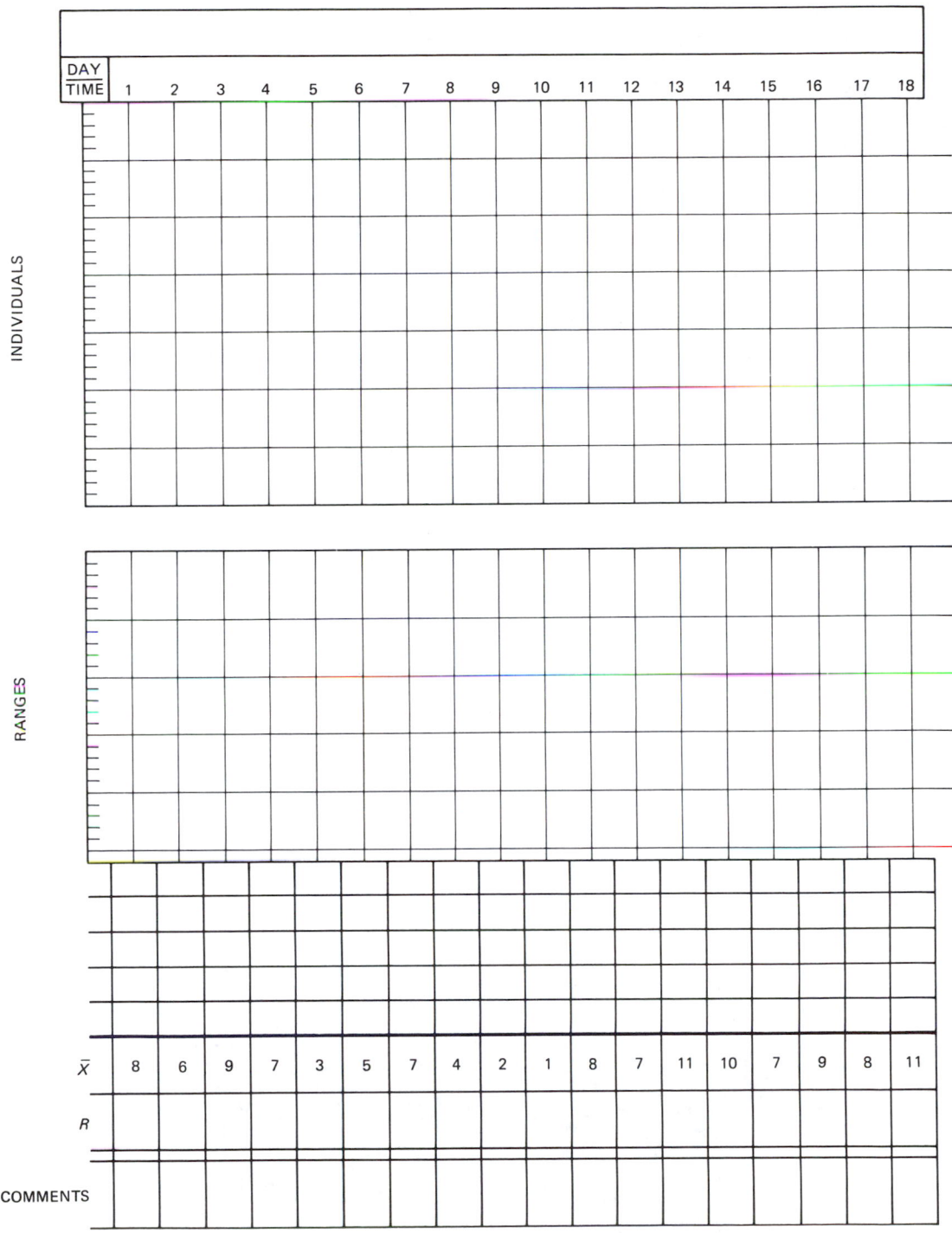

DAY / TIME	1	2	3	4	5	6	7	8	9	10	11	12	13	14	15	16	17	18
INDIVIDUALS																		
RANGES																		
$\bar{X}$	8	6	9	7	3	5	7	4	2	1	8	7	11	10	7	9	8	11
R																		
COMMENTS																		

(cont.)

FIGURE 15–3 Data for Example 15.4.1

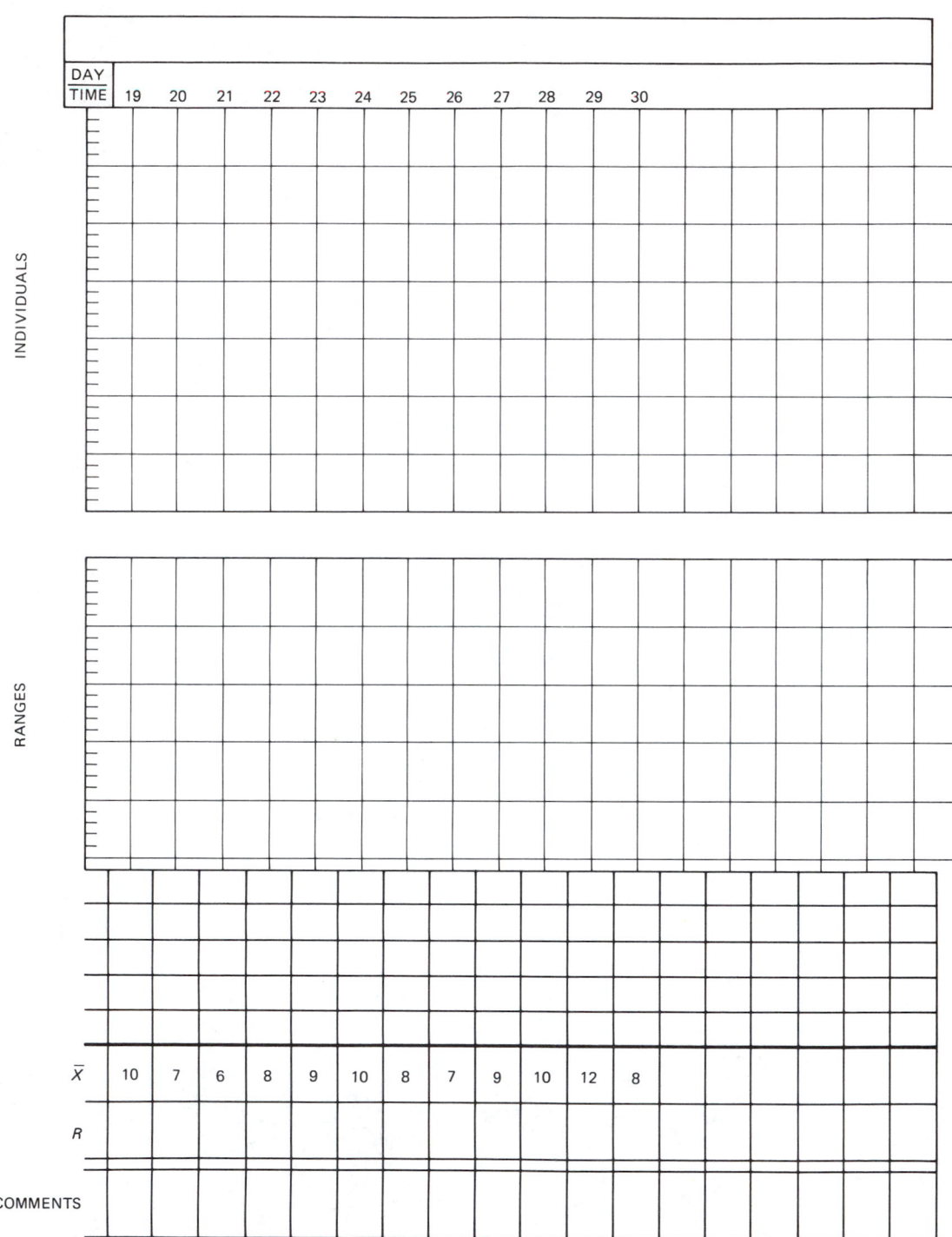

FIGURE 15–3 (*Continued*)

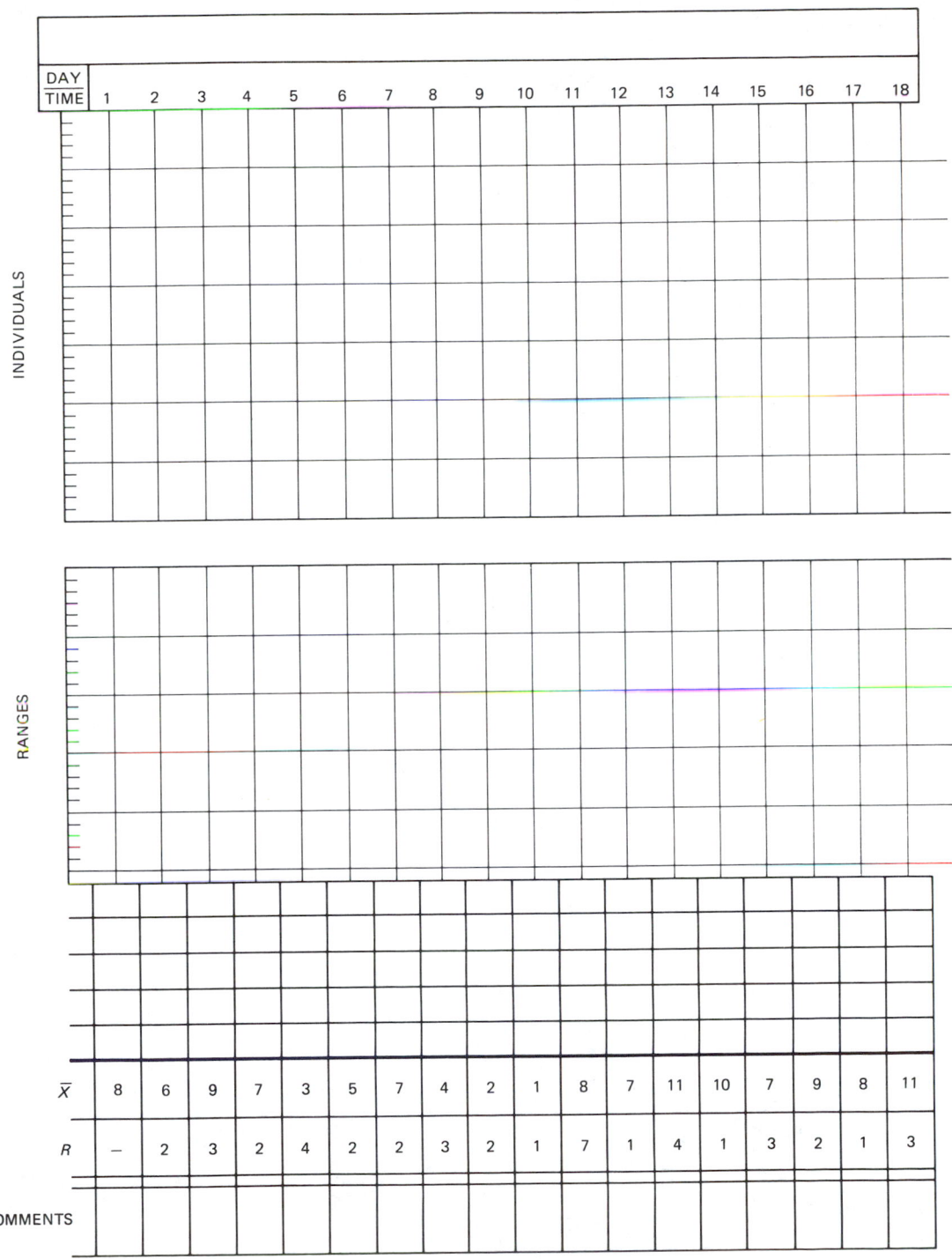

	DAY TIME	1	2	3	4	5	6	7	8	9	10	11	12	13	14	15	16	17	18
$\overline{X}$		8	6	9	7	3	5	7	4	2	1	8	7	11	10	7	9	8	11
R		—	2	3	2	4	2	2	3	2	1	7	1	4	1	3	2	1	3
COMMENTS																			

FIGURE 15-4 Range for Example 15.4.1

(cont.)

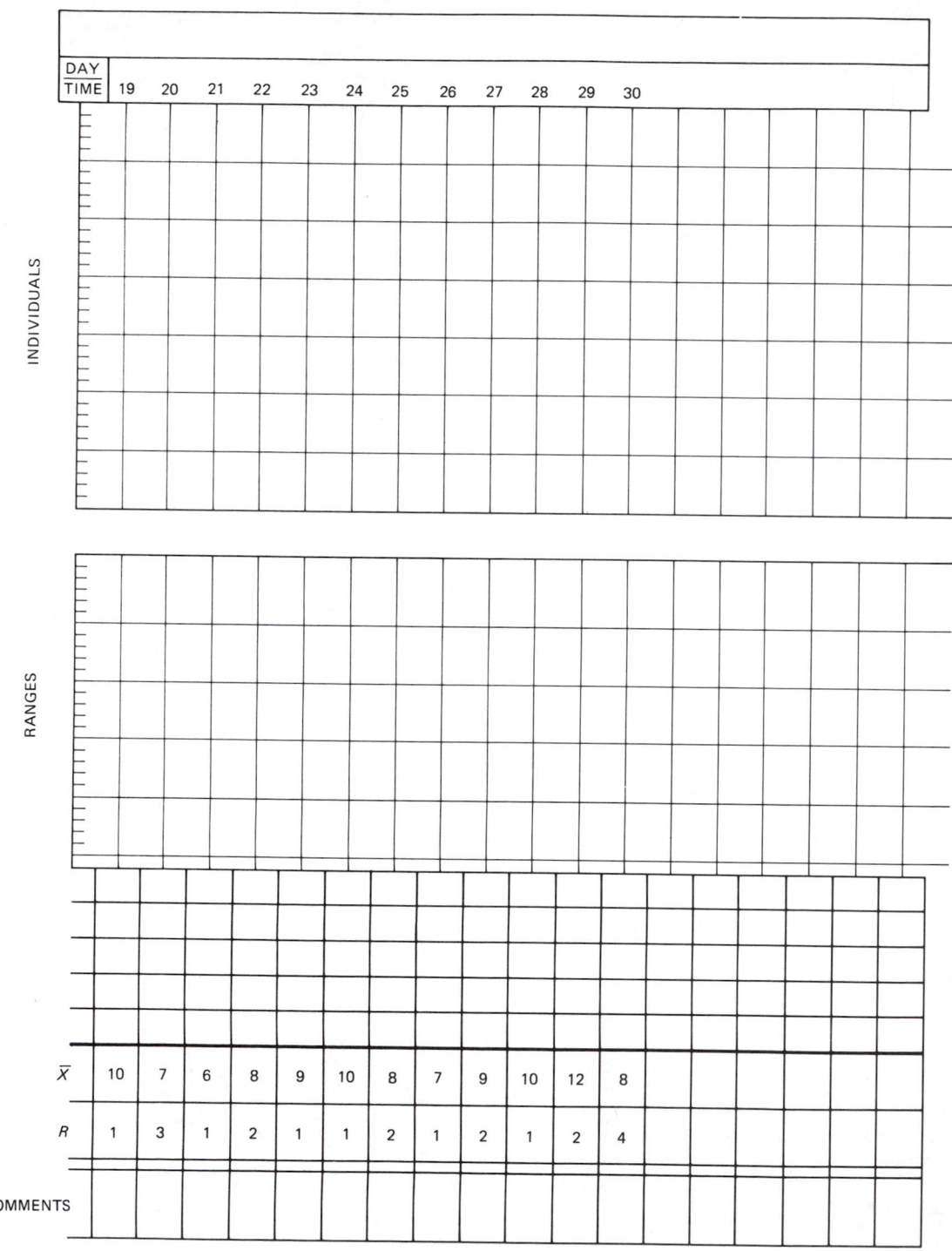

FIGURE 15-4 (Continued)

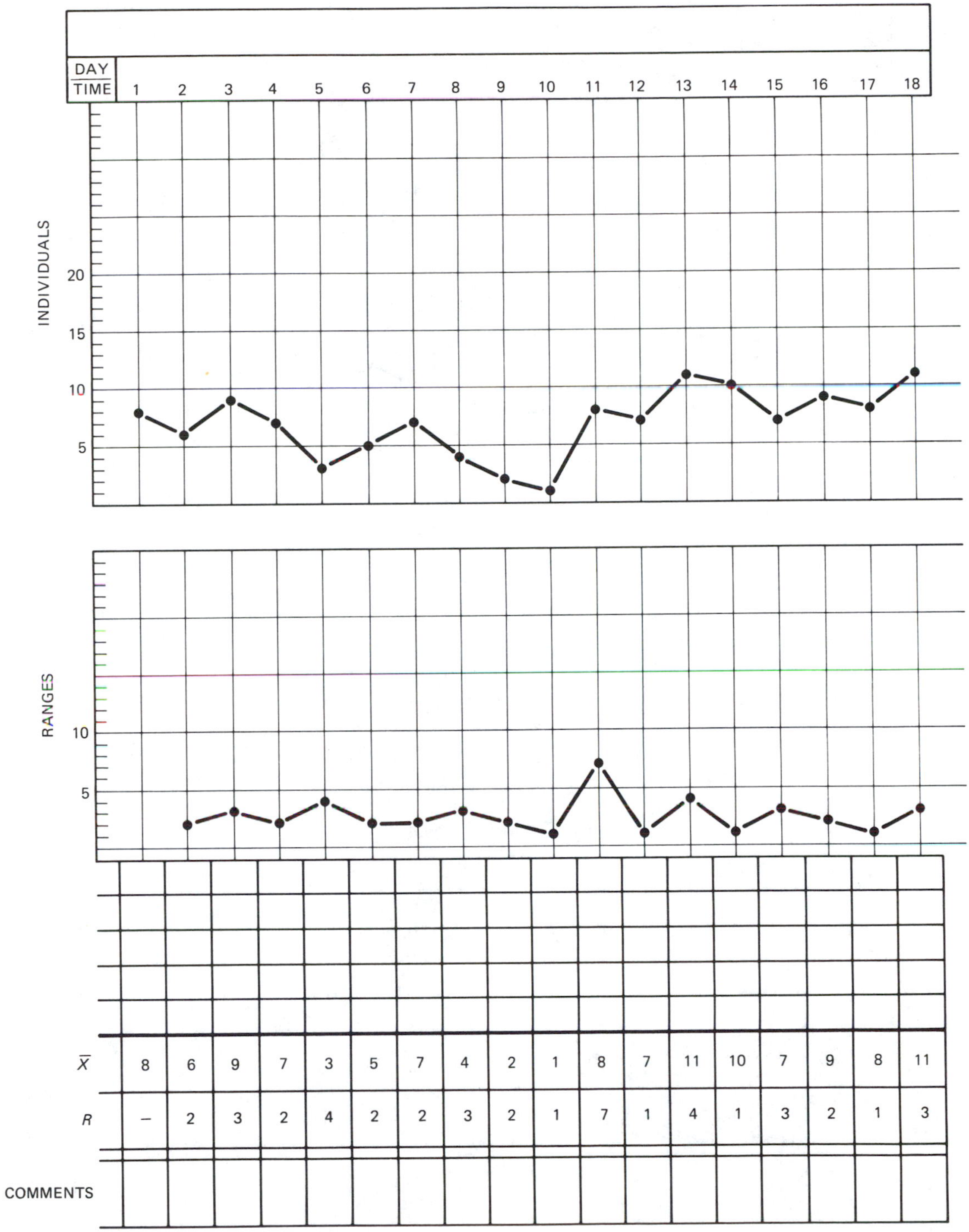
DAY
TIME
1 2 3 4 5 6 7 8 9 10 11 12 13 14 15 16 17 18
INDIVIDUALS
20
15
10
5
RANGES
10
5
$\bar{X}$
8 6 9 7 3 5 7 4 2 1 8 7 11 10 7 9 8 11
R
– 2 3 2 4 2 2 3 2 1 7 1 4 1 3 2 1 3
COMMENTS

(*cont.*)

FIGURE 15–5 Initial Plot for Example 15.4.1

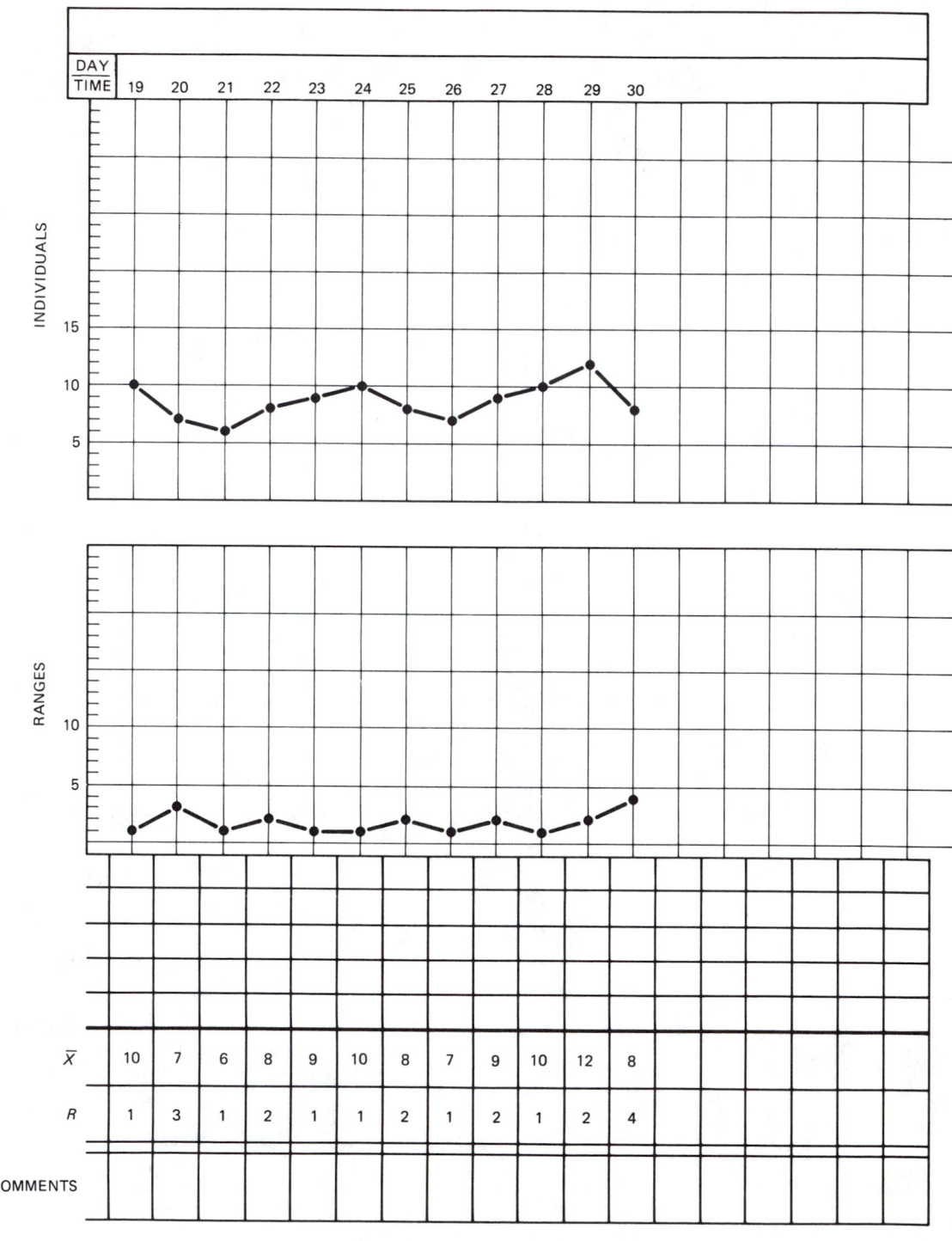

FIGURE 15–5 (*Continued*)

When these are added to the control chart for ranges, as shown in Figure 15–6, we note that all the sample ranges are in control. This means we will not have to adjust any of the range calculations at this point. At least regarding the variability between samples, we can state that the ranges are stable.

We move on now to the individuals. We calculate the limits using the formulas from Section 15.3.

$$\text{UCL}X = \overline{\overline{X}} + \frac{(3)(\overline{R})}{d_2} = 7.57 + (3)(2.79)/(1.128)$$

$$= 14.99$$

$$\text{LCL}X = \overline{\overline{X}} - \frac{(3)(\overline{R})}{d_2} = 7.57 - (3)(2.79)/(1.128)$$

$$= 0.15$$

These are added to the form in Figure 15–7. All the individual values are between the limits, so we believe that the process is in control with respect to individuals. The only variation that is present in the process is normal variation. The process is now a candidate for improvement. The improvement, in this case, may be the extension of time to failure. The nature of the improvement might be an increase in the grand average, as well as a reduction in the variability of the process. ■

Example 15.4.2 The tolerance on a slot that is critical to the assembly of a surgical instrument has been causing the manufacturer problems. Twenty measurements of this characteristic, in thousandths of an inch, are shown on the chart in Figure 15–8. The moving range for these values is also shown.

The average for the individuals is calculated:

$$\overline{X} = \frac{6.36}{20} = 0.318$$

The average range is also calculated:

$$\overline{R} = \frac{0.95}{19} = 0.05$$

The observed values and the control lines are shown on the chart in Figure 15–9.

The control limits for ranges are calculated first.

$$\text{UCL}R = (3.27)(0.050) = 0.1635$$

$$\text{LCL}R = 0$$

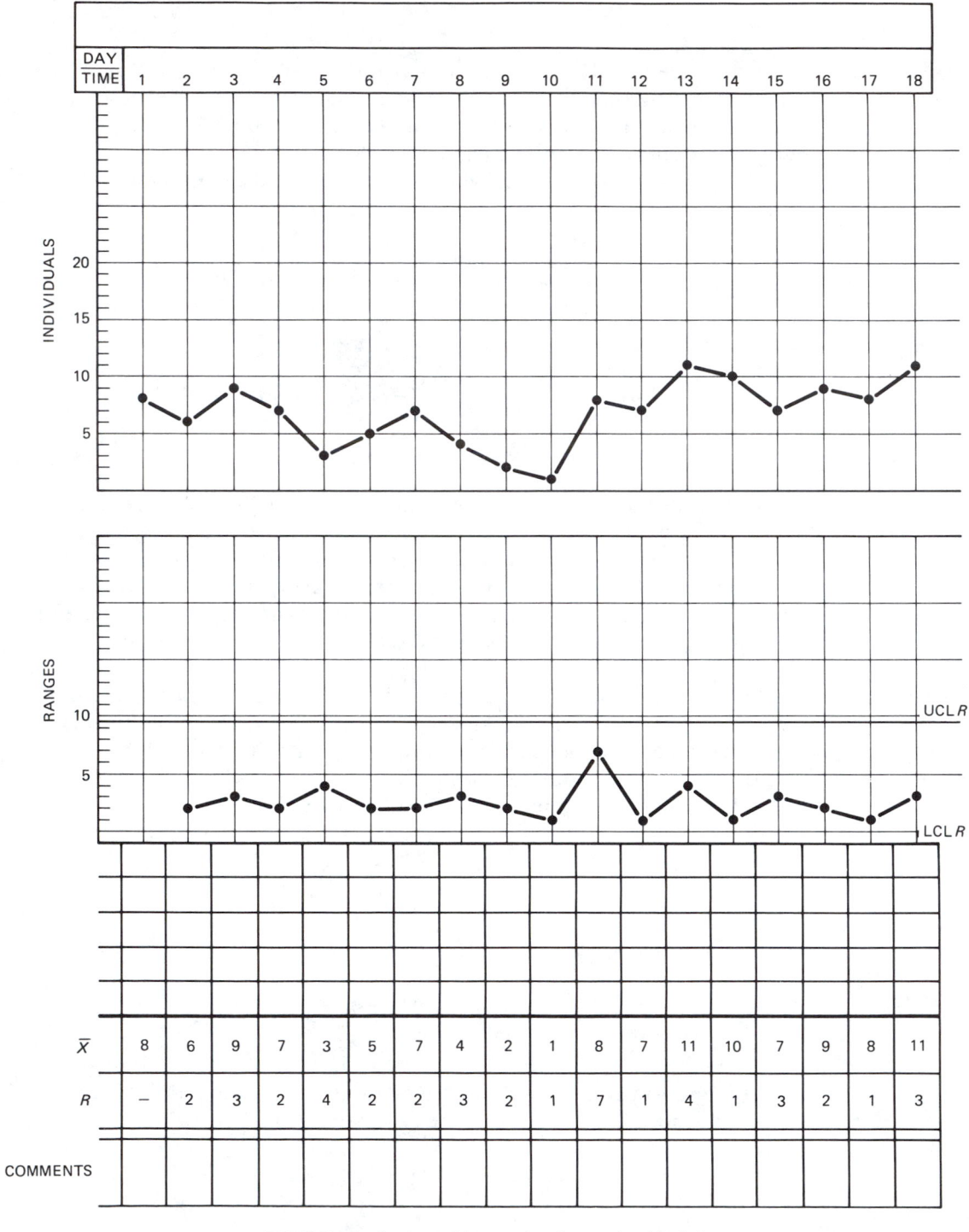

FIGURE 15–6 Initial Limits for Example 15.4.1

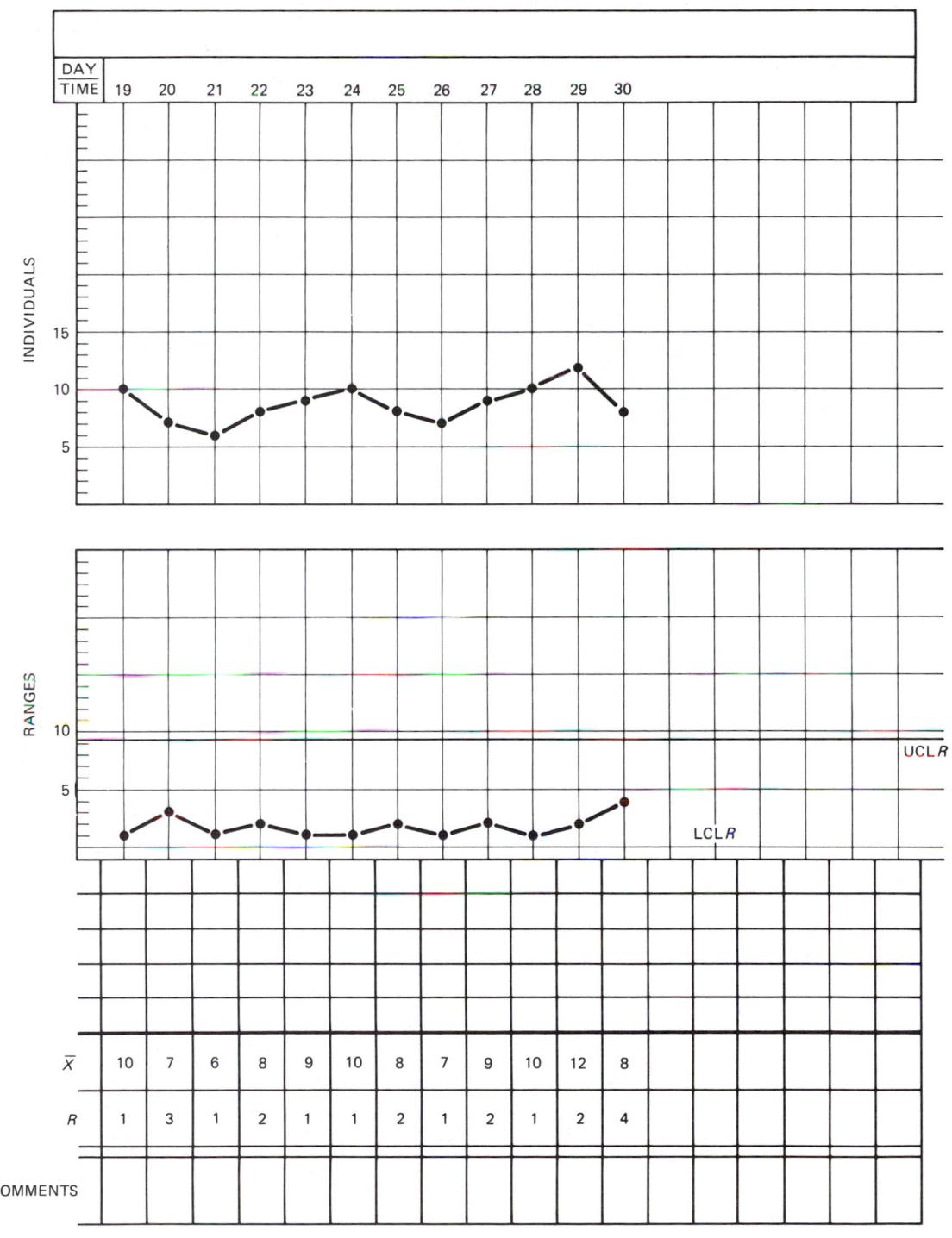

FIGURE 15–6 (*Continued*)

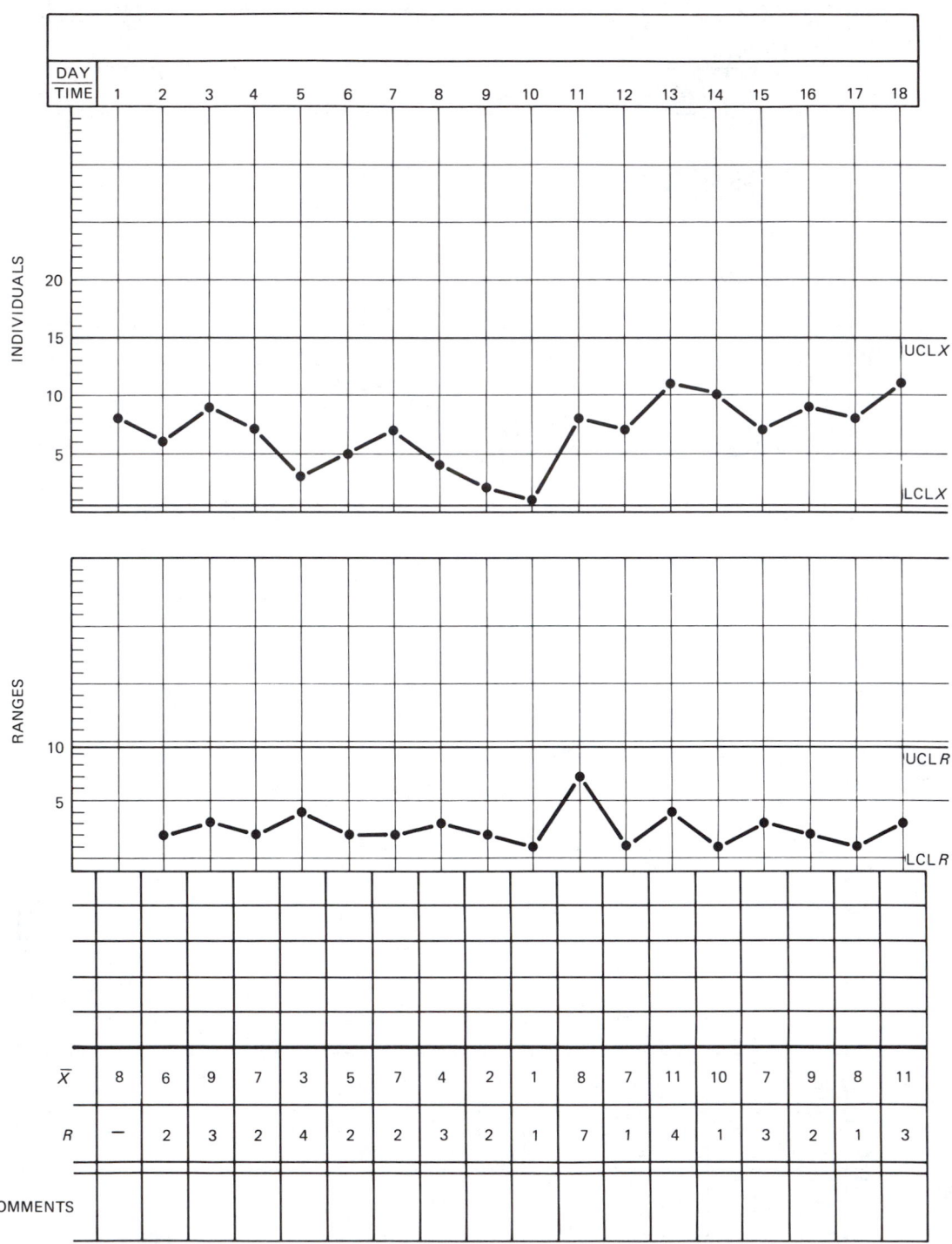

FIGURE 15–7 Additional Limits for Example 15.4.1

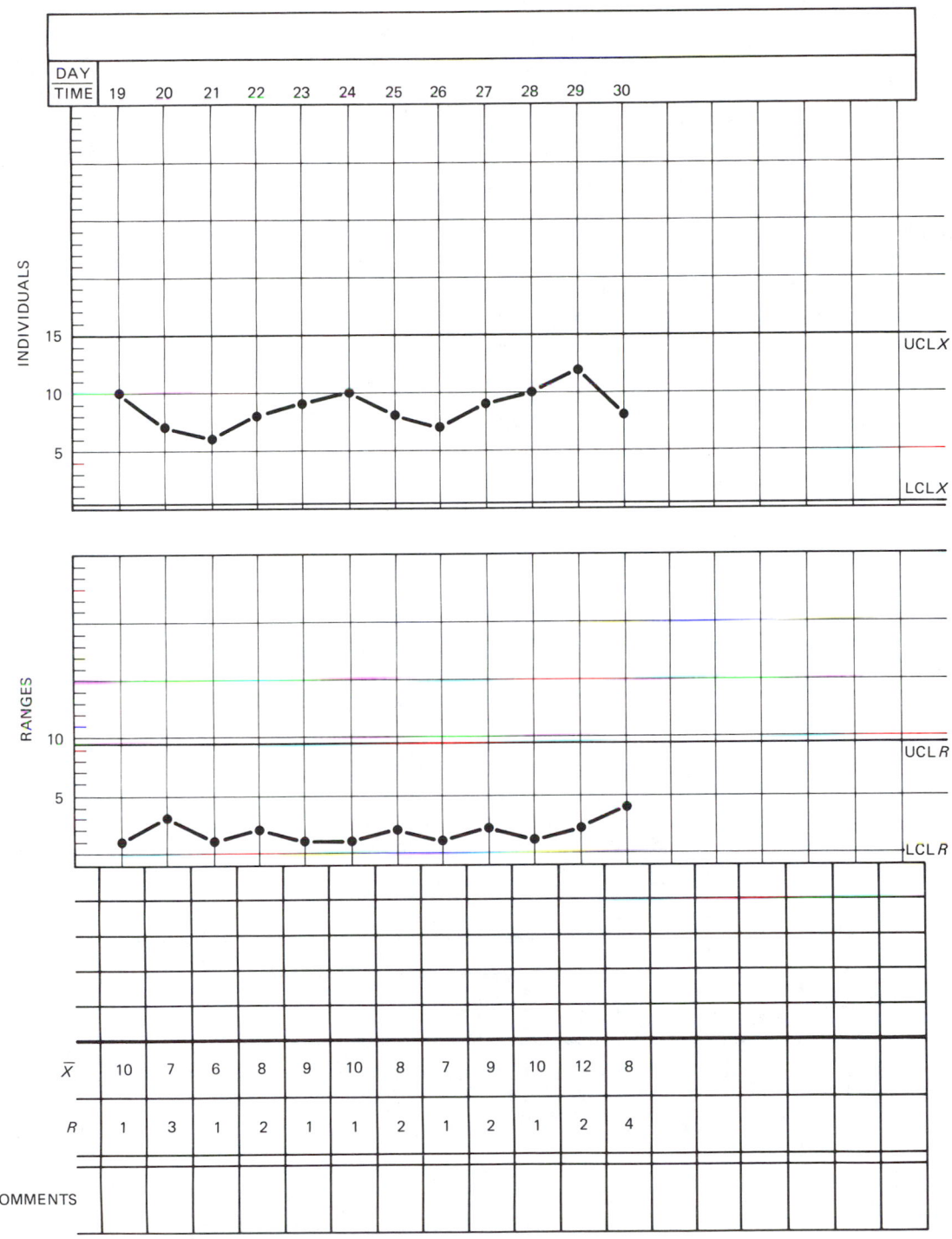

FIGURE 15–7 (*Continued*)

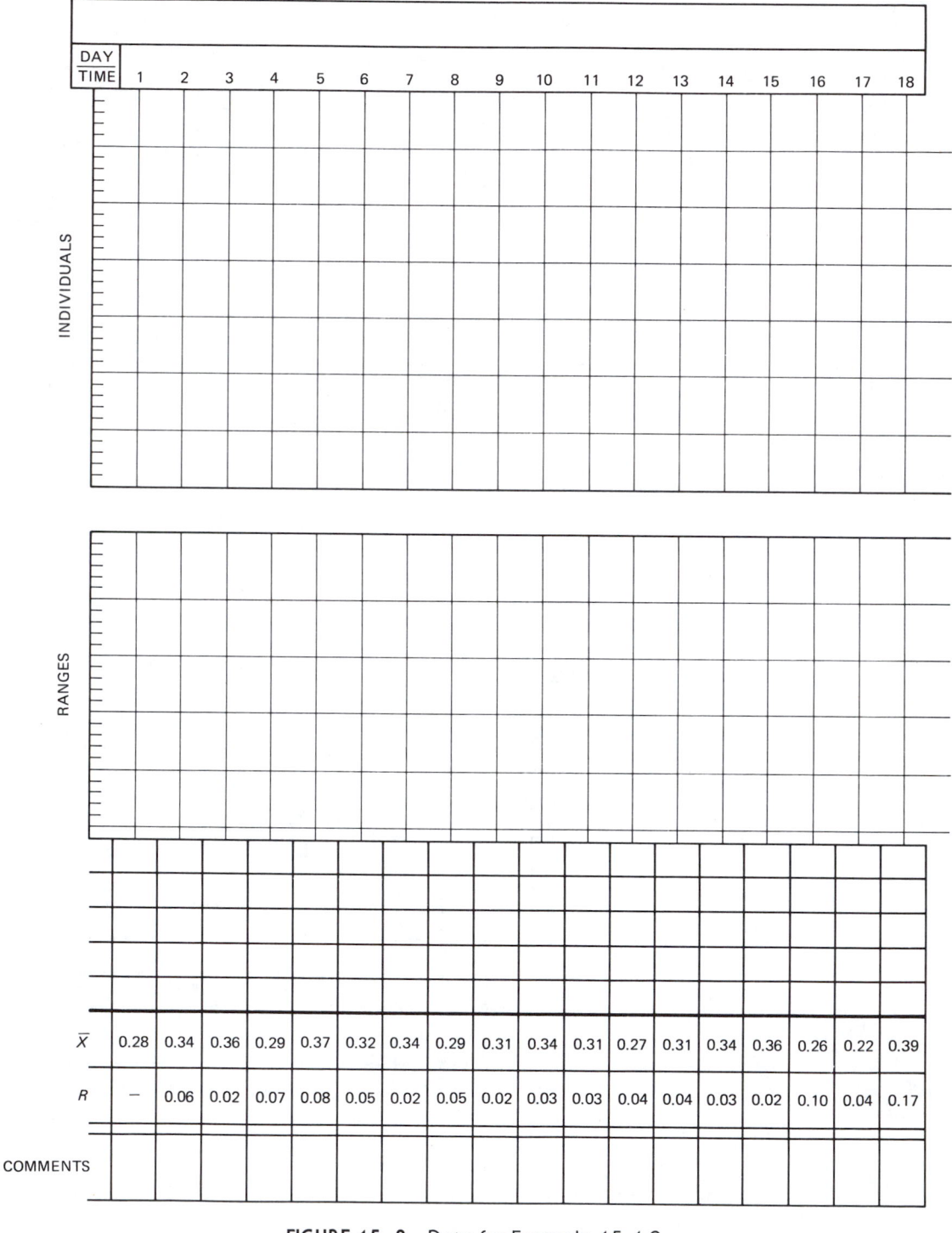

The data table at the bottom of the figure:

		1	2	3	4	5	6	7	8	9	10	11	12	13	14	15	16	17	18
$\overline{X}$		0.28	0.34	0.36	0.29	0.37	0.32	0.34	0.29	0.31	0.34	0.31	0.27	0.31	0.34	0.36	0.26	0.22	0.39
R		—	0.06	0.02	0.07	0.08	0.05	0.02	0.05	0.02	0.03	0.03	0.04	0.04	0.03	0.02	0.10	0.04	0.17

FIGURE 15–8 Data for Example 15.4.2

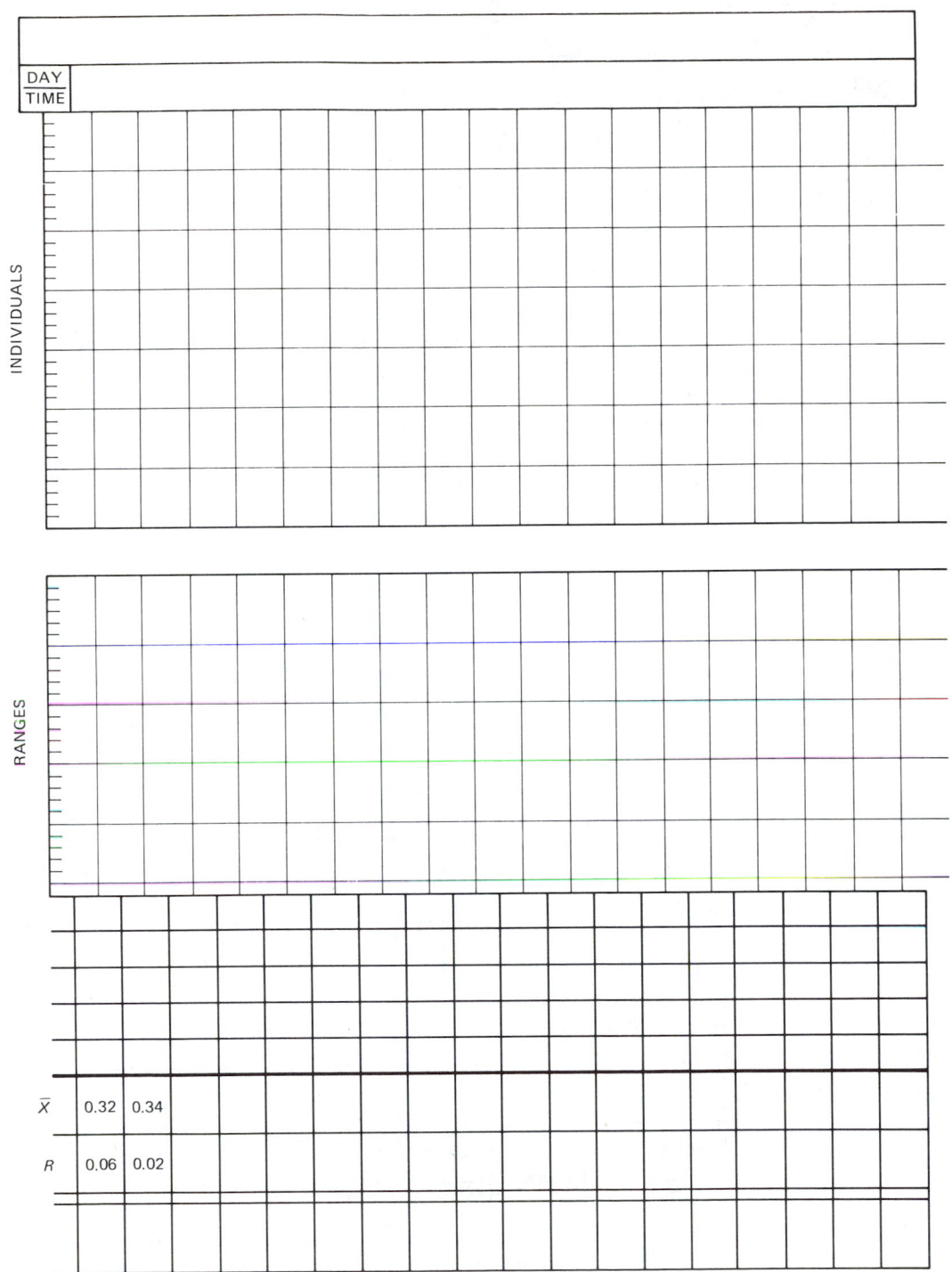

FIGURE 15–8 (*Continued*)

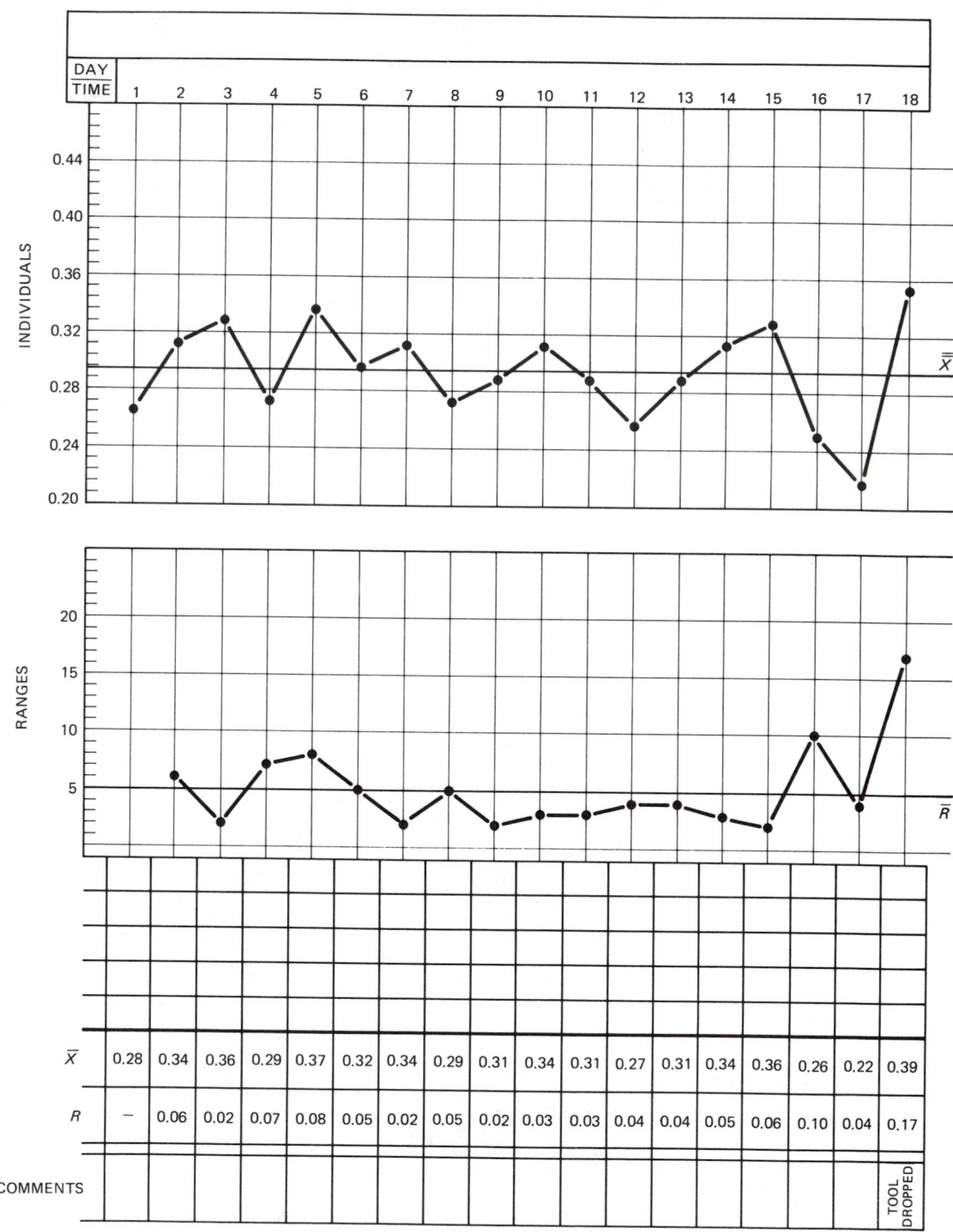

FIGURE 15-9 Initial Plot for Example 15.4.2

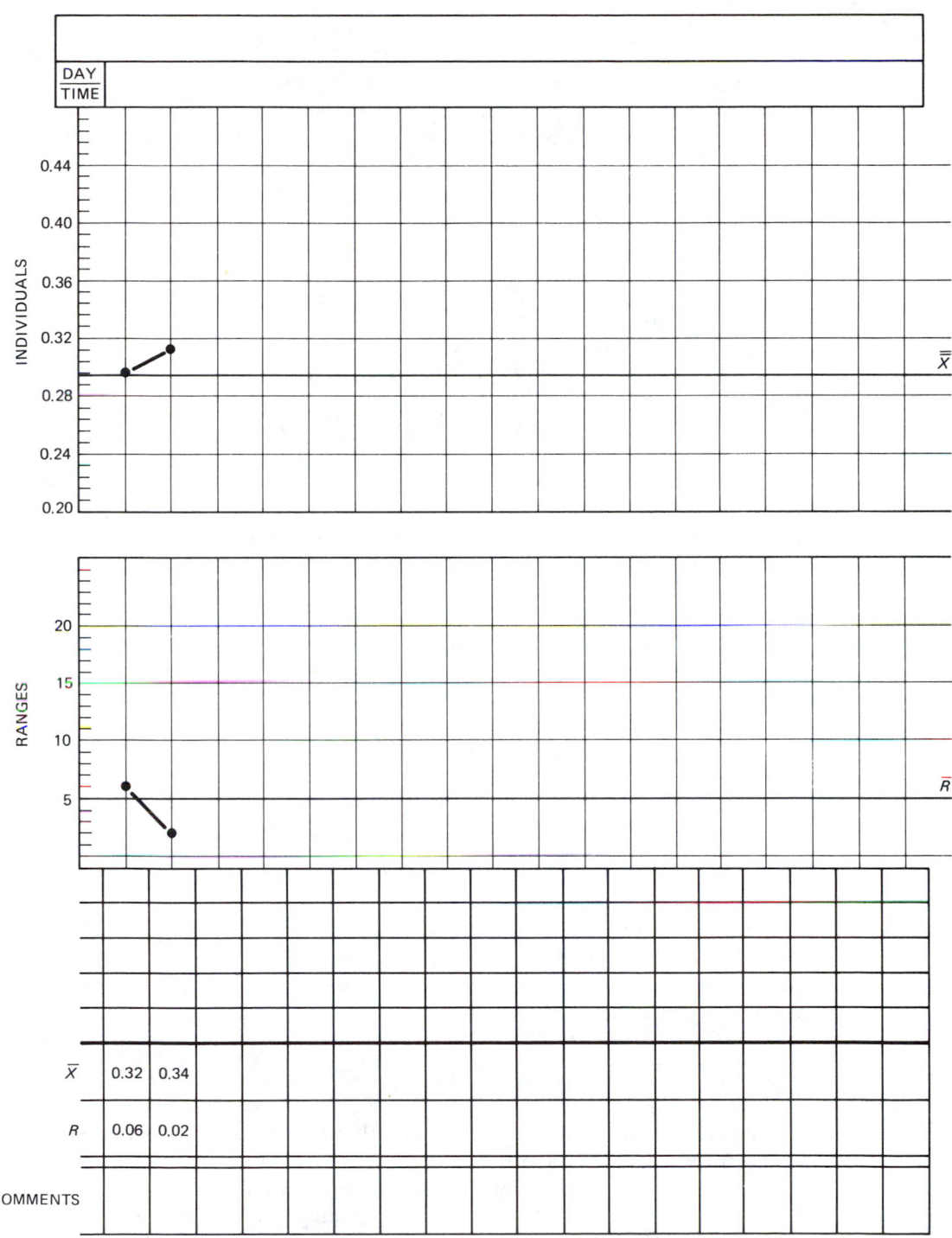

FIGURE 15–9 (*Continued*)

When these are added to the control chart, as shown in Figure 15–10, point 18 is noticed to be outside the upper limit. Upon investigating the situation, it is noted that the tool was dropped before the inspection was performed. This is an abnormal cause of variation, something that should not normally be performed, and is justification for discarding the point. This means that the grand average and average range have to be recalculated and that the limits for ranges also must be redone.

$$\overline{\overline{X}} = \frac{5.97}{19} = 0.314$$

$$\overline{R} = \frac{0.78}{18} = 0.0433$$

$$UCLR = (3.27)(0.0433) = 0.1417$$

$$LCLR = 0$$

The new limits, as calculated, are shown in Figure 15–11.

Upon examination, all the remaining moving ranges are in control. With the exception of the identified point, it appears that only normal variation is now present in the process. Attention is now directed toward the control limits for the individuals. Using the revised average range and the revised grand average, we calculate the limits to be

$$UCLX = 0.314 + \frac{(3)(0.0433)}{(1.128)} = 0.429$$

$$LCLX = 0.314 - \frac{(3)(0.433)}{(1.128)} = 0.199$$

These are added to the control chart in Figure 15–12. As can be seen, all the remaining individual values are within the limits. The process is stable, and improvement can begin. In this case, since the tolerance was a problem, the process must be improved in some way, shape, or form to get the desired fit. The process is doing as well as it can under the current conditions. ∎

Example 15.4.3 A travel agency was measuring the time required to book customer airplane reservations. They recorded the time, in seconds, to confirm travel plans for their clients. It is shown in Figure 15–13a. Having recently been through an SPC course, they also plotted the times in a frequency histogram. this is shown in Figure 15–13b. The shape appeared to be normal so they proceeded with the analysis. As a service organization, they knew that the quicker they could serve their customers, the better chance they would have in building repeat business. The individual values were re-

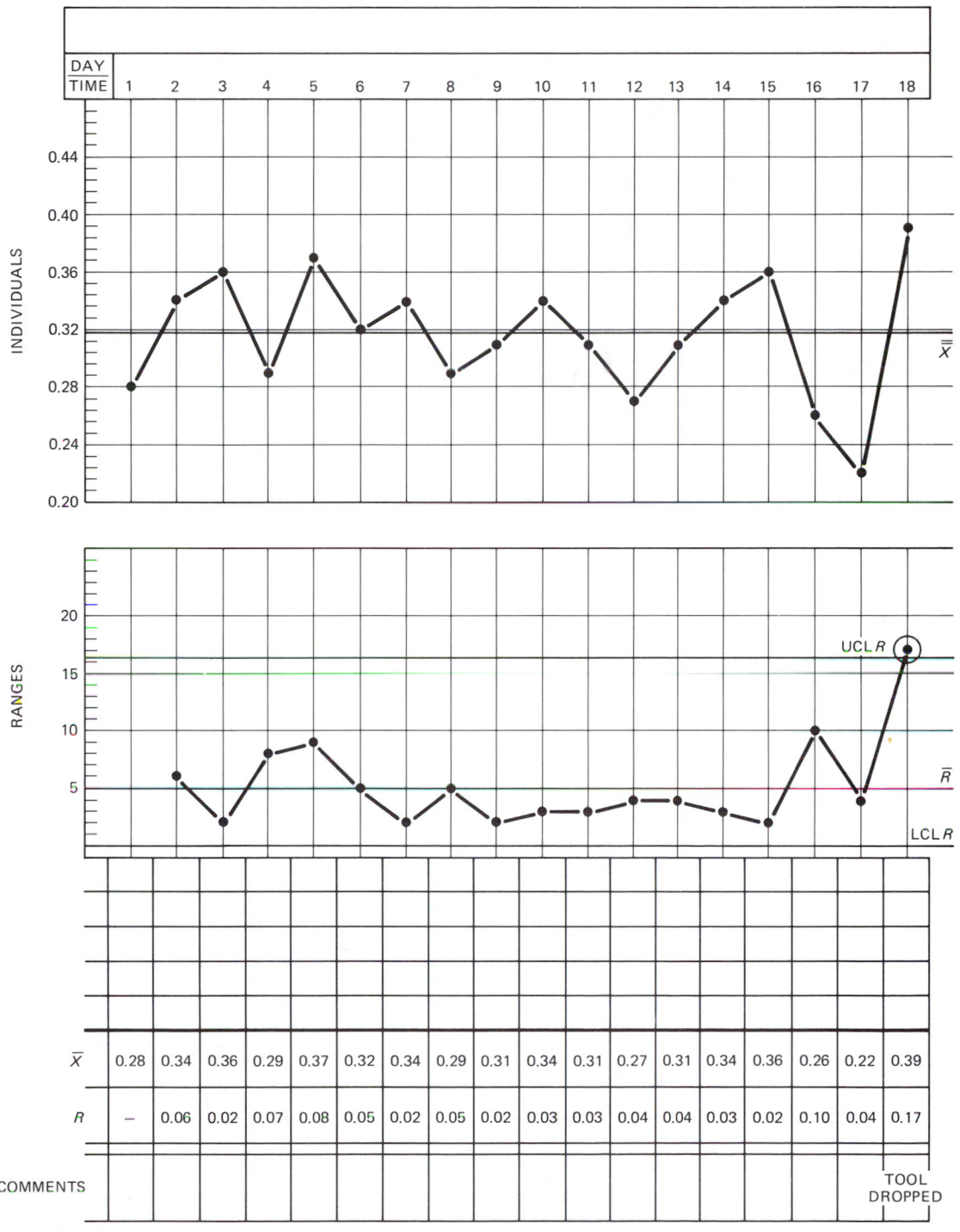

FIGURE 15–10 Initial Limits for Example 15.4.2

(cont.)

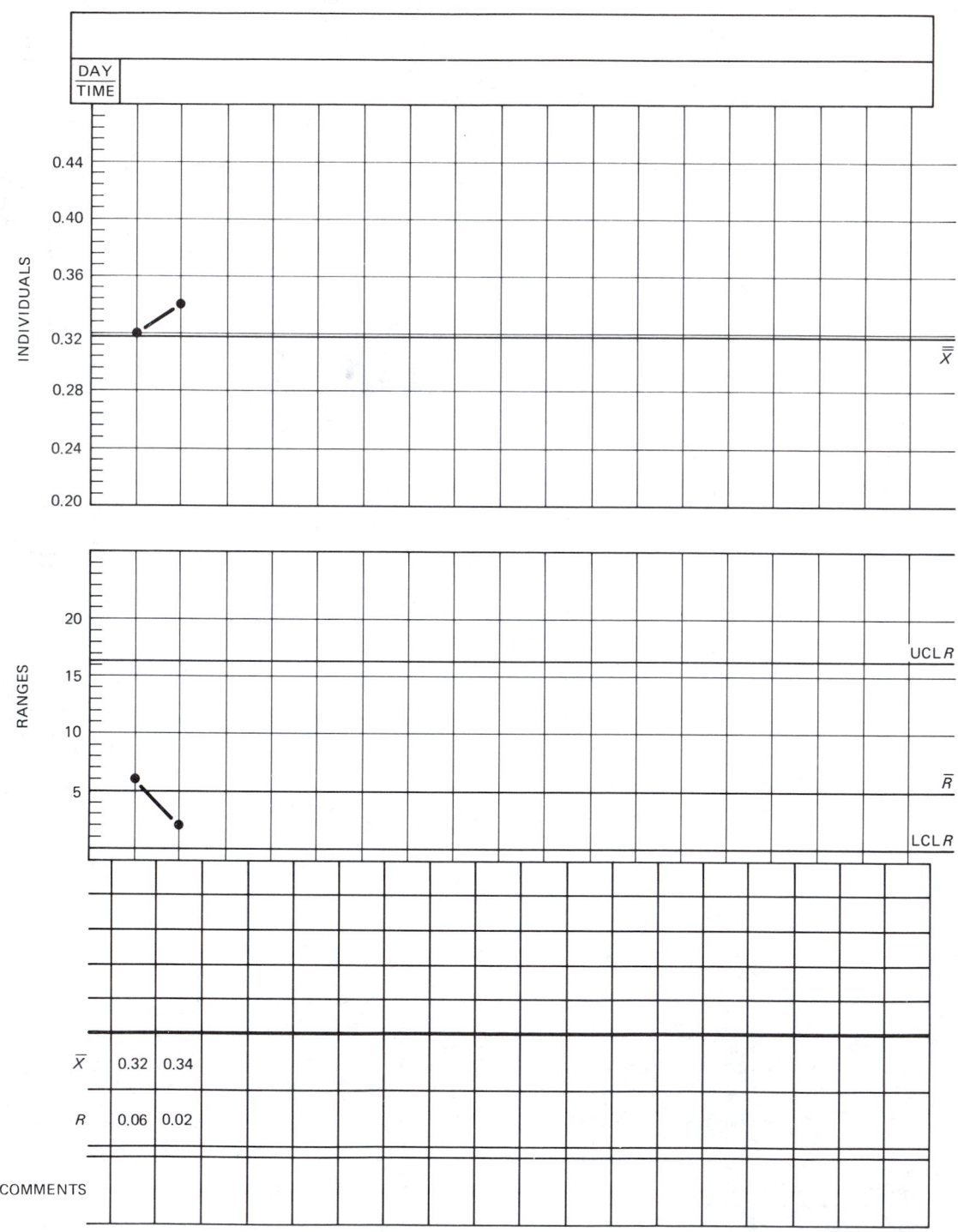

FIGURE 15–10 (*Continued*)

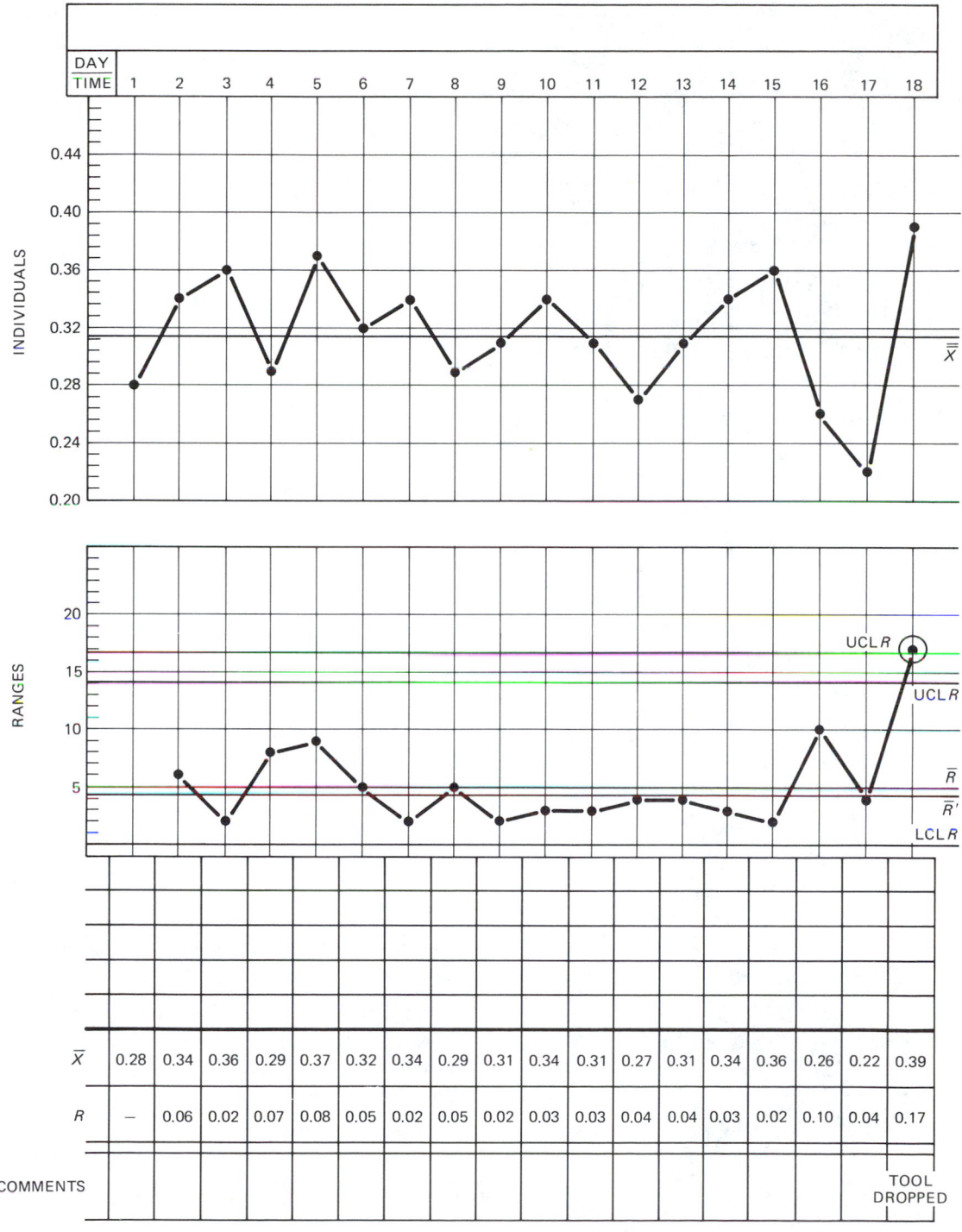

FIGURE 15–11 Revised Limits for Example 15.4.2

(cont.)

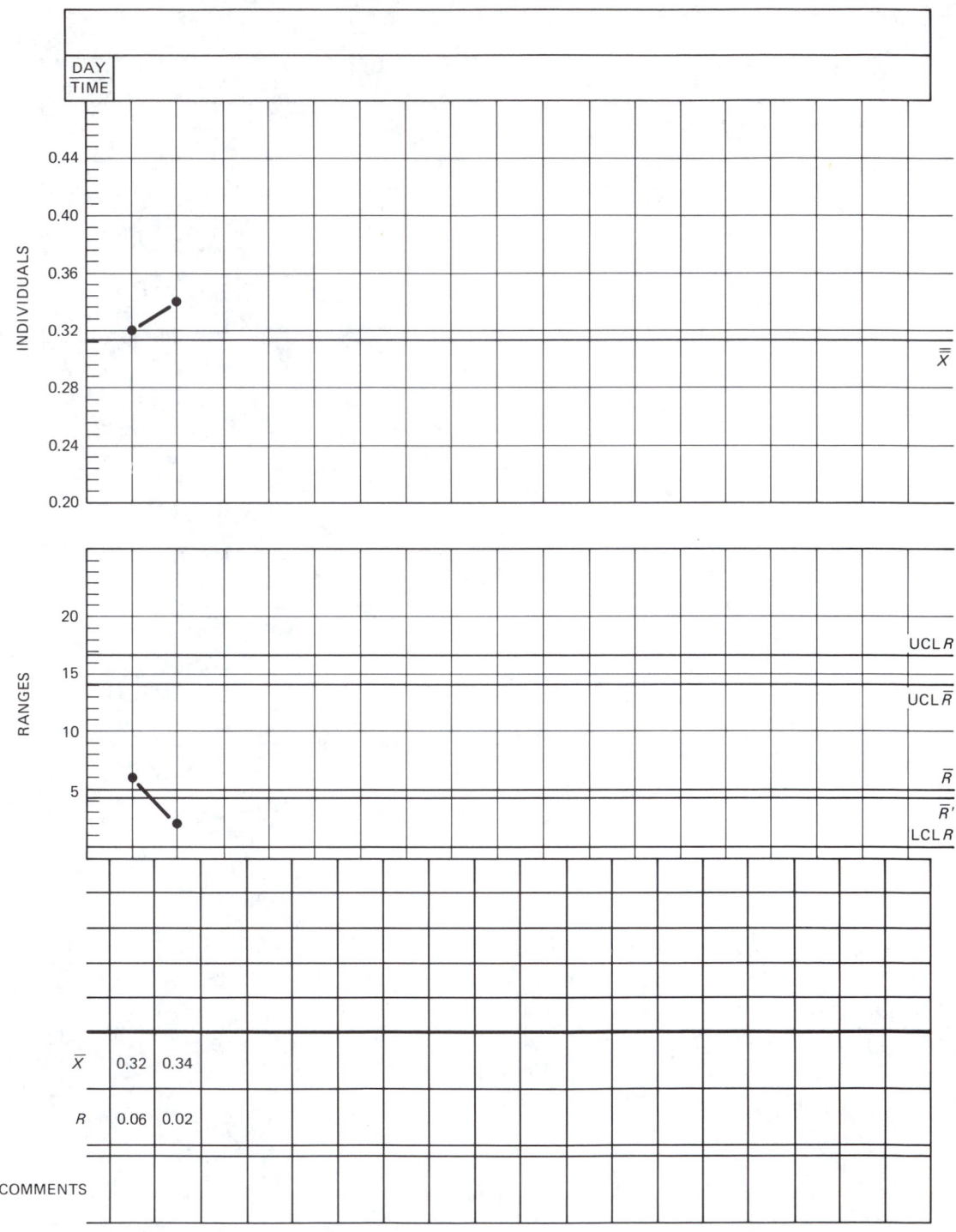

FIGURE 15–11 (*Continued*)

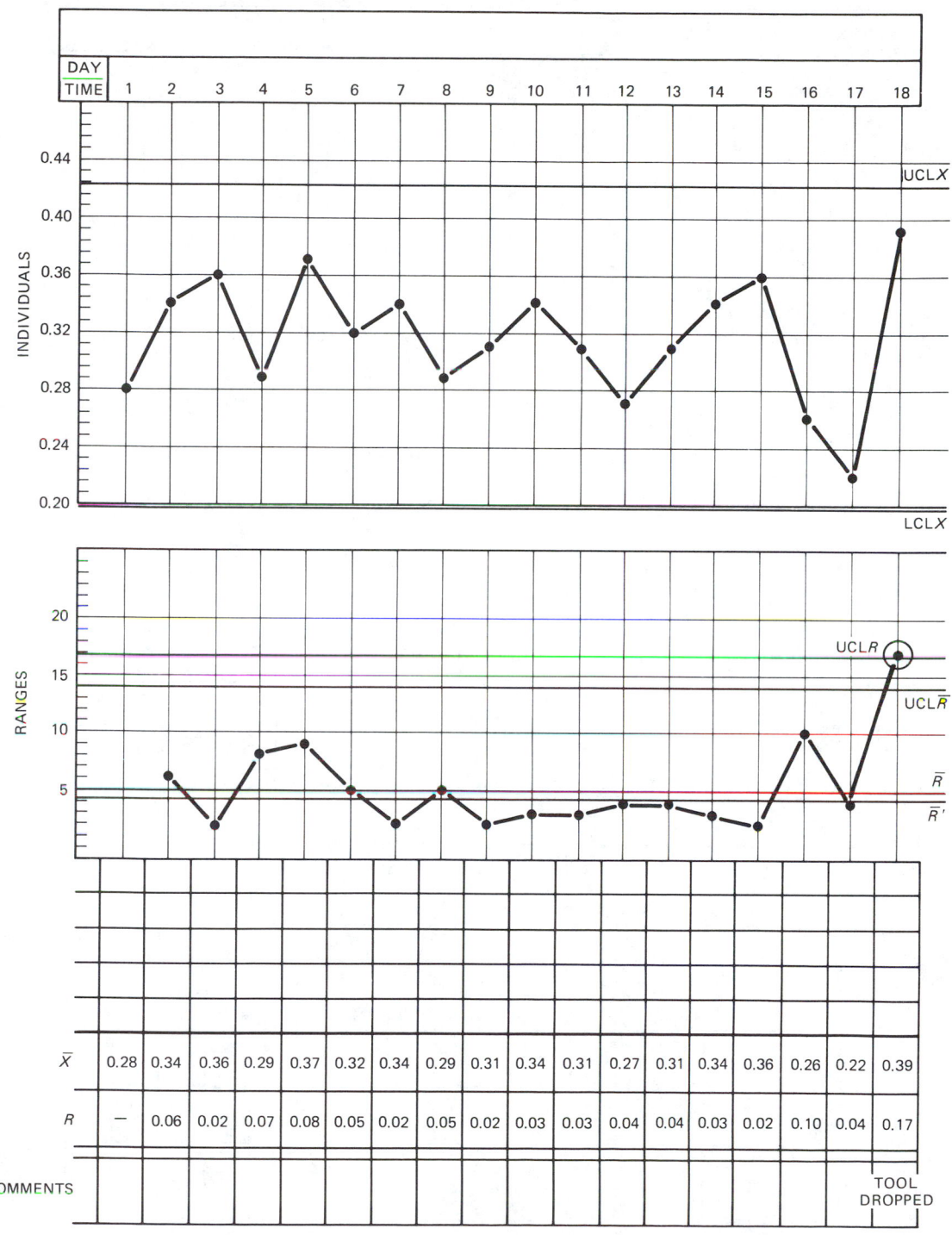

FIGURE 15-12 Completed Chart for Example 15.4.2

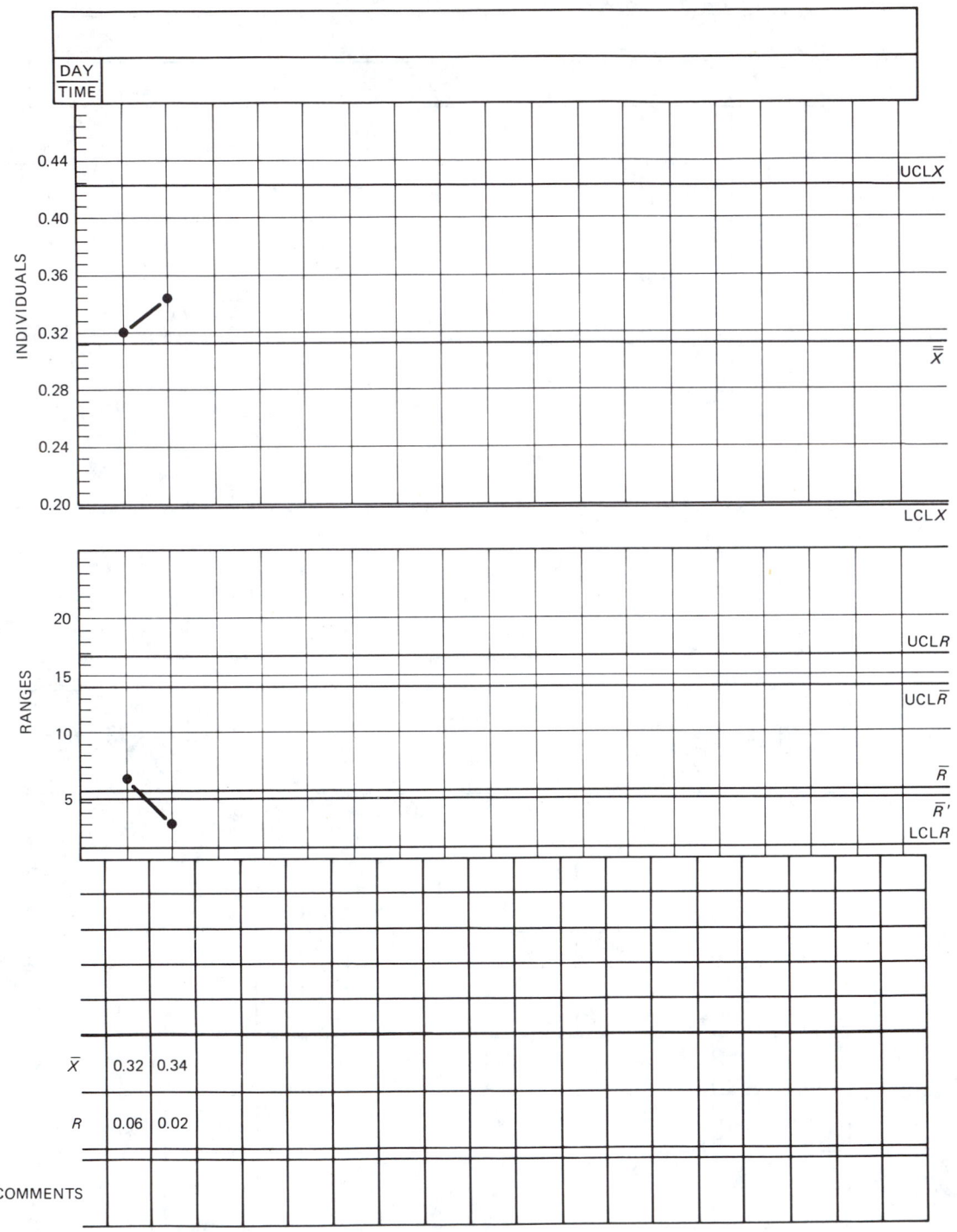

FIGURE 15–12 (*Continued*)

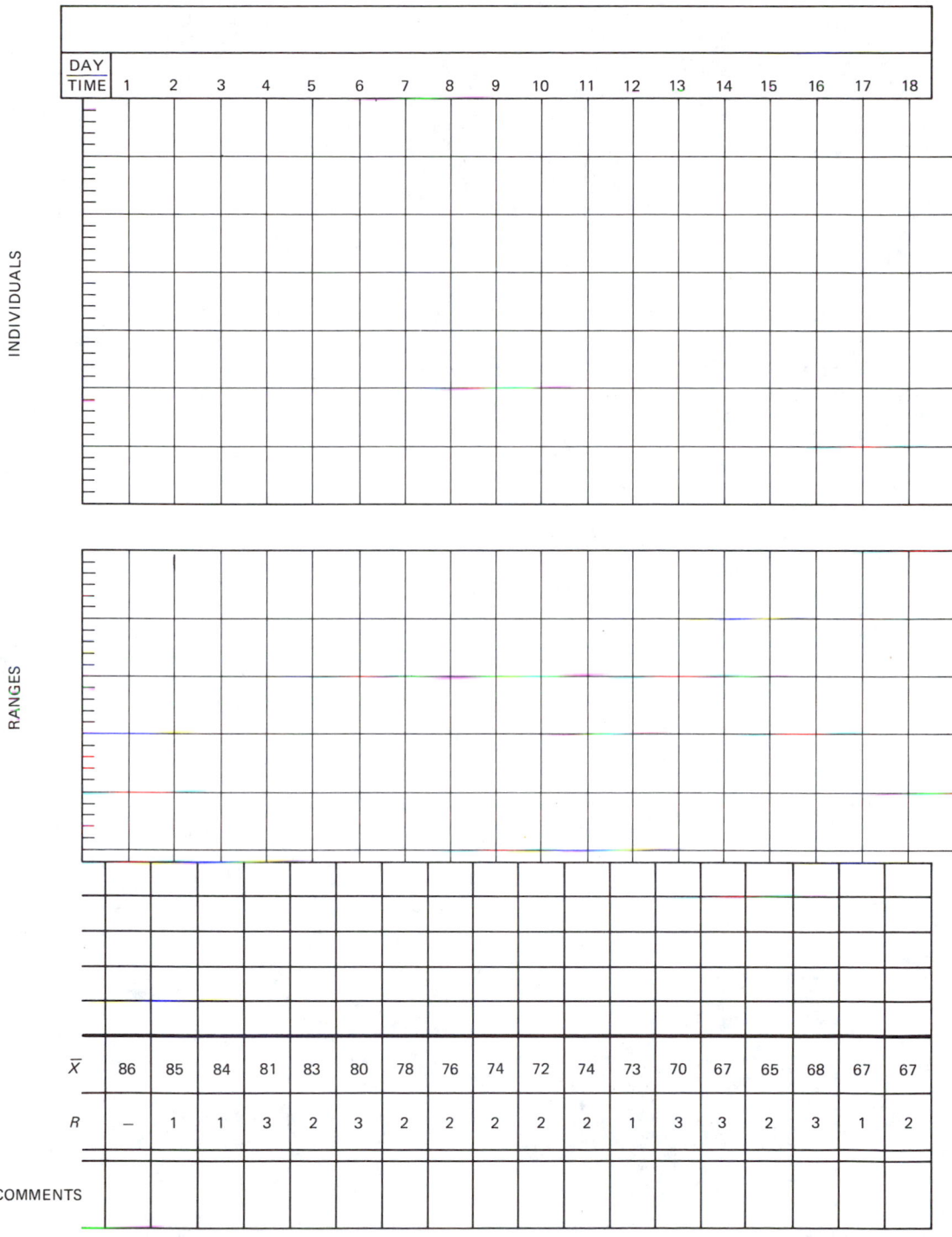

	DAY TIME	1	2	3	4	5	6	7	8	9	10	11	12	13	14	15	16	17	18
$\overline{X}$		86	85	84	81	83	80	78	76	74	72	74	73	70	67	65	68	67	67
R		—	1	1	3	2	3	2	2	2	2	2	1	3	3	2	3	1	2

INDIVIDUALS

RANGES

COMMENTS

FIGURE 15–13 (a) Data for Example 15.4.3; (b) Histogram for Example 15.4.3

(cont.)

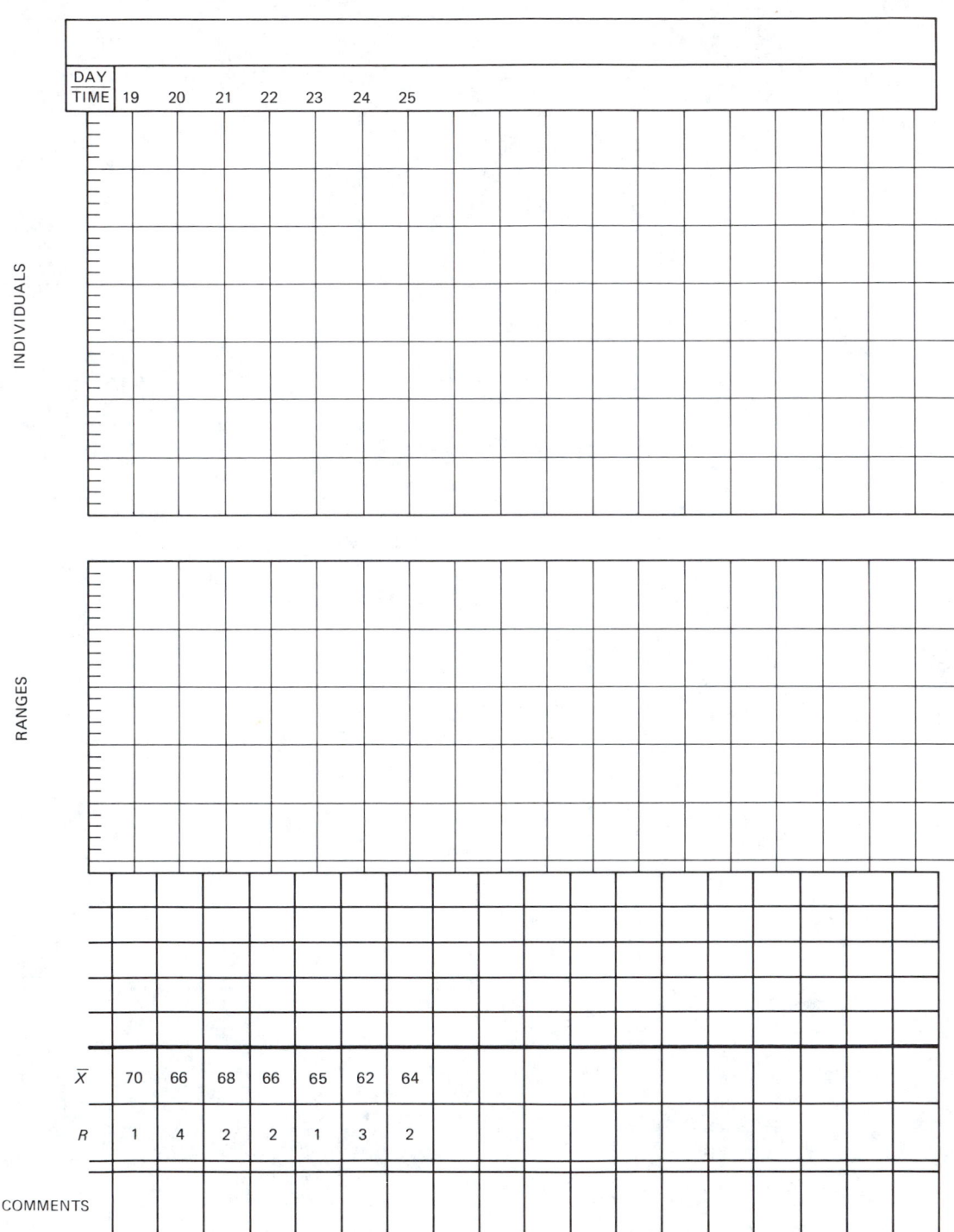

	DAY	19	20	21	22	23	24	25												
$\overline{X}$		70	66	68	66	65	62	64												
R		1	4	2	2	1	3	2												

FIGURE 15–13a (*Continued*)

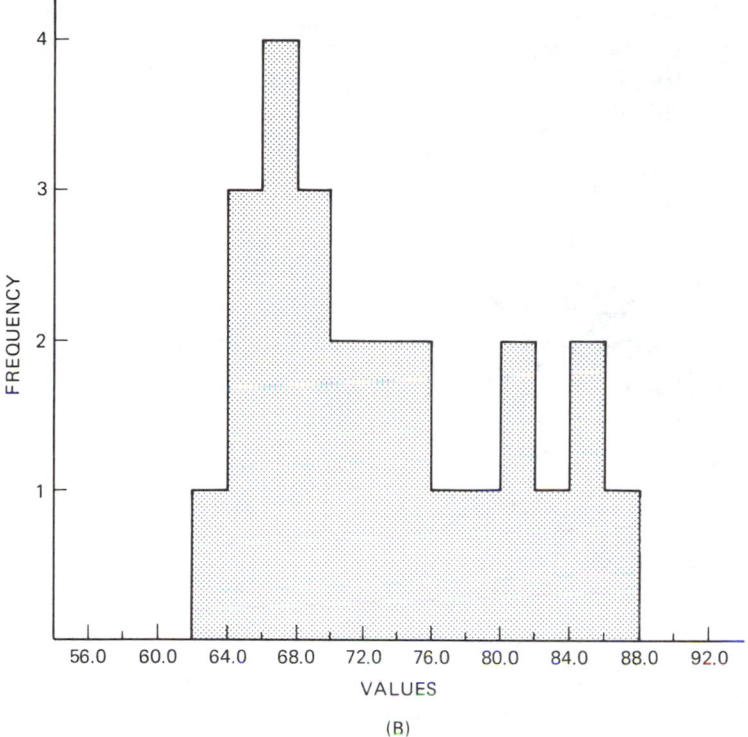

FIGURE 15-13 (b) Histogram for Example 15.4.3

corded and the moving ranges calculated. The averages for individuals and ranges were calculated as

$$\overline{\overline{X}} = \frac{1813}{25} = 72.52 \text{ seconds}$$

$$\overline{R} = \frac{53}{24} = 2.21 \text{ seconds}$$

These and the individual points are added to the control chart and shown in Figure 15–14. The control limits for ranges were calculated using the value for R calculated previously.

$$\text{UCL}R = (3.27)(2.21) = 7.23$$

$$\text{LCL}R = 0$$

When these are added to the control chart, as shown in Figure 15–15, all the values are within the limits. Again, the conclusion that we draw at this point is that the process is stable regarding the variability between times required to make an airplane reservation.

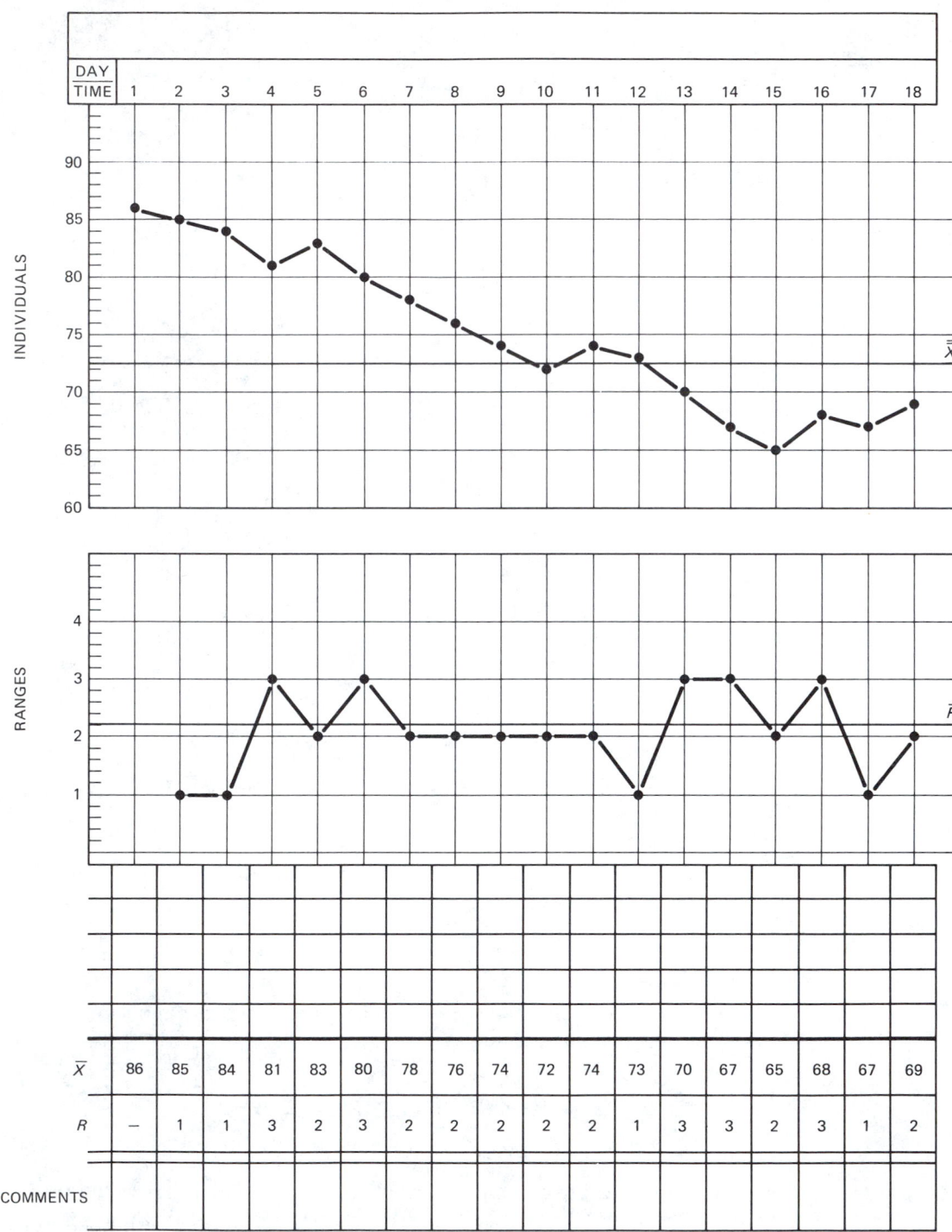

FIGURE 15–14 Initial Plot for Example 15.4.3

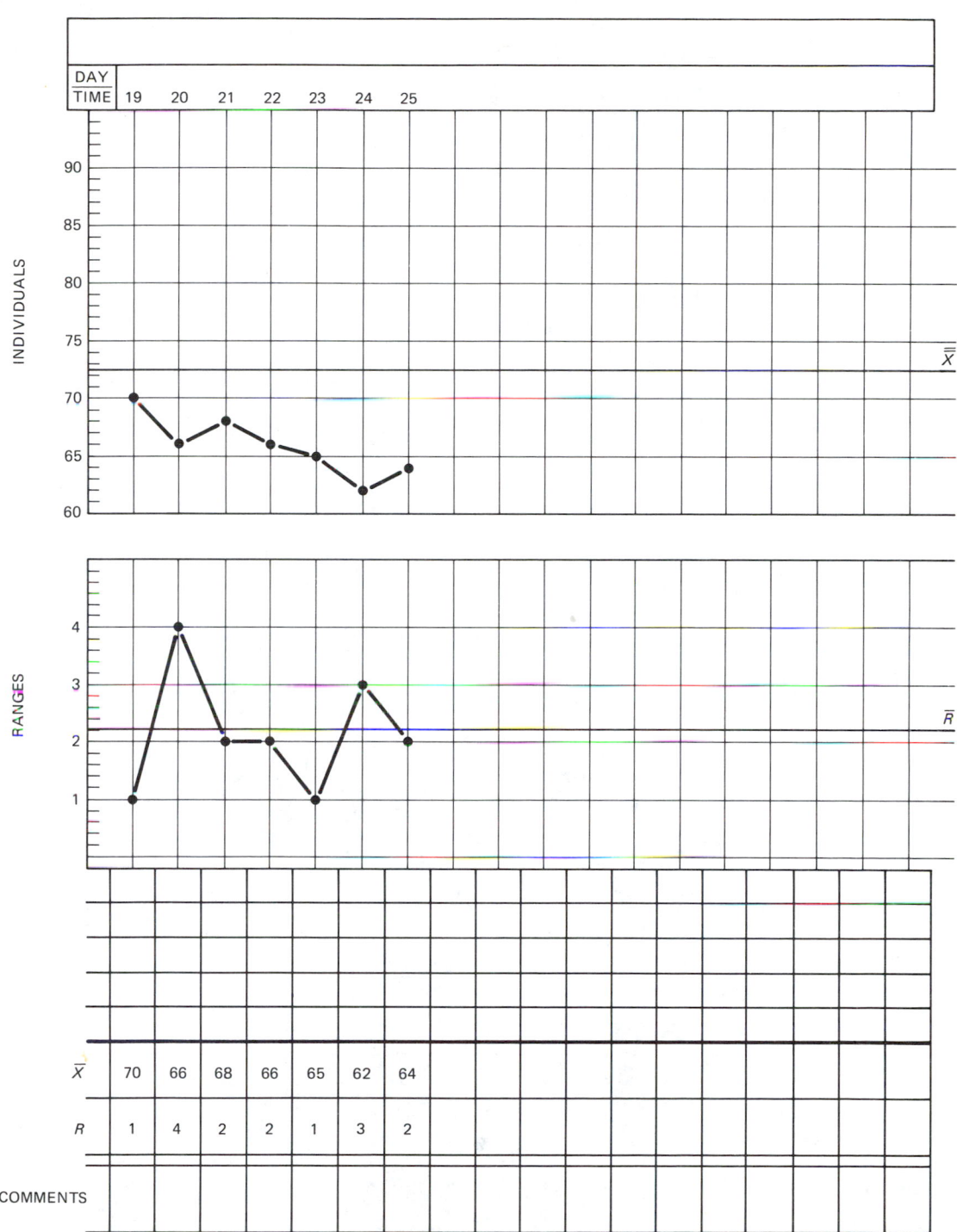

FIGURE 15–14 (*Continued*)

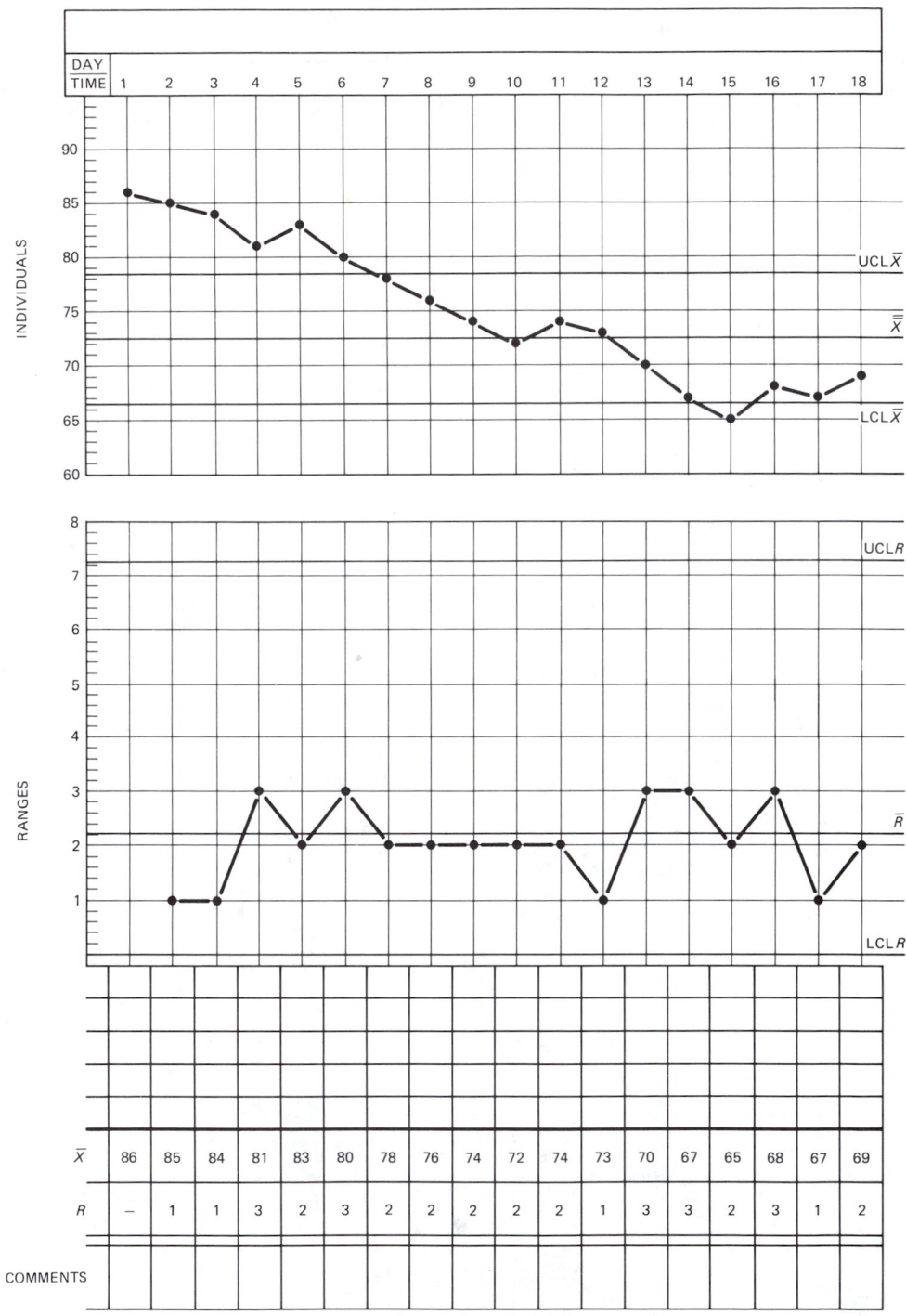

FIGURE 15–15 Initial Limits for Example 15.4.3

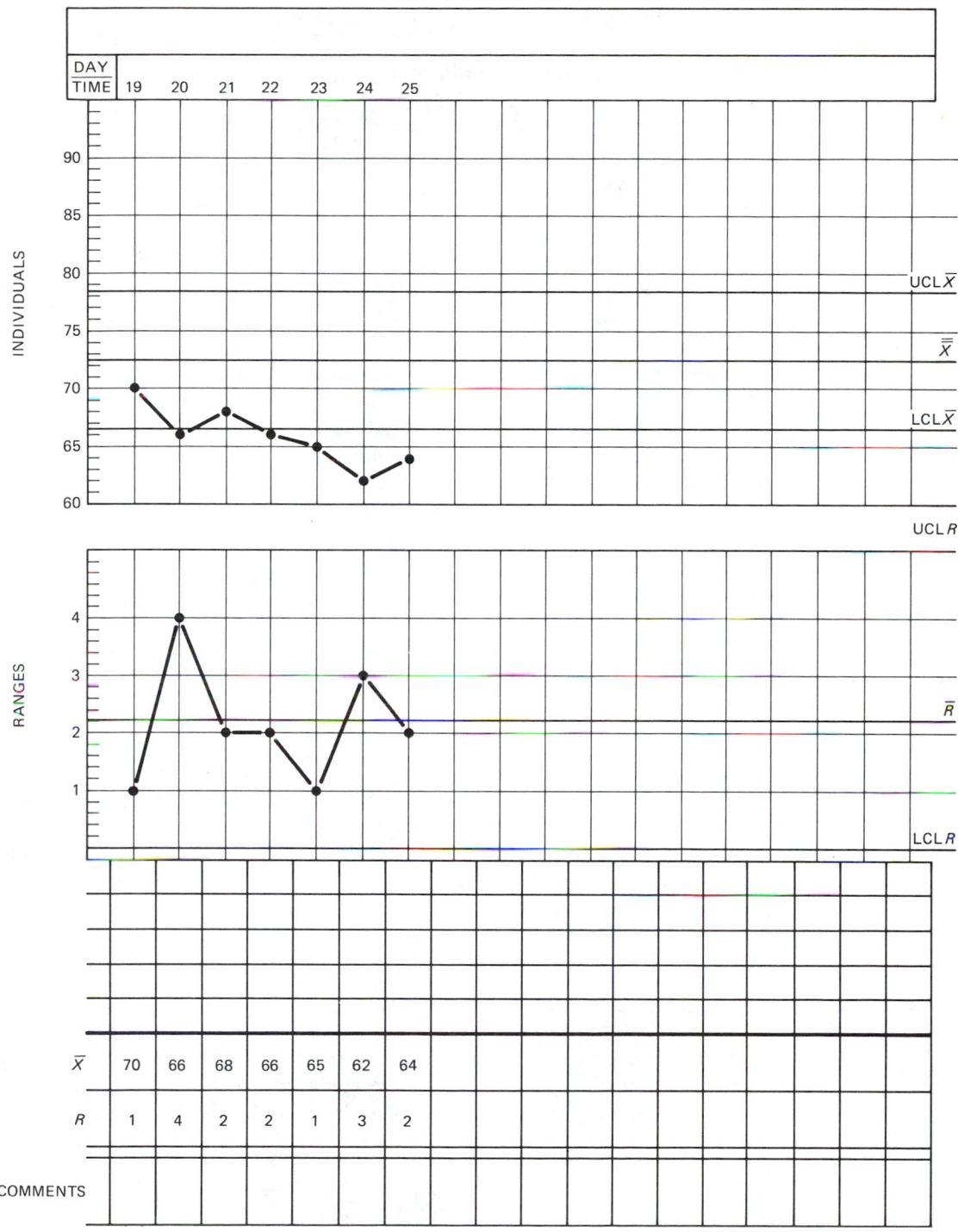

FIGURE 15-15 (*Continued*)

The limits for averages were then calculated.

$$UCLX = 72.52 + \frac{(3)(2.21)}{1.128} = 78.40$$

$$LCLX = 72.52 - \frac{(3)(2.21)}{1.128} = 66.64$$

When these are added to the control chart, as shown in Figure 15–16, it is discovered that not just one, not two, but nine of the 25 individual values do not fall within the limits. The process is not stable. There is a tremendous amount of variability that does not appear to be normal.

Further examination of the chart seems to indicate that there is an overall downward trend to the times required to book a reservation. It appears that the agent booking the flights *might* be getting faster. At this point, the only conclusion that we can draw is that we had better collect some additional data—continue to monitor this process. When so many points are out of control, something is happening that needs explaining. We need to investigate and determine what these special causes might be. It may indeed be true that the agent is getting better. Or there may be some other reason or set of reasons for the pattern that has emerged. Regardless, the chart has told us something about the process that we might not have otherwise noted. ■

15.5 CONCLUSION

The control charts for moving ranges and individuals show us what is happening to the process as time passes. Had we, in Example 15.4.3, merely used the histogram as a graphical description of the process, then we would have been less knowledge-able about the process and what was happening.

To reemphasize what we have been saying in the past few chapters, the control chart will help us to pinpoint when changes occur in our process. Control charts will not help us to identify the specific cause of the change. For that we must rely on our knowledge of the process.

EXERCISES

1. Prepare an individuals chart and a range chart for the data presented. The average times to failure for a missile guidance component were recorded as follows. The time is in hours. See Problem 1(a) in Chapter 12.

4.1	4.6	4.2	4.7	4.9	4.7	4.6	4.8
4.2	4.4	4.6	4.8	4.7	4.5	4.3	4.1
4.4	4.4	4.5	4.5	4.6	4.5	4.6	4.4
4.8	4.1	4.4	4.6	4.5	4.5	4.3	4.7
4.6	4.7	4.7	4.6	4.7	4.6	4.6	4.5
4.7	4.4	4.4	4.3	4.5	4.5	4.6	4.5

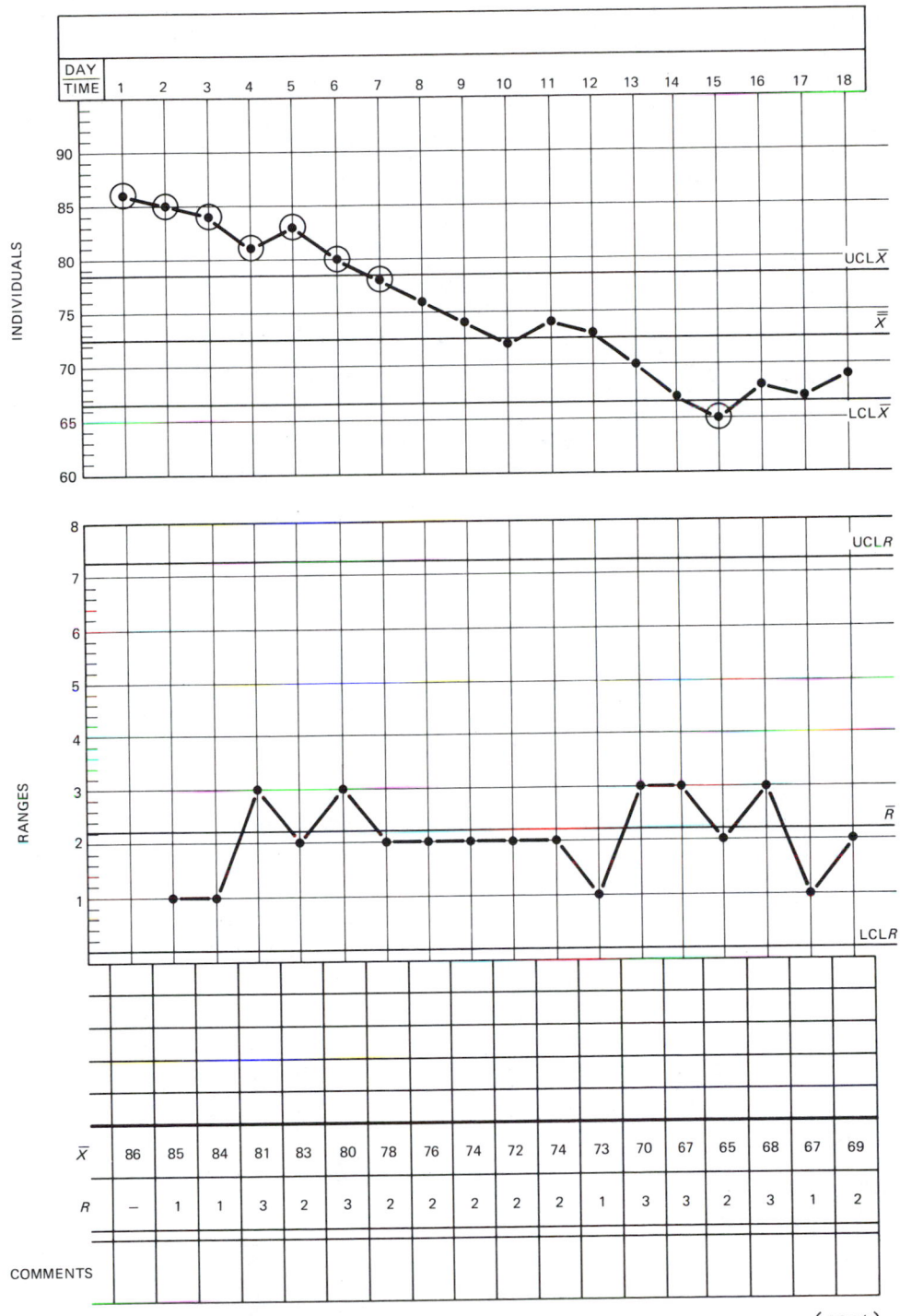

FIGURE 15-16 Revised Limits for Example 15.4.3

(cont.)

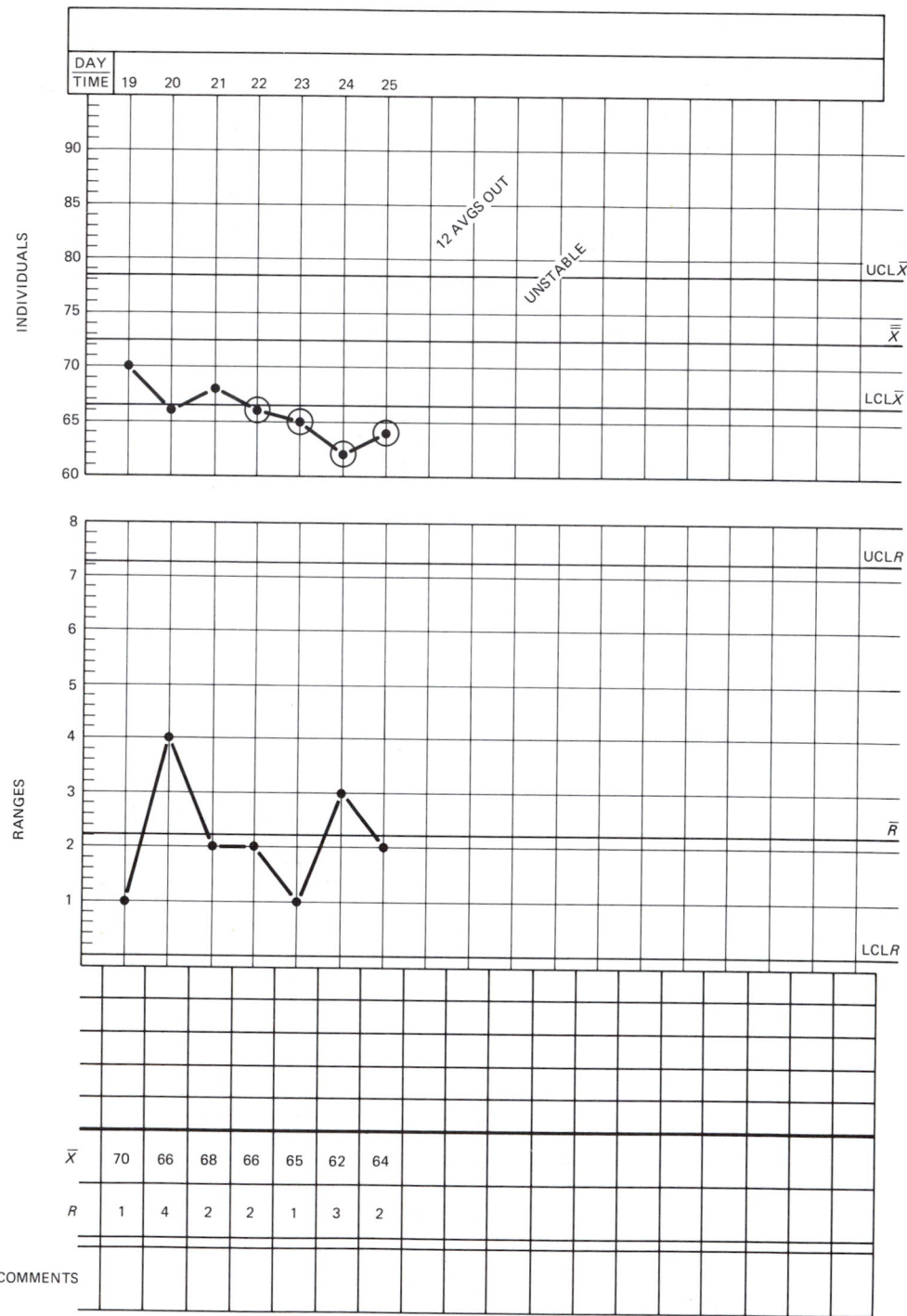

FIGURE 15-16 (*Continued*)

2. Prepare an individuals chart and a range chart for the data presented. The weather bureau collected the following barometric pressure each 2 hours for a period of 4 days. See Problem 1(b) in Chapter 12.

Time	Day			
	1	2	3	4
0100	29.95	30.01	29.95	29.91
0300	29.86	29.91	29.85	29.94
0500	29.94	30.00	29.65	30.08
0700	29.91	29.89	29.25	30.14
0900	30.00	30.04	28.95	30.18
1100	30.05	29.92	28.85	30.16
1300	30.08	30.02	28.65	30.10
1500	30.14	29.98	29.05	29.84
1700	30.10	29.89	29.18	29.88
1900	30.11	30.01	29.56	30.07
2100	30.02	30.00	30.04	29.94

3. Prepare an individuals chart and a range chart for the data presented. An SPC instructor collected the class grades as shown for a period of several terms. See Problem 1(c) in Chapter 12.

Term 1	Term 2	Term 3
88	74	77
84	78	78
91	82	79
77	86	80
86	90	77
85	88	78
70	92	79
78	82	80
94	72	77
66	62	72
85	52	82
82	77	81
70	87	80
74	91	79

Control Charts for Attributes

16.1   INTRODUCTION

Attributes, in the simplest definition, are characteristics that are counted rather than identified. Attributes may be the proportion of defects produced by a process, the number of defectives produced, the number of defects per unit, or the average number of defects per unit. Specifically, attributes may be the number of lab specimens failing a given test, the proportion of applicants passing a promotion exam, the number of defects on a bolt of cloth, the number of errors per accounting report, or the number of engineering change orders per week.

Control charts for attributes show the same information about the monitored process as the control charts for variables shows, that is, whether abnormal variation is present and, if it isn't, the limits of the normal variation.

The attributes charts are based on statistical probability distributions other than the normal curve. The specific distribution involved is not really important for our interests. For information purposes, though, the proportion defectives chart is based on the binomial distribution, while the defects per unit chart uses the Poisson distribution. What is important, though, is to remember that the control limits are three sigma control limits. *We expect to find virtually all the normal variation be-tween these limits.*

Although there are many different types of attributes charts, we will examine only two major ones in this chapter. We will look at the proportion defective chart and the closely related number of defectives chart, as well as the defects per unit chart. As in the preceding chapters, we will first present the method and then work through some example problems that illustrate the application of the specific methods.

16.2 PROPORTION DEFECTIVE CONTROL CHARTS

The first step in constructing a chart for proportion defective is to determine the characteristic to be monitored. As with the charts for ranges and averages, this is selected either as the result of a Pareto analysis, from a process flow analysis and discussions with the process's customers, or from a cause and effect diagram analysis.

After the characteristic is identified, the sampling scheme is determined. The guiding principle regarding number of samples to observe before setting limits will be whatever fits the process, whatever is reasonable. Generally, a minimum of 20 individual measurements should be recorded, although, as always, the more obser-vations the better the results will represent the process being monitored. The frequency of sampling is also considered at this point. It should fit the process and not overly interfere with the other work being performed by the operator, who should be the data collector. Again, the guiding word is reasonable. It is convenient for the samples to all be of the same size, but as long as they don't differ by too much, we are on safe ground. Generally, as long as the samples don't vary by more than 25 percent, we will not have problems. This is a check that we must make before proceeding any further. If there is more than a 25 percent difference, the method described next will not be appropriate.

Once the sampling scheme is developed, sufficient initial data should be col-lected to give meaningful results. Any and all unusual occurrences should be noted on the data-collection form. An example of a typical attribute chart and data-collection form is shown in Figure 16–1.

After the data have been collected, the initial calculations are performed. The proportion defective for each sample is the ratio of number of defectives to the number of values in each sample. Each sample proportion is designated with the symbol p.

The grand average is the average of the sample proportions defective. This is called p-bar.

Next, the sample of proportions defective is graphed or plotted on the appro-priate chart. Generally, the individual observations are connected with a solid line. This will help to show patterns later during analysis. The grand average, or average proportion defective, is drawn in to identify the location of the process.

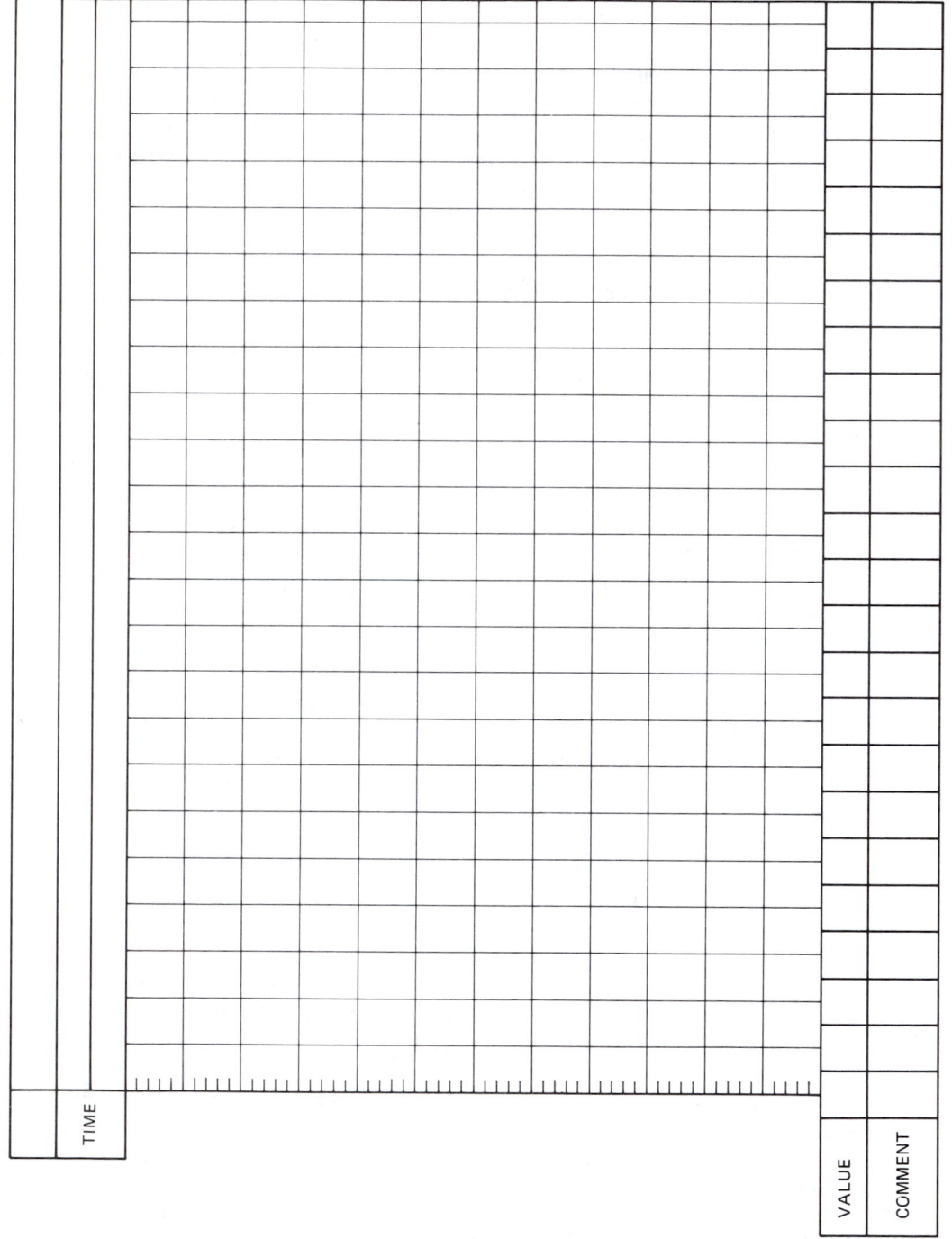

FIGURE 16-1 Typical Attributes Control Chart Form

At this point, the limits for proportion defective are calculated.

$$UCLP = \bar{p} + (3) \sqrt{\frac{(\bar{p})(1 - \bar{p})}{\bar{n}}}$$

$$LCLP = \bar{p} - (3) \sqrt{\frac{(\bar{p})(1 - \bar{p})}{\bar{n}}}$$

$\bar{n}$ is the average sample size.

After the limits for proportion defective have been calculated, they should be drawn on the chart. Each sample proportion defective should be checked to see if the values fall between the upper and lower control limits. If a sample value is not between the limits, then we should determine if there is an assignable or special cause for this abnormal variation. Often the notations made during the data-collection process will determine if there is a special reason. If there is a special cause for a sample being outside the limits and that cause has been eliminated, then that sample should be discarded.

If this is the case, then the average proportion defective must be recalculated. The sample proportions are then compared with the "new" limits, which are also drawn on the chart. If any of the remaining values of p is out of control, the process is repeated. If not, then a broken line is used to connect the points around the deleted point.

At this point the process is said to be in control. This means that only normal variation is present. A process must be in control before we can begin improving it. No mention has been made about whether or not material being produced conforms to specifications.

That is the procedure. The next section will look at some examples of the process.

One last point of emphasis, though. The process, once it is in control, generally will require a continuing monitoring. This should be done by the operator. As soon as abnormal variation occurs, the operator should first recognize it and, second, initiate action to remove it. Looking at the data after the fact, a day or week or even a month later, will not help to control the process. Chapter 17 will illustrate some of the common control chart interpretation techniques.

The number of defectives chart is very similar to the proportion defective chart. This chart differs only in the fact that it uses whole numbers instead of proportions to determine the limits. The average sample size multiplied times the p chart limits will give the limits for number of defects, or the np chart limits. These formulas are

$$UCLnp = \bar{n}\bar{p} + (3) \sqrt{\bar{n}\bar{p}(1 - \bar{p})}$$

$$LCLnp = \bar{n}\bar{p} - (3) \sqrt{\bar{n}\bar{p}(1 - \bar{p})}$$

16.3 EXAMPLES OF PROPORTION DEFECTIVE CONTROL CHARTS _____

This section includes three examples. The first two are p charts. The third is a modification of the second, in which control limits are calculated and shown as np values, rather than as just plain p charts.

Example 16.3.1 Each lawn mower that was produced at Aft Tech's Lawn Mower Division was checked to make sure that it would start before being shipped. Production was completely sampled each hour to determine the number of mowers that would not start. These data, for 25 hourly samples, are shown in Figure 16–2. The data have been collected on the typical attribute chart data-collection form.

   The sample proportion defective for each sample is calculated. This is shown in Figure 16–3. The average sample size is calculated. The sum of the 25 sample sizes is 2,503, making this average equal to 100.12. (The sample sizes are checked to make sure that they are all within approximately 25 percent of the average, or

	n	#	P
1	102	5	0.049
2	88	6	0.068
3	93	5	0.054
4	107	4	0.037
5	97	4	0.041
6	104	5	0.048
7	102	6	0.059
8	100	4	0.040
9	106	5	0.047
10	101	6	0.059
11	96	4	0.042
12	99	5	0.051
13	102	4	0.039
14	101	6	0.059
15	98	5	0.051
16	95	4	0.042
17	97	4	0.041
18	107	3	0.028
19	105	8	0.076
20	102	6	0.059
21	99	5	0.051
22	100	6	0.060
23	101	4	0.040
24	100	6	0.060
25	101	5	0.050
Σ	2503		1.192
Ave.	100.12		0.048

FIGURE 16–2 Data for Example 16.3.1

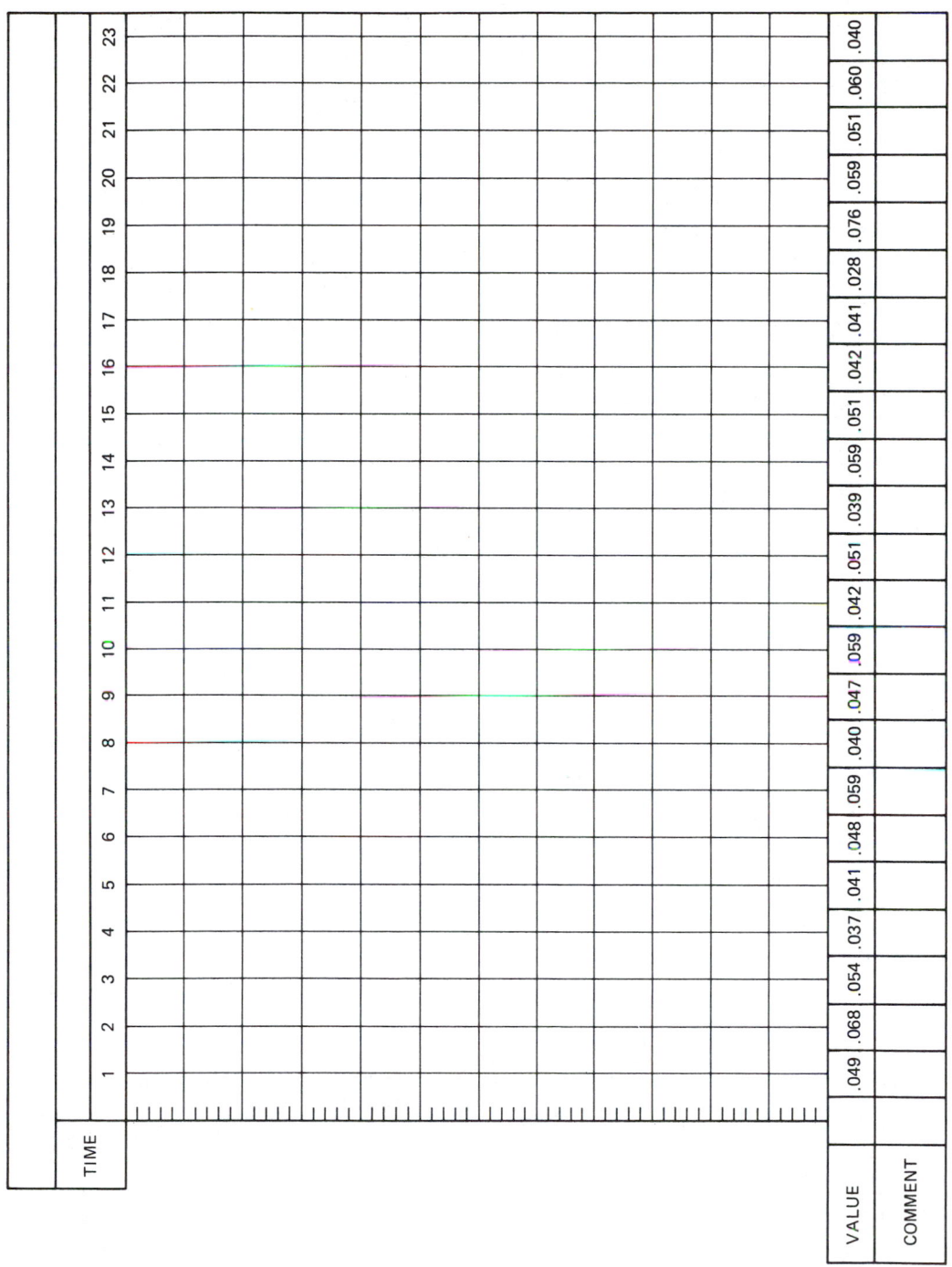

FIGURE 16–3 Initial Calculation for Example 16.3.1 (cont.)

FIGURE 16-3 (Continued)

TIME

24 25

VALUE .060 .050

COMMENT

approximately between 75 and 125.) Since they all are, the average proportion defective is then calculated. This is

$$\bar{p} = \frac{1.192}{25} = 0.048$$

The average proportion defective, along with the individual values of p, is plotted on the chart shown in Figure 16–4. The control limits for sample proportion defective are then calculated.

$$UCLP = 0.048 + (3) \sqrt{\frac{(0.048)(0.952)}{100.12}} = + 0.112$$

$$LCLP = 0.048 - (3) \sqrt{\frac{(0.048)(0.952)}{100.12}} = 0.000$$

The lower limit is negative, which is impossible. Whenever this occurs, the value is truncated at 0. It is not realistic to expect to have material that has less than 0 percent defective. Similarly, it is also impossible to have material that is worse than 100 percent defective.

The limits, 0.109 and 0, then added to the control chart as shown in Figure 16–5. As can be seen, all the sample values fall between the limits. This means that, at the time these initial data were collected, only normal variation was present in the process. It is now time to begin improving the process. The average percentage defective, 4.8 percent, may be too high, but it reflects the nature of this stable process. ∎

Example 16.3.2 The quality button manufacturing firm was producing buttons for a new promotional campaign. Every hour 250 buttons were sampled to determine the nature of the process. These data, as recorded on a p chart form, are shown in Figure 16–6. The sample proportion defective is calculated and shown on the form in Figure 16–7. The average sample size in this example is the constant sample size of 250. The average proportion defective is calculated:

$$\bar{p} = \frac{0.116}{20} = 0.0058$$

This, along with all the individual points, is drawn on the control chart in Figure 16–8. The control limits are then calculated, using the sample average proportion defective of 0.0058 and the constant sample size of 250.

$$UCLP = 0.0058 + (3) \sqrt{\frac{(0.0058)(0.9942)}{250}} = + 0.0202$$

$$LCLP = 0.0058 - (3) \sqrt{\frac{(0.0058)(0.9942)}{250}} = 0.0000$$

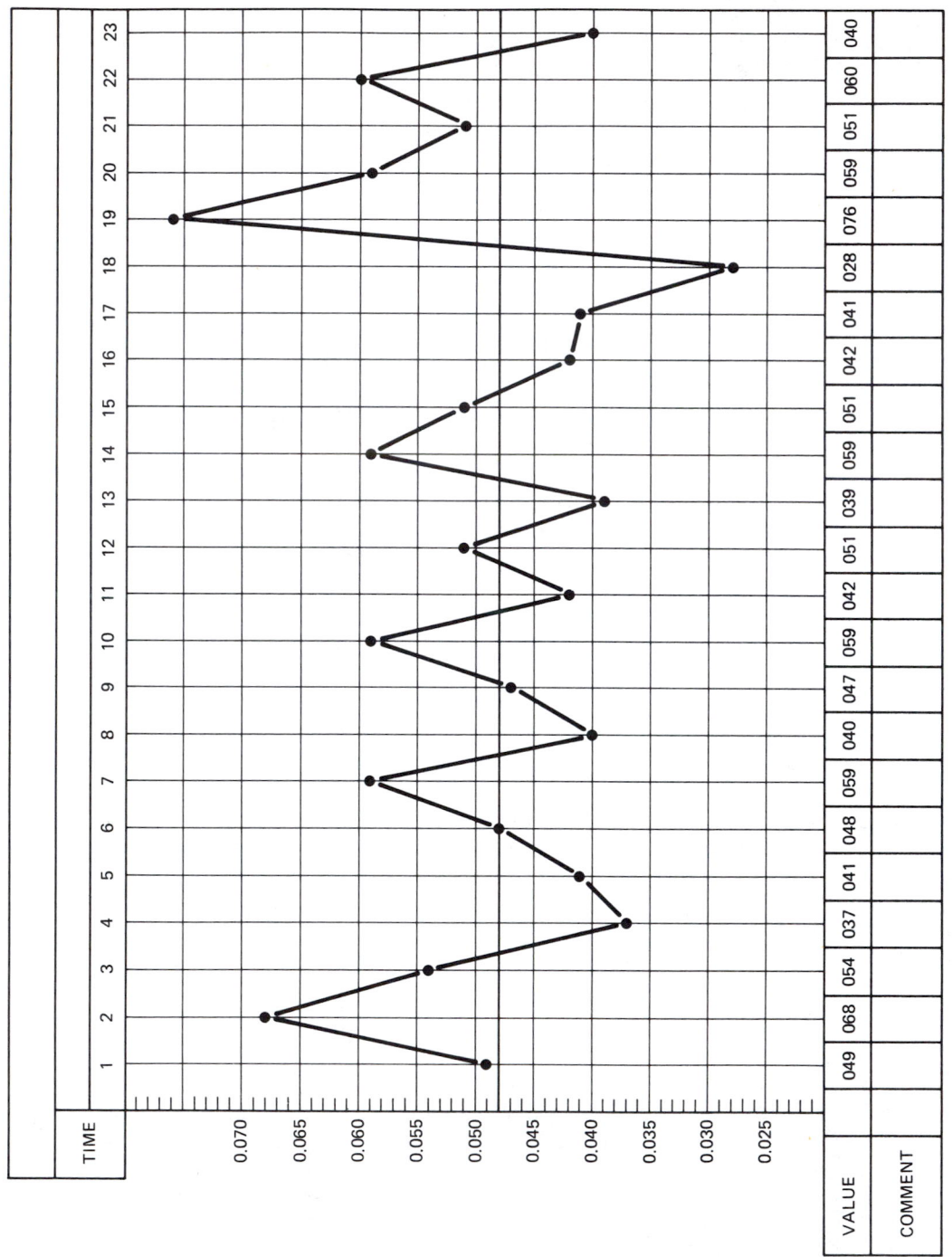

FIGURE 16-4 Initial Plot for Example 16.3.1

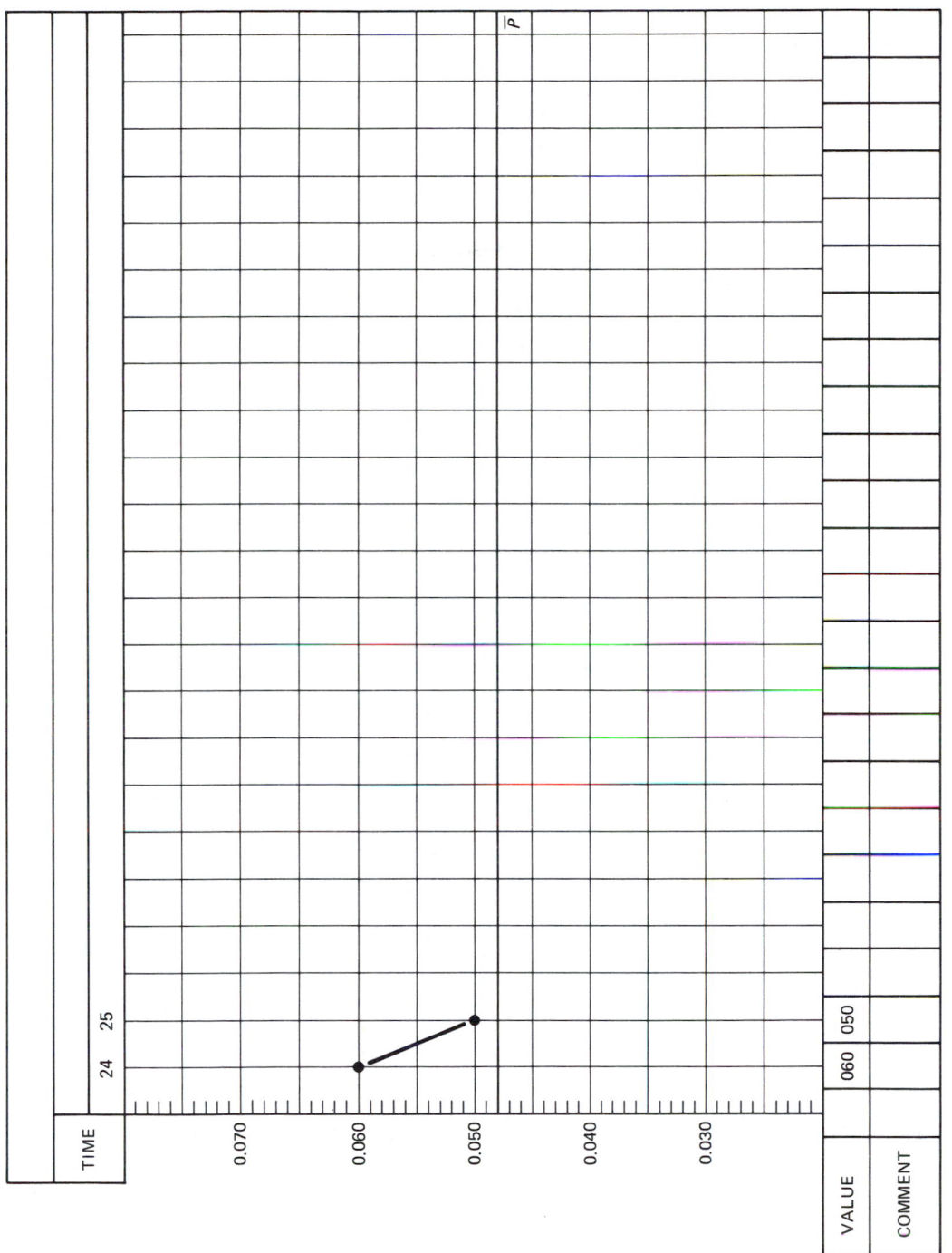

FIGURE 16-4 (Continued)

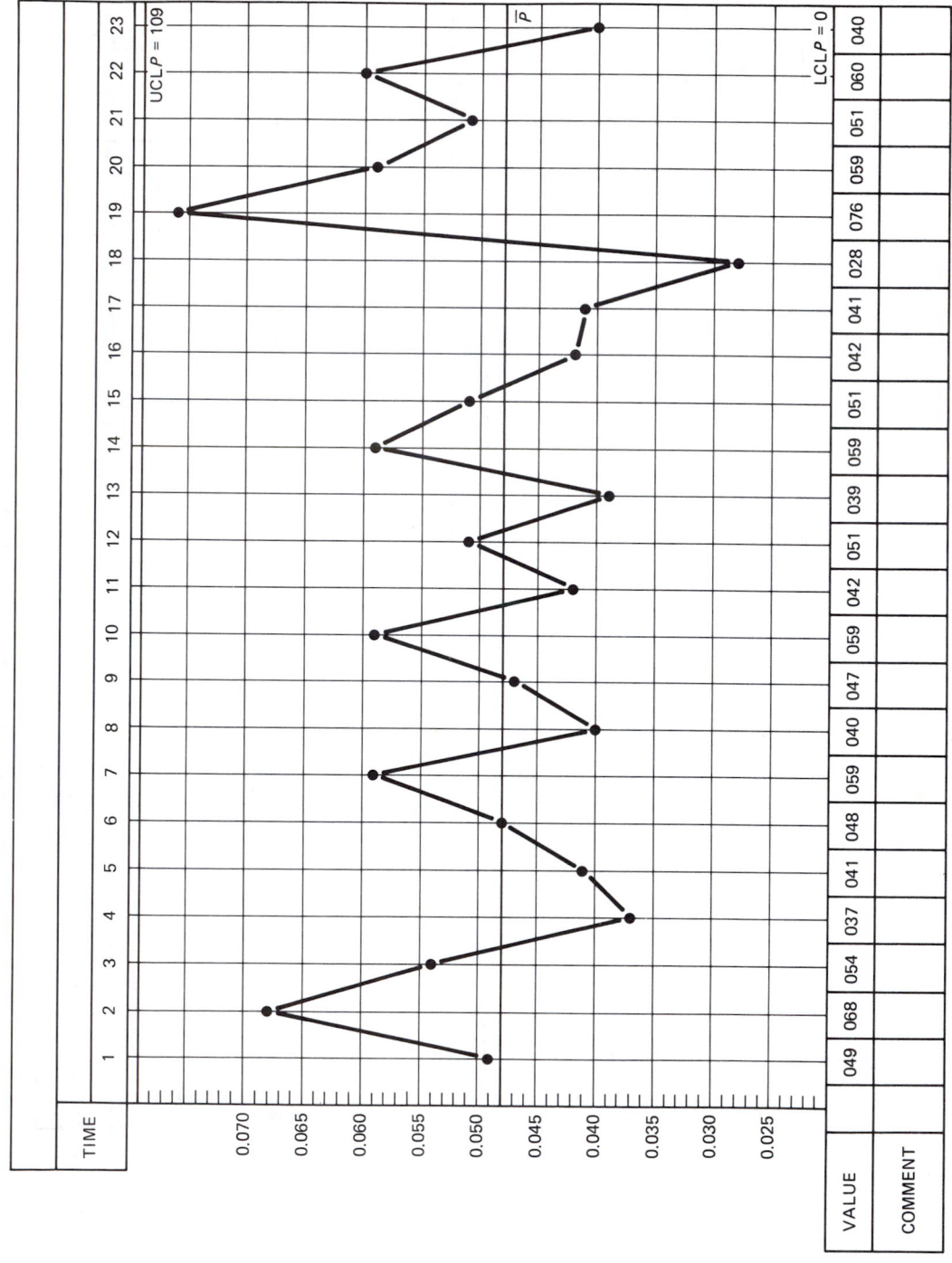

FIGURE 16-5 Initial Limits for Example 16.3.1

254

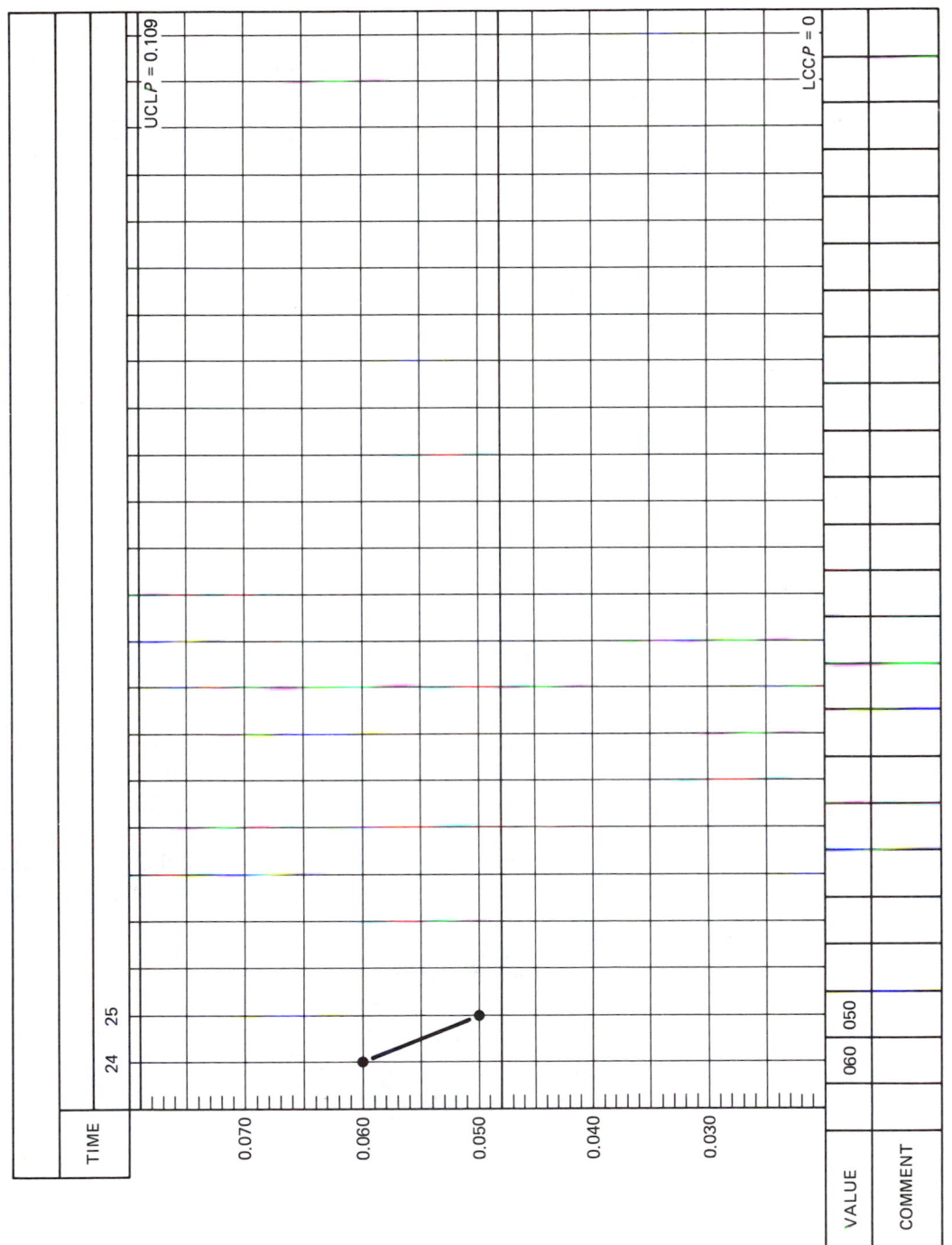

FIGURE 16-5 (Continued)

Sample No.	Sample Size	No. Defects	Proportion
1	250	1	.004
2	250	2	.008
3	250	2	.008
4	250	3	.012
5	250	0	0
6	250	2	.008
7	250	1	.004
8	250	2	.008
9	250	0	0
10	250	1	.004
11	250	0	0
12	250	0	0
13	250	1	.004
14	250	3	.012
15	250	2	.008
16	250	5	.020
17	250	2	.008
18	250	1	.004
19	250	0	0
20	250	1	.004

FIGURE 16–6   Data for Example 16.3.2

The lower limit was again truncated at 0. We cannot have fewer than 0 percent defective. These values are added to the control chart. Upon examining Figure 16-9, we see that all the sample values fall within the limits. At this point, we can say that the process is stable, only normal variation is present, and we are ready to begin improving the process. We would expect to find virtually all the samples to have between 0 and 2.02 percent defective buttons. ■

Example 16.3.3 Use the data from the preceding example to calculate control limits for number of defectives. As presented earlier, the control limits for this type of chart are calculated with the following formulas:

$$\text{UCL}np = \bar{n}\bar{p} + (3)\sqrt{\bar{n}\bar{p}(1 - \bar{p})}$$

$$\text{LCL}np = n\bar{p} + (3)\sqrt{\bar{n}\bar{p}(1 - \bar{p})}$$

For the data in Example 16.3.2, we calculated $\bar{p}$ to be equal to 0.0058 and $\bar{n}$ to be 250. The actual control limits are calculated as

$$\text{UCL}np = (250)(0.0058) + (3)\sqrt{(250)(0.0058)(0.9942)}$$

$$= 5.05$$

$$\text{LCL}np = (250)(0.0058) - (3)\sqrt{(250)(0.0058)(0.9942)}$$

$$= 0.00$$

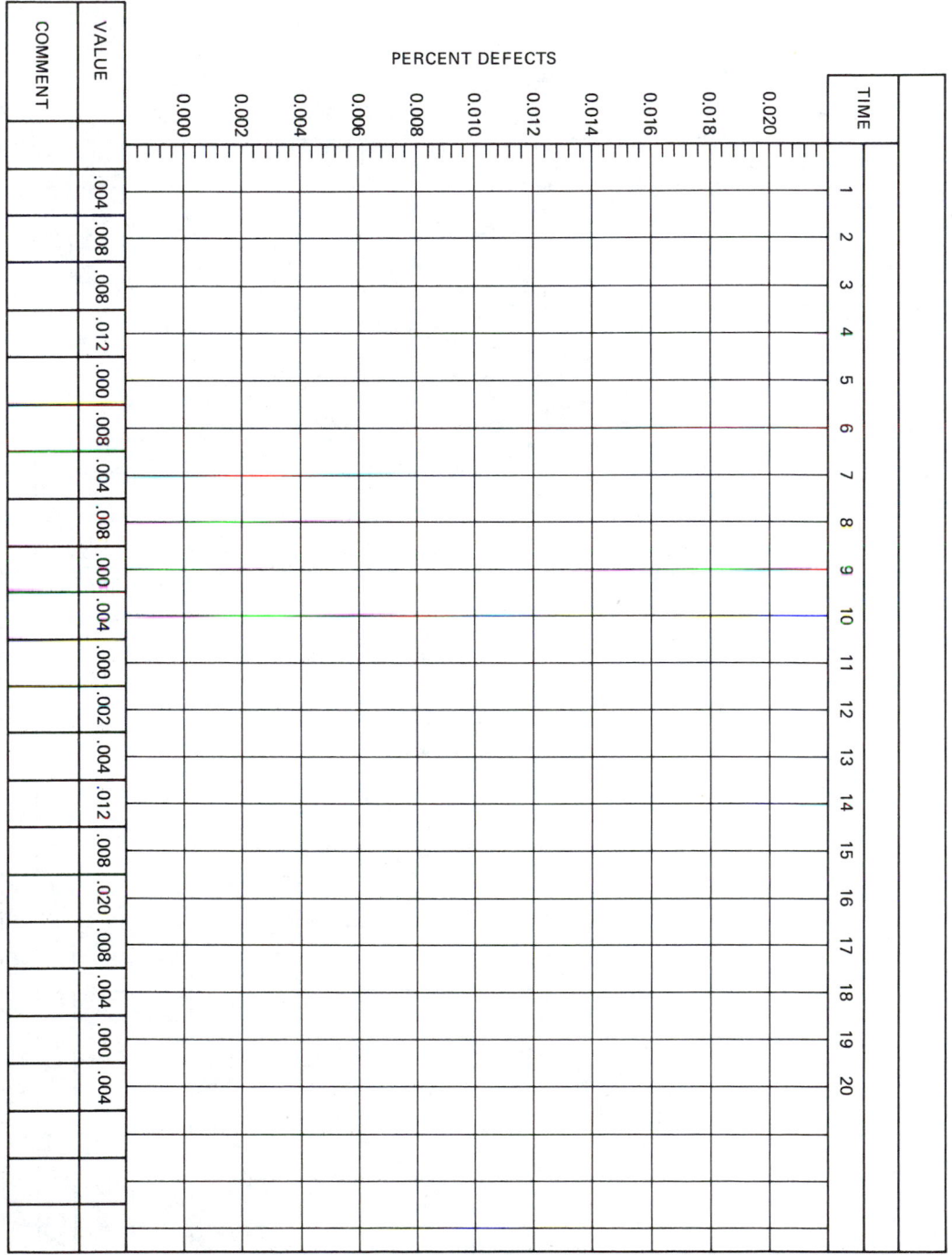

FIGURE 16-7 Initial Calculation for Example 16.3.2

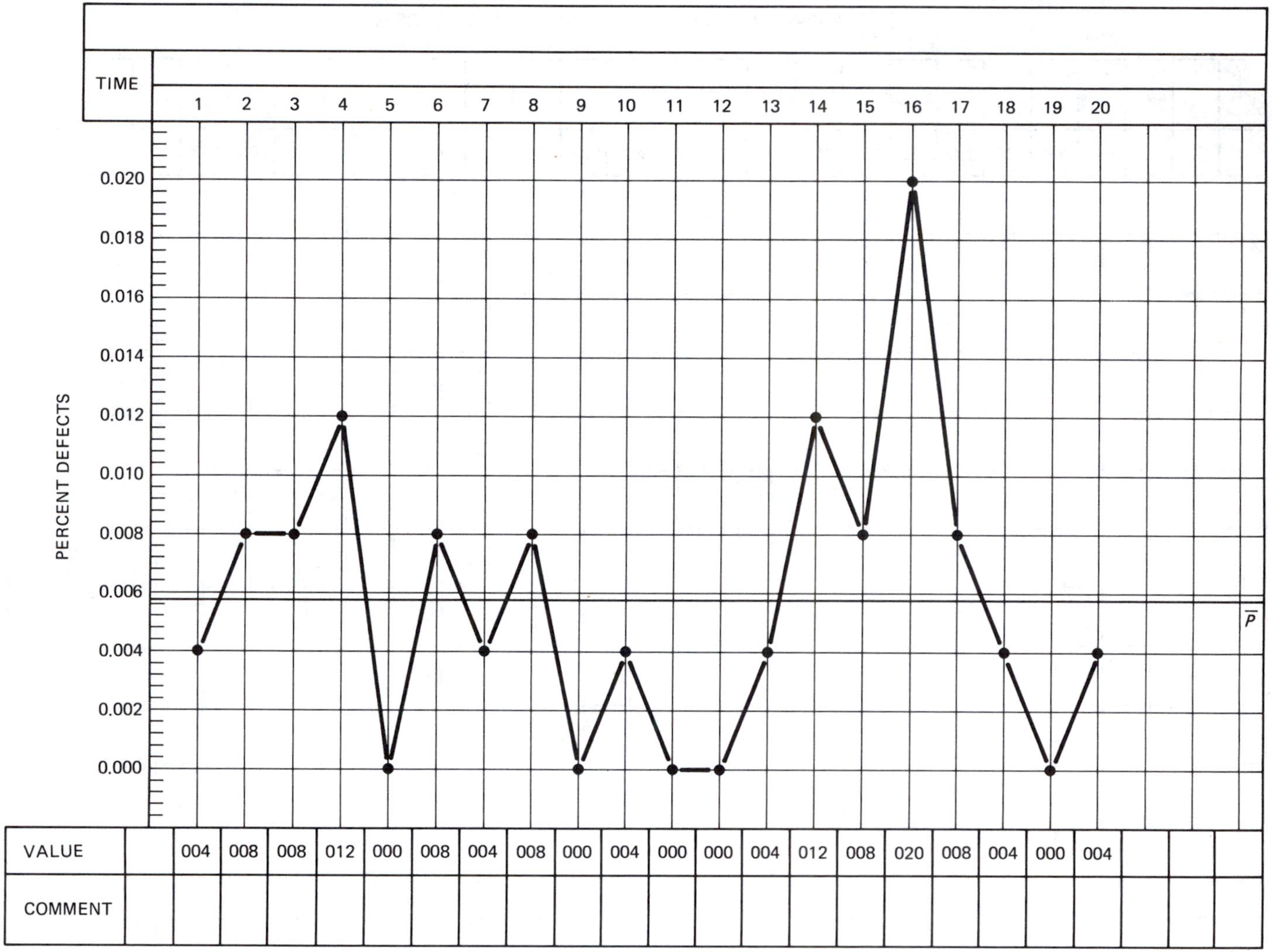

FIGURE 16–8 Initial Plot for Example 16.3.2

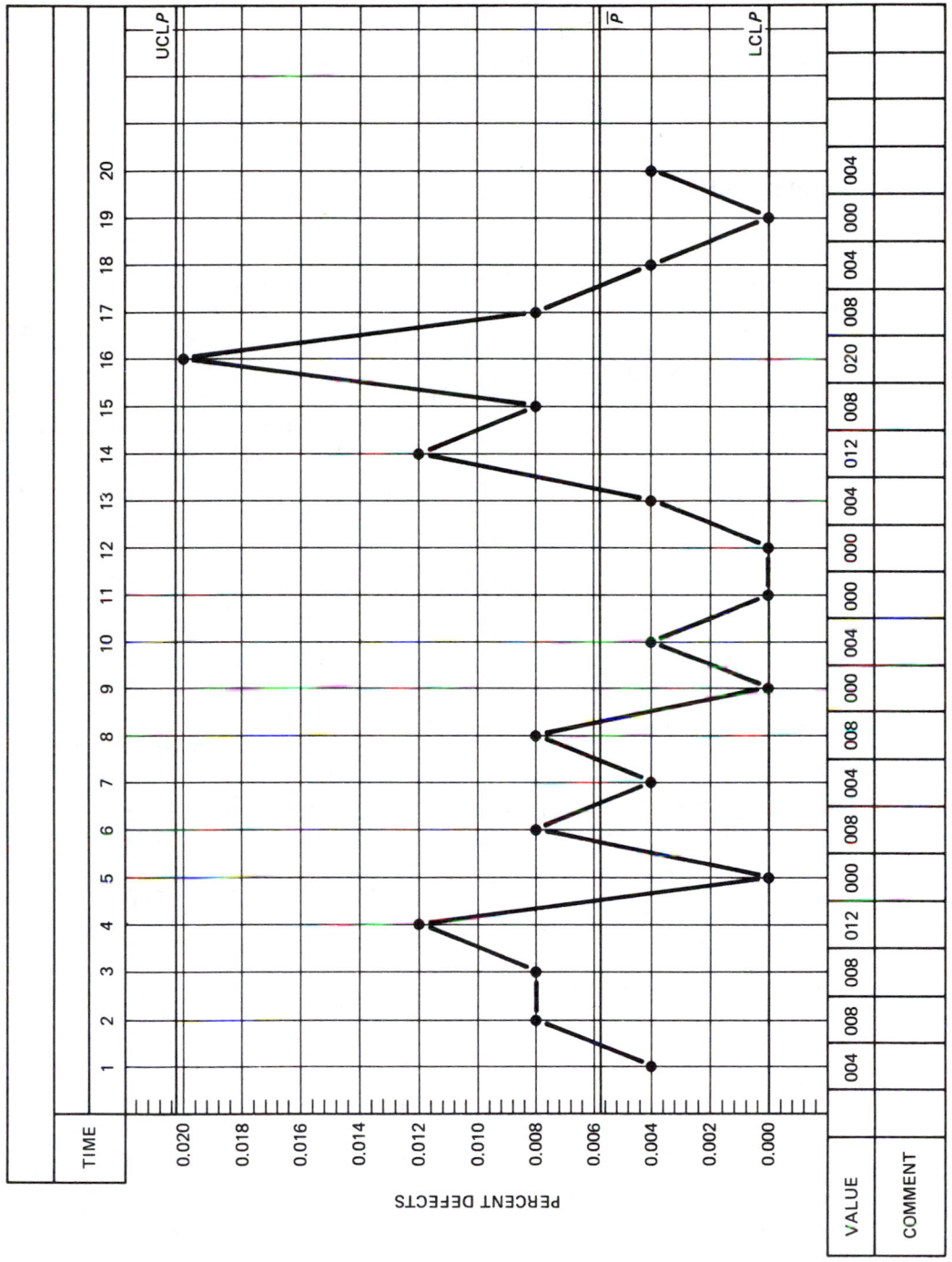

FIGURE 16–9 Initial Limits for Example 16.3.2

We would expect to find between 0 and 5.05 defectives in each sample of 250. This is exactly the same information that the p chart showed, except that we are expressing the limits as numbers of defectives rather than a percentage or proportion of defectives. ∎

16.4 DEFECTS PER UNIT DEFECTIVE CONTROL CHARTS

The first step in constructing a chart for defects per unit is to determine the characteristic to be monitored. As with the charts for ranges and averages and proportion defective, this is selected either as the result of a Pareto analysis, from a process flow analysis and discussions with the process's customers, or from a cause and effect diagram analysis.

After the characteristic is identified, the sampling scheme is determined. The guiding principle regarding the number of samples to observe before setting limits will be whatever fits the process, whatever is reasonable. Generally, a minimum of 20 individual measurements should be recorded, although, as always, the more observations the better the results will represent the process being monitored. The frequency of sampling is also considered at this point. It should fit the process and not overly interfere with the other work being performed by the operator, who should be the data collector. Again, the guiding word is reasonable.

Once the sampling scheme is developed, sufficient initial data should be collected to give meaningful results. Any and all unusual occurrences should be noted on the data-collection form. An example of a typical attribute chart and data-collection form is shown in Figure 16–1.

After the data have been collected, the initial calculations are performed. The number of defects per unit is the actual count of defects found on each individual item sampled. Each sample measurement is designated with the symbol c.

The grand average is the average of the sample defects per unit. This is called c-bar.

Next, the defects per unit are graphed or plotted on the appropriate chart. Generally, the individual observations are connected with a solid line. This will help to show patterns later during analysis. The grand average, or average number of defects per unit, is drawn in to identify the location of the process.

At this point, the limits for defects per unit are calculated.

$$UCLC = \bar{c} + 3\sqrt{\bar{c}}$$
$$LCLC = \bar{c} - 3\sqrt{\bar{c}}$$

After the limits for defects per unit have been calculated, they should be drawn on the chart. Each sample should be checked to see if the values fall between the upper and lower control limits. If a sample value is not between the limits, then we should determine if there is an assignable or special cause for this abnormal variation. Often the notations made during the data-collection process will determine if there is a special reason. If there is a special cause for a sample being outside the limits, then that sample should be discarded.

If this is the case, then the average number of defects per unit must be recalculated. The sample values are then compared with the "new" limits, which are also drawn on the chart. If any of the remaining values of c is out of control, the process is repeated. If not, then a broken line is used to connect the points around the deleted point. It is important to remember that by throwing out data we are not bringing the process into control. Only by eliminating the actual special causes of variation do we bring the process into control.

At this point, the process is said to be in control. This means that only normal variation is present. A process must be in control before we can begin improving it. No mention has been made about whether or not material being produced conforms to specifications.

That is the procedure. Section 16.5 will look at some examples of the process.

One last point of emphasis, though. The process, once it is in control, generally will require continuing monitoring. This should be done by the operator. As soon as abnormal variation occurs, the operator should first recognize it and, second, initiate action to remove it. Looking at the data after the fact, a day or week or even a month later, will not help to control the process. Chapter 17 will illustrate some of the common control chart interpretation techniques.

16.5 EXAMPLES OF DEFECTS PER UNIT CONTROL CHARTS

This section contains two examples showing the application of the c chart methods explained in Section 16.4.

Example 16.5.1 Aft Tech's television manufacturing subsidiary, known as After Vision, was interested in determining how stable its production was on a new model that was set to be introduced. They pulled 20 sets off the end of the line and had the chief technician count the number of defects on each set. These were recorded on an attribute chart as shown in Figure 16–10. The averages of these numbers of defects per unit is calculated:

$$\bar{c} = \frac{274}{20} = 13.7$$

The average and the individual points are plotted on the chart as shown in Figure 16–11. The control limits are then calculated:

$$UCLC = 13.7 + (3) \sqrt{13.7} = 24.8$$
$$LCLC = 13.7 - (3) \sqrt{13.7} = 2.6$$

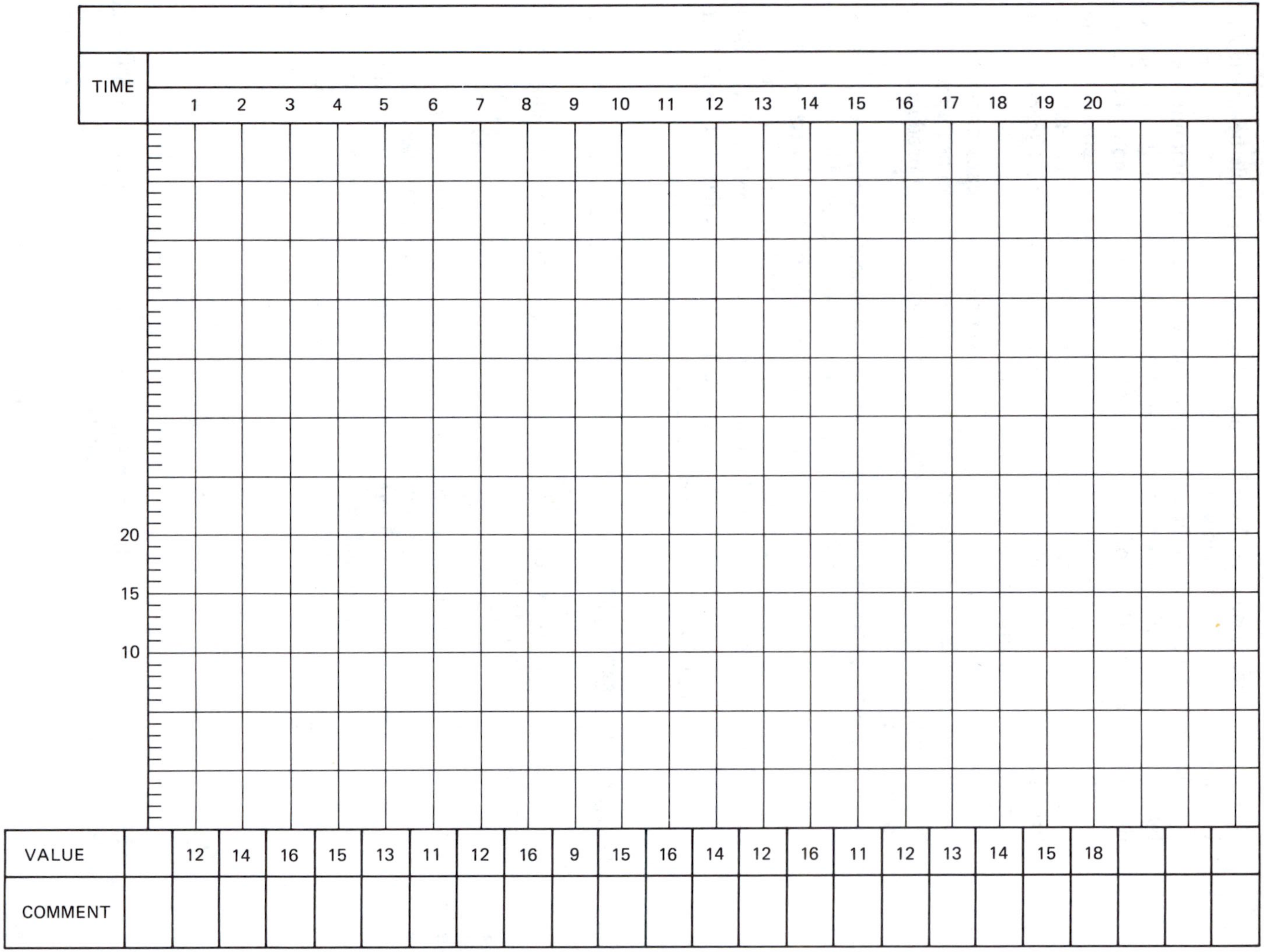

FIGURE 16–10 Data for Example 16.5.1

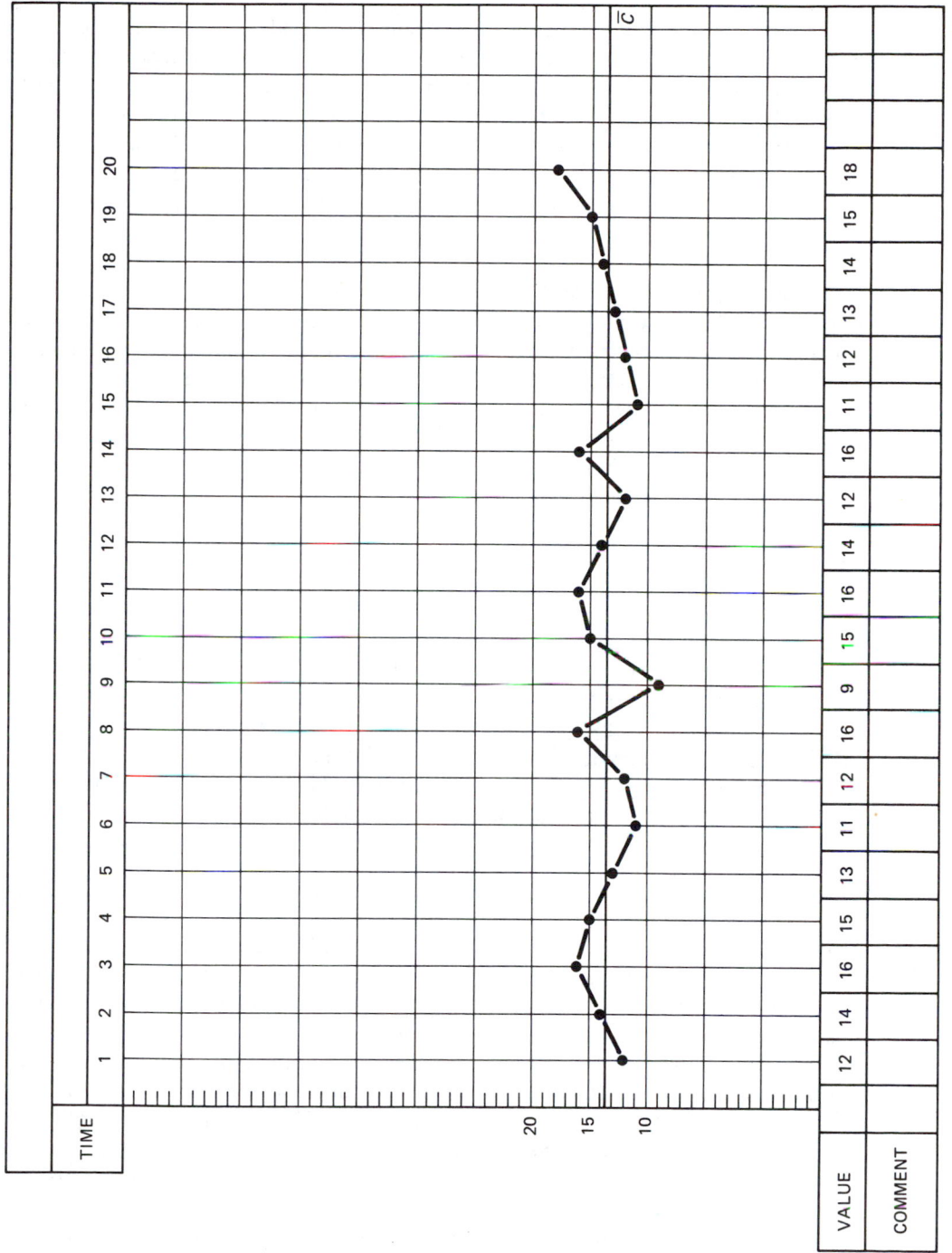

FIGURE 16–11 Initial Plot for Example 16.5.1

Although these limits are expressed as decimals, it really means that when normal variation is present we would expect to find between 3 and 25 defects per unit. When these are added to the chart in Figure 16–12, it is noted that all the values fall between the limits. Once again we note that the process is stable, only normal variation is present, and it is now time to start the improvement process. We would expect to find as many as 24.8 or as few as 2.6 defects on each television set produced by After Vision. This may or may not be acceptable, but it is descriptive of the process as it now exists. ∎

Example 16.5.2 The operations manager at After Vision was not pleased with the performance of the new television sets. She decided that the process had to be improved and invested a large sum in modernizing production methods. After the changes were made, additional data were collected, as shown in Figure 16–13. The average number of defects now found in the new television sets was reduced to 182/25 or 7.3 defects per unit. This, along with the individual points, is added to the chart and shown as Figure 16–14.

The control limits are

$$UCLC = 7.3 + (3) \sqrt{7.3} = 15.3$$
$$LCLC = 7.3 - (3) \sqrt{7.3} = -.8 = 0$$

After truncating the lower limit, because we can't have fewer than 0 defects on a unit, we note that we would expect to find between 15.3 and 0 defects on each set produced. These limits are drawn on the chart for a completed control chart (Figure 16–15). Comparing this to Figure 16–12 shows that the process has improved. At least now we are capable of producing material that is perfect. Prior to the process modification we were not even capable of that. The process may still not be good enough, but we can state that the process is stable. ∎

16.6 CONCLUSION

The control charts for attributes show us what is happening to the process as time passes. Had we merely used the histogram as a graphical description of the process, or calculated simple descriptive statistics, then we would have been less knowledgeable about the process and what was happening.

This chapter did not attempt to illustrate all the attributes charts. The many fine statistical quality control books presented in the reference list earlier in the text provide an ample selection for finding the particular limits that you might need.

To reemphasize what we have been saying in the past few chapters, the control chart will show us the variation normally found in our process and help us to pinpoint when changes occur in our process. Control charts will not help us to identify the specific cause of the change. For that we must rely on our knowledge of the process.

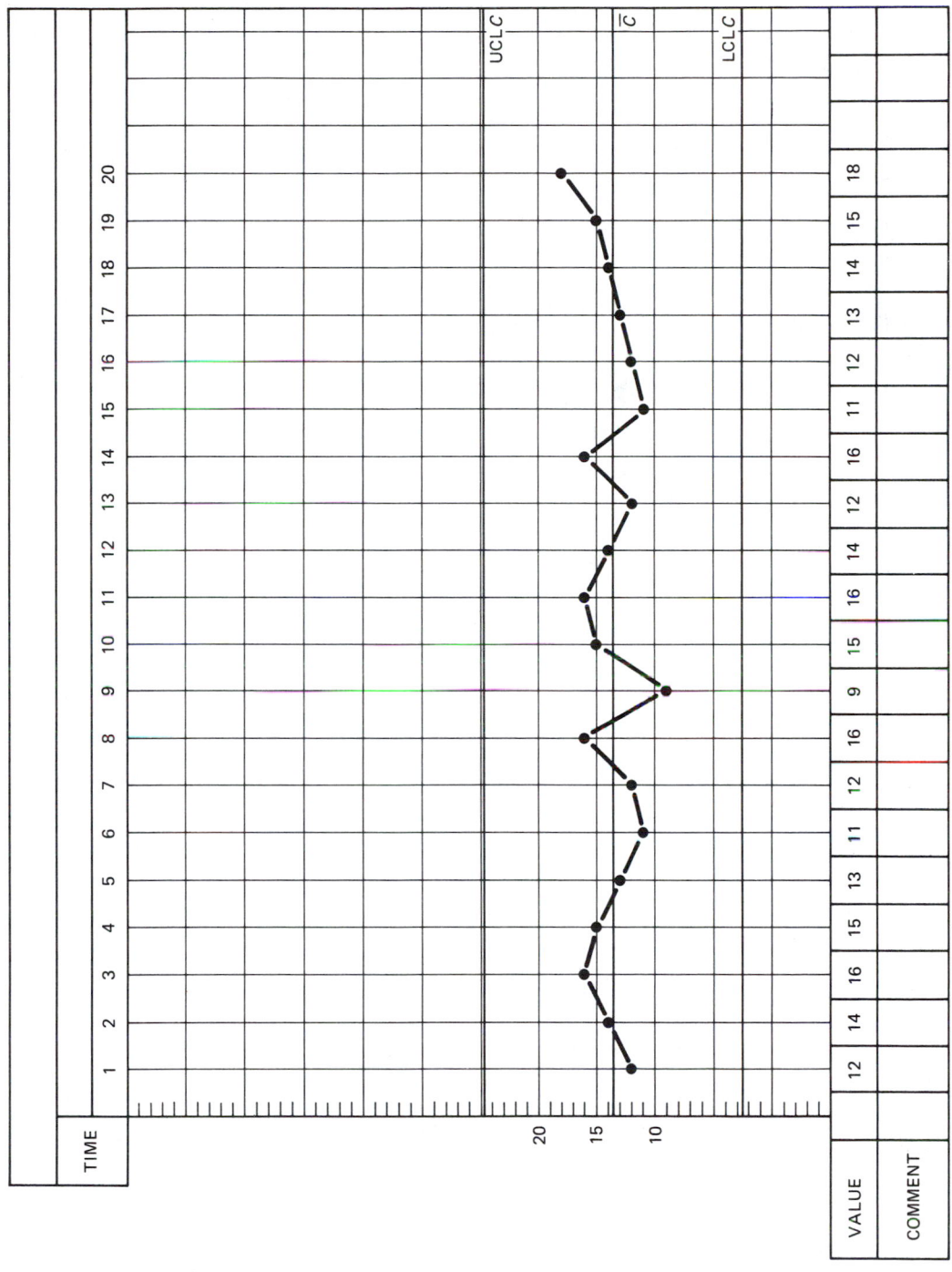

FIGURE 16–12 Initial Limits for Example 16.5.1

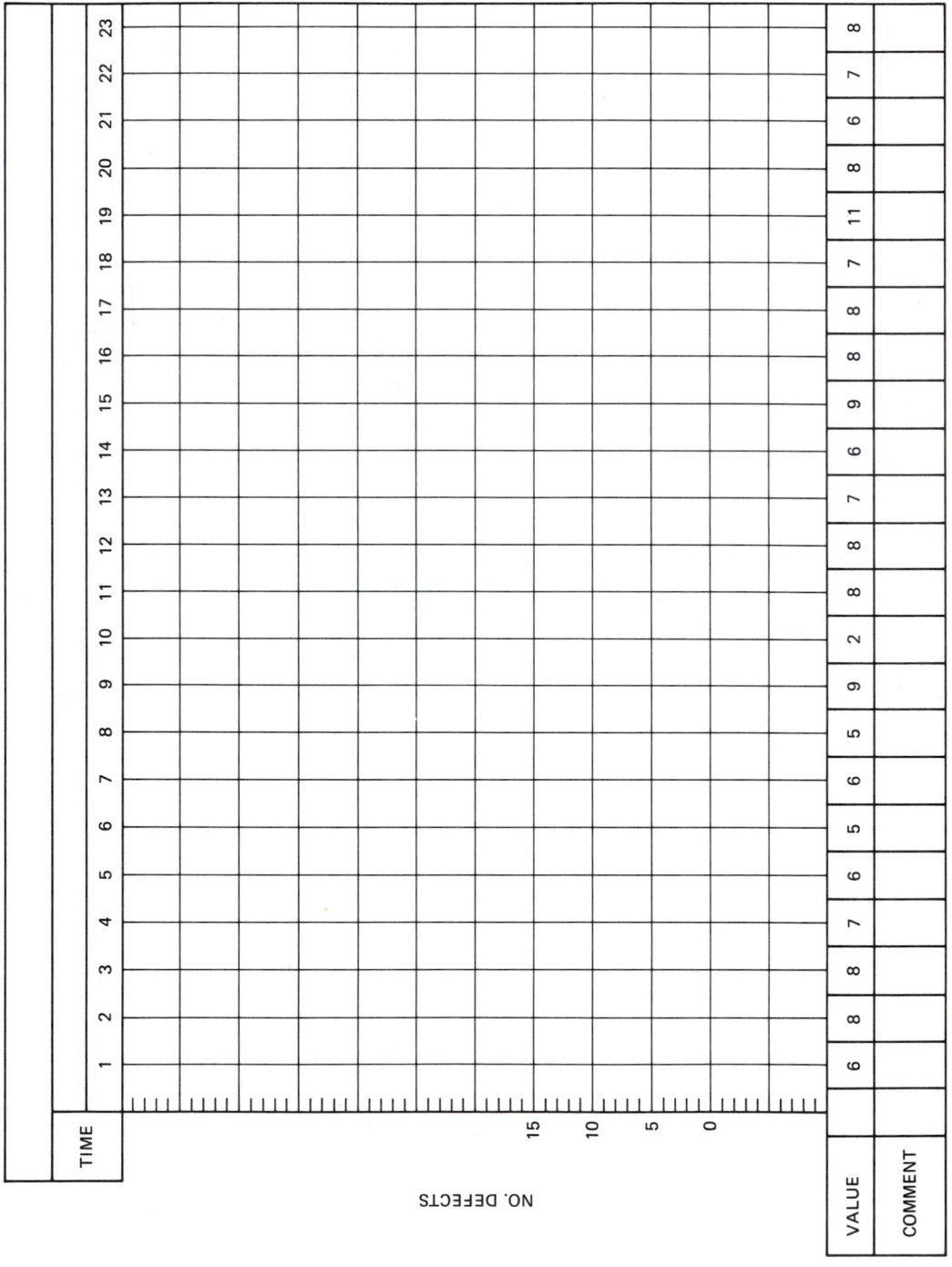

FIGURE 16–13 Data for Example 16.5.2

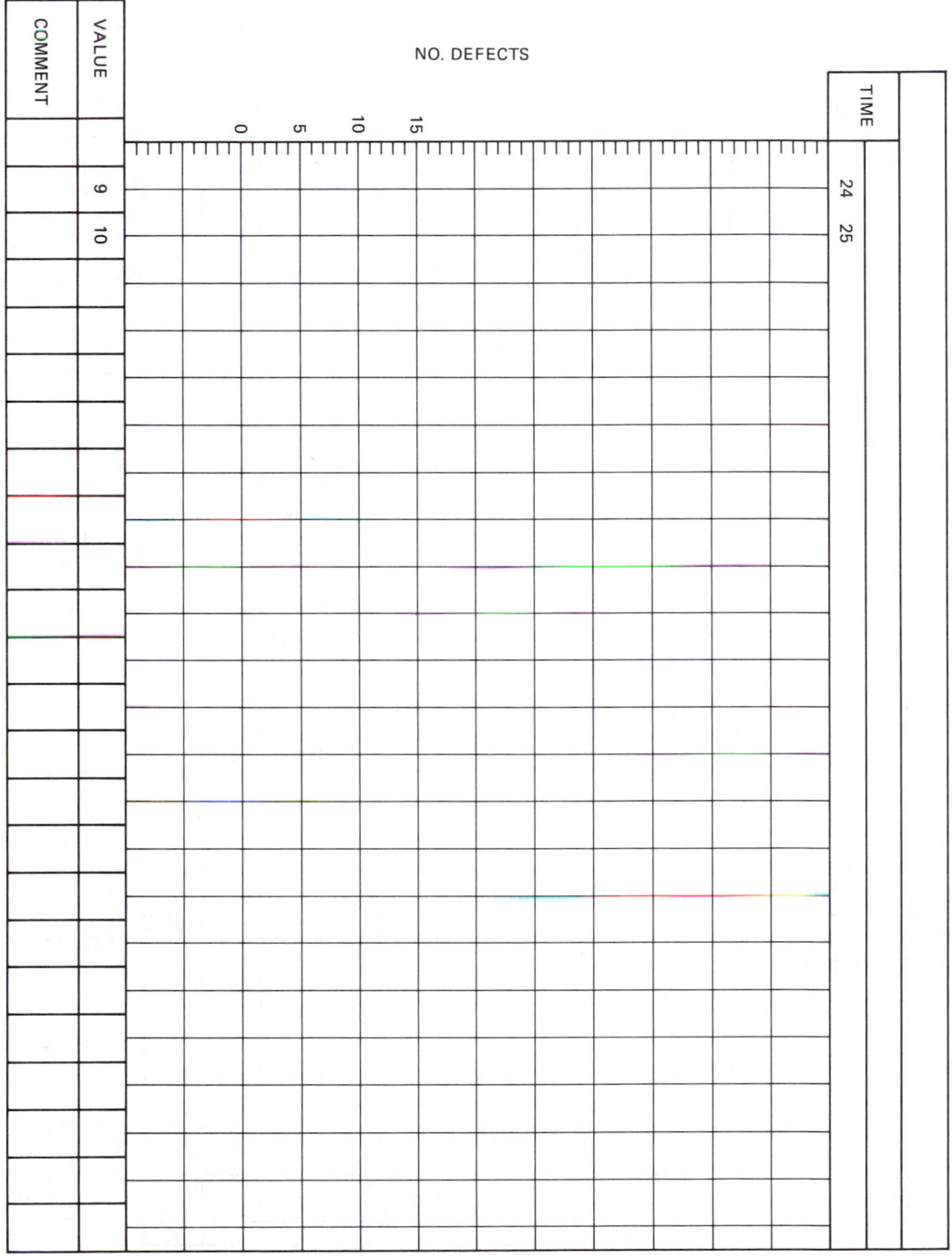

FIGURE 16-13 (Continued)

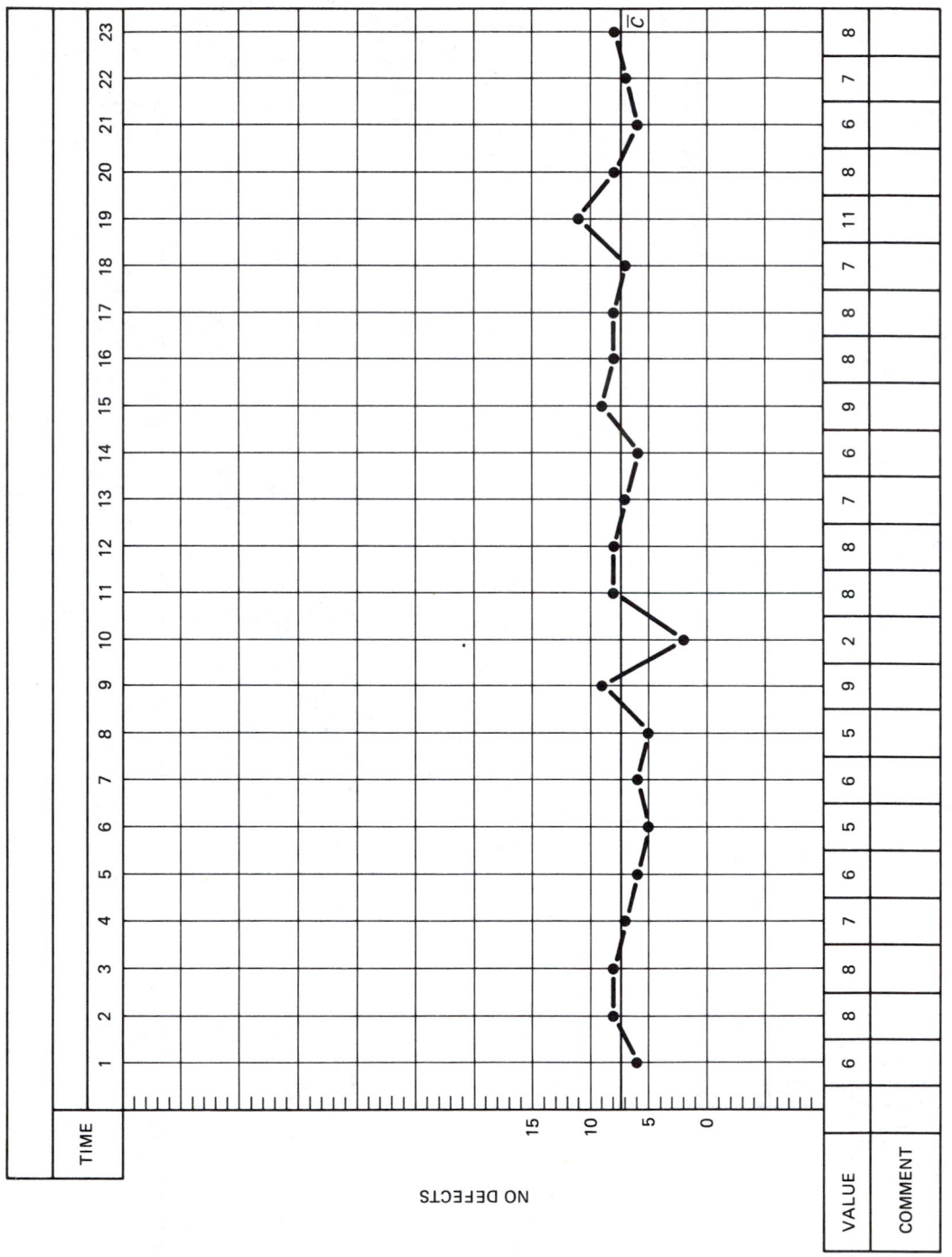

FIGURE 16–14 Initial Plot for Example 16.5.2

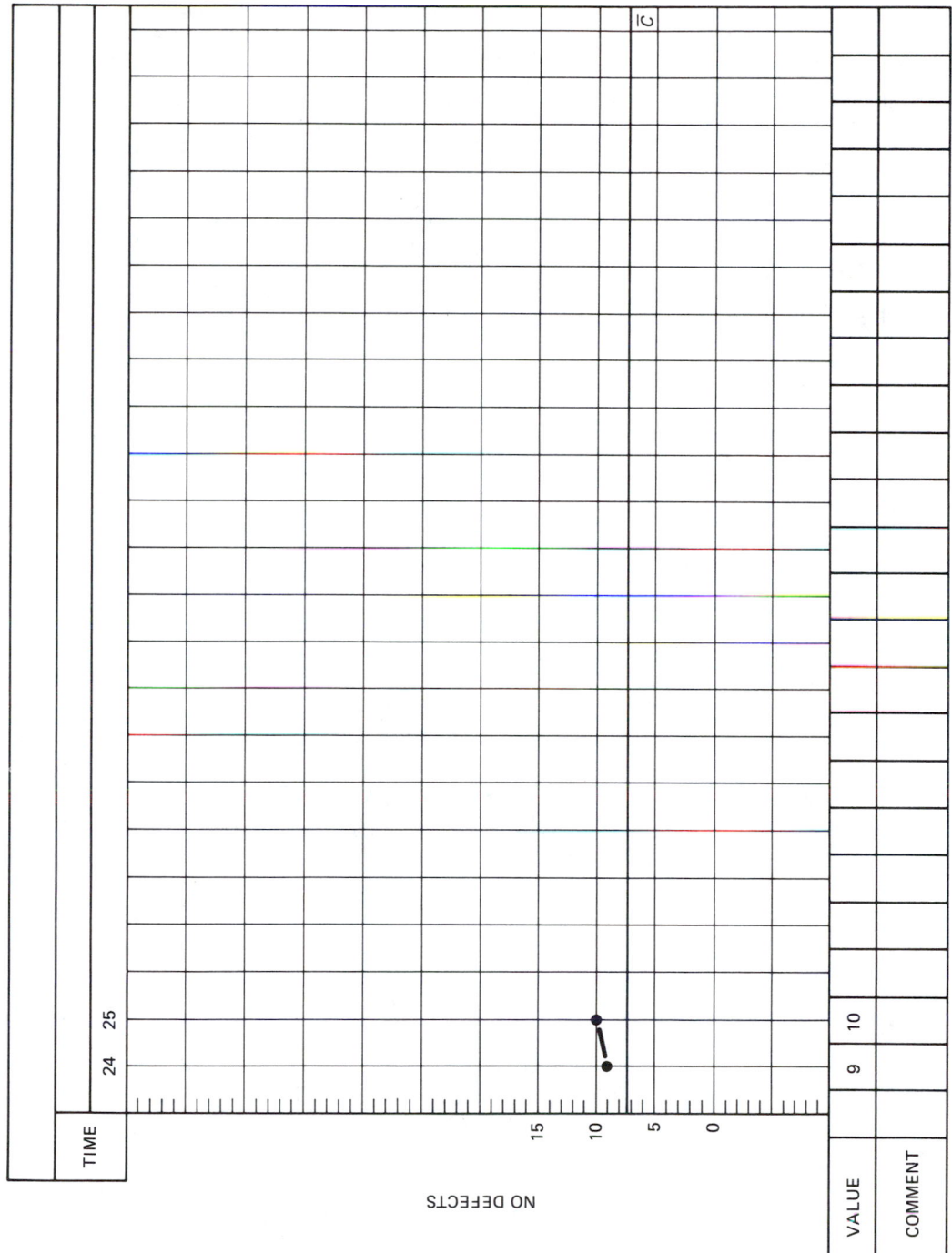

FIGURE 16-14 (Continued)

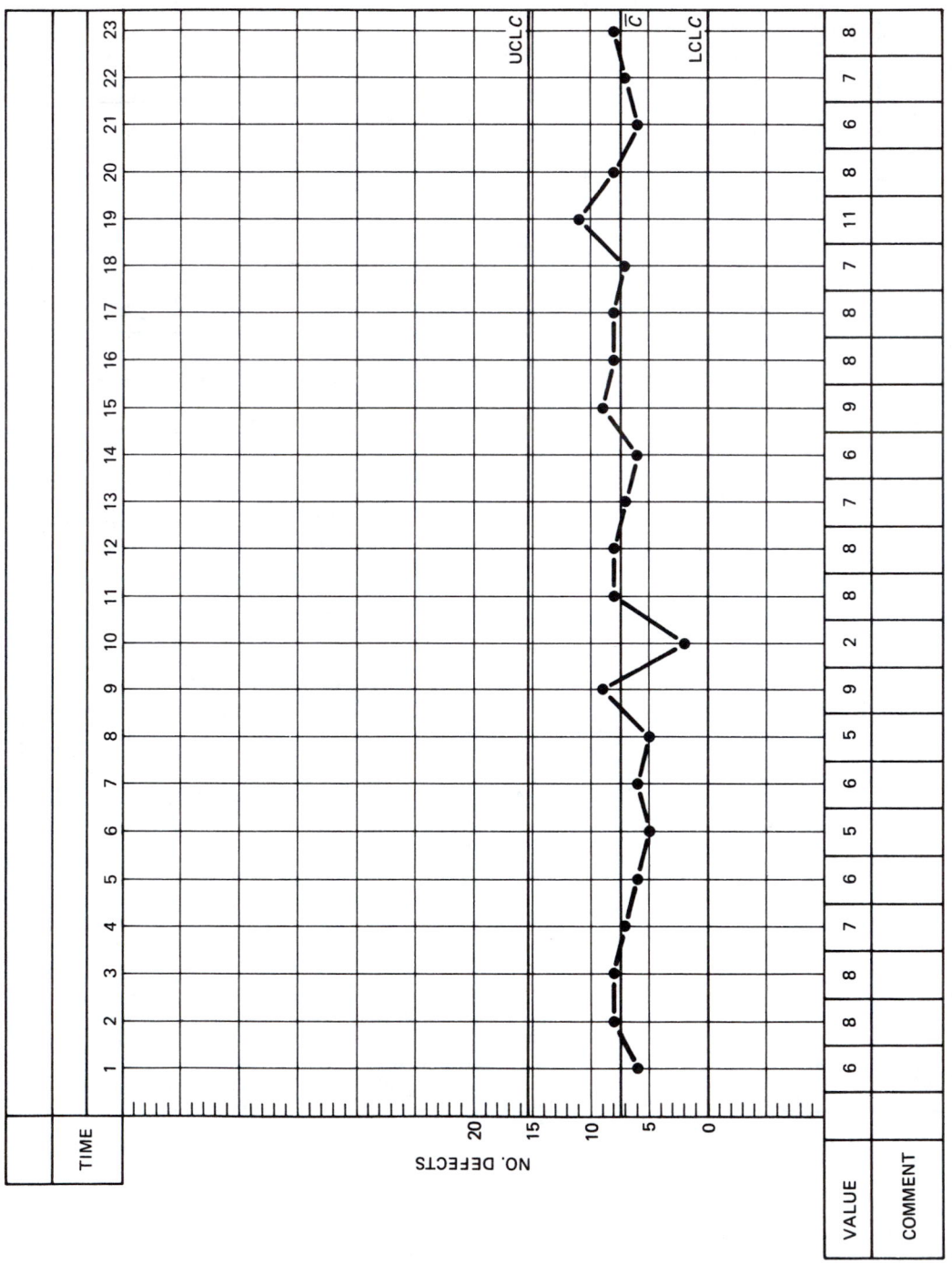

FIGURE 16–15 Initial Limits for Example 16.5.3

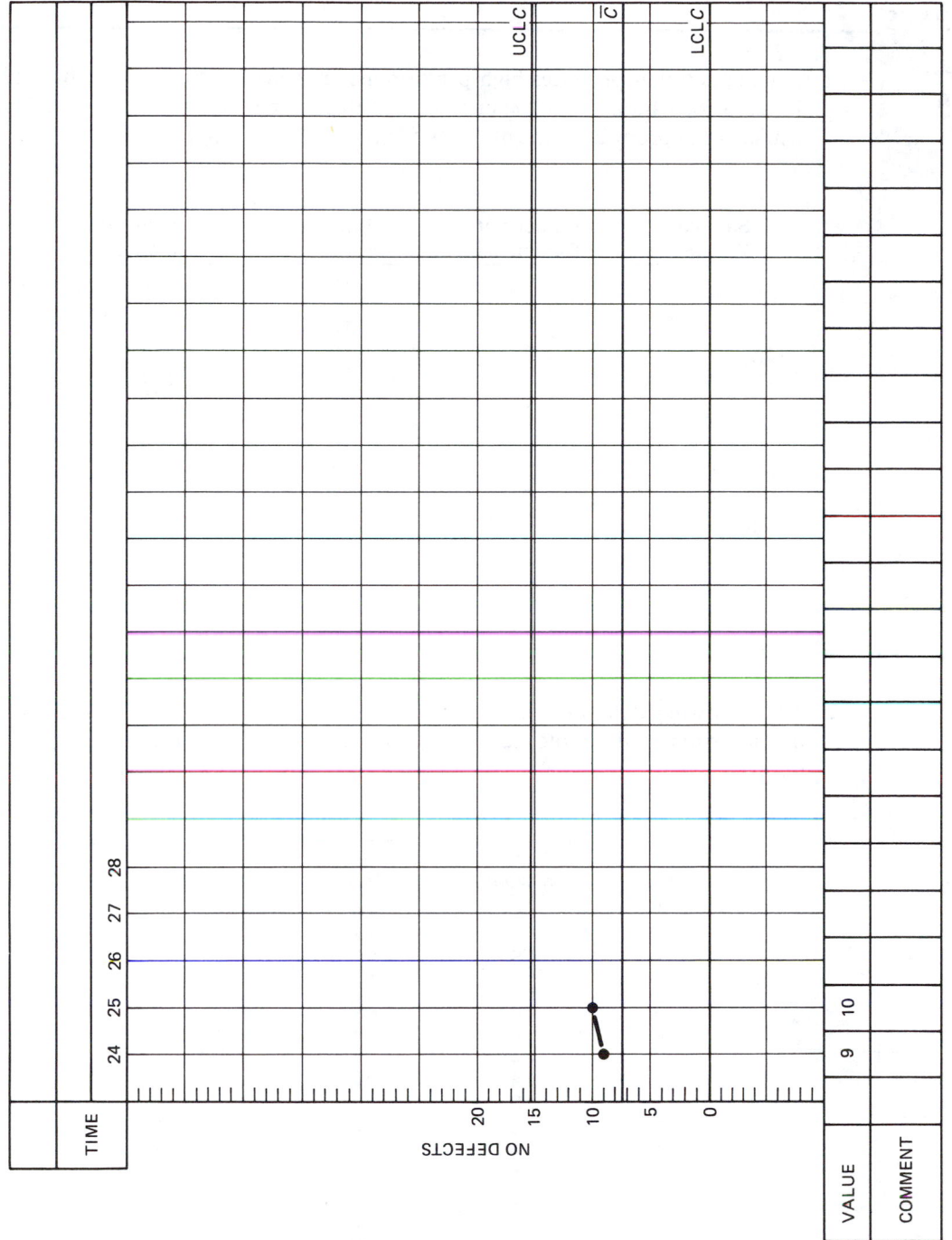

FIGURE 16–15 (Continued)

EXERCISES

1. A company that produces high-performance pistons for motorcycles has collected information about the number of defective pistons produced each day. Calculate appropriate control limits for the following data:

Sample Number	Number of Defectives	Sample Number	Number of Defectives
1	4	16	3
2	3	17	11
3	3	18	4
4	4	19	3
5	3	20	2
6	2	21	1
7	3	22	3
8	2	23	5
9	2	24	1
10	5	25	4
11	3	26	4
12	4	27	3
13	6	28	2
14	3	29	2
15	5	30	3

2. The following data were collected regarding the time required to pay each invoice submitted to the accounting office: construct appropriate control limits.

Day	Time (in weeks)	Day	Time (in weeks)
1	4	16	3
2	3	17	1
3	5	18	2
4	2	19	3
5	3	20	2
6	2	21	11
7	3	22	3
8	4	23	4
9	3	24	3
10	3	25	5
11	4	26	2
12	4	27	4
13	3	28	3
14	5	29	6
15	1	30	4

3. A microprocessor manufacturer has introduced a new integrated circuit. Three hundred are produced each day. Shown are the number of defectives found each day.

Day	Number of Defectives	Day	Number of Defectives
1	4	14	4
2	6	15	12
3	3	16	6
4	7	17	5
5	5	18	5
6	4	19	3
7	6	20	1
8	1	21	4
9	3	22	7
10	0	23	5
11	2	24	0
12	0	25	1
13	1		

4. A television manufacturer inspects television cabinets each hour. The following data show the number of cabinets made and the number of defects found in them.

Hour	n	Number of Defectives	Hour	n	Number of Defectives
1	120	6	16	80	5
2	100	4	17	100	3
3	80	3	18	85	3
4	85	2	19	110	3
5	110	3	20	80	2
6	100	3	21	100	1
7	75	3	22	100	0
8	125	5	23	85	2
9	110	5	24	100	4
10	100	4	25	110	5
11	75	1	26	120	6
12	80	2	27	110	6
13	100	4	28	100	4
14	100	4	29	100	5
15	120	6	30	85	2

CHAPTER 17

Interpreting Control Charts

In the final analysis, customers are the real arbiters of service quality because they have expectations about the service they purchase, and they compare its actual performance to those expectations. *[144: 34]*

Rita E. Collins
Bell Communication Research

17.1 INTRODUCTION

This chapter has been referenced many times during the preceding discussion of control limits. We have been using control charts to determine when our process is in control, that is, when only normal variation is present, and when the process is out of control, or unstable, because abnormal variation has entered into it.

We have used the very obvious situation of calling a process out of control when a single point is outside the control limits. This is a logical deduction. There are, however, many other indications that abnormal variation is now present within a process.

While it is possible to enumerate over 100 possible conditions that indicate that a process is no longer consistent, we will not be that specific. We will suggest in Section 17.2 several common ways that have been developed to determine whether or not our process is in control. Each will be illustrated with sample data that have been charted to be representative of the criteria that have been suggested.

Since this list is not designed to be inclusive, the key point we must stress and remember is that **when a process is out of control it means that something unusual or different has happened.** Something is happening that did not happen before. Specifically, when a process is out of control it means either (1) that the process is not stable or (2) that abnormal variation has entered the process. Whatever this something is, it may be bad, or it may be good. All the chart will show us is that it is happening.

Section 17.3 will suggest some typical causes for a process going out of control, and Section 17.4 will suggest some action to be taken with control charts, depending on the nature of the inconsistency.

17.2 IDENTIFYING OUT OF CONTROL PROCESSES

To provide a complete record of the potential out of control criteria, we will start out with the already cited way to recognize that a process is out of control.

A process may be out of control if a single point is outside the control limits (Figure 17–1). The chance of finding a single point that far from the mean is so slim that we are surprised at finding a value there. Thus a point outside the limits certainly merits investigation for its cause.

A process may be out of control if more than 50 percent of the values are on one side of the mean (Figure 17–2). The mean, by its definition, implies that half the values are larger and half are smaller. A major difference with that is suspicious and should be indicative that *something* is happening to the process.

Before describing any additional criteria, the concept of a run has to be defined. A **run** is a set of consecutive ascending or descending points. It is closely related to a long-term trend. A point is counted in a run if it continues increasing (decreasing) in the same direction as the preceding point. **A process may be out of control if a run of 6 points occurs** (Figure 17–3). Normal variation is supposed to be random. Six consecutive increasing or decreasing points is not likely to occur. Therefore, it is worth investigating.

A process may be out of control if there exists a pattern or cycle that regularly recurs. Again, the normal variation that is always present in a process is random. If a pattern or cycle emerges, then it is quite possible that the variation is not random. Figure 17–4 shows a very obvious pattern or cycle.

Obvious short trends with adjustments may be an indication that the process is out of control. Rather than fixing the process, sometimes the process is merely adjusted everytime there appears to be a change. The overadjustment of the process can cause as much as twice the variation normally expected. The pattern shown in Figure 17–5 shows that something unusual is occurring. That is sufficient reason to investigate.

While the control limits that have been calculated thus far have been three sigma limits, it is entirely possible to calculate both two sigma and even one sigma limits. The actual calculation is a simple procedure. It involves only using a different constant, in the case of the Shewhart charts, and substituting a 2 or 1 for the 3 in the attributes formulas. If these limits are calculated, then we can use them to help recognize other out of control processes that initially are not as obvious as the ones we have cited thus far.

A percentage of values other than 68 percent within the one sigma limits may

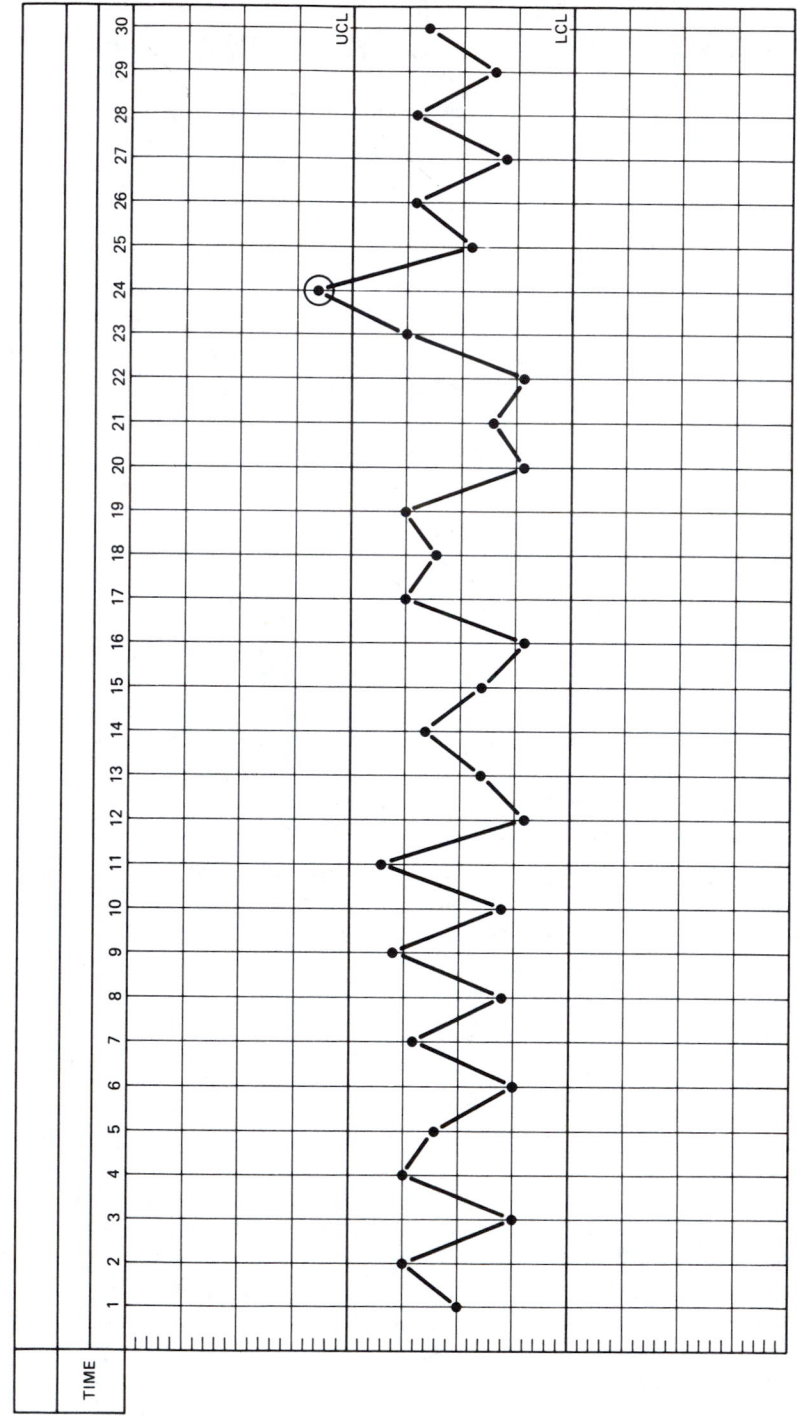

FIGURE 17-1 Single Point out of Control

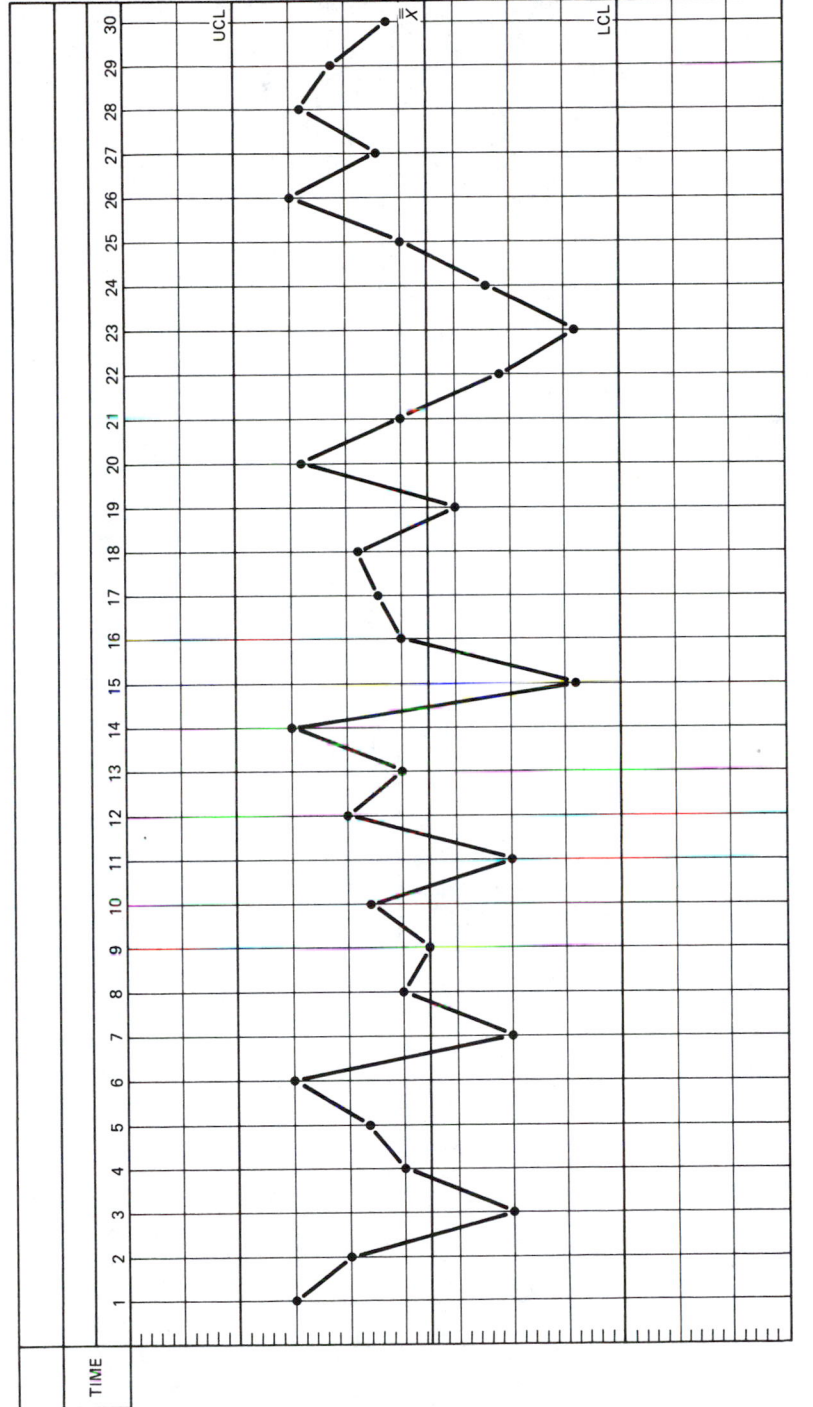

FIGURE 17–2 Fifty Percent above/below Mean

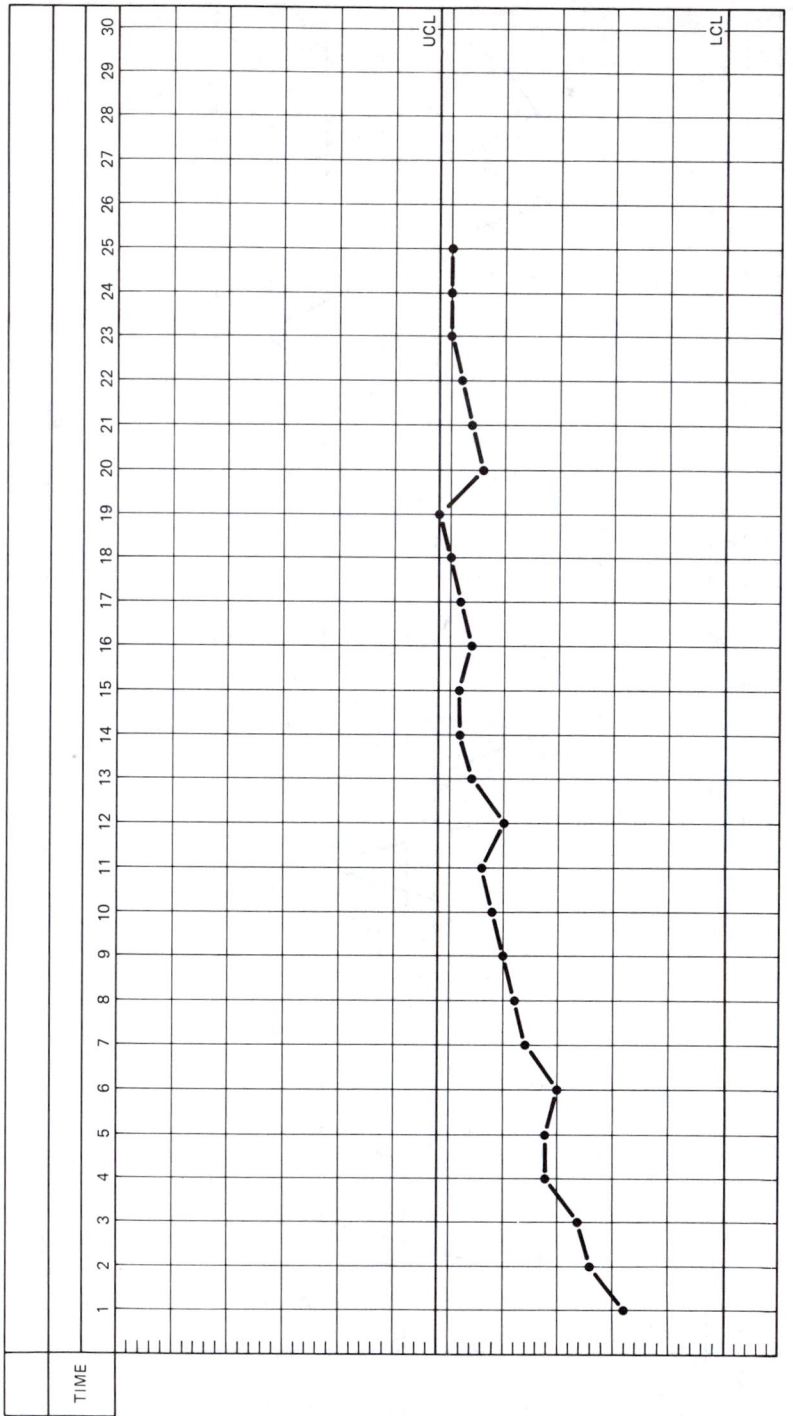

FIGURE 17-3 Run of 6 Points

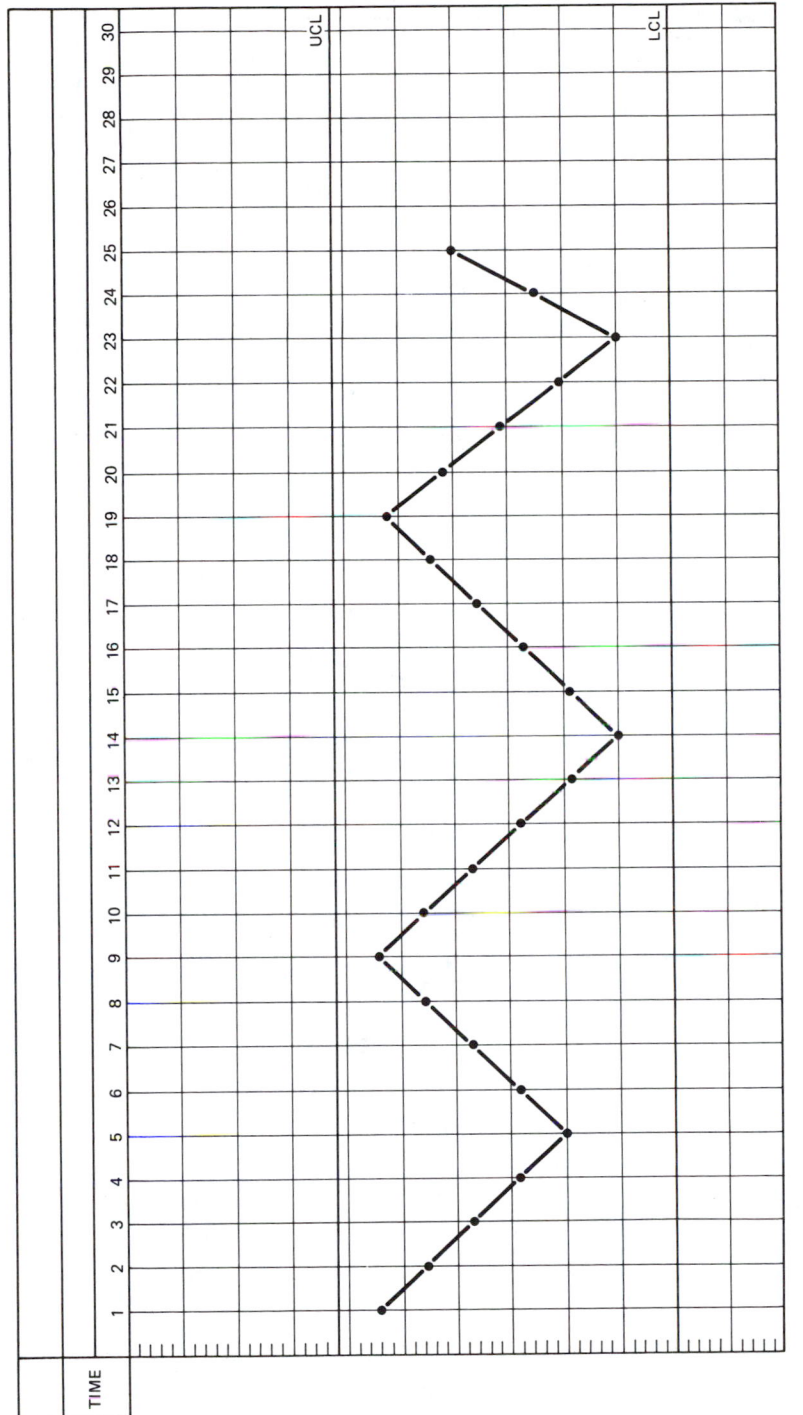

FIGURE 17-4 Cyclical Pattern

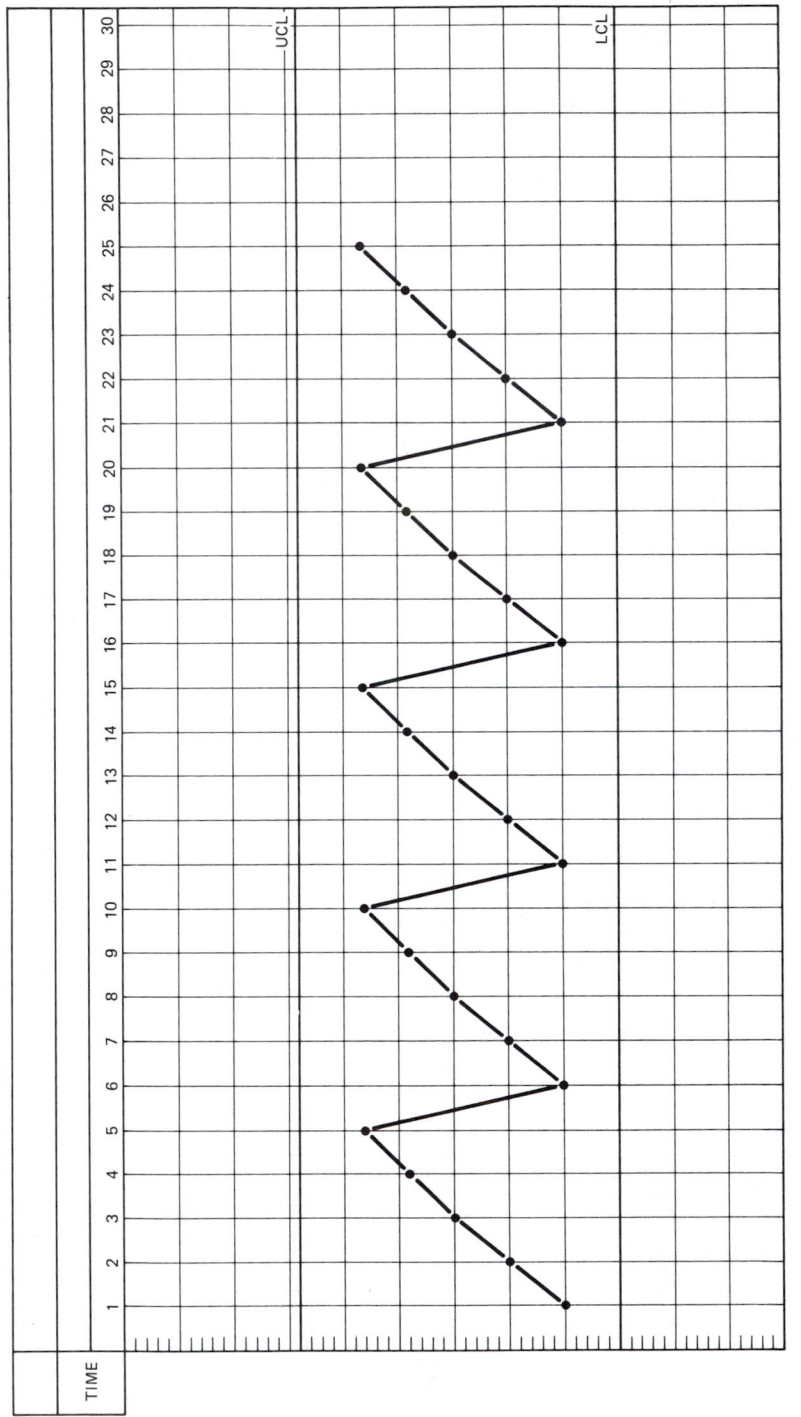

FIGURE 17–5 Short-term Trends with adjustments

indicate that the process is not in control (Figure 17–6). Either too many points too close to the mean or not enough points close to the mean indicates that something abnormal may be happening to the process.

A percentage of values other than 95 percent within the two sigma limits may indicate that the process is not in control (Figure 17–7). Either too many points too close to the mean or, more likely, too many points too far away from the mean indicates that something unusual is happening. In both this and the preceding suggested criteria, the percentages 68 and 95 are a suggested guideline. If the actual count gives a percentage of 65, this is probably close enough not to raise any undue concern. Remember, it is an overall trend that we are looking for.

Three consecutive points between two and three sigma limits may indicate that the process is out of control (Figure 17–8). The likelihood of three consecutive points that far from the mean is very small. When that situation occurs, it should be investigated.

Sometimes the pattern that emerges is indicative that the process is totally unstable. Figure 17–9 is an example of such a process. It is totally out of control. Immediate steps should be taken to bring the process into control before any steps are taken to improve it.

Example 17.2.1 Use the control chart shown in Figure 17–10. For what reason(s) might this process be considered out of control? This process violates a number of the conditions described, as follows:

1. The first six points increase. This means that we start out with a run of six ascending points.

2. This chart shows a total of 30 points. Of these 30 points, only 8 are below the mean. With only 26.67 percent of the points this low, we can point to the 50/50 guideline.

3. Three consecutive points, in about the middle of the chart, fall between the two and three sigma limits.

4. Of the 30 points on the chart, 27 are between the two sigma limits. We would have expected, perhaps, some additional points; however, this is a close distinction. However, since all these points occurred sequentially, it is just another indication that the process is not stable. ■

17.3 POSSIBLE CAUSES OF ABNORMAL VARIATION

Although we have discussed possible causes of abnormal variation, this is an opportune time to repeat these assignable causes. The listing provided will by no means be comprehensive. As soon as we think we have listed everything, another method will surely crop up.

Preventive maintenance, or, really, lack of preventive maintenance, is a common cause of abnormal variation. This is often responsible for long-term trends.

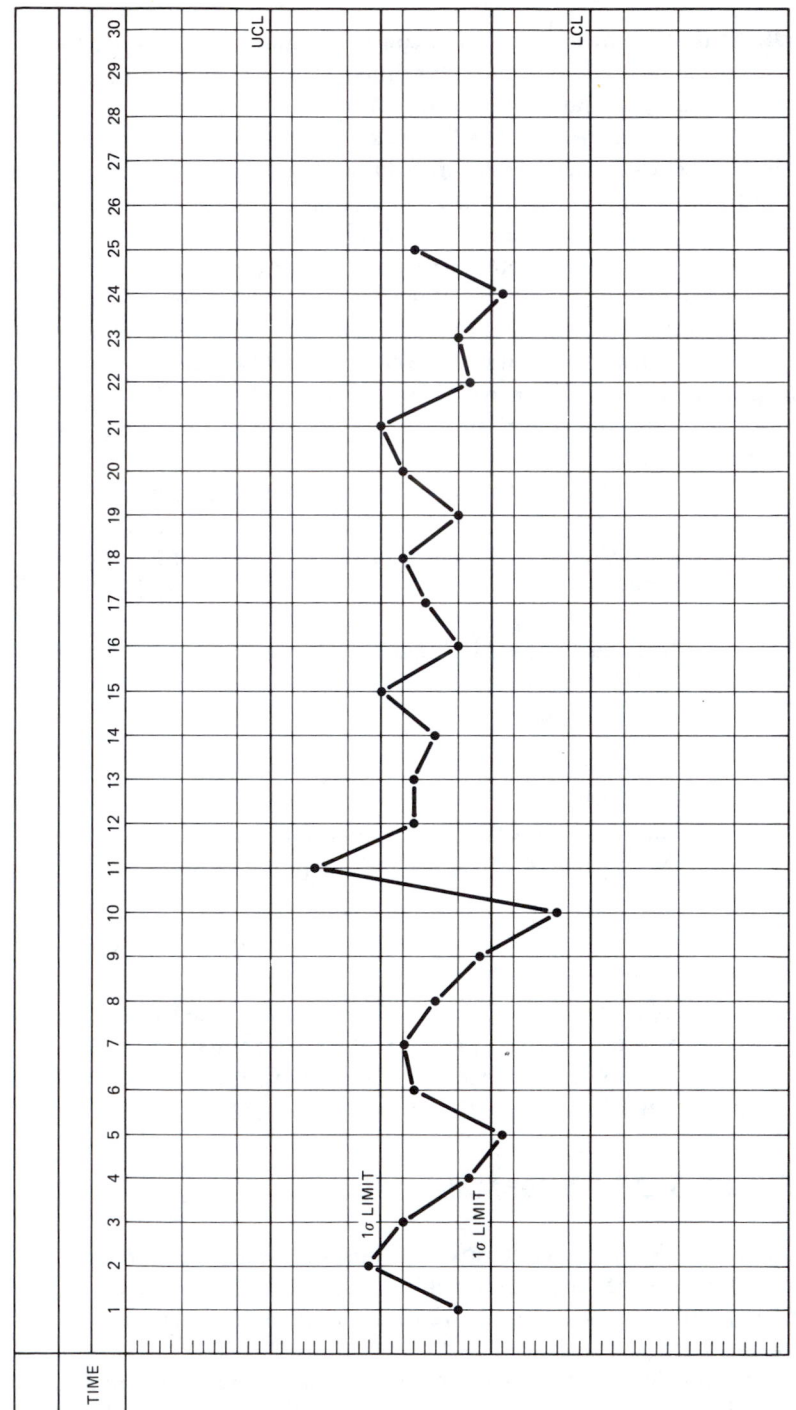

FIGURE 17-6 Sixty-eight percent within one sigma

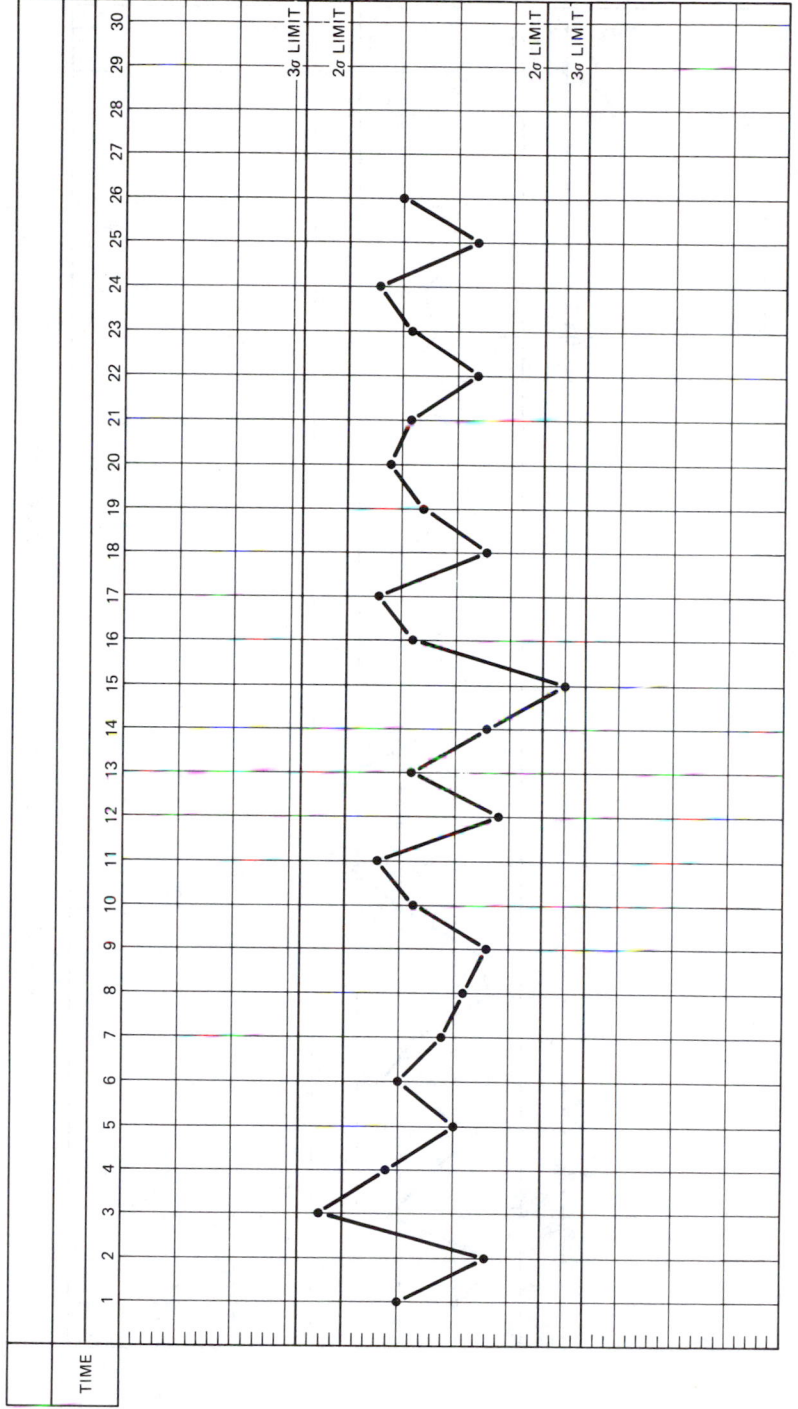

FIGURE 17-7 Ninety-five percent within two sigma

283

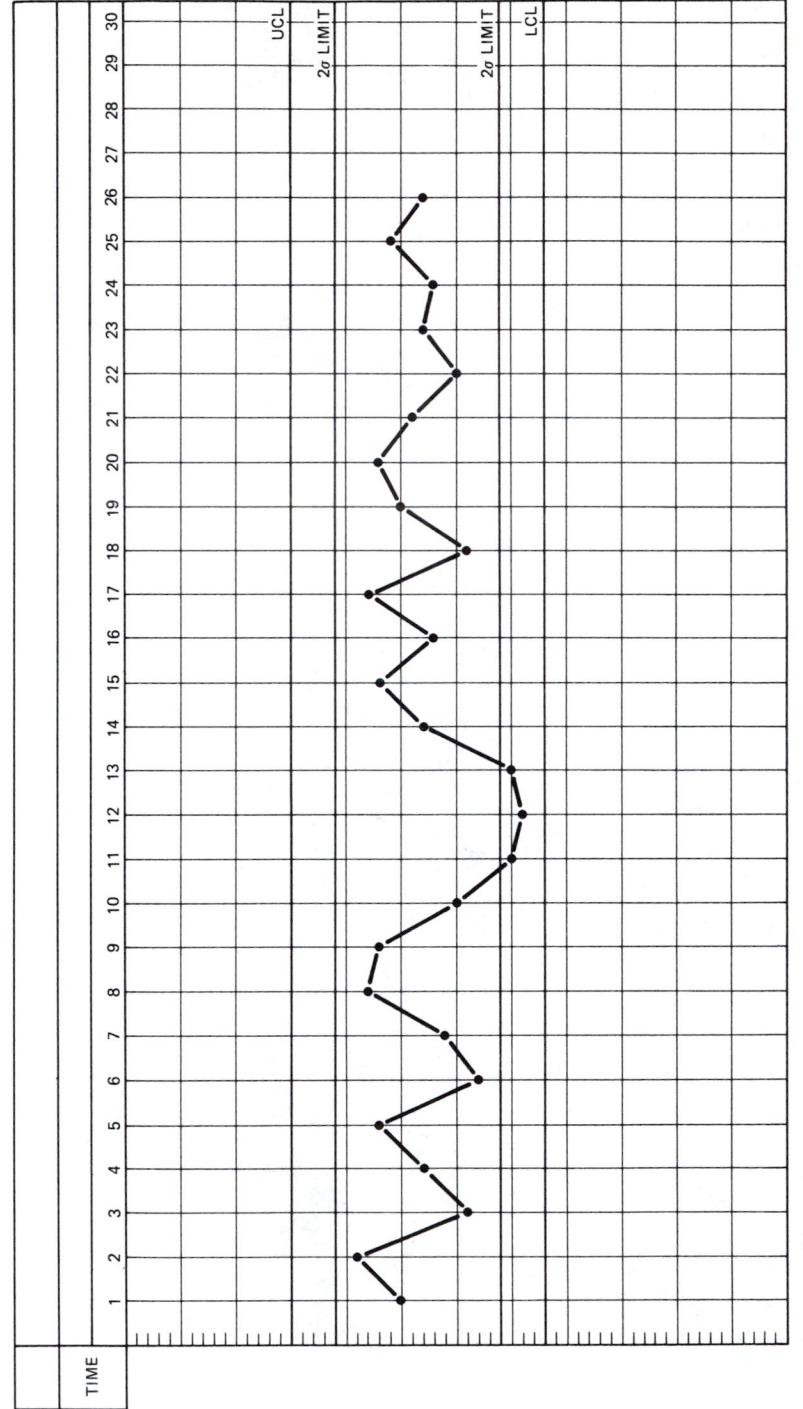

FIGURE 17–8 Points between two and three sigma

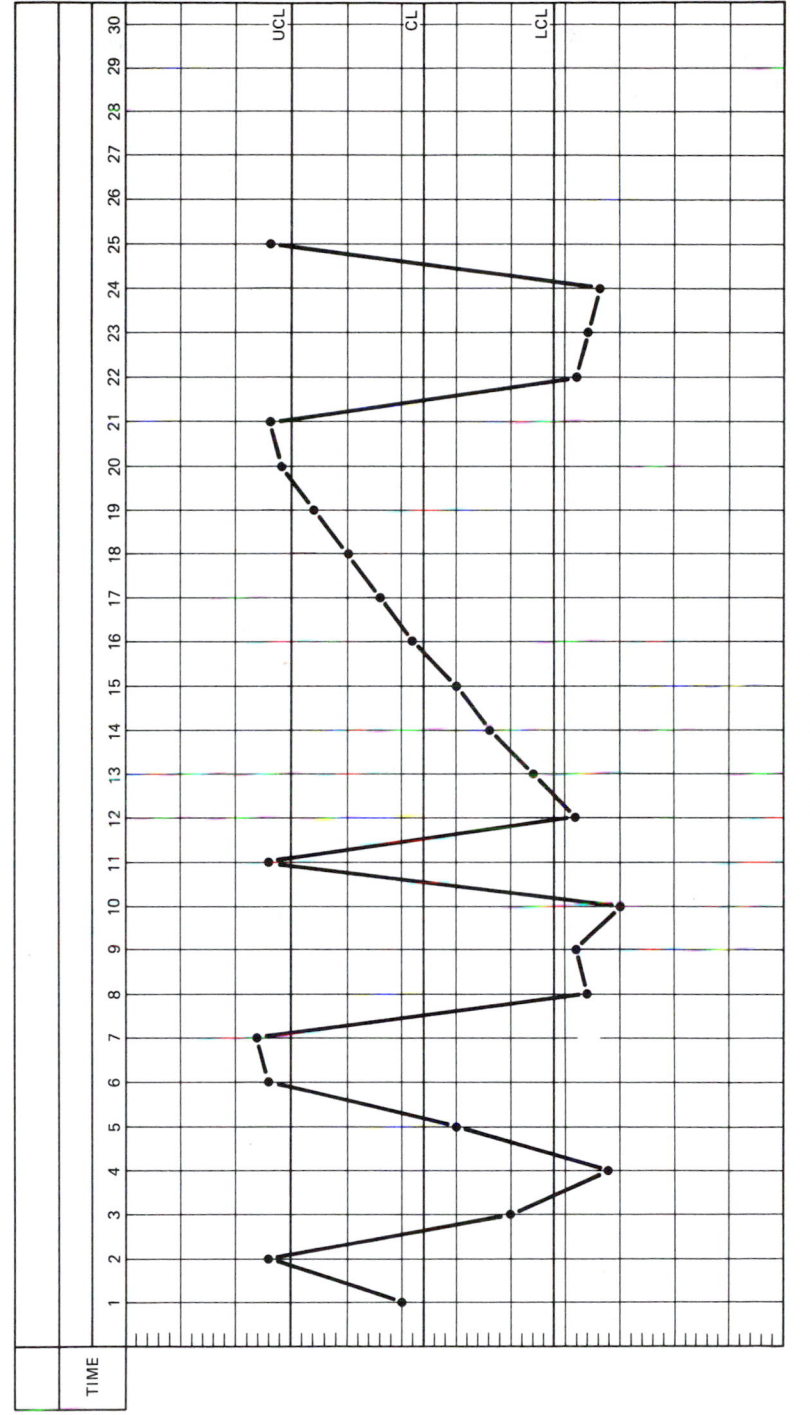

FIGURE 17-9 Chaos

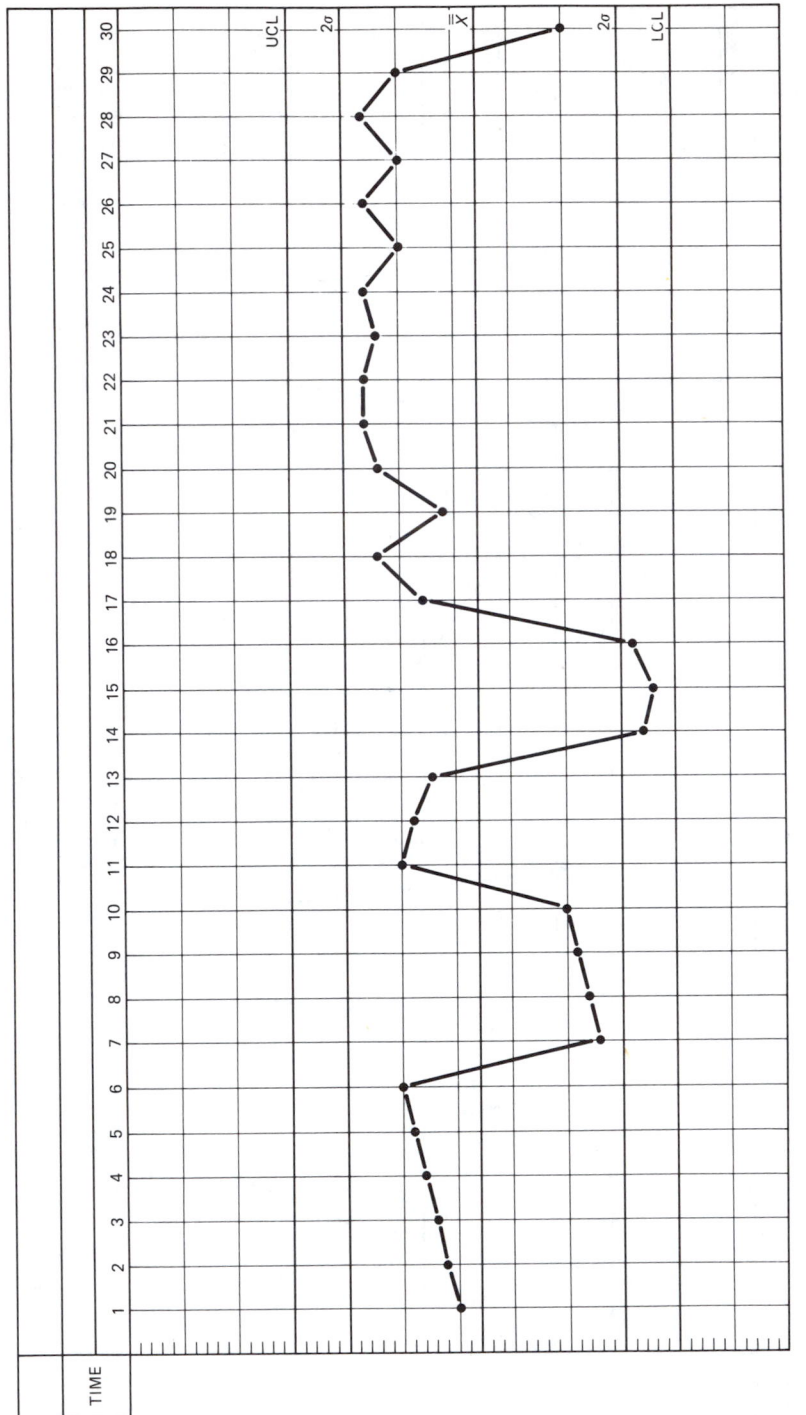

FIGURE 17–10 Data for Example 17.2.1

Another cause of abnormal variation is *worn tools.* This is closely related to preventive maintenance. Often, though, the process is such that the problem is not noted until it is literally too late.

Operator performance, often fatigue, is an easily identifiable cause of unexpected variation. Once fatigue sets in, the output of the worker-controlled process can show very obvious signs of abnormalities or inconsistencies.

There will often be assignable reasons due to *shift differentials, machine differentials, inspector differentials,* or even *day of the week differentials.* As one shift replaces another, the new operator will often adjust the process to fit his or her own personal preferences. These adjustments are usually not necessary, but occur all the time. It is comparable to the husband or wife adjusting the furnace thermostat every time he or she comes home from work. It is a characteristic that is part of human nature, but should not be permitted. It increases process variability.

We have alluded to *overadjustment.* This happens so often that some organizations have created "dummy" controls just to placate the human urge to adjust.

Environmental changes are a frequent cause of abnormal variation. Airflow, temperature, or humidity levels can change and cause serious problems. Some organizations have to change specifications in response to some of these kinds of changes, but unless they are recognized, they cannot be accommodated.

One last potential cause that we will call *sorting practices* may be responsible for assignable abnormal variation. This occurs when different evaluators or inspectors apply the same criteria differently. Borderline calls will occur and, depending on other influences, may or may not be consistent from evaluation to evaluation. This is especially noticeable on the proportion defective type of control chart.

17.4 CONTROL AND SPECIFICATIONS

Up to this point we have been intentionally ignoring the process specifications. We have been talking about how the process is actually performing, not how it should perform. We are now ready to address this. We will introduce the concept in this section, and then devote all of Chapter 18 to this important aspect of process monitoring.

As we will use it, specifications refer to those values between which some measured process characteristic must lie in order to perform as intended. Ideally, the specification will be a single target value and every item measured will be right on target. In reality, this is rarely the case. Specifications have traditionally developed a tolerance about the target that defines an acceptable range. Our goal, of course, is to continually reduce the size of that target range.

As we monitor our process and determine the limits of the normal variation, we should, at some point, compare this natural variation with the desired values. This we will do in a formal basis in Chapter 18. This chapter will present some general guidelines regarding the action that should be taken regarding the observed relationship between control limits and specification limits.

There are a number of possible relationships between variability of a stable process and specifications.

- One possibility is that the process that was stable has had abnormal variation suddenly enter it. The process is now out of control. When this happens, there are two possible ramifications regarding the process specifications.

  —If the process remains within specifications, all due haste should be made to find the causes of the abnormal variation. That which is deemed to be negative should be eliminated. That which is deemed to be positive should be replicated.

  —If the process has gone out of specifications and defective material is being produced the causes of the abnormal variation should be identified and eliminated as soon as possible.

- The second possibility is that the process that was stable does not have any abnormal variation present. Again, there are two possibilities.

  —First is that the process is not able to meet the specifications. This leads to three courses of action.

  (1) The specifications should be investigated to see if they can be changed. Sometimes specs just evolve over time or are a matter of standard company policy, and there is no real reason for having the values where they are. In this case they should be changed.

  (2) A second possibility is that the process will have to be changed so that it will be able to meet the specifications. This involves improving the process by reducing the variability or changing the adjustments to try to compensate for the normal variation that is present within the process.

  (3) The third course of action is recognition that the situation cannot be easily changed. When that happens, it may be necessary to develop a sorting procedure to divide the acceptable from the unacceptable.

  —Second is that the process is able to meet the specifications. When this happens, we might want to sit back and grin. But we dare not rest on our laurels. Instead, we have to continue to work at improving the process. Remember, as our improvement model has shown, this is a never ending process. As sure as we are able to meet the process specifications, someone will come along who will be able to exceed the specifications, that is, offer a more consistent product at the same or lower cost.

17.5   CONCLUSION

We called this chapter Interpreting Control Charts. It is an important aspect of the process-monitoring procedure. We use the charts to determine if the process is stable. If it is, then we begin the improvement process. If it is not, we stabilize the process and then begin the improvement process.

There are no absolutes regarding the interpretation of the process's stability.

We use the control charts to find any sign of any unusual behavior. We want to find out as much as we can about the process. It is only by careful monitoring that we can identify problem areas and methods to improve.

An excellent article expanding this topic has been written by Lloyd S. Nelson, "Interpreting Shewhart X Bar Control Charts," and appeared in the April 1985 issue of the *Journal of Quality Technology*. This article cites additional technical references.

CHAPTER 18

Process Capability

18.1 INTRODUCTION

Thus far in our discussion of process monitoring and control, we have intentionally limited our focus to the observation of the variation normally found in the process under study. Control limits show the range of normal variation that should be expected from a stable process. Control limits do not show the limits that are necessary for proper operation. These are, defined in Chapter 17, the specification limits, or just plain specs.

We must define, at some point, how we should be doing. We must also, at some point, be able to answer the question, "How are we doing?" The answer to that question is provided by examining the process capability.

The process capability is determined as the result of actual measurements on the process characteristics. Besides answering the "how are we doing?" question, some additional uses for measuring the process capability include: [26: 318]

- As a basis of specifying quality characteristics.
- To make reliable decisions about product specifications as supplied by the customers.

- To select among competitive processes those that will give the most desired tolerances.

- To plan future sequences of production in view of customer requirements.

- To find various causes of defects during production.

18.2 PROCESS CAPABILITY DEFINED

The definition for process capability should sound very familiar. Process capability is the limits between which we would expect to find all the values when only normal variation is present. This is the same as the definition for three sigma control limits.

The capability of any process is determined by the inputs to the process and the transformation process itself. Let us briefly examine each of these.

The inputs to any process include the people, materials, procedures, machinery, and environment. Each of these interacts with each of the others in some fashion during the actual "magic" that is the transformation itself. Thus, the process capability is more than the sum of the inputs. It reflects the consistency of each input as well as the interaction.

As we have seen, people vary, materials vary, and procedures or methods always seem to change, especially over time. Our goal is to minimize, reduce, and eventually eliminate the amount of change that occurs. We strive toward this continuous improvement.

As we minimize the variability within the inputs, we also try to minimize variability added by the transformation. The net result of this will be reduced variability within the output. This output, as we have seen, is the input for the next process. Our extended-process concept can serve to compound the problem.

Although we try to reduce this variability, we cannot always do it. Our goal may be zero variability at each of our internal processes, but that is only our goal.

We measure how we are doing by calculating a statistical measure of process capability. To do this, we use one of the statistics we learned in Chapter 12, the standard deviation. Mathematically, we define the process capability as six times the standard deviation. That defines virtually all the normal variation that we will find for any process.

The definition was easy. A caution about the process capability, though. *The process capability defines what is, not what we would like.* The specifications define what we would like. *We cannot change the process capability without changing the process in some way.* This change to the process is the responsibility of the management. We also must remember that merely meeting the specifications isn't good enough. We are always striving to improve. That has been our guiding definition of quality.

As long as we remember this, process capability is easy. The next section will look at answering the question we posed earlier, "How are we doing?"

18.3 CAPABILITY INDEX

A common used statistic to answer the question just raised is known as the capability index. The capability index has been defined as the ratio of the total specification width to the process capability. The symbol Cp_k is used to designate this index. The higher this index, the better, or more consistent, the process is. This index provides organizations ways to measure improvement. Figure 18–1 shows the relationship of process capability to process specifications for three situations, those of Cp_k greater than 1, equal to 1, and less than 1.

Example 18.3.1 A process capability study has determined that a particular process is centered right on the target value of 1600 psi. The standard deviation for individuals for the data

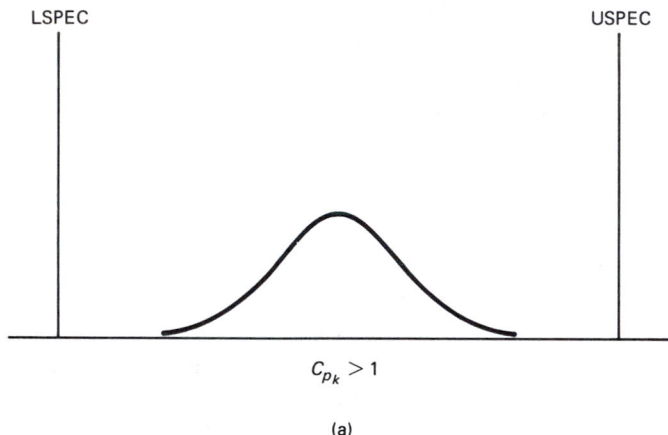

(a)

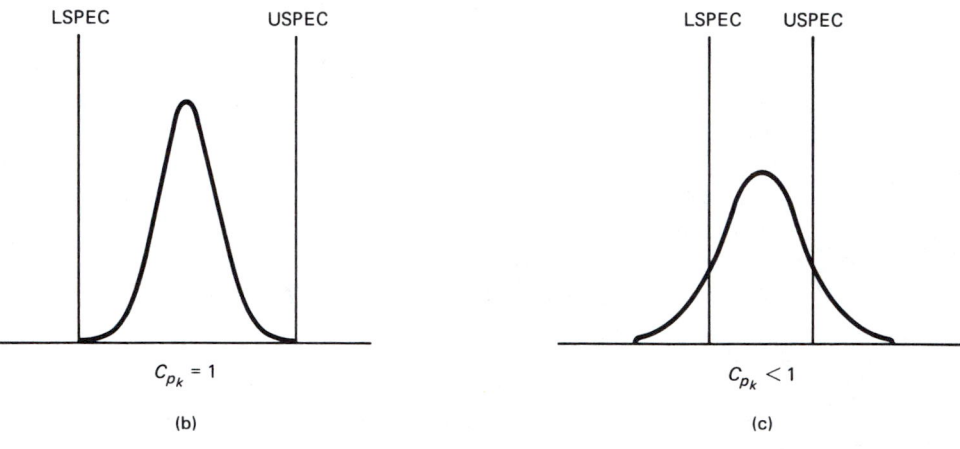

(b)   (c)

FIGURE 18–1   (a) $Cp_k > 1$; (b) $Cp_k = 1$; (c) $Cp_k < 1$

collected during the study was 22 psi. Specifications for this process indicate that the psi should be between 1550 and 1650 for the process to operate as it should. The Cp_k index for this process is calculated:

$$Cp_k = \frac{\text{spec width}}{\text{process capability}}$$

$$\text{Spec width} = 1650 - 1550 = 100 \text{ psi}$$

$$\text{Process capability} = 6 \text{ sigma} = (6)(22) = 132$$

$$Cp_k = \frac{100}{132} = 0.758$$

Because the value is less than 1, we know that the process is not capable of meeting specifications. ∎

Example 18.3.2 For the situation described in the preceding example, the management, when informed of the low capability index, took positive action. The process was changed so that, when subsequent data were collected, the standard deviation became 14 psi. The new index is calculated:

$$Cp_k = \frac{100}{84} = 1.190$$

This ratio now exceeds 1 and the process is capable of meeting current specification limits. ∎

The Cp_k index values provide a common way to measure and communicate performance. "In Japan, the minimum acceptable Cp_k is 1.33; there is a tighter requirement for quality characteristics that carry a Cp_k of 1.66. In general, however, you see many quality characteristics with Cp_k values of 3.00, 5.00, and even 8.00." [8: 17]

While it would seem that an index value of 1.00 would be the goal, this puts the process right on the edge of conformance. Within the philosophy we have developed within this book, it should be obvious that the enlightened manager will strive to continue increasing the index value.

> Most of the managers in American Industry feel that the ultimate is achieved when they are able to meet specifications. At the same time a revolution is happening in Japan, with the adoption of a mentality of Continuous Improvement and the redefining of quality as "product uniformity around the target, rather than conformance to specification." [102: 102]

18.4 CONCLUSION

Process capability is a powerful concept in that it provides a measurement tool for assessing the performance of a process. As with all the statistical tools we have described in the book, the numbers merely focus our attention on the difficulties. Some of the problems and possible solutions that relate to the relationship of process capability and specifications, and are pointed out by the analysis procedure, include the following. [80: 296]

- **Process capability inadequate to meet the tolerance.** When this is the case, there are four possible courses of action:

  1. Shift to a process that is capable of meeting and exceeding the requirements.
  2. Improve the process's capability by improving the consistency of the inputs and/or the performance of the transformation.
  3. Determine if the specifications can or should be modified. Change them if necessary.
  4. Inspect the output of the process until the process can be improved.

- **Process capability just meets the specifications.** This situation is not all that different from the preceding situation. Any small change in process variability may have a significant impact on the acceptability of the output.

- **Process capability exceeds the specifications.** Exceeds is a vague word. There are different ways to exceed specifications.

  1. The ideal situation is when the Cp_k index is in the vicinity of 1.33 and 1.50. This means that virtually all the output of the process will be acceptable and there is not a critical need for immediate process improvement.
  2. If the Cp_k index is 2.00 or greater, there may be justification for reducing the specification. This means that significantly better output than initially required is available. This can be useful either in the extended process or as a marketing device.

- One last caution when looking at process capability. All the calculations that we have looked at assume that a stable process exists. We can only project when the process is behaving normally.

CHAPTER 19

Implementing the Philosophy

We had been concerned with keeping rejects down instead of quality up. We had been busy keeping imperfection under control rather than trying for perfection. We had sometimes burnt the toast and then scraped it clean, instead of fixing the toaster. Some of us had even learned to like burnt toast. [161: 17]

Marshall McDonald, President
FPL Group, Inc.

19.1 INTRODUCTION

This book has developed a model for quality improvement. This model stresses process orientation and develops methods for defining every activity within and external to the organization as a process with customers and suppliers. The model is based on the premise that we can and must identify the critical inputs to these processes. By improving the consistency, that is, by reducing the variability of the inputs and the outputs, we work toward continually improving our quality. The model also stresses the use of basic statistical measurement techniques, including control charts, to monitor and control our processes. This leads to the identification of areas that require improvement. All these are very important. But the philosophy that we have modeled will not work without the driving force of management commitment.

Management commitment must be present if the successful implementation of the philosophy is to work. Management is responsible for demonstrating the commitment, both through personal actions and by developing and using a management system that encourages, no, *demands* the continuous improvement of every process.

While each organization is unique, there are several elements that appear to be present in every organization that has shown it is serious about this continuous improvement process. First and foremost is commitment to improvement by management. Second is a sense of ownership by all employees, no matter what their position. Third is communication with all process customer and suppliers.

There are no easy answers for the organizations that wish to implement the philosophy. This chapter will suggest a way, from the author's perspective, to implement the philosophy. It will start out with a discussion of management commitment, including ways to demonstrate that commitment. Proper organization is essential, and that will be addressed as well. For most organizations this philosophy represents a change in attitude or corporate culture. This change is difficult, and we will make some comments regarding the change and the resistance that will normally occur. Following this chapter, the book will conclude with several lengthy examples of different aspects of quality improvement taken from organizations that have, thus far, been successful.

19.2 NEED FOR COMMITMENT

The first step in the improvement process is the active demonstration that the organization is committed to improving. This must be from the top down. Improvements are possible from the bottom up, but, since we have shown earlier that about 85 percent of the problems are caused by the management system, the commitment to improve must come from the top. This is the only way it will work.

> At Motorola, SPC has been integrated with the corporate culture. We realize that SPC cannot succeed unless everyone from upper management to engineering and operators believes that SPC works. SPC is being applied in all areas of the plant; its benefits apply to marketing and document control as much as to the fabrication and assembly areas.   [160: 23]

Motorola is not alone. Table 19–1 shows that this is found in many companies. The table also includes some other consultants' words of wisdom about commitment.

No question about it. Commitment is the key. "Once top management accepts its overall responsibilities and sees quality as part of them, the organization has taken the first step towards quality management as a total system." [148: 40] The statement of commitment is important. It is the first step in a journey that lasts forever. That statement must be communicated to everyone in the organization's extended process. That is done via a mission statement, statement of purpose, or organizational goal statement. The next section will examine the requirements for the goal statement that communicates that the first step has been taken.

19.3 MISSION STATEMENTS

> A commitment is a pledge: when upper management makes a quality commitment and formulates a policy statement, they pledge their support by

TABLE 19–1
Commitment to Commitment

If top executives don't require excellence, you won't get it. *[142: 23]*

Arthur Thompson
TRW

Let me emphasize that where top management does not understand and does not get personally involved, nothing will happen. *[135: 17]*

William Conway
Nashua

Quality is an ethic, a course of action to govern everything we do. We therefore established the principle of striving for continuous improvement in the quality of everything our company does. *[139: 69]*

Kenneth Harrigan
Ford

Establishment of corporate quality goals . . . upper management participation in setting the goals, in planning, in review of performance. *[126: 20]*

J. M. Juran

Top management must be openly and actively committed to improving quality as a strategic necessity. Quality considerations must figure centrally in their strategic planning. *[133: 168]*

Frank Sasser
Harvard School of Business

Total quality control calls for total involvement in quality improvement, from top management to the janitor and including both line and staff personnel. *[104: 140]*

Richard Schonberger

The first indispensable is top management's commitment to quick detection of quality troubles at the earliest possible point in the process after defectives have been generated. *[42: 19]*

Edward Schrock

not only honoring the philosophy contained therein, but by providing active leadership to implement the intent of the policy as well. [123: 27]

Thus, the mission statement, which reflects this policy, must be one that the organization can live with. Mission statements are not that difficult to prepare. They should be short, to the point, and allow absolutely no doubt in the reader's mind that the organization is committed. The statement must also be believable.

The mission statement establishes a goal. Such a statement was made by David Kearns, CEO of Xerox.

We must create a Xerox team of employees whose energies and talents are channeled toward a common goal: that goal is quality in meeting the needs of internal and external customers. Quality is the basic business principle for Xerox and quality improvement is the job of every Xerox employee. [159: 16]

This mission statement fits our criteria. It sets the tone. It does not make any unrealistic claims.

Perhaps one of the most widely cited mission statements is that developed by Ford Motor Company. Their statement sets the tone. "Our mission is to improve continually our products and services to meet our customers' needs, allowing us to prosper as a business and to provide a reasonable return for our stockholders, the owners of our business." [17: 1a] This sounds good, but is it believable? According to *Autoweek* (April 20, 1987, p. 4), it is. According to the magazine, Ford is replacing, rather than repairing, engines in some of its Ford Taurus and Mercury Sable cars and Aerostar vans to correct a piston-scuffing problem. According to the magazine, it would have been less expensive and simpler for Ford to replace the cylinder involved rather than the entire engine. However, John King, manager of Ford Parts and Services, said that the replacement program reflects a recent Ford concentration on quality and consumer satisfaction. "We are more concerned about satisfying the customer than the dollars involved."

While we can't speak publicly for Ford, we do recognize that the action the manager took is consistent with the policy expressed in the mission statement. The statement won't create quality, but it does, pardon the expression, "show where Ford is coming from."

Another example of a corporate policy is Motorola's. It states,

> It is the policy of Motorola Semiconductor Products Sector to produce products and provide services exactly according to specification and delivery schedule. The system will be based on prevention using statistical process control. The standard will be error free performance. These results will be derived from the participative effort of each employee in conjunction with supportive participation from all levels of management. [172: 22]

Is it believable? Does it work? In the May 1987 issue of *Quality,* Jack Germain, senior vice-president and director of quality went on the record by stating,

> We have a plant in Mt. Pleasant, Iowa, that hasn't had a delivery delinquency in six years. That doesn't mean that there aren't paperwork errors from time to time, but the people in that facility are dedicated to the zero delinquency goal. They assume paper problems, they assume material difficulties, but they also anticipate these and prevent delinquencies. It was a culture change. They changed their culture—their whole process of anticipating things—and they have a flawless record. [172: 23]

In summary, a goal statement, a mission statement, or a quality philosophy statement should provide clear guidance regarding what the company is trying to accomplish. It should: [102: 103]

- Specify long-term commitments
- Be customer oriented
- Involve employees

The mission statement is almost a given. For this statement to be believed, it must be demonstrated by the top management of the organization. "People will be watching top management very closely. How do *they* conduct meetings? What level of quality do *they* tolerate?" [184: 345]

19.4 DEMONSTRATING COMMITMENT

It is very easy to ask top management to show commitment. I've never met a top official who wasn't committed to quality improvement. Often these top officials are also willing to issue a mission statement. Failure to do so would be like failing to support motherhood and apple pie. But, quite frankly, if an organization's commitment, as demonstrated by the top official, is limited to a mission statement, then the entire improvement process is doomed, if not to failure, then to a very slow process of improvement.

> A commitment is a pledge; when upper management makes a quality commitment and formulates a policy statement, they pledge their support by not only honoring the philosophy contained therein, but by providing active leadership to implement the intent of the policy as well. [123: 27]

Managers must do more than simply state that they are committed. They must demonstrate that commitment. They must lead the charge to improving quality. There have been all kinds of definitions of leadership. Some of the characteristics of a leader that readily come to mind are listed here:

- A leader works at developing the people who work for him or her.
- The leader has time for the important parts of the job.
- The leader is secure in his or her position and lets his or her followers know where they stand.
- A leader helps his or her followers to produce.
- A leader uses teamwork to accomplish tasks.
- A leader inspires his or her followers, unlike a "boss," who generates fear.
- Leaders help to find solutions to problems and don't worry about assigning personal blame.
- Leaders plan for the future.

A word that comes to mind that really translates leadership into action is involvement or, better yet, *active involvement*.

Managers must become involved in performing the actions required for continuous quality improvement. Managers must know how to create partnerships across areas, between suppliers and the company, with the customers as joint ventures, and with the union. We know, for example, the use of statistical methods for process monitoring and control is an essential part of statistical process control. We know that we can only improve stable processes. The involved manager will use these methods in improving his or her own job. Look at the commitment that Robert D.

Cadieux, president of Amoco Chemicals, shows to their use. An important process that Cadieux performs is the chairing of corporate meetings. He maintains, in his office, a nonconformance graph that shows, on a daily basis, the number of times meetings start late. Because these changes can be disruptive to the company, the goal, Cadiux says, is "to get that number down to zero." [112: 4]

Some specific steps that management can take that will show its involvement and commitment include allocating resources, demanding that everyone in the organization understand the quality disciplines, setting quality improvement goals, and including quality within the reward and/or evaluation system. [21: 47] A few comments on each of these.

Quality improvement is an investment. Quality does not cost; it pays for itself. Management must make available resources for implementing and maintaining the quality improvement system. Common wisdom indicates that an effective quality improvement program will require between 5 and 10 percent of the typical organization's sales dollars. The ongoing training required will demand 5 to 10 percent of all employees' time. Allocating this level of resource demonstrates a commitment. It also demands some organizational, not individual, accountability. This accountability can be reflected via the setting of improvement goals. Once these goals are met, then new goals have to be stated and strived for. The cycle, remember, never ends.

A way to motivate the members of the organization toward attaining these ever upwardly mobile goals is by including them in the evaluation scheme. When goals are met, the rewards should be obvious. The rewards don't necessarily have to be financial, although that does not hurt. Sometimes simple recognition via newsletters, certificates, and so forth, works just about as well. And the impact on a visitor of seeing numerous public citations for quality performance also has a very positive effect.

To accomplish these, a formal organizational structure is recommended. The following section will describe the essentials of such an organizational system.

19.5   ORGANIZATIONAL STEPS

The commitment and involvement begin at the top of the organization. That is where the organizational development and change must also start.

A top management committee should be formed to implement the continuous improvement philosophy. The head of this committee should report directly to the chief operating official of the organization. This steering committee should hold frequent meetings, examine progress, discuss problems, and remove barriers that develop as the improvement process develops.

By holding frequent meetings, the committee will come to understand that quality improvement is an important element of everybody's job. Included in these meetings must be training for the individuals on the committee. To examine progress, the committee must set goals. Initially, they may be training goals; but unless the training is put into regular use, it will soon be forgotten. As the training progresses, it will focus on more and more specifics relating to continuous improvement. Making top management part of this committee will also show the employees that there is a commitment.

Training will not by itself improve quality. Cooperation between individuals in the organization will. A top management committee is in a position to break down the barriers that normally exist in a typical pyramid organization. Focusing on improvement rather than on going through channels is an important message that will come out of the management committee.

In a larger organization, similar committees have to be developed at each location. The key management personnel at each location must also go through this same process. As this proceeds down through the organization, all levels have to be involved.

At this new awareness moves through the organization, we find that people start viewing their roles in the organization differently. This is the customer/supplier relationship. Every member of the organization must know who his or her customers are and who his or her suppliers are. The key words describing this new organization are as follows: [56: 55]

- It has a customer focus, an obsession with quality.
- It recognizes you have both external customers and internal customers.
- It demands improved relations with suppliers—a true working partnership.
- It emphasizes process improvement rather than individual accountability.

Remember that our process orientation showed that the overall transformation, as shown in Figure 19–1, is really a system of interconnected processes, as shown in Figure 19–2. This means that the organization chart is not really pyramidal anymore. Instead of the chart shown in Figure 19–3, we have one that more closely resembles that shown in Figure 19–4, where the responsibility is to the customer. "Probably the most important management fundamental that is being ignored today is staying close to the customer to satisfy his needs and anticipate his wants." [140: 20]

When discussing the implementation of the quality improvement effort at the

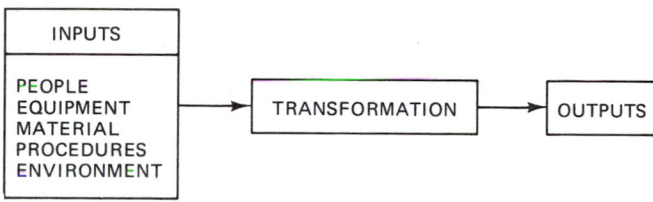

FIGURE 19–1 Overall System

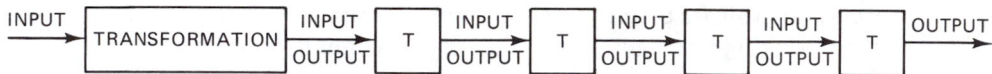

FIGURE 19-2 Interconnected Processes

First National Bank of Chicago, CEO Richard Thomas stated, "Our next task was to identify in concrete terms those customer requirements: by asking and listening, we learned that prominent among our clients' needs and expectations are timeliness, accuracy, efficiency, responsive service, and good communication." [92: 28] Tom Williams, CEO of First Wachovia, echoed that: "In the business world today, we hear a lot about quality and excellence. But as slogans, neither can substitute for the simple process of knowing your customers needs and wishes and seeing that those needs and wishes are met consistently and efficiently." [169: 11c] Another executive stated it similarly, "Our goal is to be recognized by our customers as an innovative, cost-effective, high quality supplier. This requires thorough understanding of our customers' present and future needs." [156: 21] We could fill page after page with quotes. What we need to look at, in terms of organizational strategy, is motivating our workers to adopt or "buy" this customer/supplier viewpoint. "Dealing with this phase is more than a management responsibility; it is a leadership responsibility." [181: 419]

19.6 OWNERSHIP

To understand the concept of ownership we must understand the philosophy James Houghton, CEO of Corning Glass Works, expressed when keynoting the 41st Annual ASQC Quality Congress,

> We always thought of ourselves as enlightened managers, but we found that we had vastly underestimated our people. We found our people want more responsibility on the job; they want more responsibility for their contribution and more involvement in how problems and tasks are defined and solved. [176: 5B]

The majority of workers want, quite simply, the opportunity to be heard and recognition of their contribution. They want to feel part of the organization.

Using the term ownership sums this up. It sounds a bit corny, but old expressions like teamwork fit. Paul Smith, vice-president and general manager of Rockwell Missile Systems Division, addressed this as Southern College of Technology's First Quality Forum*: "WE the people are in the company, THEY are the defects that are produced by the process."

When we speak of ownership, we mean ownership of the process. We remem-

---

*This forum, sponsored by the School of Technology of Southern College of Technology, was held in Marietta, Georgia, on April 23, 1987. The theme of the forum was *Product Excellence: Industry's Challenge to Higher Education.*

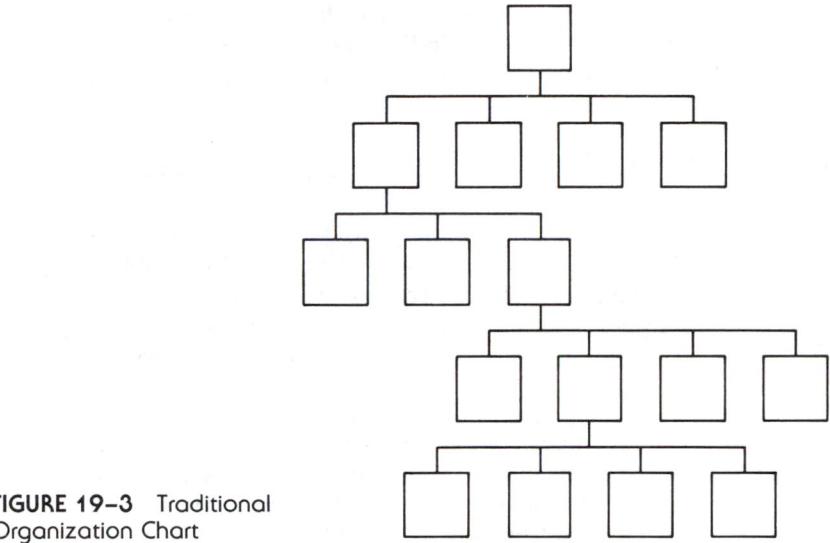

FIGURE 19–3 Traditional Organization Chart

ber that in our view of processes, as illustrated in Figure 19–2, processes flow throughout the entire organization. This is generally fairly well defined within a manufacturing organization where the flow can readily be seen. Each piece of the process is clearly defined; the point at which the output of one process becomes the input of the next is easy to identify. In the service arena, this is sometimes a little harder to see. Often, one process will have more than one person who feels responsible. There can be a blurring of inputs and outputs. A supplier can also be the customer for the same process.

Regardless of the difficulty, though, it is management's job to assign an owner to each process. The owner of a process is "fully responsible for yield, cost, and quality as well as schedule. In addition, he or she has to balance the process to the targets set on these characteristics." [108: 303] When the owner of the process is given these responsibilities, it effectively removes them from the manager who used to have control. This turns the entire organization upside down. It is a new role for the manager, especially the middle manager. In our customer supplier language, "subordinates are the customers of their manager, and the manager's role then becomes one of providing the environment and resources to the subordinates so that they can achieve the agreed upon goals." [167: 213]

This can cause a number of problems in that it reflects a whole new way of

SUPPLIERS INTERNAL PROCESSES CONSUMERS

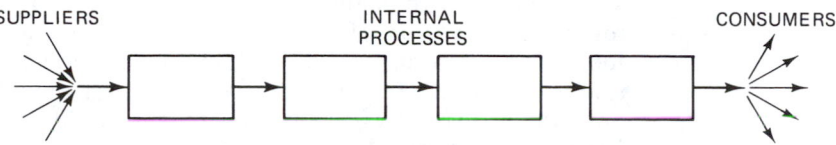

FIGURE 19–4 Process Organization Chart

doing business. It means that the culture of the organization is changing and that the attitudes of the individuals in the organization also have to change. When changes like these occur, the organization faces considerable resistance.

19.7 RESISTANCE TO CHANGE

Adopting the new philosophy essentially means that the organization is now extremely sensitive and responsive to valid customer requirements and expectations; individuals think in terms of processes and customer/supplier relationships; and people derive their authority for action from their skills and knowledge, rather than from their position on an organization chart. Specifically,

> Adopting the new philosophy requires changing attitudes. This is difficult for many people because it involves moving from something that is known to something that is unknown. This creates mistrust, fear, and anxieties, particularly for people who are satisfied with the status quo. Top and middle managers have the most to fear. [156: 33]

How then can this be overcome? Several positive steps must be taken. First among these is communication of the new goal. Everyone in the organization must understand that there is a real change taking place. Everyone must also believe that the change is really necessary. In terms of the quality problems, these changes will require significant education. There is still a vast misconception about the nature and cause of the quality problem facing U.S. industry and business.

Second, for the change to be effective, there must be a management organization in place to handle the change. "One doesn't simply announce, 'We want to change.' Rather you manage change and make a clearly identifiable set of people responsible for them. [97: 50]

Third, and this goes back to the ownership concepts introduced earlier in this chapter, the owners of the processes must be encouraged to find their own quality improvements. This has to be done under the direction of the organization's leaders, but it cannot be so structured as to be viewed as just another management edict. Employees become wary of management directed changes. Without the ownership, they view the change as simply another BOHICA (an acronym that stands for bend over, here it comes again).

Rosabeth Moss Kanter, author of *The Change Masters,* says this can be encouraged in a number of different ways.

> We found that high innovation companies have a different attitude towards reward. They not only have rewards that pay people after they do a good job, but they also have what I call investment-oriented rewards. These are rewards before the fact that somebody will perform later. . . . Challenge—opportunity—is one of the greatest untapped potential rewards that most organizations have. [97: 48]

Fourth, seek the active support of a critical mass. In any organization, there will be a small minority of people who might be termed avid supporters of the change. They need no encouragement. There is also a small minority of individuals who will fight every change tooth and nail. In the middle is a group that has no firm opinions and might be described as changeable. Figure 19–5 takes advantage of our statistical understanding and shows these three groups as portions of the area under the normal curve.

The group in the middle is what we might call the critical mass.

> In the context of organizational change, a ''critical mass'' is a dynamic and somewhat elusive quantity. It is not simply a majority. What constitutes a critical mass at one stage of innovation may be inadequate in later stages. Critical mass is a sufficient number of influential people supporting a proposed change to give the impression of a growing, formidable movement, a sense of momentum, a groundswell of interest.   [177: 207]

Perhaps a key to remember is that if change is done to me then I will view it as a threat. If I make the changes, then they become an opportunity. It isn't change that people fight, per se, it is the process of being changed that is difficult. Implementing this philosophy means that we have the opportunity to improve and get better. Handling the implementation is important.

19.8   BOTTOM-UP IMPLEMENTATION

We can talk about change from the top down. We can talk about the need for commitment. But not all organizations are that way. Ishikawa has described some organizations in which the top management is not committed. The characteristics of these organizations include the following: [58: 70–71]

1. Top managers avoid responsibility.
2. People feel that there are no problems at all.
3. People feel that there is no competition.
4. Individuals see no alternative methods.

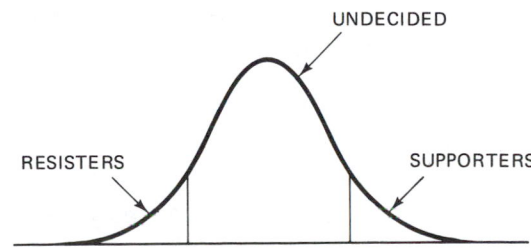

FIGURE 19–5 Distribution for Change

5. People have tunnel vision about their own organization.

6. People will not listen to other ideas.

7. Individuals are oblivious to what is happening around them.

Although it is much more difficult, these organizations can also be changed. It is much more difficult to change the organization this way, but it can be accomplished. The following specific steps have been suggested for making changes from the bottom of the organization. [177: 210–211]

First, pick improvement projects on processes that you have responsibility for. Second, select processes that, when improved, will catch the eyes of people higher up in the organization. These may be big dollar improvements focusing on reduced scrap or reduced rework. Pick the projects that will impress the skeptics and maybe start the critical mass moving.

Third, include as many people as possible in your project. Giving more people credit for the improvements will do nothing but help. Being associated with success, owning some of the success, will build up your supporters. Fourth, enter the process with a great deal of patience. It may take quite a while to convince everyone above you.

Fifth, be ready for any opportunities to spread your vision. Be especially eager to assist those higher in the organization to improve their processes. Sixth, become a source and resource of information about continuous quality improvement. Be prepared to speak about the topic to any and all audiences. Seventh, compile success stories. Keep them handy and use them to help sell the concept.

Last, "keep in mind that the efforts should always be geared at getting the attention of top management, educating them and making them believers and champions of them. Without their eventual buy-in, all of your transformation efforts will wither on the vine." [177: 211]

19.9 COST OF QUALITY

A discussion of the implementation of the philosophy of continuous improvement would not be complete without a mention of quality costs. The crucial point for every organization at some point lies in the bottom line. It is essential that quality costs be monitored.

These systems are needed to identify, define and prioritize quality improvement opportunities, to encourage long term solutions, to track the overall Total Quality Improvement Process journey, and to provide a baseline from which recognition can be given for successes. Action needed to install these systems include:

- Develop business-wide COQ [cost of quality] measurement policies and general implementation guidelines.

- Identify some initial cost of quality components for awareness and tracking purposes.

- Use the input/output model to determine the key processes that need to be monitored.
- Install in each department cost of quality measurement systems to monitor key processes and to identify, define, and prioritize quality improvement opportunities.
- Roll up departmental COQ reports into consolidated business-wide reports on a periodic basis to track overall trends. [185: 319]

The designation of quality costs is probably a misnomer. It should better be stated as the cost of nonquality. The basic concept of quality is recognition and organization of certain quality-related costs to gain knowledge of their major contributing segments and the direction of their trends. Tracking quality costs provide a guide to management, in management's language. It also provides information for justifying quality improvement programs.

The major cost categories generally used for cost of quality analysis include prevention, detection, correction, and failure. (Because there are many fine references dedicated to quality costs, this section will merely summarize. Attention is directed toward such references and the *Quality Control Handbook*.)

Prevention costs are those associated with personnel in designing, implementing, and maintaining the quality system, including auditing the system. Some specific prevention costs include:

- Vendor quality evaluations
- Procurement
- Process engineering
- Reliability engineering
- Quality engineering
- Quality planning
- Training

Appraisal costs are those associated with measuring and evaluating to assure conformance with standards and performance requirements. Some typical appraisal costs include:

- Receiving inspection
- Lab testing
- Test equipment calibration
- Inspection salaries

Internal failure costs are those associated with defective materials that cause manufacturing losses. Some typical examples of these include:

- Scrap
- Rework

- Retest
- Downtime
- Failure analysis
- Material disposition

External failure costs are those generated by defective material being shipped to the customer. External failure costs include:

- Complaint adjustment
- Returned material costs
- Warranty charges
- Marketing errors
- Installation errors

There is one other quality cost. This one is most difficult to measure. It is the cost of lost business due to poor quality. Informal surveys indicate that when a customer purchases a good product she or he will tell approximately eight people about it. If the product or service is of poor quality and does not meet consumer expectations, then as many as 22 people will hear the bad news.

It is important to remember the words of A. V. Feigenbaum when considering quality costs. As he told the keynote session of the 41st Quality Congress, "Quality and cost are a sum, not a difference."

19.10 CONCLUSION

At this point, a conclusion is almost redundant, However, whether or not it is redundant, a closing paragraph is called for.

We have spent the past pages discussing the philosophy of quality improvement using a statistical process control model as the guide. The points we want to emphasize are the following:

1. Quality is what the customer perceives it to be. It is based on the customer's expectations and perceptions.

2. Quality improvement will not just happen. It has to be worked at. It has to be worked at continuously by everyone in the organization from the CEO down.

3. Quality improvement is as essential in service as it is manufacturing. The key to competitiveness is continual quality improvement.

4. The quality improvement process is never ending. Quality is not a destination. Quality is a journey.

CHAPTER 20

Case Studies

20.1 CASE STUDY 1

STATISTICAL PROCESS CONTROL: A CASE STUDY*

Amoco Foam Products Company

Introduction

Amoco Foam Products Company, part of the Amoco Chemical Company, has embarked on the journey of continuous quality improvement. The senior management of Amoco Chemical, under the leadership of company President, Robert D. Cadieux, listened to Phil Crosby in 1983 speak at a senior management meeting. In an article published by Amoco Chemical in *The Right Chemistry,* (Volume 1, Number 1, pp. 2–4) Cadieux makes some statements about Amoco Chemical's approach to quality improvement.

1. Our goal is to foster at every location an environment in which people take pride in their work and are interested in improving the quality of everything they do.

2. As management, we're the cause of about 80 percent of the company's quality problems and not the fellow on the assembly line.

Amoco Chemical saw that part of the management responsibility was to provide their employees with the tools and skills necessary to improve their processes and improve their quality. As Cadieux stated, "As management, our belief is that improving the quality of this company will create growth opportunities that would not have been available to us otherwise."

As part of the improvement process Amoco Chemical undertook several different ap-

*Printed with permission of Amoco Corporation.

proaches to training. Many members of management attend the Crosby Quality College in Florida. Other employees receive in-plant training on the same philosophy. Amoco Foam Products Company, under the direction of the former corporate Quality Assurance Manager, Tim Gavin, instituted in-plant statistical process control training in order to directly involve the people who are directly tied to the process in the efforts to improve it.

As of this writing, Amoco Foam Products Company, which is headquartered in Metropolitan Atlanta, operates 9 manufacturing plants spread around the United States. When an individual plant manager requested the statistical process control assistance, Gavin's group provided the training and statistical support required.

Training Program Overview

While the specifics of the statistical process control training varied for each of the plants, the training can best be characterized as hands-on. Within each plant initial training was provided to several groups. The membership of each group was determined by process. Members of each group were selected by the individual plant management. Typically the groups consisted of production operators, supervisors, mechanics, inspectors, process engineers, and even representatives from accounting, training, and safety. One member in each group was given the added responsibility of being the in-plant SPC co-ordinator.

The actual training was built around the General Motors slide-tape training package. These *canned* presentations were augmented by the training leader. The training was conducted over a 6 week time frame, with the leader visiting the plant, analyzing the data with the assistance of the in-plant SPC co-ordinator, and holding the training meetings each week. At the conclusion of each training session each group was given a data collection assignment for the following week that corresponded to the material presented in the preceding sessions.

The typical training schedule included, on a weekly basis, the topics shown in the following table:

Amoco Foam Products Company SPC Training Outline

Week	Topics
1	Definition of Quality
	Check Sheets
2	Pareto Analysis
	Cause Effect Diagrams
3	Variability
	Histograms
	Location
	Spread
	Shape
	Run Charts
4	Basic Statistics
	Normal Curve Orientation
5	Control Charts for Variables
6	Process Capability
	Continuing Improvement

As was stated earlier, the training was primarily hands-on. Beginning with the initial session, each group identified problems with the quality of the output of the process. Each group calculated data which the course leader and in-plant SPC co-ordinator summarized and used as the starting point for the next training session.

Although the trainer performed all the analysis, with the assistance of the in-plant co-ordinator, the process improvement training team interpreted and recommended future action. By the completion of the 6th training session each team was able to recommend a process change that would improve the overall quality of the product selected.

The remainder of this case will illustrate the application of the statistical process control methods by one training group at one Amoco Foam Products Company plant. It is representative of the types of results achieved by the training.

Process Description

The process selected at this plant was the foam extrusion process. The output of this process is rolls of foam plastic sheet that are later formed into a variety of shapes, such as apple trays and meat trays. Foam extrusion is a complicated process, compounded by the fact that no two extrusion "machines" are exactly alike.

Inputs to the process include virgin plastic pellets, reground plastic (from trim scrap), coloring agents, blowing agent (gas), and some other material that act as catalysts in the chemical reaction of the transformation process.

These inputs are combined, according to specifications developed by process engineers. The transformation includes heating the material under pressure, mixing it, cooling it, and extruding through a die. The output is foam sheet. This is wrapped into large rolls which are aged and then used as the input for the thermoforming process which creates the specific shapes.

The complicated interaction of the inputs under the variety of temperatures and pressures, provide an ideal environment for applying statistical process control improvement techniques. Each input variable has the opportunity to vary, and the transformation process itself creates additional variability. A relatively simple process adjustment, such as changing a temperature or pressure setting or mixing rate can, due to the interaction of the inputs, cause a tremendous change in the variability of the process output.

The variability of the output was causing some quality problems. Coupled with the corporate objective of continuous quality improvement, the SPC application was started.

The training outline presented earlier highlighted the week by week training topics. The following sections will highlight the objectives of each weeks' training and summarize the significant results.

Week 1

The training discussions in the first week centered on quality, productivity, and Amoco's response to these. Specifically, possible quality problems on the selected extrusion line were discussed. Brainstorming developed a list of 29 potential characteristics that *might* be problems, along with ways to measure an agreed upon rational frequency of measurements. This information for the check sheet is shown in Figure C–1. The team was instructed in the use of the check sheet and asked to collect data for a 1 week period. This was done either by production operators or by quality control technicians for the more technical tests.

Week 2

The training leader, upon his return to the plant, collected the check sheets and summarized the data. The total count was converted to a relative frequency which was rank ordered. This is shown in Figure C–2. The training the second week included Pareto analysis, so the Pareto chart of Figure C–3 was developed and explained. The 6–inch seal leak problem was discarded as a topic of SPC application because the replacement part already had been ordered. Of the

IDENTIFICATION: CHECKSHEET

CHARACTERISTICS: PROBLEMS: DEFECTS OR UNDESIREABLE EFFECTS:	WAY TO MEASURE	WHEN TO MEASURE	DATE: COUNT/TALLY
CHEVRONS TALLY IF PRESENT	VISUAL Y/N	ROLL CUT	
SHEET COLOR TALLY IF ANY OFF COLOR	VISUAL	ROLL CUT	
SWRAP SPEED TALLY IF OUT OF RANGE	LINE SPEED INDICATOR	ROLL CUT	
PREFOAMING TALLY IF PRESENT	VISUAL Y/N	ROLL CUT	
GAS FLOW OUT OF RANGE	DIGITAL FLOW METER	2 HRS	
CELL SIZE OUT OF RANGE	QC CHECK	2 HRS	
SHEET THICKNESS OUT OF RANGE	QC CHECK	2 HRS	
ORIENTATION MD OUT OF RANGE	QC CHECK	2 HRS	
ORIENTATION TD OUT OF RANGE	QC CHECK	2 HRS	
MELT TEMP # 1 OUT OF RANGE	DIGITAL TEMP GAGE	2 HRS	
MELT TEMP # 2 OUT OF RANGE	DIGITAL TEMP GAGE	2 HRS	
POST EXPANSION LESS THAN 60%	QC CHECK	2 HRS	
4 1/2" AMPS OUT OF RANGE	OPERATOR ANALOG GAGE	2 HRS	
6" AMPS OUT OF RANGE	OPERATOR ANALOG GAGE	2 HRS	
CROSSOVER PRESSURE OUT OF RANGE	OPERATOR ANALOG GAGE	2 HRS	
GAS RETENTION OUT OF RANGE	QC CHECK	2 HRS	
4 1/2 RPM OUT OF RANGE	OPERATOR DIGITAL GAGE	2 HRS	

FIGURE C–1 Initial Check Sheet

CHECKSHEET

DATE:

CHARACTERISTICS: PROBLEMS: DEFECTS OR UNDESIREABLE EFFECTS:	WAY TO MEASURE	WHEN TO MEASURE	COUNT/TALLY
6" RPMS OUT OF RANGE	OPERATOR DIGITAL GAGE	2 HRS	
LBS/HR OUT OF RANGE	OPERATOR CALCULATION	2 HRS	
6" BARREL PRESSURE OUT OF RANGE	OPERATOR DIGITAL GAGE	2 HRS	
DIE PRESSURE OUT OF RANGE	OPERATOR DIGITAL GAGE	2 HRS	
CROSS SECTION WT. OUT OF RANGE	QC CHECK	2 HRS	
6" SEAL LEAK	OPERATOR Y/N	1/SHIFT	
SHEET WIDTH WITHIN RANGE	OPERATOR MEASURE	1/SHIFT	
BUTANE PUMP TALLY IF BLEEDING REQ.	OPERATOR	TALLY IF IT OCCURS	
4 1/2 AMP FALSE ALARM	OPERATOR	TALLY IF IT OCCURS	
WINDER STOPS	OPERATOR	TALLY IF IT OCCURS	
FEED SYSTEM STOPS	OPERATOR	TALLY IF IT OCCURS	
WATER IN MATERIAL	OPERATOR	TALLY IF IT OCCURS	

FIGURE C-1 (Continued)

IDENTIFICATION: COMBINED   CHECKSHEET

CHARACTERISTICS: PROBLEMS: DEFECTS OR UNDESIREABLE EFFECTS:	WAY TO MEASURE	WHEN TO MEASURE	TOTAL COUNT	REL. FREQ.	RANK ORDER
				DATE:	
CHEVRONS TALLY IF PRESENT	VISUAL Y/N	ROLL CUT	31	31/104 = .298	4
SHEET COLOR TALLY IF ANY OFF COLOR	VISUAL	ROLL CUT	5	.048	13
S WRAP SPEED TALLY IF OUT OF RANGE	LINE SPEED INDICATOR	ROLL CUT	2	.019	17
PREFOAMING TALLY IF PRESENT	VISUAL Y/N	ROLL CUT	11	.106	10
GAS FLOW OUT OF RANGE	DIGITAL FLOW METER	2 HRS	15	15/52 = .288	5
CELL SIZE OUT OF RANGE	QC CHECK	2 HRS	10	.192	8
SHEET THICKNESS OUT OF RANGE	QC CHECK	2 HRS	5	.096	11
ORIENTATION MD OUT OF RANGE	QC CHECK	2 HRS	14	.269	7
ORIENTATION TD OUT OF RANGE	QC CHECK	2 HRS	7	.135	9
MELT TEMP # 1 OUT OF RANGE	DIGITAL TEMP GAGE	2 HRS	0	0	20
MELT TEMP # 2 OUT OF RANGE	DIGITAL TEMP GAGE	2 HRS	0	0	20
POST EXPANSION LESS THAN 60%	QC CHECK	2 HRS	26	.500	2
4 1/2" AMPS OUT OF RANGE	OPERATOR ANALOG GAGE	2 HRS	0	0	20
6" AMPS OUT OF RANGE	OPERATOR ANALOG GAGE	2 HRS	2	.038	14
CROSSOVER PRESSURE OUT OF RANGE	OPERATOR ANALOG GAGE	2 HRS	15	.288	5
GAS RETENTION OUT OF RANGE	QC CHECK	2 HRS	1	.019	17
4 1/2 RPMS OUT OF RANGE	OPERATOR DIGITAL GAGE	2 HRS	2	.038	14

FIGURE C–2 Completed Check Sheet

CHARACTERISTICS: PROBLEMS: DEFECTS OR UNDESIREABLE EFFECTS:	WAY TO MEASURE	WHEN TO MEASURE	TOTAL COUNT	REL. FREQ.	RANK ORDER
6" RPMS OUT OF RANGE	OPERATOR DIGITAL GAGE	2 HRS	0	0	20
LBS/HR OUT OF RANGE	OPERATOR CALCULATON	2 HRS	24	0.461	3
6" BARREL PRESSURE OUT OF RANGE	OPERATOR DIGITAL GAGE	2 HRS	1	0.019	17
DIE PRESSURE OUT OF RANGE	OPERATOR DIGITAL GAGE	2 HRS	2	0.038	14
CROSS SECTION WT. OUT OF RANGE	OPERATOR Y/N	2 HRS	3	0.057	12
6" SEAL LEAK	OPERATOR MEASURE	1/SHIFT	11	0.086	1
SHEET WIDTH WITHIN RANGE	OPERATOR	1/SHIFT	0	0	20
BUTANE PUMP TALLY IF BLEEDING REQ.	OPERATOR	TALLY IF IT OCCURS	3		
4 1/2 AMP FALSE ALARM	OPERATOR	TALLY IF IT OCCURS	4		
WINDER STOPS	OPERATOR	TALLY IF IT OCCURS	1		
FEED SYSTEM STOPS	OPERATOR	TALLY IF IS OCCURS	1		
WATER IN MATERIAL	OPERATOR	TALLY IF IT OCCURS	0		

FIGURE C-2   (*Continued*)

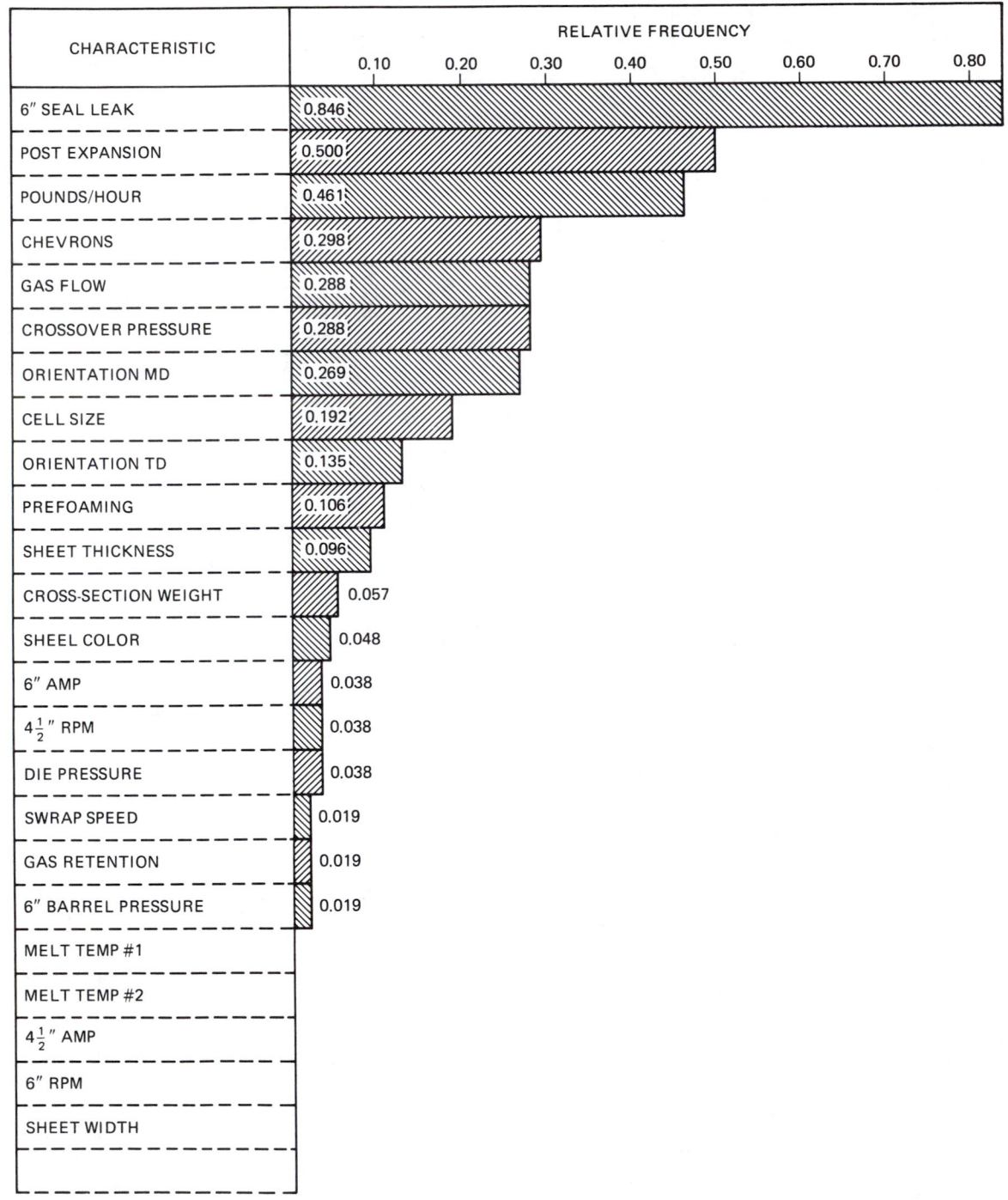

FIGURE C–3 Pareto Chart

remaining high frequency problems a team consensus was reached deciding to study the post expansion less than 60 percent problem. Post expansion refers to the aging process wherein the material expands after extrusion. The 60 percent requirement was necessary for the material to thermoform properly.

A second topic of the week's training was the cause and effect diagram. Figure C–4 shows the diagram that the training group developed for the post expansion problem. Six characteristics out of the many suggested were identified as being the most likely causes of the post expansion problem. These were outside temperature, gas flow rate [flow rate], gas retention, melt 2 temperature, die pressure, and machine direction [md] orientation. It was decided that data would be collected on these characteristics based on the specific type of material produced that week, such as light (weight) white or medium (weight) colored foam. Figure C–5 shows the data collection form.

Week 3

The third week's training session focused on variability, histograms, and run charts. When the trainer returned he prepared the histograms shown in Figure C–6 and run charts shown in Figure C–7.

Conclusions reached by the training group were that the process had lots of natural or normal variability and that more data on the same characteristics would be helpful.

Week 4

The fourth week's training continued an analysis of the data and covered the basic statistics—the measures of location, spread, and shape. The conclusions focused on the gas flow, gas temperature, die pressure, and gas retention rates. Figure C–8 shows the second week's histograms and Figure C–9 shows the run charts.

It was decided that the melt 2 data and the md orientation were no longer pertinent to the problem solving, so the collection of that information was halted. The analyst also agreed at this time to start providing the mean and standard deviations of the characteristics that were being measured.

Week 5

The data collected this week, as shown in the run charts of Figure C–10 continued to show variability, but some patterns were emerging. A problem with rapid gas flow rate fluctuations provided a convenient transition mechanism to introduce control charts for variables. The relationship of process variability and sample averages was discussed, and for the last week of data collection tied directly to the training program, it was decided that gas temperature as measured in the gas line right before the process begins, the average flow rate, using a sample size of 3, and die pressure would be monitored.

Week 6

The data collected for the final week of training proved to be very interesting. Figure C–11 shows the cyclic pattern associated with the gas temperature.

A similar pattern showed up for the gas flow rate and the die pressure. These charts are shown in Figure C–12.

Figure C–13 shows the run chart for gas temperature and the control chart for flow rate and the run charts for gas temperature and die pressure on the same time scale. These charts led to some interesting analysis and provided the transition to talk about the analysis of control charts and process capability.

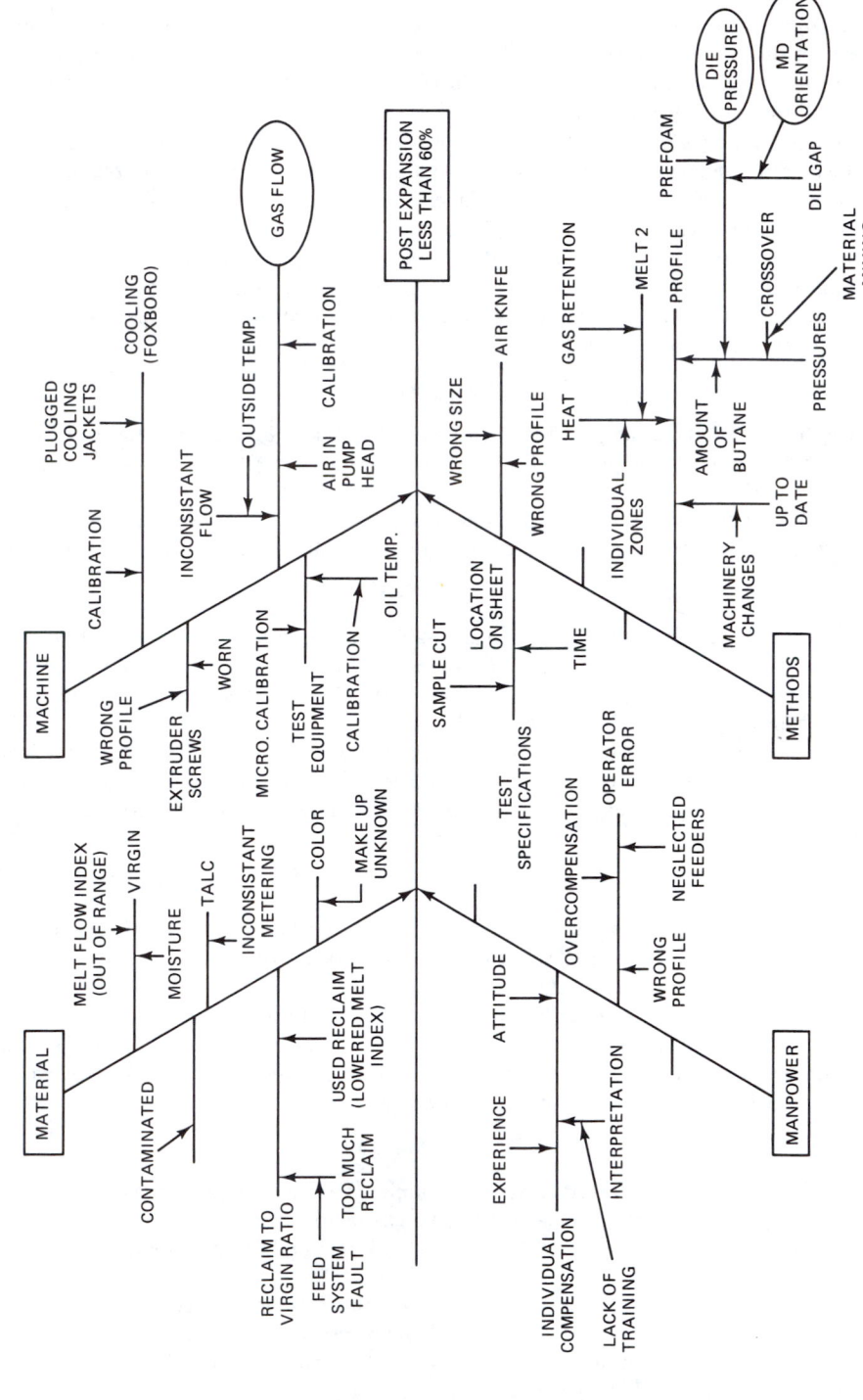

CAUSE AND EFFECT DIAGRAM

FIGURE C-4 Cause/Effect Diagram for Post Expansion

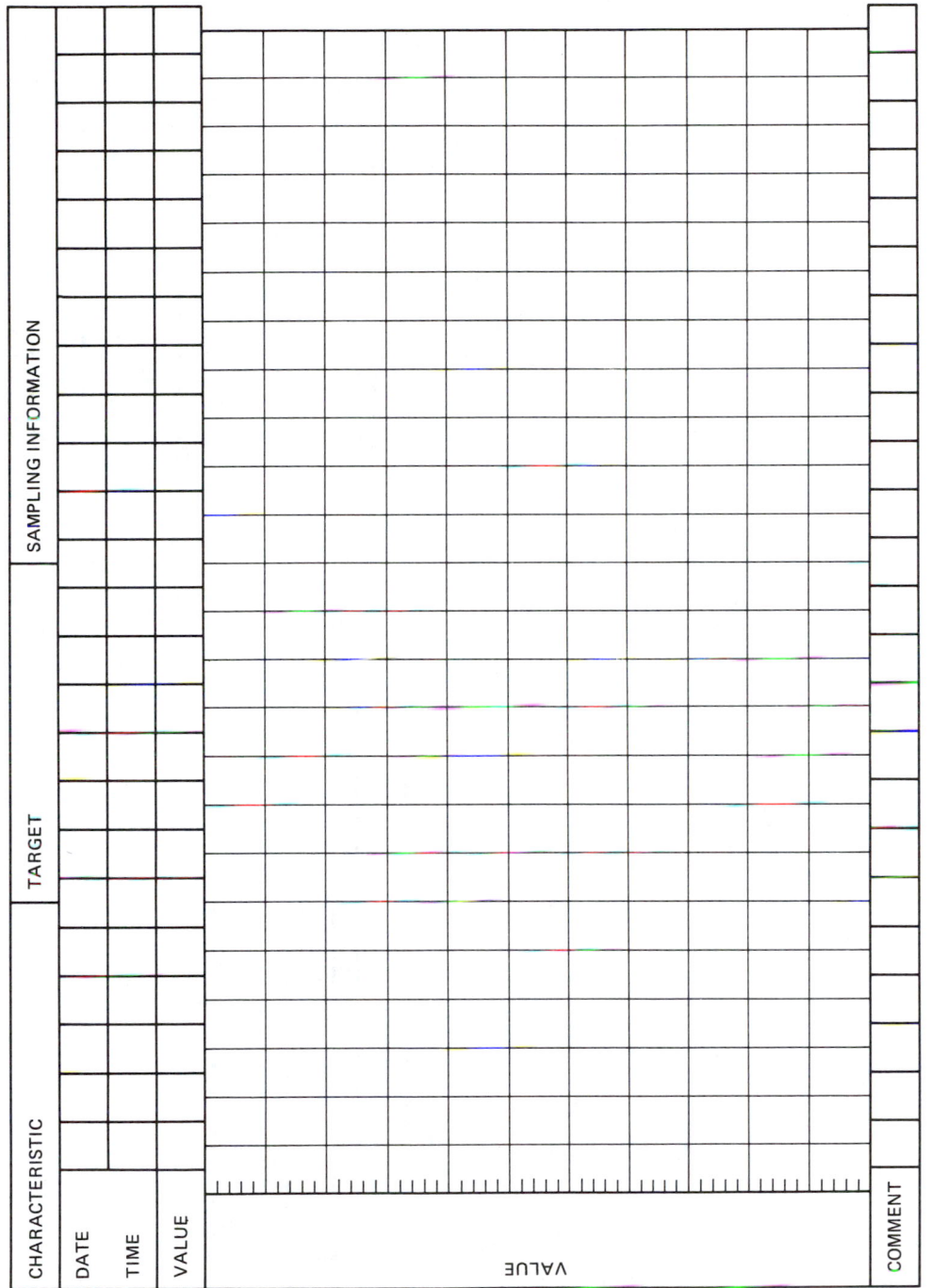

FIGURE C-5 Run Chart/Data Collection Form

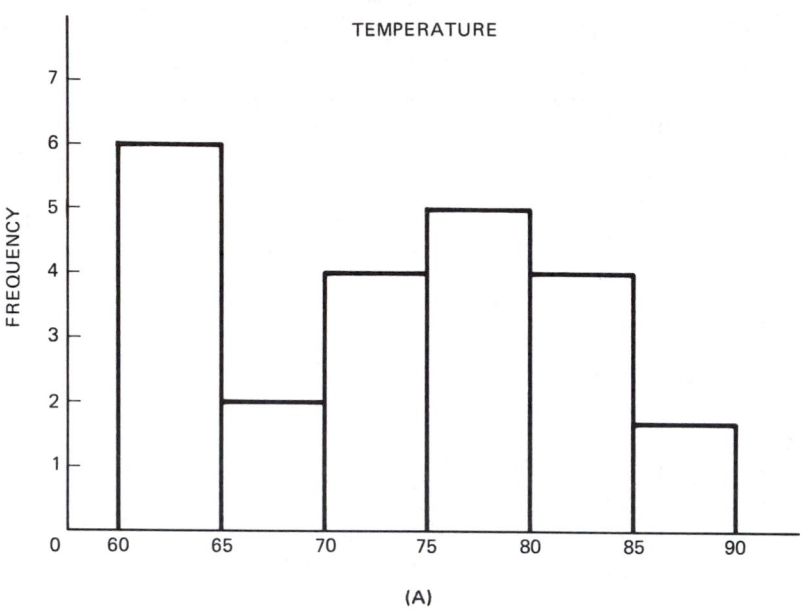

(A)

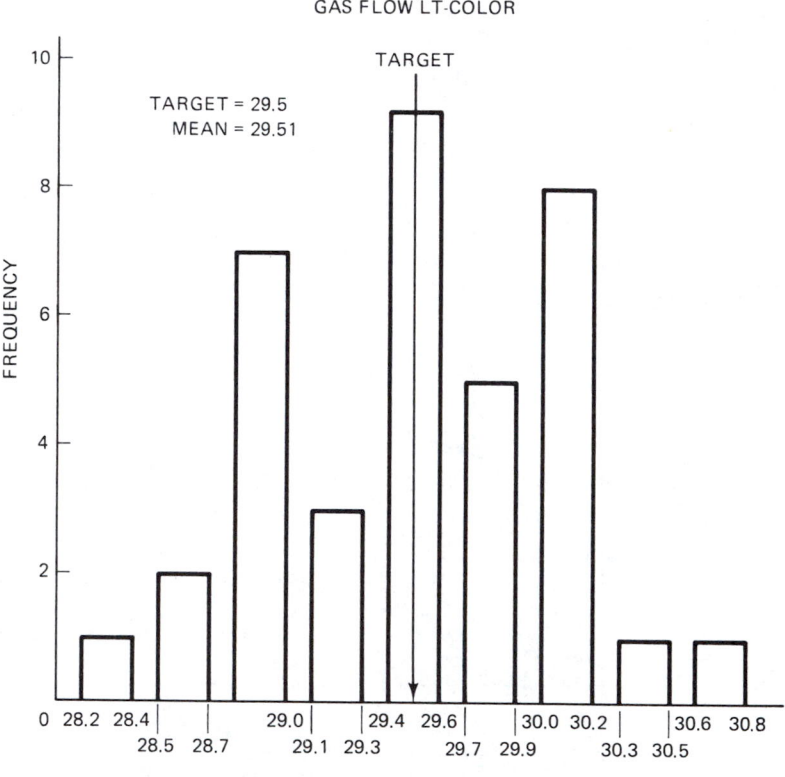

(B)

FIGURE C–6a–g Histograms

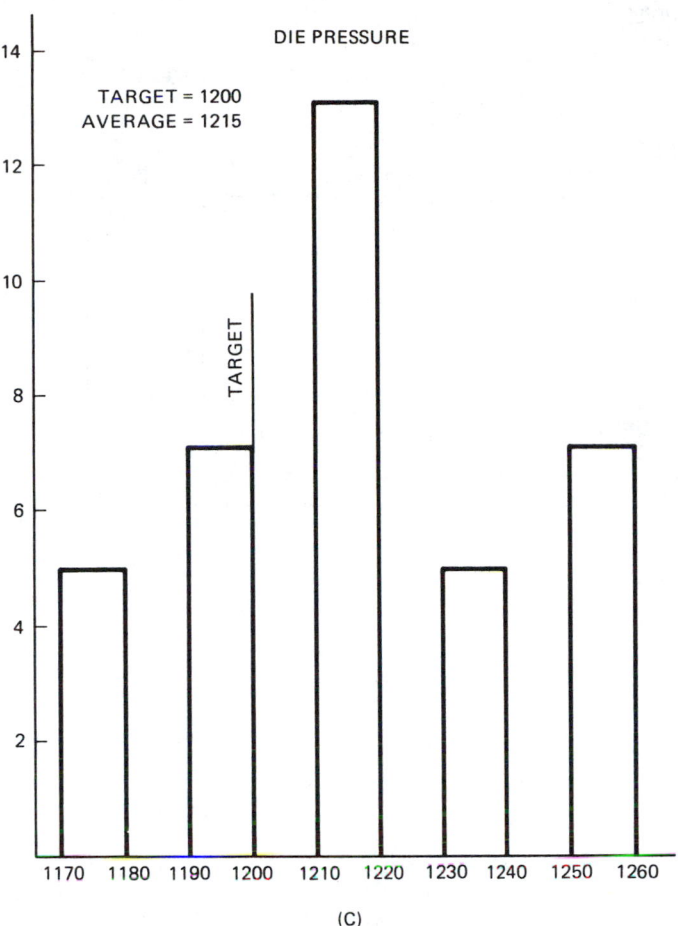

(C)

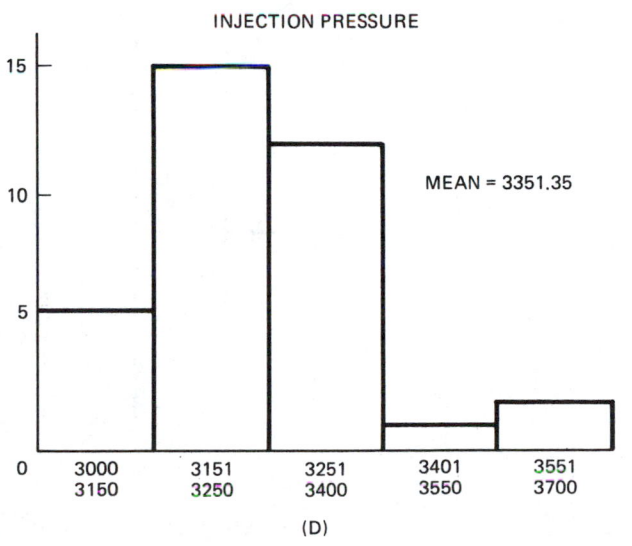

(D)

FIGURE C–6a–g *(Continued)* *(cont.)*

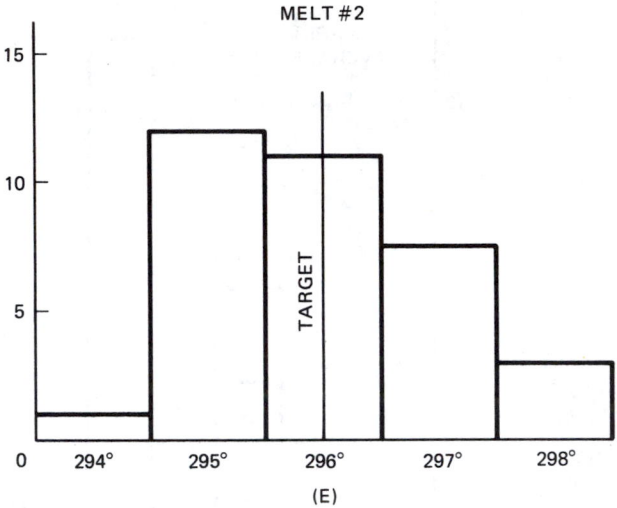

(E)

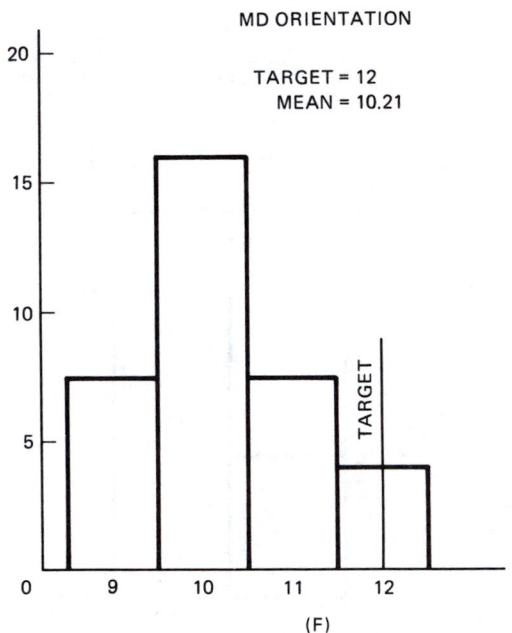

(F)

FIGURE C–6a–g (*Continued*)

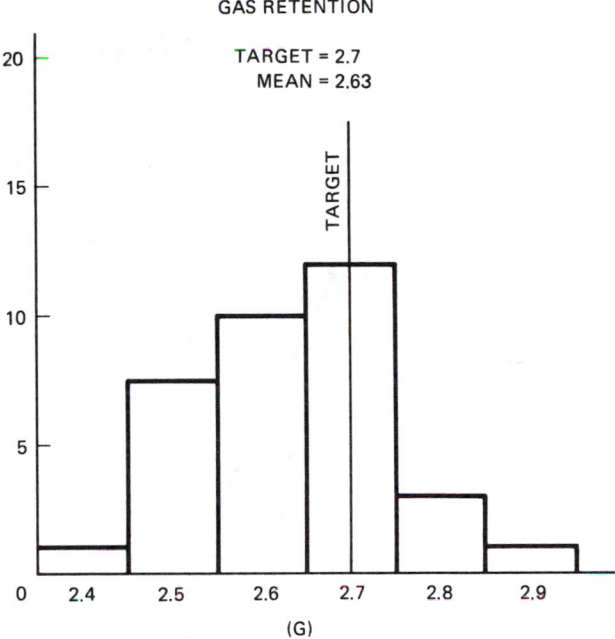

FIGURE C–6a–g (*Continued*)

Listing and discussing indicators of abnormal variation, such as the appearance of cycles, immediately pinpointed a possible problem for some of the participants and confirmed a hunch for some of the others. It appeared that the cyclical variation in gas temperature was causing the variation in the other characteristics. The gas flow rate and the die pressure were believed to have a causal relationship with the post expansion quality problem.

The final training session formed an in-plant statistical process control team to continue working on improving this process. The members were selected from all the personnel receiving the training in the plant. The ground rules for the in-plant team's operation are presented as an attachment to this case.

After Week 6

The plant SPC team continued to work on the post expansion problem. The training led them in the direction of a solution, or possible solution, and they were anxious to continue. As the team continued to work on the problem it became obvious that the process would have to be modified to stabilize the gas temperature variability. An experiment was designed to wrap the gas line with a cool water line. The variability of the characteristics, as shown by the decrease in standard deviations, shown in Figure C–14, before and after the installation of the water line, led the team to believe they had identified a viable solution to the problem.

Consultations with the plant engineer led to the recommendation that a heat exchanger be installed on the gas line. Figure C–15 shows the gas temperature, die pressure, and average gas flow rate after the heat exchanger was installed.

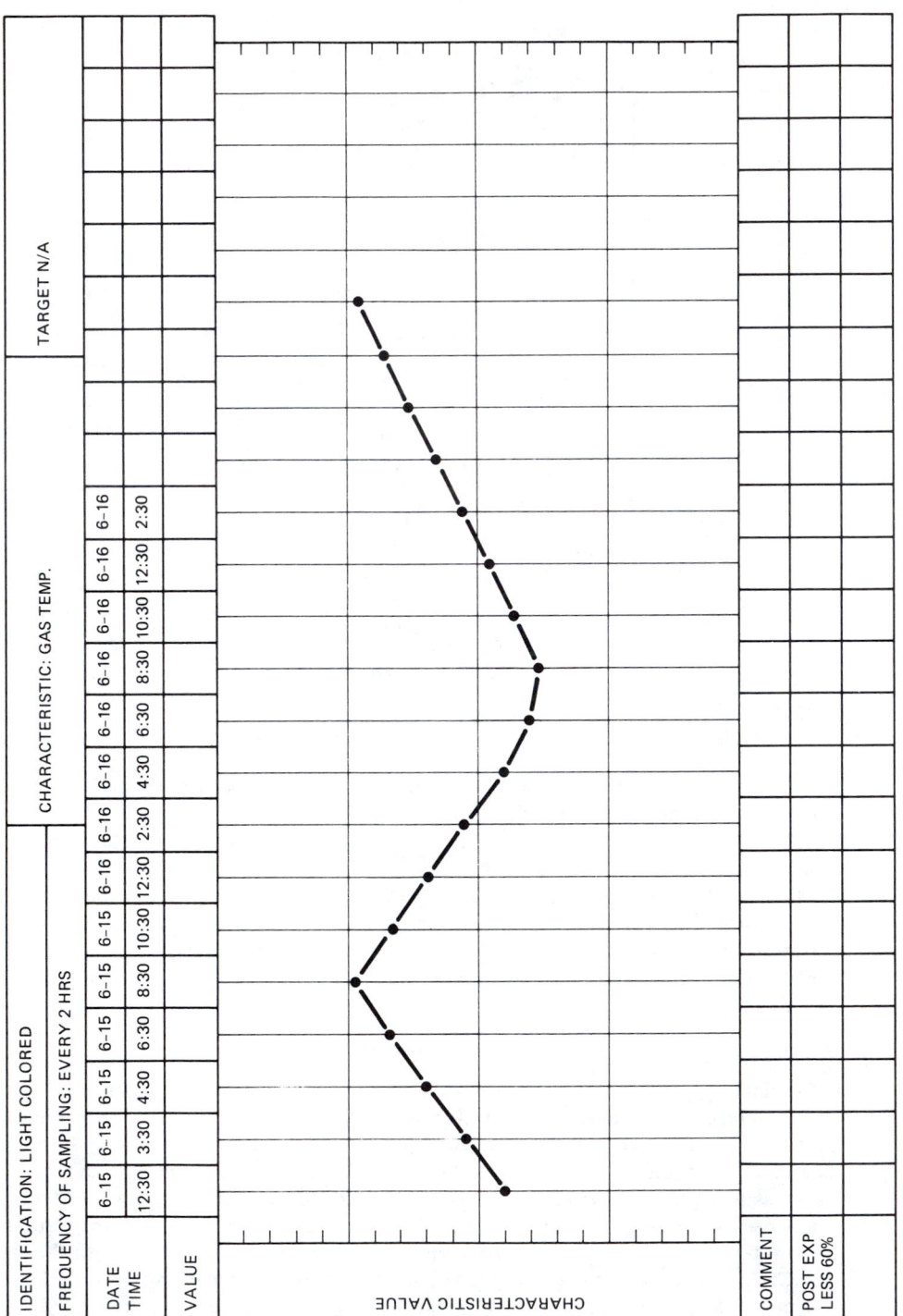

FIGURE C-7a-f Run Charts

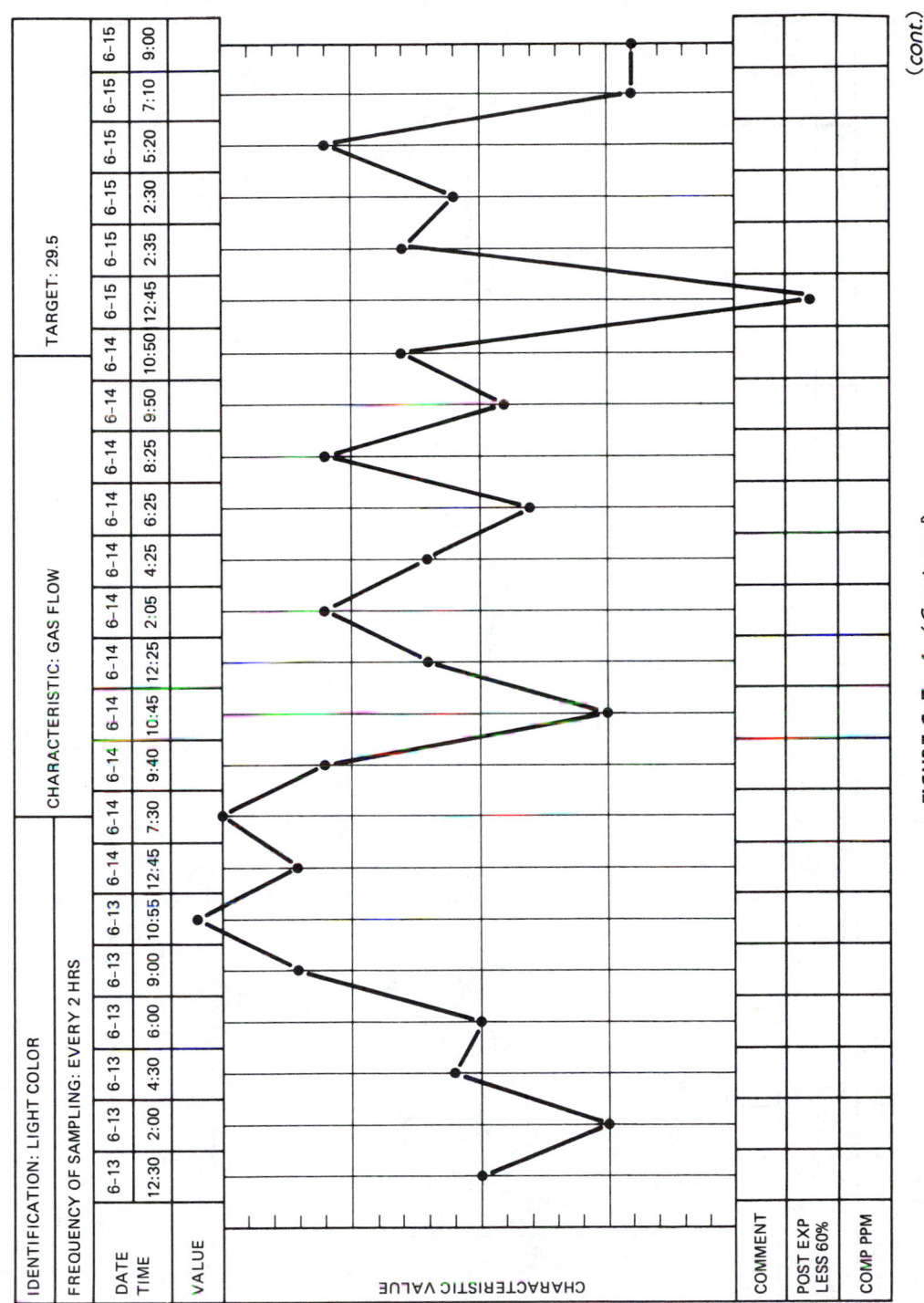

FIGURE C-7a-f (Continued)

IDENTIFICATION: LIGHT COLOR							CHARACTERISTIC: GAS RETENTION									TARGET:						
FREQUENCY OF SAMPLING: EVERY 2 HRS																						
DATE	6-13	6-13	6-13	6-13	6-13	6-13	6-14	6-14	6-14	6-14	6-14	6-14	6-14	6-14	6-14	6-14	6-14	6-15	6-15	6-15	6-15	6-15	6-15
TIME	12:55	3:45	4:20	6:00	9:00	10:55	12:45	7:50	9:40	10:35	12:25	2:25	4:25	6:25	8:25	9:50	10:50	12:45	2:45	3:30	3:20	7:10	9:00
VALUE																							

COMMENT																							
POST EXP LESS 60%																							

FIGURE C–7a–f (*Continued*)

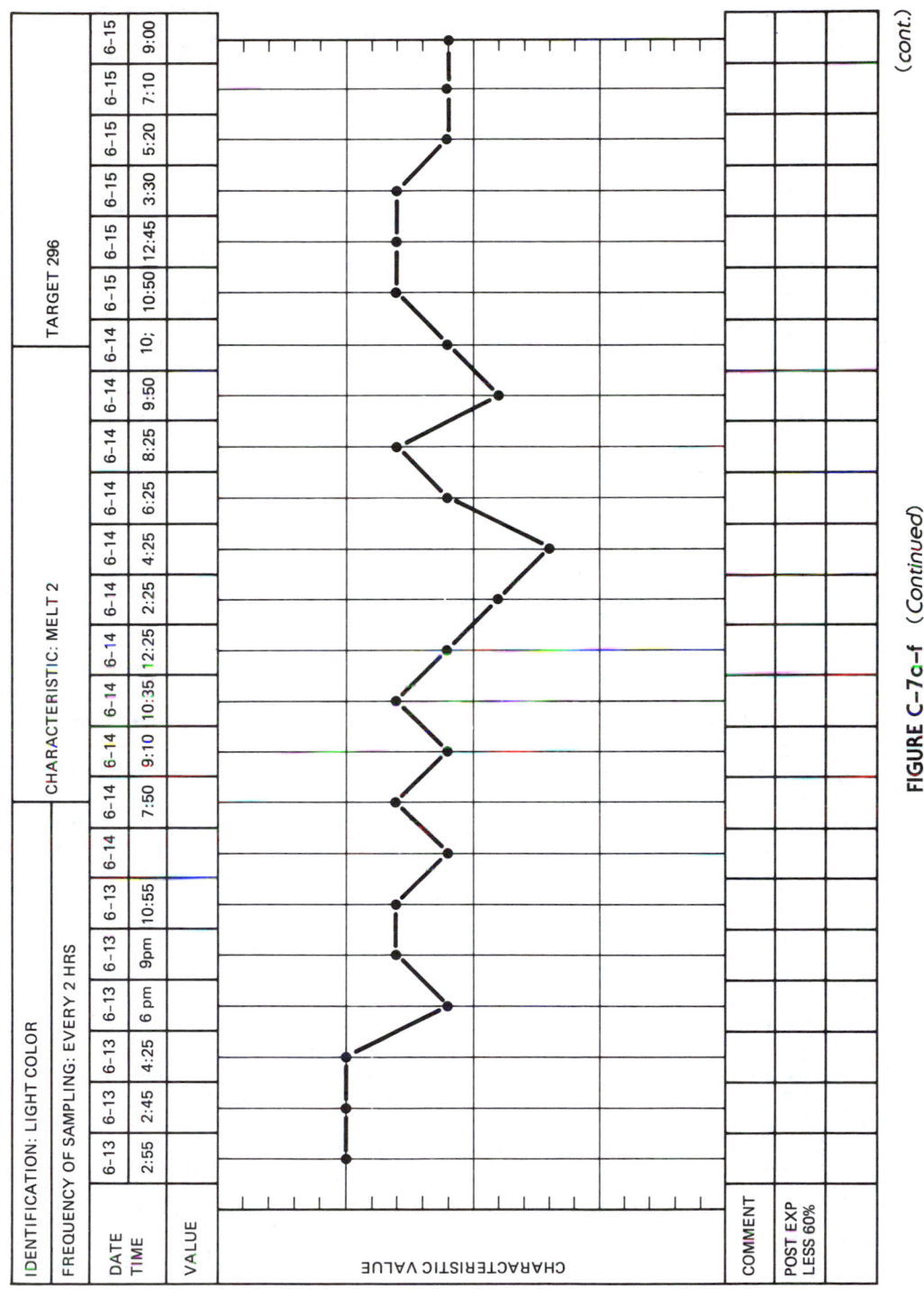

FIGURE C-7a-f *(Continued)*

(*cont.*)

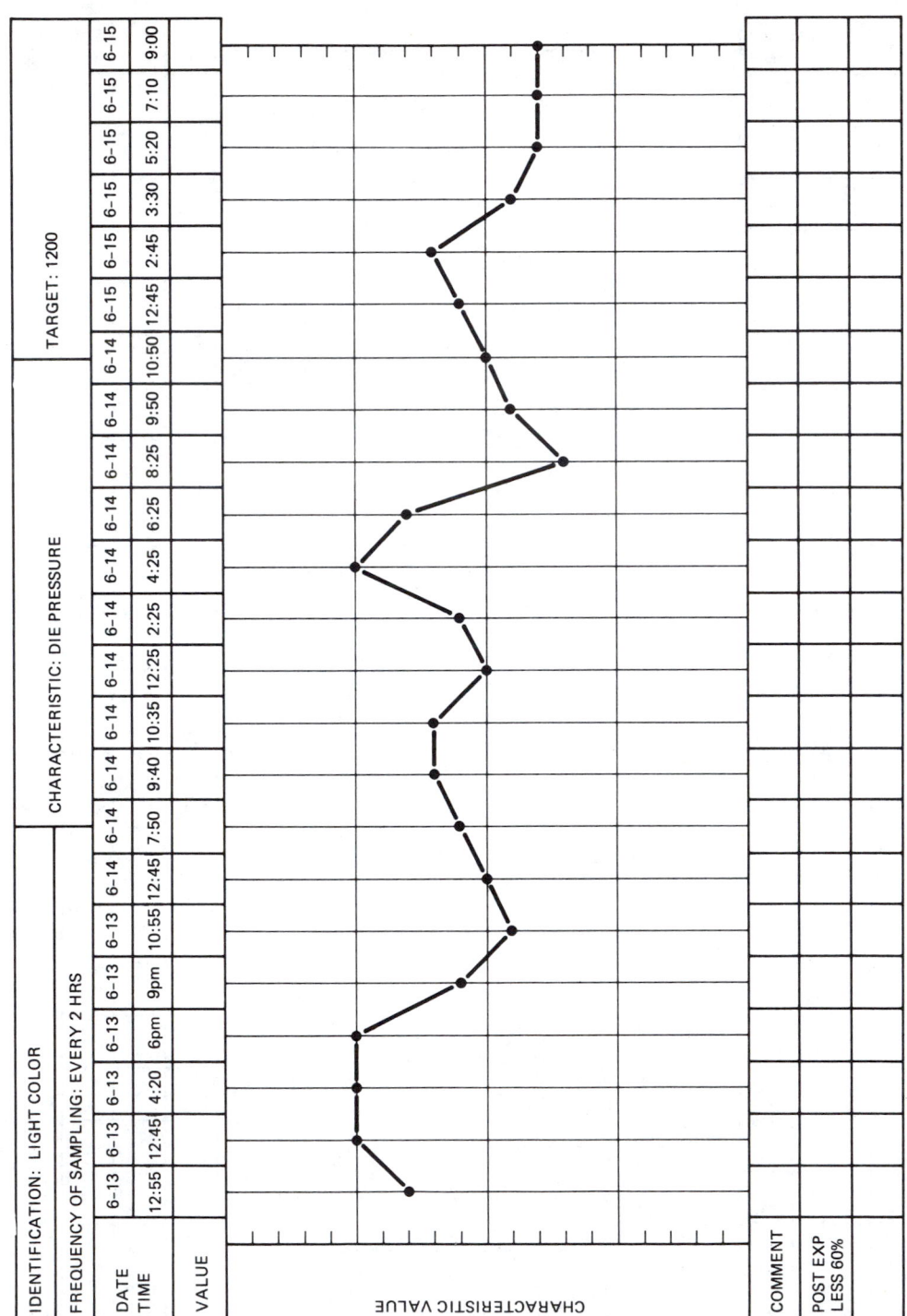

FIGURE C-7a-f (*Continued*)

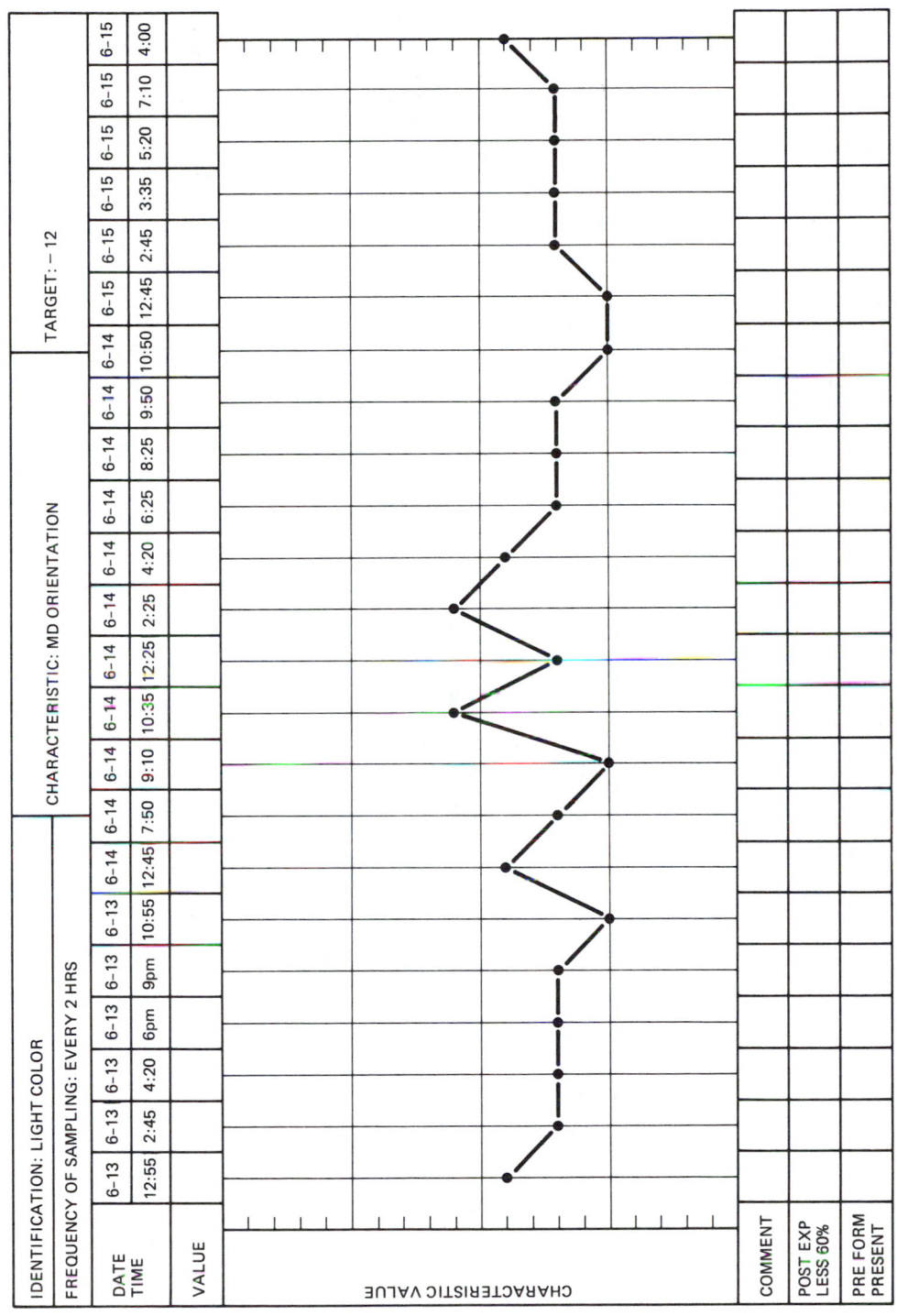

FIGURE C-7a-f *(Continued)*

329

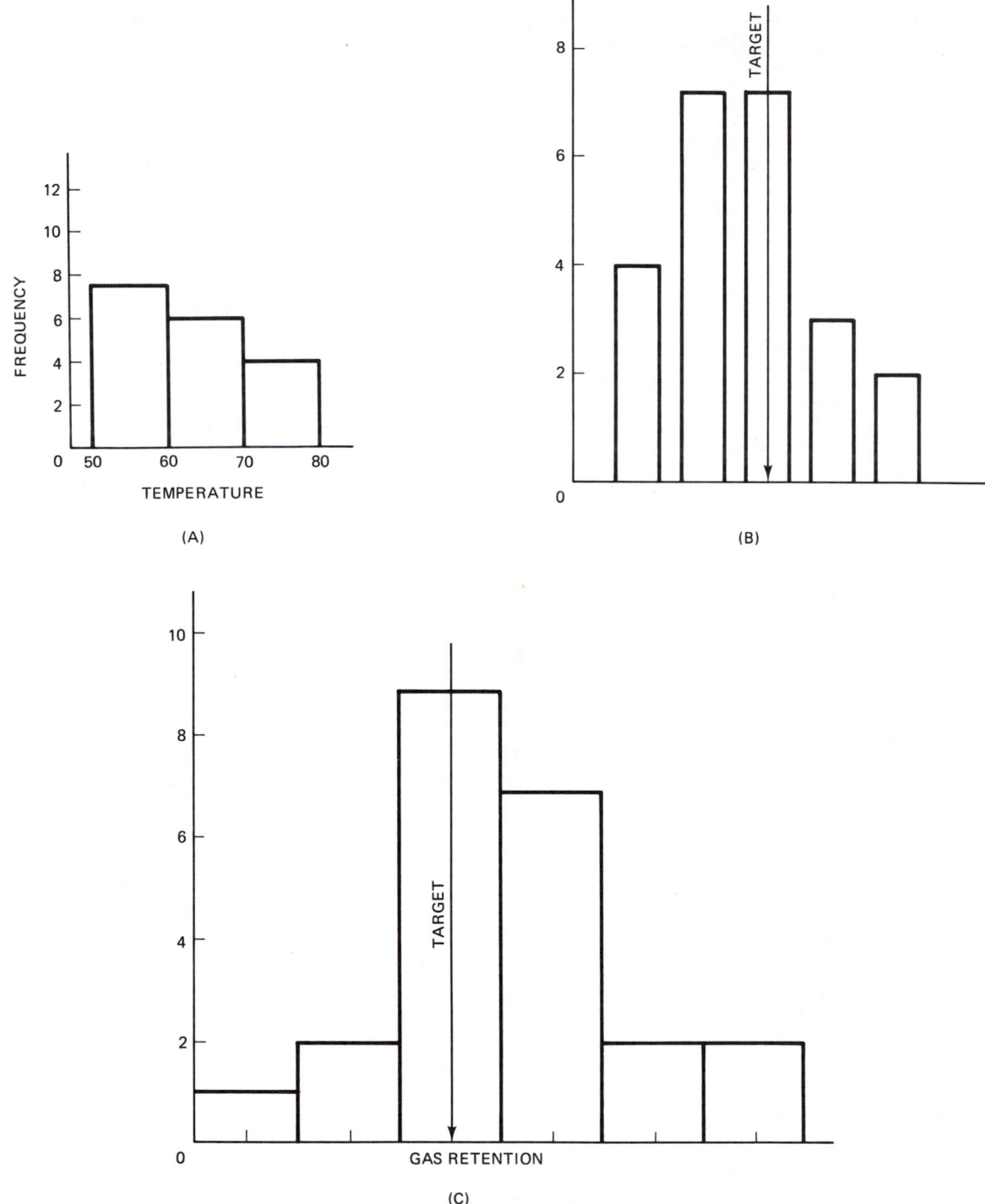

FIGURE C–8a–f Histograms

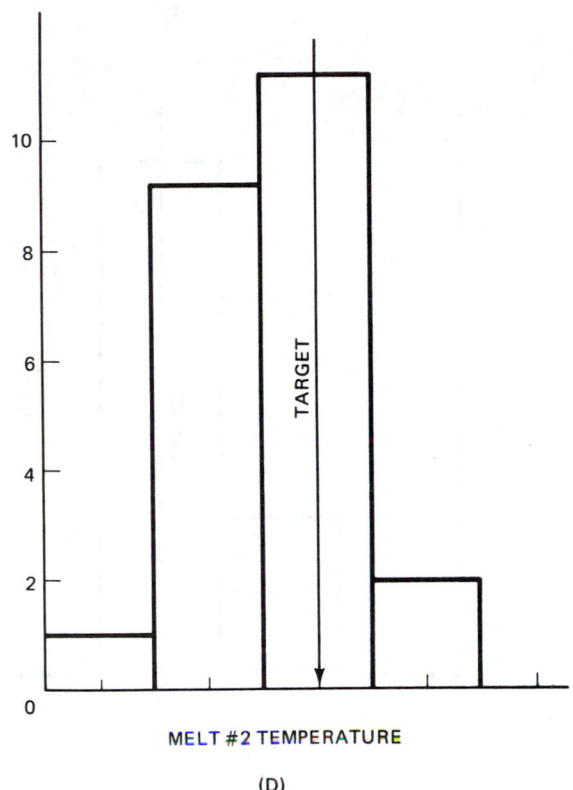

MELT #2 TEMPERATURE

(D)

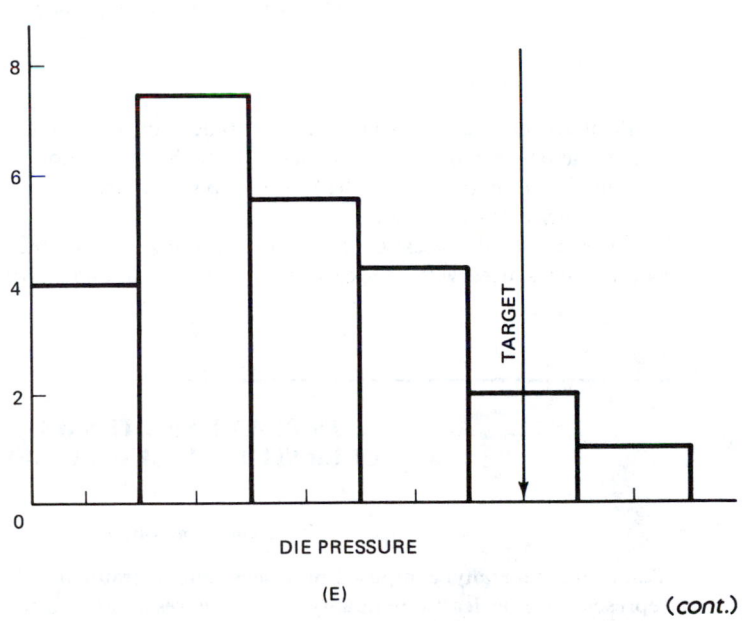

DIE PRESSURE

(E)

(cont.)

FIGURE C–8a–f (*Continued*)

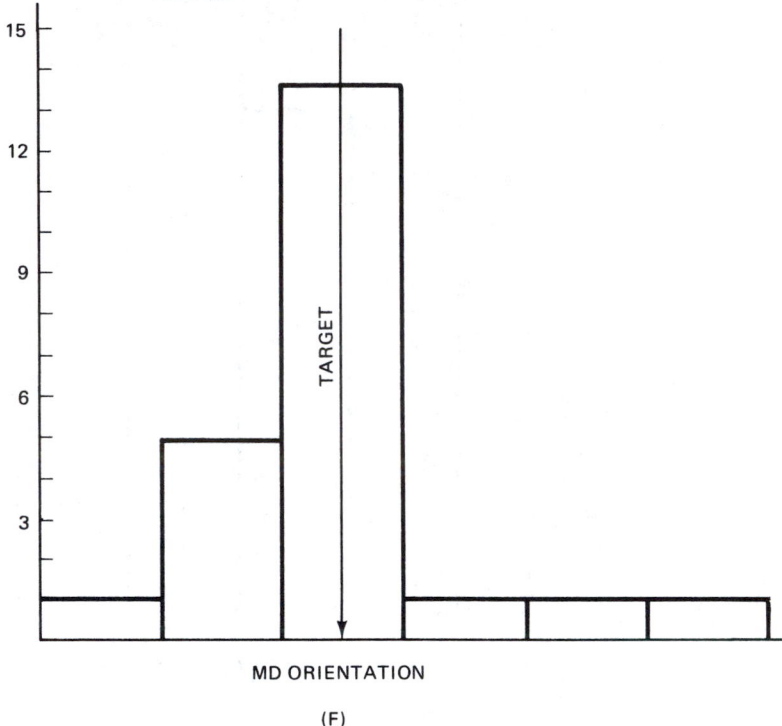

MD ORIENTATION

(F)

FIGURE C–8a–f *(Continued)*

Prior to the heat exchanger being installed, over 75 percent of the rolls checked were failing the post expansion requirement. After the installation this was reduced to virtually 0 percent. Based on the success the SPC group recommended that heat exchangers be installed on the other extrusion lines.

Since statistical process control is a continuing process, the team then began the process again. They started with check sheets and identified a new problem to begin solving.

IN-PLANT SPC TEAMS
OPERATIONAL GUIDELINES

Team Composition

Teams are (generally) composed of at least one operator per shift, at least one maintenance representative, at least one quality control representative, a process engineering representative, and a management representative. Also included is the in-plant SPC co-ordinator to

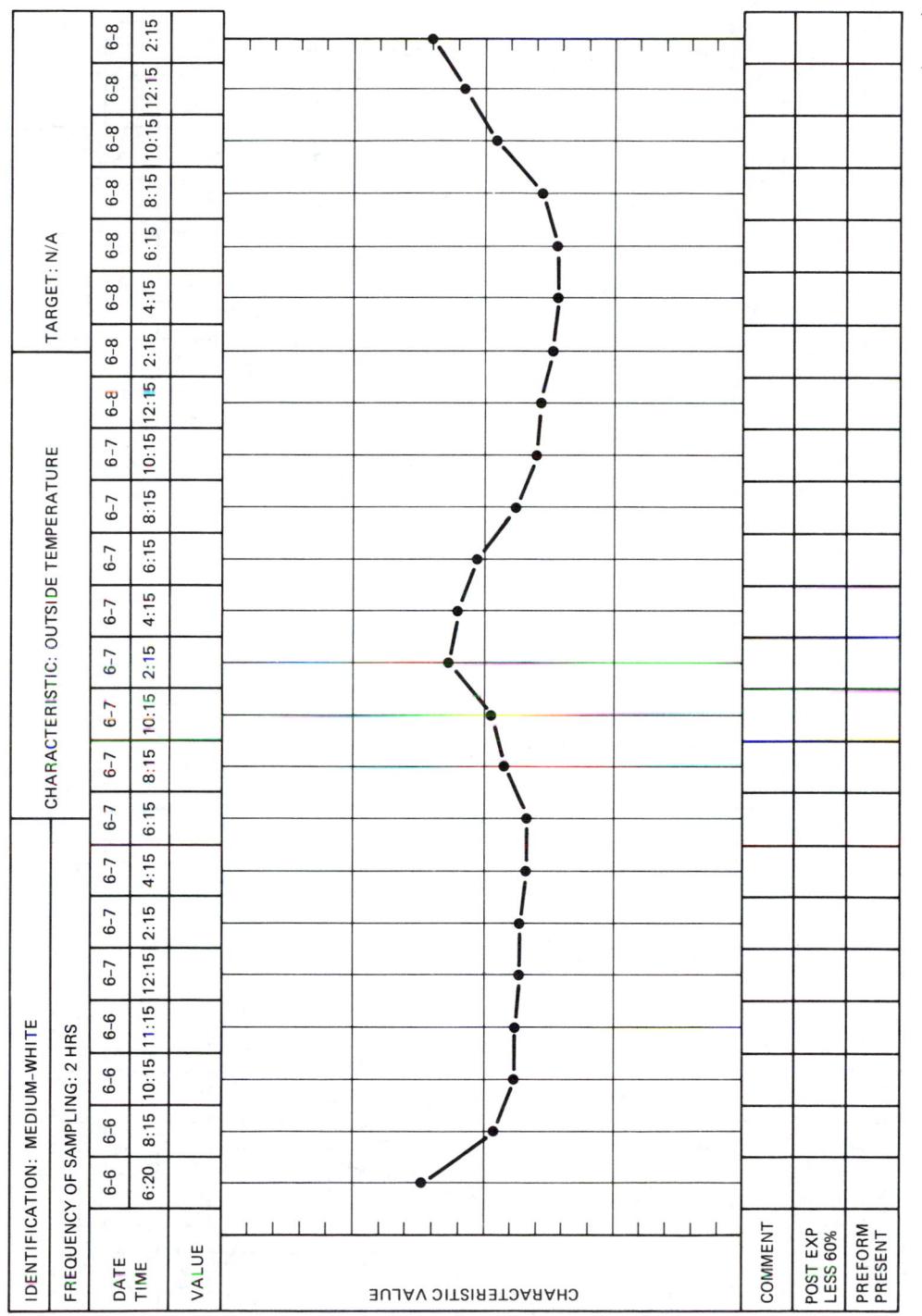

FIGURE C-9a-f Run Charts

(cont.)

334

IDENTIFICATION: MEDIUM – WHITE								CHARACTERISTIC: GAS FLOW								TARGET: 31.0							
FREQUENCY OF SAMPLING: 2 HRS																							
DATE	6-6	6-6	6-6	6-6	6-7	6-7	6-7	6-7	6-7	6-7	6-7	6-7	6-7	6-7	6-7	6-8	6-8	6-8	6-8	6-8	6-8	6-8	6-8
TIME	6:20	8:15	10:15	11:15	12:15	2:15	4:15	6:15	7:15	10:15	2:15	4:15	6:15	8:15	10:15	12:15	2:15	4:15	6:15	8:15	10:15	12:15	10:15
VALUE																							

COMMENT																							
POST EXP LESS 60%																							
PRE FORM PRESENT																							

FIGURE C–9a–f *(Continued)*

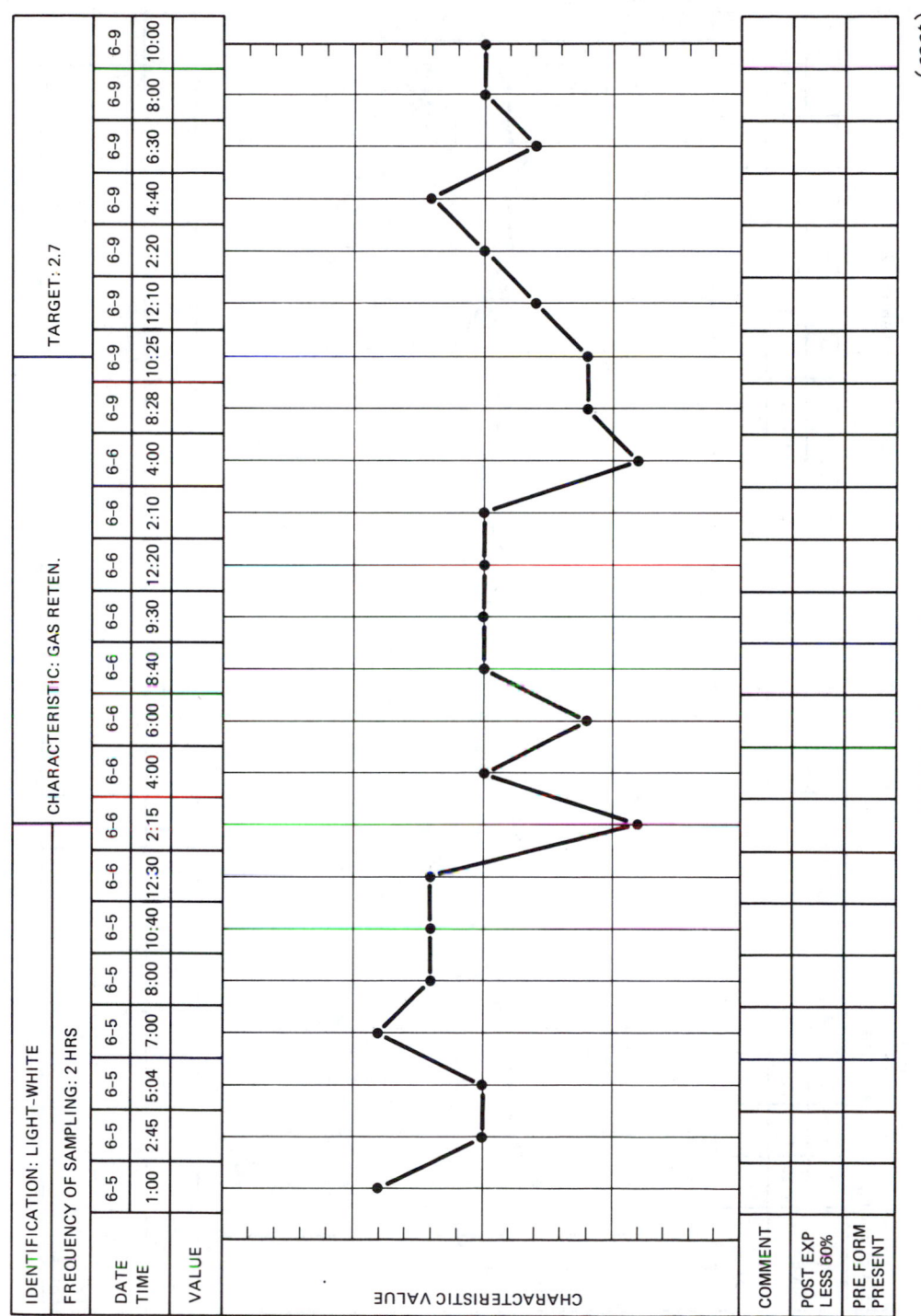

FIGURE C-9a-f (*Continued*)

(cont.)

IDENTIFICATION: MEDIUM WHITE								CHARACTERISTIC: MELT # 2								TARGET: 297						
FREQUENCY OF SAMPLING: EVERY 2 HRS																						

DATE	6-6	6-6	6-6	6-6	6-7	6-7	6-7	6-7	6-7	6-7	6-7	6-7	6-7	6-7	6-7	6-8	6-8	6-8	6-8	6-8	6-8	6-8	6-8
TIME	6:20	8:15	10:15	11:15	12:15	2:15	4:15	6:15	8:15	10:15	2:15	4:15	6:15	8:15	10:15	12:15	2:15	4:15	6:15	8:15	10:15	12:15	2:15
VALUE																							

COMMENT																							
POST EXP LESS 60%																							
PRE FORM PRESENT																							

FIGURE C-9a-f (*Continued*)

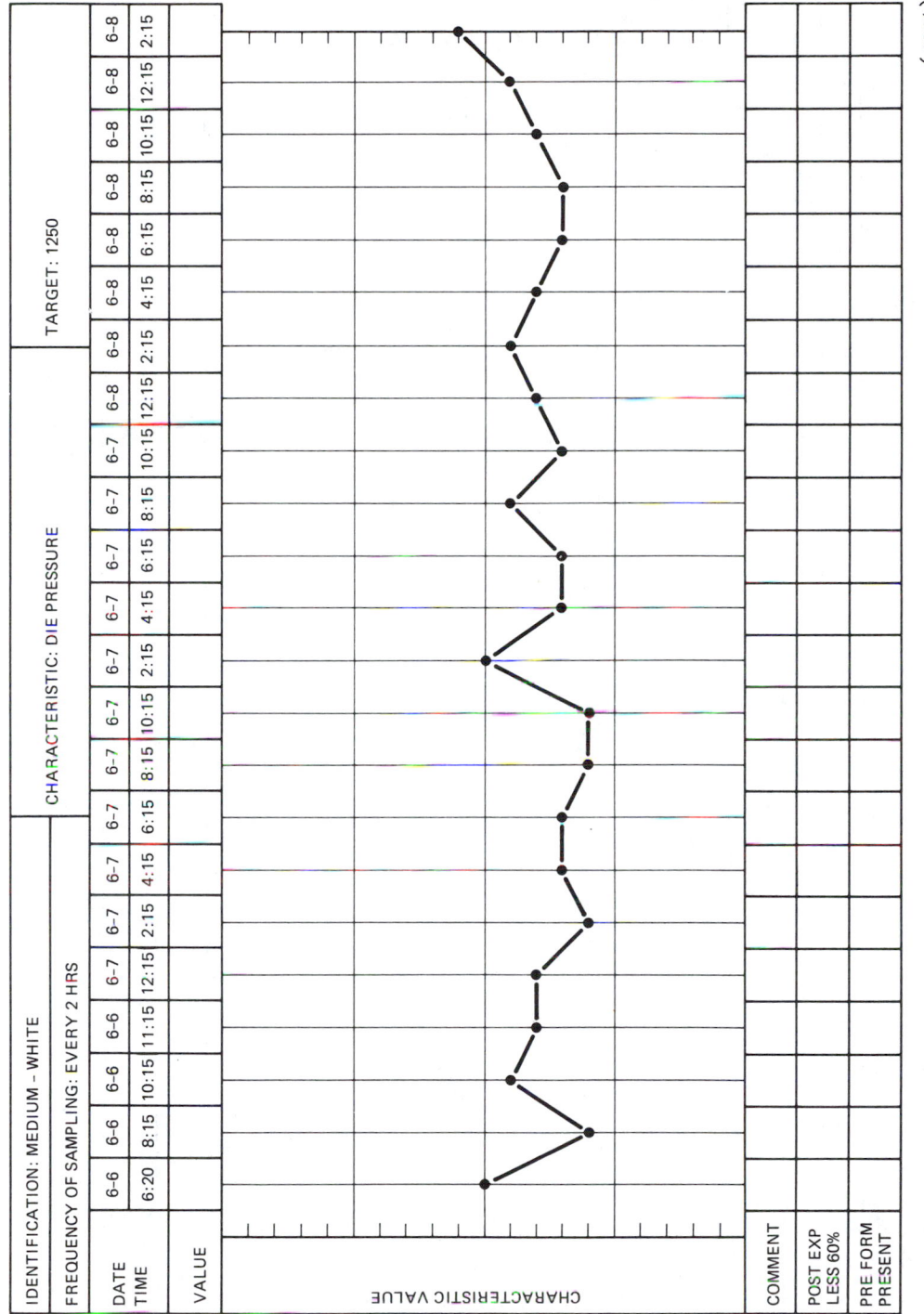

IDENTIFICATION: MEDIUM – WHITE

CHARACTERISTIC: DIE PRESSURE

TARGET: 1250

FREQUENCY OF SAMPLING: EVERY 2 HRS

DATE	6-6	6-6	6-6	6-6	6-7	6-7	6-7	6-7	6-7	6-7	6-7	6-7	6-8	6-8	6-8	6-8	6-8	6-8	6-8
TIME	6:20	8:15	10:15	11:15	12:15	2:15	4:15	6:15	8:15	10:15	12:15	2:15	4:15	6:15	8:15	10:15	12:15	2:15
VALUE																		

CHARACTERISTIC VALUE

COMMENT

POST EXP LESS 60%

PRE FORM PRESENT

FIGURE C–9a–f (Continued)

(cont.)

337

| IDENTIFICATION: MEDIUM –WHITE | | | | | | | | | CHARACTERISTIC: MD ORIENTATION | | | | | | | | TARGET: – 10 | | | | | | | |
| FREQUENCY OF SAMPLING; EVERY 2 HRS | | | | | | | | | | | | | | | | | | | | | | | | |

DATE	6-6	6-6	6-6	6-6	6-7	6-7	6-7	6-7	6-7	6-7	6-7	6-7	6-7	6-7	6-7	6-8	6-8	6-8	6-8	6-8	6-8	6-8	6-8
TIME	6:20	8:15	10:15	11:15	12:15	2:15	4:15	6:15	8:15	10:15	2:15	4:15	6:15	8:15	10:15	12:15	2:15	4:15	6:15	8:15	10:15	12:15	2:15
VALUE																							
CHARACTERISTIC VALUE																							
COMMENT																							
POST EXP LESS 60%																							
PRE FORM PRESENT																							

FIGURE C–9a–f (*Continued*)

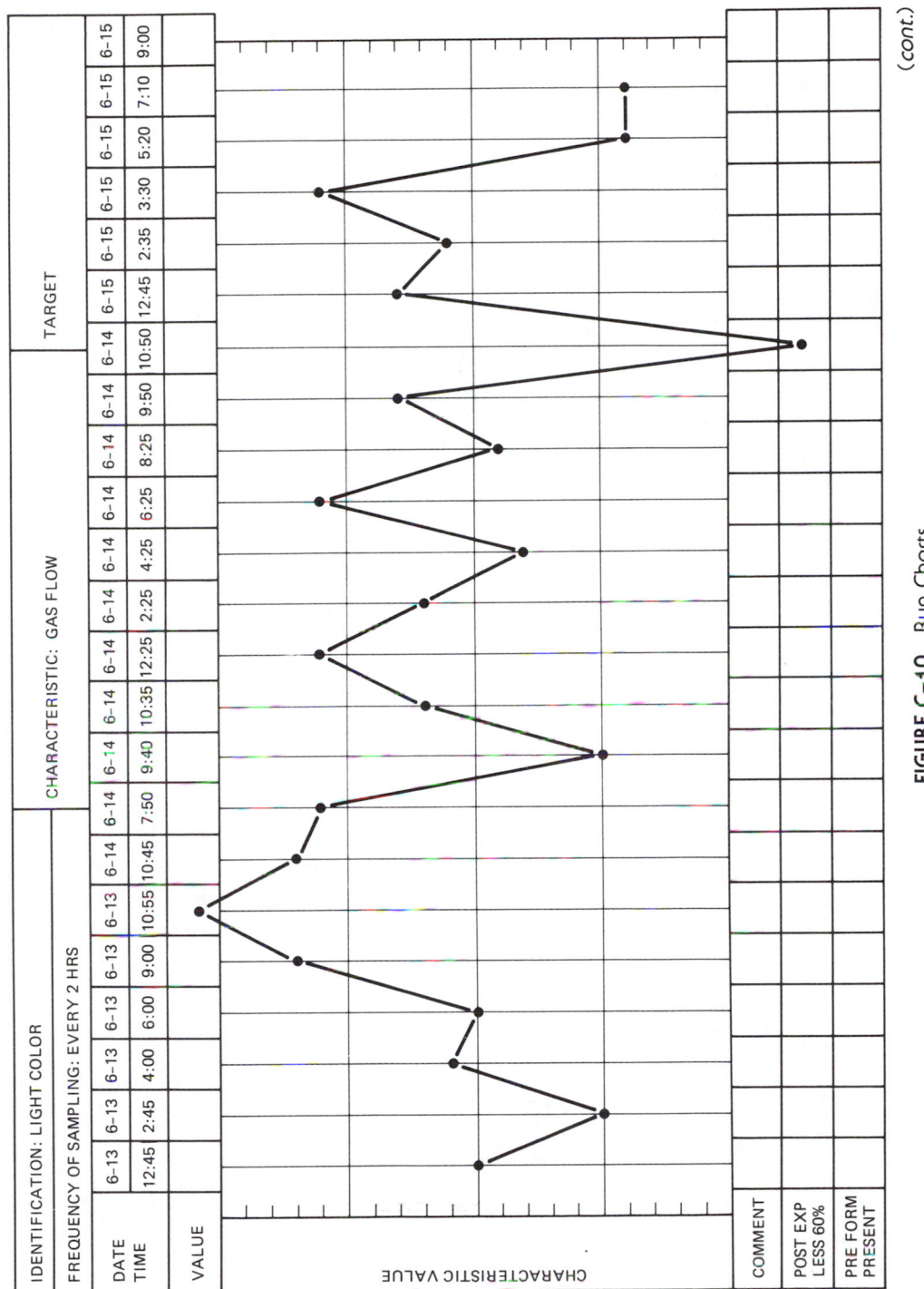

FIGURE C-10 Run Charts

(cont.)

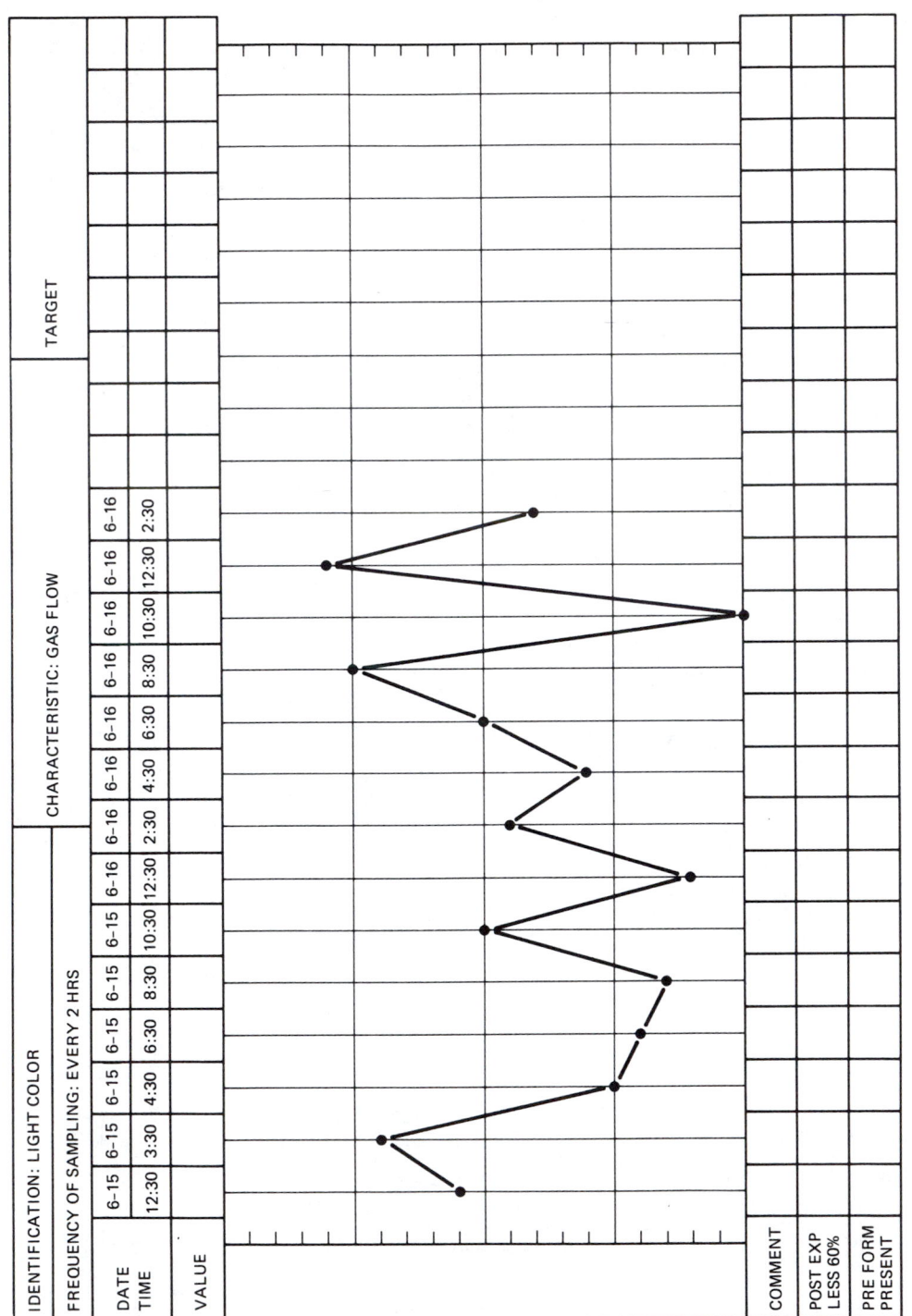

FIGURE C-10 (Continued)

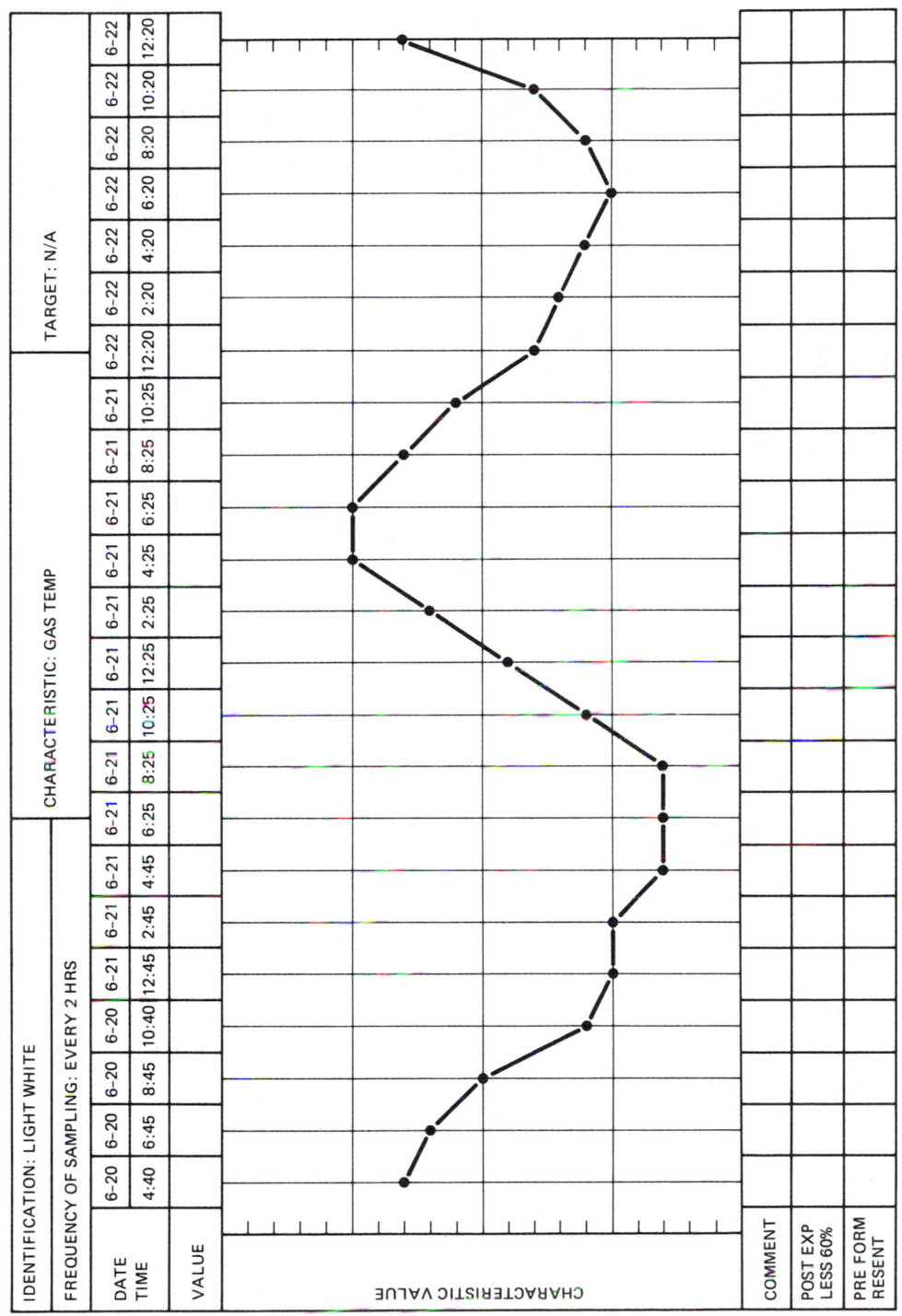

FIGURE C–11 Gas Temperature over Time

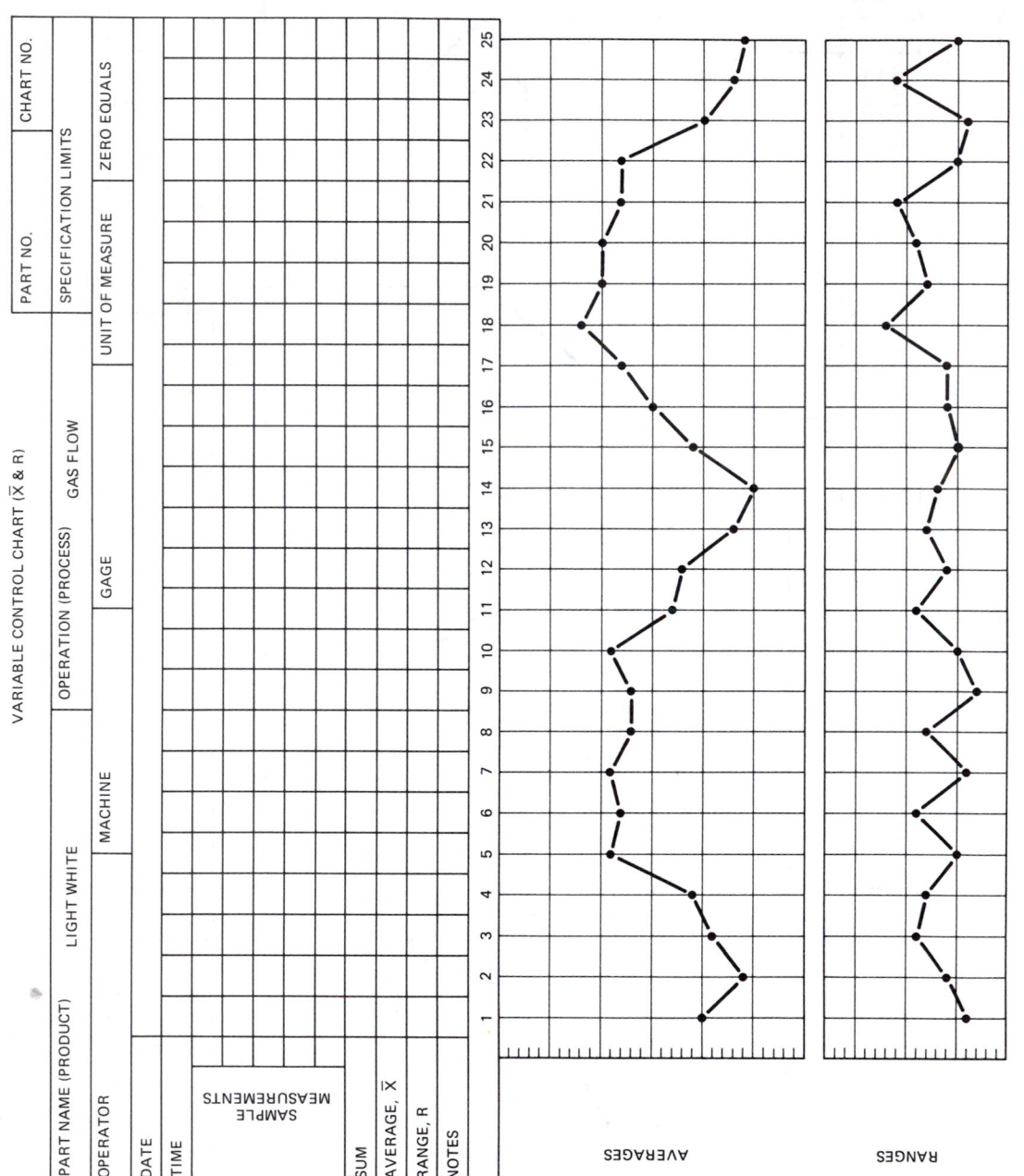

FIGURE C–12a,b Control/Run Charts

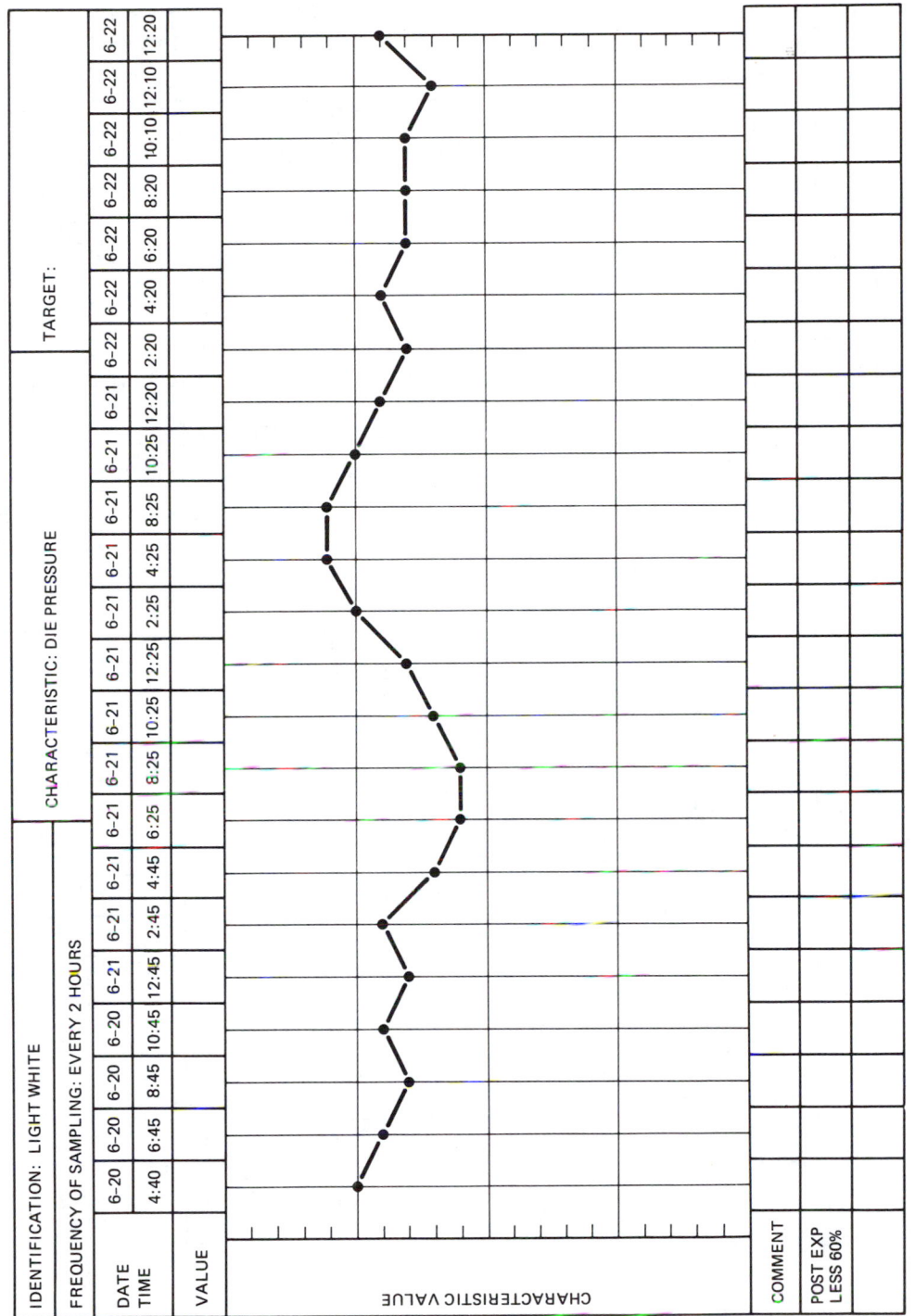

FIGURE C–12a,b (*Continued*)

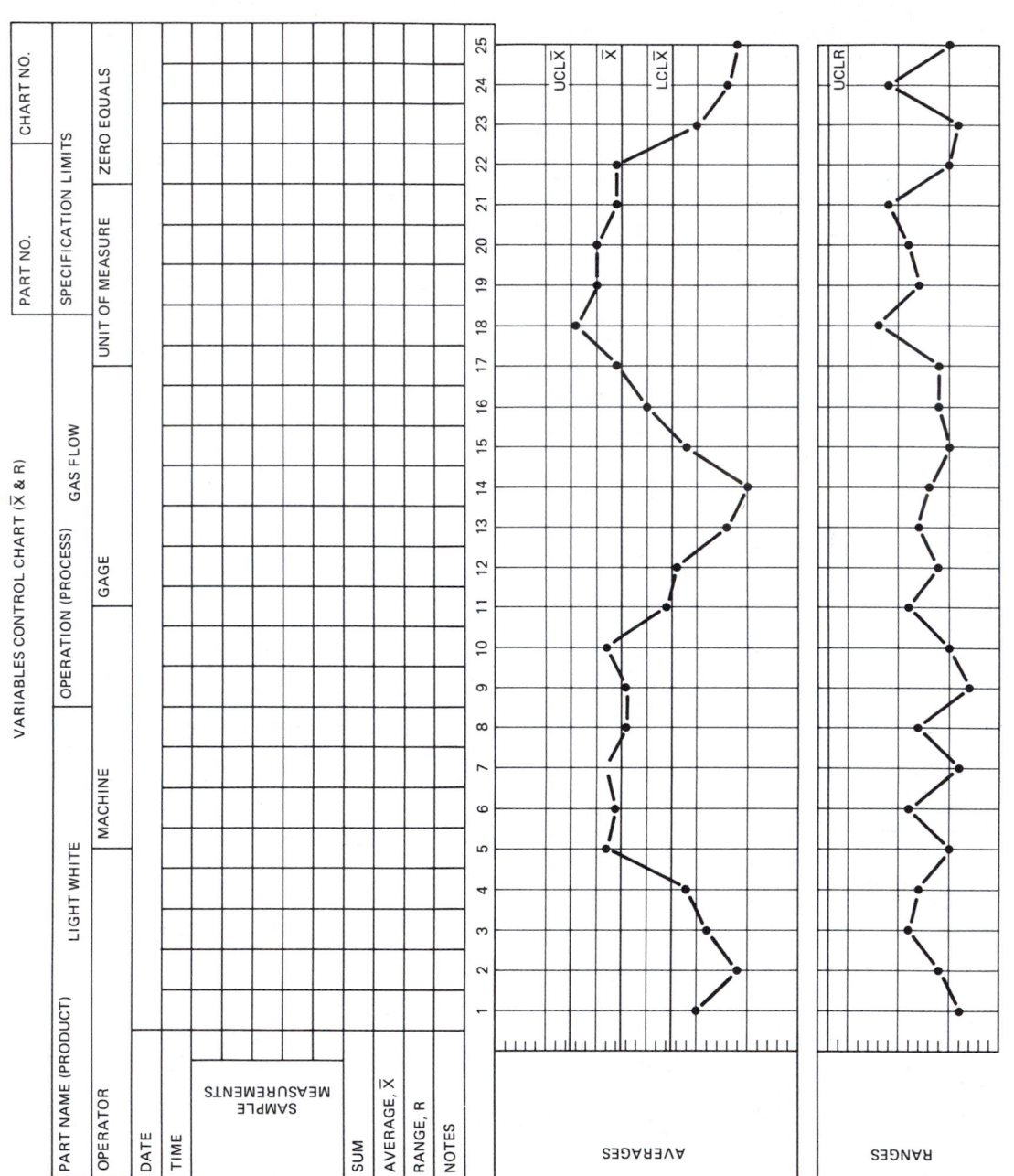

FIGURE C-13a,b Control Charts

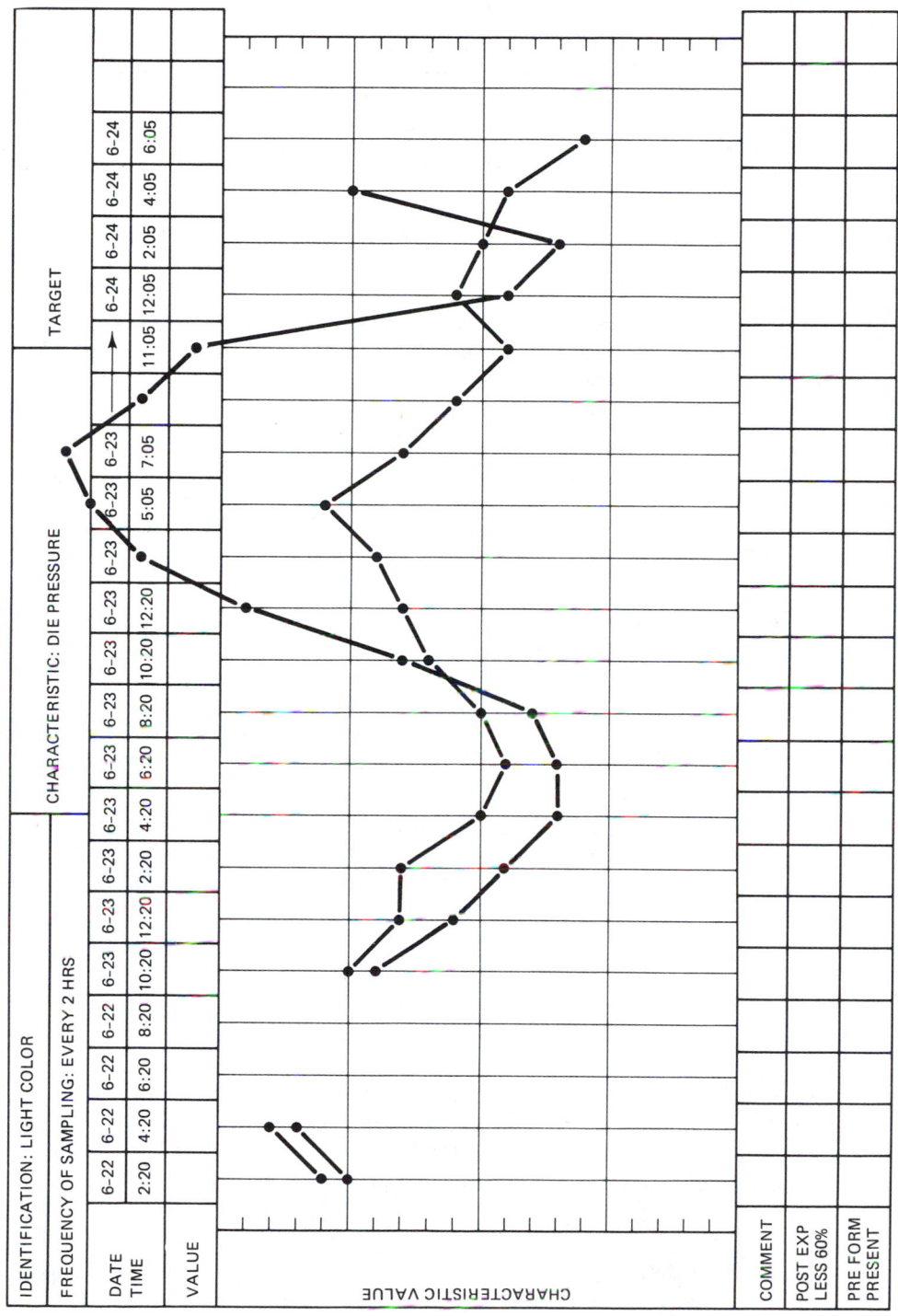

FIGURE C–13a,b Run Charts

CHARACTERISTIC	S BEFORE	S AFTER
GAS TEMPERATURE	6.76	2.43
DIE PRESSURE	27.89	0.00
GAS FLOW	11.64	0.73

FIGURE C–14 Descriptive Statistics

provide necessary technical assistance. Team members volunteer with the approval of management. The team leader may either be selected by management or elected by the team members at the first team meeting.

Goals

While each group or team will establish its own goals, the following are suggested as generic goals.

1. Continue the initial SPC project (from training) to conclusion.
2. Update check sheet for the initial line.
3. Develop list of related quality problems that must be addressed.
4. Long term goal is to apply SPC on all lines.

Initial Meeting

The following activities occur at the first meeting of the In-Plant SPC team.

1. Elect team leader
2. Assign team leader to take and publish meeting minutes. These are to be posted for all people in the plant to see. The minute taker will rotate among all members of the team.
3. Establish length of membership for individual team members. Typical terms are 3–6 months. Membership is rotated so that there are always experienced members on the team.

Specific Responsibilities

The following activities should be specifically performed by team members.

1. Update charts and report data on the team at each meeting. (In-plant SPC Coordinator is suggested for this.)
2. Maintain check sheets so that current problems are evident.
3. Track status of long term problems/recommendations.

Meeting Schedules

Meetings are to be held regularly at a time convenient to the members of the group. Generally one meeting every two weeks is sufficient.

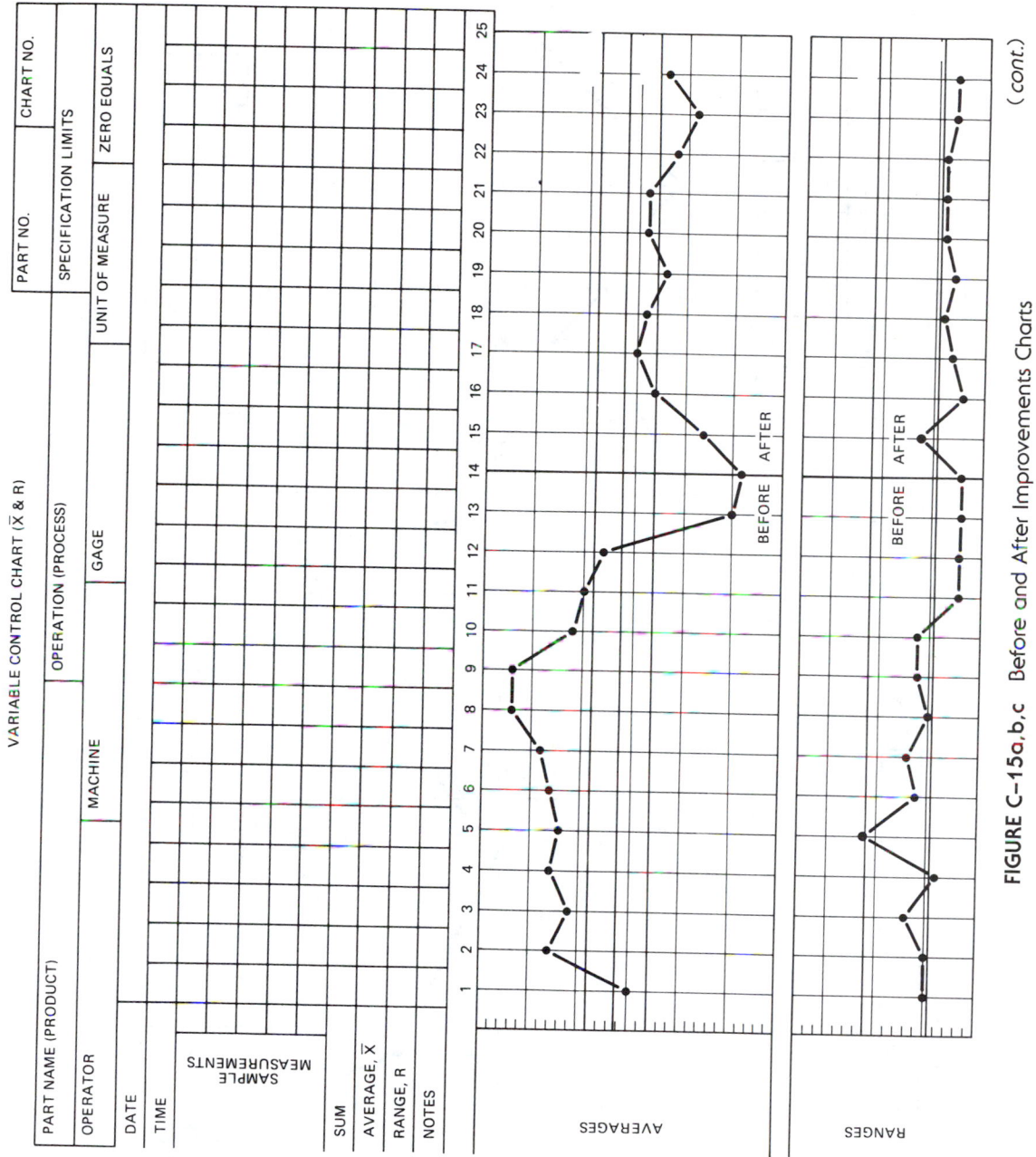

FIGURE C-15a,b,c Before and After Improvements Charts

(cont.)

347

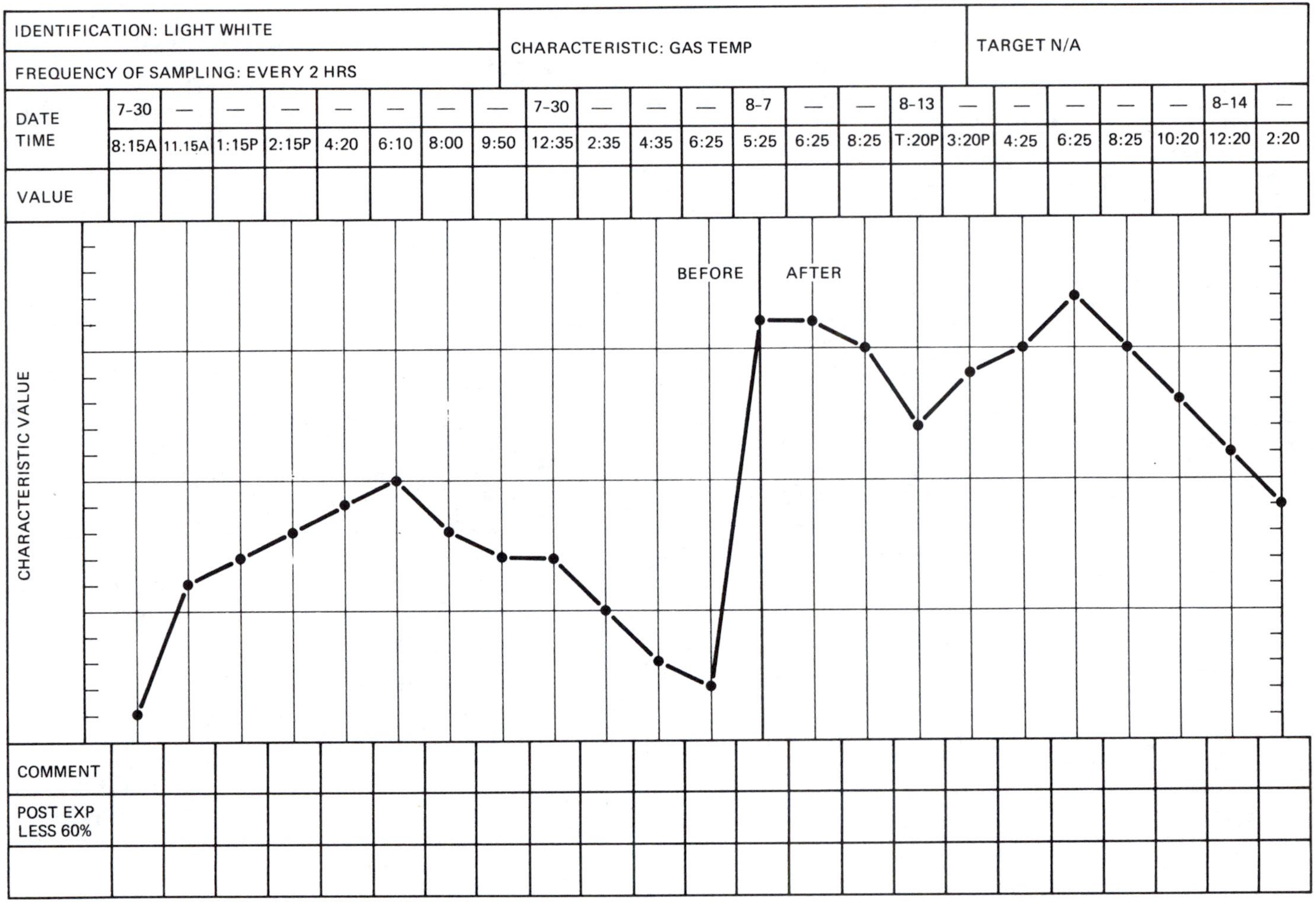

	7-30	—	—	—	—	—	—	—	7-30	—	—	—	8-7	—	—	8-13	—	—	—	—	—	8-14	—
DATE / TIME	8:15A	11.15A	1:15P	2:15P	4:20	6:10	8:00	9:50	12:35	2:35	4:35	6:25	5:25	6:25	8:25	T:20P	3:20P	4:25	6:25	8:25	10:20	12:20	2:20
VALUE																							

IDENTIFICATION: LIGHT WHITE

FREQUENCY OF SAMPLING: EVERY 2 HRS

CHARACTERISTIC: GAS TEMP

TARGET N/A

BEFORE   AFTER

CHARACTERISTIC VALUE

COMMENT

POST EXP LESS 60%

FIGURE C–15a,b,c (*Continued*)

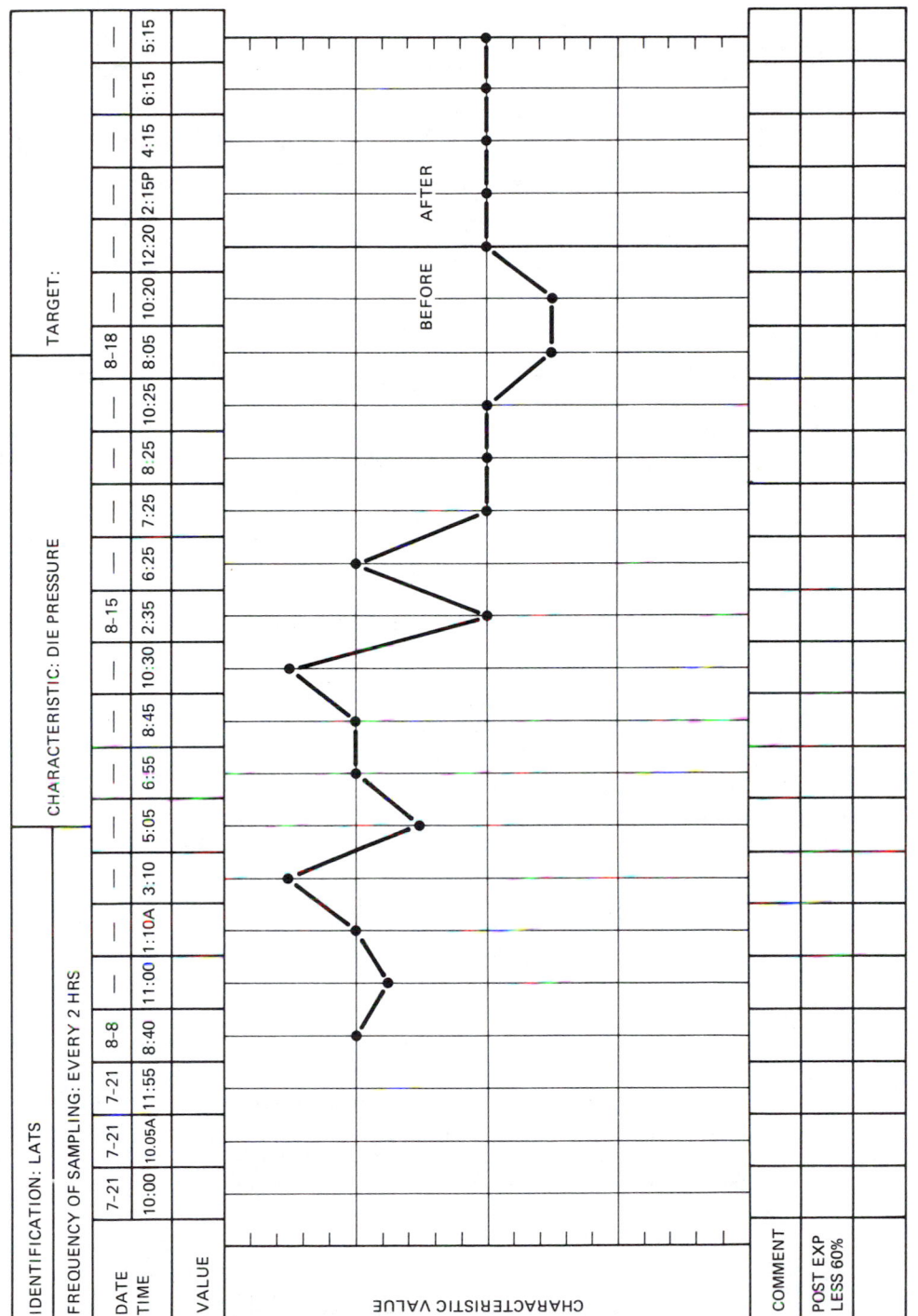

FIGURE C-15a,b,c (Continued)

20.2 CASE STUDY 2

INTRODUCTION TO THE CEDAC*

A system that pinpoints the causes of problems and generates ways
to improve quality

Ryuji Fukuda

Sumitomo Electric Industries, a Japanase manufacturer of wires and cables with $2 billion in sales in 1980, experienced an amazing decline in the ratio of losses due to quality defects against sales from 1976 through 1979. As can be seen from Figure 1, the rate dropped to almost half during the four-year period.

What helped to achieve this remarkable result was the "CEDAC," cause and effect diagram with addition of cards, developed by the QC problem-study group at Sumitomo Electric. In order to manufacture goods continuously with satisfactory quality, it is important that we examine each factor in the complete production process, such as materials, machines, manufacturing conditions,and workers' performance, and then make sure that each factor is functioning effectively and efficiently for the purpose. In other words, quality should be woven into a product during the production process.

The relationship between causes and a characteristic quality as an effect can be illustrated as in Figure 2, which is called a "Cause and Effect Diagram" or, because of its shape, a "Fish Bone." All factors considered to be causes for an effect (fracture surface of cast material in Figure 2) are written out on the left of the diagram to clarify the relationship between causes and effect. Major causes such as casting temperature, mold coating, composition of molten metal, and mold temperature are put down at the main lines of the diagram. And detailed factors of each major cause, for example, coated volume for fine coal mixing ratio for mold coating, are written at the sub-lines. The CEDAC is a modification of this diagram, which had already been well known and widely used in Japan. This modification has three points:

1. The Cause and Effect Diagram expresses factors such as "temperature" or "skill" with a single word. But behind these simple words lie engineers' knowledge and workers' know-how. To solve quality control problems, the valuable information each person has must be integrated. For this reason, the CEDAC uses short sentences to express its information.

2. Each person can, at any time, write out his observations, ideas, and know-how on small cards and put them on a diagram. This information is then available to be read by anyone at any time. Thus the use of cards enables all persons concerned to participate in solving problems without holding any special meetings. Further modification and addition of information becomes much easier since new cards can easily replace old cards or be placed over them.

*Reprinted with permission of the American Society for Quality Control.

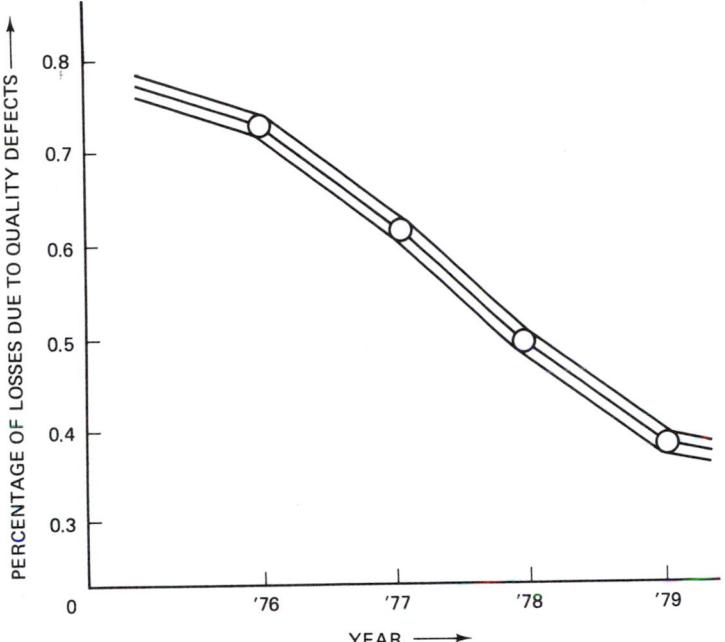

Figure 1 Decrease in Quality Defect Rate

3. When the effect is written on the CEDAC diagram, a qualitative expression, such as a "Fracture" in Figure 2, is eliminated and a quantitative expression is used instead, e.g., indication of the degree, use of a control chart, or other numerical expressions. A characteristic quality without a target is like a sport without score-keeping. If a characteristic quality cannot be kept within a control limit, then there is room for improvement in the "causes." The main purpose of the CEDAC is to clarify the relationship between causes described in short sentences and an effect written in a quantitative expression.

Preparation and Application

Following are steps for preparing and applying the CEDAC.

1) Select a major quality problem that you want to improve, and specify the target.

2) Write out all manufacturing conditions and technical know-how needed to achieve good quality. From this, a selection of needed information is made by workers, foremen, production engineers, plant engineers, and all other persons concerned. Put the selected information into diagram form.

3) Hang the diagram on a wall of the plant to show the "cause" and "effect" to all persons concerned.

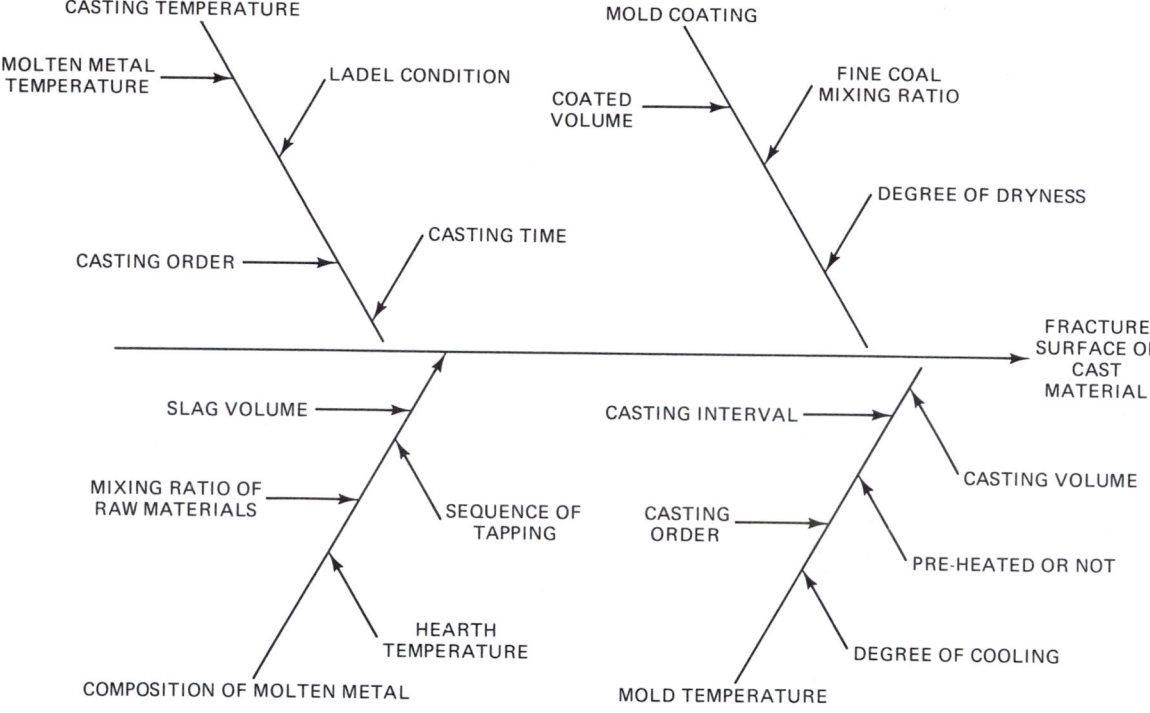

Figure 2 Example of Cause and Effect Diagram (Japan Industrial Standard Z-8101)

4) If the quality cannot be kept within the control limits, there is room for improvement in the "causes." Thus the root of the problem is sought by gathering and analyzing more "facts," and then further improvement of the technique or equipment is made.

5) The content of the improvement is written on a new card, which is put over the corresponding old card. As a group of cards is gradually accumulated, they show not only the past record of the production process but also the effects of each improvement.

Everyone participates in the process from points 2 through 5. With such a system, previously unknown information is brought up and necessary improvements are made, so that the standard operation is formed step by step without any regression.

Figure 4 shows the process of integrating into one CEDAC card the various affecting affecting quality defects.

In step 4, there are two approaches for analyzing the relationship between cause and effect.

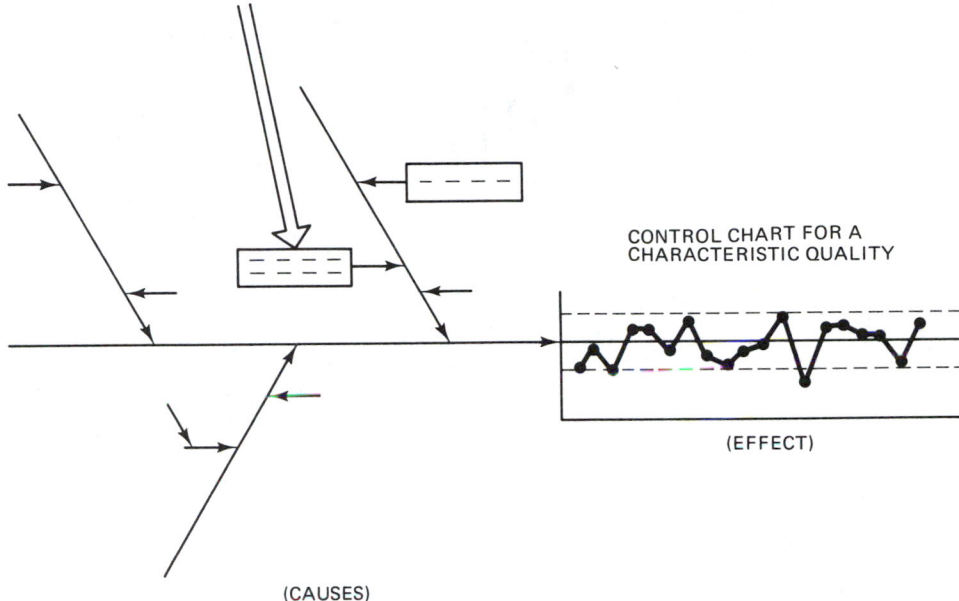

CONTROL CHART FOR A
CHARACTERISTIC QUALITY

(EFFECT)

(CAUSES)

ONE SHORT SENTENCE DESCRIBING THE NECESSARY CONDITIONS AND TECHNICAL KNOW-
HOW FOR CONTROLLING THE CHARACTERISTIC QUALITY IDENTIFIED AT RIGHT.

Figure 3   Basic Structure of the CEDAC

- When the effect varies, look for a change in the causes.
- Make a change in the causes, and observe how the effect varies.

The latter approach is more effective than the former because it produces more accurate and more plentiful knowledge within a shorter time period, and with less effort. Through this we can find out not only those causes that decrease the quality, but also those which increase it and those which have no effect. And the most advantageous point is that it is a much more "creative" approach. This active approach is much more interesting for all persons concerned than the former passive one.

The CEDAC can be called Shewart Control Chart with additional functions. We learned this approach through practice.

The CEDAC has a great variety of forms and functions, developed by users to fit their respective quality control problems.

Not only the "Fish Bone," but many other types of diagrams using pictures of equipment, machines, products, and processes were devised. But each variation has something in common with the others, as shown in Figure 5.

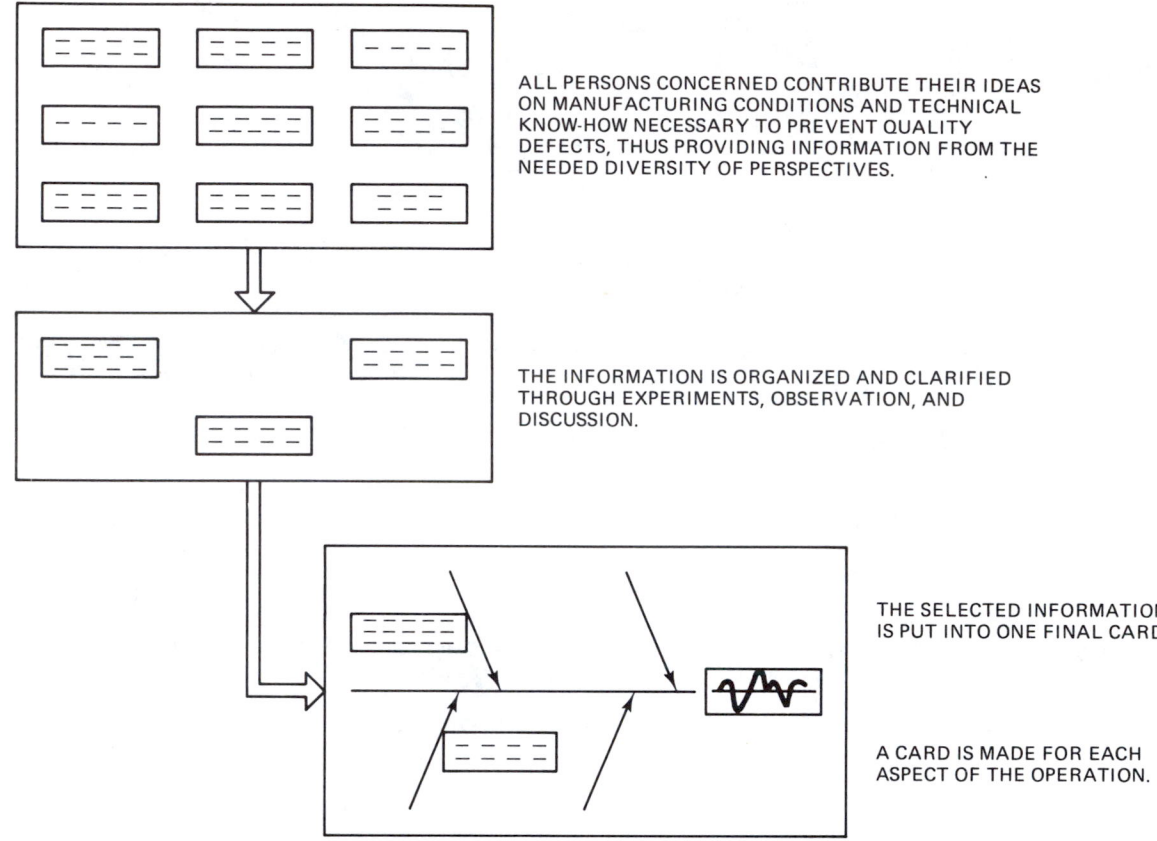

ALL PERSONS CONCERNED CONTRIBUTE THEIR IDEAS ON MANUFACTURING CONDITIONS AND TECHNICAL KNOW-HOW NECESSARY TO PREVENT QUALITY DEFECTS, THUS PROVIDING INFORMATION FROM THE NEEDED DIVERSITY OF PERSPECTIVES.

THE INFORMATION IS ORGANIZED AND CLARIFIED THROUGH EXPERIMENTS, OBSERVATION, AND DISCUSSION.

THE SELECTED INFORMATION IS PUT INTO ONE FINAL CARD.

A CARD IS MADE FOR EACH ASPECT OF THE OPERATION.

Figure 4 Process for Filling in the Cards

Results

As mentioned before, Sumitomo Electric reduced its losses due to defects by almost half within four years. Table I shows the results in the plants where all QC circles applied the CEDAC system to their respective quality control problems.

These results were achieved within eight months; some were even achieved within four days. Such rapid and remarkable effects of the CEDAC had not been expected by anyone, so it was decided to investigate the cause.

In order to explain the reason why such remarkable results had been achieved, we formulated a hypothesis, as illustrated in Figure 6.

Category A–1 means both the managerial-technical staff and workers "know and practice" the correct production methods for preventing defects. Category A–2 means they "know but do not practice them." Categories B and C mean either the staff or workers, respectively, know the method, but the other group does not. Category D means neither

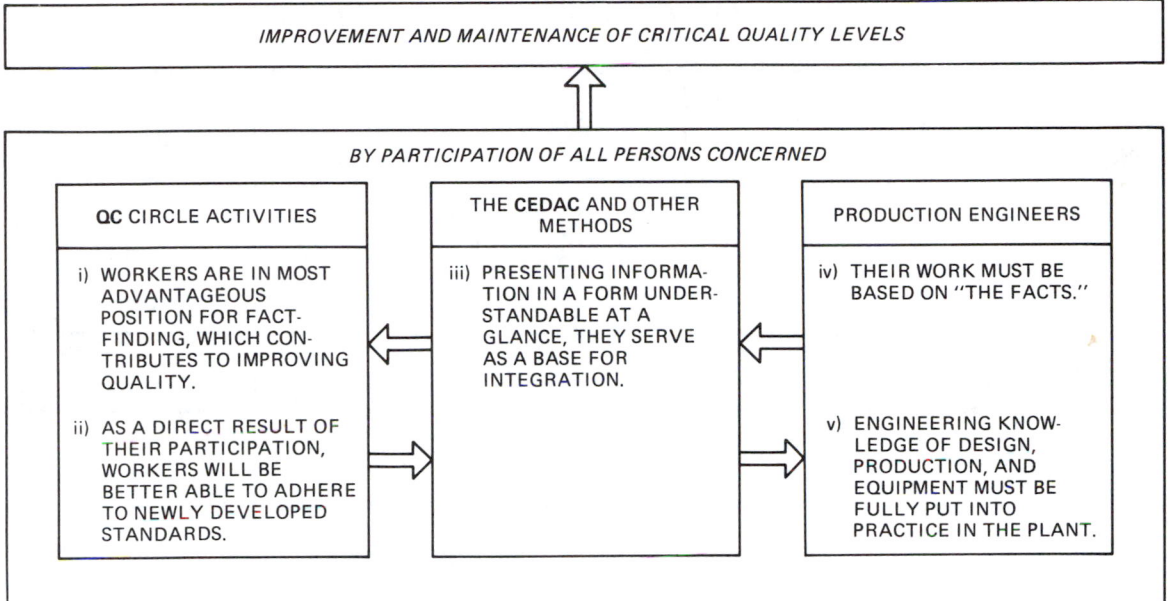

Figure 5 Basic Conceptual Frame of the CEDAC System

group knows. Under Category D circumstances, it is necessary to find and solve machine or technical problems which are unknown at the moment and to alter the conditions of the production process.

Let us apply the CEDAC actions to Figure 6:

1. Category A–1 comprises matters known and correctly practiced. With respect to standard operations, all persons should be in this category. This means that every worker knows and correctly practices the best and most effective operations known at that time.

2. To solve quality control problems we must follow the cycle

$$(1) \rightarrow (2) \rightarrow (3) \rightarrow (4) \rightarrow (1) \rightarrow .$$

If any one step is overlooked, good results cannot be expected. The key for success is not how to use the CEDAC, but how to follow this cycle using the CEDAC's great effectiveness.

This approach can be divided into two steps for solving quality control problems. At first, established adherence to existing standards (i.e., Category A–1) and then, if quality defects are still not reduced, find new manufacturing methods from Category D. The hypothesis is that the most effective way is to move to Category A–1 first and then, if the problem remains unsolved, to move into Category D on the basis of what has been established in Category A–1.

RESULTS OF CEDAC APPLICATIONS

Results / Problems	excellent	good	poor	total no. of problems
A	I problem	5	0	6
B	5	3	I	9
C	10	2	4	16
total no. of problems	16	10	5	31
percentage	52%	32%	16%	100%

Problems:
A: had been dealt with by engineers but remained unsolved
B: had been dealt with by a QC circle but remained unsolved
C: had not been dealt with at all

Results
excellent: more than a 90% decrease in defect rate
good: a 50 ~ 90% decrease in defect rate
poor: less than a 50% decrease in defect rate

TABLE I

Figure 7 classifies data from 86 QC circles into two categories from the standpoints of complete adherence and discovery of new methods within a specific time period.

A. Circles which used the CEDAC to establish adherence to existing standards and also to find more effective methods
B. Circles which established adherence to existing or revised standards by use of the CEDAC but couldn't find more effective methods

The percentage of reduction for Circle B was less than that of Circle A. Therefore, of the two approaches, it is evident that finding new methods is more effective.

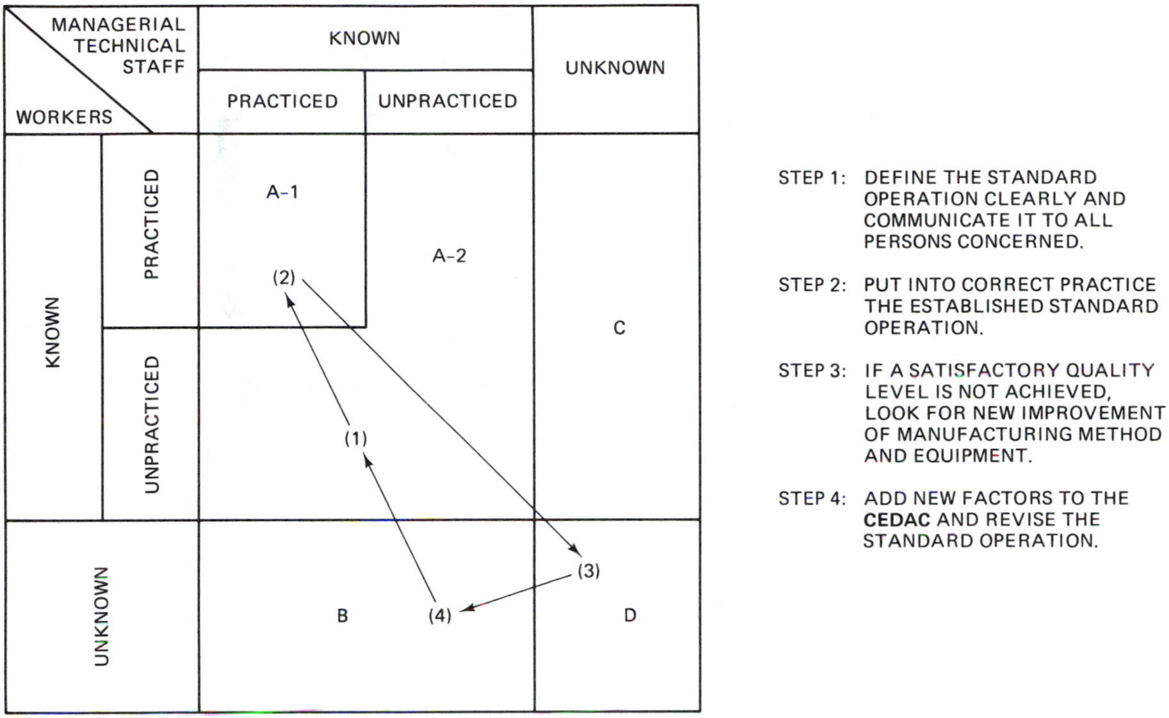
MANAGERIAL TECHNICAL STAFF
WORKERS
KNOWN
UNKNOWN
PRACTICED
UNPRACTICED
A-1
A-2
B
C
D
(1)
(2)
(3)
(4)
STEP 1: DEFINE THE STANDARD OPERATION CLEARLY AND COMMUNICATE IT TO ALL PERSONS CONCERNED.
STEP 2: PUT INTO CORRECT PRACTICE THE ESTABLISHED STANDARD OPERATION.
STEP 3: IF A SATISFACTORY QUALITY LEVEL IS NOT ACHIEVED, LOOK FOR NEW IMPROVEMENT OF MANUFACTURING METHOD AND EQUIPMENT.
STEP 4: ADD NEW FACTORS TO THE CEDAC AND REVISE THE STANDARD OPERATION.

Figure 6 Model for Analyzing the CEDAC System

An interesting conclusion can be drawn when Group A is divided into two categories (see Figure 8):

A–1. Those Circles which have always closely adhered to established standards

A–2. Those Circles which did not completely adhere to standards

Thus, even if the circle had found improved methods, an important factor for the circle's effectiveness was in adherence to the method.

In conclusion, establishing adherence (Category A–1) does not in itself have as great an effect as establishing adherence first and also finding new methods, but the probability of finding new methods and the effectiveness of the methods will be increased by the factor of complete adherence.

No "Magic Wand"

Although the CEDAC is an effective tool for use as a basic step in quality control, it is not a magic wand which creates something from nothing.

1. QC activity starts with collecting various "bare" facts.
   Lieutenant Columbo in the TV series goes to the scene of a murder, collects many facts, and finds important clues about the killer. In some case an important clue is a five-minute discrepancy somewhere, or just a hair. Columbo hunts for the criminal by

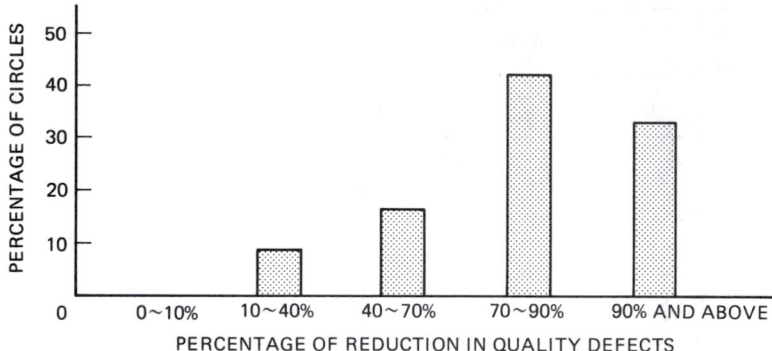

PERCENTAGE OF REDUCTION IN QUALITY DEFECTS

(A) CIRCLES WHICH FIRST ESTABLISHED ADHERENCE AND ALSO FOUND MORE EFFECTIVE METHODS

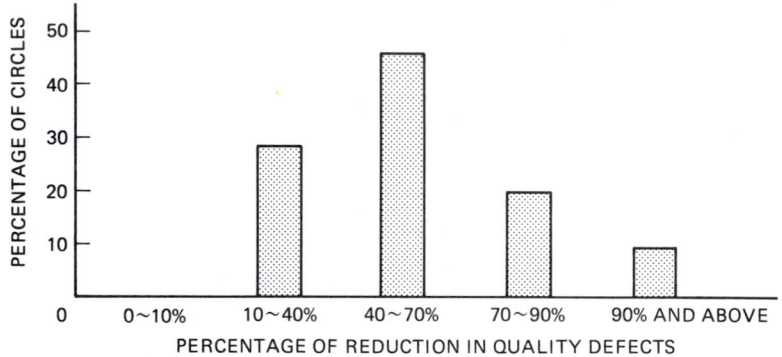

PERCENTAGE OF REDUCTION IN QUALITY DEFECTS

(B) CIRCLES WHICH ESTABLISHED ADHERENCE BUT COULDN'T FIND NEW METHODS

Figure 7 Adherence to Existing Standards and Discovery of New Methods

himself, but in the CEDAC the whole circle hunts for the criminal which causes quality defects. Gathering facts in the actual workshops by people who are doing different functions at their work is challenging and exciting.

2. QC is a practical science; therefore, it requires repeated practice by the persons who study it. At the beginning, when the CEDAC was first introduced to our workshops, we suffered from problems as well: workers' resistance to the tool, lack of active participation in meetings for collecting information, and, as a result, a CEDAC with very few cards. QC, like football, requires team play. The only way to be strong and successful is to practice repeatedly so that the team can overcome many difficulties.

3. Drawing a cause and effect diagram and using cards is just one of the available media to implement points 1 and 2. In short, it is not a matter of what tool to use; what is important is to have a basic QC philosophy. Therefore, the selection of a tool merely depends on the place, people, and situation.

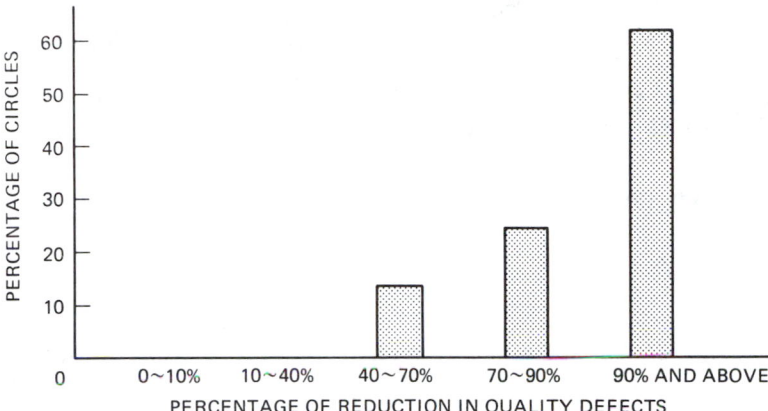

(A-1)   CIRCLES WHICH HAVE ALWAYS ADHERED CLOSELY
TO STANDARDS.

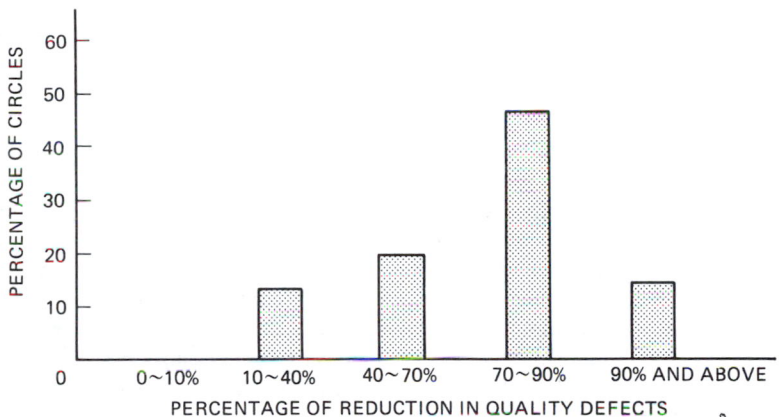

(A-2)   CIRCLES WHICH DID NOT COMPLETELY ADHERE
TO STANDARDS

Figure 8   Classification of Circles Which Found New Methods

4.   One of the most important factors for motivation of workers and the technical staff in their work is for them to have the same amount of information, which is made possible through using the CEDAC system. This is vital for people to work independently and with high morale. Sharing information should be one of our goals in this information-oriented era.

The world is continuously changing and advancing at accelerated speed, yet we human beings have to start our lives from the illiterate infant stage in the same way as people who lived thousands of years ago. How to cope with this rapidly changing world in a way harmonious to people will always be a serious question we have to solve.

The same is true with respect to Quality Control. Therefore, we QC engineers need to develop tools, such as the CEDAC, for integrating the knowledge, wisdom, and experiences of many individuals, thereby increasing the intellectual stimulation of the activities of workers and others. We must not make mistakes when selecting the direction to follow in developing such tools and systems.

20.3   CASE STUDY 3

THE VIEW FROM THE TOP*

A CEO's long-term commitment proves vital to the growth of an organization-wide major quality program

Charles C. Harwood

We felt pretty smug at Signetics in 1979. Sales were running at an annual rate of over $250 million, double our 1976 rate. We felt that we did not have any major quality problems or reliability problems. The quality of our products delivered to customers was okay, though spotty. There were no customers threatening us with dire consequences if we did not improve our product quality.

But even in 1979, we saw that a new attitude toward quality was emerging in the market-place.

We had all started to hear about Japanese quality and productivity, and we began to ponder such statements as "quality will be the battleground of the future."

For example, we were selling a particular product in Japan and we had to reinspect and retest all these parts in our Japanese operation, after they were manufactured to the same spec in our U.S. assembly plant. We also had a major customer—a U.S. automaker—that was putting our parts into an ignition control system. That company started talking about parts per million quality levels—levels much beyond our current performance. These cases raised our level of interest and concern about quality but there was no clarion call to action.

In the fall of 1979, after sales growth plans were set, our quality department started work on its four-year plan. At that time, our quality people were responsible for quality, and everyone else was responsible for output. Our quality people were "policemen."

Our quality department plan came to three conclusions.

- The requirements of the future clearly called for quality performance levels possible only through more sophisticated prevention programs.
- The number of quality personnel operating as "policemen" would have to expand exponentially to keep pace with our forecasted growth in volume.
- We had to give the quality responsibility to the people who make the product.

Our quality people felt that a prevention philosophy and a reorganization of their group were essential. In early 1980, after some discussion throughout the company and within my staff, we agreed to reorganize the corporate quality and reliability group by putting certain

*Reprinted with permission of the American Society for Quality Control.

functions under the operating management of the company. This reorganization was started slowly, division by division, so we could test acceptance as we went along.

At this point I was asked to start making positive noises about the organizational change and the new look in quality. In staff meetings, we discussed the pros and cons of adopting the program described by Philip Crosby in *Quality Is Free.*[1] I was urged to require that quality objectives be part of our "Responsibilities, Measures and Objectives" (RMOs)—in the management-by-objectives program designed by our organization development group. The upshot was a meeting in April 1980 of the top 250 people in the company. The subject: quality. The agenda included an outline of the complete quality program. I opened the meeting by stating that we were going to adopt the program, and that quality objectives were to be part of each person's RMO.

At the beginning of 1980 we had started a quality program on some selected products for an automotive customer. It was called a "flagship" project. It involved striving for zero defects on wafers made in our Orem plant and assembled in our Korean plant. It was a project we would monitor to see if attention to "making it right the first time" would markedly reduce our rate of nonconformity. A member of the quality organization was promoted to the line organization to manage the project.

Then we sat back to watch the miracle take place. We had planted some seeds, set up some models, passed down the word; we expected this to flower in the rest of the company.

What happened? Not much.

We did a critique at the end of 1980. Here is what we said about ourselves.

- The Quality group understood the new emphasis and accepted the organization change well. We had begun to work on determining the "cost of quality." This proved to be very difficult. We had difficulty getting the controllers and managers to accept the concept. There was disagreement about defining the cost. The controllers felt overworked. The line people couldn't see a way to determine a measurable number, and were concerned about showing a cost of quality figure in the 20% range; they feared that their bosses would have a new club with which to hit them.

- Orem showed some impressive improvement. They documented lower nonconformities, higher yields, and sharply reduced rework. Orem already had semiautonomous work teams, from a program installed by the organization development department. This enhanced the installation of the program. However, progress in installing the complete program was very slow. Commitment was the hang-up. The people at Orem held lengthy debates about the idea that better quality meant higher productivity.

But Orem finally did come up with a cost of quality figure of $7.6 million per year—and that represented only 10% of our activities. I began to see the large cost of quality for the company, and therefore a large opportunity for cost reduction.

I was not happy with our progress. A survey at the end of 1980 showed that some people thought the new program was great; others thought it was baloney; and others knew that, if they just hunkered down, this program would go away. At this point, I decided to appoint a quality program manager, full time, reporting to me. This person could be anybody but a current member of the quality group. Fortunately, our head of Q&R agreed that the program wouldn't go into place being managed by quality people. That insight and unselfishness made our task much easier.

In February 1981 we put together the corporate quality improvement team which was made up of the corporate staff (the people who report directly to me), the head of quality and reliability, the new corporate quality program manager, and me.

The corporate staff meets once a week for three hours. We realized that if we were going to prove that we meant it when we said quality, we were going to have to put some time into it. We knew about the "managers' apparent-interest index," which says, in effect, "people watch your feet, not your lips." If the boss does a lot of preaching, but doesn't invest a lot of hours of effort himself, people see through it.

We therefore decided to devote one hour a week—out of three-hour staff time—to quality. We also sent the head of quality and reliability and the quality program manager to a one-week course on quality.

In April 1981, we established a 1,000-ppm average outgoing quality (AOQ) program. It started with a meeting that bought in all the product test managers, worldwide. We told them to set an objective of getting to 1,000 ppm on product shipped. At this time we were at about 7,000 ppm. We focused on product test for two major reasons.

- We wanted to make clear to the test managers that this was their project—they had to spearhead the effort.
- We needed to show our customers that our outgoing quality was improving because we had started to brag about our big internal program.

This task was formidable, if only because we have a catalog of over 3,000 types, and a product master file with over 10,000 active types, counting special tests for major customers.

On July 24, 1981, the staff issued the corporate quality policy. This was step number one in the program[2] and it took us about two years to get there.

We also set up a two-day course in Sunnyvale for our top 25 people. We knew we didn't have real commitment from our top 25. So on Aug. 31 and Sept. 1, 1981, 23 all went through the two-day course. Nobody came out unchanged. Everybody was moved positively, and all came out committed to giving the program their best shot.

Commitment comes from involvement. Changing our perceptions, assumptions, and interpretations of the program took a great deal of involvement. But it was not wasted time. I believe commitment is key. It may not have to be done just the way we did it, but public, clear, strong commitment is vital to any endeavor if it is to be a success.

The impact of the course on our team convinced us that it is impossible to introduce the complete program to our people if we did not have them attend a similar program. We therefore designed our own quality college of two days duration, and by the end of 1981 over 100 people had gone through the program.

At the end of 1981 we had learned some lessons. One was that the great majority of the nonconformities could be traced back to management's mistakes. Likewise, we observed that our production people were eager to do an error-free job. They had realized for some time that the materials they were given, the tools, and the procedures were not error-free. How delighted they were to realize that their bosses had finally awakened, had taken responsibility and had installed a program to fix the problems. Needless to say, the morale of all our people, and their commitment to high-quality objectives, had risen markedly.

We also discovered that administrative problems were much more difficult than product problems to fix, and in the long run just as important. It is much easier to install a program on product nonconformities than on administrative nonconformities.

The commitment of the corporate staff—including me—was continually tested by various groups and people. Would we approve a piece of capital equipment? Would we add people where necessary? Would we ship product that was marginally out of spec?

I didn't record my views on the subject at the end of 1981, but to the best of my recollection they went something like this: I was committed to the program. I began to see great progress in reducing AOQs and customer returns. But I felt we could no doubt improve to a level quite acceptable to our customers without the full-blown program we had been talking about. People on the program were enthusiastic about their work, but couldn't we do this with other programs?

I decided to go ahead with the full program.

Why? The real clincher was the cost of quality. The cost of quality was found to be 30% of sales. This is a staggering figure. But we are probably no different than other manufacturers in the high-tech area. Talking with others, we have established that 30% cost of quality is normal. And when your pretax margins are 10% of sales, a 30% cost—one that doesn't do a thing for you—is something to attend to.

I also came to the realization that a zero-defect program is the key to productivity, and that perhaps what the Japanese have discovered through their zero-defect programs is this kernel of truth. Quality and productivity go hand in hand. When you think about it, it is as plain as the nose on your face. If you do it right the first time, and do it on time, your costs must be lower. No rework, no scrap, no customer returns, no reschedules, and no management time spent on these issues.

On the basis of these ideas, the staff and I established the three major focus items for the company in 1982. They were: "Meet our quality objective, our new product objectives, and our financial objectives." We had previously established a major program to revamp our logistics system. Our major purpose was to design a system to meet our promised delivery dates every time. We decided that this was also a program to have zero defects at those promised dates, so we included this program under our quality tasks.

We made a positive decision not to start any other programs to compete with our quality program—we did not want to lose our focus.

At the beginning of 1982 I wrote my RMO for quality. It included the following:

- Meet corporate program dated 10/22/81.
- Achieve outgoing quality less than 1,000 ppm.
- Achieve acceptance rates of 98% for seven key customers.
- Key quality returns under .65% and administrative returns under 1.00%.
- Fix three specific reliability issues.

Then I had to put action steps in place to be sure we met these objectives.

Each major unit (there were 33) formed a quality improvement team (QIT) and appointed a chairperson and a program manager. The quality improvement teams were mirrors of the corporate team. Each major unit manager was the chairperson and staff personnel were the team members.

In October 1982 we faced an important decision. Our corporate quality program manager left our company to join a company that was just starting up. Our profits were nonexistent. We debated whether to replace the program manager, and decided it was important to the program and a signal to the company that we meant what we said. We appointed one of our senior product engineering managers to the job.

In December 1982, the first issue of our corporate quality publication was produced. By then, over 20 bootleg—but officially encouraged—quality newsletters were being published by various groups. All exempt employees had gone through our two-day quality college—over 2,000 people by the end of 1982.

In April 1983 we had our first QIT Recognition Day. We gave out awards to key performers. The program was now moving broadly across the company. There were many spontaneous groups being formed, like ZD teams and a few quality circles. Department slogans appeared. By September of 1983 massive corrective-action programs had begun. All employees signed a pledge to work toward zero defects. Each QIT held a ZD day. A quality college for nonexempt employees was started.

The program was now four years old. We still had open issues. For example, some people still were not comfortable with the cost of quality measurement, and we had differences of opinion on the application of quality measures in the administrative area. But the program had become part of us.

In December 1983 we had an off-site staff meeting and, like almost everybody else I know, we took a look at ourselves in light of Peters' and Waterman's book, *In Search of Excellence.*[3] The book stresses the importance of having a superordinate goal. It was a quick and unanimous decision that quality was our superordinate goal. We selected the phrase, "People Committed to Quality." And you can change that phrase from the plural to the singular: "I am committed to zero defects."

When people ask me what Signetics does, I say that we make integrated circuits for our customers, with special emphasis on new products. They then say, "Yes, I know, but what is important to you, what do you stand for?" I then say, "What we stand for is 'People Committed to Quality' . . . and that starts with me." Five years after starting we have really just laid the quality foundation. More hard work lies ahead—and more opportunities.

References

1. Philip B. Crosby, *Quality is Free,* New York: McGraw-Hill, 1979.
2. Ibid.
3. Thomas J. Peters and Robert H. Waterman, Jr., *In Search of Excellence,* New York; Harper & Row, 1982.

20.4 CASE STUDY 4

A CALL FOR LEADERSHIP*

Quality depends as much on a vision of excellence as on management technique

Dana M. Cound

In an article published a year ago in *Quality Progress,*[1] I asserted that the secret of Japan's success in the international arena was not cultural advantage or QC circles or even statistical methods—as important as all of these are. Rather, I asserted, the secret of Japan's success is an unrelenting, some might say fanatical, adherence to what amounts to a de facto national industrial policy. That policy is quality first. Centralized planning might dictate which industries will be encouraged to flourish and which allowed to decline, but within the markets in which they choose to compete, it's strictly quality first. An operations executive in a Japanese firm has but two objectives: improve quality and reduce costs—but quality first. All other business goals, objectives, and systems are congruent with that policy.

That article carried a number of controversial ideas and I expected to be challenged. Interestingly, there was little debate over what I thought were the more controversial assertions, while the most thoughtful and reasoned challenges were directed at a statement which I thought was beyond question: "American managements in growing numbers are recognizing the quality issue for exactly what is—a strategic business issue of the first order. And they are responding to this issue as management responds to any strategically critical issue: by applying their personal energy, effort, and leadership to the improvement of quality in America."

Several colleagues whose opinions I respect challenged that observation: they did not see executives applying their personal leadership in any convincing way, notwithstanding the growing recognition of quality as a strategically critical issue in American business and industry. I found these remarks troubling. Almost a year having elapsed, I am more confident than ever of the validity of approximately half of that statement. "American managements in growing numbers are recognizing the quality issue for exactly what it is—a strategic business issue of the first order. And they are responding . . . ."

The problem has to do with personal leadership. I believe this is a fundamental issue to be faced if we are to achieve the future we all want.

In our society we tend to think that leaders are born, not made; that leadership is a function of personality and not an acquired skill. As a consequence—and operating under the scientific management mentality of Frederic Taylor, Henri Fayol, et al.—we have substituted the hard skills of management for the more elusive characteristics of leadership.

The quality issue is a good example. Quality unquestionably has management's attention: they are convinced that it is critical; they are applying energy and effort, both their own and others'; they have voiced their commitment to quality values; they have assigned the resources of the organization—in other words, they have taken all the management actions learned about in school and believed necessary and sufficient to alter the course of the organization. Yet in too many cases, quality initiatives sincerely launched and desperately needed are born without a heartbeat, or lack the vitality to survive. While leadership without management can lead to chaos, management without leadership is sterile.

Consider the golf swing. The setup and backswing are vitally important; the physical resources are gathered and put in place to execute the perfect swing; you might call this the management phase. During the downswing and follow through, however, many parts of the body are entering and leaving the process too fast to be managed consciously—this is analogous to the leadership phase. And unless all of these actions and reactions are totally harmonious and consistent and almost automatic, you're in for a walk in the woods. The trouble for many a quality improvement initiative begins when management "pulls the trigger."

If management's release and follow through are often tentative or inconsistent, it may not be a result of a lack of commitment; rather, it may indicate that managers don't understand how to create shared values in an organization. But in the absence of consistency and harmony among all of the goals, objectives, and values of the organization, the natural consequence is confusion among the rank and file about what the executive really wants—today, right now, if he can't have everything he wants and instantly. This perceived ambiguity is reflected in the organization's behavior: people mouth the words, hang the posters, and form the committees, but all the while behave as they perceive the boss to be behaving—tentatively and with a lack of commitment. This is not failure in management but failure in leadership.

This failure has especially serious consequences in the circumstances that confront us. The quality first movement is taking us into what amounts to a new era—one fraught with promise but also uncertainty and danger. We're asking people to forget many of the lessons they've learned over the past 40 years and to accept a new set of guiding principles—principles that are often diametrically opposed to the model of successful behavior they've grown up with. In some cases, the implications of these principles are not even totally clear, let alone second nature. For a while—perhaps a long while—we'll have to be quick on our feet if we're going to handle the unexpected situations that are sure to arise. The only force that will cause whole organizations to follow into this area of uncertainty is excellent, compelling leadership.

The economic conditions we find ourselves in today—symbolized by the closed factory and measured in terms of massive trade deficits—offer compelling reasons to leave behind old behaviors. Yet even among people of pioneer stock, trailblazers aren't always easy to find. Perhaps that's why our popular culture is full of figures like Daniel Boone. Dan'l didn't become a hero by sending somebody else out to fight the bear; charting a course through unexplored territory wasn't a job to be delegated, it was a way of life—it was what he did, dangerous or not. Now as then, leadership means going first. If an executive is unwilling to do that—to stick his personal neck out—then he has forfeited his role as a leader, and shouldn't be surprised if the people who work for him seem unwilling to accept his marching orders.

Furthermore, to be a leader—the one in the lead—the executive must unequivocally understand why the trip is worth making. Before sending anyone else, the executive must undertake a journey himself—the personal, intellectual journey required to adopt a new set of values. Squarely facing fundamental issues and coming away with unequivocal answers, values, and standards one is wiling to be measured by is an essential prerequisite to the caliber of leadership this issue requires.

What the quality movement needs today is effective, coherent leadership. Leadership is not the application of technique, management or otherwise, and results do not inevitably flow from the application of technology. A review of the *In Search of Excellence* companies reveals some excellent managements; more importantly, these organizations are characterized by excellent leadership. Frito Lay cannot defend its service call rate on a cost/benefit basis— nor do they choose to. It's not a question of management or analysis or technique; it's a question of values and leadership. That's the way they do it at Frito Lay—period.

In *A Passion for Excellence*—the follow-up to *In Search of Excellence*—Tom Peters and Nancy Austin devote an entire chapter to this idea; "Quality is Not a Technique" is its title. The authors observe: "The heart of quality is not technique. It is commitment by management to its people and product—stretching over a period of decades and lived with persistence and passion." Stew Leonard's Dairy Store of Norwalk, CT, is celebrated in Tom Peters' works, and properly so. I know; the Counds have shopped there on many occasions. But you know, Akron, OH, has an operation to match it in every way—with maybe a few tricks to teach Stew. It's the locally famed West Point Market that does more things superbly (and routinely) than any operation of its type I've ever seen. Tom Peters would love it. So would Stew Leonard. But neither Stew Leonard's nor the West Point Market are what they are because of superior technique. They are what they are because of superior leadership—a leadership that is focused, so unambiguous that it infects all who are exposed to it.

Leadership is not cheerleading or symbolic behavior; it is not merely commitment; it is not even just participation. These are manifestations of leadership in action but they are not leadership.

In a speech delivered to the Veer Foundation in the Netherlands in 1982, Joseph Jaworski, chairman and CEO of the American Leadership Forum, cited five elements that he felt were key to excellent leadership.

1. The successful leader must have a compelling vision. Excellent leaders are concerned with the organization's basic purpose: why it exists; what it should achieve. They are not preoccupied with the "how to" or nuts and bolts aspects of the operation; they see themselves as leaders, not as managers. The driving vision has an almost spiritual quality to it.

2. The successful leader must be powerful. This doesn't mean dominion or control or manipulation but rather the capacity to mobilize people and resources to get things done. Rosabeth Moss Kanter of Yale and more recently Harvard, one of our leading sociologists, describes the powerful leader not as an autocrat but rather as a sensitive, empathetic, compassionate, empowering person. Leaders are not so much exercisers of power as providers of power—dynamos.

3. The successful leader must exemplify the highest values of the organization. To earn trust, a leader has to be authentic. He comes across as a good musical composition does—the words and music match.

4. The leader must provide breadth and risk-taking entrepreneurial imagination for the organization. He must be able to see things in a fresh and different context—to "recontextualize" a situation.

5. The effective leader is a transforming leader. Transforming leaders are capable of directing people through fundamental change—personal, institutional, and societal. The leader "engages with his followers, brings them to heightened consciousness, and in this process converts many followers into leaders in their own right," Jaworski argued.

For an understanding of leadership, one could do worse than to refer to what is perhaps the most thought-provoking book on organization and management ever written by a practicing executive. It is more widely read today than upon its publication almost 50 years ago. It is *The Functions of the Executive* by Chester J. Barnard.

In this book, Barnard defines leadership as "the power of individuals to inspire cooperative personal decision by creating faith." We don't hear much in school today about creating faith. In fact, we probably find the idea mildly embarrassing. Management is about harder stuff.

Barnard goes on. "Faith in common understanding, faith in the probability of success, faith in the ultimate satisfaction of personal motives, faith in the integrity of objective authority and faith in the superiority of common purpose." Leaders create faith. Barnard speaks of morals, not meaning any particular set of ethical values but rather the personal forces or propensities in individuals that tend to control behavior that is inconsistent and to reinforce behavior that is consistent with personal values. In other words, personal flywheels that resist being detoured or redirected by the continual bombardment of short-term forces.

When this tendency is strong and stable, there exists a condition of responsibility. Responsibility, as Barnard defines it, is the power of a particular private code to control the conduct of the individual in the presence of strong contradictory impulses. Responsibility thus equals steadfastness—Deming's constancy of purpose. Barnard asserts that all of us possess several if not many moral codes: religious, patriotic, familial, business, etc. Persons differ not only as to the quality, complexity, and relative importance of their moral codes, but also as to the strength of their sense of responsibility toward them. Leaders have the faculty—and the responsibility—of creating moral codes for the organization; value structures, organizational flywheels.

I find it interesting that the words moral and morale have a common root. Organizations with strong, coherent value systems have excellent morale.

Barnard asserts that the important distinctions of rank lie in the fact that the higher the grade, the more complex the moralities involved and hence the greater the need for skill in resolving the conflicts implicit in the positions. When various sets of values come into conflict, as they inevitably must, the manager chooses: he places one above the other, thereby strengthening one value and depreciating the other. The leader, however, invokes creativeness; that is, he invents a moral basis for the solution of moral conflicts. He either substitutes a different action that avoids the conflict or provides a moral justification for exception or compromise. In other words, the leader resolves value conflicts by eliminating them if possible; but if that is not possible, the leader creates overarching values, so that conflicts are resolved instead of one value being subordinated to the other. Resolution is a win–win between opposing values; choosing between is a win–lose.

This creative function as a whole is the essence of leadership. The structure of organizational values provides the spirit that overcomes the centrifugal forces of individual interests. It infuses the subjective aspect of countless decisions with consistency in a changing environment.

William Ouchi observed in his remarks at the 1986 Annual Quality Congress in Anaheim that leadership, which he defined as the ability to cause others to follow the leader into areas of uncertainty, was based in all cases on the personal integrity of the leader. Referring to Barnard's work and paraphrasing only slightly, he observed that integrity didn't imply any particular set of values but rather a coherence of personality—the state of being together. A person who is together—integrated—has a kind of transparency of personality that always shows the same face to all people in all situations. This quality is an essential prerequisite to leadership ability.

One of several definitions for integrity, the one to which Ouchi referred, is "the quality of being whole or undivided; completeness." It is also the logical outcome of a process of integration: "to make whole by bringing all parts together." It follows that an executive cannot provide outstanding coherent leadership to the quality effort until his set of quality values (or morals, as Barnard would say) has been integrated with his other moral sets—probably by creating an overarching algorithm that reconciles inevitable conflicts to the satisfaction of both value systems. In the presence of this coherent system, ambiguity disappears. People don't have to make choices between which of the conflicting value systems are to be served. The value systems have been integrated and can be served as a whole.

Barnard observes that when codes of substantially equal validity come into conflict, one of two things can happen: either paralysis of action or conformance to one code and violation of the other. Further, behavior that continually violates a code leads to the eventual destruction of that code. Isn't that exactly what's at the root of many of the quality problems faced by American industry? Repeatedly, the values of quality, cost, and schedule are perceived to be in conflict. Repeatedly, decisions are made that have the effect of subordinating one code to the satisfaction of the others. Eventually the violated code is destroyed as an organizational value.

Why are the quality values that an individual exercises during his hours as consumer often so different from the values the same person exercises on the job as a producer? The codes are often diametrically opposed, yet the hypocrisy isn't perceived. The reason? There is no hypocrisy. As consumers they are following their personal codes; as producers they are following the organizational code.

The management process, in a technology sense, has two unfortunate outcomes. First, that process subordinates the individual to the system; then the system chooses between alternative conflicting outcomes to the corrosion of the subordinated values. Leadership, by contrast, insists that the systems serve the organization and creates integrated value systems that are holistic in nature. Management subordinates. Leadership exalts.

To see how various value systems are integrated in an organization, one must take a hard look at the organization's reward systems. What behavior is rewarded with approval, bonuses, promotions, and centrality within the organization? What behavior is met with frowns, scoldings, demotion, dismissal—or with winks? What behavior is sanctioned by the informal organization? Is it consistent with the type of behavior solicited publicly by the formal organization? Coherent leadership can never be achieved until both the formal and informal reward systems are brought into alignment with the express value systems. A classic example of value conflict is when management calls for quality first or quality improvement in the presence of an incentive program that rewards raw production, mitigating against the very behavior management is calling for.

The would-be leader must also examine the organization's measurement systems. The measurement system is so closely linked to the reward system that they cannot be considered apart. Take baseball as an example: I'm not sure whether batting averages are measured because they're important or are important because they're measured. It makes little difference—measurement imputes importance. If, for example, the quality policy involves products and services, then both areas must be measured. If quality judgments are to be customer-based, then so must the measurement system. Most quality information systems deal with production efficiency, not customer satisfaction. Those limited attempts to measure customer satisfaction ultimately measure degree of dissatisfaction and confuse absence of expressed dissatisfaction with the presence of satisfaction—a potentially fatal mistake.

Finally, the would-be leader should take a hard look at the award system. While I will grant that the award system is an integral part of the reward system, it has some unusual properties. Does the award in question implicitly shift to the worker a responsibility that properly belongs to management—like safety or housekeeping? Does the award create a lottery wherein someone will win, no matter how poor, and someone will lose, no matter how good? Does the award divide team effort and create frictions within the system? (Consider the effect on you and your peers if your workers were to set up an award for supervisor or manager of the month, and make the presentation the way employee-of-the-month presentations are often made.) Does the award exalt and dignify or does it perhaps demean and reinforce a caste system? Are you better off with it or would it be better to discontinue what may be an organizational beauty contest and substitute a day-by-day environment characterized by dignity and respect? Maybe we should stop giving awards and plaques to each other and take our awards in the form of shared values and team jobs well done.

The measurement, reward, and award systems play important roles in communicating organizational values. But even properly aligned, they are not enough. It will be almost impossible for anyone—leader or manager—to integrate quality values within an organization if the organization doesn't know what the term "quality" means. Thus, the leader must develop a set of principles and a quality definition with which he is willing, with unequivocal fervor, to inculcate the organization.

Why should the executive have the responsibility for implanting quality in the organization? The answer is clear. It is now widely agreed that quality is not just a manufacturing issue; if the executive believes this, then he believes that quality crosses through every function in the company. Since the least common denominator among all the functions is the chief executive, then it follows that he must personally provide the leadership. It's not a functional issue, it's a business issue.

The final question is "So what?" We have adopted some principles, formulated a definition, and explored the scope of the issue. What is the leader going to do about it—if anything? That course of action is the organization's quality policy. Policy, according to my dictionary, is a practical course of action. It is very different from most quality policies we see. It is modest in tone. It is devoid of hyperbole. It is not self-aggrandizing. It may even be a little dull. It is also credible and it probably shows the linkage back to the underlying principles and forward to some fundamental business objectives.

Notice several important differences in the process described here and the usual policy development process. First, the policy is not developed by a committee and presented to the leader for signature; the primary role is played by the leader. After all, that's what leadership is all about. Granted, the leadership may consult with many people and use many sounding boards, but the contacts will probably be made individually or in small groups, not in committee.

Second, the policy is the last thing developed and, when the time comes to write it, the policy almost writes itself: the course of action for the organization flows naturally from the principles, definitions, and product deliberations. When finally given voice, the policy comes forth as a decision, a direction—and yes, perhaps as a vision. It connects a value system both moral and visionary with practical business objectives and serves as an organizational guidon.

So where are we after all of this? Yes, the hard skills of management practiced in a polished and professional manner are necessary, but not sufficient to cause organizations to take on new and threatening challenges. That takes leadership. While leadership may be enhanced by a charismatic personality, it is to a more important degree the consequence of a coherent integration of all the values of an organization into a cohesive totality that all people can sense and relate to. As such, it is an acquired skill and the product of hard personal work. It is not sufficient for management to give voice to goals and philosophical values, as important as these are. In addition, management must also consider all the day-by-day decisions of the organization and its members and provide answers to the important question: "What do they want me to do with this problem, this conflict of values that is sitting on my desk here right now? I know they want quality. They also want a lot of other important things. But the decision must be made—now."

The ultimate leader can't sit and solve all of the problems of the organization one by one. Moses learned that in the 18th Chapter of Exodus. Yet if all the decision makers are to march to the same drummer they must all hear the same beat. It is the specific and personal responsibility of the leader to assure that all of the systems of the enterprise, and specifically the reward system, channel the decision making to the same end. Most important, the leader, through his personal efforts, must assure that the value system of the enterprise is integrated and holistic in nature so that values do not have to be sacrificed to values.

Reference

1. Dana M. Cound, "Quality First," *Quality Progress,* March 1986, pp. 19–22.

Glossary

The following terms have been used in the text. A brief definition follows each term.

Attribute. Characteristic that can be counted for data recording and analysis.

Average. The statistic that indicates, numerically, the location of a sample or population of data. The average of a single sample is designated with the title x-bar and the average of a group of averages, or a population average, is designated x-double bar.

Capability. Also known as process capability, this is a numerical measure indicating the expected limits of normal variation for a process. Statistically, it is the average plus or minus three standard deviations.

Cause and effect diagram. A tool for individual or group problem solving that uses a graphical representation of process elements to identify potential sources of variation. Also known as Ishikawa diagram and fishbone diagram.

Central limit theorem. A statistical rule that assures the normality of the distribution of sample data when sufficient numbers of samples or subgroups are measured.

Central line. A line on the control chart that shows the location of the center of the data.

Control chart. A graphical representation of the variation of a process characteristic over time. The control chart shows the central tendency of the data, as well as control limits for the characteristic. The control chart differentiates between normal and abnormal variation within the process.

Control limit. Lines on a control chart that establish the limits of normal variation for the process. Generally, the limits are called three sigma limits.

Detection. Acting on process variation after nonconforming material is produced.

Frequency distribution. A graphical representation of the number of times that a certain characteristic or certain value of a characteristic occurs. Sometimes this is called a frequency histogram.

Individual. A single unit of a characteristic.

Inputs. Part of a process that is transformed with other inputs to create the outputs of the process. Typical inputs include people, equipment, material, procedures, and environment.

Location. Synonymous with the central location of the sample data and described by the average.

Mean. The arithmetic average of a sample of measurements. A measure of location.

Median. The middle value in a sample of rank-ordered data or measurements. There are as many values in the sample larger than the median as there are smaller. The median is a measure of location.

Mode. The most frequently occurring value in a sample. The mode is a measure of location.

Normal distribution. A continuous bell-shaped frequency distribution for variables data. Normally, distributed data has approximately 68 percent of the points with ± 1 standard deviation of the mean; 95.5 percent of the points within ± 2 standard deviations of the mean; and approximately 99.7 percent of the points within ± 3 standard deviations of the mean.

Outputs. Part of a process that results from the transformation. The output of one stage of the process often acts as the input for the next.

Pareto chart. A problem-solving tool that involves ranking all potential problem areas or sources of variation according to their contribution to cost or to total variation. Typically, the chart will show that very few of the causes are responsible for most of the variation.

Prevention. Acting on process variation before nonconforming material is produced.

Process. The combination of inputs, such as people, equipment, environment, procedures, and materials, in a transformation to produce some related outputs. Every aspect of every business can be viewed as both a complete process and a series of related/dependent processes, where the output from one process is the input to the next.

Randomness. A condition in which individual values are not predictable even though they may come from a known distribution.

Range. The difference between the largest and smallest value within a sample. A measure of spread.

Run. Consecutive number of points consistently increasing or decreasing on a control chart.

Run chart. A control chart for individual values of a measurable characteristic of a process.

Sample. A subgroup of values taken from a process at a designated time and measured using a designated measuring procedure.

Shape. The overall pattern formed by the distribution of values.

Sigma. The Greek letter used to designate standard deviation.

Specification. The engineering requirement for a characteristic so that the output of the process functions as intended.

Spread. The width of a distribution of values.

Stability. A process is said to be stable when only normal variation is present. This is also called statistical control.

Standard deviation. A mathematical measure of the variability or spread of a sample of data. It is designated with the letter S or the lowercase Greek letter sigma.

Statistic. A mathematical measure of one of the characteristics of sample data, such as location, spread, or shape. Statistics are used to describe data and help draw conclusions about the data.

Statistical control. A process is said to be in statistical control when it is stable and only normal variation is present.

Statistical process control. The use of statistical methods to identify the variation within a process. The objective is to first achieve statistical control and then to improve the process by continually reducing the amount of variation in the process.

Subgroup. One of more sample values used to analyze the performance of a sample.

Variable. Characteristic that can be measured for data recording and analysis.

Variation. The always present differences between individual characteristics. Two types of variation are of concern. Normal variation is always present and is a function of the process. Abnormal variation is present only when special or assignable causes are present. Normal variation can be reduced by modifying the process.

APPENDIX A
Normal Value Curves

TABLE A1
Proportions of Area under the Normal Curve

(A) z	(B) Area between Mean and z	(C) Area beyond z	(A) z	(B) Area between Mean and z	(C) Area beyond z	(A) z	(B) Area between Mean and z	(C) Area beyond z
0.00	0.0000	0.5000	0.40	0.1554	0.3446	0.80	0.2881	0.2119
0.01	0.0040	0.4960	0.41	0.1591	0.3409	0.81	0.2910	0.2090
0.02	0.0080	0.4920	0.42	0.1628	0.3372	0.82	0.2939	0.2061
0.03	0.0120	0.4880	0.43	0.1664	0.3336	0.83	0.2967	0.2033
0.04	0.0160	0.4840	0.44	0.1700	0.3300	0.84	0.2995	0.2005
0.05	0.0199	0.4801	0.45	0.1736	0.3264	0.85	0.3023	0.1977
0.06	0.0239	0.4761	0.46	0.1772	0.3228	0.86	0.3051	0.1949
0.07	0.0279	0.4721	0.47	0.1808	0.3192	0.87	0.3078	0.1922
0.08	0.0319	0.4681	0.48	0.1844	0.3156	0.88	0.3106	0.1894
0.09	0.0359	0.4641	0.49	0.1879	0.3121	0.89	0.3133	0.1867
0.10	0.0398	0.4602	0.50	0.1915	0.3085	0.90	0.3159	0.1841
0.11	0.0438	0.4562	0.51	0.1950	0.3050	0.91	0.3186	0.1814
0.12	0.0478	0.4522	0.52	0.1985	0.3015	0.92	0.3212	0.1788
0.13	0.0517	0.4483	0.53	0.2019	0.2981	0.93	0.3238	0.1762
0.14	0.0557	0.4443	0.54	0.2054	0.2946	0.94	0.3264	0.1736
0.15	0.0596	0.4404	0.55	0.2088	0.2912	0.95	0.3289	0.1711
0.16	0.0636	0.4364	0.56	0.2123	0.2877	0.96	0.3315	0.1685
0.17	0.0675	0.4325	0.57	0.2157	0.2843	0.97	0.3340	0.1660
0.18	0.0714	0.4286	0.58	0.2190	0.2810	0.98	0.3365	0.1635
0.19	0.0753	0.4247	0.59	0.2224	0.2776	0.99	0.3389	0.1611

TABLE A1 Continued

(A) z	(B) Area between Mean and z	(C) Area beyond z	(A) z	(B) Area between Mean and z	(C) Area beyond z	(A) z	(B) Area between Mean and z	(C) Area beyond z
0.20	0.0793	0.4207	0.60	0.2257	0.2743	1.00	0.3413	0.1587
0.21	0.0832	0.4168	0.61	0.2291	0.2709	1.01	0.3438	0.1562
0.22	0.0871	0.4129	0.62	0.2324	0.2676	1.02	0.3461	0.1539
0.23	0.0910	0.4090	0.63	0.2357	0.2643	1.03	0.3485	0.1515
0.24	0.0948	0.4052	0.64	0.2389	0.2611	1.04	0.3508	0.1492
0.25	0.0987	0.4013	0.65	0.2422	0.2578	1.05	0.3531	0.1469
0.26	0.1026	0.3974	0.66	0.2454	0.2546	1.06	0.3554	0.1446
0.27	0.1064	0.3936	0.67	0.2486	0.2514	1.07	0.3577	0.1423
0.28	0.1103	0.3897	0.68	0.2517	0.2483	1.08	0.3599	0.1401
0.29	0.1141	0.3859	0.69	0.2549	0.2451	1.09	0.3621	0.1379
0.30	0.1179	0.3821	0.70	0.2580	0.2420	1.10	0.3643	0.1357
0.31	0.1217	0.3783	0.71	0.2611	0.2389	1.11	0.3665	0.1335
0.32	0.1255	0.3745	0.72	0.2642	0.2358	1.12	0.3686	0.1314
0.33	0.1293	0.3707	0.73	0.2673	0.2327	1.13	0.3708	0.1292
0.34	0.1331	0.3669	0.74	0.2704	0.2296	1.14	0.3729	0.1271
0.35	0.1368	0.3632	0.75	0.2734	0.2266	1.15	0.3749	0.1251
0.36	0.1406	0.3594	0.76	0.2764	0.2236	1.16	0.3770	0.1230
0.37	0.1443	0.3557	0.77	0.2794	0.2206	1.17	0.3790	0.1210
0.38	0.1480	0.3520	0.78	0.2823	0.2177	1.18	0.3810	0.1190
0.39	0.1517	0.3483	0.79	0.2852	0.2148	1.19	0.3830	0.1170
1.20	0.3849	0.1151	1.60	0.4452	0.0548	2.00	0.4772	0.0228
1.21	0.3869	0.1131	1.61	0.4463	0.0537	2.01	0.4778	0.0222
1.22	0.3888	0.1112	1.62	0.4474	0.0526	2.02	0.4783	0.0217
1.23	0.3907	0.1093	1.63	0.4484	0.0516	2.03	0.4788	0.0212
1.24	0.3925	0.1075	1.64	0.4495	0.0505	2.04	0.4793	0.0207
1.25	0.3944	0.1056	1.65	0.4505	0.0495	2.05	0.4798	0.0202
1.26	0.3962	0.1038	1.66	0.4515	0.0485	2.06	0.4803	0.0197
1.27	0.3980	0.1020	1.67	0.4525	0.0475	2.07	0.4808	0.0192
1.28	0.3997	0.1003	1.68	0.4535	0.0465	2.08	0.4812	0.0188
1.29	0.4015	0.0985	1.69	0.4545	0.0455	2.09	0.4817	0.0183
1.30	0.4032	0.0968	1.70	0.4554	0.0446	2.10	0.4821	0.0179
1.31	0.4049	0.0951	1.71	0.4564	0.0436	2.11	0.4826	0.0174
1.32	0.4066	0.0934	1.72	0.4573	0.0427	2.12	0.4830	0.0170
1.33	0.4082	0.0918	1.73	0.4582	0.0418	2.13	0.4834	0.0166
1.34	0.4099	0.0901	1.74	0.4591	0.0409	2.14	0.4838	0.0162
1.35	0.4115	0.0885	1.75	0.4599	0.0401	2.15	0.4842	0.0158
1.36	0.4131	0.0869	1.76	0.4608	0.0392	2.16	0.4846	0.0154
1.37	0.4147	0.0853	1.77	0.4616	0.0384	2.17	0.4850	0.0150

(*cont.*)

TABLE A1 Continued

(A) z	(B) Area between Mean and z	(C) Area beyond z	(A) z	(B) Area between Mean and z	(C) Area beyond z	(A) z	(B) Area between Mean and z	(C) Area beyond z
1.38	0.4162	0.0838	1.78	0.4625	0.0375	2.18	0.4854	0.0146
1.39	0.4177	0.0823	1.79	0.4633	0.0367	2.19	0.4857	0.0143
1.40	0.4192	0.0808	1.80	0.4641	0.0359	2.20	0.4861	0.0139
1.41	0.4207	0.0793	1.81	0.4649	0.0351	2.21	0.4864	0.0136
1.42	0.4222	0.0778	1.82	0.4656	0.0344	2.22	0.4868	0.0132
1.43	0.4236	0.0764	1.83	0.4664	0.0336	2.23	0.4871	0.0129
1.44	0.4251	0.0749	1.84	0.4671	0.0329	2.24	0.4875	0.0125
1.45	0.4265	0.0735	1.85	0.4678	0.0322	2.25	0.4878	0.0122
1.46	0.4279	0.0721	1.86	0.4686	0.0314	2.26	0.4881	0.0119
1.47	0.4292	0.0708	1.87	0.4693	0.0307	2.27	0.4884	0.0116
1.48	0.4306	0.0694	1.88	0.4699	0.0301	2.28	0.4887	0.0113
1.49	0.4319	0.0681	1.89	0.4706	0.0294	2.29	0.4890	0.0110
1.50	0.4332	0.0668	1.90	0.4713	0.0287	2.30	0.4893	0.0107
1.51	0.4345	0.0655	1.91	0.4719	0.0281	2.31	0.4896	0.0104
1.52	0.4357	0.0643	1.92	0.4726	0.0274	2.32	0.4898	0.0102
1.53	0.4370	0.0630	1.93	0.4732	0.0268	2.33	0.4901	0.0099
1.54	0.4382	0.0618	1.94	0.4738	0.0262	2.34	0.4904	0.0096
1.55	0.4394	0.0606	1.95	0.4744	0.0256	2.35	0.4906	0.0094
1.56	0.4406	0.0594	1.96	0.4750	0.0250	2.36	0.4909	0.0091
1.57	0.4418	0.0582	1.97	0.4756	0.0244	2.37	0.4911	0.0089
1.58	0.4429	0.0571	1.98	0.4761	0.0239	2.38	0.4913	0.0087
1.59	0.4441	0.0559	1.99	0.4767	0.0233	2.39	0.4916	0.0084
2.40	0.4918	0.0082	2.75	0.4970	0.0030	3.10	0.4990	0.0010
2.41	0.4920	0.0080	2.76	0.4971	0.0029	3.11	0.4991	0.0009
2.42	0.4922	0.0078	2.77	0.4972	0.0028	3.12	0.4991	0.0009
2.43	0.4925	0.0075	2.78	0.4973	0.0027	3.13	0.4991	0.0009
2.44	0.4927	0.0073	2.79	0.4974	0.0026	3.14	0.4992	0.0008
2.45	0.4929	0.0071	2.80	0.4974	0.0026	3.15	0.4992	0.0008
2.46	0.4931	0.0069	2.81	0.4975	0.0025	3.16	0.4992	0.0008
2.47	0.4932	0.0068	2.82	0.4976	0.0024	3.17	0.4992	0.0008
2.48	0.4934	0.0066	2.83	0.4977	0.0023	3.18	0.4993	0.0007
2.49	0.4936	0.0064	2.84	0.4977	0.0023	3.19	0.4993	0.0007
2.50	0.4938	0.0062	2.85	0.4978	0.0022	3.20	0.4993	0.0007
2.51	0.4940	0.0060	2.86	0.4979	0.0021	3.21	0.4993	0.0007
2.52	0.4941	0.0059	2.87	0.4979	0.0021	3.22	0.4994	0.0006
2.53	0.4943	0.0057	2.88	0.4980	0.0020	3.23	0.4994	0.0006
2.54	0.4945	0.0055	2.89	0.4981	0.0019	3.24	0.4994	0.0006
2.55	0.4946	0.0054	2.90	0.4981	0.0019	3.25	0.4994	0.0006
2.56	0.4948	0.0052	2.91	0.4982	0.0018	3.30	0.4995	0.0005

TABLE A1 Continued

(A) z	(B) Area between Mean and z	(C) Area beyond z	(A) z	(B) Area between Mean and z	(C) Area beyond z	(A) z	(B) Area between Mean and z	(C) Area beyond z
2.57	0.4949	0.0051	2.92	0.4982	0.0018	3.35	0.4996	0.0004
2.58	0.4951	0.0049	2.93	0.4983	0.0017	3.40	0.4997	0.0003
2.59	0.4952	0.0048	2.94	0.4984	0.0016	3.45	0.4997	0.0003
2.60	0.4953	0.0047	2.95	0.4984	0.0016	3.50	0.4998	0.0002
2.61	0.4955	0.0045	2.96	0.4985	0.0015	3.60	0.4998	0.0002
2.62	0.4956	0.0044	2.97	0.4985	0.0015	3.70	0.4999	0.0001
2.63	0.4957	0.0043	2.98	0.4986	0.0014	3.80	0.4999	0.0001
2.64	0.4959	0.0041	2.99	0.4986	0.0014	3.90	0.49995	0.00005
						4.00	0.49997	0.00003
2.65	0.4960	0.0040	3.00	0.4987	0.0013			
2.66	0.4961	0.0039	3.01	0.4987	0.0013			
2.67	0.4962	0.0038	3.02	0.4987	0.0013			
2.68	0.4963	0.0037	3.03	0.4988	0.0012			
2.69	0.4964	0.0036	3.04	0.4988	0.0012			
2.70	0.4965	0.0035	3.05	0.4989	0.0011			
2.71	0.4966	0.0034	3.06	0.4989	0.0011			
2.72	0.4967	0.0033	3.07	0.4989	0.0011			
2.73	0.4968	0.0032	3.08	0.4990	0.0010			
2.74	0.4969	0.0031	3.09	0.4990	0.0010			

Shewhart Control Chart Constants

n	A_2	D_3	D_4	d_2
2	1.88	0	3.27	1.128
3	1.02	0	2.57	1.693
4	.73	0	2.28	2.059
5	.58	0	2.11	2.326
6	.48	0	2.00	2.534
7	.42	.08	1.92	2.704
8	.37	.14	1.86	2.847
9	.34	.18	1.82	2.970
10	.31	.22	1.78	3.078

REFERENCES

1. "Draft Report of the Panel on Product and process Quality," *White House Conference on Productivity,* Pittsburgh, Pa., August 1–4, 1983.

2. "Interim report on Quality and Productivity," *American Productivity Center Computer Conference, White House Pre-conference on Private Sector Initiatives,* Pittsburgh, Pa., August 2–4, 1983.

3. Hall, Robert W., *Zero Inventories,* Dow Jones-Irwin, Homewood, Il., 1983.

4. Crosby, Phil, *Quality Without Tears,* McGraw-Hill, New York, 1984.

5. Reid, Robert P., "SPC—America's Quality Revolution," *Quality,* August 1985, pp. Q3–Q5.

6. Houston, Jerry, "SPC—Start Small for Successful SPC," *Quality,* August 1985, pp. Q12–Q17.

7. Karabatsos, Nancy A., "World Class Quality," *Quality,* January 1986. pp. 14–23.

8. Sullivan, L. P., "Reducing Variability: A New Approach to Quality," *Quality Progress,* July, 1984. pp. 15–21.

9. Fukuda, Ryuji, "Introduction to the CEDAC," *Quality Progress,* November 1981. pp. 14–21.

10. Kane, Edward J., "IBM's Quality Focus on the Business Process," *Quality Progress,* April 1986. pp. 26–34.

11. Sullivan, Edward, "A Common Commitment to Total Quality," *Quality Progress,* April 1986. pp. 15–17.

12. Beels, Gregory J., "It's Time to Get Back to the Basics," *Quality,* May 1986. pp. 14–21.

13. Kobayashi, Joji, "Quality Management at NEC Corporation," *Quality Progress,* April 1986. pp. 18–25.

14. Feigenbaum, Armand V., "Total Quality Leadership," *Quality,* April 1986, pp. 26–31.

15. Sullivan, L. P., "Japanese Quality Thinking at Ford," *Quality,* April 1986, pp. 32–37.

16. Walton, Mary, "Making America Work Again," *The Philadelphia Inquirer Magazine,* March 11, 1984, pp. 20–27.

17. *Continuing Process Control and Process Capability Improvement,* Statistical Methods Office Operations Support Staffs, Ford Motor Company, Dearborn, Mich., 1984.

18. "The State of Quality in the U.S. Today," *Quality Progress,* October 1984, pp. 32–37.

19. Harwood, Charles, "The View from the Top," *Quality Progress,* October 1984, pp. 26–31.

20. Williams, Harry E., "Quality plus Productivity plus Cost Equals Profit," *Quality Progress,* October 1984. pp. 17–21.

21. Hagan, John T., "The Management of Quality: Preparing for a Competitive Future," *Quality Progress,* October 1984, pp. 44–51.

22. Joiner, Brian L., "Using Statisticians to Help Transform Industry in America," *Quality Progress,* May 1986, pp. 46–50.

23. Goldstein, Raymond, "Theories X and Y Revisited—An Engineer's Viewpoint," *Quality Progress,* May 1986, pp. 42–45.

24. Sullivan, L. P., "The Seven Stages in Company Wide Quality Control," *Quality Progress,* May 1986, pp. 77–83.

25. Wadsworth, H. M., Stephens, K. S., and Godfrey, A. B., *Modern Methods for Quality Control and Improvement,* Wiley, New York, 1986.

26. Sinha, M. N., and Willborn, W. O., *The Management of Quality Assurance,* Wiley, New York, 1986.

27. Turner, T. E., "Do You Measure Up," *Quality Progress,* May 1, 1973, p. 14.

28. ReVelle, Jack B., "Training Programs Help Ensure Continual Improvement in Levels of Product or Service Quality," *IE,* July 1986, pp. 68–76.

29. Anderson, Robert, "The Ratchet Effect on Quality," *Quality Progress,* July 1986, pp. 16–20.

30. Kenworthy, Harry W., "Total Quality Concept: A Proven Path to Success," *Quality Progress,* July 1986, pp. 21–24.

31. McBryde, Vernon E., "In Today's Market, Quality Is Best Focal Point for Upper Management," *IE,* July 1986, pp. 51–55.

32. Kukla, Bob, "Meeting Customer Needs," *Quality Progress,* June 1986, pp. 15–18.

33. Snee, Ronald D., "In Pursuit of Total Quality," *Quality Progress,* August 1986, pp. 25–31.

34. Hammond, Joshua, "Quality Is the Measure of Value," *Quality Progress,* August 1986, pp. 12–15.

35. "Industry Steels for a Transformation," *USA TODAY,* August 1, 1986, p. 1B.

36. Sargent, Terry R., "The Pygmalion Effect on Quality," *Quality Progress,* August 1986, pp. 34–38.

37. Platt, Adam, "U.S. Productivity's Stunted Growth," *Insight,* August 18, 1986, pp. 8–11.

38. Platt, Adam, "Training the Paper Shufflers to Push the Right Buttons," *Insight,* August 18, l986, pp. 12–14.

39. Platt, Adam, "New Mold for U.S. Industry," *Insight,* August 18, 1986, pp. 15–17.

40. Lowe, Ted, and Mazzeo, Joseph, "Three Preachers, One Religion," *Quality,* September 1986, pp. 22–25.

41. Chaparian, Albert P., "Teammates: Design and Quality Engineers," *Quality Progress,* April 1977, pp. 16–17.

42. Schrock, Edward M., "How to Manufacture a Quality Product," *Quality Progress,* August 1977, pp. 25–27.

43. Freund, Richard A., "Saying What You Mean to Say," *Quality Progress,* February 1977, pp. 16–20.

44. Stockbower, E. A., "Consumer–Supplier: An Advantageous Relationship," *Quality Progress,* (advertising supplement).

45. Gagne, James, "America's Quality Coaches," *CPI Purchasing,* March 1986.

46. Houghton, James R., "The Old Way of Doing Things Is Gone," *Quality Progress,* September 1986, pp. 15–18.

47. Juran, J. M., "The Taylor System and Quality Control," *Quality Progress,* May 1973, pp. 42.

48. Juran, J. M., "The Emerging Quality Control Department," *Quality Progress,* December 1973, pp. 31–32.

49. Shillif, K. A., and Bodis, M. A., "How to Pick the Right Vendor," *Quality Progress,* January 1975, pp. 12–15.

50. Juran, J. M., "Vendor Relations—An Overview," *Quality Progress,* July 1968, pp. 10–13.

51. Mihalsky, J., "The Vendor: A Neglected Quality Improvement Tool," *ASQC** Annual Quality Congress Transactions, 1982, pp. 212–216.

52. Aft, Lawrence, *Fundamentals of Industrial Quality Control,* Addison-Wesley, Reading, Mass., 1986.

53. Ryan, John, "Spokesman for a Century Old Quality Culture," *Quality Progress,* October 1986, pp. 22–26.

54. McDonald, F. James, and others, "The Quality Guidance System, *Quality Progress,* October 1986, pp. 35–42.

55. Marr, Jeffrey, "Letting the Customer Be the Judge of Quality," *Quality Progress,* October 1986, pp. 46–49.

*American Society for Quality Control, 310 W. Wisconsin Ave., Milwaukee, Wisconsin 53203.

56. Joiner, Brian and Scholtes, Peter, "The Quality Manager's New Job," *Quality Progress,* October 1986, pp. 52–56.

57. Thurow, L. C. (editor), *The Management Challenge,* MIT Press, Cambridge, Mass., 1985.

58. Ishikawa, Kaoru, *What Is Total Quality Control? The Japanese Way,* Prentice-Hall, Englewood cliffs, N.J., 1985.

59. Peters, Tom, and Austin, Nancy, *A Passion for Excellence,* Random House, New York, 1985.

60. Mohr, W. L., and Mohr, H., *Quality Circles,* Addison-Wesley, Reading, Mass., 1983.

61. Feigenbaum, A., *Total Quality Control,* McGraw-Hill, New York, 1983.

62. Lester, R. H., Enrick, N. L., and Mottley, Jr., H. E., *Quality Control for Profit,* Marcel Dekker, New York, 1985.

63. Klippel, W. H. (editor), *Statistical Quality Control,* Society for Manufacturing Engineers, Dearborn, Mich., 1984.

64. Skrabec, Quentin R., "Process Diagnostics," *Quality Progress,* November 1986, pp. 40–44.

65. *Criteria for Accrediting Programs in Engineering Technology,* Accreditation Board for Engineering and Technology, New York, 1985.

66. Gast, Bruce M., "Quality Control Swedish Style," *Quality,* December 1986, pp. 14–17.

67. Squires, Frank H., "Tark's Truths," *Quality,* December 1986, p. 74.

68. Mahalanobis, P. C., "Why Statistics," *Sankhya,* volume 10, 1950, pp. 195–228.

69. Osborn, Alex F., *Applied Imagination,* Scribners, New York, 1961.

70. Aft, Lawrence S., *Productivity Measurement and Improvement,* Reston Publishing Company (Prentice-Hall, Inc.), Englewood Cliffs, N.J., 1983.

71. Barker, Thomas B., "Quality Engineering by Design," *Quality Progress,* December 1986, pp. 32–42.

72. Kackar, Raghu N., "Taguchi's Quality Philosophy: Analysis and Commentary," *Quality Progress,* December 1986, pp. 21–29.

73. "Gallup Survey: Top Executives Talk about Quality," *Quality Progress,* December 1986, pp. 48–54.

74. Kohut, Andrew, "What the Survey Means: The Pollster's Perspective," *Quality Progress,* December 1986, p. 55.

75. Cound, Dana M., "Leadership Called for . . . ," *Quality Progress,* December 1986, p. 56.

76. Houghton, James R., " . . . and Called on the Carpet," *Quality Progress,* December 1986, p. 57.

77. Burgess, J. A., "Developing a Supplier Certification Program," *Quality,* January 1987, pp. 36–38.

78. Juran, J. M., *Managerial Breakthrough,* McGraw-Hill, New York, 1964.

79. Ishikawa, Kaoru, *Guide to Quality Control,* Asian Productivity Organization, Tokyo, 1982.

80. Juran, J. M., and Gryna, Frank M., *Quality Planning and Analysis,* McGraw-Hill, New York, 1980.

81. "Federal Beat," *IE,* January 1987, pp. 9–10.

82. Nemac, M. M., "Work Force 2000: Dramatic Changes and a Shortage of Skilled Workers," *IE,* January 1987, pp. 26–31.

83. Starr, Stephanie, "IE's Share Thoughts on Productivity and Quality," *IE,* January 1987, pp. 70–74.

84. Guaspari, John, *I Know It When I See It,* Amacom, New York, 1985.

85. Harrington, H. J., *The Improvement Process,* McGraw-Hill, New York, 1986.

86. Squires, Frank, "Macho Managers, Japan, and SPC," *Quality,* February 1987, p. 80.

87. Marcum, Billie Ruth, "Manufacturing's Quality System," *Quality,* February 1987, pp. 30–32.

88. Walton, Richard E., "From Control to Commitment in the Workplace," *Harvard Business Review,* March–April 1985, pp. 77–84.

89. "We've Traded Quality of Product for Profits," *USA Today,* February 11, 1987, p. 11A.

90. Danforth, Douglas D., "The Quality Imperative," *Quality Progress,* February 1987, pp. 17–19.

91. Brown, Clarence, "Trade Barriers, New Markets, and Quality," *Quality Progress,* February 1987, pp. 22–24.

92. Thomas, Richard L., "Bank on Quality," *Quality Progress,* February 1987, pp. 27–29.

93. Taylor, Claude I., "No Boundaries to Quality," *Quality Progress,* February 1987, pp. 30–31.

94. Feigenbaum, Armand V., "ROI: How Long Before Quality Improvement Pays Off," *Quality Progress,* February 1987, pp. 32–35.

95. Tallon, Robert, "How Long Before Quality Improvement Pays Off?" *Quality Progress,* February 1987, pp. 36–37.

96. Samuel, Howard, "A Labor Perspective on Participative Management," *Quality Progress,* February 1987, pp. 38–39.

97. Kanter, Rosabeth Moss, "Quality Leadership and Change," *Quality Progress,* February 1987, pp. 45–51.

*98. Garvin, David A., "Quality on the Line," *Harvard Business Review,* September–October 1983, pp. 7–12.

*Asterisks indicate that the articles have been reprinted in *Quest for Quality,* published by Institute of Industrial Engineers, Norcross, Ga., 1986. The pages refer to the pages in this publication.

*99. Garvin, David A., "What Does Product Quality Really Mean," *Sloan Management Review,* Fall 1984, pp. 34–48.

*100. Bean, Ed, "Cause of Quality-Control Problems Might Be Managers—Not Workers," *Wall Street Journal,* April 10, 1985, p. 65.

101. Fine, Charles H., and Brjidge, David H., "Managing Quality Improvement," *Quest for Quality,* Institute of Industrial Engineers, Norcross, Ga., 1986, pp. 66–74.

*102. Zubairi, Mazhar, "Statistical Process Control: Management Issues," *Proceedings, 1985 Fall Industrial Engineering Conference,* Norcross, Ga., 1985, pp. 100–108.

*103. Wortham, A. William, "Problem-Solving in Quality Control Areas Creates Synergistic 'Ripple Effect,'" *Industrial Engineering,* July 1986, pp. 117–121.

*104. Schonberger, Richard J., "Production Workers Bear Major Quality Responsibility in Japanese Industry," *Industrial Engineering,* December 1982, pp. 140–145.

*105. Nelson, Lloyd S., "Interpreting Shewhart-$\overline{X}$ Control Charts, *Journal of Quality Technology,* April 1985, pp. 161–163.

*106. Shetty, Y. K., and Ross, Joel E., "Quality and Its Management in Service Businesses," *Industrial Management,* November–December 1985, pp. 187–192.

*107. Roth, H. P., and Morse, W. J., "Let's Help Measure and Report Quality Costs," *Management Accounting,* August 1983, pp. 226–229.

*108. Melan, E. H., "Process Management in Service and Administrative Operations," *Quality Progress,* June 1985, pp. 302–309.

*109. Main, Jeremy, "Ford's Drive for Quality," *Fortune,* April 18, 1983, pp. 310–312.

110. Townsend, Patrick L., *Commit to Quality,* Wiley, New York, 1986.

111. Groocock, J. M., *The Chain of Quality,* Wiley, New York, 1986.

112. "The Best That We Can Be," *The Right Chemistry,* 1986, No. 1, pp. 2–4.

113. Mann, Nancy, *The Keys to Excellence,* Prestwick Books, Los Angeles, 1985.

114. Oliver, Thomas, "Studies: Both Workers, Management at Fault," *Atlanta Journal-Constitution,* March 1, 1987, pp. 1E, 4E.

115. Bajaria, H. J., "SPC Training, Is Your Investment Paying Off," *Quality,* March 1987, pp. 27–30.

116. Sease, Douglas R., "Japanese Firms Export U.S. Made Goods," *Wall Street Journal,* March 3, 1987, p. 6.

117. Scherkenbach, William W., *The Deming Route to Quality and Productivity,* ASQC Quality Press, American Society for Quality Control, Milwaukee, Wisc., 1986.

118. Cound, Dana M., "A Call for Leadership," *Quality Progress,* March 1987. pp. 11–15.

119. Karabatsos, Nancy, "The Chairman Doesn't Blink," *Quality Progress,* March 1987, pp. 19–24.

120. Shewhart, Walter, *Economic Control of Quality of Manufactured Product,* Van Nostrand Reinhold, New York, 1931.

121. Rice, William B., *Control Charts,* Wiley, New York, 1947.

122. Cannestra, K. W., and Rogers, H. B., *Case Studies in Quality Assurance,* Assurance Science Publishing, Campbell, Calif., 1972.

123. Hayes, Glenn E., *Quality and Productivity: The New Challenge,* Hitchcock Executive Book Service, Wheaton, Il., 1985.

124. Main, Jeremy, "Under the Spell of the Quality Gurus," *Fortune,* August 18, 1986, pp. 31–34.

125. "Juran's Industrial Revolution: Still Developing at a Rapid Pace," *International Management,* August 1986, pp. 34–36.

126. Juran, J. M., "Catching Up: How Is the West Doing?" *Quality Progress,* November 1985, pp. 18–22.

127. Juran, J. M., "The Quality Trilogy," *Quality Progress,* August 1986, pp. 19–24.

128. Cole, Robert E., "The Japanese Lesson in Quality," *Technology Review,* July 1981, pp. 29–40.

129. Irving, Robert R., "Quality in Design," *Iron Age,* August 1, 1983, pp. 35–40.

130. Lerner, Eric, "Quality Control: U.S. and Japan," *IIIE Spectrum,* October 1981, pp. 97–101.

131. Manoochehri, G. H., "Building Quality into the Product," *Business,* July–September 1985, pp. 47–50.

132. Reddy, Jack and Berger, Abe, "Three Essentials of Product Quality," *Harvard Business Review,* July–August 1983, pp. 153–159.

133. Leonard, F. S., and Sasser, W. E., "The Incline of Quality," *Harvard Business Review,* September–October 1982, pp. 163–170.

134. Burt, David W., "Understanding Quality Control," *Journal of Purchasing* 9, No. 2, May 1973, pp. 12–24.

135. Deming, W. E., "Improvement of Quality and Productivity through Action by Management," *National Productivity Review* 1, No 1, Winter 1981–82, pp. 12–22.

136. Ebrahimpour, Maling, "An Examination of Quality Management in Japan: Implications for Management in the United States," *Journal of Operations Management* 5, No. 4, August 1985, pp. 419–431.

137. Friesecke, Raymond F., "The Quality Revolution: A Challenge to Management," *Managerial Planning* 32, No. 1, July–August 1983, pp. 7–9,26.

138. Guiniven, John, "How to Compete by Quality," *Management Today,* December 1985, pp. 78–80.

139. Harrigan, Kenneth W., "Making Quality Job One—A Cultural Revolution," *Business Quarterly* 49, No. 4, Winter, 1984/1985, pp. 68–71.

140. Ross, Joel, "The Quality Gap: Causes and Cures," *Industrial Management* 26, No. 5, September–October 1984, pp. 19–24.

141. Smith, Ray, "Quality—Commitment to the Future," *Telephone Engineer and Management* 89, No. 21, November 1, 1985, pp. 12–14.

142. Tuttle, Howard C., "The Quality Push Is On," *Production* 87, No. 4, April 1981, pp. 88–94.

143. Williams, Harry E., "Quality Control: A Communications Function," *Advanced Management Journal* 44, No. 1, Winter 1979, pp. 45–51.

144. Collins, Rita E., "Service Quality—Measuring the Network and the Customer," *Telephony* 209, No. 24, December 9, 1985, pp. 32–34.

145. Crosby, Philip B., "The Management of Quality," *Research Management* 15, No. 4, July 1982, pp. 10–12.

146. Doran, P. K., "A Total Quality Improvement Programme," *Quality Assurance* 11, No. 4, December 1985, pp. 106–109.

147. McMillan, Charles J., "From Quality Control to Quality Management: Lessons from Japan," *Business Quarterly* 47, No. 1, May 1982, pp. 31–40.

148. Rehder, R., and Ralston, F., "Total Quality Management: A Revolutionary Management Philosophy," *Advanced Management Journal* 49, No. 3, Summer 1984, pp. 24–33.

149. "A Case Study of Quality Control and Productivity at Toshiba," *Electronics and Communications* 30, No. 6, December 1982, pp. 10, 35.

150. Griffith, Gary K., "SPC and Mil-Q–9858A," *Quality,* April 1987, pp. 54–55.

151. Hashim, M., "The Application of Total Socio-Technical Approach to Achieve Optimum Quality," 3rd Annual Southeastern Quality Conference, Marietta, Ga., 1984.

152. Mast, G. W., "Dealing with Interpretation Errors in Shewhart Control Charts," 3rd Annual Southeastern Quality Conference, Marietta, Ga., 1984.

153. Johnson, R. H., and Weber, R. T., *Buying Quality,* Franklin Watts, New York, 1985.

154. Shingo, Shigeo, *Zero Quality Control,* Productivity Press, Stamford, Conn., 1986.

155. Gitlow, H. S., and Gitlow, S. J., *The Deming Guide to Quality and Competitive Position,* Prentice-Hall, Englewood Cliffs, N.J., 1987.

156. Latzko, Willilam, *Quality and Productivity for Bankers and Financial Managers,* Marcel Dekker, New York, 1986.

157. Western Electric Company, *Statistical Quality Control Handbook,* Western Electric, New York, 1956.

158. DeToro, Irving, "Strategic Planning for Quality at Xerox," *Quality Progress,* April 1987, pp. 16–20.

159. Praveen, G., and others, "A Systematic Approach to SPC Implementation," *Quality Progress,* April 1987, pp. 22–25.

160. McDonald, Marshall, "Why FPL Pursued Quality Improvement," *The Juran Report,* No. 8, Juran Institute, Wilton, Conn., pp. 17–19.

161. Walden, James C., "Integrating Customer Satisfaction into Daily Work," *The Juran Report,* No. 8, Juran Institute, Wilton, Conn., pp. 30–34.

162. Kenworthy, Harry W., "Top Management's Part in Quality Improvement," *The Juran Report,* No. 8, Juran Institute, Wilton, Conn., pp. 40–42.

163. Nickell, W. L., and McNeil, J. S., "Process Management in a Marketing Environment," *The Juran Report,* No. 8, Juran Institute, Wilton, Conn., pp. 71–78.

164. Stevens, Eric R., "Implementing an Internal Customer Satisfaction Improvement Process," *The Juran Report,* No. 8, Juran Institute, Wilton, Conn., pp. 140–145.

165. Leonard, James, "Implementing the QI Process: A Structured Approach to Planning and Measuring Progress," *The Juran Report,* No. 8, Juran Institute, Wilton, Conn., pp. 166–172.

166. Parikh, Anil, "Quality Culture: What it Is and How to Achieve It," *The Juran Report,* No. 8, Juran Institute, Wilton, Conn., pp. 212–223.

167. Crowe, Lisa, "Why Are Workers' Attitudes So Rotten?" *Atlanta Journal-Constitution,* April 27, 1987, pp. 1c, 16c.

168. Williams, Thomas R., "In a Deregulated Market, You Simply Can't Forget the Customer's Needs," *Atlanta Journal-Constitution,* April 27, 1987, p. 11c.

169. "Ford Replaces Taurus/Sable V6s," *Autoweek,* April 20, 1987, p. 4.

170. Atkinson, P., "Managing Total Quality," *Management Services,* October 1985, pp. 18–21.

171. Wolak, Jerry, "Motorola Revisited," *Quality,* May 1987, pp. 18–23.

172. Hagan, J., *The Management of Quality,* ASQC, Milwaukee, 1984.

173. Ingle, Sud, *In Search of Perfection,* Prentice-Hall, Englewood Cliffs, N.J., 1985.

174. Shetty, Y. K., and Buehler, V. M. (editors), *Quality and Productivity Improvements,* Utah State University, Logan, 1983.

175. Peters, Dave, "Quality Failures Laid to Management," *St. Paul Pioneer Press Dispatch,* May 5, 1987, p. 5B.

176. Scholtes, Peter, and Hacquebord, Heero, "A Practical Approach to Quality," *Proceedings, 41st Annual Quality Congress,* Minneapolis, Minn., May 1987, ASQC, pp. 202–222.

177. Deming, W. Edwards, *Quality, Productivity, and Competitive Position,* MIT Press, Cambridge, Mass., 1982.

178. King, Josph P., "Executive Survival Guide to Meeting Requirements," *Proceedings, 41st Annual Quality Congress,* Minneapolis, Minn., May 1987, ASQC, pp. 827–832.

179. Adam, Paul R., "Quality—A Giant Step into the White-Collar World," *Proceedings, 41st Annual Quality Congress,* Minneapolis, Minn., May 1987, ASQC, pp. 441–447.

180. Luther, David B., "Introducing Quality in Large Organizations," *Proceedings, 41st Annual Quality Congress,* Minneapolis, Minn., May 1987, ASQC, pp. 419–423.

181. Dobbins, Richard K., "Service Quality: When Friendly Skies Are Cancelled," *Proceedings, 41st Annual Quality Congress,* Minneapolis, Minn., May 1987, ASQC, pp. 415–418.

182. Hagan, Jack, and Scanlon, Frank, "Maturing of Service Industry Quality," *Proceedings, 41st Annual Quality Congress,* Minneapolis, Minn., May 1987, ASQC, pp. 404–414.

183. Schneier, C. E., "Performance Management: Quality Becomes a Reality," *Proceedings, 41st Annual Quality Congress,* Minneapolis, Minn., May 1987, ASQC, pp. 341–347.

184. Lucht, Lee H., "The Quality/Excellence Connection at Jostens," *Proceedings, 41st Annual Quality Congress,* Minneapolis, Minn., May 1987, ASQC, pp. 315–320.

185. Stratton, A. D., "Improving Quality in a White Collar Environment," *Proceedings, 41st Annual Quality Congress,* Minneapolis, Minn., May 1987, ASQC, pp. 310–314.

186. McBride, Ronald C., "The Selling of Quality," *Proceedings, 41st Annual Quality Congress,* Minneapolis, Minn., May 1987, ASQC, pp. 236–239.

187. Thornton, M. P., "SPC for Administrative Systems," *Proceedings, 41st Annual Quality Congress,* Minneapolis, Minn., May 1987, ASQC, pp. 287–292.

188. Deming, W. Edwards, *Out of the Crisis,* MIT Press, Cambridge, Mass., 1986.

189. Tribus, Myron, "The Quality Imperative," *The Bent,* Spring 1987, pp. 24–27.

190. Walton, Mary, *The Deming Management Method,* Dodd, Mead Publishing, New York, 1986.

191. Kanter, Rosabeth Moss, *The Change Masters,* Simon and Schuster, New York, 1983.

192. Matthews, William, "Dismal Future Forecast for U.S. Shipbuilding," *Navy Times,* June 1, 1987, p. 37.

193. Allen, Larry G., "A Measure of SPC," *Quality,* June 1987, pp. 62–63.

194. Brown, Mark, "Bridging the Quality Gap," *Quality,* June 1987, pp. 40–44.

195. Matthews, Richard, "Japanese Demand Quality in Imported Goods," *Atlanta Journal-Constitution,* June 14, 1987, p. 8A.

196. Ford, Susan, *Toronto Sun,* April 25, 1983, p. 6.

197. Kendrick, John, "Total Quality," *Quality,* September 1987, pp. 20–25.

198. Rudin, Bruce, "Automated SPC," *Quality,* September 1987, pp. 40–42.

199. Stanula, Richard, "A Process Improvement Tool," *Quality,* September 1987, pp. 59–60.

200. Wurster, Ralph, "Must Quality be an Import," *Quality,* September 1987, p. 54.

201. Horton, Thomas, "The Global Factory," *Quality,* September 1987, p. 68.

202. Adams, Tom, "Customers Know Quality," *Quality Progress,* August 1987, pp. 14–20.

203. Van Koevering, A.R., "Transformation of Quality," *Quality,* August 1987, pp. 24–26.

204. Cervenka, Robert, "Start with Quality—Grow with Quality," *Quality,* August 1987, pp. Q18–20.

205. Prikso, Paul, "Production and Quality Inseparable," *Quality,* August 1987, pp. Q21–Q22.

206. Williams, Roy H., and Zigli, Ronald M., "Ambiguity Impedes Quality in the Service Industries," *Quality Progress,* July 1987, pp. 14–17.

207. Squires, Frank, "Human Fallibility and Process Variability," *Quality Progress,* July 1987, pp. 31–34.

208. Davis, William W., et al., "Successfully Communicating Can Pay High Dividends," *Quality Progress,* July 1987, pp. 36–39.

209. Hunter, William, et al., "Doing More with Less in the Public Sector," *Quality Progress,* July 1987, pp. 19–26.

210. King, Carol, "A Framework for a Service Quality Assurance System," *Quality Progress,* September 1987, pp. 27–32.

211. Ryan, John, "This Company Hates Surprises," *Quality Progress,* September 1987, pp. 12–16.

212. Ryan, John, "High Tech, High Touch," *Quality Progress,* September 1987, pp. 19–23.

213. Horn, S. M., "Sitmar Cruises," *Cruise Travel,* July/August, 1987, pp. 20–22.

Index